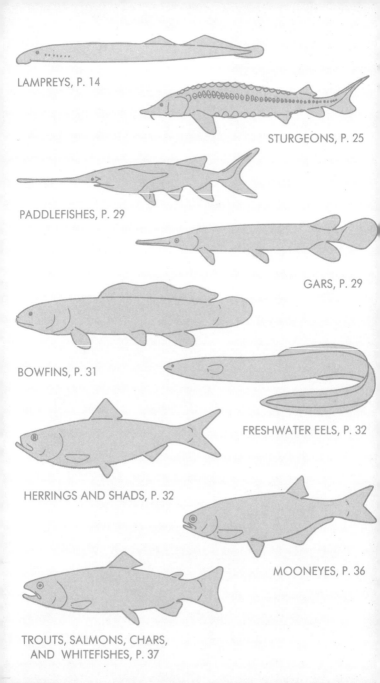

LAMPREYS, P. 14

STURGEONS, P. 25

PADDLEFISHES, P. 29

GARS, P. 29

BOWFINS, P. 31

FRESHWATER EELS, P. 32

HERRINGS AND SHADS, P. 32

MOONEYES, P. 36

TROUTS, SALMONS, CHARS,
AND WHITEFISHES, P. 37

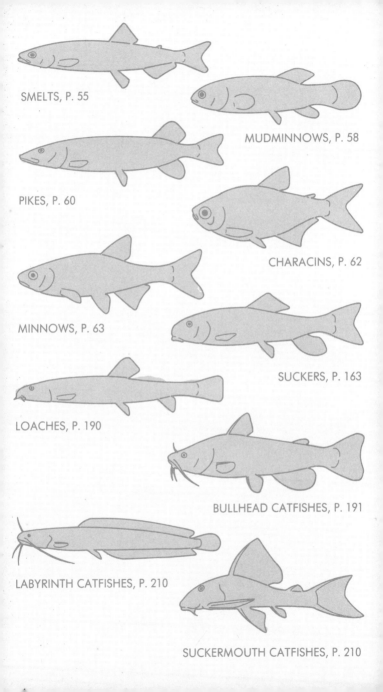

SMELTS, P. 55

MUDMINNOWS, P. 58

PIKES, P. 60

CHARACINS, P. 62

MINNOWS, P. 63

SUCKERS, P. 163

LOACHES, P. 190

BULLHEAD CATFISHES, P. 191

LABYRINTH CATFISHES, P. 210

SUCKERMOUTH CATFISHES, P. 210

THE PETERSON FIELD GUIDE SERIES®

Edited by Roger Tory Peterson

A Field Guide to Freshwater Fishes

North America
North of Mexico

LAWRENCE M. PAGE
Illinois Natural History Survey

BROOKS M. BURR
Southern Illinois University at Carbondale

Illustrations by
Eugene C. Beckham, III
John Parker Sherrod
Craig W. Ronto

*Sponsored by the National Audubon Society,
the National Wildlife Federation,
and the Roger Tory Peterson Institute*

HOUGHTON MIFFLIN COMPANY
Boston   New York

For information about permission to reproduce selections from
this book, write to Permissions, Houghton Mifflin Company,
215 Park Avenue South, New York, New York 10003

PETERSON FIELD GUIDES and PETERSON FIELD GUIDE SERIES
are registered trademarks of Houghton Mifflin Company.

For information about this and other Houghton Mifflin
trade and reference books and multimedia products, visit
The Bookstore at Houghton Mifflin on the World Wide Web at
http://www.hmco.com/trade/.

Library of Congress Cataloging-in-Publication Data

Page, Lawrence M.
    A field guide to freshwater fishes of North America north of
Mexico / Lawrence M. Page, Brooks M. Burr; illustrations by
Eugene C. Beckham III, John Parker Sherrod, Craig W. Ronto.
        p.   cm. — (The Peterson field guide series®; 42)
    "Sponsored by the National Audubon Society, the National
Wildlife Federation, and the Roger Tory Peterson Institute."
    Includes bibliographical references and index.
    ISBN 0-395-35307-6 (cl.)
    ISBN 0-395-53933-1 (pa.)
    1. Fishes, Freshwater—United States—Identification.   2.
Fishes, Freshwater—Canada—Identification.   I. Burr, Brooks,
M.   II. National Audubon Society.   III. National Wildlife
Foundation.   IV. Roger Tory Peterson Institute.   V. Title.   VI.
Series.
QL627.P34   1991
597.092'973--dc20   90-42049
                                                                        CIP
            Printed in the United States of America

                        VB 10 9 8 7 6

EDITOR'S NOTE

The publication of this long-awaited volume completes the trilogy of Peterson Field Guides to North American fishes. The guide to Pacific Coast fishes was published in 1983, the guide to Atlantic Coast fishes in 1986, and this, the guide to freshwater fishes, in 1991. Each is comprehensive, providing information necessary to identify all species of fishes within their respective domains. Collectively, they provide the resources to identify *all* fishes known in North America north of Mexico.

That guides to the fishes appeared so much later than guides to the other groups of vertebrates — the reptiles and amphibians, birds, and mammals — is mainly because fishes are not nearly as well known. Changes in taxonomy, new information on distribution, and other factors relating to species identifications make the "completion" of a guide such as this nearly impossible. Still, it is of paramount importance, especially to an environmentally conscious society, that the information necessary to understand the diversity of life be available to the public. With this goal in mind, Lawrence Page and Brooks Burr have produced the first field guide to all North American freshwater fishes.

Peterson Field Guides have long gestation periods. The one for this book was not as long as some, but longer than the authors anticipated. When William N. Eschmeyer completed his *Field Guide to Pacific Coast Fishes*, he felt that completion of a freshwater fish guide could be done relatively quickly, given his experience with the various tasks that go into the production of a field guide. One thing he needed to accomplish early was to find a coauthor for the guide who was familiar with freshwater fishes.

Eschmeyer chose Lawrence M. Page. Page had just published the *Handbook of Darters* and knew that group (one-fifth of the North American fish fauna) intimately. He also knew minnows, the other large group (one-third of the fish fauna) as well as anyone. Eschmeyer and Page thought they could complete the book in two years.

Eugene C. Beckham III learned of the project and asked to do the artwork. The samples he sent to the authors and to me were excellent, and the team of Eschmeyer, Page, and Beckham was off and running. However, the imperfect state of our knowledge (undescribed, transplanted, and introduced species) as well as the other obligations of the team members slowed the project. At the end of two years, Page had written accounts for about 300 species, Beckham had painted 12 of the 48 plates, and Eschmeyer had returned to his first love, marine fishes.

It became clear to Page and Beckham that a second author and additional artists were needed. Brooks M. Burr, a long-time colleague of Page and an expert on catfishes, lampreys, and other fishes, agreed to help write the guide. John P. Sherrod, an artist known for his excellent renderings of insects, submitted some superb fish paintings. Craig W. Ronto, an artist with experience in the illustration of fishes and in map production, agreed to draw the maps and to do some of the black-and-white illustrations.

Working in different parts of the country, the new team met every six months to plan, critique work, and harangue one another for not making more progress. At last, the project begun in 1983 was completed in 1990.

Our freshwater fishes are fascinating and, unfortunately, in trouble. Page and Burr note that 11 species already are extinct, and another 83 species and subspecies are federally listed as threatened and endangered. Use this guide to study the wonderful diversity we have, and use it also to educate others as to what we will lose if we continue to pollute, dam, and channelize our aquatic habitats out of existence.

ROGER TORY PETERSON

ACKNOWLEDGMENTS

Many colleagues and friends contributed information and otherwise helped in the preparation of this guide. We are extremely grateful for their help; the finished product is much more accurate and useful than it would have been without their assistance.

We are especially grateful to William N. Eschmeyer for initiating this project (in fact, for inviting us to participate), and to Mary Lou Williamson for typing the manuscript and for keeping us on track and organized through its many revisions.

Other contributors deserving special thanks are those who reviewed portions of the manuscript, loaned photographs, and provided information on undescribed species.

Accounts were reviewed as follows: Amblyopsidae: David L. Swofford; Catostomidae: Robert E. Jenkins, Gerald R. Smith; Centrarchidae: Robert C. Cashner, Fred C. Rohde, Melvin L. Warren, Jr.; Clupeidae: George H. Burgess, Frank J. Schwartz; Cottidae: Carl E. Bond, Robert E. Jenkins; Cyprinidae: Miles M. Coburn, Carter R. Gilbert, Richard L. Mayden; Cyprinodontidae: Anthony A. Echelle, Robert R. Miller; Elassomatidae: Robert C. Cashner, Fred C. Rohde, Melvin L. Warren, Jr.; Eleotrididae and Gobiidae: Ray S. Birdsong, David G. Lindquist; Fundulidae: Robert C. Cashner, Jamie E. Thomerson; Ictaluridae: David A. Etnier, James M. Grady, William H. LeGrande, William R. Taylor; Percidae: David A. Etnier; Petromyzontidae: F. William H. Beamish, Fred C. Rohde, Philip A. Cochran; Poeciliidae: Clark Hubbs, Alex E. Peden; Salmonidae: Robert J. Behnke, Robert R. Miller; *Semotilus:* Carol E. Johnston; exotic species: Walter R. Courtenay, Jr. General comments and suggestions on the Cyprinidae and Percidae accounts were made by Reeve M. Bailey.

Slides and photographs for preparation of the plates were provided by Thomas M. Baugh, Jacques F. Bergeron, Carl E.

Bond, Noel M. Burkhead, George H. Burgess, Anthony A. Echelle, David A. Etnier, Robert E. Jenkins, Richard L. Mayden, Robert R. Miller, Paul J. Monaco, Peter B. Moyle, David L. Propst, John N. Rinne, Henry W. Robison, Fred C. Rohde, William N. Roston, Wayne C. Starnes, Harold M. Tyus, and Ralph W. Yerger. Camm C. Swift provided color notes on southeastern U.S. fishes. Maps for the Starhead Topminnow (*Fundulus notti*) species-group were updated by James S. Rogers. Michael E. Retzer wrote first drafts of the *Semotilus* and *Phoxinus* accounts. Steve W. Kelsch and Robert R. Miller provided information on characters useful in separating *Ictalurus* species.

Information on undescribed species was provided by Herbert T. Boschung, Jr., David A. Etnier, Robert E. Jenkins, Richard L. Mayden, Robert R. Miller, and John S. Ramsey. Suggestions on drainage nomenclature were made by Robert E. Jenkins.

CONTENTS

PLATES

(Grouped after p. 208)

A FIELD GUIDE TO
FRESHWATER FISHES
NORTH AMERICA

HOW TO USE THIS GUIDE

Naturalists, fishermen, and aquarists derive pleasure and knowledge from observing and catching fishes. Ichthyologists and other scientists are using fishes to learn more about the evolution of life, about the history of our continent, and about how new food sources can be developed. For all these interests and endeavors, accurate identification of fishes is essential. This guide is the first to include all fishes found in the fresh waters of North America north of Mexico.

Fishes are aquatic, cold-blooded animals with backbones and have fins and gills throughout life. This definition covers a wide variety of species and, consequently, a great diversity of forms and habits. Currently recognized as valid are about 22,000 species of fishes, of which 790 species (4% of the total) are known from the fresh waters of the United States and Canada. Of the 445 families of fishes, 36 (8%) are represented by one or more species native to the freshwater lakes and streams of the United States and Canada, and another 10 families have marine species that occasionally enter our rivers. Four other families are represented by introduced (exotic) species. Although our fish fauna represents a small fraction of the world's total, it is the most diverse temperate freshwater fish fauna in the world.

All freshwater fishes known from North America north of Mexico are included in this guide. A few marine fishes that have become established in fresh water, such as the Sea Lamprey, are included here. Information on the families of marine and brackish-water species that are most likely to be encountered in fresh water can be obtained from the *Peterson Field Guide to Atlantic Coast Fishes* and the *Peterson Field Guide to Pacific Coast Fishes*.

Marine species most likely to be encountered in fresh water on the Atlantic and Gulf slopes are:

Bull Shark *Carcharhinus leucas*
Atlantic Stingray *Dasyatis sabina*
Tarpon *Megalops atlanticus*
Ladyfish *Elops saurus*
Atlantic Thread Herring *Opisthonema oglinum*
Scaled Sardine *Harengula jaguana*
Bay Anchovy *Anchoa mitchilli*
Hardhead Catfish *Ariopsis felis*
Atlantic Needlefish *Strongylura marina*
Mummichog *Fundulus heteroclitus*
Gulf Killifish *Fundulus grandis*
Marsh Killifish *Fundulus confluentus*
Saltmarsh Topminnow *Fundulus jenkinsi*
Blackspotted Stickleback *Gasterosteus wheatlandi*
Gulf Pipefish *Syngnathus scovelli*
Opossum Pipefish *Oostethus brachyurus*
Snook *Centropomus undecimalis*
Fat Snook *Centropomus parallelus*
Tarpon Snook *Centropomus pectinatus*
Swordspine Snook *Centropomus ensiferus*
Gray Snapper *Lutjanus griseus*
Striped Mojarra *Diapterus plumieri*
Spotfin Mojarra *Eucinostomus argenteus*
Pigfish *Orthopristis chrysoptera*
Sheepshead *Archosargus probatocephalus*
Pinfish *Lagodon rhomboides*
Silver Perch *Bairdiella chrysoura*
Spotted Seatrout *Cynoscion nebulosus*
Spot *Leiostomus xanthurus*
Atlantic Croaker *Micropogonias undulatus*
Red Drum *Sciaenops ocellatus*
Striped Mullet *Mugil cephalus*
White Mullet *Mugil curema*
Mountain Mullet *Agonostomus monticola*
Bigmouth Sleeper *Gobiomorus dormitor*
Spinycheek Sleeper *Eleotris pisonis*
Fat Sleeper *Dormitator maculatus*
River Goby *Awaous tajasica*
Crested Goby *Lophogobius cyprinoides*
Violet Goby *Gobioides broussoneti*
Freshwater Goby *Gobionellus shufeldti*
Darter Goby *Gobionellus boleosoma*
Clown Goby *Microgobius gulosus*
Green Goby *Microgobius thalassinus*

Naked Goby *Gobiosoma bosc*
Code Goby *Gobiosoma robustum*
Southern Flounder *Paralichthys lethostigma*
Bay Whiff *Citharichthys spilopterus*
Hogchoker *Trinectes maculatus*

Marine species most likely to be encountered in freshwater on the Pacific slope are:

Machete *Elops affinis*
Surf Smelt *Hypomesus pretiosus*
California Killifish *Fundulus parvipinnis*
Pacific Staghorn Sculpin *Leptocottus armatus*
Sharpnose Sculpin *Clinocottus acuticeps*
Bairdiella *Bairdiella icistia*
Striped Mullet *Mugil cephalus*
Pacific Fat Sleeper *Dormitator latifrons*
Yellowfin Goby *Acanthogobius flavimanus*
Tidewater Goby *Eucyclogobius newberryi*
Arrow Goby *Clevelandia ios*
Longjaw Mudsucker *Gillichthys mirabilis*
Chameleon Goby *Tridentiger trigonocephalus*
Starry Flounder *Platichthys stellatus*

Names. Most fish names in this guide are those in the American Fisheries Society's *A List of Common and Scientific Names of Fishes from the United States and Canada*, published in 1980.

Scientific names of species consist of two Latinized and italicized words (e.g., *Etheostoma sagitta*). The first is the genus, which always begins with a capital letter. The second word, the "specific epithet," is not capitalized. A subspecies has a third descriptor; e.g., *Etheostoma sagitta spilotum*. Genera are grouped into families (with names that end in *idae*), families into orders (ending in *iformes*), and orders into classes.

Illustrations. The color plates were painted from live fishes or, more often, from color photographs of live or freshly killed fishes. Black and white plates depict fishes that lack bright colors or that show little variation in coloration among species. Fishes are not drawn to scale, but much larger species usually are shown larger than smaller species on a plate. The 48 plates (33 in color, 15 in black and white) show 702 individuals representing 598 species. An additional 19 species are illustrated in black-and-white figures.

Measurements. Although ichthyologists use the metric system (centimeters, kilograms, etc.), many people remain more familiar with inches, feet, and pounds. This Field Guide gives measurements according to both systems. A short rule comparing metric and U.S. units appears below and on the back cover. The maximum total length known (tip of snout, lip, or chin — whichever is farthest forward — to end of longer caudal fin lobe) is given for each species. For small fishes, this number is given in tenths of centimeters and quarter-inches, for intermediate fishes in centimeters and inches, and for very large fishes in meters and feet.

If the maximum length recorded was given originally in centimeters, it was converted to inches; if in inches, it was converted to centimeters. Rounding from centimeters to quarter-inches can give various results; for example, 7.4 through 7.9 cm all are given as equivalent to 3 in.

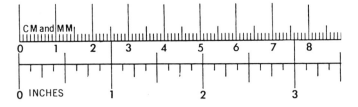

Accounts. Family accounts provide information on distinguishing characteristics (often anatomical) and distribution. The number in parentheses following the family name is the number of species found in the United States and Canada.

Generic accounts are given for large genera and for small genera in which all of the species share characteristics useful in their identification. *If a characteristic is described in a family or generic account it usually is not repeated in a species account.*

Species accounts begin with the common and scientific names. In the upper right-hand corner of each account is the number of the plate or figure in this guide where the species is illustrated, or "Not shown" if not illustrated. A species is not illustrated if it is similar to another species.

Every species account contains the following 4 sections. A **Remarks** section is added if the species has subspecies or noteworthy life history characteristics.

Identification: This section describes the most useful characteristics for identification. Usually these are color descriptions such as "black stripe along body," shape descriptions such as "dorsal fin origin behind pelvic fin origin," and unusual features such as "barbel at corner of mouth." The best field characteristics are *italicized* and usually appear early in the account. Accurate field identifications sometimes will require a consideration of locality and habitat. Large specimens, especially colorful males, are easiest to identify. Positive identification of small or single individuals may require close examination; for that reason, we give some characteristics useful in the identification of preserved fishes but not live fishes (e.g., numbers of scales, fin rays, and pharyngeal teeth).

A color description is included unless a species is noted to be similar or nearly identical to another species. Unless stated otherwise, the description is of an adult fish, and the fish is white below (breast and belly) and has clear fins, conditions that pertain in the vast majority of species. In many fishes, the female retains colors similar to those of the young, but males become notably brighter or darker as they age. During the spawning season, males of many species become much brighter in color than at any other time. When known to differ, both "average" and "breeding male" descriptions are given. In some fishes (e.g., darters), large males retain bright colors through much of the year; in others (e.g., most minnows), bright colors are present only during the spawning season.

Counts provided are those considered to be most important for identification. Counts are known ranges unless they are preceded by "usually" or identified as modes (i.e., number[s] occurring most frequently) in the family account.

Counts of bilateral characteristics are given for one side only; for example, 6 branchiostegal rays means 6 on each side. Pectoral and pelvic fins come one to a side and are referred to collectively (i.e., all four of them) as the paired fins. We discuss these fins and other paired structures (e.g., eyes) in the singular (e.g., pectoral fin, eye) to simplify comparisons between species.

Range: A description of each species' range (geographic distribution) is followed by a comment on abundance (e.g.,

"Rare"). All species vary in abundance with locality, and the statement on abundance is meant to apply to the species over its entire range. The statement is not a relative comparison among species. For example, the Fountain Darter is common in its area but is an endangered species because it occurs in only one small area. *Abundant* means a species is almost certain to be found in its preferred habitat within its range (see How to Observe Fishes, below); *common* indicates a species is likely to be found; *fairly common,* may be found; *uncommon,* is unlikely to be found; *rare,* is very unlikely to be found. Species and subspecies protected as *threatened* or *endangered* are those appearing on the official lists of Canada and the United States as of 1 January 1990.

Habitat: Fishes vary widely in their restriction to particular habitats. Some are extremely limited (e.g., to springs); others can occupy habitats as different from one another as gravel riffles and swamps. For a stream-inhabiting species, the habitat description includes a statement on the size of stream the species generally occupies. Terms used are *stream* (any body of running water), *headwater* (a stream less than 1 m wide during average conditions), *creek* (1–5 m), *small river* (5–25 m), *medium river* (25–50 m), and *large river* (more than 50 m). A *basin* is a major drainage unit (i.e., the Arctic, Hudson Bay, Great Lakes–St. Lawrence, Atlantic, Gulf, Pacific, Mississippi R., Ohio R., and Missouri R. basins) or an independent endorheic drainage unit (e.g., Bonneville basin). The component drainages may be referred to as, e.g., the Atlantic drainages. A *drainage* is an interconnected group of streams entering an ocean or the main river of a basin (e.g., the Wabash R. drainage of the Ohio R. basin). A *system* is a subdivision of a drainage (e.g., the Embarras R. system of the Wabash R. drainage).

For convenience, we make a distinction between Atlantic and Gulf Slope drainages even though the Gulf of Mexico is part of the Atlantic Ocean. Atlantic Slope drainages are those entering the Atlantic Ocean from the Arctic Ocean to the southern tip of Florida. Gulf Slope drainages are those entering the Gulf of Mexico.

Composition of the stream or lake bottom (substrate) is of major importance in the distribution of fishes, and habitat descriptions usually include statements on the type(s) of bottom material most often associated with the species. *Mud* refers to a soft bottom (clay or silt); *rock* refers to a hard bottom (gravel, rubble, boulders, or mixtures thereof). More precise terms, in increasing order of particle size, are *clay, silt, sand, gravel, rubble, boulders,* and *bedrock.*

Similar species: Comparisons are made with species that appear most similar. These usually, but not always, are closely related forms. When there are many similar species, we compare those within or closest to the range of the species being identified.

Maps. Range maps are provided for all freshwater fishes that are *native* to North America north of Mexico. Range maps are not provided for species that were introduced from outside North America, or that are primarily marine or brackish and enter fresh water only rarely or only along coastal areas. Production of the range maps relied heavily on the *Atlas of North American Freshwater Fishes* and recent state, provincial, and regional "fish books." We stopped making additions and corrections to maps on 1 January 1989.

A map usually shows the total range of a species. However, a map may show only part of the range (e.g., if one or more populations have been established outside the original range); if so, a notation such as "Introduced elsewhere" appears on the map. These notations indicate that the reader should consult the text for information on the present range, including introductions. In many instances, we chose not to depict introduced populations on maps because of their ever-changing and unpredictable nature, in particular the rapid spread of some populations and rapid die-off of others. Although this approach may seem less informative than showing the present range of a species transplanted to a wide area outside its native range (e.g., Largemouth Bass), for many species we found it impossible to produce maps that would not be out of date as soon as they were published. On the other hand, for a few species, the original range is no longer known, and the present range, including introduced populations, is shown.

Hybridization. Crosses between species occur occasionally in nature. Identifications of hybrids (as species A × species B) usually are difficult. In making identifications, keep in mind that hybridization occurs most often between closely related species, and hybrids usually have characteristics that are intermediate between those of the parental species. As aquatic environments degrade, hybridization in fishes increases, presumably because of the difficulty fishes have in recognizing spawning partners in turbid and polluted water.

Intergrade zones are areas where individuals (known as intergrades) are intermediate in characteristics used in the recognition of two subspecies. Intergrades may be intermediate because of the mixing of genes ("gene flow") of the two subspecies or because of environmental intermediacy and hence selection for characteristics intermediate to those of the two subspecies. Intergrades are named as hybrids between two subspecies (e.g., *Etheostoma whipplei whipplei* × *E. whipplei artesiae*).

How to Observe Fishes. You can watch living fishes, just as you watch birds, by going to where they live. You can see fishes in clear water from stream banks and lake shores; and although at first they may all look the same or at best as "minnows" or "sunfishes," you can identify them by knowing what species occur in the area and noting their distinguishing morphological and behavioral traits. Binoculars and polarized sunglasses that eliminate surface glare greatly facilitate fish watching from above water.

Serious fish watchers enter the water and join their subjects. With a snorkel and mask, you can view fishes at amazingly short distances and observe their feeding, spawning, etc. Although fishes tend to swim away from fish watchers on stream banks, humans in the water seem much less threatening to them, and they remain close by. In fact, fishes are curious and readily approach underwater observers.

In areas where many similar species occur, removing fishes from the water may be the only positive way to identify them. Many species can be obtained readily by seining, dipnetting, or angling, and examined while on shore or transferred to aquariums for long-term observation. State or provincial laws concerning the removal and keeping of native fishes may apply.

Making Identifications. For most identifications, it is best to begin with the family outlines on the endpapers and proceed to the plate(s) depicting those families. The plates are located in the middle of the guide. Locate the plate with fishes that look most like the one you wish to identify (see "How to Use the Plates" on the page preceding the plates), and read the short descriptions of distinguishing features on the legend page opposite the plate. Arrows on the plates pinpoint these features. When you believe that you have located the correct species, go to the longer text description (page number given on legend page) and compare the characteristics of the fish with those given in the species account and, if necessary, in generic and family accounts. At some point, you will need to refer to the distribution map (number given on legend page and at the end of the text description). "Similar species" descriptions near the end of each account identify the most likely alternatives to the species you originally selected and should always be consulted before you decide that you have made the correct identification.

If you know from past experience that the fish you are working with is one of a few similar species (e.g., a sand darter), you can start with the maps. Eliminating species outside your area can often speed identification. The maps are placed together rather than distributed throughout the text to expedite this maps-first procedure.

Fish Morphology. Fig. 1 illustrates various structures, counts, and measurements used to identify fishes. Most are self-explanatory. The following comments and the Glossary explain the others.

Fishes have single median fins (dorsal, caudal, and anal) and paired fins (pectoral and pelvic). The dorsal fin in primitive fishes is supported by flexible segmented rays. In advanced fishes, the front section of the fin contains only inflexible spiny rays ("spines") and may be contiguous with or separated from the soft rayed part; when this section is separated (or nearly separated) the fish is said to have 2 dorsal fins. Likewise, the anal fin may be spineless or have spines (usually only 1–3) preceding the rays.

Throughout the evolution of fishes, the pelvic fins have tended to move forward on the body, and their position is a quick way to judge whether a fish is primitive or advanced. If the pelvic fins are abdominal, the fish is primitive (e.g., a sturgeon) and you can expect to find it near the front of the guide. If the pelvic fins are thoracic (on the breast) or jugular (on the throat), you will find the fish (e.g., a sunfish) closer to the rear of the guide.

The mouth is described as *terminal* if it opens at the front end of the head with the upper and lower jaws being equally far forward, *upturned* if it opens above that point, and *subterminal* if it opens on the underside of the snout. You can see the gill rakers, on the gill arches, by lifting the gill cover (Fig. 3); gill raker counts are those for the entire 1st arch (including rudiments) unless upper or lower limb only is specified. The largest bone in the gill cover is the opercle (Fig. 1).

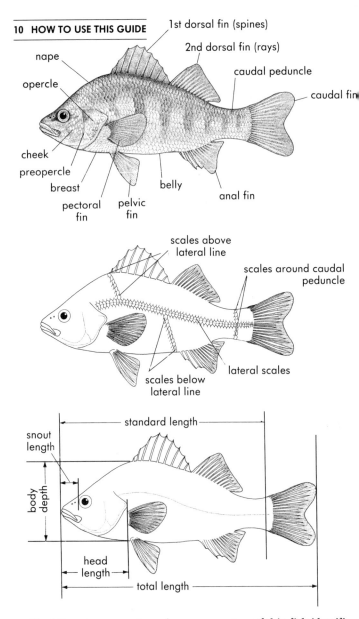

Fig. 1 Structures, counts, and measurements useful in fish identification. See Glossary for definitions of terms.

Measurements and counts used in this guide are shown in Fig. 1. Measurements of body parts (e.g., snout length) or fins occasionally are used to separate similar species. These measurements, which are always made in a straight line (not along a contour of the body), usually are compared to another measurement (e.g., total length). We may make a comparison such as snout length into total length by dividing one measurement into the other, or by physically "stepping off" one measurement into the other using dividers.

The lateral scale count (also known as lateral-line scale count) begins just behind the head and continues along the lateral line (or along the midside if lateral line is absent) to the origin of the caudal fin (which we locate by bending the caudal fin to either side). Scales on the caudal fin are not included in the lateral scale count even if they are pored. Scales above and below the lateral line begin at the origin of the dorsal or anal fin, respectively, and continue diagonally to the lateral line (but do not include the lateral-line scale). A transverse scale count is a continuation of the count of scales below the lateral line diagonally upward (including the lateral-line scale) to the dorsal fin. Scales around the caudal peduncle are those around the narrowest part. Predorsal scales are those along a straight line from the rear of the head along the midline to the dorsal fin origin.

Fig. 2 shows how dorsal and anal rays are counted. In pectoral and pelvic fins, all rays are counted. Fig. 3 shows how to count gill rakers. Branchiostegal rays are long slender bones supporting the branchiostegal membranes; all (short and long) rays are counted.

To examine the pharyngeal teeth, it is necessary to remove the 1st pharyngeal arch. To remove the arch, place the fish on its side and lift the gill cover (slit along bottom if necessary to loosen from body). The arch lies just to the rear of the gills. Insert a scalpel or strong forceps between the arch and the shoulder girdle, beginning at the upper angle of the gill opening and cutting down along the shoulder girdle. Carefully sever the fleshy tendons that hold the upper and lower ends of the arch in position. Lift out the arch and remove the attached flesh to expose the teeth.

Conservation. Pets, bait, and other fishes should never be released into a stream, lake, or pond other than the one from where they were originally obtained. If non-native fishes reproduce, their offspring may outcompete or feed on fishes or

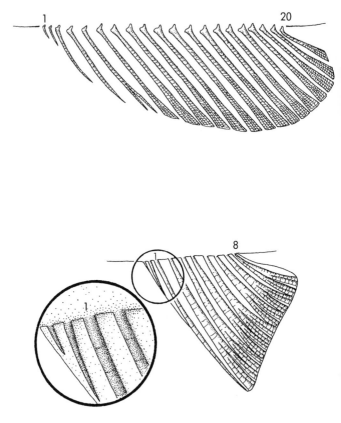

Fig. 2 How to count dorsal and anal rays. In catfishes, trouts, and other fishes in which the rudimentary rays at the beginning of the fin grade gradually in size into branched rays, count all rays. In other fishes, including minnows, suckers, and darters, there is a sharp break in size between rudimentary and long rays; count only the long rays. Count the last ray as one even if its branches are separated to the fin base; that is, if the branches of the ray look as if they will join just below the surface, they probably do and are counted as one ray.

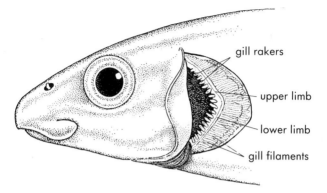

Fig. 3 How to count gill rakers. Count rakers on the 1st arch exposed as the gill cover is lifted. All rakers, including rudiments, are counted unless "upper limb" or "lower limb" of arch is specified.

other organisms and do tremendous harm to native populations.

No objective of this guide is more important than that of increasing humanity's appreciation of fishes and their environments. We often fail to give adequate consideration to the vast and varied forces over millions of years that have forged our present-day biodiversity. Each species on Earth is the product of millions of years of evolution and as such is fine-tuned to its environment. Only a few species (e.g., dog, starling, carp) can long survive the enormous changes in the environment that humankind currently is causing. Unless the human race succeeds in making major changes in its values and lifestyles, conservation efforts now underway can at best only delay the extinction of most of the species on Earth. To conserve the diversity of life, we must reduce our own population, reduce our consumption, and set aside large ecosystems as preserves. We will be able to accomplish those changes only through education and an awareness of the value of diversity. It is our greatest hope that this guide to the amazing diversity of North American fishes will contribute to that end.

1

JAWLESS FISHES: CLASS AGNATHA

■ **LAMPREYS: Family Petromyzontidae (19)**

Primitive, eel-like fishes that *lack jaws, scales, paired fins, and bone.* Lampreys occur in both fresh and salt water in North America, Europe and Asia. A total of 38 species is known, of which 19 are found in the fresh waters of North America north of Mexico.

Lampreys excavate pits in stream riffles (rarely in wave-swept areas of lakes) to be used as spawning sites by removing stones with their suction-disc mouths and by fanning out fine particles with vibrations of the body. Eggs hatch into blind larvae called ammocoetes (Fig. 4) which later metamorphose into adults. The larva may last 3–8 (or, rarely, more) years; it lives in mud- or sand-bottomed pools and feeds by filtering microorganisms from the water. Some species, the so-called brook or nonparasitic lampreys, do not feed as adults and spawn the spring following their metamorphosis. Other species are parasitic and feed by attaching to and rasping a hole in the side of a large fish. Adults of several parasitic species migrate to the ocean but must return to fresh water to spawn.

Adults have a cartilaginous skeleton, *1 median nostril, 7 pairs of porelike gill openings, 1 or 2 dorsal fins* continuous with the caudal fin, and a *circular mouth* with rasping teeth on the tongue and oral disc (Fig. 4). The kind and arrangement of teeth are the best characteristics to use in identifying lampreys. In the species descriptions, a "2" in a tooth formula (e.g., 2–2–2–2) refers to a bicuspid tooth; a "1" refers to a unicuspid tooth (Fig. 4). The count given is the usual condition. Some variation in dentition occurs within species, and tooth development may be incomplete in newly transformed individuals. Ammocoetes lack most of the characteristics used to identify adults, and they seldom can be identified to species with confidence; however, myomere counts are constant throughout life, and in some geographic areas the counts given below can be used to identify ammocoetes as well as adults.

SEA LAMPREY *Petromyzon marinus* **Pl. 1**
Identification: 2 dorsal fins. Expanded oral disc *as wide or wider* than head. *Large, sharp disc teeth;* 2 supraoral teeth; usually 2–2–2–2 lateral circumoral teeth, 8–10 posterior circumoral teeth, 7–8 infraoral teeth (Fig. 4). Usually 66–75 trunk myomeres. Unpigmented lateral

line organs. *Round or spatulate caudal fin* in adult. *Prominent black mottling* on blue-gray to olive-brown back, side, and fins; cream or yellow-white below. Breeding adult is olive to orange above and on side, white below; spawning male has prominent rope-like ridge on nape. Parasitic. To 47 in. (120 cm); landlocked individuals rarely exceed 25 in. (64 cm).

Range: Atlantic Coast from Labrador to Gulf of Mexico, FL; landlocked in Great Lakes and several NY lakes. Also along Atlantic Coast of Europe and Mediterranean Sea. Locally common. **Habitat:** Individuals with access to ocean are anadromous. Spawning adults in gravel riffles and runs of streams; feeding adults in ocean and lakes; ammocoetes most common in flowing areas of streams.

Remarks: Considered a serious pest in landlocked areas where Lake Trout and whitefish fisheries have been severely decimated.

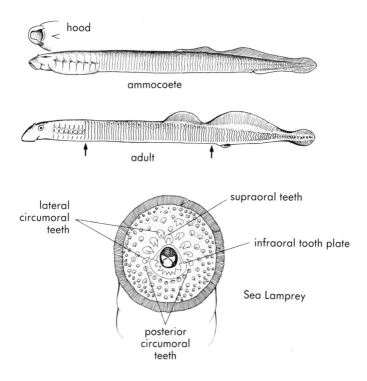

Fig. 4 Lamprey ammocoete and hood surrounding toothless mouth; adult (arrows indicate 1st and last trunk myomere); and Sea Lamprey disc

Similar species: (1) Silver (Fig. 5) and (2) Chestnut Lampreys (Pl. 1; Fig. 5) have *1* slightly notched *dorsal fin*, usually fewer than 56 trunk myomeres, *no* prominent black mottling on body. **Map 1**

SILVER LAMPREY *Ichthyomyzon unicuspis*   Not shown

Identification: 1 slightly notched dorsal fin. Expanded oral disc *as wide or wider* than head. *Large, sharp disc teeth;* usually 2 supraoral teeth, *1–1–1 or 1–1–1–1 lateral circumoral teeth* (Fig. 5). Usually 49–52 trunk myomeres. Black lateral line organs. Gray-brown to yellow-tan above; light yellow or tan below; yellow fins. Parasitic. To 15½ in. (39 cm).

Range: St. Lawrence–Great Lakes basin from QU to sw. ON and south through upper Mississippi and Ohio R. basins to cen. TN. Records from Nelson R., MB, Missouri R., NE, and Mississippi R., MS. Uncommon. **Habitat:** Feeding adults usually found attached to other fishes in large rivers, lakes, and impoundments; as many as 61 Silver Lampreys have been found on one Lake Sturgeon. Adults migrate upriver to spawn in gravel riffles and runs; ammocoetes inhabit sandy or muddy pools and backwaters.

Similar species: See Fig. 5. (1) Chestnut (Pl. 1) and (2) Ohio Lampreys have 2–2–2–2 or 2–2–2–2–2 lateral circumoral teeth, usually more than 51 trunk myomeres. (3) Northern Brook Lamprey has *blunt* disc teeth, pale line along back, no black lateral line organs. **Map 2**

NORTHERN BROOK LAMPREY *Ichthyomyzon fossor*   Not shown

Identification: 1 slightly notched dorsal fin. Expanded oral disc *narrower* than head. Small, *blunt disc teeth;* usually 2 supraoral teeth, *1–1 or 1–1–1 lateral circumoral teeth* (Fig. 5). Usually 50–52 trunk myomeres. Lateral line organs *not* black. Dark gray or brown above; often a *pale line* along back; pale gray, yellow, or silver-white below; gray, yellow, or tan fins. Nonparasitic. To 6¾ in. (17 cm).

Range: St. Lawrence R., QU, west through Great Lakes and n. Mississippi R. basins to Red R. (Hudson Bay basin), s. MB; localized in Ohio R. basin of nw. PA, w. WV, e. KY, n. and s.-cen. OH, and n. IN; Missouri R. basin, Ozark Uplands, MO. Locally common. **Habitat:** Clean, clear gravel riffles and runs of small rivers; ammocoetes occupy quiet water over sand, silt, and debris.

Similar species: (1) Silver Lamprey (Fig. 5) has *large, sharp disc teeth, black* lateral line organs, *no* pale line on back. (2) Other nonparasitic lampreys in this genus have 2–2–2 or 2–2–2–2 lateral circumoral teeth (Fig. 5), *black* lateral line organs, *no* pale line on back. **Map 3**

CHESTNUT LAMPREY *Ichthyomyzon castaneus*   Pl. 1

Identification: 1 slightly notched dorsal fin. Expanded oral disc *as wide as or wider* than head. Large, sharp disc teeth; usually 2–3 supraoral teeth, *2–2–2–2 or 2–2–2–2–2 lateral circumoral teeth* (Fig. 5). Usually *51–56 trunk myomeres. Yellow or tan* above; white to light olive-yellow below; olive-yellow fins. Parasitic. To 15 in. (38 cm).

Range: Great Lakes (primarily Lake Michigan) and Mississippi R. basins from MI, WI, and MN south to LA, and from e. TN west to e. KS and OK; Red R. (Hudson Bay basin), MB, MN, and SD; Gulf Coast drainages from Mobile Bay, GA and AL, to Sabine Lake, TX. Locally common. **Habitat:** Lakes and streams. Adults ascend streams to spawn, ammocoetes occupy sand- and silt-bottomed pools and backwaters.

Similar species: See Fig. 5. (1) Silver Lamprey has 1–1–1–1 lateral circumoral teeth; usually 49–52 trunk myomeres. (2) Ohio Lamprey has usually *56–62 trunk myomeres;* is gray above and on fins. (3) Southern Brook Lamprey has blunt disc teeth, expanded oral disc *narrower* than head, nonfunctional digestive tract in adult; reaches only 6½ in. (17 cm). **Map 4**

SOUTHERN BROOK LAMPREY *Ichthyomyzon gagei*   Not shown

Identification: 1 slightly notched dorsal fin. Expanded oral disc *narrower* than head. *Blunt,* poorly developed disc teeth; usually 2–3 supraoral teeth, *2–2–2 or 2–2–2–2 lateral circumoral teeth* (Fig. 5). Usually *52-56 trunk myomeres.* Black lateral line organs. Gray or tan above, white to cream below; cream or yellow fins. Nonparasitic. To 6½ in. (17 cm).

Range: Mississippi R. basin of s. MO, e. OK, AR, and LA; Tennessee R. drainage, w. KY and n. AL; Gulf Coast drainages from Ochlockonee R., FL, to Galveston Bay, TX. Disjunct population in St. Croix R. drainage, n. WI and n. MN. Locally common, except rare in Tennessee and St. Croix drainages. **Habitat:** Gravel and sand riffles and runs of creeks and small rivers; ammocoetes in flowing water near sand bars and debris.

Similar species: (1) Chestnut Lamprey (Pl. 1; Fig. 5) has *sharp,* well-developed *disc teeth,* expanded oral disc *wider* than head, functional digestive tract in adult; reaches 15 in. (38 cm). (2) Mountain Brook Lamprey (Fig. 5) has usually *57–60 trunk myomeres,* larger teeth; *lacks* black lateral line organs below. **Map 5**

OHIO LAMPREY *Ichthyomyzon bdellium*   Not shown

Identification: 1 slightly notched dorsal fin. Expanded oral disc as *wide or wider than head.* Sharp, well-developed disc teeth; usually 2–3 supraoral teeth, *2–2–2–2 or 2–2–2–2–2 lateral circumoral teeth* (Fig. 5). Usually *56–62 trunk myomeres.* Black lateral line organs. Blue to lead gray above; white to slightly mottled below; gray fins. Parasitic. To 12 in. (30 cm).

Range: Ohio R. basin from extreme sw. NY west to n. IN and e. IL, and south to n. AL. Uncommon. **Habitat:** Large rivers; sometimes creeks and small rivers. Ammocoetes live near debris in muddy pools and backwaters.

Similar species: (1) Chestnut Lamprey (Pl. 1; Fig. 5) has usually *51–56* trunk myomeres; is yellow or tan in life. (2) Mountain Brook Lamprey (Fig. 5) has smaller teeth, expanded oral disc *narrower* than head, reaches only 7¾ in. (20 cm); *lacks* functional digestive tract as adult. **Map 6**

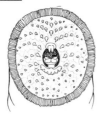

Silver

Northern Brook

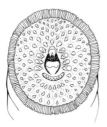

Chestnut

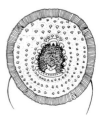

Southern Brook

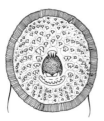

Ohio

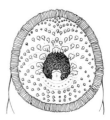

Mountain Brook

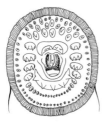

Pacific

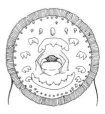

Miller Lake

Fig. 5 Lamprey oral discs

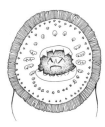

Pit-Klamath Brook

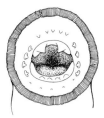

Kern Brook

Arctic

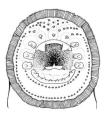

American Brook

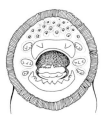

River

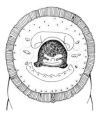

Western Brook

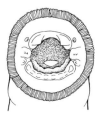

Pacific Brook

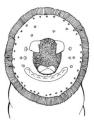

Least Brook

MOUNTAIN BROOK LAMPREY *Ichthyomyzon greeleyi* **Not shown**
  Identification: 1 slightly notched dorsal fin. Expanded oral disc *narrower* than head. Moderately well-developed disc teeth; usually 2–3 supraoral teeth, *2–2–2 to 2–2–2–2 lateral circumoral teeth* (Fig. 5). Usually *57–60 trunk myomeres.* Black lateral line organs above, *not* below. Gray-brown to olive-tan above, olive to tan with small dark flecks on side, white or cream below; cream or yellow fins. Nonparasitic. To 7¾ in. (20 cm).
  Range: Ohio R. basin from sw. NY to n. AL. Locally common. **Habitat:** Gravel riffles and sandy runs of clean, clear high-gradient streams; ammocetes in sand, mud, and debris in pools and backwaters.
  Similar species: See Fig. 5. (1) Ohio and (2) Chestnut Lampreys (Pl. 1) have *large, sharp disc teeth*, lateral line organs black *below*, reach 11 in. (28 cm) or more, have functional digestive tract in adult. (3) Southern Brook Lamprey has usually *52–56 trunk myomeres*, smaller disc teeth, lateral line organs black above and *below*. **Map 5**

PACIFIC LAMPREY *Lampetra tridentata* **Not shown**
  Identification: 2 dorsal fins. Expanded oral disc *as wide or wider* than head. *Medium-sized eye.* Large, sharp disc teeth; 3 supraoral teeth; usually 2–3–3–2 lateral circumoral teeth; usually 17–20 posterior circumoral teeth, 0–15 bicuspid; usually 5–6 infraoral teeth (Fig. 5). Usually 64–71 trunk myomeres. Short disc averages 6.7% of total length. Unpigmented lateral line organs. Dark blue or brown above, *light or silver below*, dusky dorsal and caudal fins. Parasitic; anadromous. To 30 in. (76 cm). Dwarf, nonfeeding populations to 10¾ in. (27 cm).
  Range: Pacific Coast from AK south to Santa Ana R., CA; also off Baja California and along Pacific Coast of Asia. Common. **Habitat:** Spawning adults in gravel riffles and runs of clear coastal streams; feeding adults usually in ocean; ammocoetes in silt, mud, and sand of shallow eddies and backwaters of streams.
  Remarks: Dwarf, nonanadromous, and nonparasitic populations landlocked in OR and n. CA require further taxonomic study. This is the only species of lamprey in which some individuals (from WA) are known to spawn more than once. The Miller Lake Lamprey, *Lampetra minima*, formerly endemic to Miller Lake, Klamath Co., OR (Map 8), had 13–17 posterior circumoral teeth (Fig. 5), usually 60–65 trunk myomeres, and reached 5 in. (13 cm). It was purposely exterminated from Miller Lake because of its predation on introduced trout.
  Similar species: See (1) Lake and (2) Klamath River Lampreys. **Map 7**

LAKE LAMPREY *Lampetra macrostoma* **Not shown**
  Identification: Nearly identical to Pacific Lamprey but has *larger eye*; expanded oral disc *much wider* than head; *uniformly dark*, almost black, body and fins. To 10 in. (25 cm).
  Range: Mesachie Lake and Lake Cowichan on s. Vancouver Island,

BC. Common. **Habitat:** Spawns on shallow gravel bars in freshwater lakes or the mouths of creeks flowing into lakes; ammocoetes in silt, mud, or sand in quiet water.
Similar species: See Pacific Lamprey (Fig. 5). **Map 8**

KLAMATH RIVER LAMPREY *Lampetra similis* **Not shown**
Identification: Similar to Pacific Lamprey but has usually *60-63 trunk myomeres*, longer disc averaging 9.2% of total length, smaller eye. Parasitic. To 10½ in. (27 cm).
Range: Klamath R. drainage and Klamath Lake, s. OR and n. CA. Rare. **Habitat:** Large rivers, impoundments, and lakes.
Similar species: (1) See Pacific Lamprey (Fig. 5). (2) Miller Lake Lamprey (Fig. 5) has shorter disc averaging 6.3% of total length; reaches only 5 in. (13 cm). **Map 8**

PIT-KLAMATH BROOK LAMPREY *Lampetra lethophaga* **Not shown**
Identification: 2 dorsal fins. Expanded oral disc *narrower* than head. Disc teeth reduced in size and number; 2 or 3 supraoral teeth; usually *1–2–2–1 or 2–3–3–2 lateral circumoral teeth*; 9–15 posterior circumoral teeth (10–15 usually unicuspid); usually 5 infraoral teeth (Fig. 5). Usually *60–70 trunk myomeres*. Unpigmented lateral line organs. Slate gray above; brass or silver below; wax yellow fins. Nonparasitic. To 8¾ in. (22 cm).
Range: Klamath R., s.-cen. OR, and Pit R., ne. CA. **Habitat:** Riffles and runs of clear streams; ammocoetes near weed beds and sand bars. Common.
Similar species: See Fig. 5. (1) Kern Brook Lamprey has usually *52–56 trunk myomeres*, usually *1–1–1–1 lateral circumoral teeth*. (2) Pacific Lamprey has large, sharp disc teeth, functional digestive tract in adult; reaches 30 in. (76 cm). **Map 9**

KERN BROOK LAMPREY *Lampetra hubbsi* **Not shown**
Identification: 2 dorsal fins. Expanded oral disc *narrower* than head. Usually blunt disc teeth; 2 supraoral teeth; usually *1-1-1-1 lateral circumoral teeth*; 9-12 unicuspid posterior circumoral teeth; 5 infraoral teeth (Fig. 5). Usually *52-56 trunk myomeres*. Unpigmented lateral line organs. Gray to olive-brown above; white below; black specks on dorsal and caudal fins. Nonparasitic. To 5½ in. (14 cm).
Range: Known only from Friant-Kern Canal, Kern Co., CA, and Merced R., Merced Co., CA. Rare; Merced R. is now about 85% concrete-lined. **Habitat:** Unknown; probably similar to other western nonparasitic lampreys.
Similar species: See Fig. 5. (1) Pit-Klamath Brook Lamprey has usually *60–70 trunk myomeres*; *1–2–2–1 or 2–3–3–2 lateral circumoral teeth*. (2) Pacific Lamprey has large, sharp disc teeth, usually *64-71 trunk myomeres*, functional digestive tract in adult; reaches 30 in. (76 cm). **Map 10**

ARCTIC LAMPREY *Lampetra japonica* **Not shown**
Identification: 2 dorsal fins. Expanded oral disc *as wide or wider* than

head. Large, sharp, disc teeth; 2 supraoral teeth; usually *2–2–2 lateral circumoral teeth;* 15–24 posterior circumoral teeth; 5–10 infraoral teeth (Fig. 5). Usually 67–72 trunk myomeres. Unpigmented lateral line organs. Dark brown to blue-black above, yellow to light brown below; light tan to gray dorsal fins; dark blotch on tail. Parasitic. To 24½ in. (62 cm).

Range: Arctic and Pacific drainages of NT, YU, and AK, from Artillery Lake, Great Slave Lake, Mackenzie R., and Anderson R. west to Pacific Coast. Also in n. Europe and Asia. Common. **Habitat:** Spawning adults in gravel riffles and runs of clear streams; feeding adults usually in ocean or lakes; ammocoetes in muddy margins and backwaters of rivers and lakes.

Similar species: (1) American Brook Lamprey (Pl. 1; Fig. 5) has usually blunt disc teeth, nonfunctional digestive tract in adult; reaches only 11¾ in. (30 cm). (2) Pacific Lamprey (Fig. 5) has 3 supraoral teeth, usually 2–3–3–2 lateral circumoral teeth. **Map 11**

AMERICAN BROOK LAMPREY *Lampetra appendix* **Pl. 1**

Identification: 2 dorsal fins. Expanded oral disc *narrower* than head. Usually *blunt disc teeth;* 2 supraoral teeth; usually 2–2–2 lateral circumoral teeth; usually *20–24 posterior circumoral teeth;* usually 7–8 infraoral teeth (Fig. 5). Usually *67-73 trunk myomeres.* Unpigmented lateral line organs. Lead gray to slate blue above, white or silver-white below; yellow fins; dark gray to black blotch on tail. Breeding adult is olive green or pink-purple to shiny black above, black stripe at base of dorsal fins. Nonparasitic. To 13¾ in. (35 cm).

Range: Atlantic, Great Lakes, and Mississippi R. basins from St. Lawrence R., QU, west to MN, and south to Roanoke R. system, VA, Tennessee R. system, n. AL, and St. Francis and White R. systems, MO and AR; Martin R. (Arctic basin), NT to Ugashik and Chatanika R. (Pacific basin), AK. Uncommon. **Habitat:** Adults in gravel/sand riffles and runs of creeks and small to medium rivers with strong flow and usually clear water. Ammocoetes in sandy or silty pools.

Remarks: 2 subspecies: *L. a. appendix,* on Atlantic Slope, usually reaches only 5¾ in. (15 cm) and has 17–21 posterior circumoral teeth; *L. a. wilderi,* throughout St. Lawrence-Great Lakes and Mississippi basins, and in Roanoke R., VA, reaches 8½ in. (22 cm) and has 19–26 posterior circumoral teeth. *L. a. alaskense,* in NT and AK, may be a third North American subspecies.

Similar species: See Fig. 5. (1) Arctic Lamprey has large, *sharp* disc teeth, functional digestive tract in adult; reaches 24½ in. (63 cm). (2) Least Brook Lamprey has extremely degenerate disc teeth; *usually 52–59 trunk myomeres;* usually *lacks* posterior circumoral teeth. (3) River Lamprey *lacks* posterior circumoral teeth; has usually 2–3–2 lateral circumoral teeth. **Map 12**

RIVER LAMPREY *Lampetra ayresi* **Not shown**

Identification: 2 dorsal fins. Expanded oral disc *as wide or wider* than head. Large, *sharp disc teeth;* 2 widely separated supraoral teeth; usually *2–3–2 lateral circumoral teeth; no* posterior circumoral teeth; 7–10 infraoral teeth (Fig. 5). Usually *65–70 trunk myomeres.* Unpigmented lateral line organs. Yellow to silver-gray above, white below; yellow fins; dark gray blotch on tail. Parasitic. To 12¼ in. (31 cm).

Range: Pacific Slope from Tee Harbor, AK, south to Sacramento-San Joaquin drainage, CA. Uncommon. **Habitat:** Spawning adults in clear gravel riffles of streams; feeding adults in estuaries and ocean. Ammocoetes in sandy and muddy pools of spawning streams.

Similar species: (1) Pacific Brook Lamprey (Fig. 5) has small *blunt disc teeth;* usually *53–58 trunk myomeres,* nonfunctional digestive tract in adult. (2) Western Brook Lamprey (Fig. 5) has small, *blunt disc teeth,* usually *58–67 trunk myomeres,* nonfunctional digestive tract in adults.   **Map 10**

WESTERN BROOK LAMPREY *Lampetra richardsoni*   **Not shown**
Identification: 2 dorsal fins. Expanded oral disc *narrower* than head. Small, blunt disc teeth; 2 widely separated supraoral teeth; usually *1–2–1* or *2–3–2 lateral circumoral teeth; no* posterior circumoral teeth; 7–10 infraoral teeth (Fig. 5). Usually *58–67 trunk myomeres.* Unpigmented lateral line organs. Gray above; white below; gray fins; dark spot on tail. Nonparasitic. To 6 in. (15 cm).

Range: Pacific Slope from McDonald Lake, se. AK, to Umpqua R. drainage, OR. Uncommon. **Habitat:** Gravel riffles and runs of clear, cool streams; ammocoetes in muddy and sandy backwaters and pools of spawning streams.

Similar species: (1) See Pacific Brook Lamprey (Fig. 5). (2) River Lamprey (Fig. 5) has usually *65–70 trunk myomeres;* large, *sharp* disc teeth, functional digestive tract in adult, expanded oral disc *as wide or wider* than head; reaches 12¼ in. (31 cm).   **Map 9**

PACIFIC BROOK LAMPREY *Lampetra pacifica*   **Not shown**
Identification: Similar to Western Brook Lamprey but has usually *53–58 trunk myomeres,* 6–9 infraoral teeth (Fig. 5). Gray-brown above; white below; salt-and-pepper caudal fin; dark gray spots in oral cavity. Nonparasitic. To 6¾ in. (17 cm).

Range: Willamette R. (Columbia R. drainage), OR; Sacramento–San Joaquin R. drainage, CA. Uncommon. **Habitat:** Clear, gravel riffles and runs; ammocoetes in silt-bottomed pools and backwaters.

Similar species: (1) See Western Brook Lamprey (Fig. 5). (2) River Lamprey (Fig. 5) has usually 65–70 trunk myomeres; *sharp,* well-developed disc teeth; expanded oral disc *wider* than head; functional digestive tract in adult; reaches 12¼ in. (31 cm).   **Map 8**

LEAST BROOK LAMPREY *Lampetra aepyptera*   **Not shown**
Identification: 2 dorsal fins. Expanded oral disc *narrower* than head. *Blunt, extremely degenerate disc teeth;* 2 widely separated supraoral teeth; usually *1–2–1* or *1–1–1* lateral circumoral teeth; usually no posterior circumoral teeth — if present usually 4–9 (range 1–22) and unicuspid; usually 7–12 infraoral teeth (Fig. 5). Usually *52-59 trunk myomeres.* Unpigmented lateral line organs. Light tan to silver-gray

above; yellow or white below; yellow or gray fins. Breeding adult has mottled gray-brown back, black stripe on side of body through eye and at base of 1st dorsal fin; dusky black edges on dorsal fins, gold stripe from caudal fin through middle of dorsal fins; dark-tipped caudal fin. Nonparasitic. To 7 in. (18 cm); on Atlantic Slope to only 4¾ in. (12 cm).

Range: Atlantic Slope from Susquehanna R. drainage, se. PA to Neuse R. drainage, NC; Mississippi R. basin from w. PA to s.-cen. MO and n. AR, south to n. AL; Mobile Bay and Pascagoula R. drainages, GA, AL, and MS. Common. **Habitat:** Clean, clear gravel riffles and runs of creeks and small rivers; ammocoetes in spring-fed wetlands and quiet pools and backwaters of small, sand- or mud-bottomed streams.

Remarks: The Coastal Plain population of w. KY and TN exhibits characteristics of neoteny. Spawning adult from Atlantic Slope lacks black stripe through eye, gold stripe on dorsal fin, and dark-tipped caudal fin.

Similar species: No other eastern North American *Lampetra* species has so few, minute, and degenerate disc teeth. **Map 13**

2

BONY FISHES: CLASS OSTEICHTHYES

All fishes except jawless ones and jawed cartilaginous ones (e.g., sharks) are bony fishes. They have jaws and, except in some with reduced ossification, a bony skeleton. There is a single gill opening on each side. Bony fishes occur in virtually all waters of the world. There are about 21,000 species, of which about 8,000 (40%) occur in fresh water.

STURGEONS: Family Acipenseridae (7)

Sturgeons are large ancient fishes with a cartilaginous skeleton, *heterocercal tail*, and spiral valve. A total of 23 species survive today. All of them enter fresh water, at least to spawn, but some species spend most of their lives in the ocean. The greatest diversity occurs in Europe, with fewer species in Asia and North America.

Sturgeons are easily recognized by the *shovel-shaped snout, large fleshy barbels, ventrally located mouth,* and *large bony scutes* (or plates) on the head and along the back and side. Sturgeons are large fishes (up to 3–30 ft.) that are commercially important, both for their flesh and for their ripe eggs (caviar). Unfortunately, populations of sturgeons have been depleted badly in the United States as a result of overharvesting and the detrimental effects of dams and pollution.

ACIPENSER

Genus characteristics: Cone-shaped snout; *spiracle*; upper lobe of caudal fin *lacks* long filament; fairly short caudal peduncle, round in cross section and only partly covered by scutes; smooth barbels; 2 fleshy lobes on lower lip.

HORTNOSE STURGEON *Acipenser brevirostrum*   **Pl. 1**
Identification: *Short snout,* bluntly V-shaped, not upturned at tip. *Anal fin origin beneath dorsal fin origin.* Caudal peduncle relatively short, tip of anal fin reaching caudal fin origin. 1 row of preanal scutes; 2 scutes between dorsal fin and caudal fulcrum; 1 large scute between anal fin and caudal fulcrum. Dark brown to black above and

on upper side, light brown to yellow on lower side; scutes on back and side *paler* than skin; white below; gray or brown fins; white edges on paired fins. Black viscera. Young (under 24 in.) have black or dusky blotches on snout and body. 19–22 anal rays; 22–29 gill rakers; 8–13 scutes on back; 22–33 scutes along side. To 43 in. (109 cm).

Range: Atlantic Coast from St. John R., NB, to St. Johns R., FL. Uncommon; protected as an *endangered species.* **Habitat:** River mouths, lakes, estuaries, and bays; occasionally enters open sea.

Similar species: See Pl. 1. (1) See Lake Sturgeon. (2) Green Sturgeon is green; has 1 scute between dorsal fin and caudal fulcrum, 22–28 anal rays, 18–20 gill rakers; white viscera. (3) Atlantic Sturgeon has *long,* sharply V-shaped *snout;* 2 rows of preanal scutes; white viscera.

Map 14

LAKE STURGEON *Acipenser fulvescens* **Pl. 1**

Identification: Similar to Shortnose Sturgeon (above) but *anal fin origin is behind dorsal fin origin;* caudal peduncle longer, tip of anal fin reaching only to anterior edge of fulcral caudal scute; olive-brown to gray above and on side; scutes on back and along side *same color as skin;* white below; dark gray or brown fins. 25–30 anal rays; 25–40, usually 32–35, gill rakers; 9–17 scutes on back; 29–42 scutes along side. To 9 ft. (274 cm).

Range: St. Lawrence–Great Lakes, Hudson Bay, and Mississippi R. basins from QU to AB and south to AL and LA; Coosa R. system (Mobile Bay drainage), AL. Rare and nearing extinction in Coosa, Missouri, Ohio, and middle Mississippi drainages; more common at northern latitudes. **Habitat:** Bottom of lakes and large rivers, usually those 16–30 ft. (5–9 m) in depth, over mud, sand, and gravel. Occasionally enters brackish water in Hudson Bay and Gulf of St. Lawrence.

Similar species: (1) See Shortnose Sturgeon (Pl. 1). (2) Green Sturgeon (Pl. 1) is *green;* has scutes along side *paler* than skin, 18–20 gill rakers, 23–30 scutes along side, white viscera.

Map 14

GREEN STURGEON *Acipenser medirostris* **Pl. 1**

Identification: Moderately blunt snout in adults; sharper and more shovellike in young; *barbels usually closer to mouth than to snout tip.* 1 row of preanal scutes. 1 large scute between anal fin and caudal fulcrum. *Olive to dark green above and on side;* white-green below; gray or green fins; scutes along side *paler* than skin. Some northern fish have stripes on belly and lower side. White viscera. 22–28 anal rays; 18–20 gill rakers; 9–11 scutes on back; 23–30 scutes along side. To 7 ft. (213 cm).

Range: Pacific Coast from Aleutian Islands to cen. CA. Also in China, n. Japan, Korea, and Soviet Union north to Amur R. **Habitat:** Estuaries, lower reaches of large rivers, and salt or brackish water off river mouths. Ascends far up Trinity and Klamath rivers, CA.

Similar species: See Pl. 1. (1) Shortnose Sturgeon is *brown or black;* has 2 scutes between dorsal fin and caudal fulcrum, 19–22 anal rays, 22–29 gill rakers, black viscera. (2) Lake Sturgeon is *olive or gray;* has

2 scutes between dorsal fin and caudal fulcrum, 25–40 gill rakers, 25–30 anal rays, black viscera. (3) White Sturgeon (below) is *gray;* has barbels *closer to snout tip than to mouth,* no scutes behind dorsal and anal fins, 2 rows of preanal scutes, 38–48 scutes along side, black viscera. **Map 15**

WHITE STURGEON *Acipenser transmontanus* **Pl. 1**
Identification: Moderately blunt snout in adult, sharper in young; *barbels closer to snout tip than to mouth. No obvious scutes behind dorsal and anal fins* (other than fulcra). 2 rows (6–9 scutes) of preanal scutes. Gray, pale olive, or gray-brown above and on upper side, white to pale gray on lower side; all scutes light in color; white below; gray fins. Black viscera. 28–30 anal rays; 34–36 gill rakers; 11–14 scutes on back; 38–48 scutes along side. To 20 ft. (6.1 m).
Range: Pacific Coast from Alaska Bay, AK, to cen. CA. Introduced into lower Colorado R., AZ. Common. **Habitat:** Estuaries of large rivers; moves far inland to spawn. Landlocked in Columbia R. drainage, MT, and perhaps Lake Shasta, CA.
Remarks: This is the largest freshwater fish in North America.
Similar species: All other *Acipenser* species (Pl. 1) have obvious scutes behind the dorsal or anal fins. **Map 16**

ATLANTIC STURGEON *Acipenser oxyrhynchus* **Pl. 1**
Identification: *Long, sharply V-shaped snout.* Snout tip upturned in young. 2 rows of preanal scutes; *4 small scutes, usually as 2 pairs, between anal fin and caudal fulcrum* (1st pair may overlap anal fin base, 2nd pair may look like 1 scute); 6–9 scutes, mostly in pairs, behind dorsal fin. Blue-black above, paler on side; white below; gray to blue-black fins; white leading edge on paired fins, lower lobe of caudal fin, anal fin. White spines on scutes on back and side contrast with dark skin. White viscera. 26–28 anal rays; 15–27 gill rakers; 7–16 scutes on back; 24–35 scutes along side. To 14 ft. (4.3 m).
Range: Atlantic Coast from Hamilton R., Labrador (NF), to ne. FL; Gulf of Mexico from Tampa Bay, FL, to Lake Pontchartrain, LA. Uncommon; greatly depleted throughout most of range. **Habitat:** Shallow waters of continental shelf; ascends coastal rivers to spawn.
Remarks: 2 subspecies. *A. o. oxyrhynchus,* along Atlantic Coast, has a relatively short head, pectoral fin, and spleen; scutes on back longer than wide. *A. o. desotoi,* along Gulf Coast, has a longer head, pectoral fin, and spleen; scutes on back much shorter than wide.
Similar species: See Pl. 1. (1) Shortnose Sturgeon has *shorter snout, 1 large scute* between anal and caudal fins, 2 scutes between dorsal fin and caudal fulcrum, 1 row of preanal scutes. (2) White Sturgeon *lacks* obvious scutes between anal and caudal fins, and between dorsal and caudal fins. (3) Green Sturgeon is green; has *1 large scute* between anal and caudal fins, 1 row of preanal scutes. **Map 17**

SHOVELNOSE STURGEON *Scaphirhynchus platorynchus* **Pl. 1**
Identification: *Flat, shovel-shaped snout.* 4 fleshy lobes on lower lip. 4 fringed barbels. Long, slender caudal peduncle flat in cross section and covered with bony scutes. Long filament on upper lobe of caudal

fin (sometimes broken off). No spiracle. Scalelike scutes on belly (except in smallest young). Bases of outer barbels *in line with, or ahead of*, inner barbels (Fig. 6). Light brown or buff above and on side, white below; fins similar in color to surrounding body parts. 30–36 dorsal rays, 18–23 anal rays. To 43 in. (108 cm).

Range: Mississippi R. basin from w. PA to MT and south to LA; Mobile Bay drainage, AL and MS; upper Rio Grande, NM. Common in Mississippi basin, rare in Mobile Bay drainage, extirpated in Rio Grande. **Habitat:** Bottom of main channels and embayments of large, turbid rivers; frequently in flowing water over sand mixed with gravel and mud.

Similar species: See Pallid Sturgeon (Pl. 1). **Map 18**

PALLID STURGEON *Scaphirhynchus albus* **Pl. 1**

Identification: Similar to Shovelnose Sturgeon (above) but has *no scalelike scutes* on belly, bases of outer barbels usually *behind* bases of inner barbels (Fig. 6), larger head, wider mouth, shorter inner barbels, longer and sharper snout, smaller eye; usually lighter in color, gray-white above and on side; 37–43 dorsal rays, 24–28 anal rays. To 73 in. (185 cm).

Range: Nearly restricted to main channels of Missouri R. and lower Mississippi R. from MT to LA. Uncommon. **Habitat:** Large, deep, turbid river channels; usually in strong current over firm sand or gravel.

Similar species: See Shovelnose Sturgeon (Pl. 1). **Map 17**

Pallid   Shovelnose

Fig. 6 Pallid and Shovelnose Sturgeons — underside of head

■ PADDLEFISHES: Family Polyodontidae (1)

The paddlefishes are a family composed of two strange and ancient species of fishes having a skeleton of cartilage, *heterocercal tail, spiral valve* and *long paddle-shaped snout.* One species, *Polyodon spathula,* inhabits the Mississippi and adjacent Gulf Coast drainages in North America. The other, *Psephurus gladius,* is China's largest freshwater fish (to 21 ft.) and inhabits the Yangtze River system of eastern China. The paddlefish's huge snout is covered with taste buds that may aid the fish in locating concentrations of plankton and other food organisms.

PADDLEFISH *Polyodon spathula*   **Pl. 2**

Identification: Large, *sharklike* fish; *long snout shaped like a canoe paddle;* snout length about ⅓ body length. Huge mouth; toothless jaws. Unscaled except for tiny scales on caudal peduncle. Large, *fleshy, pointed flap* on rear edge of gill cover. Tiny eye. Gray to blue-gray (nearly black), often mottled, above and on upper side; white below. Many long, slender gill rakers. To 87 in. (221 cm).

Range: Mississippi R. basin from sw. NY to cen. MT and south to LA; Gulf Slope drainages from Mobile Bay, AL, to Galveston Bay, TX. Formerly Lake Erie drainage, OH (and possibly lakes Huron and Michigan). Extirpated from Great Lakes basin, Galveston Bay and Sabine R. drainages, TX, and Calcasieu drainage, LA. Common. **Habitat:** Slow-flowing water of large rivers; usually in water deeper than 4 ft. (130 cm).

Similar species: No other North American fish remotely resembles the Paddlefish.   **Map 19**

■ GARS: Family Lepisosteidae (5)

Gars are a group of 7 North American species of primitive fishes easily recognized by their *long sharply-toothed jaws, diamond-shaped and non-overlapping ganoid scales,* and dorsal and anal fins placed *far back* on the body. The primitiveness of gars is demonstrated by the retention in living species of a spiral valve, a lunglike gas bladder used to assist the gills in breathing, ganoid scales, and an abbreviated (rounded externally) heterocercal tail. Small gars (less than 10 in.) have a rayless fleshy filament extending above the caudal fin. Gars once occurred in Africa, India, and Europe, as well as North America.

In addition to the five species found north of the Rio Grande are the Tropical Gar, *Atractosteus tropicus,* found from s. Mexico to Costa Rica, and the Cuban Gar, *A. tristoechus,* native to w. Cuba and the Isle of Pines.

ALLIGATOR GAR *Atractosteus spatula*   **Pl. 2**

Identification: *Giant of the gars* — to nearly 10 ft. (3 m). *Short, broad snout;* upper jaw shorter than rest of head. *2 rows of teeth* on upper jaw. Young has light stripe along back from tip of snout to upper base of caudal fin. Dark olive-brown (sometimes black) above and on side, occasionally spotted; white to yellow below; dark brown fins, few dark spots on median fins. 58–62 lateral scales; 48–54 predorsal scales; 59–66 gill rakers.

Range: Mississippi R. basin from sw. OH and s. IL south to Gulf of Mexico; Gulf Coastal Plain from Enconfina R., FL, to Veracruz, Mexico. Uncommon, except locally in swamps and bayous in extreme southern U.S. **Habitat:** Sluggish pools and backwaters of large rivers, swamps, bayous, and lakes. Rarely in brackish and marine water.

Similar species: Shortnose Gar (Pl. 2) has upper jaw *longer than rest of head, 1 row* of teeth on upper jaw, 33 or fewer gill rakers.   **Map 20**

SHORTNOSE GAR *Lepisosteus platostomus*   Pl. 2

Identification: *Short* (relative to those of other gars), *broad snout;* upper jaw longer than rest of head. 1 row of teeth on upper jaw. Olive or brown above and on side; white below; black spots on median fins; paired fins usually lack spots (some spots on head and paired fins of individuals from clear water). Young has fairly broad dark brown stripes along back and side. 59–65 lateral scales; 50–60 predorsal scales; 16–25 gill rakers. To 33 in. (83 cm).

Range: Mississippi R. basin from s.-cen. OH, n. IN, and WI to MT and south to n. AL and LA; Lake Michigan drainage, WI; Calcasieu and Mermentau rivers on LA Gulf Coast. Common. **Habitat:** Quiet pools and backwaters of creeks and small to large rivers, swamps, and lakes. Often found near vegetation and submerged logs.

Similar species: (1) Florida and (2) Spotted Gars (both Pl. 2) have many dark spots on body, head, and *all* fins, 53–59 lateral scales.   **Map 21**

LONGNOSE GAR *Lepisosteus osseus*   Pl. 2

Identification: *Long, narrow snout,* more than twice as long as rest of head. 1 row of teeth on upper jaw. Olive-brown above and on side; white below; dark spots on median fins and, in individuals from clear water, on body. Young has narrow brown stripe along back and broad dark brown stripe along side. 57–63 lateral scales; 47–55 predorsal scales; 14–31 gill rakers. To 72 in. (183 cm).

Range: Atlantic Slope from Delaware R., NJ, to cen. FL; St. Lawrence R., QU, through Great Lakes (except Superior), and Mississippi R. basin to Gulf Coast; Gulf Slope drainages from cen. FL to Rio Grande drainage, TX and Mexico. Locally common, especially in clear lakes and impoundments. **Habitat:** Sluggish pools, backwaters and oxbows of medium to large rivers, lakes. Usually near vegetation. Occasionally in brackish waters.

Similar species: Other gars (Pl. 2) have much shorter, wider snouts.   **Map 22**

SPOTTED GAR *Lepisosteus oculatus*   Pl. 2

Identification: *Many olive-brown to black spots on body, head, and all fins.* Moderately long snout; upper jaw longer than rest of head. 1 row of teeth on upper jaw. A few *bony plates on underside of isth-*

mus. Olive-brown to black above and on side; white to yellow below. Young has dark stripes along back and side. 53–59 lateral scales; 45–54 predorsal scales; 15–24 gill rakers. To 44 in. (112 cm).
Range: Lake Erie and s. Lake Michigan drainages south through Mississippi R. basin to Gulf Coast; Gulf Slope drainages from lower Apalachicola R., FL, to Nueces R., TX. Locally common. **Habitat:** Quiet, clear pools and backwaters of lowland creeks; small to large rivers, oxbow lakes, swamps, sloughs; ditches with an abundance of vegetation or debris. Occasionally enters brackish water.
Similar species: (1) See Florida Gar (Pl. 2). (2) Shortnose Gar (Pl. 2) *lacks* dark spots on top of head, body, and paired fins; has usually 60–63 lateral scales. **Map 23**

FLORIDA GAR *Lepisosteus platyrhincus* Pl. 2

Identification: Similar to Spotted Gar but *lacks* bony plates on underside of isthmus; has shorter, broader snout and lower jaw. 54-59 lateral scales; 47-51 predorsal scales; 19-33 gill rakers. To 52 in. (132 cm).
Range: Savannah R. drainage, GA, to Ocklockonee R. drainage, FL and GA; throughout peninsular FL. Common. **Habitat:** Sluggish mud- or sand-bottomed pools of quiet lowland streams and lakes; usually near vegetation.
Similar species: (1) See Spotted Gar (Pl. 2). (2) Other gars (Pl. 2) usually *lack* large dark spots on anterior part of body, head, and paired fins. **Map 23**

■ BOWFINS: Family Amiidae (1)

Now represented by one living species, the bowfin family previously (as far back as the Jurassic) was distributed in Europe, Asia, Africa, South America, and North America. A primitive fish, the bowfin retains an abbreviated (rounded externally) heterocercal tail, lunglike gas bladder, and vestiges of a spiral valve. On the underside of the head is a large, bony gular plate.

BOWFIN *Amia calva* Pl. 2

Identification: *Long, nearly cylindrical body;* large head. *Long dorsal fin* extends more than half length of back; 42–53 rays. *Tubular nostrils.* Large mouth with many teeth; upper jaw extends beyond eye. Rounded pectoral, pelvic, and caudal fins. Cycloid scales. *Large, bony gular plate.* Mottled olive above; cream-yellow to pale green below. Black bands on dark green dorsal and caudal fins; turquoise-green ventral fins. Yellow to orange halo around prominent *black spot* near base of upper caudal fin rays in young; less distinct spot in adult. Brilliant turquoise-green lips, throat, belly, and ventral fins on breeding male. To 43 in. (109 cm).
Range: St. Lawrence R.–Great Lakes (including Georgian Bay and Lakes Nipissing and Simcoe, ON) and Mississippi R. basins from QU to n. MN and south to Gulf; Atlantic and Gulf Coastal Plain from

Susquehanna R. drainage, se. PA, to Colorado R., TX. Introduced sparingly elsewhere. Locally common. **Habitat:** Swamps, sloughs, and pools, and backwaters of lowland streams. Usually near vegetation. **Map 24**

■FRESHWATER EELS: Family Anguillidae (1)

Freshwater eels occur on every continent except Antarctica. They *lack* pelvic fins and have scales so small that they appear to be absent. Adults of the American (*Anguilla rostrata*) and European (*A. anguilla*) eels migrate from fresh water to a place in the Atlantic Ocean (usually assumed to be in the Sargasso Sea between Bermuda and the West Indies) where they spawn and die. From the egg hatches a leptocephalus (leaflike larva) that migrates to the shores of North America or Europe. The trip to North America takes 1 year; that to Europe takes 3 years. After arrival the larva transforms, in sequence, into a "glass-eel" (small and transparent but with the adult morphology), an elver (darkly pigmented but still small), and finally an adult. Males remain in brackish water and in streams along the coasts; females may migrate far upstream and remain there for as long as 15 years.

AMERICAN EEL *Anguilla rostrata* **Pl. 1**
Identification: Slender, *snakelike body*; small, pointed head. *Long dorsal fin* extends more than half of body, *continuous with caudal and anal fins*. Small, single gill slit just in front of pectoral fin. Lower jaw projects well beyond upper jaw. Yellow to olive-brown above; pale yellow to white below; fins similar in color to adjacent body. To 60 in. (152 cm).
Range: Catadromous species that spawns in the Atlantic Ocean and ascends streams in North and South America. Found in Atlantic, Great Lakes, Mississippi, and Gulf basins from NF to SD and south to South America. Common near sea; uncommon in more inland streams and lakes. **Habitat:** Usually in permanent streams with continuous flow. Hides during daylight in undercut banks and in deep pools near logs and boulders. **Map 25**

■HERRINGS AND SHADS: Family Clupeidae (8)

Most herrings and shads are marine, but a few species live only in fresh water, and some marine species frequently enter fresh water. These fishes are strongly *compressed; lack* a lateral line and scales on the head; and have cycloid scales on the body, 1 dorsal fin, a conspicuous adipose eyelid (Fig. 7), abdominal pelvic fins, an axillary process just above the base of the pelvic fin, no adipose fin, and no spines in the fins. Belly has sharply pointed scales, creating a *saw-*

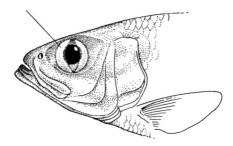

Fig. 7 Clupeid — adipose eyelid

tooth edge. Included among the nearly 200 species of clupeids are sardines, menhaden, shads, and other economically important fishes.

BLUEBACK HERRING *Alosa aestivalis*   **Pl. 3**
  Identification: *Strongly oblique mouth* (about 45° to horizontal);
  lower jaw *equal to or projecting only slightly beyond* snout. Cheek
  longer than or about equal to its depth (Fig. 8). *Blue above;* silver
  side, usually 1 small blue-black spot near upper edge of gill opening.
  Adult has thin dark stripes on back and upper side; light green or yellow fins. Teeth on lower jaw. Fairly small eye, diameter about equal
  to snout length. Usually 44–50 rakers on lower limb of 1st gill arch.
  Black peritoneum. To 15¾ in. (40 cm).
  Range: Atlantic Coast from Cape Breton, NS, to St. Johns R., FL. Ascends lower reaches of coastal rivers during spring spawning season;
  young move to ocean at about 1 month of age (1–2 in. [3–5 cm]). Introduced into VA reservoirs. Common; dams have reduced freshwater range and abundance. **Freshwater habitat:** Usually in current over
  rocky bottom.
  Similar species: See Pl. 3. (1) See Alewife. (2) Hickory Shad and (3)
  Skipjack Herring have lower jaw projecting *far beyond* snout, usually
  fewer than 23 rakers on lower limb of 1st gill arch; are *gray-green*
  above. (4) American Shad has cheek deeper than long (Fig. 8), less oblique mouth; lacks jaw teeth.   **Map 26**

ALEWIFE *Alosa pseudoharengus*   **Pl. 3**
  Identification: Similar to Blueback Herring but is *blue-green above;*
  has *larger eye* (diameter greater than snout length), deeper body, usually *39–41 rakers* on lower limb of 1st gill arch. Gray peritoneum. To
  15 in. (38 cm), but usually less than 10 in. (25 cm) in landlocked populations.
  Range: Atlantic Coast from Red Bay, Labrador, to SC; many landlocked populations. Individuals with access to ocean are anadromous, ascend coastal rivers during spring spawning migrations (usually going farther upstream than Blueback Herring). Considered

native to Lake Ontario; introduced into other Great Lakes via the Welland Canal (1st taken in Lake Erie in 1931) and spread rapidly during l930s–1960s. Introduced sparingly elsewhere. Often abundant, although dams now impede upstream migrations and landlocked populations undergo extreme fluctuations. **Habitat:** Open water over all bottom types.

Similar species: See Blueback Herring (Pl. 3). **Map 27**

HICKORY SHAD *Alosa mediocris* Pl. 3

Identification: *Strongly oblique mouth* (about 45° to horizontal); lower jaw *projects beyond* snout. Cheek longer than or about equal to its depth. Blue-black spot near upper edge of gill cover followed by *row of poorly defined dusky spots* reaching to below dorsal fin. Gray-green above, *gradually shading to silver side;* clear fins, except often black edges on dusky dorsal and caudal fins. Teeth on lower jaw. 18–23 rakers on lower limb of 1st gill arch. To 23¾ in. (60 cm).

Range: Atlantic Coast from Kenduskeag R., ME (possibly Campobello Island, NB), to St. Johns R., FL; ascends coastal rivers during spring and fall. Least common of Atlantic Coast *Alosa.* **Freshwater habitat:** Open water of large rivers.

Similar species: See Pl. 3. (1) See Skipjack Herring. (2) Blueback Herring and (3) Alewife have lower jaw *equal to or projecting only slightly beyond* snout, usually 39 or more rakers on lower limb of 1st gill arch; are blue above. (4) American Shad has cheek deeper than long (Fig. 8), less oblique mouth. **Map 28**

SKIPJACK HERRING *Alosa chrysochloris* Pl. 3

Identification: Similar to Hickory Shad but *lacks* blue-black spot behind gill cover; *blue-green above ends abruptly,* not gradually shading into silver side. 20–24 rakers on lower limb of 1st gill arch. To 21 in. (53 cm).

Range: Red R. drainage (Hudson Bay basin) and Mississippi R. basin from cen. MN south to Gulf, and from sw. PA west to e. SD, NE, KS, OK, and TX; Gulf Slope drainages from Apalachicola R., FL, to Colorado R., TX. Common throughout much of range; extirpated from upper Mississippi R. following construction of dams. **Habitat:** Open water of clear to moderately turbid, medium to large rivers and large reservoirs. A schooling species usually in current over sand and gravel. Occasionally enters brackish and marine waters.

Similar species: (1) See Hickory Shad (Pl. 3). (2) Alabama Shad (Pl. 3) has cheek deeper than long, less oblique mouth; adult lacks jaw teeth. **Map 27**

AMERICAN SHAD *Alosa sapidissima* Pl. 3

Identification: Adult *lacks* jaw teeth. Cheek decidedly *deeper than long* (Fig. 8); mouth less oblique than in previous 4 species. Lower jaw equal to or projecting only slightly beyond snout. Blue-black spot near upper edge of gill opening usually followed by *1 or 2 rows of smaller spots.* Green or blue above; silver side; clear to light green fins; dusky dorsal and caudal fins; black edge on caudal fin. 59–73

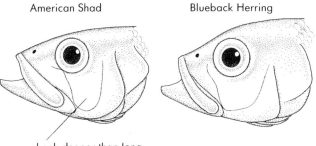

American Shad   Blueback Herring

cheek deeper than long

Fig. 8 American Shad and Blueback Herring

rakers on lower limb of 1st gill arch of adult. To 30 in. (75 cm).
Range: Atlantic Coast from Sand Hill R., Labrador, to St. Johns R.,
FL; ascends coastal rivers during spring spawning migrations. Introduced into Sacramento R., CA, in 1870s and has since spread along
Pacific Coast from Kamchatka, U.S.S.R., to Todos Santos Bay, Mexico. Landlocked in Millerton Lake, CA. **Freshwater habitat:** Open water of large rivers.
Similar species: See Pl. 3. (1) See Alabama Shad. (2) Blueback Herring,
(3) Alewife, (4) Hickory Shad, and (5) Skipjack Herring have *teeth* on
lower jaw, strongly oblique mouth, *cheek longer than deep.* **Map 29**

ALABAMA SHAD *Alosa alabamae*   **Pl. 3**
Identification: Nearly identical to American Shad, but adult has
42–48 rakers on lower limb of 1st gill arch. To 20¼ in. (51 cm).
Range: Gulf Coast from Suwannee R., FL, to Mississippi R., LA; as-
cends rivers during spawning runs in January to July. Sporadic in
Mississippi R. basin, but reported as far north as Keokuk, IA, and, in
recent years, the Cumberland, Tennessee, Missouri, Arkansas,
Ouachita, and Red rivers. Locally common; depleted in Mississippi
R. basin. **Freshwater habitat:** Open water of medium to large rivers.
Similar species: (1) See American Shad (Pl. 3). (2) Skipjack Herring
(Pl. 3) has teeth on lower jaw, strongly oblique mouth, cheek longer
than deep.   **Map 30**

GIZZARD SHAD *Dorosoma cepedianum*   **Pl. 3**
Identification: *Long, whiplike last dorsal ray. Blunt snout;* distinctly
subterminal mouth; deep notch at center of upper jaw. *No scales* on
nape. Dorsal fin origin above or behind pelvic fin origin. *Large
purple-blue spot* near upper edge of gill cover in young and small
adult; faint or absent in large adult. Silver-blue above, grading to
silver-white side, often with blue and green reflections on head and
body; 6–8 dark stripes on back and upper side; dusky fins; no black

specks on chin or floor of mouth. 52–70 lateral scales; 10–13 dorsal rays; 25–36 anal rays. To 20½ in. (52 cm).
Range: St. Lawrence-Great Lakes, Mississippi, Atlantic, and Gulf drainages from QU to cen. ND and NM, and south to cen. FL and Mexico. Introduced outside native range. Common. **Habitat:** Most common in deep, open water of medium to large rivers, lakes, and impoundments; often ascends creeks and small rivers with well-developed pools. Commonly enters brackish water.
Similar species: See Threadfin Shad (Pl. 3).   **Map 31**

THREADFIN SHAD *Dorosoma petenense*   **Pl. 3**
Identification: Similar to Gizzard Shad but has *more pointed snout, terminal mouth, black specks* on chin and floor of mouth, *yellow fins,* purple shoulder spot near upper edge of gill cover *persisting in adult, 40–48 lateral scales.* 11–14 dorsal rays; 17–27 anal rays. To 9 in. (23 cm).
Range: Ohio R., IN and IL, and Mississippi R., s. IL, south through Mississippi R. basin to Gulf; Atlantic drainages of FL; Gulf drainages from s.-cen. FL to n. Guatemala. Introduced widely as a forage fish outside native range including Atlantic drainages north to Chesapeake Bay; Colorado R. drainage, AZ, NV, and CA; and Pacific drainages, CA. Common. **Habitat:** Lakes, backwaters, and pools of medium to large rivers; usually in open water over sand, mud, and debris. Occasionally enters brackish water.
Similar species: See Gizzard Shad (Pl. 3).   **Map 32**

■ MOONEYES: Family Hiodontidae (2)

An exclusively North American family containing only two species. They resemble shad but have a *lateral line* and an *untoothed keel* along the belly. They are *strongly compressed, large-eyed fishes* with no scales on the head, cycloid scales on the body, no spines in the fins, 1 dorsal fin, an adipose eyelid, abdominal pelvic fins, and an axillary process at the base of the pelvic fin.

Mooneyes feed on aquatic insects, other invertebrates, and small fishes. The eggs, unlike those of any other native North American freshwater fish, are semibuoyant and drift downstream or into quiet water.

GOLDEYE *Hiodon alosoides*   **Pl. 3**
Identification: *Deep, compressed silver body.* Dorsal fin origin opposite or behind anal fin origin. Fleshy keel along belly extends from pectoral fin base to anal fin. Large mouth; maxillary extends behind pupil of eye. Blunt, round snout. Usually 9–10 dorsal rays, 29–34 anal rays, 57–62 lateral scales. Blue-green above with silver reflections, silver-white below; clear to dusky fins. Gold iris. To 20 in. (51 cm).
Range: Tributaries of James Bay, QU and ON; Arctic, Missouri, Mississippi, and Ohio basins from Mackenzie R. drainage, NT, to w. PA

and south to LA. Locally common. **Habitat:** Deep, open pools and channels of medium to large, often turbid, lowland rivers; lakes and impoundments.
Similar species: See Mooneye (Pl. 3).   **Map 33**

MOONEYE *Hiodon tergisus*   **Pl. 3**
Identification: Similar to Goldeye but has *dorsal fin origin in front of anal fin origin,* larger eye, deeper body, fleshy keel along belly extending from *pelvic fin base* to anal fin, maxillary extending to front or middle of pupil, more silver body and iris. Usually 11–12 dorsal rays, 26–29 anal rays, 52–57 lateral scales. To 18¾ in. (47 cm).
Range: St. Lawrence–Great Lakes (except Superior), Mississippi R., and Hudson Bay basins from QU to AB and south to Gulf; Gulf Slope drainages from Mobile Bay, AL, to Lake Pontchartrain, LA. Locally common. **Habitat:** Deep pools and backwaters of medium to large rivers; lakes and impoundments.
Similar species: See Goldeye (Pl. 3).   **Map 34**

■ TROUTS, SALMONS, CHARS, AND WHITEFISHES: Family Salmonidae (38)

Salmonids live in cool to cold streams and lakes throughout Europe, northern Asia, North America as far south as nw. Mexico, extreme n. Africa (n. slope of the Atlas Mountains), and Taiwan. The Arctic Char occurs farther north than any other freshwater fish. Because they are among the most commercially important fishes, trout and salmon have been introduced into Africa south of their native range, South America, Australia, New Zealand, New Guinea, and India.

All salmonids are freshwater or migrate into fresh water to spawn. In migratory (anadromous) species, the young migrate to sea, where they grow for a number of years, then migrate back to and spawn in the stream in which they themselves hatched.

Salmonids are characterized by having many small cycloid scales, a lateral line, 1 dorsal fin plus an *adipose fin,* abdominal pelvic fins, an axillary process at the base of the pelvic fin, and *no spines* in the fins. Many species are large, and one Asiatic species, the Taimen (*Hucho taimen*), is reported to reach 175 lb. (80 kg).

In North America, many populations of salmonids are not recognized as species even though they are reproductively isolated (often by geographic boundaries) and morphologically distinct and therefore fit the definition of biological species. The fact that they are not named as species is due in large part to the difficulty in expressing the diversity resulting from the evolutionary process in the form of biological nomenclature. The whitefishes of the Great Lakes and the trouts and chars of the western U.S. are among the most taxonomically difficult freshwater fishes in North America. Users of this guide should keep in mind that some of the recognized "species" are in fact groups of species and that geographic forms at variance with the descriptions and illustrations occasionally will be encountered. Numerous introductions of salmonids throughout much of North America also make identifications difficult; a species may appear suddenly in an area where it previously did not occur, and introduced fishes often hybridize with species already present, producing intermediate forms not fitting any species description.

Young trouts, salmons, and chars have color patterns and characteristics differing from those of adults and from one another, but are difficult to identify. The best characteristics are shown in Fig. 9.

The Great Lakes populations of whitefishes and the Lake Trout have been severely depleted by the introduction of the Sea Lamprey.

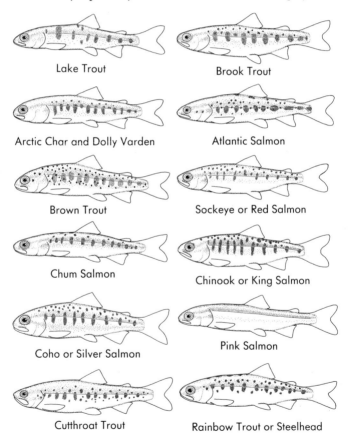

Lake Trout

Brook Trout

Arctic Char and Dolly Varden

Atlantic Salmon

Brown Trout

Sockeye or Red Salmon

Chum Salmon

Chinook or King Salmon

Coho or Silver Salmon

Pink Salmon

Cutthroat Trout

Rainbow Trout or Steelhead

Fig. 9 Young trouts, chars, and salmons 2–6 in. (5–15 cm) long

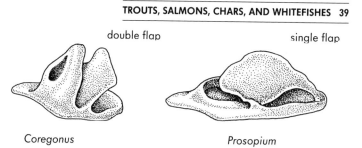

double flap single flap

Coregonus *Prosopium*

Fig. 10 *Coregonus* **and** *Prosopium* — **nostril flaps**

• *COREGONUS*

Genus characteristics: *2 small flaps* of skin between nostrils (Fig. 10); fairly *broad snout*; small subterminal to terminal mouth; body compressed to round in cross section; forked caudal fin; usually *long, slender rakers*, 18–64 on 1st gill arch; no or small teeth on jaws; 9–16 dorsal rays; *no parr marks*; usually no distinct black spots on body or fins; generally silver, silver-green or silver-blue in color. Ciscoes and whitefishes are the most difficult of all North American freshwater fishes to identify. They vary enormously within populations and seem to overlap one another in characteristics used to recognize species. The following descriptions cannot be regarded as absolute. In particular, no characteristic or combination of characteristics fully separate the "species" in the Great Lakes basin, and it is possible that only two variable species (Cisco and Lake Whitefish) are present.

BROAD WHITEFISH *Coregonus nasus* **Not shown**
Identification: *Compressed body.* Snout overhangs *subterminal mouth.* Head profile smoothly convex; *no* (or small) concavity between snout and nape (Fig. 11). Thick, white lower fins. Olive-brown to nearly black above; silver side, white to yellow below; white to gray fins. *Short, broad maxillary,* its length less than twice its width. 84–102 lateral scales. 18–25 *short rakers* on 1st gill arch (less than ⅕ as long as space between eyes). To 28 in. (71 cm).
Range: Arctic drainages from Perry R., NT, to Kuskokwim R. (Bering Sea tributary), AK. Also in Eurasia. Common. **Habitat:** Most frequently in streams; lakes, brackish water.
Similar species: See Humpback Whitefishes (*Coregonus clupeaformis* complex) (Pl. 2). **Map 35**

Next four species (Humpback Whitefishes or *Coregonus clupeaformis* complex) are extremely difficult to distinguish from one another. They differ from the Broad Whitefish in having a more distinct *concavity* between the snout and nape, a pronounced *hump* behind head in adult (Fig. 11), longer gill rakers (longest raker more than ⅕ of space between

Broad Whitefish

Lake Whitefish

Cisco or Lake Herring

Shortjaw Cisco

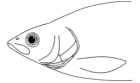

Blackfin Cisco

Kiyi

Fig. 11 *Coregonus* species

eyes), longer maxillary (its length twice the width or more), and more translucent lower fins. Humpback Whitefishes appear to differ from one another only in modal number of rakers on 1st gill arch.

LAKE WHITEFISH *Coregonus clupeaformis*   **Pl. 2**
    Identification: 24–33, usually 26 or more, gill rakers. Dark brown to midnight blue above, silver side. 70–97, usually fewer than 90, lateral scales. To 31 in. (80 cm).
    Range: Throughout AK and most of Canada south into New England, the Great Lakes basin, and cen. MN. Introduced as forage and food fish into nw. U.S. (MT, ID, and WA). Locally common. **Habitat:** Lakes and large rivers; enters brackish water.
    Remarks: The Lake Simcoe Whitefish, *C. clupeaformis* subspecies,

found only in Lake Simcoe, ON, has been found to be genetically distinct and is protected as a *threatened subspecies*.
Similar species: See (1) Alaska, (2) Humpback, and (3) Atlantic Whitefishes. **Map 36**

ALASKA WHITEFISH *Coregonus nelsoni* **Not shown**
Identification: Nearly identical to Lake Whitefish but has *22–27*, usually 24–25, gill rakers. To about 22 in. (56 cm).
Range: Not accurately known because of identification problems within the Humpback Whitefish complex. Probably restricted to n. NT, YU, and AK in Yukon R., Paxson Lake, Copper R. system, Anderson R., and Mackenzie R. delta. Locally common. **Habitat:** Small to large rivers; rarely in lakes.
Similar species: (1) See Lake (Pl. 2) and (2) Humpback Whitefishes. **Map 37**

HUMPBACK WHITEFISH *Coregonus pidschian* **Not shown**
Identification: Nearly identical to Lake Whitefish but has *17–25*, usually 21–23, gill rakers. To about 18 in. (46 cm).
Range: Tributaries of the Beaufort, Chukchi, and Bering seas, AK; upper Atlin Lake, YU. Also in Eurasia. Common. **Habitat:** Coastal waters near shore; anadromous, migrates at least 795 mi. (1280 km) inland. Overwinters near river mouths.
Similar species: (1) See Lake (Pl. 2) and (2) Alaska Whitefishes. **Map 37**

ATLANTIC WHITEFISH *Coregonus huntsmani* **Not shown**
Identification: Similar to Lake Whitefish but has nearly *terminal mouth*, less compressed body, *91–100* lateral scales. To 15¾ in. (40 cm).
Range: Known only from Yarmouth Harbour, Tusket R. drainage, and Leipsigate Lake, s. NS. Protected as a *threatened species*. Rare. **Habitat:** Nearshore coastal waters; open water of lakes and small to large rivers, often in current in rivers. Anadromous.
Similar species: See Lake Whitefish (Pl. 2). **Map 38**

Next seven species (Lake Ciscoes or *Coregonus artedi* complex) are difficult to distinguish from one another using field characters. They differ from the Humpback Whitefishes in having: *terminal mouth* or *projecting lower jaw* (except Shortjaw Cisco); *no* pronounced hump behind head; more gill rakers, usually more than 35 on 1st arch; and dusky or black lower fins (except Arctic Cisco). The most useful character to distinguish members of this complex from one another is modal number of rakers on the 1st gill arch.

CISCO or LAKE HERRING *Coregonus artedi* **Pl. 2**
Identification: Long body, almost round in cross section, deepest at middle. Lower jaw equal to or projects slightly beyond upper jaw; upper jaw reaches front of pupil (Fig. 11). Symphyseal knob at tip of lower jaw. Often *dusky* or *black-tipped* pelvic fins on fish over 6 in.

(15 cm). Pelvic fins *far back* on body; distance from snout to pelvic fin origin equal to distance from pelvic fin origin to a point on caudal fin. Dark blue to green above; silver side. 38–64, usually *46–50, long, slender rakers* on 1st gill arch. Usually 63–94 lateral scales. To 22½ in. (57 cm).

Range: Widespread through much of Canada and n. U.S. in St. Lawrence–Great Lakes, Arctic, and upper Mississippi R. basins from QU to NT and AB, and south to n. OH, IL, and MN. Introduced sparingly elsewhere. Common. **Habitat:** Open waters of lakes and large rivers; coastal waters of Hudson Bay.

Similar species: (1) See Least and (2) Arctic Ciscoes. (3) Bloater and (4) Kiyi have usually *36–47 rakers* on 1st gill arch. **Map 39**

LEAST CISCO *Coregonus sardinella* **Not shown**
Identification: Similar to Cisco but distance from snout to pelvic fin origin equal to distance from pelvic fin origin to a point *on caudal peduncle*. Rather high, *falcate dorsal fin*. Brown to dark green above. 41–53 long, slender rakers on 1st gill arch. Usually 78-98 lateral scales. To about 18½ in. (47 cm) (see Remarks).

Range: Anadromous form from Murchison R., NT, to Bristol Bay, AK; ascends Yukon R. to BC, and Mackenzie R. to Fort Simpson; also in Eurasia. Landlocked forms (see Remarks) in upper Yukon R. drainage and lakes near Bristol Bay, AK. Common. **Habitat:** Coastal waters, estuaries, large lakes and rivers.

Remarks: 4 forms: Anadromous form occurring in Arctic drainages and lower Yukon R. reaches 18½ in. (47 cm), has spotted back and dorsal fin, 48–53 rakers on 1st gill arch; dwarf, nonanadromous form (to about 7 in. [18 cm]) in Naknek and Iliamna lakes, AK, lacks spots, has 49–53 gill rakers; nonanadromous form in upper Yukon R. lakes reaches 18½ in. (47 cm), has extensively spotted back and dorsal fin, 48–52 rakers on 1st gill arch; nonanadromous form occurring elsewhere reaches 8½ in. (22 cm), lacks spots, has 41–47 rakers on 1st gill arch.

Similar species: (1) See Cisco (Pl. 2). (2) Arctic Cisco has white pelvic fins; *lower* dorsal fin. **Map 38**

ARCTIC CISCO *Coregonus autumnalis* **Not shown**
Identification: Nearly identical to Cisco but *lacks* dusky or black tips on pelvic fins. Light green to brown above; dusky dorsal and caudal fins, white lower fins. 41–48 long, slender rakers on 1st gill arch. To 25 in. (64 cm).

Range: Murchison R., NT, west along Arctic Coast to Cook Inlet, AK. Also in Eurasia. Common. **Habitat:** Anadromous, near river mouths and in brackish lagoons; ascends Mackenzie R. to Fort Simpson.

Remarks: 2 subspecies: *C. a. laurettae*, along coast of AK from Olitok, near Colville R. to Cook Inlet, has usually 18–25 rakers on lower limb of 1st gill arch; *C. a. autumnalis*, from Murchison R., NT, to Point Barrow, AK, has usually 26–31 rakers on 1st gill arch; intergrades occur in Mackenzie R., NT.

Similar species: (1) See Cisco (Pl. 2). (2) Least Cisco has higher, more falcate dorsal fin; dusky or black pelvic fins. **Map 40**

SHORTJAW CISCO *Coregonus zenithicus* Not shown

Identification: Stout lower jaw usually *shorter* than upper jaw, *lacks* symphyseal knob; upper jaw often reaches *middle of pupil* (Fig. 11). Body deepest near middle. Dark blue-green to pale pea-green above; silver side; black on most fins (darkest on large individual). Usually 34–42 medium rakers (about length of gill filaments) on 1st gill arch. To 16 in. (40 cm).

Range: Great Slave Lake, NT, southeast through Hudson Bay and Great Lakes basins (except Lakes Ontario and Erie). Declining in Lakes Superior and Nipigon; uncommon outside Great Lakes basin. Legally protected in Canada as a *threatened species.* **Habitat:** Usually in deep (65–589 ft. [20–180 m]) water of large lakes.

Similar species: (1) See Blackfin Cisco. (2) Kiyi and (3) Bloater have slender lower jaw, *symphyseal knob* at tip of lower jaw, longer paired fins. (4) Cisco (Pl. 2) has slender lower jaw; lower jaw equal to or projecting beyond upper jaw. **Map 38**

BLACKFIN CISCO *Coregonus nigripinnis* Not shown

Identification: Similar to Shortjaw Cisco (above) but has body *deepest under nape,* jaws *equal* in length, upper jaw reaches *front* of pupil (Fig. 11). Dusky upper lip. Blue-green to blue-black above; silver side. Usually *blue-black fins.* Usually *46–50 long rakers* (longest usually longer than gill filaments) on 1st gill arch. To 15¼ in. (39 cm).

Range: Endemic to Lakes Nipigon, Huron, and Michigan. Rare; extant only in Lake Nipigon. Legally protected in Canada as a *threatened species.* **Habitat:** Formerly in deep waters (294–523 ft. [90–160 m]) of lakes Michigan and Huron; in 6½–327 ft. (2–100 m) in Lake Nipigon.

Similar species: (1) See Shortjaw Cisco. (2) Cisco (Pl. 2) has more elongate body *deepest at middle,* slender lower jaw, symphyseal knob at tip of lower jaw. (3) Kiyi and (4) Bloater have lower jaw projecting slightly beyond upper jaw, symphyseal knob at tip of lower jaw. **Map 41**

KIYI *Coregonus kiyi* Not shown

Identification: Pointed snout; lower jaw projecting slightly beyond upper jaw (Fig. 11); slender, darkly pigmented lower jaw; *black upper lip;* symphyseal knob at tip of lower jaw. *Long paired fins;* pelvic fin usually reaches to anus or beyond. *Large eye* nearly equal to snout length. Body deepest under nape. Silver with faint pink to purple iridescence; black edges on dorsal and caudal fins. Usually *36–41 medium rakers* (about length of gill filaments) on 1st gill arch. To 13¾ in. (35 cm).

Range: Endemic to Great Lakes (except Lake Erie). Common in Lake Superior; extremely rare, possibly extirpated, in Lakes Huron and Ontario; endangered in Lake Michigan. **Habitat:** Open water; generally at depths of 327–589 ft. (100–180 m) in Lake Superior.

Similar species: (1) See Bloater. (2) Cisco (Pl. 2) has more elongate body, rounder in cross section, deepest at middle; usually *46–50 long rakers* on 1st gill arch. **Map 41**

BLOATER *Coregonus hoyi*   **Not shown**
Identification: Nearly identical to Kiyi but has *less dusky upper lip, smaller eye* (eye usually less than snout length), body deepest at middle, pelvic fin seldom reaching anus, usually 40–47 long rakers (longer than longest gill filament) on 1st gill arch. To 14½ in. (37 cm).
Range: Endemic to Great Lakes (except Lake Erie) and Lake Nipigon. Probably extirpated from Lakes Ontario and Nipigon, threatened in Lake Michigan, declining in Lakes Superior and Huron. **Habitat:** Large lakes; generally at depths of 98–618 ft. (30–189 m).
Remarks: When fish is brought up from depths, the gas bladder expands, giving the fish a bloated appearance, hence its name.
Similar species: See Kiyi. **Map 41**

INCONNU *Stenodus leucichthys*   **Fig. 12**
Identification: *Large, wide mouth* extends to rear of pupil; *lower jaw projects* beyond upper jaw. 2 small flaps of skin between nostrils. Forked caudal fin. High, pointed dorsal fin; 11–19 rays. Green, blue, or pale brown above; silver-white side and below, dusky-edged dorsal and caudal fins. *No* parr marks. 90–115 lateral scales. 13–17 rakers on lower limb of 1st gill arch. Small, velvetlike bands of teeth on both jaws. To 49 in. (125 cm).
Range: Arctic drainages from Anderson R., NT, to Kuskokwim R. (Bering Sea tributary), AK. Upstream in Mackenzie R. and Yukon R. drainages to n. BC. Also in Asia. Abundant. **Habitat:** Anadromous near coasts; landlocked in inland lakes.
Similar species: Whitefishes (Pl. 2) have *smaller mouth*, usually more than 20 rakers on lower limb of 1st gill arch. **Map 42**

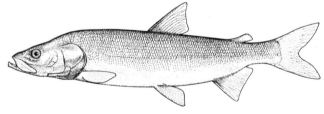

Fig. 12 Inconnu *Stenodus leucichthys*

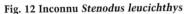

• *PROSOPIUM*

Genus characteristics: *1 flap* of skin between nostrils (Fig. 10); *pinched snout* (when viewed from above); small, subterminal mouth; body round in cross section; forked caudal fin; *short, stout* *rakers*, 13–45 on 1st gill arch; no teeth on jaws; 10-14 dorsal rays; *parr marks* on young; silver to silver-white.

BONNEVILLE CISCO *Prosopium gemmiferum*   **Not shown**
 Identification: *Long, sharply pointed snout* (Fig. 13); *long maxilla.* Long, slender body; forked caudal fin. Pale moss green above; pearl iridescence on silver side. Brassy side on large male. 69–76 lateral scales; 10–11 dorsal rays; 9–12 anal rays. 37–45 rakers on 1st gill arch. To 8½ in. (22 cm).
 Range: Endemic to Bear Lake, se. ID and n. UT. Introduced into several other western states, but transplants apparently have been unsuccessful. Common. **Habitat:** Open water. Widely scattered when lake is colder than 58°F (14.4°C). As water warms, Bonneville Cisco descends into deeper, colder water.
 Similar species: Other *Prosopium* species (Pl. 2; Fig. 13) have *short blunt snout,* fewer than 26 rakers on 1st gill arch.   **Map 43**

Next five species: short blunt snout (Fig. 13).

PYGMY WHITEFISH *Prosopium coulteri*   **Pl. 2**
 Identification: *Large eye;* diameter about same as snout length (Fig. 13). Transparent membrane surrounding eye has distinct notch be-

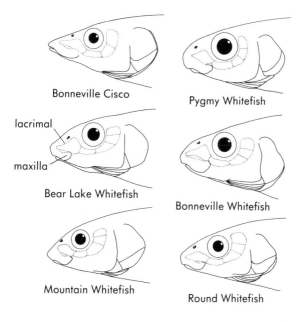

Bonneville Cisco

Pygmy Whitefish

lacrimal

maxilla

Bear Lake Whitefish

Bonneville Whitefish

Mountain Whitefish

Round Whitefish

Fig. 13 *Prosopium* species

low rear edge of pupil. Large scales; *54–70* along lateral line, 31–40 around body, 16–20 around caudal peduncle. Dark brown above; silver or white below. Young have 7–14 oval parr marks on side. Usually 11–12 dorsal rays, 12–14 anal rays; 13–20 rakers on 1st gill arch; *13–33* pyloric caeca. To 11 in. (28 cm).
Range: 3 disjunct areas: (a) Lake Superior, ON and MI; (b) Yukon R. drainage, YU, to Columbia R. drainage, w. MT and WA; (c) Chignik, Naknek, and Wood R. drainages, sw. AK. Abundant in western areas; uncommon in Lake Superior. **Habitat:** Swift, cold streams; below 20 ft. (6 m) in lakes; in Lake Superior at depths of 60–220 ft. (18–89 m).
Similar species: (1) Mountain (Fig. 13) and (2) Round Whitefishes (Pl. 2, Fig. 13) have *smaller eye* (diameter less than snout length), *more than 70* lateral scales, 20 or more scales around caudal peduncle, 50 or more pyloric caeca; reach 22 in. (56 cm). **Map 43**

BEAR LAKE WHITEFISH *Prosopium abyssicola* **Not shown**
Identification: Maxilla *short and deep,* not reaching end of lacrimal (Fig. 13). Silver-white; *no* dark spots on body. 67–78 (usually *69–74*) lateral scales; *38–43 scales* around body; usually 11 dorsal rays, 10 anal rays; 19-23 rakers on 1st gill arch. To 11 in. (28 cm).
Range: Endemic to Bear Lake, se. ID and n. UT. Common. **Habitat:** Usually near the bottom in cold Bear Lake; rarely near shore.
Similar species: (1) See Bonneville Whitefish (Fig. 13). (2) Mountain Whitefish (Fig. 13) has maxilla reaching *end* of lacrymal, 76–89 lateral scales, usually 12–13 dorsal rays. **Map 44**

BONNEVILLE WHITEFISH *Prosopium spilonotus* **Not shown**
Identification: Similar to Bear Lake Whitefish but has somewhat blunter snout; maxilla reaches *end of lacrimal* (Fig. 13); usually *76–86* lateral scales, *44 or more scales* around body. Upper jaw usually *more* than ½ length of dorsal fin base. Young have *dark spots* on body (to 10 in. [25 cm]). Usually 10–12 dorsal rays, 9–11 anal rays, 18–22 rakers on 1st gill arch. To 22 in. (56 cm).
Range: Endemic to Bear Lake, se. ID and n. UT. Common. **Habitat:** Frequently at depths of 40–100 ft. (12–30 m); more often in shallow water than are Bonneville Cisco and Bear Lake Whitefish.
Similar species: See (1) Bear Lake (Fig. 13) and (2) Mountain Whitefishes (Fig. 13). **Map 43**

MOUNTAIN WHITEFISH *Prosopium williamsoni* **Not shown**
Identification: Similar to Bonneville Whitefish (above) but has *12–13* dorsal rays, *11–13* anal rays; upper jaw *less* than ½ length of dorsal fin base (Fig. 13). Olive green to dark brown above; silver or white below; dusky dorsal fin. Young has 7–11 large oval dark parr marks. 76–89 lateral scales; 20–23 scales around caudal peduncle; 19–26 rakers on 1st gill arch, 50–146 pyloric caeca. To 22½ in. (57 cm).
Range: Mackenzie R. drainage (Arctic basin), NT, south through w. Canada and nw. U.S. in Pacific, Hudson Bay, and upper Missouri R. basins, to Truckee R. drainage, NV, and Sevier R. drainage, UT. Common. **Habitat:** Lakes (to depth of at least 30 ft. [10 m]) and fast, clear or silty streams.

Similar species: See Fig. 13. (1) See Bonneville Whitefish. (2) Bear Lake Whitefish (above) has short, deep maxilla *not* reaching end of lacrimal, usually 69–74 lateral scales, 38–43 scales around body; usually *11 dorsal rays, 10 anal rays.* **Map 45**

ROUND WHITEFISH *Prosopium cylindraceum*   Pl. 2
Identification: Brown to bronze above, *dark-edged scales;* silver-white side; amber lower fins; dusky dorsal and caudal fins. Young (2–3 in. [51–76 mm]) are silver, have 2 or more rows of *black spots* on side that may coalesce with row of black spots on back. Fairly pointed snout (Fig. 13). 76–89 lateral scales; usually 22–24 scales around caudal peduncle; 14–21 rakers on 1st gill arch; 50–117 pyloric caeca. To 22 in. (56 cm).
Range: Disjunct: Arctic and Pacific drainages from western shore of Hudson Bay to AK and n. BC; Arctic and Atlantic drainages from Labrador to CT and west through St. Lawrence–Great Lakes basin (absent from Lake Erie). Also in Arctic drainages of Asia. Common.
Habitat: Shallow areas (usually less than 150 ft. [46 m]) of lakes and clear streams; rarely in brackish water.
Similar species: (1) Mountain Whitefish (Fig. 13) *lacks* dark-edged scales (may be dusky-edged); has larger but less distinct spots on side of young; 19–26 rakers on 1st gill arch. (2) Pygmy Whitefish (Pl. 2, Fig. 13) has larger eye, 54–70 lateral scales, 16–20 scales around caudal peduncle; 13–33 pyloric caeca; reaches 11 in. (28 cm). **Map 44**

ARCTIC GRAYLING *Thymallus arcticus*   Pl. 4
Identification: Rows of red to green spots on *huge purple to black* (on adult) *dorsal fin;* 17–25 rays. *Small mouth;* small teeth on both jaws. *Forked caudal fin.* Fairly large (77–103 lateral) scales. Dark blue-gray above; scattered black spots (darkest on young) on silver-gray to blue, sometimes pink, side; sometimes a black stripe on lower side between paired fins; orange-yellow stripes on pelvic fin; other fins dusky to dark gray. Narrow, vertical parr marks on young. To 30 in. (76 cm).
Range: Widespread in Arctic drainages from Hudson Bay to AK and in Arctic and Pacific drainages to cen. AB and BC; upper Missouri R. drainage, MT. Formerly in Great Lakes basin, MI. Widely introduced elsewhere, especially in w. U.S. Also in Asia. Locally common. **Habitat:** Open water of clear, cold, medium to large rivers and lakes; enters rocky creeks to spawn (May-June).
Similar species: Young whitefishes have no, or round, parr marks. **Map 46**

• *SALVELINUS*

Genus characteristics: Troutlike body. *Light* (pink, red, or cream) *spots* on body; *minute* (about 105–200 lateral) *scales; snow-white leading edge* on lower fins; scales along lateral line *smaller* than surrounding scales with little or no overlap with scales in front and behind; teeth on front (head) of vomer, not on shaft; 8–12 dorsal rays; 7–12 anal rays; dark parr marks on young.

LAKE TROUT *Salvelinus namaycush*   **Pl. 4**
Identification: *Deeply forked caudal fin.* Many small, often bean-shaped, *cream or yellow spots* on dark green to gray head, body, and dorsal and caudal fins. Narrow white edge on orange-red lower fins. (Individuals in large lakes may be silver overall.) No bright orange or red on body. Breeding male has dark stripe along side. 7–12 narrow, often interrupted parr marks on young (Fig. 9). 93–208 pyloric caeca. To 49½ in. (126 cm).
Range: Widely distributed from n. Canada and AK (missing in southern prairie provinces) south to New England and Great Lakes basin. Introduced widely outside native range to many parts of w. U.S. and other areas, including New Zealand, South America, and Sweden. Common in north, uncommon in Great Lakes except where maintained by artificial propagation. **Habitat:** Restricted to relatively deep lakes in southern part of range; in shallow and deep waters of northern lakes and streams.
Remarks: An exceedingly fat form of Lake Trout from deep waters of Lake Superior is called Siscowet. A hybrid between Lake Trout and Brook Trout is called a Splake. Splakes have been successfully introduced into many parts of North America.
Similar species: (1) Other *Salvelinus* species (Pl. 4) *lack* deeply forked caudal fin, have orange or red on body. (2) Pacific salmons and trouts (*Oncorhynchus* species, Pls. 4 & 5) have black spots on body or fins.
      Map 47

BROOK TROUT *Salvelinus fontinalis*   **Pl. 4**
Identification: *Slightly forked* to nearly straight-edged caudal fin. *Light green or cream wavy lines or blotches* on back and dorsal fin, broken into spots on side; *blue halos* around *pink or red spots* on side. Olive to black above; black lines on caudal fin; black line behind white edge on red lower fins. Anadromous individual is dark green above; has pale pink spots on silver side. Breeding male is brilliant orange or red below, has black belly. 8–10 regularly arranged parr marks on side of young (Fig. 9). 14–22 (usually 16–21) rakers with marginal teeth on 1st gill arch; 23–55 pyloric caeca. To 27½ in. (70 cm).
Range: Native to most of e. Canada from NF to w. side of Hudson Bay; south in Atlantic, Great Lakes, and Mississippi R. basins to MN and (in Appalachian Mountains) n. GA; introduced widely in North America and temperate regions of other continents. Common. **Habitat:** Clear, cool, well-oxygenated creeks, small to medium rivers, and lakes. Some populations are anadromous.
Remarks: The Aurora Trout, maintained only as hatchery stocks in lakes in the Temiskaming District of Ontario, may be a distinct subspecies, *S. f. timagamiensis,* and is considered *endangered* by the Canadian Government. The extinct Silver Trout, *S. f. agassizi,* of Dublin Pond, NH, is sometimes considered a distinct species.

Similar species: (1) Lake Trout (Pl. 4) has *deeply forked caudal fin, cream spots* on dark green or gray body. (2) Other *Salvelinus* species (Pl. 4) *lack* wavy dark green lines on dorsal fin. **Map 48**

ARCTIC CHAR *Salvelinus alpinus* Pl. 4

Identification: *Slightly* forked caudal fin. *Pink to red spots* (largest usually larger than pupil of eye) *on back and side.* No dark, wavy lines on dorsal and caudal fins. Color highly variable; in general, green to brown above, pink to red spots on side, lighter below. Silver overall in landlocked, nonspawning adult; some landlocked populations retain brilliant spawning colors year round. Breeding male is dark green to blue-green above; has silver-blue with scattered orange or red spots on side, white or brilliant orange-red below. Adult from estuaries is steel blue above; silver-blue on side with numerous large red, pink, or cream spots. Fins similar in color to body; white front edge on lower fins. Young has 10–15 irregularly arranged parr marks on side (Fig. 9). Usually *23–32* rakers on 1st gill arch; no marginal teeth. *35–75* pyloric caeca. To 38 in. (96 cm).
Range: Circumpolar; has the most northern distribution of any North American freshwater fish. Coastal areas in Atlantic, Arctic, and Pacific drainages from NF to AK; south along Atlantic Slope to New England. Seldom more than 186 mi. (300 km) from ocean. Also in Eurasia. Locally abundant. **Habitat:** Deep runs and pools of medium to large rivers; lakes. Anadromous populations enter rivers to spawn in fall and winter.
Similar species: See Dolly Varden (Pl. 4). **Map 49**

DOLLY VARDEN *Salvelinus malma* Pl. 4

Identification: Similar to Arctic Char, but has usually *14–21 rakers* on 1st gill arch, usually *21–29 pyloric caeca* (rarely as many as 40). Color variable. In fresh water, olive green to brown above; yellow, orange, or red spots (largest spots usually *smaller* than pupil of eye) on side. Anadromous individual usually dark blue above; has pale or pink spots on silver side. Breeding male is green-black above, has bright orange or red lower side, white front edge followed by black or red line on lower fins; breeding female is similar but less brilliant. Young have 8–12 parr marks (Fig. 9). Usually 11–12 branchiostegal rays, 6 mandibular pores. To about 25 in. (63 cm); many dwarf populations under 12 in. (31 cm).
Range: Arctic and Pacific drainages from AK to Puget Sound, WA; formerly in McCloud R. drainage, CA. Also in Asia. Common. **Habitat:** Deep runs and pools of creeks and small to large rivers; lakes. Typically anadromous, but many populations landlocked. Anadromous individuals may spend 2–3 years at sea, evidently near shore; migrate upstream usually in fall, spawn in spring.
Remarks: 2 subspecies in North America: *S. m. malma,* from Mackenzie R. to n. side of Alaska Peninsula, has usually 21–23 rakers on 1st gill arch, 66–68 vertebrae; *S. m. lordi,* south of the Alaska Peninsula, has usually 17–18 rakers on 1st gill arch, 62–64 vertebrae.

Similar species: See (1) Arctic Char (Pl. 4), (2) Bull Trout, and (3) Angayukaksurak Char.   **Map 50**

BULL TROUT *Salvelinus confluentus*   **Not shown**
Identification: Nearly identical to Dolly Varden but has slightly flatter and *longer head* — length usually *less than 4* times into standard length (more than 4 times in Dolly Varden); eye *higher* on head; usually 14–20 rakers on 1st gill arch; *large marginal teeth*; usually *13–15 branchiostegal rays, 7–9 mandibular pores*, 22–34 pyloric caeca. To about 3 ft. (91 cm).
Range: Coastal and mountain streams of Arctic, Pacific, and Missouri R. drainages from extreme s. YU to headwaters of Columbia R. drainage, n. NV, and McCloud R. drainage, n. CA. Locally common; rare in southern part of range. **Habitat:** Deep pools in large cold rivers and lakes; most common in high mountainous areas where snowfields and glaciers are present. Rarely anadromous.
Similar species: (1) See Dolly Varden (Pl. 4). (2) Arctic Char (Pl. 4) *lacks* marginal teeth on gill rakers; has usually 23–32 rakers on 1st gill arch, 35–75 pyloric caeca.   **Map 49**

ANGAYUKAKSURAK CHAR *Salvelinus anaktuvukensis*   **Not shown**
Identification: Similar to Dolly Varden but has *fire-red spots* on *velvet black* (on adult) or brown side (on young), usually *10 pelvic rays* (9 in Dolly Varden). To about 11¾ in. (30 cm).
Range: Restricted to streams on crest of Brooks Range, AK, from Romanzoff Mountains west to Howard Pass. Uncommon. **Habitat:** Cold headwaters; near springs in lake bottoms.
Similar species: See Dolly Varden (Pl. 4).   **Map 51**

ATLANTIC SALMON *Salmo salar*   **Pl. 5**
Identification: *Black spots* on head and body, *2-3 large spots* on gill cover; usually *unspotted* caudal fin (no rows of black spots). No white edge on pelvic and anal fins. Upper jaw reaches below *center of eye*; behind eye only in large male. Slightly forked caudal fin. At sea, brown, green, or blue above; silver side (often with X-marks). In fresh water, adult loses silver appearance and becomes darker; breeding adult is bronze and dark brown (often with red spots). *Hooked lower jaw* on male. 8–11 narrow parr marks along side of young (Fig. 9); *1 red spot* between each pair. 109–121 lateral scales; usually 12 branchiostegal rays, 11 dorsal rays. To 55 in. (140 cm).
Range: Atlantic Coast drainages from n. QU to Housatonic R., CT (possibly formerly to DE); inland to Lake Ontario (where now extirpated). Widely introduced elsewhere but seldom successfully. Also eastern Atlantic drainages from the Arctic Circle to Portugal. Locally common; depleted or extirpated from western and southern parts of range. **Habitat:** Rocky runs and pools of small to large rivers; lakes. The Atlantic Salmon is a classic example of an anadromous fish (although several lake populations are landlocked). It spawns in the fall in rocky streams; most young remain in fresh water for 2–3 years,

then migrate to the ocean for 1 or more years before returning to fresh water to spawn. Unlike Pacific salmon, the Atlantic Salmon does not die after spawning but returns to the ocean.

Remarks: Few animals have attracted as much attention as the Atlantic Salmon, a game fish par excellence and an overly exploited commercial species. It was one of the first North American fishes to disappear from parts of its range because of humankind's careless use of natural resources.

Similar species: (1) Brown Trout (Pl. 4) has *many* black spots on gill cover, usually rust-red spots on adult, usually red or orange adipose fin; upper jaw reaches *well beyond* eye in fish over 5 in. (13 cm). (2) Brook and (3) Lake Trouts (both, Pl. 4) have *light pink, red, or cream spots* on dark body; white edge on pelvic and anal fins.   **Map 46**

BROWN TROUT *Salmo trutta*   **Pl. 4**
Identification: *Red and black spots* on head and body, *many spots* on gill cover; usually unspotted or vaguely spotted caudal fin (no rows of black spots). No white edge on pelvic or anal fins. Upper jaw reaches below center of eye in 5-in. (13-cm) fish, *well beyond eye* in larger fish. Nearly straight-edged caudal fin. In streams, olive to dark brown above; silver sheen on yellow-brown side, white to yellow below; bold black spots on head, back, dorsal, and adipose fins, and extending below lateral line on side (*spots often surrounded by pale halos*); rust-red spots on side; usually *orange or red adipose fin.* Silver overall, often with X-marks above in large lakes and ocean. Breeding male has hooked upper jaw, rounded anal fin; female has falcate anal fin. 9–14 short, narrow parr marks along side of young (Fig. 9); few red spots along lateral line. 120–130 lateral scales; usually 10 branchiostegal rays, 9 dorsal rays. To 40½ in. (103 cm).
Range: Native to Europe, n. Africa, and w. Asia. Introduced to North America in 1883 (NY and MI) and now widely stocked throughout s. Canada and much of the U.S. Locally common. **Habitat:** Most stockings have been into cool, high gradient streams and cold lakes. In streams, adults live in pools; young occupy pools and riffles. Some sea-run populations have become established.
Similar species: Atlantic Salmon (Pl. 5) has *2–3 large black spots* on gill cover, *no* red spots on body, *no* red or orange on adipose fin; upper jaw reaches *only* to below center of eye (except on large male).

● *ONCORHYNCHUS*

Genus characteristics: Salmon- or troutlike body. Usually *black spots or specks* on body or caudal fin (or both); tiny (about 100–200 lateral) scales; *no* snow-white leading edge on lower fins; scales along lateral line *as large* as or larger than scales in adjacent rows, overlap with scales in front and behind; teeth on front (head) and shaft of vomer; 8–16 dorsal rays; 8–12 anal rays in trouts, 13–19 in salmons; dark parr marks on young (except Pink Salmon); to 58 in. (147 cm).

SOCKEYE or RED SALMON *Oncorhynchus nerka* **Pl. 5**

Identification: Small black specks but *no large black spots* on back or caudal fin. At sea, metallic blue-green above; silver below. Breeding male has *green head, bright red body,* yellow-green caudal fin, white lower jaw; female is similar but often has green or yellow blotches on side. 28–40 long, thin, serrated, closely spaced rakers and rudiments on 1st gill arch. 8–14 elliptical to oval parr marks along side of young (Fig. 9). To 33 in. (84 cm).

Range: Arctic and Pacific drainages from Point Hope, AK, to Sacramento R. drainage, CA. Landlocked populations in AK, YU, BC, WA, and OR. Widely stocked, but most transplants unsuccessful. Also in ne. Asia. Common in north; rare south of Columbia R. drainage. **Habitat:** Open ocean; lakes; migrates up coastal streams to spawn. **Remarks:** Lake populations known as Kokanee.

Similar species: Chum Salmon (Pl. 5) also lacks black spots, has 18–28 short, stout, smooth rakers and rudiments on 1st gill arch. **Map 52**

CHUM SALMON *Oncorhynchus keta* **Pl. 5**

Identification: *Black specks,* but *no large black spots* on back or caudal fin. At sea, metallic blue above; silver below. Breeding individual is black or dark olive above; has *red or dusky bars or fused blotches* along *dull green side,* white-tipped (brightest on male) anal and pelvic fins. Front teeth of males become more enlarged than in other salmons. 6–14 narrow, short parr marks along side of young (Fig. 9). 18–28 short, stout, smooth rakers and rudiments on 1st gill arch. To 40 in. (102 cm).

Range: Arctic and Pacific drainages from Anderson and Mackenzie rivers, NT, through much of AK south to Sacramento R. drainage, CA; rarely to San Lorenzo R., s. CA. Also in ne. Asia. Common. **Habitat:** Anadromous; ocean and coastal streams.

Similar species: (1) Sockeye Salmon (Pl. 5) has *no* white tips on fins, usually more than 30 long, thin, serrated rakers and rudiments on 1st gill arch. (2) Other salmons (Pl. 5) have *large black spots* on back and caudal fin. **Map 53**

CHINOOK or KING SALMON *Oncorhynchus tshawytscha* **Pl. 5**

Identification: *Largest salmon;* salmon over 30 lb. (14 kg) are almost always this species. *Irregular black spots* on back, *both lobes of caudal fin* and dorsal and adipose fins. *Gums black* at base of teeth. At sea, blue, green, or gray above; silver below. Small male often dull yellow; larger male often blotchy, *dull red* on side. Breeding individual dark olive-brown to purple. 6–12 large parr marks along side of young (Fig. 9). To 58 in. (147 cm); rarely over 50 lb. (23 kg); 1 specimen from AK reportedly weighed 126 lb. (57 kg).

Range: Arctic and Pacific drainages from Point Hope, AK, to Ventura R., CA. Occasionally strays south to San Diego, CA. Widely stocked outside native range, somewhat successfully in Great Lakes. Also in ne. Asia. Uncommon; least abundant of Pacific salmons. **Habitat:** Anadromous; ocean and coastal streams.

Similar species: See Pl. 5. (1) Sockeye and (2) Chum Salmons have *no* large black spots. (3) Coho Salmon has no black spots on *lower lobe* of caudal fin; *gums white* at base of teeth. (4) Pink Salmon has large *oval black spots* on back and caudal fin; does not exceed 30 in. (76 cm).   **Map 54**

COHO or SILVER SALMON *Oncorhynchus kisutch*   **Pl. 5**
Identification: *Black spots on back* and *upper lobe* of caudal fin. *Gums white* at base of teeth. At sea, metallic blue above; silver below. Breeding male has dusky green on back and head, *bright red side,* black belly; female has bronze to *pink-red* side. 8–12 narrow parr marks along side of young (Fig. 9). To 38½ in. (98 cm).
Range: Arctic and Pacific drainages from Point Hope, AK, to Monterey Bay, CA; infrequently as far south as Chamalu Bay, Baja California. Also in ne. Asia. Generally common; rare south of cen. CA. **Habitat:** Anadromous; ocean and coastal streams.
Similar species: Chinook Salmon (Pl. 5) has black spots on *both lobes* of caudal fin, *gums black* at base of teeth.   **Map 55**

PINK SALMON *Oncorhynchus gorbuscha*   **Pl. 5**
Identification: *Large,* mostly *oval, black spots* on back and *both lobes* of caudal fin. At sea, metallic blue or blue-green above; silver below. Breeding male develops *humped back* and hooked upper jaw; *pink to brown stripe along side.* Female lacks hump, markedly hooked jaw. Young *lack* parr marks (Fig. 9). Usually more than 169 lateral scales (usually fewer than 155 in other salmons). To 30 in. (76 cm).
Range: Arctic and Pacific drainages from Mackenzie R. delta, NT, to Sacramento R. drainage, CA; occasionally as far south as La Jolla, s. CA. Introduced in upper Great Lakes and e. NF. Also in ne. Asia. Common. **Habitat:** Anadromous; ocean and coastal streams.
Similar species: (1) Coho Salmon (Pl. 5) *lacks* black spots on lower lobe of caudal fin. (2) Chinook Salmon (Pl. 5) has small *irregular black spots* on back and caudal fin.   **Map 56**

CUTTHROAT TROUT *Oncorhynchus clarki*   **Pl. 4**
Identification: *Red "cutthroat" mark* under lower jaw (usually pale in sea-run fish); *many black spots on body.* No or faint red stripe on side (some populations have narrow copper-orange stripe). Upper jaw reaches *well behind* eye in adult (except in some fast-growing females). Extremely variable in color. Inland populations have olive-yellow, blue-green, or red body. Coastal populations are olive to dark green above, silver-blue to pale olive on side, silver-olive to white below; have many black spots on body and fins. Young have black spots on about 10 oval parr marks on side (Fig. 9). 110–130 lateral scales. Small teeth on floor of mouth between gill arches. To 39 in. (99 cm).
Range: Pacific Coast drainages from Prince William Sound, AK, to Eel R., n. CA (generally not more than 100 mi. [161 km] inland). Freshwater populations range through Rocky Mountains in Hudson Bay, Mississippi R., Great (including Lahontan, Bonneville, and Alvord basins) and Pacific basins from s. AB to Rio Grande drainage, NM. Widely transplanted within and outside native range. Estab-

lished in Laurentian lakes, QU. Locally common. **Habitat:** Gravel-bottomed creeks and small rivers; lakes. Anadromous in many coastal streams.

Remarks: At least 14 subspecies (some very distinctive) historically, but indiscriminate stocking has obscured recognition. Three subspecies are protected as *threatened subspecies: O. c. stomias*, the "Greenback Cutthroat Trout," in CO; *O. c. henshawi*, the "Lahontan Cutthroat Trout," in NV and CA; and *O. c. seleniris*, the "Paiute Cutthroat Trout," in CA. Hybridizes with Rainbow and Golden Trouts.

Similar species: (1) Gila Trout (Pl. 4), has *yellow "cutthroat" mark*, rose stripe on side, white tips on fins. (2) Rainbow Trout (Pl. 4) *lacks* red "cutthroat" mark; has pink to red stripe on side, no teeth on floor of mouth between gill arches. **Map 57**

GILA TROUT *Oncorhynchus gilae* Pl. 4

Identification: Many *small, irregular black spots* on side (mostly above lateral line), head, and dorsal and caudal fins. Olive-yellow to brassy side; faint *rose stripe* along side of adult; *yellow "cutthroat" mark* under lower jaw; white or yellow tips on dorsal, anal, and pelvic fins. To 12½ in. (32 cm).

Range: Gila R. system, NM and AZ. Introduced into other streams in w. NM and mountain streams in cen. AZ. Rare; protected as an *endangered species.* **Habitat:** Clear, cool mountain creeks (above 6540 ft. elevation [2000 m]).

Similar species: (1) See Apache Trout. (2) Cutthroat Trout (Pl. 4) has *red "cutthroat" mark, no* rose stripe on side, usually no white tips on fins. **Map 58**

APACHE TROUT *Oncorhynchus apache* Not shown

Identification: Similar to Gila Trout but has bright *yellow body and fins; large black spots* on body, top of head, and dorsal, adipose, and caudal fins; *no* rose stripe on side. Iris has *2 small black spots* on either side of pupil, creating *black stripe* through eye. To about 6¾ in. (17 cm) in streams; 19¼ in. (49 cm) in lakes.

Range: Upper Salt R. and Little Colorado R. systems (Colorado R. drainage), AZ. Introduced into several surrounding streams and lakes but rare in pure (nonhybrid) form. Protected as a *threatened species.* **Habitat:** Clear, cool mountain headwaters and creeks (generally above 8175 ft. elevation [2500 m]); mountain lakes.

Remarks: Hybridization with Rainbow Trout and competition from Brook and Brown Trouts have resulted in 95% (stream km) reduction in range.

Similar species: See Gila Trout (Pl. 4). **Map 57**

RAINBOW TROUT or STEELHEAD *Oncorhynchus mykiss* Pl. 4

Identification: *Small, irregular black spots* on back and most fins. *Pink to red stripe* on side (except in sea-run form). Distinct *radiating rows of black spots* on caudal fin. Often black edge on adipose fin. Upper jaw reaches barely behind eye in young and female, well behind eye in large male. Highly variable: steel-blue, yellow-green, or brown above; silver to pale yellow-green below. Stream and spawning fish have intense dark colors; lake fish are light and silvery. Young has 5–10 widely spaced, short, dark, oval parr marks (Fig. 9). Usually 115–130 lateral scales; 8–12 anal rays. No teeth on floor of mouth between gill arches. To 45 in. (114 cm).

Range: Native to Pacific Slope from Kuskokwim R., AK, to (at least) Rio Santa Domingo, Baja California; upper Mackenzie R. drainage (Arctic basin), AB and BC ; endorheic basins of s. OR. Widely introduced in cold waters elsewhere in North America and rest of the world. Common. **Habitat:** Cold headwaters, creeks, and small to large rivers; lakes. Anadromous in coastal streams.

Remarks: The sea-run Rainbow Trout is called a Steelhead, and interior populations often are referred to as Redband Trout. One of the most important game fishes in North America. Unlike salmon, adults usually survive spawning.

Similar species: (1) See Golden Trout (Pl. 4). (2) Cutthroat Trout (Pl. 4) has orange or red "cutthroat" mark on underside of lower jaw, small teeth on floor of mouth between gill arches. (3) *Salvelinus* species (Pl. 4) have *light spots* on dark body, white leading edges on lower fins. (4) Salmons (Pl. 5) have 13 or more anal rays. **Map 59**

GOLDEN TROUT *Oncorhynchus aguabonita* **Pl. 4**

Identification: Similar to Rainbow Trout but has usually about *10 parr marks* on adult (as well as young), usually 175–210 lateral scales; brilliant *red-orange to bright red belly, cheek, and branchiostegal membranes; gold lower side; red-orange stripe* along side; *large black spots* on dorsal and caudal fins. Orange lower fins have white tips preceded by dusky black stripe; white to orange tip on dorsal fin. To 28 in. (71 cm).

Range: Endemic to upper Kern R. basin, Tulare and Kern cos., CA. Introduced into more than 300 mountain lakes and streams in the Sierra Nevada, CA, and other Rocky Mountain states and provinces. Common. **Habitat:** Clear, cool headwaters, creeks, and lakes at elevations above 6867 ft. (2100 m).

Remarks: Most transplanted populations hybridize with Rainbow and Cutthroat Trouts. 2 subspecies: *O. a. gilberti*, in Main and Little Kern rivers, has usually 140–170 lateral scales, 60–63 vertebrae, 30–50 pyloric caeca; *O. a. aguabonita* in S. Fork Kern R. and Golden Trout Cr., has usually 150–210 lateral scales, 58–61 vertebrae, 25–40 pyloric caeca.

Similar species: (1) See Rainbow Trout (Pl. 4). (2) Cutthroat Trout (Pl. 4) has red or orange "cutthroat" mark on lower jaw; small teeth on floor of mouth behind tongue; no white tips on dorsal, pelvic, or anal fins. **Map 58**

■ SMELTS: Family Osmeridae (7)

Smelts live in cold and temperate coastal waters, both marine and fresh, of the Northern Hemisphere. Small, *slender* fishes with a *large mouth*, cycloid scales, a lateral line, abdominal pelvic fins, 1 rayed dorsal fin and an *adipose fin,* and no spines in the fins. Unlike the similar-looking salmonids, they *lack* a pelvic axillary process. They feed mainly on crustaceans. Spawning occurs in spring over gravel or sand in streams or on gravel shoals of lakes.

POND SMELT *Hypomesus olidus*   **Not shown**
Identification: *Small mouth;* upper jaw ends *before* middle of eye. Dorsal fin origin *above or in front* of pelvic fin origin. *Incomplete lateral line; 51–62 lateral scales.* Small, pointed teeth on jaws; none enlarged. Olive to light brown above; purple iridescence on silver stripe along side; clear fins. Breeding male has gold cast. 8–10 dorsal rays; 12–16 anal rays; 10–13 pectoral rays, 31–36 rakers on 1st gill arch; 0–3 pyloric caeca. To 8 in. (20 cm).
Range: Arctic and Pacific drainages from Rae R. (Coronation Gulf) and Great Bear Lake, NT, to Copper R., AK. Also Pacific Coast of Asia. Common to abundant. **Habitat:** Middle and surface water of ponds, lakes, and streams; over a variety of bottom types. Enters brackish water.
Similar species: (1) See Delta Smelt. (2) Wakasagi has *4–7 pyloric caeca.*   **Map 60**

DELTA SMELT *Hypomesus transpacificus*   **Not shown**
Identification: Nearly identical to Pond Smelt (above) but has *9–10 dorsal rays, 4–5 pyloric caeca.* Steel blue above and on side, almost translucent; silver-white below; dusky fins. Faint black specks on silver stripe along side. 0–1 black specks between mandibles. 53–60 lateral scales, 15–17 anal rays, 10–12 pectoral rays; 27–33 rakers on 1st gill arch. To 4¾ in. (12 cm).
Range: Sacramento–San Joaquin Delta region, cen. CA. **Habitat:** Open brackish and fresh water of large channels.
Similar species: (1) See Pond Smelt and (2) Wakasagi.   **Map 60**

WAKASAGI *Hypomesus nipponensis*   **Not shown**
Identification: Nearly identical to Delta Smelt, but has *10 or more black specks* between mandibles, 12–14 pectoral rays, *7–9 dorsal rays,* 13–15 anal rays. Yellow-brown above; black specks on back and side; 54–60 lateral scales, 4–7 pyloric caeca; 29–37 rakers on 1st gill arch. To 6¾ in. (17 cm).
Range: Native to Japan. Introduced successfully into several n. CA impoundments and can be expected anywhere in lower Klamath and Sacramento R. drainages. **Habitat:** Open water of impoundments and their tributaries.
Similar species: See Delta Smelt.

RAINBOW SMELT *Osmerus mordax*   **Pl. 3**
Identification: *Huge mouth,* upper jaw reaches *middle of eye* or beyond. *2 large canine teeth* (and sometimes smaller ones) in roof of mouth; large teeth on tongue. Dorsal fin origin *above or in front* of pelvic fin origin. Olive above; blue or pink iridescence on silver side; usually a silver stripe along side, dark specks on upper side; dusky

fins. Landlocked individual may have black head, back, and fins. Incomplete lateral line, 62–72 lateral scales; 11–16 anal rays; usually 28–32 rakers on 1st gill arch. To 13 in. (33 cm).
Range: Atlantic drainages from Lake Melville, NF, to Delaware R., PA, and west through Great Lakes; Arctic and Pacific drainages from Bathurst Inlet, NT, to Vancouver Island, BC. Also Pacific drainages of Asia. Introduced into many impoundments and lakes in e. North America including Great Lakes; seasonally present in main channels of Missouri, Mississippi, Ohio, and Illinois rivers from KY to MT and south to LA. Common; locally abundant. **Habitat:** Cool clear lakes, medium to large rivers, and nearshore coastal waters. Often in schools in midwater. Coastal populations are anadromous.
Remarks: 2 subspecies, *O. m. mordax* of e. North America and *O. m. dentex* of North Pacific–Arctic drainages, sometimes recognized but in need of study.
Similar species: (1) See Pygmy Smelt. (2) Longfin Smelt has pectoral fin reaching to pelvic fin, *no* large teeth in roof of mouth, 15–21 anal rays. **Map 61**

PYGMY SMELT *Osmerus spectrum* **Not shown**
Identification: Nearly identical to Rainbow Smelt (above) but has usually *33–36 rakers* on 1st gill arch, reaches only 6¾ in. (17 cm).
Range: Native to Heney Lake, s. QU, Lake Utopia, s. NB, Wilton Pond and Green Lake, s. ME. Introduced into Meach and Ouimet lakes, s. QU. May be present in other lakes in e. Canada and New England. **Habitat:** Small, deep, thermally stratified lakes.
Remarks: When it occurs with Rainbow Smelt, the Pygmy Smelt usually spawns later in the year, eats smaller food items, grows more slowly, matures earlier in life, and has a shorter life span.
Similar species: See Rainbow Smelt (Pl. 3). **Map 41**

LONGFIN SMELT *Spirinchus thaleichthys* **Not shown**
Identification: Pectoral fin almost *reaches or extends past* pelvic fin origin. *Huge mouth;* upper jaw extends *to middle of eye* or beyond. *Large canine teeth* on tongue; small jaw teeth. Dorsal fin origin above or behind pelvic fin base. Dusky or olive-brown to iridescent pink-green above; dusky fins. No silver stripe on side. Breeding male has large, rounded anal fin; moss green back; many black specks on head. Incomplete lateral line; 55–62 lateral scales; 15–21 anal rays; 38–47 rakers on 1st gill arch. To 6 in. (15 cm).
Range: Pacific Coast from Prince William Sound, AK, to Monterey Bay, CA. Landlocked in Harrison Lake, BC, and Lakes Washington and Union, WA. Locally and seasonally abundant. **Habitat:** Nearshore; bays and estuaries. Ascends coastal streams from October to December to spawn.
Similar species: Other smelts have pectoral fin *not* reaching pelvic fin. **Map 62**

EULACHON *Thaleichthys pacificus* **Not shown**
Identification: Concentric bony *striations* on gill cover. *Huge mouth;*

upper jaw extends to *rear* of eye. Usually no enlarged jaw teeth. Dorsal fin origin behind pelvic fin origin. Blue-brown above, small black specks on back; shading to silver-white below; no silver stripe along side; dusky pectoral and caudal fins. Breeding male has a thick ridge along side. *Complete lateral line;* 70–78 scales. 18–23 anal rays; 17–23 rakers on 1st gill arch. To 11¾ in. (30 cm).

Range: Pacific Coast from Pribilof Island (Bering Sea) and Nushagak R., AK, to Monterey Bay, CA. Seasonally abundant. **Habitat:** Nearshore; coastal inlets. Young apparently in deeper water. Ascends rivers in spring to spawn, but seldom penetrates more than a few miles inland.

Remarks: Eulachons were a source of food and cooking oil for Indians, who also dried specimens, inserted wicks, and used them as torches; hence, the alternate name Candlefish.

Similar species: Other smelts *lack* striations on gill cover.   **Map 42**

■ MUDMINNOWS: Family Umbridae (4)

Mudminnows are fairly obscure small fishes with a long, slender body, cylindrical in front and compressed at rear; cycloid scales; 1 dorsal fin; no fin spines; and dorsal and anal fins *far back* on the body. Pelvic fins are small and abdominal.

Mudminnows have a highly disjunct North American and European distribution. Only *Umbra krameri* occurs naturally in Europe, but the Eastern Mudminnow (*U. pygmaea*) has been introduced. Mudminnows can breathe atmospheric oxygen and thereby survive in poorly oxygenated water unsuitable for other fishes.

OLYMPIC MUDMINNOW *Novumbra hubbsi*   **Pl. 6**
Identification: Dorsal fin origin *above or only slightly in front of* anal fin origin. Anal fin base about as long as dorsal fin base. *Small pelvic fins, with 6–7 rays.* Straight-edged or slightly indented caudal fin. Fairly small pectoral fins, with 18–25 rays. *No* lateral line. Green to dark brown above and on side; *10-15 cream to yellow, interrupted narrow bars on side;* white to yellow below; pale olive to dark brown median fins, sometimes with light narrow bands. No black bar at base of caudal fin. Breeding male is dark chocolate brown to black; has iridescent blue-green to white bars on side, sky-blue edges on dorsal and anal fins. Fairly small (52–58 lateral) scales. 12–15 dorsal rays; 10–13 anal rays. To 3 in. (8 cm).

Range: Coastal lowlands of Olympic Peninsula, WA, from Ozette Lake and Queets R. drainage, to upper Chehalis R. drainage. Locally common. Occasionally found in lower Deschutes R. (Puget Sound drainage), apparently as a result of floodwater exchange with Chehalis R. **Habitat:** Quiet water with dense vegetation or other cover over mud and debris; cool, brown waters of bogs and swamps.

Similar species: See Pl. 6. (1) Central and (2) Eastern Mudminnows

have black bar on caudal fin base, *no* narrow yellow bars on side, dorsal fin origin *far in front* of anal fin origin, 30–37 lateral scales.
Map 63

ALASKA BLACKFISH *Dallia pectoralis*   Pl. 6
Identification: *Black mottling and blotches* on dark brown to olive back and side; yellow-white below with black specks; *black specks on red-brown fins;* white to clear edge on median fins of adult become pale red on large male. *Tiny pelvic fins, with 2–3 rays.* Broadly rounded pectoral fins, with *32–36 rays.* Dorsal fin origin *above* anal fin origin. Anal fin base about as long as dorsal fin base. *Tiny (76–100 lateral) scales.* Short, flat snout. Rounded caudal fin. Lateral line present but inconspicuous. 10–14 dorsal rays; 11–16 anal rays. To 13 in. (33 cm).
Range: AK; Colville R. delta south to cen. Alaska Peninsula near Chignik; upstream in Yukon-Tanana drainage to near Fairbanks. Introduced into Hood and Spenard lakes near Anchorage. Also Bering Sea islands and ne. Siberia. Common to abundant. **Habitat:** Usually in heavily vegetated swamps and ponds; occasionally in medium to large rivers and lakes with abundant vegetation. **Map 64**

CENTRAL MUDMINNOW *Umbra limi*   Pl. 6
Identification: *Black bar* on caudal fin base. Dorsal fin origin *far in front* of anal fin origin. Anal fin base about *half as long* as dorsal fin base. *No* lateral line. Rounded caudal fin. Small pelvic fins, with 6–7 rays. Fairly small pectoral fins, with 11–16 rays. Green to brown-black above and on side; white to yellow below; up to *14 dark brown bars* occasionally on side; no spots on dusky brown fins. Breeding male has iridescent blue-green anal and pelvic fins. Fairly large (30–37 lateral) scales. 13–17 dorsal rays; 7–10 anal rays. To 5½ in. (14 cm).
Range: St. Lawrence–Great Lakes, Hudson Bay (Red R.), and Mississippi R. basins from QU to MB and south to cen. OH, w. TN, and ne. AR; Hudson R. drainage (Atlantic Slope), NY. Isolated populations in Missouri R. drainage of e.-cen. SD and w. IA. Common. **Habitat:** Quiet areas of streams, sloughs, swamps, and other wetlands over mud and debris. Often in dense vegetation. Tolerant of drought, low oxygen levels, and extremes in water temperature.
Similar species: See Eastern Mudminnow (Pl. 6). **Map 65**

EASTERN MUDMINNOW *Umbra pygmaea*   Pl. 6
Identification: Similar to Central Mudminnow (above) but has *10–14 dark brown stripes* with pale interspaces (about as wide as stripes) on back and side. To 4½ in. (11 cm).
Range: Atlantic and Gulf slopes from se. NY (including Long Island) to St. Johns R. drainage, FL, and west to Aucilla R. drainage, FL and GA. Common except at extremes of range. **Habitat:** Quiet streams, sloughs, swamps, and other wetlands over sand, mud, and debris; often in dense vegetation.
Similar species: See Central Mudminnow (Pl. 6). **Map 65**

■ PIKES: Family Esocidae (4)

Highly distinctive, large, predatory fishes with a green body, a yellow eye, a large *duckbill-like snout*, many small cycloid scales, *forked caudal fin*, and dorsal and anal fins that are located *far back* on the long cylindrical body. Pikes have one dorsal fin, pelvic fins located on the abdomen, and no spines in the fins. They live in e. and n. North America, Europe, and n. Asia. One species, the Northern Pike, *Esox lucius*, is one of the few species of freshwater fishes to occur in both North America and Eurasia. The Amur Pike, *Esox reicherti*, is endemic to Siberia.

Pikes are voracious predators, feeding on a wide variety of fishes. Because of their large size and fighting behavior, they (especially the Muskellunge and Northern Pike) are favorite sport fishes.

GRASS or REDFIN PICKEREL *Esox americanus*   Pl. 6
Identification: *Fully scaled cheek and opercle* (Fig. 14). Black (darker in female) suborbital bar *slanted* toward rear. Dark olive to brown above; 15–36 dark green to brown wavy bars along side of adult; amber to white below. Red, yellow, or dusky fins (see Remarks). 11–13 branchiostegal rays; 4 (rarely 3–5) submandibular pores; 92–118 lateral scales. To 15 in. (38 cm).
Range: Atlantic Slope from St. Lawrence R. drainage, QU, to Lake Okeechobee, FL; Gulf drainages east to Brazos R., TX; Mississippi R. and Great Lakes basins north to NE, WI, MI, and s. ON. Common; absent in Appalachian Highlands. Introduced elsewhere, including into sw. WA, CA, and CO. **Habitat:** Lakes, swamps, and backwaters, and sluggish pools of streams. Usually among vegetation in clear water.
Remarks: 2 subspecies: *E. a. americanus* (Redfin Pickerel) has red lower and caudal fins, a short broad snout with a convex profile, and occupies the Atlantic Slope drainages to s. GA. Intergrades (with amber fins) occupy the Gulf Slope drainages west to Pascagoula R. *E. a. vermiculatus* (Grass Pickerel) has yellow-green to dusky lower fins and a long narrow snout with a concave profile; it occupies rest of range.
Similar species: See Pl. 6. (1) Chain Pickerel has chainlike pattern on side, vertical suborbital bar, longer snout, 14–17 branchiostegal rays. (2) Northern Pike and (3) Muskellunge *lack* scales on lower half of opercle; have 13 or more branchiostegal rays, 5 or more submandibular pores.   **Map 66**

CHAIN PICKEREL *Esox niger*   Pl. 6
Identification: *Fully scaled cheek and opercle* (Fig. 14). *Green chainlike pattern* on yellow side (adult), wavy bars on young. *Vertical* black suborbital bar. Very long snout, distance from tip of snout to middle of eye greater than distance from middle of eye to rear edge of gill cover. 14–17 branchiostegal rays; 3–5 submandibular pores; 110–138 lateral scales. To 39 in. (99 cm).
Range: Atlantic Slope from NS (where introduced) to s. FL; Gulf

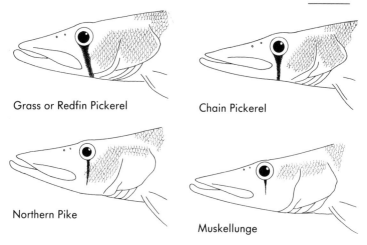

Grass or Redfin Pickerel Chain Pickerel

Northern Pike Muskellunge

Fig. 14 *Esox* species

Coast west to Sabine Lake drainage, LA; Mississippi R. basin north to
KY and MO (mostly Former Mississippi Embayment but also upland
streams in se. MO). Introduced into Lakes Ontario and Erie drainages, and other scattered localities as far west as CO. **Habitat:** Vegetated lakes, swamps, and backwaters and quiet pools of creeks and
small to medium rivers.
Similar species: Grass Pickerel (Pl. 6) *lacks* chainlike pattern on side,
has *slanted* suborbital bar, shorter snout (distance from tip of snout
to middle of eye about equal to distance from middle of eye to rear
edge of gill cover), 11–13 branchiostegal rays.   **Map 67**

NORTHERN PIKE *Esox lucius*   **Pl. 6**
Identification: *Partly scaled opercle; fully scaled cheek* (Fig. 14). *Rows
of yellow bean-shaped spots* (on adult), yellow to white wavy bars
(on young) on green back and side; large individuals dark gray above.
No suborbital bar. Usually black spots on all fins except pectoral;
median fins dusky green, yellow or pale red. 13–16 branchiostegal
rays; 5–6 submandibular pores; 105–148 lateral scales. To 53 in. (133
cm).
Range: Atlantic, Arctic, Pacific, Great Lakes, and Mississippi R. basins from Labrador to AK and south to PA, MO, and NE. Widely introduced elsewhere. Also occurs in n. Eurasia as far south as n. Italy.
Common. **Habitat:** Clear vegetated lakes; quiet pools and backwaters
of creeks and small to large rivers.
Remarks: The "tiger musky" is a hybrid Northern Pike–Muskellunge
(recognizable by the strong barring pattern on the side) that is con-

sidered a superior sport fish and often is introduced in impoundments and lakes.

Similar species: Muskellunge (Pl. 6) has pattern of *dark marks* on light background, *no* scales on lower half of cheek, 16–19 branchiostegal rays, 6–10 submandibular pores. **Map 68**

MUSKELLUNGE *Esox masquinongy* **Pl. 6**

Identification: *Partly scaled cheek and opercle* (Fig. 14). *Dark spots, blotches, or bars* on light yellow-green back and side; cream to white below with small brown to gray blotches; large individuals dark gray above. No suborbital bar. 16–19 branchiostegal rays; 6-10 submandibular pores; 130–167 lateral scales. To 72 in. (183 cm).

Range: Originally St. Lawrence R.–Great Lakes, Hudson Bay (Red R.), and Mississippi R. basins, from QU to se. MB and south in the Appalachians to GA and in the west to IA. Introduced into Atlantic drainages as far south as s. VA; introduced elsewhere in s. and w. U.S. but seldom successfully. **Habitat:** Clear vegetated lakes; quiet pools and backwaters of creeks and small to large rivers.

Remarks: The "musky" is a solitary hunter, lurking about cover and lunging after suitable prey. It begins feeding on other fishes at about 4 days of age and may reach 12 in. (30 cm) in only 4 months. Its large size and fighting spirit make it one of North America's favorite sport fishes.

Similar species: Northern Pike (Pl. 6) has pattern of *light marks* on *dark* background, *fully scaled cheek,* 13–16 branchiostegal rays, 5–6 submandibular pores. **Map 69**

■ CHARACINS: Family Characidae (1)

Characins comprise 800 or so species of mostly small fishes, closely related to minnows, found mainly in Central America, South America, and Africa. Unlike minnows, characins have an *adipose fin* and *teeth* on the jaws. Many are brightly colored and popular aquarium fishes (e.g., tetras). One species, the Mexican Tetra, occurs in s. TX and NM.

MEXICAN TETRA *Astyanax mexicanus* **Pl. 32**

Identification: *Adipose fin. Black stripe* on caudal peduncle and fin. *2-3 dusky black spots* on silver side above pectoral fin. Deep, compressed body; blunt snout; terminal mouth; large, sharp teeth on jaws. Large individual has yellow fins, red on caudal and at front of anal fin. 35–40 lateral scales; 10–11 dorsal rays; 21–23 anal rays. To 4¾ in. (12 cm).

Range: Originally restricted to the Nueces, lower Rio Grande, and the lower Pecos R. drainages, TX; now established elsewhere in TX (primarily streams on Edwards Plateau) and NM (throughout Pecos R. system). Also native to e. and cen. Mexico. Common. **Habitat:** Rock- and sand-bottomed pools and backwaters of creeks and small to large rivers; springs. **Map 70**

■MINNOWS: Family Cyprinidae (238)

The minnow family is the largest family of fishes, containing about 2100 species, and is present on all continents except South America, Australia, and Antarctica. The greatest diversity is in Southeast Asia; as many as 600 species may occur in China. Our native North American fauna north of Mexico includes about 231 species.

The term *minnow* is sometimes applied to any small fish, but properly it refers only to members of the family Cyprinidae. Minnows have *1 dorsal fin, abdominal pelvic fins*, a lateral line (rarely absent), and cycloid scales on the body. They have no true spines in the fins, although some (e.g., carp and spinefins) have soft rays that harden embryologically to give rise to spinelike structures (referred to below as spines). They lack teeth in the mouth but have 1–3 rows of teeth on the pharyngeal bone, which grind food against a horny pad on the basioccipital bone. Although not useful on live minnows, the numbers and configuration of the "pharyngeal teeth" can be quite helpful in the identification of preserved specimens. A notation of "2,5–4,2," for example, means that the teeth are in 2 rows on each side of the head, with 2 teeth in each outer row, 5 in the inner row on the left side, and 4 in the inner row on the right side.

In the genus and species accounts, *anal ray and pharyngeal tooth counts are modes;* other counts are ranges unless stated otherwise.

Minnows are as varied ecologically as they are morphologically. The speciose genus *Notropis* consists mostly of small midwater carnivores that feed mainly on small crustaceans and insects. Herbivorous minnows, feeding predominantly on algae, include the stonerollers (*Campostoma*), Chiselmouth (*Acrocheilus alutaceus*), some of the silvery minnows (*Hybognathus*), and a few species of *Notropis* (e.g., the Cape Fear Shiner). Plant material takes longer than meat to digest, so herbivorous species have longer intestines. The long and usually coiled gut is often visible through the belly of these species. The lining of the body cavity (peritoneum) is usually white in carnivorous minnows and black in herbivorous ones. The color of the peritoneum sometimes can be seen through the body wall; unless stated otherwise a species has a white peritoneum.

GRASS CARP *Ctenopharyngodon idella*   **Pl. 7**
Identification: *Wide head;* terminal mouth. *Large (34–45 lateral) scales, dark-edged,* with *black spot* at base. Slender (especially adult), fairly compressed body; dorsal fin origin in front of pelvic fin origin. Gray to brassy green above; white to yellow below; clear to gray-brown fins. 7 dorsal rays; 8 anal rays; pharyngeal teeth 2,5–4,2 or 2,4–4,2. To 49 in. (125 cm).
Range: Native to east Asia. Introduced into AR in 1960s; now known in at least 34 states. Uncommon but increasing in lower Mississippi R. **Habitat:** Lakes, ponds, pools, and backwaters of large rivers.
Remarks: Because of its appetite for vegetation, the grass carp is being introduced into the U.S. to control aquatic weed problems in lakes and ponds. However, many fishes, waterfowl, and other native spe-

cies are dependent upon aquatic vegetation, and the introduction of the grass carp may prove to be more costly than beneficial.

Similar species: (1) Goldfish and (2) Common Carp (both, Pl. 14) have long dorsal fin, deeper body, spines in dorsal and anal fins; common carp has barbels; goldfish *lacks* dark-edged scales.

GOLDFISH *Carassius auratus* Pl. 14

Identification: *Large scales,* 25–31 along lateral line. *Long dorsal fin,* 15–21 rays. *Stout, saw-toothed spine* (and 2 smaller spines) at front of dorsal and anal fins. Deep, thick body; terminal mouth; large caudal fin. Gray-green above, brassy sheen on back and side; white to yellow below; gray to brown dorsal and caudal fins (see Remarks). 5–6 anal rays; pharyngeal teeth 0,4–4,0. To 16 in. (41 cm).

Range: Native to Asia; first introduced into U.S. in late 1600s. Now established in much of U.S., s. ON, s. AB, and s. BC. Sporadic; locally common. **Habitat:** Shallow, muddy pools and backwaters of sluggish rivers, ponds, and lakes. Most common in warm turbid or vegetated water; more tolerant than most fishes of some forms of pollution.

Remarks: A recently released goldfish with "pet-store" colors (red, white, blue, black) may occasionally be encountered in the wild. However, because of natural selection, reproducing populations quickly revert back to their natural cryptic coloration. Hybridizes readily with the Common Carp; in some areas, especially ones suffering from major pollution, hybrids (which are fertile) outnumber either parent species.

Similar species: Common Carp (Pl. 14) has barbels, 32–38 lateral scales, pharyngeal teeth 1,1,3–3,1,1; is more flattened below.

COMMON CARP *Cyprinus carpio* Pl. 14

Identification: *2 barbels,* rear 1 much larger, on each side of upper jaw. *Long dorsal fin,* 17–21 rays. *Stout, saw-toothed spine* (and 2 smaller spines) at front of dorsal and anal fins. Deep, thick body, strongly arched at dorsal fin, flattened below. Mouth terminal on young, subterminal on adult. Gray (young) to brassy green (adult) above; scales on back and upper side dark-edged, with black spot at base; white to yellow below; clear to dusky fins. Large adult has red-orange caudal and anal fins. Large scales (32–38 lateral scales); 5–6 anal rays; pharyngeal teeth 1,1,3–3,1,1. To 48 in. (122 cm).

Range: Native to Eurasia; first introduced to North America in 1831 and now widely distributed in s. Canada and most of U.S. Common. **Habitat:** Muddy pools of small to large rivers; lakes and ponds. Most common in manmade lakes and in turbid, sluggish streams containing large amounts of organic matter.

Remarks: Individuals known as "mirror carp" (with few, enlarged scales) or "leather carp" (scaleless) are fairly common. Because it roots in mud and increases turbidity, the presence of the Common Carp can result in decreased populations of native fishes. It now is considered, as are many introduced species, a nuisance.

Similar species: (1) Goldfish (Pl. 14) *lacks* barbels, dark-edged scales; is less flattened below; has 25–31 lateral scales, pharyngeal teeth 0,4–

4,0. (2) Grass Carp (Pl. 7) has slender body, *short* dorsal fin; *lacks* barbels, spines in dorsal and anal fins.

IDE *Leuciscus idus*   **Not shown**
  Identification: Slender body, somewhat compressed, *humped* (adult) behind head. *Red fins,* especially anal and paired fins of adult. Rounded snout, terminal mouth. Dorsal fin origin behind pelvic fin origin. Gray to gold-brown above, silver side. 53–63 lateral scales; 8 dorsal rays; 9–10 anal rays; pharyngeal teeth 3,5–5,3. To 40 in. (102 cm).
  Range: Native to Eurasia. Reproducing in 1 lake in ME. **Habitat:** Clear pools of medium to large rivers; ponds and lakes.

RUDD *Scardinius erythrophthalmus*   **Fig. 15**
  Identification: *Deep, compressed body; scaled bony keel* along belly from pelvic to anal fin. *Bright red* anal, pelvic, and pectoral fins; red-brown dorsal and caudal fins. Small head; terminal oblique mouth; dorsal fin origin behind pelvic fin origin. Concave margin on dorsal and anal fins (tips of front rays reach beyond fin when depressed). Brown-green above, brassy yellow side; gold eye with red spot at top. 36–45 lateral scales; usually 9–11 dorsal rays, 10–11 anal rays; 10–13 rakers on 1st gill arch; pharyngeal teeth 3,5–5,3. To 19 in. (48 cm).
  Range: Native to Eurasia. Reproducing populations in lower Hudson R. drainage, NY, and in ME. **Habitat:** Lakes; sluggish pools of medium to large rivers.
  Similar species: Golden Shiner (Pl. 7) *lacks* red on fins (young may have light red-orange median fins); has scaleless keel; has usually 7–9 dorsal rays, 11–14 anal rays, 17–19 rakers on 1st gill arch; pharyngeal teeth 0,5–5,0.

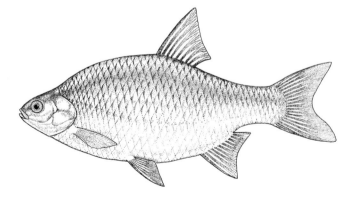

Fig. 15 Rudd *Scardinius erythrophthalmus*

TENCH *Tinca tinca*   **Pl. 7**
Identification: *Small scales,* 95–105 in lateral line; thick, *leatherlike skin. Short, deep caudal peduncle.* Square (barely forked) caudal fin. *Long barbel* at corner of terminal mouth. Dorsal fin origin over or behind pelvic fin origin. Olive to dark green above; white to bronze below with gold reflections; gray fins. Eight dorsal rays; 7–8 anal rays; pharyngeal teeth 0,5–4,0, or 0,5–5,0. To 33 in. (84 cm).
Range: Native to Eurasia. Introduced into U.S. in 1880s; now reproducing in CT, CO, BC, WA, CA, and possibly NY, DE, and MD. Localized and uncommon. **Habitat:** Mud-bottomed, usually vegetated lakes; backwaters of small to large rivers.

BITTERLING *Rhodeus sericeus*   **Not shown**
Identification: *Incomplete lateral line,* confined to 1st 4–10 scales. *Orange to red fins* on adult. Fairly deep, compressed body; dorsal fin origin behind pelvic fin origin. Rounded snout, terminal to slightly subterminal mouth. Gray-green above, metallic blue stripe along rear half of silver side; dusky orange fins. Breeding male has iridescent blue side, bright red dorsal and anal fins. 34–40 lateral scales; 9–10 dorsal rays; 8–9 anal rays; pharyngeal teeth 0,5–5,0. To 4¼ in. (11 cm).
Range: Native to Eurasia. Introduced and possibly established in Bronx R. (lower Hudson R. drainage), NY. **Habitat:** Ponds, lakes, marshes; muddy and sandy pools and backwaters of rivers.
Remarks: Female develops an extremely long ovipositor for insertion of eggs within the shells of living mussels.

GOLDEN SHINER *Notemigonus crysoleucas*   **Pl. 7**
Identification: *Extremely compressed body;* strongly *decurved* lateral line; *scaleless keel* along belly from pelvic to anal fin (Fig. 16). Small, *upturned mouth* on pointed snout; dorsal fin origin behind pelvic fin

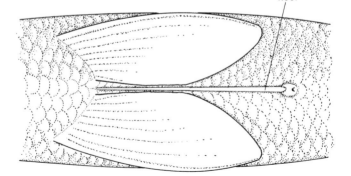

Fig. 16 Golden Shiner — belly

origin. Silver in clear and turbid water; gold side and fins in coffee-colored water. Dusky stripe along side, *herringbone lines* on upper side of young. 44-54 lateral scales; 7–9 dorsal rays; 8–19, usually 11–14, anal rays; 17–19 rakers on 1st gill arch; pharyngeal teeth 0,5–5,0. To 12 in. (30 cm).
Range: Atlantic and Gulf Slope drainages from NS to s. TX; Great Lakes, Hudson Bay (Red R.), and Mississippi R. basins west to AB, MT, WY, and w. OK. Widely introduced (via bait buckets) elsewhere in U.S. Common except in mountain areas. **Habitat:** Vegetated lakes, ponds, swamps, backwaters and pools of creeks and small to medium rivers.
Similar species: (1) Rudd (Fig. 15) has red fins, *scaled keel,* usually 9–11 dorsal rays, 10–11 anal rays, 10–13 rakers on 1st gill arch; 3,5–5,3 pharyngeal teeth. **Map 71**

HITCH *Lavinia exilicauda* **Pl. 7**
Identification: *Deep, compressed body,* tapering to narrow caudal peduncle; large caudal fin; strongly *decurved lateral line.* Small compressed head, terminal (slightly upturned) mouth. Dorsal fin origin behind pelvic fin origin. Brown-yellow above, scales on back and silver side darkly outlined (cross-hatched pattern on small individuals); dusky fins. Small individuals have black caudal spot. 54–62 lateral scales, 10–13 dorsal rays, 11–13 anal rays; pharyngeal teeth 0,5–4,0 or 0,5–5,0. To 14 in. (36 cm).
Range: Clear Lake (Lake Co.), Russian R., Sacramento–San Joaquin, San Francisco, and Monterey Bay drainages, CA. Common. **Habitat:** Lakes, ponds, sloughs, backwaters, and sluggish sandy pools of small to large rivers.
Similar species: Golden Shiner (Pl. 7) has keel on belly, 8 dorsal rays, more compressed body. **Map 72**

SPLITTAIL *Pogonichthys macrolepidotus* **Pl. 7**
Identification: Upper lobe of *large caudal fin longer* than lower lobe. *Barbel* at corner of slightly subterminal mouth. Long, slender, compressed body; dorsal fin origin in front of pelvic fin origin; small head; large eye. Olive-gray above, silver-gold side. Large individual has hump on nape, red-orange caudal and paired fins. 9–10 dorsal rays; 57–64 (usually 60–62) lateral scales; 14–18 rakers on 1st gill arch; pharyngeal teeth 2,5–5,2. To 17½ in. (44 cm).
Range: Formerly throughout Sacramento–San Joaquin R. drainage, CA; now restricted to San Francisco Bay Delta and lower Sacramento R. Common in reduced range. **Habitat:** Backwaters and pools of rivers; lakes. Tolerant of brackish water.
Similar species: See Clear Lake Splittail. Other minnows have symmetrical caudal fin. **Map 73**

CLEAR LAKE SPLITTAIL *Pogonichthys ciscoides* **Not shown**
Identification: Similar to Splittail but *no* (or small) *barbel on terminal mouth,* less asymmetrical caudal fin; usually 62–65 lateral scales; 18–23 rakers on 1st gill arch. To 14 in. (36 cm).

Range: Clear Lake and tributaries, Lake Co., CA. Formerly common but now extremely rare, possibly extinct. **Habitat:** Shoreline (as young) and open water of Clear Lake; formerly spawned in tributaries of lake.
Similar species: See Splittail (Pl. 7).   **Map 73**

● *PTYCHOCHEILUS*

Genus characteristics: Long conical head, flattened between the eyes; *very large, horizontal, terminal mouth* extending to or past front of eye; slender, barely compressed body; large *deeply forked caudal fin;* dorsal fin origin slightly behind pelvic fin origin; *narrow caudal peduncle,* appears pinched near caudal fin; moderately decurved, complete lateral line. Gray-green above, silver side; fins clear to slate with yellow to orange margins on large individuals. Large male has bright orange anal, pelvic, and pectoral fins. Young have dusky stripe on rear half of side, black caudal spot. Pharyngeal teeth 2,4–4,2 to 2,5–5,2. Squawfishes are the largest North American minnows. They differ from one another mainly in the relative sizes of their scales, which can be difficult to determine on live specimens. However, no river system contains more than 1 species, so the distribution maps facilitate identification to species.

COLORADO SQUAWFISH *Ptychocheilus lucius*   **Pl. 7**
Identification: *Very small scales:* 76–97 (usually 80–87) lateral scales, 18–23 scales above lateral line; usually 9 dorsal rays, 9 anal rays. To 6 ft. (180 cm).
Range: Colorado R. drainage, WY, CO, UT, NM, AZ, NV, CA, and Mexico. Now mostly restricted to UT and CO; extirpated from s. portion of range by construction of large dams on Colorado and Gila rivers. Protected as an *endangered species.* **Habitat:** Pools of medium to large rivers. Large individuals usually in deep, flowing rocky or sandy pools.
Similar species: (1) Other Squawfishes (Pl. 7) have *larger scales* (usually fewer than 75 lateral scales), *deeper caudal peduncle,* usually 8 anal rays; reach a smaller maximum size (1½ to 4½ ft.). (2) Roundtail Chub (Pl. 14) has mouth extending only to *front* of eye; juvenile lacks black spot on caudal fin base.   **Map 74**

SACRAMENTO SQUAWFISH *Ptychocheilus grandis*   **Pl. 7**
Identification: 38–44 scales on back from head to dorsal fin, 65–78 (usually 67–75) lateral scales, 12–15 scales above lateral line; usually 8 dorsal rays, 8 anal rays. To 54 in. (140 cm).
Range: Sacramento–San Joaquin, Pajaro-Salinas, Russian, Clear Lake, and upper Pit R. drainages, CA. **Habitat:** Rocky and sandy pools and runs of small to large rivers. Common in clear, warm streams.
Similar species: Other squawfishes (Pl. 7) have 48 or more scales on back from head to dorsal fin, 9 dorsal rays.   **Map 74**

NORTHERN SQUAWFISH *Ptychocheilus oregonensis* **Pl. 7**
Identification: 48–72 (usually 51–62) scales on back from head to dorsal fin, 64–79 (usually 66–75) lateral scales, 12–20 scales above lateral line; usually 9 dorsal rays, 8 anal rays. To 25 in. (63 cm).
Range: Pacific drainages from Nass R., BC, to Columbia R., NV; Harney R. basin, OR; Peace R. system (Arctic basin), BC and AB. Common; locally abundant. **Habitat:** Lakes, pools, and sometimes runs of small to large rivers. Largest individuals found in deep water.
Similar species: (1) Umpqua Squawfish has usually 18–20 scales above lateral line, 60–83 scales on back from head to dorsal fin. (2) Sacramento Squawfish (Pl. 7) has 38–44 scales on back from head to dorsal fin, usually 12–14 scales above lateral line, 8 dorsal rays. **Map 74**

UMPQUA SQUAWFISH *Ptychocheilus umpquae* **Not shown**
Identification: 60–83 scales on back from head to dorsal fin, 66–81 (usually 68–75) lateral scales, 16–22 scales above lateral line; usually 9 dorsal rays, 8 anal rays. To 17½ in. (44 cm).
Range: Umpqua and Siuslaw R. drainages, OR. Common. **Habitat:** Pools and sluggish runs of creeks and small rivers; lakes.
Similar species: See Pl. 7. (1) Northern Squawfish has usually 14–18 scales above lateral line, 51–62 scales on back from head to dorsal fin. (2) Sacramento Squawfish has usually 38–44 scales on back from head to dorsal fin, 12–15 scales above lateral line, 8 anal rays.
Map 74

HARDHEAD *Mylopharodon conocephalus* **Pl. 7**
Identification: *Premaxillary frenum;* long pointed snout; large terminal mouth reaches front of eye. Long slender body; dorsal fin origin behind pelvic fin origin. Brown to dusky bronze above (darkest on large individual); silver side. 69–81 lateral scales; 8 dorsal rays; pharyngeal teeth 2,5–4,2. To 39½ in. (1 m).
Range: Sacramento–San Joaquin and Russian R. drainages, CA. Fairly common, but becoming increasingly localized. **Habitat:** Deep, rock- and sand-bottomed pools of small to large rivers.
Similar species: (1) Sacramento Squawfish (Pl. 7) and (2) Sacramento Blackfish (Pl. 7) *lack* premaxillary frenum; Sacramento Squawfish has mouth extending under eye; Sacramento Blackfish has dorsal fin origin in front of pelvic fin origin, 90–105 lateral scales. **Map 75**

SACRAMENTO BLACKFISH *Orthodon microlepidotus* **Pl. 7**
Identification: *Small* (90–105 lateral) *scales. Wide head,* flat above; slightly upturned mouth. Slender, compressed body; long *narrow caudal peduncle;* dorsal fin origin in front of pelvic fin origin. Light to dark gray above, often with olive sheen; silver side. 9–11 dorsal rays; pharyngeal teeth 0,6–6,0 or 0,6–5,0. To 21½ in. (55 cm).
Range: Native to Sacramento–San Joaquin, Pajaro, and Salinas R. drainages; Clear Lake, CA. Introduced into Russian and Carmel R. drainages, CA, and Truckee Meadows area, w.-cen. NV. Common within native range (abundant in Clear Lake). **Habitat:** Lakes, back-

waters, and sluggish pools of small to large rivers; usually in warm, turbid water.

Similar species: (1) Hardhead (Pl. 7) has premaxillary frenum, *larger* (69–81 lateral) *scales,* dorsal fin origin behind pelvic fin origin. (2) Sacramento Squawfish (Pl. 7) has more *compressed head,* longer snout, larger mouth reaching below eye, *larger* (73–86 lateral) *scales.*

Map 76

PEAMOUTH *Mylocheilus caurinus* **Pl. 14**

Identification: Dark gray-brown to green above; *2 dark stripes, lower one ending before anal fin,* on silver-yellow side; yellow to brown fins. Slender body, somewhat compressed; large eye; long rounded snout; *barbel* at corner of slightly subterminal mouth; large forked caudal fin; dorsal fin origin over or in front of pelvic fin origin. *Axillary process* at pelvic fin base. Large male has red on side, belly, mouth, gill cover, and pectoral fin base. Complete lateral line; 66–84 lateral scales; 8 dorsal rays; 8 anal rays; short intestine; molarlike pharyngeal teeth 1,5–5,1. To 14 in. (36 cm).

Range: Nass (Pacific Slope) and Peace R. (Arctic basin) systems, BC, south to Columbia R. drainage, OR and ID; also on Vancouver and other coastal islands. **Habitat:** Lakes and slow-flowing areas of small to medium rivers; most common in vegetation. Common; locally abundant.

Similar species: Species of *Ptychocheilus* (Pl. 7) have larger mouth, *no barbel,* usually no stripes along side, no red coloration; pharyngeal teeth 2,4–4,2 or 2,5–5,2 (not molarlike). **Map 75**

CHISELMOUTH *Acrocheilus alutaceus* **Pl. 7**

Identification: *Large forked caudal fin.* Wide head; subterminal mouth, *hard plate* on lower jaw (Fig. 17); large eye. Moderately com-

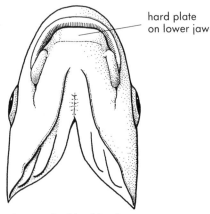

hard plate
on lower jaw

Fig. 17 Chiselmouth — underside of head

pressed body, deepest in front of dorsal fin, strongly tapering to *narrow* caudal peduncle; dorsal fin origin over pelvic fin origin; rounded, protruding snout. Gray above, brassy silver side; yellow to brown fins. Large individual has gray dorsal and caudal fins, orange at pectoral and pelvic fin bases. Decurved, complete lateral line; long intestine (at least twice length of body); black peritoneum. 85–93 lateral scales; 10–11 dorsal rays; 9–10 anal rays; pharyngeal teeth 0,4–4,0 to 0,5–5,0. To 12 in. (30 cm).

Range: Fraser and Columbia R. drainages, BC, WA, ID, OR, and NV; Harney R. basin, OR. Fairly common in Columbia R. drainage. **Habitat:** Flowing pools and runs over sand and gravel in creeks and small to medium rivers; margins of lakes.

Remarks: Sharp, cartilaginous plates on upper (concealed under lip) and lower jaws (Fig. 17) are used to scrape food from rocks.

Similar species: (1) Redside Shiner (Pl. 14) and (2) Lahontan Redside (Pl. 14) *lack* protruding snout and hard plates on jaws, have dorsal fin origin well *behind* pelvic fin origin. **Map 77**

REDSIDE SHINER *Richardsonius balteatus* **Pl. 14**
Identification: Deep, compressed body; *dorsal fin origin far behind pelvic fin origin. Narrow caudal peduncle;* deeply forked caudal fin. Short snout, terminal mouth, large eye. *Axillary process* at pelvic fin base. Olive-gray to brown above, clear to yellow streak above dark stripe along side. Red above pectoral fin base on large individual; clear to yellow-brown fins. Breeding male is brassy yellow, bright red along lower side. Decurved, complete lateral line; 52–67 lateral scales; 8-12 (usually 10) dorsal rays; 10–24 (usually 15) anal rays; long intestine; silver peritoneum; pharyngeal teeth 2,4–4,2 to 2,5–5,2. To 7 in. (18 cm).

Range: Pacific Slope drainages from Nass R., BC, to Rogue, Klamath, and Columbia R. drainages, OR, ID, NV, and WY; Bonneville basin, s. ID, w. WY, and UT; Peace R. system (Arctic basin), AB and BC. Introduced into upper Missouri R. basin, MT, and upper Colorado R. drainage, WY, UT, and AZ. Common; often abundant. **Habitat:** Runs and flowing to standing pools of headwaters, creeks, and small to medium rivers; lakes and ponds. Usually over mud or sand, often near vegetation.

Similar species: See Lahontan Redside (Pl. 14). **Map 78**

LAHONTAN REDSIDE *Richardsonius egregius* **Pl. 14**
Identification: Similar to Redside Shiner but has longer snout, more slender body, less slender caudal peduncle, 8–9 (rarely 10) anal rays. To 6½ in. (17 cm).

Range: Lahontan and other interior basins in n. and w. NV, and n. CA, including Humboldt, Walker, Carson, Truckee, Susan, Quinn, and Reese R. systems; Walker, Tahoe, and Pyramid lakes. Also in upper Sacramento R. system, CA, where possibly introduced. **Habitat:** All types of stream habitats but most common in pools and slow runs; margins of lakes. Common; locally abundant.

Similar species: See Redside Shiner (Pl. 14). **Map 78**

CALIFORNIA ROACH *Hesperoleucus symmetricus*   **Pl. 14**
 Identification: *Slightly subterminal mouth* on fairly short snout.
Deep compressed body tapering to *narrow caudal peduncle*; dorsal
fin origin behind pelvic fin origin; large caudal fin. Dusky gray to
steel blue above; dark stripe along side; silver-white below. Breeding
individual has red-orange chin, gill cover, and anal and paired fin
bases. 47–63 lateral scales; 7–10 dorsal rays; pharyngeal teeth 0,5–
4,0. To 4¼ in. (11 cm).
 Range: Sacramento–San Joaquin and Pajaro-Salinas R. drainages, CA.
Introduced into Cuyama and Eel R. drainages, CA. Common, but less
so than historically. **Habitat:** Rocky pools of headwaters, creeks, and
small to medium rivers.
 Similar species: (1) Lahontan Redside (Pl. 14) and (2) Redside Shiner
(Pl. 14) have bright red side on adult, *terminal upturned mouth* on
pointed snout, axillary process at pelvic fin base; pharyngeal teeth in
2 rows. (3) Hitch (Pl. 7) has deeper, more compressed body, *terminal
mouth*, 10–13 dorsal rays, no red coloration.   **Map 77**

• *GILA*

Gila species are a diverse group of primitive minnows in the western
U.S. Dorsal fin origin over or slightly behind pelvic fin origin. Most
have small scales and pharyngeal teeth in two rows (2,5–4,2 or 2,5–
5,2). All except Borax Lake Chub have complete lateral line.
    The Thicktail Chub, *Gila crassicauda*, presumably extinct but
formerly common in the backwaters and marshes of the
Sacramento–San Joaquin R. drainage, Clear Lake (Lake Co.), and
Coyote Cr. (San Francisco Bay drainage), CA (Map 79), had a *thick,
deep caudal peduncle*; a deep, compressed body with *high nape* rising steeply from short, pointed head; and 49–60 lateral scales.

ROUNDTAIL CHUB *Gila robusta*   **Pl. 14**
 Identification: Deep, compressed body; flat head; slender caudal
peduncle; large forked caudal fin; angle along anal fin base continues
into *middle* of caudal fin (Fig. 18). Terminal mouth extends to front
of eye. Dark olive-gray above; silver side. Breeding male may develop
red or orange on lower half of cheek and paired fin bases. 80–99 lateral scales, usually 9 dorsal rays, 9 anal rays; pharyngeal teeth 2,5–
4,2. To 17 in. (43 cm).
 Range: Colorado R. drainage, WY, CO, UT, NV, NM, and AZ; also
Rio Yaqui south to Rio Piaxtla, nw. Mexico. Locally common. **Habitat:** Rocky runs, sometimes pools, of creeks and small to large rivers;
sometimes common in impoundments.
 Remarks: 4 subspecies in U.S.; others in Mexico. *G. r. jordani* (protected as an *endangered subspecies*), in Pluvial White R., NV, often
has black blotches on back and side, exposed scales on back, breast,
and belly. *G. r. seminuda* (protected as an *endangered subspecies*), in
Virgin R., sw. UT, s. NV, and nw. AZ, has usually more than 85 lateral scales, no or deeply embedded scales on back, breast, and belly.

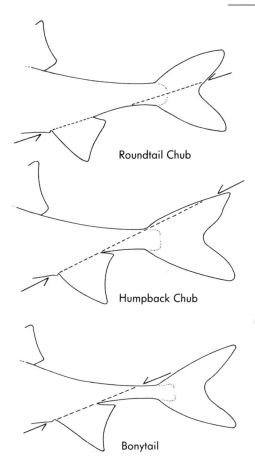

Roundtail Chub

Humpback Chub

Bonytail

Fig. 18 Roundtail Chub, Humpback Chub, and Bonytail — angle along anal fin base

G. r. grahami, in Gila R., NM and AZ, often has black blotches on back and side, usually 80–85 lateral scales, exposed scales on back, breast, and belly. *G. r. robusta*, in rest of U.S. range, has usually more than 85 lateral scales, only slightly embedded scales on back, breast, and belly.

Similar species: (1) Humpback Chub (Pl. 14) and (2) Bonytail (Pl. 14) have extremely slender caudal peduncles, smaller eyes, angle along anal fin base continuing *above* caudal fin (Fig. 18); large individuals have hump on nape, depressed head. Roundtail and Humpback Chubs hybridize throughout their shared range except in the Yampa R. (3) Colorado Squawfish (Pl. 7) has mouth extending to rear of eye; juvenile has black spot on caudal fin base.   **Map 79**

HUMPBACK CHUB *Gila cypha*   **Pl. 14**
Identification: Deep, compressed body; *long, extremely slender caudal peduncle;* falcate fins; large forked caudal fin; angle along anal fin base continues along *upper edge* of caudal fin (Fig. 18). Large individual has large, nearly scaleless *hump* behind *small, depressed head. Subterminal mouth* extends to front of small eye. Dark olive-gray above; silver side. Large individual has orange lower side, pectoral and anal fin bases. 73–90 lateral scales; usually 9 dorsal rays, 10 anal rays; pharyngeal teeth 2,5–4,2. To 15 in. (38 cm).
Range: Green and Colorado rivers (Colorado R. drainage), WY, CO, UT, and AZ. Rare; restricted to middle river basin; formerly more common and widespread (perhaps including lower Colorado R.). Protected as an *endangered species.* **Habitat:** Swift, rocky runs and flowing pools.
Remarks: The hump at the back of the head directs the water current down on the Humpback Chub's flat head and enables the fish to maintain position in the swift Colorado R. Similar humps are found on other Colorado R. fishes, the Bonytail and Razorback Sucker (Pl. 21). Large falcate fins and narrow caudal peduncle are also found in other fast-swimming fishes.
Similar species: (1) See Bonytail (Pl. 14). (2) Roundtail Chub (Pl. 14) *lacks* hump on nape; has *deeper head, deeper caudal peduncle,* larger eye, *more terminal mouth;* angle along anal fin base continues into *middle* of caudal fin (Fig. 18).   **Map 80**

BONYTAIL *Gila elegans*   **Pl. 14**
Identification: Similar to Humpback Chub but has *terminal mouth,* angle along anal fin base continues *well above* caudal fin (Fig. 18), more slender caudal peduncle, smaller hump on nape, usually 10 or more dorsal rays. Breeding male has red lower side and pectoral and anal fin bases. 75–99 lateral scales. To 24½ in. (62 cm).
Range: Colorado R. drainage, WY, CO, UT, NM, AZ, CA, and Mexico. Extremely rare; extant only in Green R., UT, and perhaps in some large impoundments of the Colorado R. Protected in U.S. as an *endangered species.* **Habitat:** Flowing pools and backwaters, usually over mud or rocks. Streamlined body suggests at least occasional occupation of swift runs.
Similar species: (1) See Humpback Chub (Pl. 14). (2) Roundtail Chub (Pl. 14) has larger eye, deeper head, deeper caudal peduncle; *lacks* hump on nape; angle along anal fin base continues into *middle* of caudal fin (Fig. 18).   **Map 81**

CHIHUAHUA CHUB *Gila nigrescens*   **Pl. 14**
Identification: Deep, compressed body; long, fairly slender caudal peduncle. *Terminal mouth on rounded snout.* Olive-gray above; sil-

ver side; clear to slate gray fins. Breeding individual has *red-orange mouth* and paired and anal fin bases. 67–78 lateral scales, 9 dorsal rays, 8 anal rays, 9–14 rakers on 1st gill arch; pharyngeal teeth 2,5–4,2. To 9½ in. (24 cm).

Range: Mimbres R., NM; also Lagunas Guzman and Bustillos, Chihuahua, Mexico. Rare. Protected in U.S. as a *threatened species.*
Habitat: Flowing pools of creeks and small rivers; usually near brush or other cover.
Similar species: (1) Rio Grande Chub (Pl. 14) and (2) Sonora Chub have shorter, deeper caudal peduncle; 2 dusky black stripes on side, blunter snout, larger eye, 8 dorsal rays, 6–10 rakers on 1st gill arch. Rio Grande Chub also has 51–67 lateral scales. (3) Yaqui Chub has deep caudal peduncle, black wedge on caudal fin base, 48–62 lateral scales, 8 dorsal rays. **Map 82**

RIO GRANDE CHUB *Gila pandora* Pl. 14

Identification: Olive-gray above; *2 dusky stripes* along silver side (darkest on large individual), upper one extending to caudal fin, lower one to anal fin; dusky to black caudal spot. Fairly deep, compressed body; deep caudal peduncle. Slightly subterminal mouth extends to front of large eye; rounded, fairly blunt snout. Breeding individual has red-orange (brightest on male) anal, dorsal, and paired fin bases and side of head; orange lower side. 51–67 lateral scales, 8 dorsal rays, 8 anal rays, 6–10 rakers on 1st gill arch; pharyngeal teeth 2,5–4,2. To 7 in. (18 cm).

Range: Upper Rio Grande and Pecos R. systems, CO and NM; isolated population in Davis Mountains (Pecos R. system), TX. Introduced into headwaters of Canadian R. (Red R. drainage), NM. Common, but less so than historically. **Habitat:** Flowing pools of headwaters, creeks, and small rivers; usually near brush.
Similar species: (1) See Sonora Chub. (2) Other *Gila* species (Pls. 7 & 14) *lack* 2 stripes on side. **Map 82**

SONORA CHUB *Gila ditaenia* Not shown

Identification: Nearly identical to Rio Grande Chub but with *smaller* (63–75 lateral) *scales.* To 10 in. (25 cm).
Range: Sycamore (Bear) Canyon, Santa Cruz Co., AZ; also in Rio de la Concepcion, Sonora, Mexico. Uncommon in extremely small area in U.S.; protected in U.S. as a *threatened species.* **Habitat:** Rocky and sandy pools (intermittent during dry season) of creeks; springs.
Similar species: See Rio Grande Chub (Pl. 14). **Map 83**

ARROYO CHUB *Gila orcutti* Pl. 7

Identification: Deep body; *deep caudal peduncle.* Small, slightly subterminal mouth; short, rounded snout; large eye. Gray-olive above; often a dusky gray stripe along silver side. 48–62 lateral scales, 8 dorsal rays, 7 anal rays; pharyngeal teeth 2,5–4,2. To 16 in. (40 cm).
Range: Native to Malibu Cr., Santa Clara, San Luis Rey, and Santa Margarita R. drainages, s. CA. Introduced into Santa Ynez, Santa Maria, Cuyama, and Mojave (Death Valley basin) R. drainages, CA.

Common. **Habitat:** Sand- and mud-bottomed flowing pools and runs of headwaters, creeks, and small to medium rivers; often in intermittent streams.
Similar species: (1) See Yaqui Chub. (2) Thicktail Chub has *deeper caudal peduncle,* high nape, 8 anal rays. **Map 79**

YAQUI CHUB *Gila purpurea* **Not shown**
Identification: Similar to Arroyo Chub (above; Pl. 7) but has *black wedge* on caudal fin base, 8 anal rays. Yellow-brown to steel blue (large male) above. To 5½ in. (14 cm).
Range: San Bernardino Cr., extreme se. AZ; also in Rios Matape, Sonora, and Yaqui, Sonora, Mexico. Introduced into Leslie Cr., extreme se. AZ. Extremely rare. Recognized in U.S. as an *endangered species.*
Habitat: Quiet pools of headwaters and creeks; usually in vegetation.
Similar species: See Arroyo Chub (Pl. 7). **Map 82**

BLUE CHUB *Gila coerulea* **Pl. 14**
Identification: Large eye; *pointed snout;* terminal mouth extends to front of eye. Fairly slender, compressed body; *slender caudal peduncle.* Dusky olive above; silver-blue side. Breeding male has blue snout, orange side and fins. 58–71 lateral scales, 9 dorsal rays, 8–9 anal rays; pharyngeal teeth 2,5–5,2. To 16 in. (41 cm).
Range: Klamath and Lost R. systems, OR and CA. Common; abundant in impoundments. **Habitat:** Rocky pools of creeks and small to large rivers; rocky shores of lakes and impoundments.
Similar species: Tui Chub (Pl. 14) has smaller mouth not extending to front of eye, deeper body, *more rounded snout,* larger (42–64 lateral) scales. **Map 84**

LEATHERSIDE CHUB *Gila copei* **Pl. 14**
Identification: *Leatherlike appearance* created by small (68–85 lateral) scales, black specks on *silver-blue back and side.* Breeding male has red paired and anal fin bases, lower lobe of caudal fin, upper edge of gill slit. Slender, barely compressed body; large eye; terminal mouth on short rounded snout. 8 dorsal rays, 8 anal rays; pharyngeal teeth 1,4–4,1 to 2,5–4,2. To 6 in. (15 cm).
Range: Upper Snake R. system, WY and ID, south to Sevier R. system, s. UT. Introduced into Colorado R. drainage, UT. Common.
Habitat: Rocky flowing pools, sometimes riffles, of creeks and small to medium rivers.
Similar species: Utah Chub (Pl. 14) has brassy side, larger (45–64 lateral) scales, 9 dorsal rays; lacks red. **Map 81**

UTAH CHUB *Gila atraria* **Pl. 14**
Identification: Olive-brown to blue-black above; *yellow to brassy side;* clear to olive-yellow fins. Large male has yellow to gold fin bases, mouth, and side of head; may be gold overall. Deep, compressed body; large eye; *short, blunt snout.* 45–65 lateral scales; usually 9 dorsal, 8 anal rays; pharyngeal teeth 2,5–4,2. To 22 in. (56 cm).
Range: Native to upper Snake R. system, WY and ID, and Lake Bonneville basin (including Great Salt Lake drainage and Sevier R. system), se. ID and UT. Introduced into e. NV, upper Missouri R. ba-

sin, MT, and Colorado R. drainage, WY and UT. **Habitat:** Lakes; quiet pools of headwaters, creeks, and small to medium rivers; often in vegetation over mud or sand.
Similar species: Leatherside Chub (Pl. 14) is *silver;* has red on lower body, larger (68–85 lateral) scales, 8 dorsal rays.   **Map 85**

TUI CHUB *Gila bicolor*   **Pl. 14**
Identification: Highly variable (see Remarks). Deep, compressed body; fairly deep caudal peduncle; *small rounded fins.* Small, terminal to slightly subterminal mouth; does *not* extend to eye. Dusky olive to dark green above; brassy brown side, often mottled in adult; silver-white to yellow below; clear to dusky olive fins. Young has dusky stripe along side. Large individual may have yellow to copper fins with pink, red, or orange bases, red-orange lower side. 41–64 lateral scales; usually 8 dorsal, 7–8 anal rays; pharyngeal teeth 0,5–5,0 to 0,4-4,0. To 17¾ in. (45 cm).
Range: Columbia R. drainage, WA, OR, and ID, south in Klamath and upper Pit R. (Sacramento R. drainage), and interior drainages of NV and CA to Mohave R., s. CA. Common; locally abundant but decreasing in some areas because of habitat degradation and introduced species. **Habitat:** Quiet, vegetated, mud- or sand-bottomed pools of headwaters, creeks, and small to large rivers; lakes.
Remarks: Many distinctive forms of the Tui Chub occupy the isolated (endorheic) drainages of the w. U.S. Many are recognized through combinations of characteristics not described here because a comprehensive study of intraspecific variation has yet to be made. Among the distinctive subspecies are *G. b. snyderi* (protected as an *endangered subspecies*) in Owens R., CA; *G. b. mohavensis* (protected as an *endangered subspecies*), Mojave R., CA; and *G. B. bicolor*, Klamath R. system, OR and CA. *G. b. obesa*, a stream- and spring-inhabiting form, and *G. b. pectinifer*, a lake-inhabiting form, both are found in the Lake Lahontan basin, NV.
Similar species: (1) Alvord (Pl. 7) and (2) Borax Lake Chubs have higher nape, usually 7 dorsal rays. (3) Blue Chub (Pl. 14) has larger mouth extending to *front of eye*, 58–71 lateral scales; is more slender.
                                                                          Map 80

LVORD CHUB *Gila alvordensis*   **Pl. 7**
Identification: *High nape* rising steeply from short pointed head; slender, fairly compressed body; deep caudal peduncle. Small eye high on head; rounded snout; terminal mouth. Dusky olive to dark green above, line of black specks along upper side; silver side; clear to dusky olive fins. 58–72 lateral scales; usually 7 dorsal rays, 7 anal rays, 14–15 pectoral rays; pharyngeal teeth 0,5–4,0. To 5¼ in. (14 cm).
Range: Alvord basin, se. OR and nw. NV. Common in small area.
Habitat: Springs and spring-fed streams; impoundments.
Similar species: (1) See Borax Lake Chub. (2) Tui Chub (Pl. 14) has usually 8 dorsal rays. (3) Other species of *Gila* (Pls. 7 & 14) have 8–9 dorsal rays; pharyngeal teeth in 2 rows.   **Map 84**

BORAX LAKE CHUB *Gila boraxobius*   **Not shown**
  Identification: Similar to Alvord Chub but *larger head is concave be-*
  tween eyes; has *incomplete lateral line,* more slender caudal
  peduncle, usually 13 pectoral rays. To 4¼ in. (11 cm).
  Range: Borax Lake (Alvord basin), Harney Co., OR. Common in extremely small range; protected as an *endangered species.* **Habitat:** Borax Lake is a small, shallow, clear lake fed by hot springs. Borax Lake
  Chub is the only fish in the lake.
  Similar species: See Alvord Chub (Pl. 7).   **Map 85**

ROSYSIDE DACE *Clinostomus funduloides*   **Pl. 15**
  Identification: *Large oblique mouth; long pointed snout.* Large,
  forked caudal fin. Compressed body; small scales. Dorsal fin origin
  behind pelvic fin origin. Olive above, dark stripe along back, dark-
  edged scales on upper side; green to yellow-gold stripe (brightest on
  large individuals) above dusky stripe along silver side; scattered dark
  blotches on side of large individual; white, orange, or red lower side.
  Breeding male is dark blue above, has bright brick red lower side.
  Complete, decurved lateral line; 43–57 lateral scales; 9 anal rays;
  pharyngeal teeth 2,5–4,2. To 4½ in. (11 cm).
  Range: Atlantic Slope (mostly above Fall Line) from lower Delaware
  R. drainage, PA, to Savannah R. drainage, GA; Ohio R. basin, WV,
  VA, s. OH, KY, TN, NC, AL, and MS. Common to abundant in up-
  land areas; absent in Ohio R. basin between cen. OH and
  Cumberland R. (including most of KY); rare in Cumberland R. drainage. **Habitat:** Rocky flowing pools of headwaters, creeks, and small
  rivers; most common in small clear streams.
  Remarks: 3 subspecies: *C. f. funduloides,* on Atlantic Slope from Delaware R. drainage, PA, to lower Savannah R. drainage, SC and GA, in
  the upper Tennessee R. drainage, TN and VA, and in Ohio R. basin, s.
  OH, e. KY, and s. WV, has usually 47–54 lateral scales, 34–43 scales
  around body, lightly pigmented lower side; *C. f. estor,* in lower and
  middle Tennessee and Cumberland R. drainages, KY, TN, and AL,
  has usually 43–50 lateral scales, 31–37 scales around body, lightly
  pigmented lower side. An undescribed subspecies, endemic to Little
  Tennessee R. system, TN and NC, has blunt snout, darkly pigmented lower side, usually 50–53 lateral scales, 36–46 scales around
  body. Intergrades between *C. f. funduloides* and the undescribed
  subspecies occur in headwaters of Little Tennessee R. system, NC
  and GA, and headwaters of the Savannah R. drainage, GA. Hiwassee
  R. may contain intergrades between *C. f. estor* and the undescribed
  subspecies.
  Similar species: (1) See Redside Dace (Pl. 15). (2) Striped and (3) Common Shiners (both, Pl. 17) have *smaller mouth, shorter rounded*
  snout, dark stripes on upper side, dorsal fin origin over pelvic fin origin, 36–43 lateral scales, pharyngeal teeth 2,4–4,2.   **Map 86**

REDSIDE DACE *Clinostomus elongatus*   **Pl. 15**
  Identification: Similar to Rosyside Dace but has *longer, more pointed*
  snout; more slender body; brighter (carmine) red on lower side (of

adult); smaller (59–75 lateral) scales. Breeding male is steel blue above, has yellow-gold stripe along side, bright red on lower side. To 4½ in. (12 cm).
Range: Upper Susquehanna R. drainage, NY and PA; Great Lakes (except Lake Superior) and Mississippi R. basins from NY and s. ON to MN and south to WV, n. KY, IN, WI, and IA. Locally common in eastern part of range (but declining in many areas); localized and rare in west. **Habitat:** Rocky and sandy pools of headwaters, creeks and small rivers; largest populations in clear, spring-fed streams.
Similar species: See Rosyside Dace (Pl. 15). **Map 86**

LONGFIN DACE *Agosia chrysogaster* Pl. 15
Identification: Large female has *elongated lower lobe* on anal fin. *Small (70–95 lateral) scales. Small barbel* at corner of mouth; long coiled intestine; black peritoneum. Rounded snout; lightly subterminal mouth. Dorsal fin origin above or slightly in front of pelvic fin origin. Dark gray above; dusky black band along silver side enlarged into black spot at caudal fin base; often gold flecks on side. Large male is light yellow below, has yellow paired fin bases, large dorsal fin. 7 anal rays; pharyngeal teeth 0,4–4,0. To 4 in. (10 cm).
Range: Lower Colorado R. drainage (primarily Gila and Bill William R. systems), NM and AZ, and south through s. AZ and Pacific drainages of w. Mexico. Introduced into Mimbres R., NM. Common. **Habitat:** Shallow sandy and rocky runs; flowing pools of creeks and small to medium rivers; often near cover.
Similar species: (1) Speckled and (2) Longnose Dace (both, Pl. 16) *lack* elongated lower lobe on anal fin of female, have dorsal fin origin behind pelvic fin origin, short intestine, pharyngeal teeth 1,4–4,1 or 2,4–4,2. (3) *Gila* species (Pls. 7 & 14) *lack* elongated lower lobe on anal fin of female, barbel; have short intestine. **Map 76**

MOAPA DACE *Moapa coriacea* Pl. 8
Identification: *Leatherlike skin* (resulting from many small embedded scales). *Large black spot* on caudal fin base. Fairly slender body, dorsal fin origin over or slightly behind pelvic fin origin; long rounded snout; slightly subterminal mouth. Olive above, broad dusky stripe along back, cream spot at dorsal fin origin, green-brown blotches along upper side; turquoise stripe above dark gold-brown stripe along side (faint at front). Complete or incomplete lateral line; 69–79 lateral scales; 8 (often 7) anal rays; pharyngeal teeth 0,5–4,0. To 3½ in. (9 cm).
Range: Endemic to headwaters of Moapa R., Clark Co., se. NV. Subject to major population fluctuations and varies from rare to common within extremely restricted range. Protected as an *endangered species.* **Habitat:** Pools of Moapa R. and feeder springs over gravel, sand, and mud.
Similar species: (1) Relict Dace (Pl. 8) has larger (50–70 lateral) scales, *less* leatherlike skin; terminal mouth. (2) Speckled Dace (Pl. 16) has barbel at corner of mouth, pointed snout overhanging mouth; pharyngeal teeth 1,4–4,1 to 2,4–4,2. **Map 87**

RELICT DACE *Relictus solitarius*   **Pl. 8**
  Identification: *Chubby; soft-bodied. Incomplete lateral line,* rarely
  reaching below dorsal fin. *Large terminal mouth,* no frenum or
  barbel. Small fins. Dorsal fin origin slightly in front of to behind pelvic fin origin; anal fin well behind dorsal fin. Color highly variable;
  dusky violet, yellow or green above, speckled with brown; yellow
  fins. 50–70 lateral scales; usually 7 anal rays; pharyngeal teeth 0,4–
  4,0. To 5 in. (13 cm).
  Range: Lakes Franklin, Gale, Waring, Steptoe, and Spring basins in e.
  NV. Common in limited range. **Habitat:** Springs and their effluents.
  Similar species: (1) Desert Dace (Pl. 8) has *small subterminal mouth,*
  hard sheath on jaws, 68–78 lateral scales. (2) Tui Chub (Pl. 14) has
  complete lateral line, dorsal fin origin over pelvic fin origin.
                                                                      Map 87

DESERT DACE *Eremichthys acros*   **Pl. 8**
  Identification: *Deep chubby body; hard sheath* on upper and lower
  jaws; *small* slightly subterminal mouth. Black lips; short blunt
  snout; no barbel or frenum. Dorsal fin origin behind pelvic fin origin.
  Olive above, bright green stripe along upper side; yellow-brass side;
  silver below; amber-white fins. Complete or incomplete lateral line;
  68–78 lateral scales; 7–8 anal rays; pharyngeal teeth 0,5–4,0. To 3 in.
  (7.7 cm).
  Range and Habitat: Warm springs of Soldier Meadows, Lahontan basin, Humboldt Co., NV. Recorded in water as warm as 100°F (38°C).
  Protected as a *threatened species.*
  Similar species: (1) Relict Dace (Pl. 8) has *large terminal mouth,* 70 or
  fewer lateral scales, *no* hard sheath on jaws. (2) Speckled Dace (Pl. 16)
  has barbel in corner of *larger* mouth, is more slender, *lacks* horny
  sheaths on lips; pharyngeal teeth 1,4–4,1 to 2,4–4,2.   **Map 87**

LEAST CHUB *Iotichthys phlegethontis*   **Pl. 8**
  Identification: *Upturned mouth;* large eye; short rounded snout. *No
  lateral line* (rarely 1–2 pores at front). *Large (34–38 lateral) scales.*
  Fairly deep, compressed body; dorsal fin origin behind pelvic fin origin; slender peduncle. Olive above; black specks on back and side;
  gold stripe along blue side; white to yellow fins. Breeding male has
  red-gold lower side, gold eye and fins. 8 anal rays; pharyngeal teeth
  2,5–4,2. To 2½ in. (6.4 cm).
  Range: Bonneville basin, n. UT. Common. **Habitat:** Marshes, ponds,
  vegetated areas of streams and lakes; usually over mud.
  Similar species: (1) Utah (Pl. 14), (2) Leatherside (Pl. 14), and (3) Tui
  Chubs (Pl. 14) have *terminal mouths, complete lateral lines, smaller
  scales,* deeper peduncle; reach much larger size.   **Map 83**

■ SPINEFINS

The following six species are the only native North American minnows having *2 large spines* at front of dorsal fin (2d spine fits into

groove on 1st), *spines* (variously developed) in pelvic and pectoral fins, and a *membrane* connecting the pelvic fin to the belly. All have extremely bright silver-white sides, a complete lateral line and usually 7 pelvic rays (most North American minnows have 8 pelvic rays).

All 6 species of this interesting group of fishes are endemic to the now modified and degraded Colorado R. drainage of the sw. U.S. and have become greatly reduced in numbers in recent years. Especially detrimental have been stream impoundments, introduced fishes, chemical manipulations of fish populations, and diversion of water for human use.

• *LEPIDOMEDA*

Genus characteristics: *Large gray-black blotches and specks* (darkest on large individuals) scattered over side. *Compressed brassy olive body,* deepest under nape; dorsal fin origin behind pelvic fin origin; large eye.

LITTLE COLORADO SPINEDACE *Lepidomeda vittata*   **Not shown**
Identification: *8 anal rays;* usually more than 90 (89–105) lateral scales; pharyngeal teeth 1,4–4,1 or 2,4–4,2. Rounded snout; large, terminal, fairly slanted mouth. Large male has faint yellow-orange at paired fin bases. To 4 in. (10 cm).
Range: Upper Little Colorado R. system, e. AZ. Uncommon and highly localized. Protected as a *threatened species.* **Habitat:** Rocky and sandy runs and pools of creeks and small rivers.
Similar species: (1) Virgin (Pl. 15) and (2) White River Spinedace have *9 anal rays,* usually fewer than 90 lateral scales, pharyngeal teeth 2,5–4,2. (3) Pahranagat Spinedace has pointed snout, large slanted mouth, large pointed dorsal fin (Fig. 19), 9 anal rays, pharyngeal teeth 2,5–4,2.   **Map 88**

VIRGIN SPINEDACE *Lepidomeda mollispinis*   **Pl. 15**
Identification: Rounded snout; large terminal mouth. Large male has red-orange at paired and anal fin bases, upper edge of gill cover, sometimes on belly. Black specks on opercle confined to upper half. 77–91 lateral scales, 9 anal rays; pharyngeal teeth 2,5–4,2. To 5¾ in. (15 cm).
Range: Virgin R. system, UT, NV, and AZ. Generally common but reduced in streams subjected to impoundment and channelization. **Habitat:** Gravel- and sand-bottomed flowing pools and runs of fast and usually clear creeks and small rivers.
Remarks: 2 subspecies: *L. m. mollispinis* and *L. m. pratensis* (protected as a *threatened subspecies*); the latter is restricted to Big Spring and surrounding area, Lincoln Co., NV, and has a higher, more pointed dorsal fin, longer pelvic fins, and smaller, more slanted mouth.
Similar species: (1) See White River Spinedace. (2) Little Colorado Spinedace has 8 anal rays, usually more than 90 lateral scales, more

slanted mouth, pharyngeal teeth 2,4–4,2. (3) Pahranagat Spinedace has pointed snout; large, slanted mouth; large, pointed dorsal fin (Fig. 19). **Map 88**

WHITE RIVER SPINEDACE *Lepidomeda albivallis* **Not shown**
Identification: Similar to Virgin Spinedace but has dark specks over *all* of opercle, much larger pharyngeal arch; red-orange bases on olive to pink-brown dorsal and caudal fins, red-orange anal and pelvic fins (colors brightest on large male). 79–92 lateral scales. To 5¾ in. (15 cm).
Range: Pluvial White R. system, NV. Highly localized in small area. Protected as an *endangered species.* **Habitat:** Springs and outflows of upper White R.; usually in shallow, cool, clear water over sand and gravel.
Similar species: See Virgin Spinedace (Pl. 15). **Map 88**

PAHRANAGAT SPINEDACE *Lepidomeda altivelis* **Fig. 19**
Identification: *Pointed snout; large, slanted mouth,* front tip of lower jaw above middle of eye; compressed head. Large, pointed dorsal fin. 84–95 lateral scales, 9 anal rays; pharyngeal teeth 2,5–4,2. To 3 in. (7.9 cm).
Range: Pluvial White R., Pahranagat Valley, NV. Rare. **Habitat:** Spring outflows.
Similar species: Other spinedace have rounded snout; front tip of mouth not extending above middle of eye; smaller, less pointed dorsal fin; wider head. **Map 88**

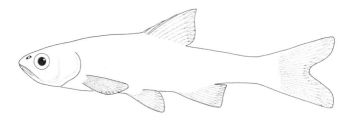

Fig. 19 Pahranagat Spinedace *Lepidomeda altivelis*

SPIKEDACE *Meda fulgida* **Pl. 15**
Identification: *No scales.* Slender body, somewhat compressed at front, strongly compressed at caudal peduncle; fairly pointed snout; slightly subterminal mouth; large eye. Dorsal fin origin behind pelvic fin origin. Olive-gray to light brown above; *brilliant silver side,* often with blue reflections; black specks and blotches on back and upper side. Breeding male has bright brassy yellow head and fin bases, yellow belly and fins. 9 anal rays; pharyngeal teeth 1,4–4,1. To 3½ in. (9.1 cm).
Range: Gila R. system, AZ and NM. Rare or extirpated over most of

range. Protected as a *threatened species*. **Habitat:** Sandy and rocky
runs and pools; often near riffles of creeks and small rivers.
Similar species: (1) Woundfin (Pl. 15) has wider, flatter head; barbel at
corner of mouth. (2) Virgin (Pl. 15) and other spinedace *have scales*,
more compressed body, large gray-black blotches on side.   **Map 87**

WOUNDFIN *Plagopterus argentissimus*   **Pl. 15**
  Identification: *No scales*. Wide, flat head; body compressed at rear.
  Long rounded snout, subterminal mouth, *barbel* at corner of mouth;
  fairly small eye high on head. Dorsal fin origin behind pelvic fin origin. Large forked caudal fin. Dusky gray above; *brilliant silver side*,
  often with blue reflections; sometimes faint yellow at paired fin
  bases. Pink lower side on breeding male. Complete lateral line; 9–10
  anal rays; pharyngeal teeth 1,5–4,1. To 3½ in. (9 cm).
  Range: Known from Virgin and Gila R. systems (both lower Colorado
  R. drainage) in UT, NV, and AZ; now believed extirpated in Gila R.
  system. Extremely rare; protected as an *endangered species*. **Habitat:**
  Fast sandy runs of small to medium rivers; usually in warm turbid
  water; sometimes in pools.
  Similar species: (1) Spikedace (Pl. 15) has *more compressed head*, dark
  specks and blotches on upper side, *lacks* barbel. (2) Virgin (Pl. 15) and
  other spinedace *have scales*, large gray-black blotches on *compressed
  body*; *lack* barbel.   **Map 83**

OREGON CHUB *Oregonichthys crameri*   **Pl. 9**
  Identification: Distinctive body compressed and deepest at dorsal fin
  origin, strongly tapering to *very narrow caudal peduncle*. Olive-tan
  above, green-brown stripe along back in front of dorsal fin; *clusters of
  large brown-black spots* scattered over back and silver side; darkly
  outlined scales on back; lines of brown specks on lower side. Small
  barbel (sometimes absent) at corner of subterminal mouth; rounded
  snout. Dorsal fin origin over or slightly behind pelvic fin origin.
  Complete lateral line; 35–40 lateral scales; 7 anal rays; pharyngeal
  teeth 1,4–4,1. To 2¾ in. (7 cm).
  Range: Willamette and Umpqua R. drainages, OR. Common in
  Umpqua; localized and rare in Willamette because of habitat alter-
  ation. **Habitat:** Sand- and gravel-bottomed pools and backwaters of
  creeks and small rivers; often in vegetation. Sometimes in ponds and
  impoundments.   **Map 84**

• *PHOXINUS*

  Genus characteristics: One of few genera of freshwater fishes (the only
  minnow genus) occurring in both North America (6 species) and
  Eurasia. Adult males are spectacularly colored. The lateral line usually ends at about the *middle* of the body, occasionally is absent.
  Scales are so small that they appear to be absent and give the fish a
  metallic look. Males have bright *silver spots* at fin bases. Slender,
  fairly compressed body; dorsal fin origin above or behind pelvic fin
  origin; 8 dorsal rays; 7–8 anal rays.

FINESCALE DACE *Phoxinus neogaeus* **Pl. 15**

Identification: *Dark brown to gray "cape" on back and upper side. Body profusely speckled with black.* Dark olive to gold stripe along side, light olive between cape and stripe; silver-white below; usually a black caudal spot; clear to yellow fins. Large male has red along side. Large head; *large terminal mouth* extending under eye; rounded snout. 63–92 lateral scales; pharyngeal teeth 2,5–4,2. To 4¼ in. (11 cm).

Range: Atlantic, Great Lakes, Hudson Bay, upper Mississippi, Missouri, and Peace-Mackenzie R. drainages from NB to YU and BC; south to NY, WI, and WY. Common in central part of range; sporadic in Missouri drainage. **Habitat:** Lakes, ponds, and sluggish pools of headwaters, creeks, and small rivers; usually over silt and near vegetation.

Remarks: Finescale Dace and Northern Redbelly Dace commonly hybridize. The hybrids are always females and in some areas are more common than the parental species. Apparently the hybrids breed with males of the parental species and consequently can outnumber and even replace one of the parent species. Hybrids are intermediate in characteristics.

Similar species: (1) Southern Redbelly (Pl. 15) and (2) Northern Redbelly Dace have two black stripes along side, *smaller head and mouth.* (3) Pearl Dace (Pl. 15) *lacks* dark "cape" on back; has blunter snout, *smaller mouth* (rarely reaching eye), herringbone lines on back, usually a complete lateral line, usually a barbel near corner of mouth. **Map 89**

SOUTHERN REDBELLY DACE *Phoxinus erythrogaster* **Pl. 15**

Identification: *2 black stripes* along side; upper one thin, broken into spots at rear; lower one wide, becoming thin on caudal peduncle. Olive-brown above, dusky stripe along back; *black spots* (sometimes absent) on upper side, often arranged in row; silver-yellow side; black wedge-shaped caudal spot; white, yellow, or red below. Large male is vividly colored, with bright red belly, lower head, and base of dorsal fin; yellow fins. Moderately pointed snout, longer than eye in adult; small, moderately oblique (less than 45°), slightly subterminal

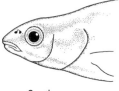

Southern

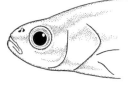

Northern

Fig. 20 Southern and Northern Redbelly Dace

mouth ending in front of eye (Fig. 20). 67–95 lateral scales; pharyngeal teeth 0,5–5,0. To 3½ in. (9.1 cm).
Range: Great Lakes and Mississippi R. basins from NY west to s. MN; south to Tennessee R. drainage, AL, and White-Arkansas R. drainage, AR and OK. Isolated populations on Former Mississippi Embayment, MS, in Kansas R. system, KS, and in upper Arkansas R. drainage, CO and NM. Common in upland and spring-fed streams; absent in lowland areas such as n. MO. **Habitat:** Rocky, usually spring-fed, pools of headwaters and creeks.
Similar species: (1) See Northern Redbelly Dace. (2) Mountain Redbelly (Pl. 15) and (3) Tennessee Dace (Pl. 15) have broken stripe along side, spots in rows on back and upper side.   **Map 90**

NORTHERN REDBELLY DACE *Phoxinus eos*   Not shown
Identification: Similar to Southern Redbelly Dace but has more rounded, *shorter* (about equal to eye diameter) snout; more upturned mouth, with chin *in front* of upper lip (Fig. 20). 70–90 lateral scales. To 3¼ in. (8 cm).
Range: Atlantic, Great Lakes, Hudson Bay, upper Mississippi, Missouri, and Peace-Mackenzie R. drainages, from NS west to NT and BC; south to n. PA, WI, NE, and CO. Common. **Habitat:** Lakes, ponds, bogs, and pools of headwaters and creeks. Usually over silt, often near vegetation.
Similar species: (1) See Southern Redbelly Dace (Pl. 15). (2) Finescale Dace (Pl. 15) has larger head and mouth, *1* stripe along side, dark "cape" on back, many small specks.   **Map 91**

MOUNTAIN REDBELLY DACE *Phoxinus oreas*   Pl. 15
Identification: Black stripe along side *broken* under dorsal fin; *large black spots* in row along back and in row along upper side. Olive to green-gold above; silver-white to red below. Large male is bright red below (including lower half of opercle), behind opercle, and at base of dorsal fin; has bright silver pectoral and pelvic fin bases, black chin and breast, yellow fins. Moderately pointed snout; slightly subterminal mouth. 64–81 lateral scales; pharyngeal teeth 0,5–5,0. To 2¾ in. (7.2 cm).
Range: Mountain and Piedmont regions of Atlantic Slope from Shenandoah R. (Potomac R. drainage), VA, to Neuse R. drainage, NC; upper New R. drainage, WV, VA, and NC. Introduced into upper Holston R. system, VA. **Habitat:** Rocky pools and runs of headwaters, creeks, and small to medium rivers.
Similar species: (1) See Tennessee Dace (Pl. 15). (2) Other *Phoxinus* species (Pl. 15) *lack* broken stripe on side.   **Map 90**

TENNESSEE DACE *Phoxinus tennesseensis*   Pl. 15
Identification: Similar to Mountain Redbelly Dace but has *smaller spots* (smaller than eye pupil) on back and upper side, usually a *thin black stripe* along side (above larger broken stripe), and red on caudal fin and below stripe along side of large male. 67–95 lateral scales. To 2¾ in. (7.2 cm).

Range: Upper Tennessee R. drainage (from lower Clinch R. system, TN, and Holston R. system, VA, to near GA border), VA and TN. Rare and localized. **Habitat:** Gravel-, sand-, and silt-bottomed pools of spring-fed headwaters.
Similar species: See Mountain Redbelly Dace (Pl. 15). **Map 90**

BLACKSIDE DACE *Phoxinus cumberlandensis* **Pl. 15**
Identification: Two dusky stripes along side *converge on caudal peduncle*, coalesce into *wide black stripe* on large male. *Many black specks on back and upper side.* Olive to green-gold above; silver-white to red below. Large male is bright red below, behind opercle, and at base of dorsal fin; has bright silver pectoral and pelvic fin bases, yellow fins. Moderately compressed body, pointed snout, slightly subterminal mouth. 66–81 lateral scales; pharyngeal teeth 0,5–5,0. To 2¾ in. (7.2 cm).
Range: Upper Cumberland R. drainage (above Big South Fork), KY and TN. Rare; protected as a *threatened species.* **Habitat:** Rocky pools of headwaters and creeks; individuals are usually found along undercut banks, around large rocks or among detritus.
Similar species: See Pl. 15. (1) Mountain Redbelly and (2) Tennessee Dace have broken stripe on side, spots in rows on upper side; are less compressed; *lack* wide black stripe on large male. (3) Southern Redbelly Dace *lacks* many black specks on upper side, has two *parallel* stripes on side. **Map 92**

FLAME CHUB *Hemitremia flammea* **Pl. 15**
Identification: Chubby, barely compressed body, *deep caudal peduncle*; short head, with extremely *short snout*; small, slightly subterminal mouth; round eye. Dorsal fin origin slightly behind pelvic fin origin. Olive above, dark stripe along back; dark streaks along upper side, then light stripe, then black stripe ending at black caudal spot or wedge; white to red below. Large individual (especially male) has bright *scarlet red* along bottom ⅓ of body and at base of dorsal fin. Silver peritoneum flecked with black. Incomplete lateral line, fewer than ½ scales pored; 38–44 lateral scales; 7–8 anal rays; pharyngeal teeth 2,5–4,2. To 2¾ in. (7.2 cm).
Range: Middle Cumberland (mostly Caney Fork) and Tennessee R. drainages, TN, GA, and AL; Kelley Cr. (Coosa R. system), ne. AL. Uncommon; extirpated from many areas because of destruction of springs. **Habitat:** Springs and spring-fed streams; usually over gravel.
Similar species: Southern Redbelly Dace (Pl. 15) has 2 black stripes along side, black spots on upper side, often has yellow on body and fins, much smaller (67–95 lateral) scales. **Map 92**

• *SEMOTILUS*

Genus characteristics: Large minnows with a thick, barely to moderately compressed body, *broad head*, small *flaplike barbel* in groove *above* (but not in) corner of mouth (Fig. 21), usually 8 anal rays, dor-

small flaplike barbel
(*Semotilus* species)

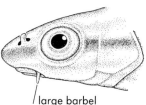

large barbel
(as in *Hybopsis*,
Erimystax species)

Fig. 21 Minnows — barbels

sal fin origin slightly behind pelvic fin origin, complete lateral line, short intestine, silver peritoneum with black specks, pharyngeal teeth usually 2,5–4,2. The most distinctive characteristic of *Semotilus*, the flaplike barbel, is most easily seen when the mouth is held open.

CREEK CHUB *Semotilus atromaculatus*   **Pl. 15**
Identification: *Large black spot* at front of dorsal fin base, black caudal spot (indistinct in large individuals). *Large terminal mouth* reaching past front of eye. Body barely compressed at front, compressed at caudal peduncle; pointed snout. Olive-brown above, dark stripe along back; herringbone lines on upper side in young; dusky black stripe (darkest on young) along green-silver side, around snout, and onto upper lip; black bar along back of gill cover. Breeding male has orange at dorsal base, orange lower fins, blue on side of head, pink on lower ½ of head and body; 6–12 large tubercles on head. 47–65 lateral scales; 8 dorsal rays. To 12 in. (30 cm).
Range: Most of e. U.S. and se. Canada in Atlantic, Great Lakes, Hudson Bay, Mississippi, and Gulf basins as far west as MB, e. MT, WY, CO, e. OK, and e. TX, but absent from s. GA and peninsular FL; isolated population in upper Pecos and Canadian R. systems, NM. Introduced in Colorado R. drainage, TX, and elsewhere in U.S. One of most common fishes in e. North America. **Habitat:** Rocky and sandy pools of headwaters, creeks and small rivers.
Remarks: In preparation for spawning, a *Semotilus* breeding male digs a pit in the stream bottom by removing mouthfuls of gravel, and then stands guard over the pit and attempts to attract females. Spawning occurs over the pit, and eggs fall into the spaces among the stones. The male guards the nest, fending off large intruders with the hornlike tubercles on his head. Some species, e.g., Rosyface and Common Shiners, prefer to spawn over the clean gravel exposed by the Creek Chub and are allowed to do so by the guarding male Creek Chub, perhaps because an increased number of eggs lessens the probability of his eggs being eaten. As eggs are deposited in the pit, the male covers them with stones and excavates another pit immediately downstream. As spawning continues and the male covers the eggs, a long

ridge of gravel develops. In the Fallfish, the ridge may be 6 ft. (2 m) long.
Similar species: (1) See Dixie Chub (Pl. 15) and (2) Sandhills Chub. (3) Fallfish (Pl. 15) *lacks* black spot at dorsal fin base; has darkly outlined, larger (43–50 lateral) scales, larger eye. **Map 93**

DIXIE CHUB *Semotilus thoreauianus* **Pl. 15**
Identification: Similar to Creek Chub (above) but has *larger* (45–52 lateral) *scales; wider, more diffuse stripe* (darker on young) along side; more robust body; less distinct dorsal and caudal spots. Breeding male has orange to pink underside, yellow fins, usually 8 large hooked tubercles on head. To 6 in. (15 cm).
Range: Gulf Slope from Ochlockonee R. system, GA and FL, to Tombigbee R. system, AL. Most populations are below the Fall Line. Common. **Habitat:** Sand- and gravel-bottomed pools of creeks and small rivers.
Similar species: (1) See Creek Chub (Pl. 15). (2) Sandhills Chub is strongly bicolored; has black caudal spot; 9, rather than 8, dorsal rays. **Map 95**

SANDHILLS CHUB *Semotilus lumbee* **Not shown**
Identification: Similar to Creek Chub but *lacks* discrete black spot at dorsal fin base (dusky spot may be present), is more strongly bicolored (dark above, white below), has 9 *dorsal rays*, larger scales (usually 18 scales around caudal peduncle; Creek Chub usually has 19–20). Breeding male has *red fins*. 42–52 lateral scales. To 9½ in. (24 cm).
Range: "Carolina Sandhills" of s.-cen. NC and ne. SC; encompassing portions of the Peedee, Yadkin, and Cape Fear R. drainages. Fairly common in small range; most common in Lumber R. system. **Habitat:** Flowing, sand- and gravel-bottomed pools and runs of headwaters, creeks, and small rivers.
Similar species: (1) See Creek Chub (Pl. 15). (2) Dixie Chub (Pl. 15) has 8 *dorsal rays*, is less strongly bicolored, lacks black caudal spot.
Map 94

FALLFISH *Semotilus corporalis* **Pl. 15**
Identification: *Large* (43–50 lateral) *scales. Large eye.* Moderately compressed body; fairly long, rounded snout slightly overhanging large mouth; dorsal fin origin over or slightly behind pelvic fin origin. Scales on back and upper side *darkly outlined* on adult; young have black stripe along side, dark caudal spot. Olive to gold-brown above, dark stripe along back; bright silver side, sometimes with purple or blue sheen; black bar along back of gill cover. Breeding male has fairly large tubercles on head. 8 dorsal rays; 8 anal rays. Largest minnow native to eastern North America; to 20¼ in. (51 cm).
Range: Atlantic Slope from NB to James R. drainage, VA; Hudson Bay, Lake Ontario, and St. Lawrence drainages, QU, ON, and NY. Common. **Habitat:** Gravel- and rubble-bottomed pools and runs of small to medium rivers; lake margins.

Similar species: (1) Creek Chub (Pl. 15) has large, black spot at front of dorsal fin base, *smaller scales* (usually more than 50 along lateral line) that are less distinctly outlined, *smaller eye*. (2) River and (3) Hornyhead Chubs (both, Pl. 16) have much *smaller eye*, larger barbel *in* corner of mouth, 7 anal rays, pharyngeal teeth 0,4–4,0 or 1,4–4,1.

Map 94

PEARL DACE *Margariscus margarita* Pl. 15

Identification: *Small* (49–78 lateral) *scales*, short head, fairly deep caudal peduncle. *Flaplike barbel* in groove above mouth (often missing on 1 or both sides). Nearly cylindrical body; rounded snout; small (seldom reaching front of eye), slightly subterminal mouth; dorsal fin origin behind pelvic fin origin. Dark olive to gray above, often with black herringbone lines, dark stripe along back; many small *black and brown specks* (absent in w. populations) on silver side; white, yellow, or red below. Black stripe along side, black caudal spot on young; stripe vague on adult. Breeding male is bright orange-red along lower side; has pale yellow stripe along belly, many small tubercles on head. Usually complete lateral line; 8 dorsal rays, 8 anal rays; pharyngeal teeth 2,5–4,2. To 6½ in. (16 cm).
Range: Atlantic, Hudson Bay, Great Lakes, and Mississippi R. basins in s. Canada and n. U.S. from Atlantic Coast to s. NT, e. BC, and MT; south to VA, MI, WI, and IA. Isolated population in upper Missouri R. basin, SD, NE, and WY. Common over most of range. **Habitat:** Pools of creeks and small rivers; ponds and lakes. Usually over sand or gravel.
Remarks: Two subspecies appear to be recognizable, although they and their ranges are poorly defined. *M. m. margarita* is a large-scaled form (about 50–62 lateral scales) found in the Allegheny region. *M. m. nachtriebi*, with about 60–75 lateral scales, occupies rest of range.
Similar species: See Pl. 15. (1) Creek Chub has black spot at front of dorsal fin base, large terminal mouth, *lacks* brown and black specks on side. (2) Lake Chub has longer, sharper snout, more compressed body; lacks red along lower side of body of large male. (3) Finescale Dace *lacks* barbel, herringbone lines; has more pointed snout, larger mouth (to below eye), incomplete lateral line. **Map 95**

LAKE CHUB *Couesius plumbeus* Pl. 15

Identification: *Barbel* at corner of large, barely subterminal mouth. *Large eye*; head flattened above and below; moderately pointed snout. Moderately compressed, slender body; dorsal fin origin over or slightly behind pelvic fin origin. Brown to green above; dark stripe along silver-gray side, darkest on young and large male; sometimes black specks on side and belly; dusky caudal spot. Large male may have red at pectoral and pelvic fin origins, corners of mouth. Complete lateral line; 53–70 lateral scales; 8 anal rays; pharyngeal teeth 2,4–4,2. To 9 in. (23 cm).
Range: Most northern minnow in North America; only minnow in AK (Yukon R. drainage). Throughout much of Canada and n. U.S.; south to Delaware R., NY, s. end of Lake Michigan, IL, Platte R. sys-

tem, CO, and Columbia R. drainage, WA. Relict population in Mississippi R. basin, IA. Common throughout much of range. **Habitat:** Virtually any body of water, standing or flowing, large or small. Most common in gravel-bottomed pools and runs of streams and along rocky lake margins.

Similar species: Pearl Dace (Pl. 15) has shorter, blunter snout; less compressed body; bright red along lower side of large male. **Map 96**

• NOCOMIS

Genus characteristics: Large, bronze-colored, stout body; *large* (36–45 lateral scales) *dark-edged scales* on back and upper side; *barbel* at corner of *large, slightly subterminal mouth.* Complete lateral line, 7 anal rays. Dorsal fin origin slightly in front of to slightly behind pelvic fin origin.

HORNYHEAD CHUB *Nocomis biguttatus*   Pl. 16
Identification: *Red* (on young) to yellow (adult) caudal fin; other fins yellow to orange. *Bright red spot* (brassy on female) behind eye on large male. Dark olive to brown above; iridescent green on yellow-brown side; white to light yellow below. Dusky iridescent yellow stripe along back, yellow streak above dusky stripe along side and around snout, black caudal spot (all darkest on young). Breeding male is pink below with pink-orange fins; has many large tubercles on top of head. Rounded snout. 38–45 lateral scales; usually 16–17 scales around caudal peduncle; pharyngeal teeth 1,4–4,1. To 10¼ in. (26 cm).

Range: Mohawk R. system, NY, west through Great Lakes and Mississippi R. basin to Red. R. drainage (Hudson Bay basin), MB and ND; south to Ohio R. and lower Kentucky R. system, KY, but rare in unglaciated areas; south into Ozarks (where common). Isolated population in Platte and Cheyenne R. systems, NB, WY, and CO. Common throughout much of range. **Habitat:** Rocky pools and runs of creeks and small to medium rivers.

Similar species: See Pl. 16. See (1) Redspot and (2) Redtail Chubs. (3) River and (4) Bull Chubs have longer snout (about same as length of head behind eye), smaller eye higher on head, usually no stripe along side, *no* red spot behind eye, *no* bright red caudal fin, large hump on head of breeding male, pharyngeal teeth 0,4–4,0. (5) Bluehead Chub *lacks* bright red caudal fin, red spot behind eye; has large loop on right side of intestine, pharyngeal teeth 0,4–4,0; breeding male has large hump on dark blue head. **Map 97**

REDSPOT CHUB *Nocomis asper*   Not shown
Identification: Similar to Hornyhead Chub, but adult and large juvenile have *rows of tubercles* (or tubercle spots) on side of body (often 2–3 tubercles/scale); spot behind eye bright red on large juveniles as well as adults. Breeding male has yellow-pink fins. 38–45 lateral

scales, usually 17–21 scales around caudal peduncle; pharyngeal teeth 1,4–4,1. To 8½ in. (22 cm).
Range: Arkansas R. drainage, sw. MO, se. KS, ne. OK, and nw. AR; isolated populations in Blue R. (Red R. drainage), OK and the upper Ouachita R. drainage, AR. **Habitat:** Rocky, usually clear, runs and pools of creeks and small to medium rivers. Locally common.
Similar species: (1) See Hornyhead Chub (Pl. 16). (2) Redtail Chub (Pl. 16) has red-orange paired fins, usually 1 tubercle/scale, pharyngeal teeth 0,4–4,0. **Map 97**

REDTAIL CHUB *Nocomis effusus* Pl. 16
Identification: Similar to Hornyhead Chub, but has *brighter red-orange fins* (especially on young), usually 19–20 scales around caudal peduncle; large juvenile and adult have *rows of tubercles* (or tubercle spots) on side of body (usually 1 tubercle/scale); pharyngeal teeth 0,4–4,0; 39–44 lateral scales. To 9 in. (23 cm).
Range: Upper Green, upper Barren, Cumberland (Little South Fork and downstream), Duck and lower Tennessee (between Cumberland and Duck rivers) R. drainages, KY and TN. **Habitat:** Clear rocky runs and pools of creeks and small rivers. Uncommon over much of range; locally common.
Similar species: (1) See Hornyhead Chub (Pl. 16). (2) Redspot Chub has less brightly colored fins, often 2–3 tubercles/scale, pharyngeal teeth 1,4–4,1. **Map 97**

RIVER CHUB *Nocomis micropogon* Pl. 16
Identification: *Long snout* (about same as length of head behind eye); *small eye* high on head. Large mouth; width greater than interpelvic width. Dark olive to brown above; brassy, iridescent green side; dark-edged scales on back and upper side; white to light yellow below; olive to light orange caudal fin; other fins light clear to yellow-pink. Dusky iridescent yellow stripe along back, sometimes a dusky stripe along side ending in darker caudal spot. Breeding male has pink-blue head, body, and fins; *large tubercles on snout* (including in front of nostrils); *large hump* on top of head. 37–43 (usually 38–41) lateral scales; more than 30 scales around body at dorsal fin origin; pharyngeal teeth 0,4–4,0. To 12½ in. (32 cm).
Range: Atlantic drainages from Susquehanna R., NY, to James R., VA; Great Lakes basin, NY to MI; Ohio R. basin, NY to e. IL and south to n. GA and AL except absent in sw. IN, w. ⅔ of KY, and most of w. TN. Introduced in Ottawa R. system, ON. Also present and possibly introduced in upper Santee R., NC, Savannah R., SC and GA; and Coosa R., GA. Common; locally abundant. **Habitat:** Rocky runs and flowing pools of small to medium rivers.
Remarks: 2 subspecies. *N. m. platyrhynchus,* in New R. drainage, WV, VA, and NC, has tubercles (on adult) extending over top of head from snout to well behind eyes. On *N. m. micropogon,* in rest of range, tubercles are larger, fewer, and usually restricted to area in front of eyes.

Similar species: See Pl. 16. (1) See Bull Chub. (2) Bluehead Chub *lacks* tubercles on snout in front of nostrils; has snout *shorter* than length of head behind eye, eye lower on head, deeper body, usually fewer than 30 scales around body, large loop on intestine (Fig. 15). (3) Hornyhead, (4) Redspot, and (5) Redtail Chubs have snout *shorter* than length of head behind eye, *larger* eye lower on head, more distinct stripe along side, red caudal fin on young, red spot behind eye on large male, *no* hump on head of breeding male. **Map 98**

BULL CHUB *Nocomis raneyi*   **Not shown**
Identification: Nearly identical to River Chub but has *smaller mouth* (width equal to or less than interpelvic width), 39–45 (usually 40–43) lateral scales. To 12½ in. (32 cm).
Range: Atlantic Slope drainages from James R., VA, to Neuse R., NC. Generally common above Fall Line. **Habitat:** Rocky pools and runs of creeks and small to medium rivers.
Similar species: See River Chub (Pl. 16).   **Map 99**

BLUEHEAD CHUB *Nocomis leptocephalus*   **Pl. 16**
Identification: *Large loop* on intestine visible through body wall of young (see Remarks). Fairly short, rounded snout, deep body. Tan-olive to dark olive above, dusky iridescent yellow stripe along back; dusky stripe along brassy iridescent green side; light yellow to red-orange fins. Breeding male has *large hump* on top of *dark blue head*, large tubercles on head *behind nostrils*, orange or blue side, orange fins. 36–43 lateral scales, usually fewer than 30 scales around body at dorsal fin origin; pharyngeal teeth 0,4–4,0. To 10 in. (26 cm).
Range: Atlantic and Gulf Slope drainages from Shenandoah R., VA, to Pearl R., MS; mostly above Fall Line except in AL and MS. Lower tributaries of Mississippi R., MS and LA; upper New R. drainage, WV, VA, and NC; Bear Cr. (Tennessee R. drainage), AL and MS. Introduced into Little Tennessee R. system, NC. **Habitat:** Rocky and sandy pools and runs of headwaters, creeks, and small to medium rivers. Common in most clear Atlantic streams; locally common in Gulf streams.
Remarks: 3 subspecies. *N. l. leptocephalus*, in the New R. and Atlantic drainages south to the Santee R., has 16 or more tubercles on the head. *N. l. interocularis*, in the Savannah, Altamaha, and Apalachicola drainages, has 7–9 tubercles on the head. *N. l. bellicus*, in Gulf Slope and Mississippi R. drainages west of the Apalachicola drainage, has only 4–6 tubercles on the head. The intestinal loop is absent in some populations of *N. l. interocularis* in the Chattahoochee R. system.
Similar species: See Pl. 16. (1) River and (2) Bull Chubs have longer snout, eye higher on head, more slender body, tubercles on snout in front of nostrils, usually more than 30 scales around body, *no* large loop on intestine. (3) Hornyhead Chub *lacks* large loop on intestine, large hump on head of breeding male; has bright red caudal fin, spot behind eye.   **Map 100**

• *CAMPOSTOMA*

Genus characteristics: *Hard* (cartilaginous) *ridge* on lower jaw (Fig. 22) of *subterminal mouth. Thick,* barely compressed body; dorsal fin origin over or slightly behind pelvic fin origin. Tan to brown above; often a dark stripe along side, dark caudal spot on young, *irregular dark brown to black blotches* on back and side of large individuals. Breeding male has *orange fins, white lips,* bright red iris. Stonerollers use the hard ridge on the lower jaw to scrape algae and other food from rocks. Algae are difficult to digest, and consequently stonerollers have a long intestine to increase exposure during digestion. To accommodate its great length (about 18 in. in a 5-in. individual) the intestine is coiled around the gas bladder (in all except the primitive Mexican Stoneroller).

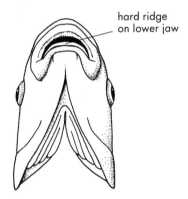

hard ridge
on lower jaw

Fig. 22 *Campostoma* — **underside of head**

CENTRAL STONEROLLER *Campostoma anomalum*　　　**Pl. 16**
Identification: Breeding male has black band on orange dorsal and *anal* fins (see Remarks), crescent-shaped row of 1–3 large tubercles on inner edge of nostril (Fig. 23), tubercles on nape and adjacent area of body, body strongly arched at nape. Complete lateral line; usually *46–55 lateral scales, 36–46 scales around body* at dorsal fin origin, 21–33 rakers on 1st gill arch; pharyngeal teeth 0,4–4,0 or 1,4–4,1. To 8½ in. (22 cm).
Range: See Remarks. Widespread across most of e. and cen. U.S. in Atlantic, Great Lakes, Mississippi R., and Hudson Bay (Red R.) basins from NY west to ND and WY, and south to SC and TX; Thames R. system (Great Lakes basin), ON; Gulf Slope drainages from Galveston Bay, TX, to Rio Grande, Mexico; isolated population in sw. MS and e. LA. Common to abundant throughout much of range but generally absent on Piedmont and Coastal Plain, uncommon on

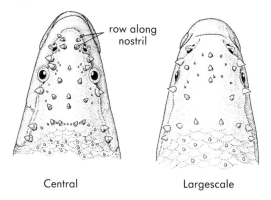

row along
nostril

Central   Largescale

Fig. 23 Central and Largescale Stonerollers – head tubercles on breeding male

Great Plains. **Habitat:** Rocky riffles, runs, and pools of headwaters, creeks, and small to medium rivers.
Remarks: The distribution and variation of the Central and Largescale Stonerollers are unclear. Tentatively, three subspecies of the Central Stoneroller are recognized: (1) *C. a. anomalum*, in the Ohio R. and upper Atlantic drainages, has usually 15–16 pectoral rays (other populations generally have 16–19 rays). (2) *C. a. michauxi*, in the Santee and Savannah R. drainages, NC and SC, uniquely lacks a black band on the anal fin of the breeding male. (3) *C. a. pullum*, apparently occupying the rest of the range, has usually 18–20 scales over the body from lateral line to lateral line at the dorsal fin origin (including lateral-line scales); other populations have 15–17 scales.
Similar species: See Pl. 16. See (1) Bluefin, (2) Largescale, and (3) Mexican Stonerollers.   **Map 101**

BLUEFIN STONEROLLER *Campostoma pauciradii*   **Pl. 16**
Identification: Similar to Central Stoneroller but has only *11–17 rakers* on 1st gill arch; *usually 33–38 scales* around body at dorsal fin origin; *blue-green dorsal and anal fins,* blue-green upper side, and brassy yellow lower side on breeding male. Usually 42–49 lateral scales; pharyngeal teeth 0,4–4,0 or 1,4–4,1. To 6¼ in. (16 cm).
Range: Apalachicola and Altamaha R. drainages (mostly above Fall Line), GA and e. AL; Alabama (Toonigh Cr., Cherokee Co., and Wirchee Cr., Haralson Co.) and Tennessee R. drainages (Toccoa R., Fannin Co.), GA. Fairly common in upper and middle Chattahoochee R. drainage; rare elsewhere. **Habitat:** Rocky riffles, runs and sometimes pools of headwaters, creeks, and small rivers.
Similar species: (1) See Central Stoneroller (Pl. 16). (2) Largescale Stoneroller (Pl. 16) has usually *19–30 rakers* on 1st gill arch; breeding male with pink-orange dorsal and anal fins, no (or a weak) black band

on anal fin, no crescent-shaped row of 1–3 large tubercles on inner edge of nostril. **Map 92**

LARGESCALE STONEROLLER *Campostoma oligolepis* Pl. 16
Identification: Similar to Central Stoneroller but has usually *31–36 scales around body* at dorsal fin origin, *43–47 lateral scales* (see Remarks). Breeding male has no (or only a weak) black band on anal fin; no crescent-shaped row of 1–3 large tubercles on inner edge of nostril (Fig. 23); body deepest near dorsal fin origin. Usually 20–28 rakers on 1st gill arch, 17–19 pectoral rays; pharyngeal teeth 0,4–4,0 or 1,4–4,1. To 8½ in. (22 cm).
Range: Upper Mississippi R. and Lake Michigan drainages of WI, e. MN, e. IA, and n. IL; Ozarkian streams of cen. and s. MO, n. AR, and ext. ne. OK; Escambia R., AL; Mobile Bay drainage, GA, AL, and e. MS; parts of Green, Cumberland, and Tennessee R. drainages of KY, TN, GA, and AL (see Remarks). Usually common; extirpated from much of cen. IL. **Habitat:** Rocky riffles and runs of clear creeks and small to medium rivers. Less tolerant of siltation than is Central Stoneroller.
Remarks: Largescale Stonerollers from more eastern drainages have higher scale counts: usually 36–42 scales around body at dorsal fin origin, 48–53 lateral scales. Largescale Stonerollers recently have been identified from the Green, Cumberland, Tennessee R. and Mobile Bay drainages, all previously thought to be inhabited only by Central Stonerollers.
Similar species: (1) See Central Stoneroller (Pl. 16). (2) Bluefin Stoneroller (Pl. 16) has usually 12–16 gill rakers on 1st arch, 15–17 pectoral rays; blue-green fins, crescent-shaped row of 1–3 large tubercles on inner edge of nostril, black band on anal fin of breeding male. **Map 102**

MEXICAN STONEROLLER *Campostoma ornatum* Pl. 16
Identification: Similar to Central Stoneroller but has usually *58–77 lateral scales, 47–60 scales around body* at dorsal fin origin, 15–19 rakers on 1st gill arch; breeding male lacks tubercles on nape and adjacent area of body; intestine rarely coiled around gas bladder (see *Campostoma* account). Pharyngeal teeth 0,4–4,0. To 6¼ in. (16 cm).
Range: Rio Grande system of Big Bend region, s. TX; Rucker Canyon and Leslie Cr., extreme se. AZ. Fairly common. Widespread and common in n. Mexico. **Habitat:** Rocky riffles and adjacent pools of headwaters and creeks.
Similar species: See Central Stoneroller (Pl. 16). **Map 101**

ROUNDNOSE MINNOW *Dionda episcopa* Pl. 16
Identification: *Strongly bicolored;* yellow-green above, silver-white below (but often with dark green belly — see Remarks). Light yellow stripe above dark stripe (*zigzagged* at front) along side and around snout, followed by *black spot* on caudal fin base. Dark green stripe along back, widest at dorsal fin origin. Yellow fins on adult. Slender, fairly compressed body; dorsal fin origin over to slightly behind pelvic fin origin; rounded snout; small subterminal mouth. Complete

lateral line; 34–45 lateral scales; 8 anal rays; pharyngeal teeth 0,4–4,0. To 3 in. (7.7 cm).
Range: Colorado, San Antonio, upper Nueces, and Rio Grande drainages, TX, NM, and Mexico. Locally common in TX, rare elsewhere; absent in Rio Grande, NM. **Habitat:** Rocky pools, sometimes runs, of headwaters, creeks and small rivers. Often among filamentous algae.
Remarks: *Dionda* species are long-gutted minnows that feed mainly on algae and other vegetation. Plant material in the gut tends to make the belly dark and discolored.
Similar species: Devils River Minnow (Pl. 16) has black wedge on caudal fin base, larger eye, dark-edged scales on back and upper side, orange fins. **Map 103**

DEVILS RIVER MINNOW *Dionda diaboli*   **Pl. 16**
Identification: *Black wedge* on caudal fin base. Black stripe along side and onto snout. Slender, fairly compressed body; *large eye*; short, blunt snout; small subterminal mouth. *Dark-edged scales* on olive back and upper side, dark stripe along back; silver-white below, often with dark green belly; orange fins. Dorsal fin origin over to slightly behind pelvic fin origin. Complete, often punctate, lateral line; 32–36 lateral scales; 8 anal rays; pharyngeal teeth 0,4–4,0. To 2½ in. (6.4 cm).
Range: Devils R. and nearby San Felipe, Sycamore, and Las Moras creeks, Val Verde and Kinney cos., TX. Common in extremely small range. **Habitat:** Rocky runs and flowing pools.
Similar species: Roundnose Minnow (Pl. 16) has *round spot* on caudal fin base, *smaller eye*, *no* conspicuous dark-edged scales on back and upper side, yellow fins. **Map 104**

• PHENACOBIUS

Genus characteristics: *Long, cylindrical body; large fleshy lips* on *subterminal mouth* (Fig. 24). Round snout; dorsal fin origin in front of pelvic fin origin. Complete, straight lateral line; pharyngeal teeth 0,4–4,0.

SUCKERMOUTH MINNOW *Phenacobius mirabilis*   **Pl. 8**
Identification: *Bicolored* (olive-brown above, silver-white below) *body*; large *fleshy lips* (Fig. 24); *intense black spot* on caudal fin base following thin dark stripe along side of body. Thin dark stripe along back; darkly outlined scales on back and upper side. Small eye; 42–51 lateral scales; 15–17 scales around caudal peduncle. To 4¾ in. (12 cm).
Range: Mississippi R. basin from OH and WV to WY, CO, and NM, and from se. MN to n. AL and s. OK; w. Lake Erie drainage, OH; isolated populations in Gulf Coast drainages (Sabine Lake, LA and TX, Galveston Bay, TX, Colorado R., TX, and upper Pecos R., NM). Common throughout most of range; rare in Gulf drainages. **Habitat:** Gravel and rubble riffles and runs of clear to turbid creeks and small to medium, sometimes large, rivers.

Similar species: See Pl. 8. (1) Kanawha Minnow *lacks* black spot on caudal fin base; is more slender; has black blotches on upper side, *larger lips.* (2) Fatlips, (3) Riffle, and (4) Stargazing Minnows *lack* black spot on caudal fin base, are much more slender, have 52 or more lateral scales.   **Map 105**

KANAWHA MINNOW *Phenacobius teretulus*   **Pl. 8**
Identification: Many papillae on *very fleshy lips* (Fig. 24). Moderate eye. Gray-brown above, *small black blotches* scattered on upper half of body; dark stripe along back; dusky stripe along silver side. 45–49 lateral scales; 16–19 scales around caudal peduncle. To 4 in. (10 cm).
Range: New (upper Kanawha) R. drainage, WV, VA, and NC. Generally uncommon. **Habitat:** Rubble and gravel riffles and runs of creeks and small to medium rivers.
Similar species: See Pl. 8. (1) Suckermouth Minnow has black spot on caudal fin base, *thinner lips* with few bumps, deeper head and body, no black blotches on upper side. (2) Fatlips, (3) Riffle, and (4) Stargazing Minnows are more slender, lack black blotches, have 52 or more lateral scales.   **Map 106**

FATLIPS MINNOW *Phenacobius crassilabrum*   **Pl. 8**
Identification: *Pelvic fins reach to or past anus.* Lips as in Suckermouth Minnow (Fig. 24). Small eye. Dark olive above; dark stripe along back wider in front of dorsal fin; light green streak above black stripe along silver side; 2 yellow spots on caudal fin base. 56–68 lateral scales; 19–20 scales around caudal peduncle. To 4¼ in. (11 cm).
Range: Upper Tennessee R. drainage (from S. Fork Holston R. south to Little Tennessee R.), w. VA, w. NC, e. TN, and ne. GA. Fairly common. **Habitat:** Gravel and rubble runs and riffles of creeks and small to medium rivers.

papillae

Suckermouth   Kanawha

Fig. 24 Suckermouth and Kanawha Minnows — underside of head

Similar species: See Pl. 8. (1) Riffle and (2) Stargazing Minnows are more slender; have larger, more upwardly directed eyes; pelvic fins *not* reaching past anus. Riffle Minnow has 15–19, Stargazing Minnow 13–16, scales around caudal peduncle. (3) Suckermouth and (4) Kanawha Minnows have pelvic fins not reaching past anus, fewer than 52 lateral scales; Suckermouth Minnow has black spot on caudal fin base; Kanawha Minnow has black blotches on upper side.

Map 105

RIFFLE MINNOW *Phenacobius catostomus*   **Pl. 8**
Identification: *Very long, cylindrical body;* lips as in Suckermouth Minnow (Fig. 24). Eyes high on head, *directed upwardly.* Dark gray-brown back; light brown upper side; silver sheen over dusky stripe along side. 56–69 lateral scales; 15–19 scales around caudal peduncle. To 4½ in. (12 cm).
Range: Mobile Bay drainage, se. TN, nw. GA, and AL. Local and uncommon in Tallapoosa and Black Warrior R. systems, fairly common in Coosa and Cahaba R. systems. **Habitat:** Gravel and rubble runs and riffles of creeks and small to medium rivers.
Similar species: See Pl. 8. (1) See Stargazing Minnow. (2) Fatlips Minnow is *less* slender, has pelvic fins reaching past anus. (3) Suckermouth Minnow is deeper bodied; has black spot on caudal fin base, 42–51 lateral scales.   **Map 106**

STARGAZING MINNOW *Phenacobius uranops*   **Pl. 8**
Identification: Similar to Riffle Minnow but has *more elongated body,* longer snout, *more elliptical eye.* 52–61 lateral scales; 13–16 scales around caudal peduncle. To 4½ in. (12 cm).
Range: Green, Cumberland, and Tennessee R. drainages, KY, VA, TN, GA, and AL. Common only in upper Tennessee and Green R. drainages. **Habitat:** Gravel and rubble runs and riffles of clear, fast creeks and small to medium rivers.
Similar species: See Riffle Minnow (Pl. 8).   **Map 106**

TONGUETIED MINNOW *Exoglossum laurae*   **Not shown**
Identification: Central *bony plate* with *fleshy lobe* to either side on lower jaw (Fig. 25). *Chubby body,* barely compressed; deep caudal peduncle; dorsal fin origin over pelvic fin origin. Rounded snout, subterminal mouth; thick upper lip thinner at middle; premaxillary frenum present; usually a small barbel near corner of mouth. Olive-gray above; silver green-purple side; clear to light olive or light red fins; small individual has dusky stripe along side and onto snout, black caudal spot. Complete lateral line; 47–53 lateral scales; 7 anal rays; pharyngeal teeth 1,4–4,1. To 6¼ in. (16 cm).
Range: 3 disjunct areas of upper Ohio R. basin: upper Allegheny R. drainage, NY and PA; upper New R. drainage, WV, VA, and NC; and Great Miami and Little Miami R. systems, OH; also in upper Genesee R. (Lake Ontario drainage), NY and PA. Fairly common, but less widespread and abundant than historically. **Habitat:** Rocky pools

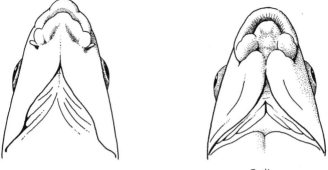

Tonguetied

Cutlips

Fig. 25 Tonguetied and Cutlips Minnows — underside of head

and runs of creeks and small to medium rivers; often near vegetation or other cover.
Remarks: Breeding male Cutlips and Tonguetied Minnows build large circular or rectangular nests by piling pebbles carried in the mouth.
Similar species: See Cutlips Minnow (Pl. 8). No other species has similar mouth structure.   **Map 107**

CUTLIPS MINNOW *Exoglossum maxillingua*   **Pl. 8**
Identification: Similar to Tonguetied Minnow, but with *a much larger fleshy lobe* on each side of lower jaw, well separated from central bony plate and followed by another fleshy lobe on underside of head (Fig. 25); no barbel near corner of mouth. To 6¼ in. (16 cm).
Range: Atlantic Slope from St. Lawrence R. drainage, QU, to upper Roanoke R., NC (absent in Connecticut R. and other rivers in northeast); Lake Ontario drainage, ON and NY. Also in upper New R. drainage, WV and VA, where believed to be introduced. Common in clear streams. **Habitat:** Rocky pools and runs of creeks and small to medium rivers; usually in quiet water near boulders.
Remarks: Cutlips Minnow plucks out the eyes of other fishes, a peculiar behavior also found in some African cichlids. It is known to fishermen in some areas as the "eye-picker."
Similar species: See Tonguetied Minnow.   **Map 107**

● *RHINICHTHYS*

Genus characteristics: *Long, slender, streamlined body,* deepest at nape, flattened below. *Small scales;* more than 40 along complete, straight lateral line. Usually *many black specks* on strongly bicolored (dark above, light below) body. Dorsal fin origin behind pelvic fin origin. Several species of *Rhinichthys* are wide-ranging and highly variable; additional populations may warrant recognition as species.

BLACKNOSE DACE *Rhinichthys atratulus*   Pl. 16
Identification: *Many brown-black specks* on back and side. *Deep caudal peduncle. Barbel* in corner of mouth; no groove separating snout from upper lip; pointed snout slightly overhangs mouth. Light brown above, black spot followed by silver spot on dorsal fin base; *black stripe* along side, through eye and onto snout, continuous in young, broken into blotches in adult; often a silver stripe above black stripe; silver-white below. Breeding male develops pads on upper surface of pectoral fin, has yellow-white pectoral and pelvic fins, white to red stripe (see Remarks) below black body stripe. 53–70 lateral scales, 7 anal rays; pharyngeal teeth 2,4–4,2. To 4 in. (10 cm).
Range: Atlantic, Great Lakes, Hudson Bay, Mississippi, and upper Mobile Bay drainages from NS to MB and south to n. GA and n. AL. Generally common, especially in mountain and spring-fed streams.
Habitat: Rocky runs and pools of headwaters, creeks, and small rivers.
Remarks: Two subspecies. *R. a. atratulus*, in n. and cen. Atlantic Slope drainages (including James and Roanoke rivers) and e. Great Lakes–St. Lawrence basin (west to e. Lake Ontario), has silver-white to gold-yellow along and below black-red stripe on side of breeding male. *R. a. meleagris*, over rest of range but apparently also inhabiting James and Roanoke River drainages, has orange to brick red stripe along and below black stripe on side of breeding male.
Similar species: See Pl. 16. (1) Speckled and (2) Leopard Dace usually have groove separating snout from upper lip; large individuals have red lips, snout, and fin bases. (3) Longnose Dace has long fleshy snout, eyes high on head.   **Map 108**

SPECKLED DACE *Rhinichthys osculus*   Pl. 16
Identification: Extremely variable — see Remarks. Usually dark olive back and side heavily *speckled with black*; gold specks on back; dusky stripe along side, through eye and onto snout; black spot on caudal fin base. (Young have black stripe along side, often lack black specks of adult.) Pointed snout slightly overhangs mouth. *Barbel* (absent in Canada and occasionally elsewhere) in corner of mouth; usually a groove separating snout from upper lip. Deep caudal peduncle (see Remarks). Silver-yellow side, white below, yellow fins. Large individual has red-orange lips, snout, and bases of pectoral, pelvic, and anal fins. 47–89 lateral scales, 7 (often 8) anal rays; pharyngeal teeth 1,4–4,1 or 2,4–4,2. To 4¼ in. (11 cm).
Range: Western drainages (Pacific and endorheic) from Columbia R., BC, to Colorado R., AZ and NM, and south into Sonora, Mexico. Most ubiquitous fish in w. U.S. **Habitat:** Rocky riffles, runs, and pools of headwaters, creeks, and small to medium rivers; rarely in lakes.
Remarks: Occupying many isolated western drainages, the Speckled Dace has diversified tremendously. Forms in swift water (e.g. in the Colorado R. drainage) are streamlined, with enlarged falcate fins and a more slender caudal peduncle; those in slower water are relatively

chubby and small-finned. At one time considered to be 12 species, the Speckled Dace now is considered to be a complex of subspecies for which the morphological variation and distributional limits are poorly known. Four subspecies, *R. o. nevadensis*, in Ash Meadows, NV, *R. o. oligoporus*, Clover Valley, NV, *R. o. lethoporus*, Independence Valley, NV, and *R. o. thermalis*, in Kendall Warm Springs, WY, are protected as *endangered subspecies*. The Las Vegas Dace, *Rhinichthys deaconi*, an extinct relative of the Speckled Dace known only from springs and outflows along Las Vegas Cr., NV (Map 109), had *very small pectoral fins* (less than ⅙ of total length of fish), anal fin with 1st and last ray of about *equal length*, and large scales (40-52 lateral).
Similar species: (1) See Leopard Dace (Pl. 16). (2) Longfin Dace (Pl. 15) has nearly terminal mouth, white spots at front and rear of dorsal fin, white bar on caudal peduncle, no scales on breast, belly, and part of back; *lacks* barbel, groove on snout. (3) Blacknose Dace (Pl. 16) lacks groove separating snout from upper lip; breeding male develops pads on pectoral fin, has white, yellow, or red stripe along lower side, no red-orange lips, snout, or fin bases. (4) Longnose (Pl. 16) and (5) Umpqua Dace have long, fleshy snout in front of mouth, no groove separating snout from upper lip. **Map 109**

LEOPARD DACE *Rhinichthys falcatus*   **Pl. 16**
Identification: Streamlined version of Speckled Dace with *falcate* (concave upper edge) *dorsal fin*, more forked caudal fin, more slender body, narrower caudal peduncle, longer and more pointed snout, bigger eye, and larger black blotches on back, side, and *fins. Long barbel* protrudes beyond corner of mouth. 51–64 lateral scales, 20–32 scales around caudal peduncle, 7 anal rays; pharyngeal teeth 2,4–4,2. To 5 in. (12 cm).
Range: Fraser and Columbia R. drainages, BC, WA, OR, and ID. Generally uncommon. **Habitat:** Flowing pools and gravel runs of creeks and small to medium rivers; rocky margins of lakes.
Similar species: See (1) Speckled Dace (Pl. 16), which has straight edge on dorsal fin, is less slender, has smaller black spots on body, and (2) Umatilla Dace. **Map 110**

UMATILLA DACE *Rhinichthys umatilla*   **Not shown**
Identification: Similar to Leopard Dace but has *short barbel not protruding beyond corner of mouth, more robust body,* 56–72 lateral scales, 29–40 scales around caudal peduncle. To 5 in. (12 cm).
Range: Columbia R. drainage, BC, ID, WA, and OR. Common. **Habitat:** Rubble riffles and runs of large rivers.
Similar species: See Leopard Dace (Pl. 16). **Map 85**

LONGNOSE DACE *Rhinichthys cataractae*   **Pl. 16**
Identification: Deep caudal peduncle; *long fleshy snout* extends in front of *subterminal mouth; barbel* in corner of mouth; no groove separating snout from upper lip. Eyes high on head; caudal fin moderately forked; straight-edged dorsal and anal fins. Olive-brown to

dark red-purple above, brown-black spots and mottling on back and side of some individuals; dark stripe along side (darkest on young); dusky spot on caudal fin base; silver to yellow below. Breeding male may have bright red on head and fin bases (see Remarks). 48–76 lateral scales, 7–9 (usually 8) anal rays, 8 dorsal rays; pharyngeal teeth 2,4–4,2. To 6¼ in. (16 cm).

Range: Widest distribution of any North American minnow. Generally distributed above 40°N from coast to coast; occurs as far north as Arctic Circle in Mackenzie R. drainage; south in Appalachian Mountains to n. GA and in Rocky Mountains south into Rio Grande drainage of TX and n. Mexico. Common in n. U.S. and along Atlantic Slope to VA; fairly common in west but absent from Alaska and from western drainages south of Columbia and Coos R. drainages. **Habitat:** Rubble and gravel riffles (sometimes runs and pools) of fast creeks and small to medium rivers; rocky shores of lakes.

Remarks: Three subspecies described; other populations probably deserve taxonomic recognition. *R. c. cataractae* occurs east of the Continental Divide, has bright red on the corners of the mouth, cheeks, and bases of the paired and anal fins; spawns during the day. *R. c. dulcis*, in the Pacific basin, spawns at night and lacks bright breeding colors. *R. c. smithi*, now extinct but formerly endemic to hot springs in Banff National Park, AB, was similar to *R. c cataractae* but had only 48–59 lateral scales and reached only 2 in. (4.8 cm).

Similar species: (1) See Cheat Minnow and (2) Umpqua Dace. (3) Blacknose, (4) Speckled, and (5) Leopard Dace — all on Pl. 16 — *lack long fleshy snout, have eye more on side of head.*   **Map 111**

CHEAT MINNOW *Rhinichthys bowersi*   **Not shown**

Identification: Similar to Longnose Dace but has much *larger (44-55 lateral) scales,* larger eye, longer head, pharyngeal teeth 1,4–4,1; is dark green above, lighter green below. To 4¾ in. (12 cm).

Range: Monongahela and Greenbrier R. systems (Ohio R. basin), s. PA, MD, and WV; possibly in Lake Erie drainage, NY and OH. Rare. **Habitat:** Rocky runs and pools of small to medium rivers.

Remarks: Long thought to be a hybrid between Longnose Dace and River Chub. Recent genetic data confirm that the Cheat Minnow is a distinct species.

Similar species: See Longnose Dace (above; Pl. 16).   **Map 113**

UMPQUA DACE *Rhinichthys evermanni*   **Not shown**

Identification: Similar to Longnose Dace but has *narrow caudal peduncle* bordered above and below by *keel* leading into caudal fin rays, concave edge on dorsal and anal fins, more deeply forked caudal fin, 9–10 dorsal rays. 57–61 lateral scales; 7–8 anal rays; pharyngeal teeth 2,4–4,2. To 4¼ in. (11 cm).

Range: Umpqua R. drainage, OR. Common. **Habitat:** Fast rocky riffles.

Similar species: See Longnose Dace (Pl. 16).   **Map 110**

LOACH MINNOW *Rhinichthys cobitis* **Pl. 16**
Identification: *Small, nearly terminal mouth; upwardly directed eyes.* Olive-brown above; many black specks and blotches on back and side; white spots at front and rear of dorsal fin; black spot in middle of *white bar* on caudal fin base. Breeding male has bright red fin bases, mouth and lower head, sometimes belly. Large female has yellow belly, fins. No scales on breast, belly, and part of back. No barbel in corner of mouth; no groove separating snout from upper lip. 65–70 lateral scales, 7 anal rays; pharyngeal teeth 1,4–4,1. To 2¼ in. (6 cm).
Range: Upper Gila R. system, NM and AZ; San Pedro R., AZ and n. Sonora. Locally common in NM; uncommon in AZ. Protected as a *threatened species.* **Habitat:** Rocky, often vegetated, riffles of creeks and small to medium rivers.
Similar species: Speckled Dace (Pl. 16) *lacks* large white spots at front and rear of dorsal fin, white bar on caudal fin base; has *subterminal mouth,* scales on nape and belly, barbel. **Map 111**

FLATHEAD CHUB *Platygobio gracilis* **Pl. 8**
Identification: *Broad, flat head* tapering to pointed snout; *small barbel* in corner of large subterminal mouth. *Large, pointed, sickle-shaped dorsal and pectoral fins* on large individuals; 1st dorsal fin ray extends beyond last ray in depressed fin. Body slightly compressed at front, more compressed along caudal peduncle; dorsal fin origin over or in front of pelvic fin origin. Fairly small eyes. Light dusky brown or olive above; silver side; lower lobe of caudal fin dusky black. 42–59 lateral scales; 8 anal rays; pharyngeal teeth 2,4–4,2. To 12½ in. (32 cm).
Range: Mackenzie, Saskatchewan, and Lake Winnipeg drainages in YU, NT, MB, SA, AB, and BC; Missouri-Mississippi R. basin from s. AB and MT to LA; upper Rio Grande (including Pecos) drainage, NM. Common in n. part of range; restricted to Mississippi R. proper in MO, IL, and south; localized in Arkansas R. drainage in OK, TX, and NM. **Habitat:** Sandy runs of small to large turbid rivers.
Remarks: Two subspecies usually recognized. *P. g. gracilis,* in the northern and eastern parts of the range, primarily is found in large rivers, has a pointed head and usually 48 or more lateral scales. *P. g. gulonella,* in the southern and western parts of the range, inhabits smaller streams; has a rounder snout, a smaller eye, usually fewer than 48 lateral scales, and is smaller (to 6 in. [15 cm]). The two forms broadly intergrade (most of the Missouri R. drainage).
Similar species: (1) Sicklefin and (2) Sturgeon Chubs (both, Pl. 8) have less flattened and pointed head, smaller eyes, small papillae on underside of head. On Sicklefin Chub, tip of pectoral fin reaches beyond pelvic fin origin. Dorsal and pectoral fins of Sturgeon Chub are straight-edged. **Map 112**

SICKLEFIN CHUB *Macrhybopsis meeki* **Pl. 8**
Identification: *Large, sharply pointed, sickle-shaped fins;* 1st dorsal fin ray extends beyond last ray in depressed fin; tip of pectoral fin reaches beyond pelvic fin origin. Lower lobe of caudal fin *black with*

white edge in large individuals. *Long barbel* in corner of subterminal mouth. Body deepest under nape, strongly tapering to narrow caudal peduncle; barely compressed at front, strongly compressed at peduncle. Dorsal fin origin over or slightly behind pelvic fin origin. Small eye high on deep head; rounded snout. Head broad with numerous small papillae on underside (gular area). Scales without bony keels. Light green to brown above, often with many dark brown and silver specks; silver side. 43–50 lateral scales; 8 anal rays; pharyngeal teeth 0,4–4,0. To 4¼ in. (11 cm).
Range: Missouri R. from MT to mouth; lower Kansas R., e. KS; Mississippi R. from mouth of Missouri R. to mouth of Ohio R. and in s. MS and n. LA. Fairly common in middle Missouri R.; rare elsewhere.
Habitat: Sand and gravel runs of large rivers.
Similar species: (1) See Sturgeon Chub (Pl. 8). (2) Flathead Chub (Pl. 8) has broad, flat head; larger eye; no papillae on underside of head; pectoral fin not reaching to pelvic fin origin.   **Map 113**

STURGEON CHUB *Macrhybopsis gelida*   **Pl. 8**
Identification: Similar to Sicklefin Chub but has *straight-edged* fins; last dorsal fin ray extends beyond 1st ray in depressed fin; *keeled scales* on back and side; snout longer and projecting well beyond upper lip; large papillae on underside of head; larger brown specks on back. 39–45 lateral scales; pharyngeal teeth 1,4–4,1. To 3¼ in. (8.4 cm).
Range: Missouri R. basin, MT and WY to IL; Mississippi R. between mouths of Missouri R. and Ohio R.; in s. MS and LA. Fairly common in middle Missouri R.; rare elsewhere. **Habitat:** Shallow sand and gravel runs of medium to large turbid rivers.
Similar species: See Sicklefin Chub (Pl. 8).   **Map 114**

SILVER CHUB *Macrhybopsis storeriana*   **Pl. 8**
Identification: *Large eye* on upper half of head; short, rounded snout; barbel in corner of *subterminal mouth*. Slender, fairly compressed body, flattened below; dorsal fin origin in front of pelvic fin origin. Light olive above; *bright silver-white side*; white edge on dusky black (absent on juveniles) lower lobe of caudal fin. Complete lateral line; 35–48 lateral scales; 8 anal rays; pharyngeal teeth 1,4–4,1. To 9 in. (23 cm).
Range: Lake Erie drainage, ON, NY, PA, OH, and MI; Assiniboine R., MB; Red R. drainage, MB, south to MN; Mississippi R. basin, NY, PA, and WV west to MN, NE, KS, and OK, and south to Gulf Coast; Gulf Coast drainages from Mobile Bay basin, AL, to Lake Pontchartrain drainages, LA; isolated population in Brazos R. drainage, TX. Common but seldom in large populations. **Habitat:** Sand-, silt-, and sometimes gravel-bottomed pools and backwaters of small to large rivers; lakes.
Similar species: Bigeye Chub (Pl. 9) has black stripe along side and onto snout, reaches only 3½ in. (9 cm).   **Map 103**

• *ERIMYSTAX*

Genus characteristics: Fast- and often deep-water-inhabiting, silvery minnows with distinctive pigment patterns. *Long, slender body* deepest at nape, *flattened below;* dorsal fin origin in front of pelvic fin origin. *Barbel* at corner of subterminal mouth; long bulbous snout; large eye; large, horizontal pectoral fins. Complete lateral line; 7 anal rays; pharyngeal teeth 0,4–4,0.

STREAMLINE CHUB *Erimystax dissimilis*   Pl. 9
Identification: 7–15 *horizontally oblong or round* dark gray blotches along side. *White to gold spot* at front and back of dorsal fin. Dark olive above, scales darkly outlined, series of dark dashes along back; often dark specks on back and upper side; often a gray stripe along silver side. 43–51 lateral scales. To 5½ in. (14 cm).
Range: Ohio R. basin from w. NY to n. IN, and south to n. AL; St. Francis and White R. drainages, MO and AR. Common in some areas (e.g., Ozark streams); localized elsewhere. **Habitat:** Riffles, runs, and current-swept pools over gravel and rubble in clear small to large rivers.
Remarks: Two subspecies: *E. d. dissimilis,* east of Mississippi R., has usually fewer than 10 blotches along side, S-shaped gut, longer head. *E. d. harryi,* west of Mississippi R., has usually more than 10, smaller, blotches along side; double-looped gut; shorter head.
Similar species: (1) See Blotched and (2) Gravel Chubs (both, Pl. 9).
         Map 114

BLOTCHED CHUB *Erimystax insignis*   Pl. 9
Identification: Similar to Streamline Chub but with 7–9 large, *vertical* dark gray blotches (obscure on young) along side; less slender body; many small dark specks on side, some in rows; iridescent yellow stripe along light green-silver side. 38–49 lateral scales. To 3½ in. (9.2 cm).
Range: Cumberland and Tennessee R. drainages, VA, NC, KY, TN, GA, and AL. Locally common. **Habitat:** Rocky riffles and runs of clear small to medium rivers.
Remarks: Two subspecies: *E. i. eristigma,* upper Tennessee R. drainage except Clinch and Powell rivers, has a large mouth (upper jaw about ⅓ head length) and the upper lip enlarged at middle. *E. i. insignis,* in the Cumberland and lower and middle Tennessee rivers (as far upstream as Sequatchie R.), has a smaller mouth (upper jaw about ¼ head length) and upper lip barely enlarged. Clinch and Powell R. populations are intergrades.
Similar species: See (1) Streamline and (2) Gravel Chubs (both, Pl. 9).
         Map 115

GRAVEL CHUB *Erimystax x-punctatus*   Pl. 9
Identification: Similar to Streamline and Blotched Chubs but *lacks* large dark gray blotches along side, dark dashes along back, has many

dark X's on back and side; less slender body; blue sheen along silver side. 38–45 lateral scales. To 4¼ in. (11 cm).
Range: Thames R. system, s. ON (where possibly extirpated); Ohio R. basin from NY and PA to IL (absent south of Ohio R. except one record in upper Green R., KY); Mississippi R. basin from s. WI and s. MN south to Ouachita R. drainage, AR, and west to e. KS and OK. Common locally but becoming less common throughout much of range. **Habitat:** Gravel riffles and runs of creeks and small to large rivers.
Remarks: Two subspecies: *E. x. trautmani*, Wabash R. drainage and eastward, has usually 12 scales around caudal peduncle, is more slender. *E. x. x-punctatus*, west of the Wabash R. drainage, has usually 16 scales around caudal peduncle, is more robust.
Similar species: See (1) Streamline and (2) Blotched Chubs (both, Pl. 9).
Map 115

SLENDER CHUB *Erimystax cahni* Pl. 9

Identification: *Large dark <'s* along rear half of side, darkest and largest on caudal peduncle. Dusky olive above; silver side; black caudal spot. 40–46 lateral scales. To 3½ in. (9 cm).
Range: Upper Tennessee R. drainage (Holston, Clinch, and Powell rivers), TN (and possibly VA). Uncommon in small range; protected as a *threatened species*. **Habitat:** Gravel runs and riffles of medium-sized rivers.
Similar species: (1) Streamline and (2) Blotched Chubs (both, Pl. 9) have dark *blotches* along side. (3) Stargazing Minnow (Pl. 8) has shorter snout, *lacks* dark <'s on side, barbel at corner of mouth.
Map 116

SPECKLED CHUB *Extrarius aestivalis* Pl. 9

Identification: *Long, bulbous snout* overhangs mouth. Usually *many small black spots* on back and side. Usually *long barbel* (see Remarks) in corner of subterminal mouth. Small, upwardly directed eyes. Slender, barely compressed body, deepest under nape, flattened below; dorsal fin origin over or in front of pelvic fin origin. Translucent; light olive to straw yellow above with silver flecks; silver side, often iridescent blue, sometimes with dusky stripe; often dusky to black stripe around snout. Complete lateral line; 34–41 lateral scales, 7–8 anal rays; pharyngeal teeth 0,4–4,0 to 1,4–4,1. To 3 in. (7.6 cm).
Range: Mississippi R. basin from OH and WV west to MN and NE and south to Gulf Coast; Gulf Coast drainages from Choctawhatchee R., AL and FL, to Rio Grande, TX, NM, and Mexico. Common. **Habitat:** Sand and gravel runs of small to large rivers.
Remarks: Highly variable over range. Several forms recognizable, including some that occur sympatrically and soon will be treated as separate species. Some populations, on both sides of the Mississippi R., have 2 barbels on each side of mouth.
Similar species: (1) Streamline, (2) Blotched, and (3) Gravel Chubs (all, Pl. 9) *lack* many black spots. **Map 118**

• *HYBOGNATHUS*

Genus characteristics: *Long, coiled intestine; black peritoneum. Small, slightly subterminal mouth* (rear edge of mouth in front of eye). Fairly deep caudal peduncle; round snout; dorsal fin origin in front of pelvic fin origin. Large male has light yellow along side and on lower fins. Complete, straight lateral line; 34–41 lateral scales; usually 8 anal rays; pharyngeal teeth 0,4–4,0. *Hybognathus* species ingest mud and organic matter, and the long intestine facilitates the digestion of algae and other plant material. The first four species of *Hybognathus* are extremely similar and can be identified accurately only by examining the basioccipital process (Fig. 26).

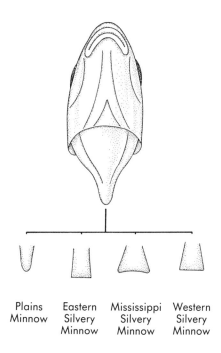

| Plains Minnow | Eastern Silvery Minnow | Mississippi Silvery Minnow | Western Silvery Minnow |

Fig. 26 *Hybognathus* species — basioccipital process

MISSISSIPPI SILVERY MINNOW *Hybognathus nuchalis* **Pl. 10**
Identification: *Stout body; moderately compressed, deepest and widest in front of dorsal fin. Moderately small eye (about ¼ head length);*

pointed dorsal fin. Light brown to yellow-olive above, wide dusky to yellow-green stripe along back; silver side (often brilliant). 15–16 pectoral rays. Basioccipital process *broad and distinctly concave at rear* (Fig. 26). To 7 in. (18 cm).

Range: Lowland areas of Mississippi R. basin, from OH to WI and MN, and south to Gulf; Gulf Coast drainages from Mobile Bay Basin, AL, to Brazos R., TX; Rio Grande drainage (including Pecos R.), TX and NM. Generally common but less so along periphery of range; now absent in MN and e. TN. **Habitat:** Pools and backwaters of low-gradient creeks and small to large rivers.

Remarks: The taxonomic status of the Rio Grande population is uncertain; usually it is considered to be a small-eyed subspecies, *H. n. amarus.*

Similar species: See (1) Eastern Silvery, (2) Western Silvery, and (3) Plains Minnows. (4) River Shiner (Pl. 10) has larger mouth, 7 anal rays; much shorter intestine. **Map 119**

EASTERN SILVERY MINNOW *Hybognathus regius* **Not shown**
Identification: Nearly identical to Mississippi Silvery Minnow but with *narrower, straight-edged basioccipital process* (Fig. 26). To 4¾ in. (12 cm).
Range: Atlantic Slope from St. Lawrence R. drainage, QU, to Altamaha R. drainage, GA; Lake Ontario drainage, ON and NY. Generally common in southern ⅔ of range; locally common in north. **Habitat:** Pools and backwaters of low-gradient creeks and small to large rivers.
Similar species: See Mississippi Silvery Minnow (Pl. 10). **Map 119**

WESTERN SILVERY MINNOW *Hybognathus argyritis* **Not shown**
Identification: Nearly identical to Mississippi Silvery Minnow but with rear edge of basioccipital process *straight* or *barely concave* (Fig. 26), slightly *smaller eye.* To 4¾ in. (12 cm).
Range: Missouri R. basin, AB and MT to IL, south in Mississippi R. basin to s. IL; South Saskatchewan R., extreme s. AB, and Souris R. (Hudson Bay basin), extreme s. MB. Common. **Habitat:** Sluggish pools and backwaters, usually over mud or sand, of small to large rivers.
Similar species: See Mississippi Silvery Minnow (Pl. 10). **Map 120**

PLAINS MINNOW *Hybognathus placitus* **Not shown**
Identification: Similar to Mississippi Silvery Minnow but has *smaller eye* (about ⅕ head length), *peglike* basioccipital process (Fig. 26), underside of head more flattened. 16–17 pectoral rays. To 5 in. (13 cm).
Range: Missouri, Arkansas, Red, Brazos, and Colorado R. drainages, from MT and ND south to NM and TX; Mississippi R. from mouth of Missouri R. to mouth of Ohio R. **Habitat:** Most common in shallow sandy runs and pools of creeks and small to large rivers. One of the most characteristic and common (sometimes abundant) fishes of the Great Plains.
Similar species: See (1) Mississippi Silvery (Pl. 10), and (2) Western Silvery Minnows. **Map 121**

BRASSY MINNOW *Hybognathus hankinsoni* **Pl. 10**
Identification: *Rounded dorsal fin. Stout, brassy-yellow body;* moderately compressed, deepest and widest in front of dorsal fin. Moderately small eye (about ¼ head length). Dusky olive above, wide dusky to yellow-green stripe along back; often with thin lines along upper side similar to those on Common and Striped Shiners (Fig. 27). Brassy yellow side (best developed on large adult; smaller individual may be dull silver); diffuse dusky stripe best developed on rear half of side. 13–15 pectoral rays. Basioccipital process *broad and straight to slightly concave* posteriorly. To 3¾ in. (9.7 cm).
Range: Upper St. Lawrence R. and Lake Champlain drainages, QU and NY, across Great Lakes, Hudson Bay, and Missouri-upper Mississippi R. basins of s. Canada and n. U.S south to KS; Fraser R. system (Pacific Slope), AB and BC. Common in many areas of range.
Habitat: Pools of sluggish, clear creeks and small rivers; usually over sand or gravel.
Similar species: (1) Mississippi Silvery (Pl. 10), (2) Western Silvery, and (3) Eastern Silvery Minnows *lack* brassy yellow color, have *pointed* dorsal fin, usually lack longitudinal lines along upper side. **Map 122**

CYPRESS MINNOW *Hybognathus hayi* **Pl. 10**
Identification: Scales on back and upper side thinly outlined with black, appearing *diamond-shaped.* Compressed body, deepest and widest at dorsal fin origin. Pointed dorsal fin. Moderately large eye (about ⅓ head length). Light to dark olive above, thin dusky to yellow-green stripe along back; silver side, sometimes overlaid by a dusky stripe usually best developed on caudal peduncle. 14–16 pectoral rays. Basioccipital process *broad and straight* to slightly concave posteriorly. To 4½ in. (12 cm).
Range: Ohio and Mississippi R. basins from sw. IN and s. IL to Gulf; Gulf Slope drainages from Escambia R., FL and AL, to Sabine R., TX (absent in Perdido and Pascagoula R. drainages); most populations occur on Former Mississippi Embayment, but a few are above Fall Line (e.g., Tennessee R. in n. AL). Locally common, but disappearing from n. part of range (at least IL and MO). **Habitat:** Swamps, oxbows, and backwaters and pools of sluggish streams; usually over mud and near detritus.
Similar species: (1) Other *Hybognathus* species (Pl. 10) *lack* diamond-appearing scales; have smaller eye and shallower, less compressed body. (2) *Notropis* species with diamond-appearing scales (Pl. 18) have dorsal fin origin behind pelvic fin rigin, much shorter intestine.
Map 122

• *LUXILUS*

Genus characteristics: Large scales; those on front half of side *much deeper than wide.* Deep, strongly compressed body; dorsal fin origin over or slightly behind pelvic fin origin. *Dusky to black bar* (often thin dusky line on juvenile) on side behind gill cover. Large, oblique terminal mouth. Large male has hooked tubercles on snout. Usually 9 anal rays; 36–46 lateral scales; pharyngeal teeth 2,4–4,2.

STRIPED SHINER *Luxilus chrysocephalus* **Pl. 17**
Identification: *Dark stripes* on upper side meet those of other side behind dorsal fin to form *large V's* (Fig. 27). Olive above, dark stripe along middle of back; silver-bronze side. Dark crescents on side, prominent on large individual. Large male and sometimes female has pink or red body and fins. Usually 24–29 scales around body at dorsal fin origin. To 7¼ in. (18 cm).
Range: Great Lakes and Mississippi R. basins, from w. NY and se. WI, south to AL, LA, and e. TX; Gulf Coast drainages from Mobile Bay, GA and AL, to Lake Pontchartrain, LA. Abundant in n., common in s. part of range. **Habitat:** Rocky pools near riffles in clear to fairly turbid creeks and small to medium rivers.
Remarks: 2 subspecies. *L. c. isolepis*, in Mississippi R. basin below confluence of White R., AR, and in Gulf drainages (except Coosa R. system), has straight dark lines on upper side (Fig. 27), usually 13–14 scales on upper side from head to beneath dorsal fin origin. *L. c. chrysocephalus*, rest of range, has crooked lines on upper side (Fig. 27), usually 14–17 scales on upper side from head to beneath dorsal fin origin.
Similar species: See Pl. 17. (1) Common Shiner has only 1 or 2 stripes on upper side parallel to stripe along back, usually 30–35 scales around body. (2) Bleeding, (3) Duskystripe, and (4) Cardinal Shiners have dark stripe along side and around snout, are less deep bodied.
Map 123

COMMON SHINER *Luxilus cornutus* **Pl. 17**
Identification: Olive above, dark stripe along middle of back; 1 or 2 dark stripes (often faint) on upper side *parallel* to stripe along back (Fig. 27); silver-bronze side. Dark crescents on side, prominent only on large individual. Breeding male (sometimes female) has pink body, pink or red fins. Usually 30–35 scales around body at dorsal fin origin. To 7 in. (18 cm).
Range: Atlantic, Great Lakes, Hudson Bay, and Mississippi R. basins, from NS to se. SA, and south to James R. drainage, VA, n. OH, cen. MO, and WY. Abundant. **Habitat:** Rocky pools near riffles in clear, cool creeks and small to medium rivers; sometimes in lakes in northern part of range.
Remarks: Hybridization between the closely related Common and Striped Shiners occurs frequently in areas where the ranges of the two species overlap.
Similar species: (1) See White Shiner (Pl. 17). (2) Striped Shiner (Pl. 17) has 3 dark stripes on upper side meeting those of other side behind dorsal fin to form V's, usually 24–29 scales around body. **Map 124**

WHITE SHINER *Luxilus albeolus* **Pl. 17**
Identification: Nearly identical to Common Shiner (above) but more silvery; *lacks* dark crescents (rarely present) on side; has usually *26–30 scales* around body at dorsal fin origin. To 5¼ in. (13 cm).
Range: Atlantic Slope from Chowan R. system, VA, to Cape Fear R. drainage, NC; upper New R. drainage (Ohio R. basin), WV, VA, and

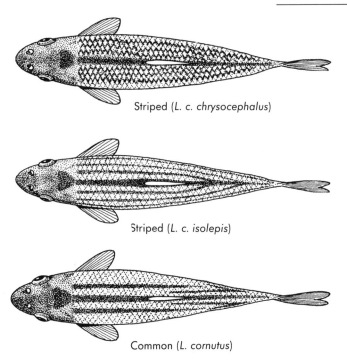

Fig. 27 Striped (*Luxilus chrysocephalus*) and Common Shiners (*L. cornutus*)

NC. Common, abundant in upper Roanoke R. drainage. **Habitat:** Rocky pools near riffles in clear creeks and small to medium rivers. **Similar species:** (1) See Common Shiner (Pl. 17). (2) Crescent Shiner (Pl. 17) has dark crescents on side, red on body and fins of large male, strongly contrasting upper and lower halves of head. **Map 124**

CRESCENT SHINER *Luxilus cerasinus* **Pl. 17**
Identification: *Large black crescents* on side. Dusky olive above, dark stripe along middle of back; silver side. Dark upper half of head strongly contrasts with light lower half. Breeding male has blue back, red on head, body, fins; large female may have red on body, fins. Usually 24–28 scales around body at dorsal fin origin. To 4½ in. (11 cm).
Range: Upper and middle Roanoke (and adjacent tributaries of Meherrin R.–Chowan R. system), James, Cape Fear, and New R. drainages, VA and NC. Common in Roanoke drainage; may be introduced in other drainages. **Habitat:** Rocky and sandy pools and runs of headwaters, creeks, and small rivers.

Similar species: (1) White Shiner (Pl. 17) *lacks* dark crescents on side, red on body and fins; has less contrasting upper and lower halves of head. (2) Common Shiner (Pl. 17) has less distinct crescents, less contrasting upper and lower halves of head, 30–35 scales around body, pink on large male. **Map 123**

BLEEDING SHINER *Luxilus zonatus* Pl. 17

Identification: *Large black bar* on side behind gill cover. *Narrow black stripe* along side and around snout; constricted behind head, not extending below lateral line. Olive above, black stripe along back; dusky stripes on upper side meet those of other side behind dorsal fin. Large individual has red head and fins (brightest on breeding male). Usually 26 scales around body at dorsal fin origin, 7 rakers on 1st gill arch. To 5 in. (13 cm).

Range: Ozark-draining tributaries of Missouri (west to Sac R.), Mississippi (including Meramec R.), Little, St. Francis, and Black rivers, s. MO and ne. AR. Common to abundant; often the most common fish present. **Habitat:** Rocky runs, riffles, and deep, flowing pools of clear, fast creeks and small to medium rivers.

Similar species: See Pl. 17. (1) See Duskystripe Shiner. (2) Cardinal Shiner *lacks* black bar on side behind gill cover, dusky stripes on upper side; has *broad black stripe* along side (not constricted behind head) extending below lateral line; blue snout and crimson red head, lower body and fins on large adult. **Map 125**

DUSKYSTRIPE SHINER *Luxilus pilsbryi* Pl. 17

Identification: Similar to Bleeding Shiner but *lacks bold* black bar behind gill cover, dusky stripes on upper side; black stripe along side *not* notably constricted behind head, *extends to lateral line* under dorsal fin; blue snout, bright red head on large individual. Usually 24–26 scales around body at dorsal fin origin, 7 rakers on 1st gill arch. To 5 in. (13 cm).

Range: White (excluding Black R. system) and Little Red R. systems, s. MO and n. AR. Common to abundant. **Habitat:** Rocky pools, runs, and deep riffles of clear, fast creeks and small to medium rivers.

Similar species: See (1) Bleeding and (2) Cardinal Shiners (both, Pl. 17). **Map 125**

CARDINAL SHINER *Luxilus cardinalis* Pl. 17

Identification: Similar to Duskystripe Shiner but has *broad black stripe* along side extending *below* lateral line; *crimson red head, lower side of body and fins* on large individual; usually 26–27 scales around body at dorsal fin origin, 8–9 rakers on 1st gill arch. To 4¼ in. (11 cm).

Range: Arkansas R. drainage, sw. MO, nw. AR, e. KS and e. OK; Red R. drainage, s. OK (west to Washita R. system). Population in upper Neosho R. system (Arkansas R. drainage), cen. KS, widely separated from population in middle Arkansas R. drainage. Common in Arkansas R. drainage; rare or extirpated in Red R. drainage. **Habitat:** Rocky runs, riffles, and flowing pools of creeks and small to medium rivers.

Similar species: (1) See Duskystripe Shiner (Pl. 17). (2) Bleeding Shiner

(Pl. 17) has black bar on side behind gill cover; dusky stripes on upper side; *narrow black stripe (constricted* behind head) along side, *not extending below* lateral line; less intense red color on head and fins.
Map 125

WARPAINT SHINER *Luxilus coccogenis* **Pl. 17**
Identification: *Black band* (red-orange on young) on yellow dorsal fin; *red bar* on opercle; wide *black edge* (darkest at fork) on caudal fin. Olive above, dark stripe along middle of back; large black bar behind gill cover on silver side. Breeding male has pink or red side, red snout, red on dorsal fin. Usually 25–29 scales around body at dorsal fin origin. To 5½ in. (14 cm).
Range: Upper Tennessee R. drainage, w. VA, w. NC, TN, n. GA, and n. AL, and adjacent tributaries of Savannah R., NC and SC, Santee R., NC, and New R., NC. Common; may be introduced in New and Santee R. drainages. **Habitat:** Gravel and rubble riffles and adjacent pools of clear, fast creeks and small to medium rivers.
Similar species: (1) Bandfin Shiner (Pl. 17) lacks wide black edge on caudal fin, has large black spot on caudal fin base. (2) Striped Shiner (Pl. 17) lacks black band on dorsal fin, wide black edge on caudal fin.
Map 125

BANDFIN SHINER *Luxilus zonistius* **Pl. 17**
Identification: *Black band* (red-orange in young) on dorsal fin, *large black spot* on caudal fin base. Olive above, dark stripe along middle of back; dusky stripe (darkest at rear) along silver-copper side; faint red bar on cheek, black (red in young) bar behind gill cover. Breeding male is blue above, has red bar on caudal fin. Usually 27–30 scales around body at dorsal fin origin, 9–10 anal rays. To 4 in. (10 cm).
Range: Apalachicola R. drainage, GA, AL, FL; adjacent tributaries of Savannah R., GA, Altamaha R., GA, Coosa R., GA, and Tallapoosa R., GA and AL. Fairly common. **Habitat:** Rocky pools near riffles in clear creeks and small rivers.
Similar species: (1) Warpaint Shiner (Pl. 17) *lacks* large black spot on caudal fin base, has wide black edge on caudal fin. (2) Striped Shiner (Pl. 17) lacks black band on dorsal fin, large black spot on caudal fin base.
Map 125

• *LYTHRURUS*

Genus characteristics: *Very small scales* on nape; dorsal fin origin *behind* pelvic fin origin. Fairly large, oblique terminal mouth. Usually 10–12 anal rays (often 9 in Rosefin Shiner); pharyngeal teeth 2,4–4,2. Large males develop bright red or yellow fins and, in some species, metallic blue bodies.

REDFIN SHINER *Lythrurus umbratilis* **Pl. 17**
Identification: *Dark blotch* at dorsal fin origin. *Deep, compressed body;* fairly large eye. Pale olive to steel blue above, dusky stripe along back; black specks on back and upper side; herringbone lines

on upper side of large individual. Breeding male has black membranes on *red fins*, blue head and body, often a large dark blotch on side. 10–11 anal rays; 37–56 lateral scales. To 3½ in. (8.5 cm).

Range: Great Lakes and Mississippi R. basins, w. NY and s. ON to se. MN and south to LA; Gulf drainages west of Mississippi R. to San Jacinto R., TX. Common; locally abundant. **Habitat:** Quiet to flowing pools (often turbid) of headwaters, creeks, and small to medium rivers.

Remarks: Two subspecies: *L. u. umbratilis*, Missouri, Arkansas, and upper Salt R. drainages, MO, e. KS, e. OK, and nw. AR, has many black specks behind gill cover (form bar in large male), dusky spot at dorsal fin origin, breeding tubercles on male's opercle. *L. u. cyanocephalus*, rest of range, has few black specks behind gill cover, black spot at dorsal fin origin, few or no tubercles on opercle. Intergrades occupy lower Salt R., MO, and Arkansas R. tributaries in w. AR.

Similar species: (1) Rosefin Shiner (Pl. 17) has dusky bars over back, no black on fin membranes; is more slender. (2) Ribbon (Pl. 17), (3) Ouachita Mountain, and (4) Mountain Shiners (Pl. 17) *lack* dark blotch at dorsal fin origin, herringbone lines, red fins; are more slender. (5) Red Shiner (Pl. 18) *lacks* dark blotch at dorsal fin origin, small scales on nape, herringbone lines on upper side; has diamond-shaped scales. **Map 126**

ROSEFIN SHINER *Lythrurus ardens* Pl. 17

Identification: *Dark blotch* at dorsal fin origin; *dusky bars* over back (often absent, especially on small individual). Fairly deep, compressed body; fairly large eye. Olive to steel blue above, dusky stripe along back; black specks on back and upper side; dusky lips and chin. Breeding male has *red fins*, orange lower side and head. 9–12 (see Remarks) anal rays; 38–53 lateral scales. To 3½ in. (8.5 cm).

Range: Atlantic Slope from York R. drainage (where probably introduced), VA, to Roanoke R. drainage, NC; Ohio R. basin from Scioto R. drainage, OH, southwest to extreme se. IL (now extirpated) and south to Tennessee R. drainage, AL; New R. drainage, VA; upper Black Warrior R. system (Gulf basin), AL. Common to abundant. **Habitat:** Rocky pools and runs of clear, fairly fast headwaters, creeks, and small rivers.

Remarks: Two subspecies: *L. a. ardens*, on the Atlantic Slope in the York, James, Chowan, and Roanoke R. drainages, and in the New R. system (Kanawha-Ohio drainage), has usually 11 anal rays and is more slender than *L. a. fasciolaris*, which has usually 10 anal rays and occupies rest of range.

Similar species: See Pl. 17. (1) See Pinewoods Shiner. (2) Redfin Shiner *lacks* dusky bars over back (rarely has faint bars); has *deeper* body, usually 11 anal rays, black on fins of breeding male. (3) Mountain, (4) Ribbon, and (5) Cherryfin Shiners *lack* black blotch at dorsal fin origin, dusky bars over back; Mountain Shiner has black stripe along side, black lips; Ribbon Shiner male has yellow fins; Cherryfin

Shiner has large black spots at tips of dorsal and anal fins, dark stripe
along rear of side. **Map 127**

PINEWOODS SHINER *Lythrurus matutinus* **Pl. 17**
Identification: Similar to Rosefin Shiner but is *more slender,* has usually 11 (range: 10–12) anal rays. Breeding male has *bright red head*
(mostly blue on Rosefin Shiner), *little or no* blue on body or red on
paired fins. 40–49 lateral scales. To 3½ in. (8.6 cm).
Range: Tar and Neuse R. drainages, NC. Common. **Habitat:** Sandy
runs and flowing pools of creeks and small to medium rivers.
Similar species: See Rosefin Shiner (Pl. 17). **Map 127**

RIBBON SHINER *Lythrurus fumeus* **Pl. 17**
Identification: Scales on nape *outlined in black. Fairly slender, compressed body;* fairly large eye. Pale olive above, dusky stripe along
back; silver-black stripe along side (darkest at rear but often weak)
and around snout; dusky lips and chin (Fig. 28). Yellow fins on large
individual. 11–12 anal rays; 35–45 lateral scales. To 2¾ in. (7 cm).
Range: Mississippi R. basin, cen. IL, sw. IN, and w. KY to nw. AL, LA,
and e. OK; Gulf drainages from Lake Pontchartrain, LA, to Navidad
R., TX. Most localities are below Fall Line, but widespread in lowlands of s. IL. **Habitat:** Quiet, usually turbid, mud- or sand-bottomed
pools of headwaters, creeks, and small rivers.
Similar species: See Pl. 17. (1) See Ouachita Mountain Shiner. (2)
Redfin Shiner has dark blotch at dorsal fin origin, herringbone lines
on upper side, red fins on large male, *deeper body.* (3) Mountain
Shiner has black lips, white chin, more slender body, blacker stripe
on side. **Map 128**

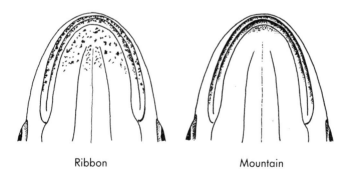

Ribbon   Mountain

Fig. 28 Ribbon and Mountain Shiners — underside of head

OUACHITA MOUNTAIN SHINER *Lythrurus snelsoni* **Not shown**
Identification: Similar to Ribbon Shiner but *lacks* black-outlined
scales on nape; has *red on head and throat* (brightest on male) during

breeding season (spring), no yellow on fins, 9–11 (usually 10) anal rays; is more slender. 27–33 scales around body at dorsal fin origin. To 2 in. (5.3 cm).

Range: Above Fall Line in Little R. system, AR and OK (Ouachita Mountains). Common. **Habitat:** Rocky pools of small to medium rivers. Often near vegetation.

Similar species: See Pl. 17. (1) See Ribbon Shiner. (2) Mountain Shiner has black stripe across lips, pink or yellow (*no red*) on head and throat. (3) Redfin Shiner has dark blotch at dorsal fin origin, deeper body, herringbone lines on upper side, red fins on large male, usually 33 or more scales around body at dorsal fin origin. **Map 128**

MOUNTAIN SHINER *Lythrurus lirus* Pl. 17

Identification: *Slender,* compressed body. *Silver-black stripe* along side (solid at rear, diffuse at front) and around snout. Fairly large eye. Pale olive above; black specks on back and upper side, often outlining scales on nape; black lips, white chin (Fig. 28). Pale pink or yellow on head and body of large individual. 10–11 anal rays; 36–49 lateral scales. To 3 in. (7.5 cm).

Range: Tennessee and Alabama R. drainages, VA, TN, nw. GA, and AL. Nearly restricted to Coosa R. system above Fall Line in Alabama R. drainage (where common). Uncommon in Tennessee R. drainage. **Habitat:** Sandy and rocky pools and runs of clear creeks and small rivers.

Similar species: See Pl. 17. (1) Ouachita Mountain Shiner has dusky lips and chin, red on head and throat of large individual. (2) Ribbon Shiner has dusky lips and chin, *deeper body,* less distinct stripe along side. (3) Rosefin Shiner has black blotch at dorsal fin origin, dusky chin, *no* black stripe along side. (4) Redfin Shiner has *deeper body,* dark blotch at dorsal fin origin, herringbone lines on upper side, *no* black stripe on side. **Map 126**

CHERRYFIN SHINER *Lythrurus roseipinnis* Pl. 17

Identification: *Black spots* at ends of 1st 2 membranes of dorsal and anal fins (Fig. 29). Deep, compressed body; fairly large eye. Pale olive above, dusky stripe along back; black specks on back and upper side, sometimes outlining scales on nape; herringbone lines rarely present; dark stripe along rear half of side; dusky lips and chin. Breeding male has pale to bright red fins. 11–12 anal rays; 36–49 lateral scales. To 3 in. (7.5 cm).

Range: Gulf drainages from Mobile Bay, AL, to Lake Pontchartrain, LA; Yazoo R., Big Black R., and Bayou Pierre drainages (Mississippi R. basin), MS. Common. **Habitat:** Sand- and gravel-bottomed pools of headwaters, creeks, and small rivers.

Similar species: See (1) Pretty and (2) Blacktip Shiners. (3) Ribbon Shiner (Pl. 17) *lacks* large black spots in dorsal and anal fins; has yellow fins. (4) Redfin Shiner (Pl. 17) has dark blotch at dorsal fin origin, *lacks* large black spots in dorsal and anal fins. **Map 129**

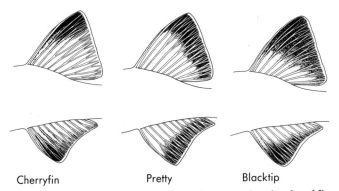

Cherryfin   Pretty   Blacktip

Fig. 29 Cherryfin, Pretty, and Blacktip Shiners — dorsal and anal fins

PRETTY SHINER *Lythrurus bellus*   **Not shown**
    Identification: Nearly identical to Cherryfin Shiner but has *broad black band* on edge of dorsal, anal, and pelvic fins (Fig. 29). 10–11 anal rays; 35–47 lateral scales. To 3 in. (7.5 cm).
    Range: Mobile Bay drainage, Bear and Yellow Cr. systems (Tennessee R. drainage), AL and MS. Common below Fall Line although avoids lower Coastal Plain. **Habitat:** Sand- and clay-bottomed pools of headwaters, creeks, and small rivers.
    Remarks: Two subspecies: *L. b. alegnotus* occurs above Fall Line in Black Warrior R. system, AL, has a dark stripe along side, usually 12–13 scales around caudal peduncle. *L. b. bellus* occupies rest of range, lacks dark stripe on side, has usually 14–15 scales around caudal peduncle, dark body on breeding male.
    Similar species: See Pl. 17. (1) See Cherryfin Shiner. (2) Blacktip Shiner has *tapering* black band on dorsal and anal fins (Fig. 29). (3) Mountain, (4) Rosefin, and (5) Ribbon Shiners *lack* black band on dorsal and anal fins, are more slender; Mountain Shiner has black stripe along side, black lips, white chin; Rosefin Shiner has black blotch at dorsal fin origin, dusky bars over back; Ribbon Shiner has yellow fins.
                                                                       Map 129

BLACKTIP SHINER *Lythrurus atrapiculus*   **Not shown**
    Identification: Nearly identical to Cherryfin Shiner but has *tapering* (wide at front, narrow at rear) *black band* on edge of dorsal, anal, and pelvic fins (Fig. 29). 10–11 anal rays; 36–45 lateral scales. To 2½ in. (6.5 cm).
    Range: Apalachicola, Choctawhatchee, Yellow, and Escambia R. drainages, w. GA, se. AL, and FL panhandle. Introduced into Old Town Cr. (Tallapoosa R. system), Bullock Co., AL. Above the Fall Line only in the Apalachicola drainage. Fairly common. **Habitat:** Sand- and gravel-bottomed pools, sometimes runs, of headwaters, creeks, and small rivers.

Similar species: (1) See Cherryfin Shiner (Pl. 17). (2) Pretty Shiner has *uniformly broad* black band in dorsal and anal fins (Fig. 29).

Map 129

• *PTERONOTROPIS*

Genus characteristics: *Broad, blue-black stripe along side; large dorsal and anal fins. Fairly deep to deep, compressed body,* deepest under dorsal fin origin; dorsal fin origin behind pelvic fin origin. Large male develops enlarged dorsal and anal fins (extremely so in Bluenose and Bluehead Shiners) and bright colors on head and body.

FLAGFIN SHINER *Pteronotropis signipinnis*   **Pl. 20**
Identification: Olive-gold above; upper side yellow at front, red at rear; *broad blue-black stripe* along side with vertical orange dashes; pale gold lower side; gold snout. Red-orange edge on yellow dorsal, caudal, anal, and pelvic fins; yellow pectoral fins. *Deep, compressed body,* strongly tapering to narrow caudal peduncle. Large dorsal and anal fins; rays at front shorter than those at rear in depressed fin. Decurved lateral line. 10–11 anal rays; 22–26 scales around body; 32–36 lateral scales; pharyngeal teeth 2,4–4,2. To 2¾ in. (7 cm).
Range: Coastal Plain streams from Apalachicola R. drainage, FL, to Pearl R. drainage, MS and LA. Common; locally abundant. **Habitat:** Flowing pools and runs of headwaters, creeks, and small rivers; usually over sand and near vegetation.
Similar species: (1) Sailfin and (2) Broadstripe Shiners (both, Pl. 20) *lack* red-orange on dorsal, caudal, and anal fins, red on upper side; have small bright red spots on caudal fin base, 27–29 scales around body.   **Map 130**

SAILFIN SHINER *Pteronotropis hypselopterus*   **Pl. 20**
Identification: Olive-gold above, dark predorsal stripe; pink upper side; *broad steel blue stripe* along side; pale gold lower side; small *red spots* on caudal fin base. Dusky middle band on clear to white dorsal fin; other fins yellow. *Deep, compressed body* strongly tapering to narrow caudal peduncle. *Large, nearly triangular dorsal and anal fins;* rays at front shorter than those at rear in depressed fin. Decurved lateral line. 10–11 anal rays; 27–29 scales around body; 33–38 lateral scales; pharyngeal teeth 2,4–4,2. To 2½ in. (6.5 cm).
Range: Below Fall Line in Atlantic and Gulf drainages from Black R. (Peedee R. drainage), SC, to Mobile Bay, AL; south in FL to Alafia R. system (Tampa Bay drainage). Common. **Habitat:** Sand- and clay-bottomed pools and runs of headwaters, creeks, and small rivers; often among debris and vegetation.
Similar species: (1) See Broadstripe Shiner (Pl. 20). (2) Flagfin Shiner (Pl. 20) has yellow to red upper side; red-orange dorsal, caudal, and anal fins; yellow on caudal fin base, 22–26 scales around body.
Map 131

BROADSTRIPE SHINER *Pteronotropis euryzonus*   **Pl. 20**
Identification: Nearly identical to Sailfin Shiner but dorsal fin is rectangular (rays at front extend *beyond* those at rear in depressed fin), dusky overall. 9–11 (usually 10) anal rays; 25–34 scales around body; 34–42 lateral scales. To 2¾ in. (7 cm).
Range: Middle Chattahoochee R. drainage, GA and AL. Locally common. **Habitat:** Clay, sand, and bedrock pools of headwaters, creeks, and small rivers; often among vegetation and debris.
Similar species: See Sailfin Shiner (Pl. 20).   **Map 130**

BLUENOSE SHINER *Pteronotropis welaka*   **Pl. 20**
Identification: *Black stripe* along side from chin and snout to caudal fin, where expanded into black spot. Slender body; fairly pointed snout; slightly subterminal mouth; dorsal fin origin slightly behind pelvic fin origin. Breeding male has *bright blue snout; huge, mostly black dorsal fin;* black band on yellow anal (also enlarged) and pelvic fins; silver on side of body. Dusky olive-brown above, scales outlined in black; dark streak along back; light yellow stripe above dark stripe along side; white below (sometimes dusky just below black stripe); clear to yellow fins. Incomplete lateral line, 5–12 pores. 34–37 lateral scales; 8 dorsal rays; 8 anal rays; pharyngeal teeth 1,4–4,1. To 2½ in. (6.5 cm).
Range: St. Johns R. drainage, FL; Gulf Coast drainages (mostly below Fall Line) from Apalachicola R., GA and FL, to Pearl R., MS and LA. Locally common. **Habitat:** Backwaters and quiet vegetated pools of creeks and small to medium rivers, over mud and sand. Usually found schooling in fairly deep (1–2 m) water.
Similar species: See Pl. 20. (1) Bluehead Shiner is *deeper bodied,* has blunter snout, 9–10 dorsal rays, pharyngeal teeth 0,4–4,0; *lacks* blue on tip of snout. (2) Dusky Shiner has broader dark stripe along side, blunt snout, terminal mouth; lacks blue snout, enlarged fins on large male. (3) Ironcolor Shiner has shorter, pointed snout, dorsal fin origin over pelvic fin origin; lacks blue snout, enlarged fins on large male; pharyngeal teeth 2,4–4,2.   **Map 132**

BLUEHEAD SHINER *Pteronotropis hubbsi*   **Pl. 20**
Identification: *Black stripe* along side from chin (but absent on upper lip and snout) to caudal fin, where expanded into spot. *9–10 dorsal* and anal rays. Breeding male has *bright blue* top of head, dorsal fin, and caudal fin; *huge dorsal and anal fins.* Deep body; short blunt snout; terminal mouth. Dusky orange-brown above, scales outlined in black; dark stripe along back from head to dorsal fin. Light orange stripe above black stripe along side. Dusky dorsal fin; other fins clear to faintly yellow or orange. Incomplete lateral line, 2–9 pores. 34–38 lateral scales; pharyngeal teeth 0,4–4,0. To 2½ in. (6 cm).
Range: Red and Ouachita R. drainage lowlands of s. AR, LA, and ne. TX; Wolf Lake in sw. IL. Local and uncommon. **Habitat:** Backwaters, oxbows, and sluggish pools of creeks and small rivers; usually near vegetation over mud or sand.

Similar species: (1) Bluenose Shiner (Pl. 20) is more slender; has more pointed snout, black stripe along side extending onto upper lip and snout, usually 8 dorsal and anal rays, pharyngeal teeth 1,4–4,1; (2) Ironcolor Shiner (Pl. 20) has more pointed snout, black stripe along side extending onto upper lip and snout, dorsal fin origin over pelvic fin origin, 8 dorsal and anal rays, pharyngeal teeth 2,4–4,2; *lacks* blue color, enlarged fins on large male. **Map 132**

• *CYPRINELLA*

Genus characteristics: Scales on side appear *diamond-shaped*, taller than wide. *Dusky to black bar* (faint on young and sometimes on adult) on chin; *white edge* on fins of large male. Strongly compressed body; dorsal fin origin slightly behind pelvic fin origin (or slightly in front or behind in Bannerfin Shiner). Pharyngeal teeth 0,4–4,0 or 1,4–4,1. Often the most abundant fishes in streams in e. North America. The success of *Cyprinella* species may be related to their habit of hiding their eggs in rock crevices and to their ability to produce sounds and (presumably) communicate with one another. Although *Cyprinella* species sometimes are difficult to separate as juveniles and females, large males develop bright colors and, in some species, enlarged fins, and are easily separated.

SPOTFIN SHINER *Cyprinella spiloptera* **Pl. 18**
Identification: *Black blotch* on rear half of dorsal fin; little or no black on membranes of front half of dorsal fin (Fig. 30) (except large males). Fairly deep body; pointed snout; terminal mouth. Dusky olive above, black stripe along back; sometimes a dusky bar on side behind head; diffuse dark stripe along rear half of silver side. Breeding male has blue back and side, yellow-white fins, dusky dorsal fin. Usually 26 scales around body, 14 around caudal peduncle; 8 anal rays. 34–41 (usually 35–39) lateral scales; pharyngeal teeth 1,4–4,1. To 4¾ in. (12 cm).
Range: Atlantic Slope from St. Lawrence drainage, QU, to Potomac R. drainage, VA; Great Lakes (except Lake Superior), Hudson Bay (Red R.), and Mississippi R. basins from ON and NY to se. ND and south to AL and e. OK; isolated populations in Ozarks. Generally common. **Habitat:** Sand and gravel runs and pools of creeks, and small to medium (sometimes large) rivers.
Similar species: See Pl. 18. (1) Steelcolor and (2) Satinfin Shiners have usually 9 anal rays, black specks on all membranes of dorsal fin (Fig. 30). (3) Red Shiner has red fins on male, deeper body, *no* black blotch on rear half of dorsal fin, usually 9 anal rays; pharyngeal teeth 0,4–4,0. **Map 133**

STEELCOLOR SHINER *Cyprinella whipplei* **Pl. 18**
Identification: Dorsal fin has black specks on *all* membranes, *black blotch* on rear half (Fig. 30). Fairly deep body; pointed snout; terminal mouth. Dusky olive above, often has blue sheen; dark stripe along

back; diffuse dark stripe along rear half of silver side. Breeding male has blue back and side, red snout, white-edged yellow fins, enlarged dusky dorsal fin. Usually 26 scales around body, 14 scales around caudal peduncle, 15 pectoral rays, 9 anal rays. 36–40 (usually 37–38) lateral scales; pharyngeal teeth 1,4–4,1. To 6¼ in. (16 cm).
Range: Mississippi R. basin, from OH and WV to IL, MO, and e. OK, and south to n. AL and n. LA; Black Warrior R. system (Mobile Bay drainage), AL. Mostly absent on Coastal Plain. Common. **Habitat:** Rocky and sandy runs, less often pools, of creeks and small to medium rivers. Most common near riffles.
Similar species: See Pl. 18. See (1) Satinfin and (2) Greenfin Shiners. (3) Spotfin Shiner has usually 8 anal rays, *little or no black* on membranes of front half of dorsal fin (Fig. 30), lacks enlarged dorsal fin on large male. (4) Bluntface Shiner has blunt snout, white bar on caudal fin base, may have pale orange or red dorsal and caudal fins on large male. (5) Red Shiner has red fins on male, *no* black blotch on rear half of dorsal fin, blunter snout; pharyngeal teeth 0,4–4,0.   **Map 134**

Spotfin   Steelcolor   Red

Fig. 30 Spotfin, Steelcolor, and Red Shiners — black pigment on dorsal fin of female and nonbreeding male

SATINFIN SHINER *Cyprinella analostana*   **Not shown**
Identification: Nearly identical to Steelcolor Shiner but has usually 13–14 pectoral rays, 33–38 lateral scales. To 4¼ in. (11 cm).
Range: Atlantic Slope from Hudson R. drainage, NY, to Peedee R. drainage, NC; Lake Ontario drainage, NY. Common. **Habitat:** Rocky and sandy pools and runs of creeks and small to medium rivers; occasionally found in headwaters and large rivers.
Similar species: See Pl. 18. See (1) Steelcolor Shiner and (2) Greenfin Shiner. (3) Spotfin Shiner has 8 anal rays, little or no black on membranes of front half of dorsal fin (Fig. 30). (4) Whitefin Shiner is more slender; has subterminial mouth, darker stripe along side, usually 8 anal rays.   **Map 134**

GREENFIN SHINER *Cyprinella chloristia*   **Not shown**
Identification: Similar to Satinfin and Steelcolor Shiners but has 8 anal rays, usually 24 scales around body, more distinct dark stripe on side. 32–36 (usually 34–36) lateral scales; pharyngeal teeth 1,4–4,1. To 3 in. (7.5 cm).
Range: Above Fall Line in Santee R. drainage, NC and SC. Common.

Habitat: Rocky and sandy pools and runs of creeks and small to medium rivers.
Similar species: See Pl. 18. See (1) Satinfin and (2) Steelcolor Shiners. (3) Whitefin is more slender; has subterminal mouth, darker stripe along side, usually 37–38 lateral scales. **Map 134**

BLACKTAIL SHINER *Cyprinella venusta* Pl. 18

Identification: *Large black spot* on caudal fin base. Dorsal fin dusky, dark blotch on rear half. Fairly deep body; pointed snout, terminal mouth. Dusky olive above, narrow black stripe along back; diffuse dark stripe along rear half of silver side. Breeding male has blue back and side, yellow-white or red-orange (in s. TX) fins, dusky dorsal fin. Usually 28–29 scales around body, 14 around caudal peduncle; 8 anal rays (often 9 in upper Chattahoochee R. system, GA). 34–48 (usually 36–43) lateral scales; pharyngeal teeth 1,4–4,1. To 7½ in. (19 cm).
Range: Gulf drainages from Suwannee R., GA and FL, to Rio Grande, TX; Mississippi R. basin (mostly on Former Mississippi Embayment) from s. IL to LA and west in Red R. drainage to w. OK. Abundant over much of range. **Habitat:** Most common in sandy pools and runs of small to medium rivers; also in creeks and rocky pools and runs.
Remarks: 3 subspecies: *C. v. venusta*, in the Mississippi R. basin and drainages to the west, has 34–39 (usually 36-38) lateral scales, and a relatively deep body. *C. v. cercostigma*, in Gulf Coast drainages (except Mobile Bay) east of Mississippi R., has 37–43 (usually 38–41) lateral scales and a slightly more diffuse spot on caudal fin base. *C. v. stigmatura*, in the upper AL and Tombigbee R. systems, has 38–48 (usually 40–44) lateral scales and a relatively slender body. Intergrades between *cercostigma* and *stigmatura* occur in the Cahaba and Tallapoosa R. systems, AL.
Similar species: See Pl. 18. (1) Tricolor and (2) Tallapoosa Shiners have black spot on caudal fin base fusing with black stripe along side, jet-black blotch on rear half of dorsal fin, orange fins on large male, usually 26 scales around body. (3) Alabama Shiner is less compressed, has red dorsal and caudal fins, more subterminal mouth, usually 24 scales around body. (Blacktail Shiner has yellow fins within range of Tricolor, Tallapoosa, and Alabama Shiners.) **Map 135**

BLUNTFACE SHINER *Cyprinella camura* Pl. 18

Identification: Usually a *clear to white bar* on caudal fin base. *Black blotch* on rear half of dorsal fin. Deep body; blunt snout; terminal or slightly subterminal mouth. Dusky olive above, narrow dark stripe along back; sometimes a dark bar on side behind head, dusky stripe along rear half of silver-blue side; dark (dusky) dorsal and caudal fins. Breeding male has pale orange or red fins and snout, enlarged dorsal fin. Usually 26 scales around body, 14 around caudal peduncle; 9 anal rays. 35–39 (usually 36–37) lateral scales; pharyngeal teeth 1,4–4,1. To 4¼ in. (11 cm).
Range: Tributaries of Mississippi and Tennessee rivers on Former Mississippi Embayment of KY, TN, MS, and e. LA; Arkansas R. drainage, sw. MO, e. KS, nw. AR, and e. OK. Generally common;

abundant in w. TN and in Neosho R. system in MO and OK. **Habitat:** Sandy and rocky pools and runs of clear to turbid creeks and small to medium rivers.
Similar species: See Pl. 18. (1) Steelcolor and (2) Spotfin Shiners *lack* clear or white bar on caudal fin base, have more pointed snout; Spotfin Shiner has usually 8 anal rays. (3) Whitetail Shiner is much more slender and has sharper snout, usually 39–41 lateral scales.
Map 136

RED SHINER *Cyprinella lutrensis* **Pl. 18**
Identification: *Deep body;* terminal mouth; rounded snout. Dusky blue triangular bar behind head on side (faint on young). Dusky olive to blue back and upper side, black stripe along back; diffuse dark stripe along rear half of silver side. Dusky dorsal fin, no black blotch on rear half (Fig. 30). Breeding male has *red fins* (except dorsal), blue back and side, dark blue bar before pink bar behind head on side. Usually 26 scales around body, 14 around caudal peduncle, 9 anal rays, 14 pectoral rays. 32–36 lateral scales; pharyngeal teeth 0,4–4,0. To 3½ in. (9 cm).
Range: Mississippi R. basin from s. WI and e. IN to SD and WY and south to LA; Gulf drainages west of Mississippi R. to Rio Grande, TX, NM, and CO. Absent in Ozark and Ouachita uplands. Widely introduced elsewhere in U.S. Also in n. Mexico. Abundant. **Habitat:** Silty, sandy, and rocky pools and runs, sometimes riffles, of creeks and small to medium rivers. Tolerant of siltation and high turbidity.
Similar species: (1) See Beautiful and (2) Edwards Plateau Shiners. (3) Proserpine Shiner (Pl. 18) has black stripe along side and on chin and throat; subterminal mouth; *yellow to orange fins.* **Map 137**

BEAUTIFUL SHINER *Cyprinella formosa* **Not shown**
Identification: Nearly identical to Red Shiner but has *orange or yellow back* and *silver side, red-orange caudal peduncle,* orange caudal and lower fins on large male. Small, crowded scales on nape. Usually 26 scales around body, 14 around caudal peduncle; 8 anal rays. 34–47 lateral scales; pharyngeal teeth 0,4–4,0. To 3½ in. (9 cm).
Range: San Bernardina Cr., sw. NM and se. AZ; also in Mexico. Presumed extirpated in U.S.; uncommon in Mexico. Recognized as a *threatened species.* **Habitat:** Sandy and rocky pools of creeks.
Similar species: See (1) Red (Pl. 18) and (2) Edwards Plateau Shiners.
Map 137

EDWARDS PLATEAU SHINER *Cyprinella lepida* **Not shown**
Identification: Similar to Red and Beautiful Shiners, but breeding male has green back, *yellow-purple side, purple bar* on side of *gold-orange head,* yellow-orange fins. To 3 in. (7.5 cm).
Range: Edwards Plateau, TX, in the upper Guadalupe and Nueces R. drainages. Common. **Habitat:** Springs and spring-fed creeks; usually in clear water over gravel.
Similar species: See (1) Red (Pl. 18) and (2) Beautiful Shiners.
Map 137

PROSERPINE SHINER *Cyprinella proserpina* **Pl. 18**
Identification: *Black stripe* on chin and throat; *black stripe* along side; yellow to orange (on male) fins. Fairly deep body; *subterminal mouth.* Dusky olive to blue back and side, dark stripe along back. Breeding male has white-edged orange fins, brassy yellow head, blue-black bar on side behind head. Usually 26 scales around body, 14 around caudal peduncle; 8 anal rays, 13 pectoral rays. 34–36 lateral scales; pharyngeal teeth 0,4–4,0. To 3 in. (7.5 cm).
Range: Devils R., lower Pecos R., and nearby tributaries of Rio Grande, TX; also Rio San Carlo (Rio Grande drainage), Coahuila, Mexico. Fairly common. **Habitat:** Rocky runs and pools of creeks and small rivers.
Similar species: (1) Red (Pl. 18), (2) Edwards Plateau, and (3) Beautiful Shiners *lack* black stripe along side and black stripe on chin and throat (may have dusky stripe on chin); have *terminal mouth,* red or orange fins. **Map 136**

WHITETAIL SHINER *Cyprinella galactura* **Pl. 18**
Identification: *2 large clear to white areas* on caudal fin base. *Black blotch* on rear half of dorsal fin. *Slender* body; moderate snout; terminal or slightly subterminal mouth. Dusky olive above, dark streak along back; silver side; dusky dorsal and caudal fins. Breeding male has blue back and side, white fins, enlarged dorsal fin; dorsal and anal fins may have red tint. Usually 26 scales around body, 14 around caudal peduncle; 9 anal rays. 38–43 (usually 39–41) lateral scales; pharyngeal teeth 1,4–4,1. To 6 in. (15 cm).
Range: Disjunct range east and west of Former Mississippi Embayment. Cumberland and Tennessee R. drainages, VA, NC, KY, TN, GA, AL, and MS; upper Savannah and Santee drainages (Atlantic Slope), NC, SC, and GA; and upper New R. drainage, VA. St. Francis and White R. drainages, MO and AR. Common; locally abundant. **Habitat:** Rocky runs, less often pools and riffles, of clear headwaters, creeks, and small rivers.
Similar species: See Pl. 18. (1) Bluntface Shiner has *deeper* body, blunt snout, usually 36–37 lateral scales. (2) Spotfin Shiner *lacks* clear or white areas on caudal fin base, dusky pigment on 1st 3 membranes of dorsal fin (except on large male); has deeper body, usually 35–39 lateral scales, 8 anal rays. (3) Steelcolor Shiner *lacks* clear or white areas on caudal fin base, has deeper body, usually 37–38 lateral scales. **Map 138**

ALABAMA SHINER *Cyprinella callistia* **Pl. 18**
Identification: *Large black spot* on caudal fin base (fusing on small individuals into black stripe on rear half of side). *Pink to red dorsal and caudal fins.* Blunt snout, *subterminal mouth,* large eye. Olive above, dark stripe along back; silver side. Breeding male has black edge on rear half of red dorsal fin, red caudal fin; other fins white. Usually 24 scales around body, 16 around caudal peduncle; 8 anal rays. 37–41 lateral scales; pharyngeal teeth 1,4–4,1. To 3¾ in. (9.5 cm).
Range: Mobile Bay drainage, se. TN, nw. GA, AL, and ne. MS; usually

above Fall Line. Generally common, but uncommon in upper Tombigbee R. system. **Habitat:** Gravel- and rubble-bottomed pools and runs of creeks and small to medium rivers.

Similar species: See Pl. 18. (1) Blacktail, (2) Tricolor, and (3) Tallapoosa Shiners have more pointed snout, more *terminal* mouth, dark blotch on rear half of dorsal fin, usually 26 or 28 scales around body, 14 scales around caudal peduncle, yellow or orange fins on large male.
Map 139

TRICOLOR SHINER *Cyprinella trichroistia*   **Pl. 18**

Identification: *Large black spot* on caudal fin base *fusing* into *black stripe* on rear half of side; *yellow to red-orange fins; jet-black blotch* on rear half of dorsal fin. Fairly deep body; moderate snout; terminal mouth. Dusky olive above, dark stripe along back; silver side. Breeding male has orange and white fins, blue side; tubercles in 1 row on lower jaw, large and in 2 rows on top of head (Fig. 31). Usually 26 scales around body, 14 around caudal peduncle; 9 anal rays. 36–44 lateral scales; pharyngeal teeth 1,4–4,1. To 4 in. (10 cm.).

Range: Alabama R. drainage (mostly Coosa and Cahaba R. systems), se. TN, nw. GA, and AL. Fairly common. **Habitat:** Rocky and sandy runs and pools of creeks and small to medium rivers.

Similar species: See Pl. 18. (1) See Tallapoosa Shiner. (2) Blue Shiner is more slender, has more subterminal mouth, less prominent spot on caudal fin base, darker stripe along side, usually 22 scales around body, 8 anal rays.
Map 138

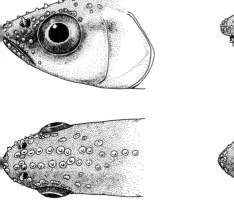
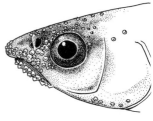

Tricolor   Tallapoosa

Fig. 31 Tricolor and Tallapoosa Shiners — head tubercles on breeding male

TALLAPOOSA SHINER *Cyprinella gibbsi*   **Not shown**
Identification: Similar to Tricolor Shiner but has longer, more over-hanging snout, subterminal mouth, tubercles in *2 rows* on lower jaw, smaller and more scattered on top of head of breeding male (Fig. 31). 37–42 lateral scales; pharyngeal teeth 1,4–4,1. To 3¾ in. (9.5 cm).
Range: Tallapoosa R. system (Alabama R. drainage), AL and GA. Most common minnow in Tallapoosa R. tributaries. **Habitat:** Sandy and rocky runs of small to medium rivers; less often in flowing pools.
Similar species: See Tricolor Shiner (Pl. 18).   **Map 138**

BLUE SHINER *Cyprinella caerulea*   **Pl. 18**
Identification: *Blue-black stripe* along side from head to caudal fin, darkest and widest at rear; expanded slightly into spot on caudal fin base. Often a *black blotch* on rear half of dorsal fin. Fairly *slender* body; *pointed snout;* slightly subterminal mouth. Light brown above, dark stripe along back; silver side. Breeding male has yellow side, yellow-white fins. Usually *22 scales* around body, 14 around caudal peduncle; 8 anal rays. 37–39 lateral scales; pharyngeal teeth 1,4–4,1. To 3½ in. (9 cm).
Range: Coosa and Cahaba R. systems, se. TN, nw. GA, and AL. Local and uncommon; possibly extirpated from Cahaba R. system. **Habitat:** Rocky runs of small to medium rivers.
Similar species: See Pl. 18. (1) Tricolor, (2) Tallapoosa, and (3) Alabama Shiners have deeper body, less diamond-shaped scales, usually 24–26 scales around body.   **Map 140**

FIERYBLACK SHINER *Cyprinella pyrrhomelas*   **Pl. 18**
Identification: *Black edge* on caudal fin of adult; *black bar* on side behind head. *Large eye.* Dark olive above, narrow black stripe along back; dusky stripe along rear half of side, often expanded into black spot on caudal fin base; silver side. Breeding male has blue back and side, *bright red snout, bright red band* after white band on caudal fin, dorsal fin red at front; other fins white. *Black blotch* on rear half of dorsal fin. Deep body; terminal mouth. Usually 26 scales around body, 14 around caudal peduncle; 10–11 anal rays. 34–39 lateral scales; pharyngeal teeth 1,4–4,1. To 4¼ in. (11 cm).
Range: Above Fall Line in Peedee and Santee R. drainages, NC and SC. Common, especially in mountain streams. **Habitat:** Rocky runs and pools near riffles of creeks and small to medium rivers.
Similar species: (1) Whitefin (Pl. 18), (2) Satinfin, (3) Greenfin, and (4) Altamaha Shiners (Pl. 18) *lack* black edge on caudal fin, bright red pigment; have smaller eye; all but Altamaha Shiner have 8–9 anal rays.   **Map 140**

ALTAMAHA SHINER *Cyprinella xaenura*   **Pl. 18**
Identification: Pointed snout; terminal or slightly subterminal mouth. Dusky olive above, dark stripe along back; silver-black stripe along rear half of side, often expanded into *spot* on caudal fin base. Breeding male has blue side, white fins; *yellow to orange dorsal, caudal, and anal fins.* Usually 26 scales around body, 16 around caudal

peduncle; 10–11 anal rays. 38–40 lateral scales; pharyngeal teeth 1,4–4,1. To 4½ in. (11 cm).
Range: Upper Altamaha R. drainage, n.-cen. GA. Fairly common.
Habitat: Rocky and sandy pools of creeks and small rivers.
Similar species: See Pl. 18. (1) Most similar to Fieryblack Shiner, which has black edge on caudal fin of adult; red on snout, dorsal and caudal fins of male; 14 scales around caudal peduncle; larger eye. (2) Ocmulgee and (3) Bannerfin Shiners, both in the Altamaha R. drainage, have distinctly subterminal mouth, 8 anal rays, 14 scales around caudal peduncle; pharyngeal teeth 0,4–4,0.   **Map 140**

OCMULGEE SHINER *Cyprinella callisema*   Pl. 18
Identification: *Deep blue stripe* along side (sometimes faint near front), often ending in darker spot on caudal fin base. *Small black blotch* at front of dorsal fin – near tip of 1st ray, middle of 2d ray. Fairly deep body; long, round snout; *subterminal mouth.* Dusky olive above; dark stripe along back to dorsal fin, dark streak behind fin; silver side. Breeding male has white lower fins, orange dorsal and caudal fins; enlarged, dusky dorsal fin. Usually 26 scales around body, 14 around caudal peduncle; 8 anal rays. 37–40 (usually 38–39) lateral scales; pharyngeal teeth, 0,4–4,0. To 3½ in. (9 cm).
Range: Altamaha and Ogeechee R. drainages, GA. Locally common in Altamaha, uncommon in Ogeechee R. drainage. **Habitat:** Sandy and rocky runs of small to medium rivers.
Similar species: See Pl. 18. (1) See Bluestripe Shiner. (2) Bannerfin Shiner has more diffuse stripe along side, more flattened underside. (3) Altamaha Shiner is deeper bodied; has terminal mouth, 10–11 anal rays, 16 scales around caudal peduncle; pharyngeal teeth 1,4–4,1.   **Map 139**

BLUESTRIPE SHINER *Cyprinella callitaenia*   Not shown
Identification: Nearly identical to Ocmulgee Shiner, but has *crescent-shaped line* of black specks from eye to mouth, *darker spot* on caudal fin base, pharyngeal teeth 1,4–4,1. 37–40 lateral scales. To 3½ in. (9 cm).
Range: Apalachicola R. drainage, GA, AL, and FL. Localized and generally uncommon. **Habitat:** Sandy and rocky runs of small to medium rivers.
Similar species: See Ocmulgee Shiner (Pl. 18).   **Map 139**

WHITEFIN SHINER *Cyprinella nivea*   Pl. 18
Identification: *Dark blue to black stripe* along side, darkest on rear half. *Black blotch* on rear half of dorsal fin. Slender body; rounded snout; *subterminal mouth.* Dusky olive above, dark stripe along back; silver side. Large male has white fins. Usually 26 scales around body, 14 around caudal peduncle; 8 anal rays. 35–41 (usually 37–38, see Remarks) lateral scales; pharyngeal teeth 1,4–4,1. To 3½ in. (8.5 cm).
Range: Atlantic Slope from Neuse R. drainage, NC, to Savannah R. drainage, GA. Common. **Habitat:** Sand and gravel runs and riffles, usually in small to medium rivers, less often in creeks.

Remarks: Savannah R. population has smaller scales (usually 39-40 lateral scales) than other populations of Whitefin Shiner.
Similar species: (1) Bluestripe and (2) Ocmulgee (Pl. 18) Shiners have black blotch on *front*, not rear, half of dorsal fin. (3) Bannerfin Shiner (Pl. 18) has small black blotch at *front*, not rear, of dorsal fin; flattened underside; pharyngeal teeth 0,4–4,0. **Map 139**

BANNERFIN SHINER *Cyprinella leedsi* Pl. 18

Identification: *Small black blotch* at front of dorsal fin — near tip of 1st ray, middle of 2d ray; outer half of fin dusky. *Subterminal mouth;* long, rounded snout. Blue to black stripe along silver side, darkest on rear half, usually faint at front. Slender body; deepest in adult near dorsal fin origin, strongly tapering to caudal peduncle and snout; *flattened underside.* Dorsal fin origin slightly in front of to slightly behind pelvic fin origin. Dusky olive above, black stripe along back (wider in front of dorsal fin); white below. Breeding male has white lower fins, orange dorsal and caudal fins, black outer half of greatly enlarged dorsal fin. Usually 26 scales around body, 14 around caudal peduncle; 8 anal rays. 35–39 lateral scales; pharyngeal teeth 0,4–4,0. To 4 in. (10 cm).
Range: Atlantic Slope from Savannah R. drainage, SC, to Altamaha R. drainage, GA; Gulf Slope in Suwannee and Ochlockonee drainages, s. GA and n. FL. Restricted to Coastal Plain; uncommon. **Habitat:** Sandy runs of medium to large rivers.
Similar species: (1) Ocmulgee (Pl. 18) and (2) Bluestripe Shiners have dark blue-black stripe along entire side; *lack* flattened underside and small black blotch at front of dorsal fin. (3) Whitefin Shiner (Pl. 18) has black blotch on *rear* half (not front) of dorsal fin; pharyngeal teeth 1,4–4,1; *lacks* flattened underside. **Map 140**

SPOTFIN CHUB *Cyprinella monacha* Pl. 19

Identification: Slender body, *flattened below,* arched above, deepest at dorsal fin origin. *Long snout overhangs mouth; small barbel* at corner of mouth; small eyes slightly directed upwardly. *Black blotch* on rear half of dorsal fin (darkest on large adult). Dorsal fin origin behind pelvic fin origin. Olive to gray above, iridescent green stripe along back, another along upper side; dark stripe along silver side, darkest on rear half, expanded into large black caudal spot. Breeding male has 2 large *white bars on blue side* (dark above, light below), white edges on blue fins. Complete lateral line; 52–62 lateral scales; 8 anal rays; 0,4–4,0 pharyngeal teeth. To 4¼ in. (11 cm).
Range: Historically in much of Tennessee R. drainage, VA, NC, TN, GA, and AL; observed recently only in Little Tennessee R., NC, Duck and Emory rivers, TN, and N. Fork Holston R., VA and TN. Rare; protected as a *threatened species.* **Habitat:** Rocky riffles and runs of clean small to medium rivers.
Similar species: Slender Chub (Pl. 9) has dark <'s along side, *no* dark blotch on dorsal fin, dorsal fin origin in front of pelvic fin origin, 7 anal rays. **Map 117**

PUGNOSE MINNOW *Opsopoeodus emiliae* **Pl. 10**
Identification: *Cross-hatched pattern* on back and upper ½ to all of side; *small, strongly upturned* mouth; *small crowded scales* on front half of nape; 9 dorsal rays; 2 dark areas (front and rear — clear area between) on dorsal fin, most prominent on large male (dark areas absent in parts of FL). Fairly slender body; dorsal fin origin over to slightly behind pelvic fin origin. Dusky olive-yellow above; dark stripe along silver side of head and body, sometimes ending in small black spot on caudal fin base; large individuals in FL have pink, red, or orange fins. Breeding male has bright white lower half of anal and pelvic fins. Usually complete lateral line, 36–40 lateral scales, 8 anal rays; pharyngeal teeth usually 0,5–5,0 (see Remarks). To 2½ in. (6.4 cm).
Range: Edisto R. drainage, SC, to s. FL, and across Gulf Slope to Nueces R. drainage, TX; north in Mississippi R. and Great Lakes basins to se. KS, se. MN, and s. ON. Generally restricted to lowlands. Common but becoming less so in parts of range. **Habitat:** Clear to turbid vegetated lakes, swamps, oxbows, and sluggish streams of all sizes.
Remarks: Two subspecies. *O. e. peninsularis,* in peninsular FL, commonly has 4 pharyngeal teeth on right side (0,4) and 5 on the left (0,5), lacks dark spots on dorsal fin; breeding male has tubercles in a cluster to either side of the upper lip. *O. e. emiliae,* in rest of range except where intergrades occur (s. GA and ne. FL west to Ochlockonee R.), has pharyngeal tooth count of 0,5–5,0, 2 dark spots on dorsal fin of adult, and breeding tubercles across snout of breeding male.
Similar species: (1) Taillight Shiner (Pl. 20), also with cross-hatched pattern and often found with Pugnose Minnow, has large black spot on caudal fin base, red on head and body (especially large male), more *horizontal* and *subterminal* mouth, smaller eye, 8 dorsal rays. (2) Pugnose Shiner (Pl. 12) has upturned mouth but *lacks* cross-hatched pattern, has black peritoneum, 8 dorsal rays, pharyngeal teeth 0,4–4,0. **Map 141**

● *PIMEPHALES*

Genus characteristics: Species of *Pimephales* are among the most common fishes in eastern North America. All have *much smaller scales on nape* (usually more than 20 in row from head to dorsal fin) than elsewhere on body; 2d ray of dorsal fin is short and stout, distinctly separated from 3d ray by a membrane.

FATHEAD MINNOW *Pimephales promelas* **Pl. 10**
Identification: Deep, compressed body; *head short, flat on top. Herringbone lines on upper side.* Blunt snout; terminal, slanted mouth; round eye on side of head. Dorsal fin origin over pelvic fin origin. Dark olive above and on side, dusky stripe along back, dusky stripe along side; dull yellow to white below with black peritoneum showing through; fins clear except often a dusky to black blotch at front of

dorsal fin (about midway). Breeding male dark with black head, 2 broad white to gold bars on side (1 behind head, 1 under dorsal fin); black fins; large gray fleshy pad on nape; about 16 large tubercles in 3 rows on snout. Intestine long, with several loops. Usually incomplete lateral line; 40–54 lateral scales; 7 anal rays; pharyngeal teeth 0,4–4,0. To 4 in. (10 cm).

Range: Over much of North America from QU to NT, and south to AL, TX, and NM. Introduced through bait-bucket releases in Mobile Bay drainage, AL, Colorado R. drainage, AZ and NM, and elsewhere. Also in n. Mexico. Most common in Great Plains. Generally absent from mountainous regions; absent on Atlantic Slope s. of Delaware R. Common over much of range. **Habitat:** Muddy pools of headwaters, creeks, and small rivers; ponds. Tolerant of conditions (e.g., turbid, hot, poorly oxygenated, intermittent streams) unsuitable for most fishes.

Remarks: The frequent use of this species as fishing bait and its ability to occupy a wide range of environments has resulted in many introduced populations of Fathead Minnow. A strain referred to as the "rosy-red" minnow has been developed primarily for the pet trade; both sexes have red-orange body and fins.

Similar species: Other *Pimephales* species (Pl. 10) are more slender, *lack* herringbone lines, have complete lateral line.   **Map 142**

BLUNTNOSE MINNOW *Pimephales notatus*   **Pl. 10**
   Identification: *Blunt snout* overhanging small, subterminal, horizontal mouth. Slender body nearly *square* in cross section, with top of head and nape *flattened*; round eye on side of head. Dorsal fin origin slightly behind pelvic fin origin. Light olive to tan above, scales darkly outlined (often with cross-hatched appearance), black streak along back; dusky to *black stripe* around snout and along silver side to conspicuous *black spot* on caudal fin base; fins clear except for dusky to black blotch at front of dorsal fin (about midway). Breeding male black with silver bar behind opercle, about 16 large tubercles in 3 rows on snout, large gray fleshy pad on nape. Intestine long with several loops; black peritoneum. Complete lateral line; 39–50 lateral scales; 7 anal rays; pharyngeal teeth 0,4–4,0. To 4¼ in. (11 cm).

Range: Great Lakes, Hudson Bay (Red R.), and Mississippi R. basins from s. QU to s. MB, and south to LA; Atlantic Slope from St. Lawrence R., QU, to Roanoke R., VA (absent from most of New England); Gulf Slope from Mobile Bay drainage, AL, to Mississippi R. Abundant; probably most common freshwater fish in eastern North America. **Habitat:** Can be found almost anywhere in its range, but most common in clear rocky streams.

Similar species: (1) Bullhead (Pl. 10) and (2) Slim Minnows have eyes higher on head, directed more upwardly; more terminal mouth; larger head; bluish sheen on side; silver-white peritoneum. **Map 143**

BULLHEAD MINNOW *Pimephales vigilax*   **Pl. 10**
   Identification: *Large eye,* directed somewhat *upwardly,* on upper half of head. *Large black spot at front of dorsal fin.* Slender body nearly

square in cross section, with top of head and nape flattened; rounded snout; small, terminal, nearly horizontal mouth; upper lip slightly thickened at middle. Dorsal fin origin over pelvic fin origin. Light to dark olive above, scales darkly outlined (often appearing cross-hatched); often a dusky to black stripe along silver-blue side, ending just before large black spot at caudal fin base; dusky stripe along underside of caudal peduncle. Breeding male dark with black head, silver bar behind opercle, 5–9 large tubercles in 1–2 rows on snout, large gray fleshy pad on nape. Intestine short. Peritoneum silvery with black specks. Complete lateral line; 37–45 lateral scales; usually 7–8 scales above lateral line, 7 anal rays; pharyngeal teeth 0,4–4,0. To 3½ in. (8.9 cm).
Range: Mississippi R. basin from w. PA to MN, and south to Gulf; Gulf Slope drainages from Mobile Bay, GA and AL, to Rio Grande, TX, NM, and Mexico. Populations in Rio Grande of NM and w. TX may be introduced. Common over much of range; locally abundant.
Habitat: Quiet pools and runs over sand, silt, or gravel, in small to large rivers. Most common in medium-sized rivers.
Similar species: (1) See Slim Minnow. (2) Bluntnose Minnow (Pl. 10) has eyes *lower* on head, directed more to side; black peritoneum; no bluish sheen on side.   **Map 144**

SLIM MINNOW   *Pimephales tenellus*   **Not shown**
Identification: Similar to Bullhead Minnow but with upper lip decidedly *thickened* at middle, narrower and darker stripe along underside of caudal peduncle, 6 (rarely 5 or 7) scales above lateral line; breeding male with usually 11–13 tubercles in 3 rows on snout. To 2¾ in. (7 cm).
Range: S. MO, e. KS, AR, and ne. OK (see Remarks). Locally common in nw. part of range. **Habitat:** Sand- and gravel-bottomed pools and runs of creeks and small rivers.
Remarks: Two subspecies. *P. t. parviceps*, in the Castor, St. Francis, Black, White, lower Arkansas, Ouachita, and Little (Red R. drainage) R. systems, is more slender and has the snout projecting slightly beyond the upper lip. *P. t. tenellus*, in the Arkansas R. drainage west of the AR-OK state line, has a terminal upper lip.
Similar species: See Bullhead Minnow (Pl. 10).   **Map 92**

• *NOTROPIS*

Genus characteristics: 8 dorsal rays; no barbel (except in Redeye Chub); short intestine with 1 loop at front (except Ozark Minnow and Cape Fear Shiner); scales on front half of side not much taller than wide (except Mimic, Cahaba, and Ghost Shiners); scales on nape about same size as those on upper side (except Mirror and Sawfin Shiners); scales usually not appearing diamond-shaped (except Taillight Shiner); pharyngeal teeth 0,4–4,0 to 2,4–4,2. *Notropis* is the 2d largest genus (71 species) of freshwater fishes in North America and includes most of our small minnows.

EMERALD SHINER *Notropis atherinoides* **Pl. 11**
Identification: *Slender compressed body;* large, terminal slanted mouth (reaching to front of eye) on fairly pointed snout; dorsal fin origin *behind* pelvic fin origin. Black lips (front half). Light olive above, narrow dusky stripe along back; partly dusky, silver stripe with emerald reflections along side. Gill rakers often (ca. 50% of individuals) T- or Y-shaped. Complete lateral line; 35–40 lateral scales; 10–12 anal rays; 8 pelvic rays; pharyngeal teeth 2,4–4,2. To 5 in. (13 cm).
Range: St. Lawrence drainage, QU, and Hudson R. drainage, NY, to Mackenzie R. drainage (Arctic basin), NT, and south through Great Lakes and Mississippi R. basins to Gulf; Gulf Slope drainages from Mobile Bay, AL, to Galveston Bay, TX. Common; probably the most abundant fish in Mississippi and other large rivers. **Habitat:** Pools and runs of medium to large rivers, lakes; most common in clear water over sand or gravel.
Similar species: See (1) Comely, (2) Rio Grande, and (3) Sharpnose Shiners (all, Pl. 11). (4) Silver Shiner (Pl. 11) has 2 dark crescents between nostrils, larger eye, 9 pelvic rays. (5) Rosyface Shiner (Pl. 19) has longer, more pointed snout, black streak just above silver stripe along side. **Map 145**

COMELY SHINER *Notropis amoenus* **Pl. 11**
Identification: Nearly identical to Emerald Shiner but has *smaller eye,* less slanted mouth, rarely has T- or Y-shaped gill rakers. Within zone of sympatry (cen. and se. NY), Comely Shiner has usually 26–31 scales around body at dorsal fin origin, 13–17 around caudal peduncle; Emerald Shiner has usually 22–27 and 12–14, respectively. 35–47 lateral scales; 11 anal rays. To 4¼ in. (11 cm).
Range: Atlantic Slope drainages from Hudson R., NY, to Cape Fear R., NC; one record each from Seneca Lake (Lake Ontario drainage), NY, and Yadkin R. system, NC. Common. **Habitat:** Runs and flowing pools, over sand, gravel, or rubble, of creeks and medium to large rivers.
Similar species: See Emerald Shiner (Pl. 11). **Map 146**

RIO GRANDE SHINER *Notropis jemezanus* **Pl. 11**
Identification: Similar to Emerald Shiner, but has *larger, less slanted mouth extending under eye;* smaller eye; deeper snout; *lacks* black lips (may be dusky), black around anal fin base and along underside of caudal peduncle. To 3 in. (7.5 cm).
Range: Rio Grande drainage, TX, NM, and Mexico. Common in lower Rio Grande; less common elsewhere. **Habitat:** Sandy and rocky runs and flowing pools of small to large rivers.
Similar species: See Emerald Shiner (Pl. 11). **Map 145**

SHARPNOSE SHINER *Notropis oxyrhynchus* **Pl. 11**
Identification: Similar to Emerald Shiner but has *sharply pointed snout;* upper jaw level with upper edge of eye. 34–37 lateral scales; 10 anal rays. To 2½ in. (6.5 cm).

Range: Brazos R. and lower portions of large tributaries, TX. Introduced into middle Colorado R., TX. Common. **Habitat:** Sand and gravel runs of medium to large rivers; less often in sand- or mud-bottomed pools.

Similar species: See Emerald Shiner (Pl. 11). **Map 145**

SILVER SHINER *Notropis photogenis* **Pl. 11**
Identification: *Slender, compressed body. 2 black crescents* (Fig. 32) between nostrils. Large, terminal mouth (reaching to front of eye) on long snout; thickened tip of lower jaw projects beyond upper jaw; large eye; dorsal fin origin behind pelvic fin origin. Light olive above, black stripe along back; partly dusky silver stripe with blue reflections along side. Black lips (front half). Complete lateral line; 36–40 lateral scales; 10–12 anal rays; 9 pelvic rays; pharyngeal teeth 2,4–4,2. To 5½ in. (14 cm).
Range: Lake Erie and Ohio R. drainages from ON and NY to MI, and south to n. GA. Common throughout eastern part of range, rare in western areas (absent in lower Wabash, lower Cumberland, and most of lower Tennessee R. drainages); rare in Lake Erie drainage. **Habitat:** Rocky runs and riffles of small to large rivers.
Similar species: (1) Emerald Shiner (Pl. 11) *lacks* black crescents; has smaller eye, shorter snout, deeper body, 8 pelvic rays. (2) Rosyface Shiner (Pl. 19) has sharper snout, black streak above silver stripe along side, red on head and body of large male; *lacks* black crescents between nostrils. **Map 146**

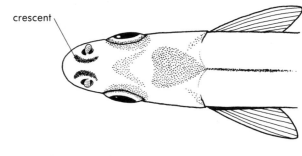

crescent

Fig. 32 Silver Shiner

ROSYFACE SHINER *Notropis rubellus* **Pl. 19**
Identification: *Sharply pointed snout* longer than eye diameter. Slender, compressed body; dorsal fin origin *well behind* pelvic fin origin (about over *middle* of pelvic fin). Olive above, often with narrow dusky stripe along back; faint *red* at base of dorsal fin; *black streak* just above silver stripe along side; blue sheen overall. Breeding male is blue above; has *orange to bright rosy red head, front half of body* and *fin bases*. Large female may have some red. Complete lateral

line; 36–45 lateral scales; 9–11 anal rays; pharyngeal teeth 2,4–4,2 or 1,4–4,1. To 3½ in. (9 cm).

Range: Atlantic Slope from St. Lawrence R. drainage, QU, to James R. drainage, VA; Great Lakes, Hudson Bay (Red R.), and Mississippi R. basins from QU to MB, and south to NC, AL, AR, and OK. Common in upland areas and clear streams with fast current. Absent in Delaware R. drainage and in lowland streams, including those on Former Mississippi Embayment, in s. IL, and in n. MO. **Habitat:** Rocky runs and flowing pools of small to medium rivers.

Similar species: (1) Emerald and (2) Comely Shiners (both, Pl. 11) have *blunter snout, no* red coloration, *no* black streak above silver stripe, dorsal fin origin over (or close) to pelvic fin origin.   **Map 147**

SILVERSTRIPE SHINER *Notropis stilbius*   **Pl. 11**
   Identification: *Horizontally oval black caudal spot. Large terminal mouth* on *pointed snout; large eye.* Slender compressed body; dorsal fin origin behind pelvic fin origin. Olive above; dusky stripe along back; darkly outlined scales on back and upper side; broad silver-black stripe along side; narrow dark stripe around snout (on both lips); punctate lateral line (Fig. 33). Complete lateral line; 35–37 lateral scales; 10–11 anal rays; 8 pelvic rays; pharyngeal teeth 2,4–4,2. To 3½ in. (9 cm).

Range: Mobile Bay drainage, GA, AL, MS, and se. TN. One record for Bear Cr. (Tennessee R. drainage), nw. AL. Locally common above Fall Line; uncommon below. **Habitat:** Gravel- and sand-bottomed runs and flowing pools of small to large rivers; often near vegetation.

Similar species: Emerald Shiner (Pl. 11) has smaller eye, no caudal spot, no punctations along lateral line.   **Map 148**

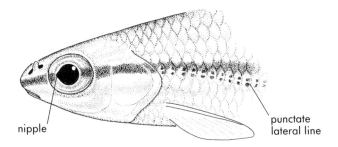

nipple

punctate
lateral line

Fig. 33 Minnow — nipple on eye and punctate lateral line

SANDBAR SHINER *Notropis scepticus*   **Pl. 11**
   Identification: *Large round eye,* diameter more than snout length. *Darkly outlined scales* on back and upper side, forming lines (often faint) meeting those of other side on caudal peduncle. *Falcate anal*

fin. Straw yellow to olive above, dark stripe along back (darker before dorsal fin); *punctate,* complete lateral line, dusky stripe (darkest at rear) on snout and along silver side, followed by small black caudal spot. Deep, compressed body; dorsal fin origin slightly behind pelvic fin origin. Large terminal mouth on fairly pointed snout. 34–38 lateral scales; 12–13 scales around caudal peduncle; 10–11 anal rays; pharyngeal teeth 2,4–4,2. To 3½ in. (9 cm).
Range: Cape Fear R. drainage, NC, to Savannah R. drainage, GA. Common on Piedmont, less common in mountain streams, uncommon on Coastal Plain. **Habitat:** Flowing, sand-bottomed pools, often near riffles, in creeks and small to medium rivers.
Similar species: (1) Telescope Shiner (Pl. 11) has slender body, *straight-edged* (barely concave) *anal fin.* (2) New River Shiner (Pl. 12) has broad snout, upwardly directed eyes, subterminal mouth, 8 anal rays.   **Map 149**

NEW RIVER SHINER *Notropis scabriceps*   **Pl. 12**
Identification: *Broad snout; large upwardly directed eye; slightly subterminal mouth. Darkly outlined scales* on back and upper side, forming lines (often faint) meeting those of other side on caudal peduncle. Olive above, dusky stripe along back before dorsal fin; *punctate lateral line,* dusky stripe (darkest at rear) on snout and along silver side. Compressed body, somewhat flattened below; large, horizontal pectoral fins; dorsal fin origin over pelvic fin origin. Complete lateral line; 35–39 lateral scales; 8 anal rays; pharyngeal teeth 2,4–4,2. To 3¼ in. (8.4 cm).
Range: New R. drainage, WV, VA, and NC. Common in upper New R. drainage, VA and NC; less common in WV. **Habitat:** Sandy and rocky runs and flowing pools of creeks and small to medium rivers.
Similar species: Sandbar Shiner (Pl. 11) has *narrower snout, eye directed to side,* deeper body, terminal mouth, 10–11 anal rays.   **Map 149**

WEDGESPOT SHINER *Notropis greenei*   **Pl. 12**
Identification: *Black wedge* on caudal fin base; large *upwardly* directed eye, nipple at front of pupil (Fig. 33). Large horizontal mouth; long rounded snout. Fairly compressed body, dorsal fin origin over pelvic fin origin. Gray above, scales on back and side outlined in black; wide dusky stripe along back in front of dorsal fin, thin stripe behind dorsal fin. Silver-black stripe along side, darkest at rear; punctate lateral line. Complete lateral line, 35–38 lateral scales, 8 (often 9) anal rays; pharyngeal teeth 2,4–4,2. To 3 in. (7.5 cm).
Range: Ozarkian tributaries of Mississippi, Missouri, White, and Arkansas rivers in s. MO, n. AR, and ne. OK. Fairly common. **Habitat:** Flowing pools and runs over sand, gravel, and rubble of creeks and small to medium rivers.
Similar species: Sand Shiner (Pl. 13) *lacks* black wedge on caudal fin base (often a dusky wedge), has small, outwardly directed eye, dark wedge at dorsal fin origin, 7 anal rays, pharyngeal teeth 0,4–4,0.   **Map 150**

POPEYE SHINER *Notropis ariommus*   **Pl. 11**
  Identification: *Huge eye* (largest eye of any member of genus *Notropis*), more than 1.5 × snout length. Fairly deep, compressed body; dorsal fin origin over to slightly behind pelvic fin origin; broad, moderately pointed snout; terminal mouth. Light brown above, *darkly outlined scales* on back and upper side; gray-black stripe along back; dusky stripe along silver side, darkest at rear and often expanded into black caudal spot. Complete lateral line; 35–39 lateral scales; usually 9 (often 10) anal rays; pharyngeal teeth 2,4–4,2. To 3¾ in. (9.5 cm).
  Range: Ohio R. basin from PA to IN and south to Tennessee R. drainage, GA and AL. One record from Maumee R. (Lake Erie drainage), OH; population now extirpated. Rare and highly localized. **Habitat:** Clear, gravel-bottomed, flowing pools and runs of creeks and small to medium rivers.
  Similar species: Telescope Shiner (Pl. 11) has dark stripes on upper side, punctate lateral line, more slender body, *smaller eye*, usually 10–11 anal rays.   **Map 148**

TELESCOPE SHINER *Notropis telescopus*   **Pl. 11**
  Identification: *Dark wavy stripes* along olive-brown back and upper side *meet* those of other side on caudal peduncle. *Large eye*, longer than moderately pointed snout; terminal mouth. *Punctate* (usually), complete lateral line; dusky stripe (darkest at rear) along silver side; often expanded into black caudal spot. Bold stripe along back gray-black to dorsal fin, then narrower and light gray. Fairly slender, compressed body; dorsal fin origin behind pelvic fin origin. 35–39 lateral scales; usually 10–11 anal rays; pharyngeal teeth 2,4–4,2. To 3¾ in. (9.4 cm).
  Range: Disjunct: Cumberland and Tennessee R. drainages, VA, NC, KY, TN, GA, and AL; Little, St. Francis, and White R. drainages, MO and AR. Introduced into upper New R. drainage, WV and VA. Fairly common. **Habitat:** Rocky runs and flowing pools, often near riffles, of clear creeks and small to medium rivers.
  Similar species: (1) Popeye Shiner (Pl. 11) *lacks* stripes on upper side and back, black punctations along lateral line; has deeper body, larger eye, usually 9 anal rays. (2) Tennessee Shiner (Pl. 19) has *smaller eye*, black rectangle on caudal fin base, red on large male, 8–9 anal rays; is more slender.   **Map 151**

TEXAS SHINER *Notropis amabilis*   **Pl. 11**
  Identification: *Large eye; black lips.* Clear stripe above *dark stripe* along side (darkest at rear) and onto caudal fin; dark stripe along back darkest in front of dorsal fin; darkly outlined scales above clear stripe. Slanted, terminal mouth; moderately pointed snout. Deep, compressed body; dorsal fin origin behind pelvic fin origin. Usually complete lateral line; 32–36 lateral scales; 9 anal rays; pharyngeal teeth 2,4–4,2. To 2½ in. (6.2 cm).
  Range: Colorado R. to Rio Grande (into lower Pecos R.) drainages, TX

and Mexico. Fairly common in some areas, especially in springs and spring-fed streams on Edwards Plateau. **Habitat:** Rocky and sandy runs and pools of headwaters, creeks, and small to medium rivers; usually in clear water.
Similar species: No similar species within range.   **Map 150**

ROUGHHEAD SHINER *Notropis semperasper*   **Pl. 11**
Identification: *Large eye. Black stripe* along side from head to caudal fin, darkest on rear half of body. Slender, compressed body; fairly pointed snout; slightly subterminal mouth. Dorsal fin origin behind pelvic fin origin. Dark green above, dusky iridescent stripe along back; silver side, thin iridescent green stripe above black stripe. Usually 38–41 lateral scales, 10–11 anal rays; pharyngeal teeth 2,4–4,2. To 3½ in. (9 cm).
Range: Upper James R. drainage, w. VA. Fairly common. **Habitat:** Clear rocky pools and backwaters of small to large rivers.
Similar species: (1) Comely (Pl. 11), (2) Rosyface (Pl. 19), and (3) Rosefin (Pl. 17) Shiners *lack* black stripe along side. Comely Shiner has longer, more pointed snout; Rosyface and Rosefin Shiners have smaller eye, red on body and fins (seasonally variable).   **Map 151**

SILVERBAND SHINER *Notropis shumardi*   **Pl. 11**
Identification: *Tall, pointed dorsal fin;* front rays extend well beyond rear rays when fin depressed. Compressed body; deep caudal peduncle; dorsal fin origin over to slightly behind pelvic fin origin, about *midway* between tip of snout and caudal fin base. Terminal, slightly upturned mouth on short pointed snout. Light olive above, dusky stripe along back; silver stripe along side (often dusky at rear). Complete lateral line; 33–39 lateral scales; 9 (often 8) anal rays; 9 pelvic rays (unusual in *Notropis*); pharyngeal teeth 2,4–4,2. To 4 in. (10 cm).
Range: Large rivers of Missouri-Mississippi basin (mainly Missouri, Mississippi, Illinois, Kaskaskia, lower Ohio, Arkansas, and Red rivers), from SD and cen. IL south to Gulf; Gulf Coast drainages, TX, from Sabine Lake (apparently introduced) to Colorado R. Fairly common. **Habitat:** Flowing pools and runs of large, often turbid, rivers; usually over sand and gravel.
Similar species: (1) See Silverside Shiner. (2) Emerald Shiner (Pl. 11) has *shorter* dorsal fin, with origin behind pelvic fin origin, *closer* to caudal fin base than to tip of snout; 10–12 anal rays; more slender body.   **Map 152**

SILVERSIDE SHINER *Notropis candidus*   **Not shown**
Identification: Nearly identical to Silverband Shiner, but has longer, more pointed snout, more slender body, larger eye, usually 8 anal rays. To 4½ in. (11 cm).
Range: Alabama and Tombigbee rivers and lower portions of their major tributaries, AL. **Habitat:** Sand-gravel runs of medium to large rivers.
Similar species: See Silverband Shiner (Pl. 11).   **Map 152**

BLUNTNOSE SHINER *Notropis simus*   **Pl. 12**
Identification: *Blunt snout,* often overhanging upper lip. *Deep, wide head;* large, slightly subterminal mouth usually ending under pupil. Small eye. Fairly deep, compressed body; deepest under nape; dorsal fin origin behind pelvic fin origin. Generally *pallid* with only small black specks on head and back and along silver side; sometimes slight concentration forming faint dusky stripe along side; clear fins. Incomplete lateral line (ending on caudal peduncle); 33–38 lateral scales; usually 9 (often 10) anal rays; 4–9 (usually 6–8) rakers on 1st gill arch; pharyngeal teeth 2,4–4,2. To 4 in. (10 cm).
Range: Upper Rio Grande (above El Paso, TX), TX and NM, and Pecos R., NM. Rare; has disappeared over much of former range, apparently because of reduced water levels in Rio Grande system. **Habitat:** Main channels of Rio Grande and Pecos R., usually over sand or gravel.
Remarks: Two subspecies. *N. s. simus,* known from Rio Grande above El Paso, TX, but now probably extinct, has embedded scales on breast (adults appear unscaled), slender caudal peduncle, usually 9–10 anal rays. *N. s. pecosensis,* recognized as a *threatened subspecies,* smaller (to 7.5 cm) and only in the Pecos R., NM, has fully scaled breast; relatively deep caudal peduncle; usually 8–9 anal rays; more pigment, including a broader dusky stripe and thin black streak along side.
Similar species: (1) See Phantom Shiner. (2) Tamaulipas Shiner (Pl. 12) has larger eye, darker stripe along side, usually 7 anal rays, pharyngeal teeth 1,4–4,1.   **Map 152**

PHANTOM SHINER *Notropis orca*   **Not shown**
Identification: Similar to Bluntnose Shiner, but has mouth ending *in front* of eye pupil, less arched back, relatively deeper caudal peduncle, usually 8 anal rays (within range of Phantom Shiner, Bluntnose Shiner usually has 9–10 rays), usually 9–10 (range is 8–11) rakers on 1st gill arch. To 3½ in. (9 cm).
Range: Rio Grande from mouth to n.-cen. NM (unknown from Pecos R.). Near extinction. **Habitat:** Main channel of Rio Grande, usually over sand and often in turbid water.
Similar species: See Bluntnose Shiner (Pl. 12).   **Map 153**

RIVER SHINER *Notropis blennius*   **Pl. 10**
Identification: Slender, fairly compressed body; mouth extends to *beneath front of eye,* uniformly dark *stripe* along back and encircling dorsal fin base. Moderately pointed snout, usually overhanging slightly subterminal mouth. Dorsal fin origin over or slightly behind pelvic fin origin. Straw-colored above, scales on upper side faintly outlined; dusky stripe along rear half of silver side. Scaled (or mostly scaled) breast. Complete lateral line; 34–41 (usually 35–36) lateral scales, 7 anal rays; pharyngeal teeth 2,4–4,2 (often 1,4–4,1). To 5¼ in. (13 cm).
Range: Hudson Bay basin from MB to AB (absent in e. SK), and south through Red R., MN and ND. Mississippi R. basin from WI and MN south to Gulf; occurs as far east as WV and as far west as e. CO. Common in cen. part of range, especially upper Mississippi and lower

Ohio rivers. **Habitat:** Pools and main channels of medium to large rivers, usually over sand and gravel.
Similar species: (1) Mississippi Silvery (Pl. 10), (2) Western Silvery, and (3) Plains Minnows have much *smaller mouth,* extending only about ½ distance from tip of snout to eye; long gut (and soft belly); dorsal fin origin in front of pelvic fin origin; 8 anal rays. (4) Sand Shiner (Pl. 13) has thin stripe along back *expanded* at dorsal fin origin, not encircling dorsal fin; punctate lateral line; smaller mouth.   **Map 154**

FLUVIAL SHINER *Notropis edwardraneyi*   **Pl. 10**
Identification: Very *large,* round eye (eye longer than snout), somewhat directed *upwardly. Pallid;* slightly dusky above with thin dark stripe along back; silver side; clear falcate fins. Fairly slender, compressed body; deepest just in front of dorsal fin. Dorsal fin origin in front of pelvic fin origin, 1st ray reaching beyond rest of fin when pressed against back. Terminal to slightly subterminal mouth; moderately pointed snout. Unscaled breast. Complete lateral line. 32–35 lateral scales, usually 7 anal rays; pharyngeal teeth 2,4–4,2. To 3¼ in. (8 cm).
Range: Mobile Bay drainage, AL and MS; mostly below Fall Line. Locally abundant. **Habitat:** Main channels, usually with current, of small to large rivers; often over sand or gravel.
Similar species: (1) River Shiner (Pl. 10) has *smaller, less upwardly directed eye;* is more darkly pigmented. (2) Skygazer Shiner (Pl. 13), with upwardly directed eye, is much more slender, has black pigment along lateral line and outlining upper scales, black wedge on caudal fin base, pharyngeal teeth 0,4–4,0.   **Map 154**

CHUB SHINER *Notropis potteri*   **Pl. 10**
Identification: *Head flat* above and below, tapering into pronounced snout (very wide viewed from above). Eye *high on head* and somewhat *directed upward.* Slightly subterminal mouth. Dorsal fin originating in front of or over pelvic fin origin; long and pointed, with 1st rays reaching beyond rest of fin when depressed against body. Moderately compressed body, deepest just in front of dorsal fin. Dull olive to tan above, thin dusky stripe along back; scales on back and upper side faintly outlined; scattered black specks along silver side, concentrated into black streak on rear half; orange along top of eye. Complete (or at least to caudal peduncle) lateral line; 34–37 lateral scales; usually 7 anal rays; pharyngeal teeth 2,4–4,2. To 4¼ in. (11 cm).
Range: Red and Brazos R. drainages, LA, AR, OK, and TX; lower Mississippi R., LA (near mouth of Red. R.), San Jacinto, Trinity, and Colorado rivers, TX. Fairly common in mainstream of Red R.; localized elsewhere. **Habitat:** Sand and gravel runs of small to large rivers; tolerant of turbidity.
Similar species: (1) Smalleye and (2) Red River Shiners (Pl. 10) have black specks concentrated in patch on side, eye directed more to side than upwardly, shorter snout, pharyngeal teeth 0,4–4,0. (3) River Shiner (Pl. 10) has larger eye located more on side of head, duskier back and side, more pointed snout.   **Map 153**

RED RIVER SHINER *Notropis bairdi* **Pl. 10**
Identification: *Broad, flat head;* large, nearly terminal mouth (ending behind front of eye); rounded snout. Round eye high on head. Black specks scattered over back and upper side, concentrated in *large patch* on front half of side. Tan above, thin dusky stripe along back; silver side, often with light blue iridescence. Compressed body, deepest under nape; arched back; dorsal fin origin in front of pelvic fin origin. Breast and nape partly unscaled. Lateral line usually with several interruptions; 33–37 lateral scales; usually 7 anal rays, 15 pectoral rays; pharyngeal teeth 0,4–4,0. To 3¼ in. (8 cm).
Range: Red R. drainage from sw. AR to w. OK and nw. TX. Abundant in w. part of range, especially sw. OK; less common elsewhere. Introduced into Cimarron R. (Arkansas R. drainage), s. KS and OK, and now more common there than related, native Arkansas River Shiner.
Habitat: Sandy, turbid channels of small to large rivers.
Similar species: See (1) Smalleye and (2) Arkansas River Shiners.
Map 155

SMALLEYE SHINER *Notropis buccula* **Not shown**
Identification: Nearly identical to Red River Shiner but has longer snout, smaller eye (mouth ends in *front* of eye); shallower head. To 2¾ in. (7.1 cm).
Range: Brazos R. drainage, TX. Apparently introduced into adjacent Colorado R. drainage, TX. Rare; sporadically distributed. **Habitat:** Sandy, turbid channels of small to large rivers.
Similar species: See (1) Red River (Pl. 10) and (2) Arkansas River Shiners.
Map 155

ARKANSAS RIVER SHINER *Notropis girardi* **Not shown**
Identification: Similar to Red River and Smalleye Shiners, but has *fully scaled* breast and nape; usually 8 anal rays, 14 pectoral rays; larger and more falcate fins. To 3¼ in. (8 cm).
Range: Arkansas R. drainage from w. AR to w. KS, w. OK, TX panhandle, and ne. NM. Introduced into Pecos R., NM. Common. **Habitat:** Flowing water over sand in creeks and small to large rivers.
Similar species: See (1) Red River (Pl. 10) and (2) Smalleye Shiners.
Map 155

ROUGH SHINER *Notropis baileyi* **Pl. 19**
Identification: *Red-brown above;* often red on side and at fin bases. Smooth, even-edged brown-black stripe along side *uniformly dark* from tip of lower jaw to caudal fin base; black caudal spot; *yellow fins;* silver-green below. Breeding male has hump behind head, bright yellow fins (sometimes washed with red), silver side; is bright red-orange below. Fairly deep, compressed body; deepest just before dorsal fin; dorsal fin origin over or in front of pelvic fin origin. Fairly long, rounded snout; terminal mouth. 33–38 lateral scales; usually 12 scales around caudal peduncle, 7 anal rays; pharyngeal teeth 2,4–4,2. To 3½ in. (9 cm).
Range: Mobile Bay and Pascagoula R. drainages, mostly below Fall

Line, AL and MS; Bear Cr. system (Tennessee R. drainage), AL and MS. Also present (and possibly introduced) in Escambia R. drainage, AL and FL, and Chattahoochee R. drainage, GA. Common. **Habitat:** Sand- and gravel-bottomed flowing pools of headwaters, creeks, and small rivers.

Similar species: See (1) Yellowfin and (2) Greenhead Shiners (both, Pl. 19).
Map 156

YELLOWFIN SHINER *Notropis lutipinnis*   **Pl. 19**
Identification: Similar to Rough Shiner, but *lacks* distinct caudal spot; has dorsal fin origin *behind* pelvic fin origin, longer snout, 8 anal rays, usually 14–16 scales around caudal peduncle. Breeding male has yellow (in Broad R. system) to red fins (in Savannah and Altamaha R. systems). Pharyngeal teeth 2,4–4,2 (see Remarks). To 3 in. (7.5 cm).
Range: Atlantic and Gulf slopes from Santee R., NC, to Altamaha R., upper Chattahoochee R., and upper Coosa R. systems, GA. Little Tennessee R. system (Tennessee R. drainage), NC. Common to abundant in mountain and upper Piedmont streams; less common on lower Piedmont. **Habitat:** Clear rocky pools of headwaters, creeks and small rivers.
Remarks: Minnows identifiable as Yellowfin Shiners in the Broad R. system are intermediate morphologically (yellow fins; high frequencies of both 1,4–4,1 and 2,4–4,2 pharyngeal tooth counts) and geographically between other populations of Yellowfin Shiners and the Greenhead Shiner. They should perhaps be considered intergrades between 2 subspecies (in which case the Yellowfin Shiner becomes *N. chlorocephalus lutipinnis*).
Similar species: See (1) Rough and (2) Greenhead Shiners (both, Pl. 19).
Map 156

GREENHEAD SHINER *Notropis chlorocephalus*   **Pl. 19**
Identification: Similar to Yellowfin Shiner but with pharyngeal teeth 1,4–4,1; breeding male is scarlet red, has green head and bright *white fins*. 36–39 lateral scales; 8 anal rays. To 2¾ in. (7.2 cm).
Range: Catawba R. system (Santee R. drainage), NC and SC. Abundant. **Habitat:** Rocky flowing pools of clear headwaters, creeks, and small rivers.
Similar species: See Yellowfin Shiner (Pl. 19).
Map 156

REDLIP SHINER *Notropis chiliticus*   **Pl. 19**
Identification: *Bright red lips; scattered black blotches* on side; black stripe on rear half of silver side leading to black caudal spot. Gold-green stripe along light green back and another along upper side; black specks on lower ⅓ of dorsal fin. Large individual has red body and eye, yellow fins; breeding male has scarlet red body, bright yellow-gold head and fins. Slender compressed body; dorsal fin origin slightly behind pelvic fin origin. Large eye; rounded snout; slightly subterminal mouth. Complete lateral line; 34–37 lateral scales; 8 anal rays. To 2¾ in. (7.2 cm).
Range: Dan R. (Roanoke R. drainage) and Peedee R. drainages, VA and

NC. Recently introduced and possibly established in New R. drainage, NC and VA. Abundant in mountain streams; common on Piedmont. **Habitat:** Rocky flowing pools of clear headwaters, creeks and small rivers.

Similar species: See Pl. 19. (1) See Saffron Shiner. (2) Greenhead and (3) Yellowfin Shiners lack red lips, black blotches on side; large male Greenhead Shiner has red head, white fins.   **Map 156**

SAFFRON SHINER *Notropis rubricroceus*   **Pl. 19**
Identification: Similar to Redlip Shiner, but has *clear spot* (absent on Redlip Shiner) on body at rear of dorsal fin, black stripe along side *dark from head to caudal fin*, darkly outlined scales (barely outlined on Redlip Shiner) *below* black stripe, *no* (or few) *black specks* on dorsal fin; is more slender. To 3¼ in. (8.4 cm).
Range: Mountainous area drained by upper Tennessee R. drainage, VA, NC, and TN; headwaters of Santee and Savannah rivers, NC. Introduced into New R. drainage, VA and NC. Common. **Habitat:** Bedrock- and rubble-bottomed pools of clear, fast headwaters and creeks.
Similar species: See Redlip Shiner (Pl. 19).   **Map 156**

RAINBOW SHINER *Notropis chrosomus*   **Pl. 19**
Identification: *Iridescent blue and pink head and body* (large individual). *Clear to red-purple stripe* above silver-black stripe along side. Dusky purple above, scales darkly outlined; white below; faint to bright red-orange fins. Breeding male has bright purple head, back, and fins; red-purple stripe above, light blue below, silver stripe along side. Compressed body; dorsal fin origin over or slightly behind pelvic fin origin. Round snout, terminal mouth, moderate eye (shorter than snout length). Lateral line complete or missing on only last 4–5 scales; 34–38 lateral scales; usually 8 anal rays; pharyngeal teeth 2,4–4,2. To 3¼ in. (8.1 cm).
Range: Coosa, Cahaba, Alabama, and extreme upper Black Warrior R. systems (all Mobile Bay drainage), nw. GA, AL, and se. TN. Fairly common, especially in spring-fed streams in Coosa R. system. **Habitat:** Gravelly riffles and pools (sometimes sandy pools) of creeks and small rivers.
Similar species: (1) Coosa Shiner (Pl. 13) *lacks* bright colors, has dark stripe along back, larger eye, 7 anal rays. (2) Burrhead Shiner (Pl. 13) *lacks* bright colors; has black stripe around longer snout, 7 anal rays; is more slender. (3) Tennessee Shiner (Pl. 19) is more slender; has pointed snout, larger eye, dark stripe along back midline, clear to white stripe above dark stripe obliterated at front, red on large male.   **Map 157**

TENNESSEE SHINER *Notropis leuciodus*   **Pl. 19**
Identification: *Dark wavy stripes* on olive back and upper side *meet* those of other side on caudal peduncle. Silver-black stripe along side often faint at front, dark at rear, and followed by distinct *black rectangle* on caudal fin base. *Punctate lateral line* extends below dark stripe on front half of body. Black stripe along back darkest before

dorsal fin, then narrower and lighter. Slender, fairly compressed body; dorsal fin origin behind pelvic fin origin. Pointed snout, terminal mouth; fairly large eye. Breeding male is *red overall*. Complete lateral line; 36–39 lateral scales; usually 8–9 anal rays; pharyngeal teeth 1,4–4,1. To 3¼ in. (8.2 cm).

Range: Green, Cumberland, and Tennessee R. drainages, VA, NC, KY, TN, GA, and AL. Abundant in upper Tennessee R. drainage, NC and e. TN; less common elsewhere. Absent in Cumberland R. drainage above Big South Fork; in Green R. drainage restricted to extreme upper Green and upper Barren systems. Also in extreme upper Savannah R. drainage, NC and GA, and New R. drainage, VA and NC (the latter may be a bait-bucket introduction). **Habitat:** Rocky pools and runs of creeks and small to medium rivers.

Similar species: (1) Rainbow Shiner (Pl. 19) *lacks* punctate lateral line; has more rounded snout and pink, purple, and blue on head and body. (2) Telescope Shiner (Pl. 11) *lacks* black rectangle at base of caudal fin; often has dark oval just before caudal fin, red on large male; has larger eye, deeper body, 10 anal rays. **Map 157**

OZARK MINNOW *Notropis nubilus* Pl. 19

Identification: *Strongly bicolored*, dark olive-brown above, white to yellow-orange below. Thin pale stripe above *black stripe* along silver side and around snout; punctate lateral line; often a small black spot on caudal fin base. *Black lining* of body cavity often visible through belly. Gold spots on dark stripe along back; clear fins. Large individual is yellow-orange below, has yellow fins (brighter on male). Slender body, barely compressed; slightly subterminal mouth; large eye; dorsal fin origin over pelvic fin origin; long, coiled gut (at least twice length of body). 33–38 lateral scales; 8 anal rays; pharyngeal teeth 0,4–4,0. To 3¾ in. (9.3 cm).

Range: Disjunct populations in upper Red Cedar R. system, n. WI; Mississippi R. tributaries in se. MN, e. IA, s. WI, and n. IL; Ozark Mountain drainages (Mississippi, Missouri, White, and Arkansas R. drainages) in s. MO, se. KS, n. AR, and ne. OK; and Boggy Cr. system, OK. Common (locally abundant) in southern part of range (except perhaps extinct in Boggy Cr. system); uncommon in north. **Habitat:** Gravel- and rubble-bottomed flowing pools and backwaters of creeks and small to medium rivers; rarely in large rivers. **Map 157**

LONGNOSE SHINER *Notropis longirostris* Pl. 19

Identification: *Small, upwardly directed eyes; long rounded snout; large, subterminal mouth.* Slender compressed body, *flattened below;* dorsal fin origin in front of pelvic fin origin. Straw yellow to gray above, faintly outlined scales, dark streak along back; silver side (blue iridescence); *yellow fins.* Large male has bright yellow to orange fins and snout. Complete lateral line; 34–37 lateral scales; 7 anal rays; pharyngeal teeth 1,4–4,1. To 2½ in. (6.5 cm).

Range: Upper Altamaha R. drainage (Atlantic Slope), GA; Gulf Slope drainages from Apalachicola R., GA and FL, to Mississippi R., LA (except Mobile Bay — see Remarks); north in Mississippi R. basin to Big Black R., MS, and lower Ouachita R. drainage, LA. Common; locally

abundant. **Habitat:** Sandy, sometimes muddy, shallow runs and pools of creeks and small to medium rivers.
Remarks: A closely related, undescribed species occurs in the Yazoo R. system, MS.
Similar species: (1) See Orangefin Shiner (Pl. 19). (2) Sabine Shiner (Pl. 19) has deep, arched body; pharyngeal teeth 0,4–4,0.   **Map 158**

ORANGEFIN SHINER *Notropis ammophilus*   Pl. 19

Identification: Similar to Longnose Shiner, but has dorsal fin origin *over* pelvic fin origin; *orange snout and fins* on large male; pharyngeal teeth 0,4–4,0. To 2¼ in. (6 cm).
Range: Mobile Bay drainage (primarily below the Fall Line), AL and MS; Yellow Cr. (Tennessee R. drainage), MS; Hatchie R. and Skuna R. drainages, TN and MS. Common. **Habitat:** Shallow sandy runs and pools of creeks and small to medium rivers.
Similar species: See Longnose Shiner (Pl. 19).   **Map 158**

SABINE SHINER *Notropis sabinae*   Pl. 19

Identification: Deep, compressed, *strongly arched body*; deepest at dorsal fin origin, *flattened below*. Large, horizontal, *subterminal mouth; long rounded snout*. Small eye directed slightly upwardly. Dorsal fin origin in front of pelvic fin origin. Olive-yellow above, faintly outlined scales, dark streak along back; silver side; punctate (often faint) lateral line; head dark above and under eye; white cheek. Complete lateral line; 31–37 lateral scales; 7 anal rays; pharyngeal teeth 0,4–4,0 (often 1,4–4,1). To 2¼ in. (5.7 cm).
Range: Disjunct: St. Francis and lower White (including lower Black) R. drainages, MO and AR; Little R. system (lower Red. R. drainage), LA; and Gulf Coast drainages from Calcasieu R., LA, to San Jacinto R., TX. Locally common. **Habitat:** Sandy runs and flowing pools of creeks and small to medium rivers.
Similar species: (1) Longnose and (2) Orangefin Shiners (both, Pl. 19) have much more *slender body*; yellow or orange snout and fins; lack dark area under eye. Longnose Shiner has pharyngeal teeth 1,4–4,1. (3) Chub Shiner (Pl. 10) has *pointed snout*, head flattened *above* and below, nearly terminal mouth, black specks on side.   **Map 158**

BIGMOUTH SHINER *Notropis dorsalis*   Pl. 13

Identification: *Upwardly directed eyes*; head *flattened* below; long snout; large subterminal mouth. Slender, *strongly arched body*; dorsal fin origin over pelvic fin origin. Punctate lateral line (front half). Light tan to olive above, dark stripe along back; faintly outlined scales on back and upper side; silver side. Complete lateral line; 33–39 lateral scales; 8 anal rays; pharyngeal teeth 1,4–4,1. To 3¼ in. (8 cm).
Range: Great Lakes, Hudson Bay (Red R.), and Mississippi R. basins from n. MI to s. MB, and from e. IL to Platte R. system, e. WY and n. CO; disjunct populations in w. NY and PA, n. WV, n. OH, and w. MI. Common over much of range. **Habitat:** Shallow sandy and silty runs and pools of headwaters, creeks, and small to medium rivers.

Remarks: Three subspecies sometimes recognized but in need of study. *N. d. piptolepis*, in Platte R. system, WY and CO, has no, or embedded, scales on nape. *N. d. keimi*, in Lake Ontario and Allegheny R. drainages, NY and PA, has relatively short snout and small mouth. *N. d. dorsalis*, elsewhere in range, has exposed scales on nape, a long snout and large mouth.

Similar species: (1) Silverjaw Minnow (Pl. 9) has pearl organs on cheek and underside of head. (2) Sand Shiner (Pl. 13) *lacks* upwardly directed eyes, flattened head; has dark wedge at dorsal fin origin, 7 anal rays.   **Map 158**

BLACKCHIN SHINER *Notropis heterodon*   Pl. 13

Identification: *Black stripe* along side and around short, *pointed snout;* concentrations of blackest pigment at lateral-line pores give a *zigzag* appearance to black stripe, at least on front half of body. Dusky to black lips and chin (Fig. 34). Olive to pale yellow above,

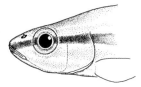

Blackchin

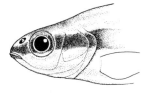

Ironcolor

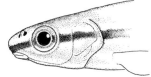

Blacknose

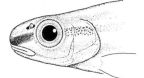

Whitemouth

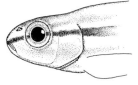

Pugnose

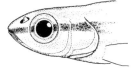

Bridle

Fig. 34 Blackchin, Ironcolor, Blacknose, Whitemouth, Pugnose, and Bridle Shiners

scales darkly outlined except pale stripe above dark stripe along side; dusky stripe along back darker and much wider in front of dorsal fin; silver side. Fairly compressed body; slender caudal peduncle; dorsal fin origin over to slightly in front of pelvic fin origin. Oblique mouth (rear edge to below nostril). Lateral line usually incomplete. 34–38 lateral scales; 8, often 7, anal rays; pharyngeal teeth 1,4–4,1. To 2¾ in. (7.1 cm).

Range: S. QU and VT west to MN and IA. Mostly restricted to Great Lakes and upper Mississippi R. basins but localized in a few Atlantic drainages (St. Lawrence, Hudson, Susquehanna rivers), upper Ohio R. basin, and Hudson Bay basin (Red R., MN). Generally common. **Habitat:** Clear, vegetated lakes; pools and slow runs of creeks and small rivers. Usually over sand.

Similar species: (1) Bigeye Shiner (Pl. 13) has larger mouth — rear edge almost to front of eye; larger eye, black peritoneum, complete lateral line. (2) Blacknose Shiner (Pl. 12) is more slender; has a smaller subterminal mouth, no black on lower lip and chin, dorsal fin origin behind pelvic fin origin; pharyngeal teeth 0,4–4,0. **Map 159**

BIGEYE SHINER Notropis boops Pl. 13

Identification: *Large eye*, much longer than snout. *Clear stripe* above *black stripe* along silver side and *around snout* (on both lips); lateral line punctate on front half of body. Slender, fairly compressed body; dorsal fin origin over pelvic fin origin. Fairly long, moderately pointed snout; large terminal mouth (rear edge almost to eye). Olive-yellow above, thin dark stripe along back; darkly outlined scales on back and upper side. Complete lateral line; 34–40 lateral scales; black peritoneum; 8 anal rays; pharyngeal teeth 1,4–4,1. To 3½ in. (9 cm).

Range: Lake Erie drainage, nw. OH; Mississippi R. basin from cen. OH to e. KS and south to n. AL, n. LA, and s. OK. Mostly confined to upland areas. Common; abundant in Ozark-Ouachita drainages; absent from most of Former Mississippi Embayment. Disappearing from large areas, including most of OH and IL, because of increased siltation. **Habitat:** Flowing, usually clear and rocky, pools of creeks and small to medium rivers; often near emergent vegetation along the stream margin.

Similar species: (1) Blackchin Shiner (Pl. 13) has smaller mouth (to below nostril), smaller eye, incomplete lateral line, silver peritoneum. (2) Coosa Shiner (Pl. 13) has large black caudal spot, 7 anal rays, pharyngeal teeth 2,4–4,2. **Map 159**

COOSA SHINER Notropis xaenocephalus Pl. 13

Identification: *Clear to yellow stripe* above dark stripe along side; dark stripe extends onto side of head, expanded into *large black caudal spot*. Large eye (about as long as snout); fairly long, fairly blunt snout; black lips; terminal mouth. Fairly slender, compressed body; dorsal fin origin over pelvic fin origin. Dusky straw yellow above, darkly outlined scales; dark stripe along middle of back in front of dorsal fin, dark streaks behind dorsal fin; silver side. Complete lateral line; 33–38 lateral scales; 7 anal rays; pharyngeal teeth 2,4–4,2. To 3 in. (7.9 cm).

Range: Above Fall Line in Coosa and Tallapoosa R. systems (Mobile Bay drainage), se. TN, nw. GA, and e. AL. Common. One (apparently introduced) population in Chestatee R. (upper Chattahoochee R. drainage), GA. **Habitat:** Clear, gravel-bottomed pools and runs; common in spring-fed streams.

Similar species: (1) Rainbow Shiner (Pl. 19) is bright purple and blue; lacks dark stripe along back; has *smaller eye,* 8 anal rays. (2) Burrhead Shiner (Pl. 13) has black stripe around longer snout, is more slender, lacks (or has only faint) dark stripe along back. **Map 159**

BURRHEAD SHINER *Notropis asperifrons* Pl. 13

Identification: *Clear to yellow-orange stripe* above dark stripe along side; dark stripe extends around *long rounded snout* (and lips and chin) and expands into black spot on caudal fin base. Slightly subterminal mouth; large eye. Slender, compressed body; dorsal fin origin over to slightly behind pelvic fin origin. Dusky yellow above, darkly outlined scales; black specks above and below lateral-line pores; silver-white below. Complete lateral line; 33–39 lateral scales; usually 7 anal rays; pharyngeal teeth 2,4–4,2. To 3 in. (7.5 cm).

Range: Alabama and Black Warrior R. systems, se. TN, nw. GA, and AL. Mostly above Fall Line; fairly common but localized. **Habitat:** Rocky and sandy pools and runs of creeks and small rivers.

Similar species: (1) Coosa Shiner (Pl. 13) *lacks* dark stripe around snout (but has black lips); has shorter snout, dark stripe along back; is deeper bodied. (2) Rainbow Shiner (Pl. 19) is bright purple and blue (when large); lacks dark stripe around *shorter snout;* has 8 anal rays. **Map 160**

SKYGAZER SHINER *Notropis uranoscopus* Pl. 13

Identification: Large *elliptical eye,* high on head. Small *black wedge* on caudal fin base; punctate lateral line (obscured by dark stripe along rear half of side). 2 dark crescents between nostrils (see Fig. 32). Slender, compressed body; dorsal fin origin slightly behind pelvic fin origin. Somewhat flattened head; long, fairly pointed snout; slightly subterminal mouth. Straw yellow above, scales fairly darkly outlined; silver-white below. Gold stripe above dark stripe along side in large individual. Complete lateral line; 34–37 lateral scales; 7 anal rays; pharyngeal teeth 0,4–4,0. To 2¾ in. (7.1 cm).

Range: Alabama R. drainage, AL. Restricted to Cahaba R., Uphapee Cr. (Tallapoosa R. system), and Alabama R. in Dallas and Wilcox cos. Fairly common in Cahaba R., uncommon elsewhere. **Habitat:** Gravelly runs, often near riffles, of small to large rivers. **Map 131**

HIGHSCALE SHINER *Notropis hypsilepis* Pl. 13

Identification: *Small black wedge* on caudal fin base. Large round eye high on head. *Blunt snout;* small, subterminal, nearly horizontal mouth. Clear to white stripe above dusky to black stripe along side. Exposed area of scales near front of lateral line much deeper than wide. Slender, compressed body; dorsal fin origin over (or slightly behind) pelvic fin origin. Dusky above, darkly outlined scales, dark streaks along midline of back in front of dorsal fin; silver side. Complete lateral line; usually 35–36 lateral scales, 7 anal rays; pharyngeal teeth 2,4–4,2. To 2½ in. (6.4 cm).

Range: Appalachicola R. drainage, GA and e. AL; one locality in upper Savannah R. drainage, ne. GA. Most common on Piedmont; rarely found in large populations. **Habitat:** Sandy runs and pools of creeks and small rivers.

Similar species: Clear Chub has dorsal fin origin in front of pelvic fin origin; longer, *more pointed snout;* smaller, more subterminal mouth; *lacks* black wedge on caudal fin base. **Map 160**

WEED SHINER *Notropis texanus* **Pl. 13**

Identification: *Black stripe* along side and around snout (on both lips); some *black-edged scales* below black stripe; often a clear stripe between black stripe and black-edged scales on upper side and back. Black spot on caudal fin base connected to, or barely separated from, black stripe; often streaking to end of caudal fin. Dark stripe along back much *wider in front of* than behind dorsal fin; often expanded into blotch in front of dorsal fin. Fairly compressed body; dorsal fin origin in front of pelvic fin origin. Fairly blunt snout; small (rear edge under nostril) terminal mouth. Olive-yellow above, silver side; clear to light red (in southern populations) fins; in Gulf Slope populations *last 3–4 anal rays lined with black* (other rays clear). Complete or nearly complete lateral line; 32–39 lateral scales; usually 7 anal rays; pharyngeal teeth 2,4–4,2. To 3½ in. (8.6 cm).

Range: Lowlands in Great Lakes, Hudson Bay (Red R.), and Mississippi R. basins from MI, WI, and MN south to Gulf; Gulf Slope drainages from Suwannee R., GA and FL, to Nueces R., TX. Common in south, uncommon and localized in north. **Habitat:** Sandy runs and pools of creeks and small to medium rivers. Usually in clear water; in north often found near vegetation.

Remarks: Individuals in north tend to be deeper bodied and more yellow, to have black spot on caudal fin base continuous with black stripe along side, and to lack black along anal fin rays.

Similar species: (1) See Coastal Shiner (Pl. 13). (2) Coosa Shiner (Pl. 13) is more slender, has large black spot on caudal fin base, no black along anal rays. (3) Blackchin and (4) Bigeye Shiners (both, Pl. 13) have pointed snout, dorsal fin origin over pelvic fin origin, usually 8 anal rays; pharyngeal teeth 1,4–4,1. **Map 161**

COASTAL SHINER *Notropis petersoni* **Pl. 13**

Identification: Similar to Weed Shiner but *lacks* black-edged scales on side below black stripe, has *all* anal rays lined with black, a wedge-shaped spot on caudal fin base, a longer, more overhanging snout; is more compressed. Individuals from tannin-colored ("black") water are darkly pigmented, pink below; have light yellow to light pink stripe on upper side. To 3¼ in. (8.2 cm).

Range: Atlantic and Gulf Slope drainages from Cape Fear R., NC, to

Jordan R., MS. Restricted to Coastal Plain on Gulf Slope; more widespread on Atlantic Slope; throughout FL except extreme s. tip. Common. **Habitat:** Over sand in pools and backwaters of creeks and small to large rivers, spring effluents, lakes.
Similar species: See Weed Shiner (Pl. 13).   **Map 160**

KIAMICHI SHINER *Notropis ortenburgeri*   **Pl. 11**
Identification: Light olive above, *pale stripe* above silver-black stripe along side; black stripe continues around snout (across chin); *dark-edged scales* on back. *Strongly upturned mouth.* Compressed body, deepest at dorsal fin origin; strongly tapering to narrow caudal peduncle. Dorsal fin origin slightly behind pelvic fin origin; large eye. 35–37 lateral scales; 9–10 anal rays; pharyngeal teeth 0,4–4,0. To 2¼ in. (5.5 cm).
Range: Upper Ouachita, Arkansas, and Red R. drainages; sw. AR and e. OK. Uncommon. **Habitat:** Rocky, flowing pools of clear creeks and small rivers.
Similar species: (1) See Blackmouth Shiner. (2) Bigeye Shiner (Pl. 13) has less arched body, *more horizontal mouth*, bigger eye, 8 anal rays, pharyngeal teeth 1,4–4,1.   **Map 162**

BLACKMOUTH SHINER *Notropis melanostomus*   **Not shown**
Identification: Nearly identical to Kiamichi Shiner but has *usually 10–12 anal rays*. To 1½ in. (3.8 cm).
Range: Blackwater–Yellow R. system (Pensacola Bay drainage), FL. Uncommon. **Habitat:** Backwaters and quiet pools of creeks and small rivers. Usually found over mud near vegetation.
Similar species: See Kiamichi Shiner (Pl. 11).   **Map 162**

PEPPERED SHINER *Notropis perpallidus*   **Pl. 12**
Identification: Mostly translucent but with *many black spots* on back, head, and along side; 2 parallel *black dashes* just in front of dorsal fin; black on lips, base of dorsal (rear half) and anal fins, along rear half of side; some black along dorsal, caudal, and pectoral fin rays. Slender, compressed body; pointed snout; dorsal fin origin well behind pelvic fin origin. 9–10 anal rays, 32–35 lateral scales; pharyngeal teeth 2,4–4,2. To 2 in. (5 cm).
Range: Ouachita and Red R. drainages, s. AR and se. OK; in Red R. drainage restricted to Little and Kiamichi R. systems. Uncommon. **Habitat:** Pools and sluggish runs of small to medium rivers; often in quiet water near vegetation.
Similar species: Other small minnows with black spots are (1) Chihuahua Shiner (Pl. 12), with rounded snout, black wedge on caudal fin base, 7–8 anal rays, less compressed body; and (2) Speckled Chub (Pl. 9), with large barbels, wide body, dorsal fin origin over pelvic fin origin.   **Map 150**

IRONCOLOR SHINER *Notropis chalybaeus*   **Pl. 20**
Identification: *Black stripe* from spot on caudal fin base along side and *around snout*, covering both lips and chin (Fig. 34); *black inside*

mouth. Large eye (longer than snout). Compressed body, deepest (and usually arched) at dorsal fin origin, which is over pelvic fin origin; slender caudal peduncle. Pointed snout; small, oblique terminal mouth. Straw yellow above, dusky stripe along back widest and darkest in front of dorsal fin. Scales above darkly outlined except just above black stripe where gold-orange streak may be present. Silver-white below. Breeding male has orange-gold body and fins. Usually incomplete lateral line; 31–37 lateral scales; 8 anal rays; pharyngeal teeth 2,4–4,2. To 2½ in. (6.5 cm).

Range: Lowlands of Atlantic, Gulf, and Mississippi R. basins, from Hudson R., NY, to s. FL, and across Gulf Slope to Pearl R., LA; also in Sabine R., LA and TX, and north in Former Mississippi Embayment (on west side of Mississippi R. only) to se. MO; extends up Red R. drainage to se. OK. Isolated populations in San Marcos R., TX, Illinois R. drainage, IL and IN, Cedar R., IA (now extirpated), Wisconsin R., WI, Lake Winnebago system, WI, and the Lake Michigan drainage of s. MI and n. IN. Generally common. **Habitat:** Clear, vegetated, sand-bottomed pools and slow runs of creeks and small rivers.

Similar species: Often collected with Weed Shiner (Pl. 13) which also has black stripe on side but has black-edged scales above and *below* lateral line, less compressed and arched body, blunter snout, 7 anal rays. **Map 163**

DUSKY SHINER *Notropis cummingsae* **Pl. 20**

Identification: Wide *black stripe* along silver side from tip of snout and lips to caudal fin where expanded into black spot *streaking* backward on caudal fin; lower edge of stripe fuzzy (not sharply defined), extending below lateral line throughout. *Compressed* body; dorsal fin origin behind pelvic fin origin; mouth slightly subterminal. Dusky yellow-brown above, scales barely outlined in dark brown; dark stripe along back, darkest in front of dorsal fin. Light yellow to orange (on large male) stripe above dark stripe along side. Fins clear to pale orange (on large male). Usually 37–39 lateral scales, 10–11 anal rays; pharyngeal teeth 1,4–4,1. To 2¾ in. (7.2 cm).

Range: Atlantic and Gulf slopes in three disjunct areas: Tar R. drainage, NC, to Altamaha R. drainage, GA; St. Johns R. drainage, FL; Aucilla R. drainage to Choctawhatchee R. drainage, FL and AL. Generally common on Coastal Plain, uncommon on Piedmont. **Habitat:** Pools and runs over sand and mud, usually in clear or tannin-stained creeks and small rivers.

Similar species: (1) Highfin Shiner (Pl. 20) has narrower, *more diffuse* dark stripe along side not extending below lowest part of lateral line; no dark stripe (thin streaks may be present) along back in front of dorsal fin; boldly outlined scales on back; pharyngeal teeth 2,4–4,2. (2) Ironcolor Shiner (Pl. 20) has narrower blacker stripe along side with upper and lower edges sharply defined, is less compressed, has dorsal fin origin over pelvic fin origin; usually 8 anal rays. **Map 164**

REDEYE CHUB *Notropis harperi* **Pl. 20**

Identification: *Pink-tan above; red eye;* dark stripe along side and around snout and upper lip, followed by black spot on caudal fin base; light stripe above dark stripe extends onto snout as a *yellow arc*; dusky stripe along back; dark-edged scales on back and upper side; white to cream below. Small barbel (often absent) at corner of subterminal mouth. Slender, fairly compressed body; rounded snout; dorsal fin origin slightly behind pelvic fin origin. 30–38 lateral scales; 8 anal rays; pharyngeal teeth 0,4–4,0. To 2¼ in. (6 cm).

Range: Below Fall Line in Atlantic and Gulf Slope drainages from Altamaha R., GA, to Escambia R., AL; south in FL to St. Johns and Withlacoochee R. drainages. Locally common; absent from some drainages within range; abundant in prime habitat. **Habitat:** Springs, spring-fed headwaters, and creeks.

Similar species: Other minnows *lack* light-colored arc on snout.
Map 165

HIGHFIN SHINER *Notropis altipinnis* Pl. 20

Identification: *Boldly outlined scales* on back, separated from *diffuse silver-black stripe* along side of body by sharply edged, clear to yellow stripe. Dark stripe extends from lips to base of caudal fin, where slightly darkened into black spot streaking backward on caudal fin. Stripe not extending below lowest part of lateral line. Compressed body; deepest at dorsal fin origin which is slightly behind pelvic fin origin. *Large eye* (longer than snout); terminal mouth; somewhat rounded snout. Olive-brown above, thin dark streaks along midline of back; clear to amber fins. Yellow snout on large individual. Usually 34–38 lateral scales; 9–11 anal rays; pharyngeal teeth 2,4–4,2. To 2½ in. (6.1 cm).

Range: Atlantic Piedmont and Coastal Plain from Roanoke R. drainage, VA, to Savannah R. drainage, SC. Common on Piedmont; uncommon (in north) to rare (in south) on Coastal Plain. **Habitat:** Pools, sometimes runs, of sandy and rocky creeks and small to medium rivers.

Similar species: Dusky Shiner (Pl. 20) has *darker* stripe along side extending *below* lateral line throughout its length; dark stripe along back; scales on back barely outlined in black; pharyngeal teeth 1,4–4,1.
Map 165

SAND SHINER *Notropis ludibundus* Pl. 13

Identification: Complete, decurved, *punctate* (front half of body) *lateral line*. Dusky stripe along back expanded into dark *wedge* at dorsal fin origin. Slender, fairly compressed body; dorsal fin origin over to slightly behind pelvic fin origin. Rounded snout; small, slightly subterminal mouth; nipple at front of pupil (Fig. 33). Straw yellow above, faintly outlined scales on back and upper side; silver side (often a dusky stripe on rear half); small black caudal spot or wedge; clear fins tinged with white on large individuals. 31–38 lateral scales; 7 anal rays; pharyngeal teeth 0,4–4,0. To 3¼ in. (8.1 cm).

Range: St. Lawrence-Great Lakes, Hudson Bay (Red R.), and Mississippi R. basins from St. Lawrence R., s. QU, to e. SA, and south to TN and TX; west to e. MT, WY, CO, and NM; Gulf Slope from Trinity R. to Rio Grande, TX, NM, and Mexico. One of the most common shiners. **Habitat:** Sand and gravel runs and pools of creeks and small to

large rivers; sandy margins of lakes. Usually in clear creeks and small rivers; rarely found in upland areas.
Similar species: (1) See Swallowtail Shiner (Pl. 13). (2) Palezone Shiner has clear stripe above black stripe along side, less decurved lateral line; is more slender. (3) Mimic Shiner (Pl. 13) *lacks* dark stripe along back, wedge at dorsal fin origin; has broader snout, wide scales along back, deep scales along side, 8 anal rays. (4) Bigmouth Shiner (Pl. 13) has upwardly directed eyes, 8 anal rays; lacks dark wedge at dorsal fin origin. **Map 166**

SWALLOWTAIL SHINER *Notropis procne* **Pl. 13**
Identification: Similar to Sand Shiner but has *longer snout,* more subterminal mouth, nearly straight lateral line, blacker caudal wedge, often a darker stripe (black in some populations) along side and around snout, *yellow body and fins* on breeding male. To 2¾ in. (7.2 cm).
Range: Atlantic drainages, above and below Fall Line, from Delaware and Susquehanna rivers, NY, to Santee R., SC; Lake Ontario drainage, NY. Generally common but localized in n. and s. parts of range. Apparently introduced into New R. drainage, VA. **Habitat:** Sandy, sometimes rocky, pools and runs of creeks and small to large rivers.
Similar species: (1) See Palezone and (2) Sand Shiners (Pl. 13). (3) Cape Fear Shiner (Pl. 13) has long coiled gut, black peritoneum, black lips, 8 anal rays. **Map 166**

PALEZONE SHINER *Notropis* species **Not shown**
Identification: Similar to Swallowtail Shiner but is more slender; has *clear stripe* above *black stripe* along side; black stripe extends around snout. To 2¾ in. (7.2 cm).
Range: Little South Fork and Marrowbone Cr. (Middle Cumberland R. drainage), KY and TN; Cove Cr. and Paint Rock R. system (upper Tennessee R. drainage), TN and AL. Uncommon and extremely localized. **Habitat:** Rocky and sandy, usually flowing, pools of creeks and small rivers.
Similar species: (1) See Swallowtail Shiner (Pl. 13). (2) Sand Shiner (Pl. 13) *lacks* well-defined clear and black stripes along side, is deeper bodied, has more decurved lateral line. **Map 161**

CAPE FEAR SHINER *Notropis mekistocholas* **Pl. 13**
Identification: *Long coiled dark gut* visible through belly wall; *black peritoneum.* Black stripe along side of body and side of snout, absent on front of snout; black lips. Black wedge on caudal fin base, usually detached from dark stripe along body. Olive above, scales outlined in black, thin dusky stripe along midline; light stripe above dark stripe along side. Clear to yellow fins (large individuals). Compressed body; dorsal fin origin over or slightly before pelvic fin origin. Nearly horizontal, subterminal mouth. Complete lateral line; 34–37 lateral scales; 8 anal rays; pharyngeal teeth 0,4–4,0. To 3 in. (7.7 cm).
Range: Cape Fear drainage near Fall Line, Chatham and Harnett cos., NC. Rare; recognized as an *endangered species.* **Habitat:** Sandy and rocky pools and runs of small to medium rivers.

Remarks: A highly specialized detritus- and plant-eating species, the Cape Fear Shiner has the smallest range of any species of *Notropis.*
Similar species: No other shiner (genus *Notropis*) except Ozark Minnow has long coiled gut; few have black peritoneum. (1) Swallowtail (Pl. 13) and (2) Whitemouth Shiners (Pl. 12) have 7 anal rays, little or no black on lips. **Map 167**

CHIHUAHUA SHINER *Notropis chihuahua* Pl. 12

Identification: *Many black spots* on back and upper side of body and head; *black wedge* on caudal fin base. Lateral-line pores at front outlined in black. Yellow to pale orange lips and dorsal, caudal, and pectoral fins. Stout, barely compressed body, deepest under nape; dorsal fin origin over pelvic fin origin; rounded snout. Straw yellow above, often a dusky stripe along back; dusky (at front) to black (at rear) stripe on silver side; white below. Usually 7, often 8, anal rays. 33–37 lateral scales; pharyngeal teeth 0,4–4,0. To 3¼ in. (8 cm).
Range: Rio Grande drainage in Big Bend region of sw. TX; and n. Mexico. Uncommon in TX, common in Mexico. **Habitat:** Sandy and rocky pools and runs of creeks and small rivers.
Similar species: Speckled Chub (Pl. 9) has large barbel at corner of mouth, flattened body, *no* black wedge on caudal fin base. **Map 168**

TAMAULIPAS SHINER *Notropis braytoni* Pl. 12

Identification: *Dusky stripe* along side from opercle (where diffuse) to caudal peduncle, followed by *clear area,* then small *black wedge* on caudal fin base. Straw-colored above; scales above dusky stripe along side darkly outlined, creating cross-hatched appearance; often a dusky stripe along back. Silver side; white below; clear fins. Body compressed, deepest at origin or in front of dorsal fin; dorsal fin origin over pelvic fin origin. Bluntly rounded snout; subterminal mouth; round eye. Complete lateral line; 32–39 lateral scales; usually 7 anal rays, 15–16 pectoral rays; pharyngeal teeth 1,4–4,1. To 2¾ in. (6.9 cm).
Range: Rio Grande drainage from near mouth upstream to mouth of Rio Conchos and lower Pecos R., TX. Also in Rio Grande drainage, n. Mexico. Common in Rio Grande mainstream. **Habitat:** Rocky and sandy channels of large creeks and small to medium-sized rivers.
Similar species: Within its range, the Tamaulipas Shiner is most similar to the Phantom Shiner, which has a smaller eye, usually 8 anal rays, pharyngeal teeth 2,4–4,2; is more pallid, with only a faint stripe along side. **Map 169**

GHOST SHINER *Notropis buchanani* Pl. 13

Identification: Aptly named, the Ghost Shiner is *translucent milky white* overall. Body compressed, arched at front, deep at dorsal fin origin, *strongly tapering to thin caudal peduncle. Large pointed fins;* depressed pelvic fins reach anal fin origin. In turbid water, individuals lack dark pigment; in clear water, scales on back may be faintly outlined; black specks may be present on snout, along lateral line, and along underside of caudal peduncle. Fairly large eye; rounded snout; small, subterminal mouth; dorsal fin origin over pelvic fin origin. Lateral-line scales on front half of body deeper than wide (Fig. 35). Complete lateral line; 30–35 lateral scales; 8 anal rays; no infraorbital canal (rarely short segment present); pharyngeal teeth 0,4–4,0. To 2½ in. (6.4 cm).

Range: Mississippi R. basin from PA to se. NB, e. KS, and w. OK, and from MN and WI south to n. AL and LA; Gulf Slope drainages from Calcasieu R., LA, to Rio Grande, TX and Mexico. Common in w. part of range; absent in Ozarks; uncommon to rare in east. **Habitat:** Quiet pools and backwaters, usually over sand, of small to large rivers.

Similar species: Mimic Shiner (Pl. 13) *lacks* arched, deep body at dorsal fin origin; has infraorbital canal, deeper caudal peduncle; pelvic fins do *not* reach anal fin. **Map 168**

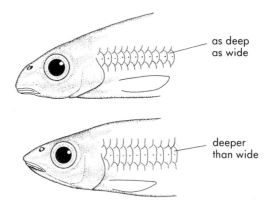

as deep
as wide

deeper
than wide

Fig. 35 Minnows — lateral-line scales

MIMIC SHINER *Notropis volucellus* **Pl. 13**
Identification: Scales along back in front of dorsal fin *wider* than those on upper side. Scales along side (front half of body) *much deeper than wide* (Fig. 35). *Broad rounded snout;* small, slightly subterminal mouth; large eye. Fairly slender, compressed body; dorsal fin origin over to slightly behind pelvic fin origin. Transparent gray to olive-yellow above (see Remarks), faintly to darkly outlined scales on back and upper side; dusky stripe (darkest at rear and in individuals from clear, vegetated habitats) along silver side; stripe expanded just in front of caudal fin (Fig. 36). Complete lateral line; 32–38 lateral scales; 8 anal rays; pharyngeal teeth 0,4–4,0. To 3 in. (7.6 cm).
Range: St. Lawrence–Great Lakes, Hudson Bay, and Mississippi R. basins from QU and VT to w.-cen. MB, and south to Gulf; Atlantic Slope drainages from James R., VA, to Neuse R., NC (introduced into Connecticut and Housatonic rivers, MA and CT); Gulf Slope drain-

ages from Mobile Bay, GA and AL, to Nueces R., TX. Common. **Habitat:** Sandy pools of headwaters, creeks, and small to large rivers; quiet areas of lakes.

Remarks: A highly variable species badly in need of study. *N. volucellus wickliffi*, with a deeper and broader body, deeper caudal peduncle, and no or only a faint stripe along midline of nape, usually is treated as a large-river subspecies of the Mimic Shiner, but may be a distinct species.

Similar species: (1) See Cahaba Shiner. (2) Sand Shiner (Pl. 13) has dusky stripe along back, black wedge at dorsal fin origin, narrower snout, 7 anal rays; *lacks* wide scales along back and deep scales along side. **Map 169**

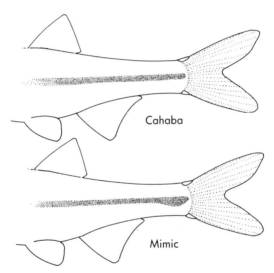

Fig. 36 Mimic and Cahaba Shiners — dark stripe on caudal peduncle

CAHABA SHINER *Notropis cahabae*   **Not shown**
  Identification: Similar to Mimic Shiner, but dark stripe along side *straight-edged* (rather than expanded) near caudal fin base (Fig. 36). To 3 in. (7.5 cm).
  Range: Main channel of Cahaba R., Shelby and Bibb cos., AL. Rare.
  Habitat: Flowing pools, usually over sand or gravel; less often near rocky riffles.
  Similar species: See Mimic Shiner (Pl. 13).   **Map 166**

MIRROR SHINER *Notropis spectrunculus*   **Pl. 20**
  Identification: Scales on front half of nape *absent* ("mirror-like") or *small and crowded. Broad head;* rounded snout; somewhat up-

wardly directed eyes; small subterminal mouth. Slender body, usually *arched* throughout; *black wedge* on caudal fin base. Dorsal fin origin behind pelvic fin origin. Olive above, thin black stripe along back; darkly outlined scales on back and upper side; dusky stripe (darkest at rear) on silver side. Large male has white edges on *red-orange* fins. Complete lateral line; 36–39 lateral scales; 8–9 anal rays; pharyngeal teeth 0,4–4,0. To 3 in. (7.5 cm).
Range: Upper Tennessee R. drainage, VA, NC, TN, and GA. Common to abundant in NC; more localized elsewhere. **Habitat:** Rocky, sandy, and muddy pools and backwaters of high-gradient creeks and small rivers.
Similar species: (1) See Sawfin Shiner (Pl. 20). (2) Ozark Shiner (Pl. 20) has *normal scales* on nape, black *spot* at dorsal fin origin, *no* bold black wedge on caudal fin base, narrower head. **Map 170**

SAWFIN SHINER *Notropis* species   Pl. 20

Identification: Similar to Mirror Shiner but has black specks along only the *1st 4*, rather than all, dorsal fin rays. Large male has orange and black specks on *front half* of dorsal fin. To 2½ in. (6.6 cm).
Range: Upper and middle Cumberland R. drainage, KY and TN; Tennessee R. drainage, VA, TN, and AL. Locally common. **Habitat:** Rocky and sandy pools and backwaters of creeks and small to medium rivers.
Similar species: See Mirror Shiner (Pl. 20).   **Map 170**

OZARK SHINER *Notropis ozarcanus*   Pl. 20

Identification: *Very slender*, usually arched body. *Small dusky to black spot* at dorsal fin origin. Rounded snout; small subterminal mouth; fairly large eye. Dorsal fin origin slightly behind pelvic fin origin. Light yellow above, dark-edged scales; thin black stripe along back; dusky stripe (darkest at rear) along silver side; often a small black caudal spot. Fins clear to dusky in adult; black on breeding male. Complete lateral line; 34–38 lateral scales (those at front much deeper than adjacent scales); 8 anal rays; pharyngeal teeth 0,4–4,0. To 3 in. (7.5 cm).
Range: Above Fall Line in White and Black R. systems, MO and AR. Formerly in upper St. Francis R. drainage, MO, but now extirpated. Locally common (especially in upper Current R.). **Habitat:** Rocky and sandy runs and flowing pools, often near riffles, of clear fast-flowing small to medium rivers.
Similar species: Mirror Shiner (Pl. 20) has no or crowded scales on nape, a broader head, black wedge at caudal fin base, *no* spot at dorsal fin origin.   **Map 170**

BLACKNOSE SHINER *Notropis heterolepis*   Pl. 12

Identification: *Black stripe* along side and around snout, but barely onto upper lip and absent on chin; *black crescents* within stripe. Rounded, somewhat elongated snout; small, nearly horizontal, subterminal mouth; round eye (Fig. 34). Slender, slightly compressed body; dorsal fin origin slightly behind pelvic fin origin. Olive to

straw-colored above; often a faint streak before dorsal fin; scales darkly outlined except above dark stripe along silver side. Incomplete lateral line; 32–39 lateral scales; 13 or more predorsal scales; 8 anal rays; pharyngeal teeth 0,4–4,0. To 3¾ in. (9.8 cm).
Range: Atlantic, Great Lakes, Hudson Bay, and Mississippi R. basins from NS to SA, south to OH, IL, s.-cen. MO, and KS (where extremely localized). Common in some parts of range (especially ON, MI, and WI) but disappearing from southern part. **Habitat:** Clear vegetated lakes and pools of creeks and small rivers; usually over sand.
Similar species: (1) See Bedrock Shiner (Pl. 12). (2) Pallid Shiner (Pl. 9) has a larger horizontally elliptical eye, dorsal fin origin slightly in *front* of pelvic fin origin, body notably arched at dorsal fin origin, *no* black crescents in dark stripe along side, pharyngeal teeth 1,4–4,1.
Map 171

BEDROCK SHINER *Notropis rupestris*   **Pl. 12**
Identification: Similar to Blacknose Shiner but has *complete lateral line* (except small young), *more arched back*, dorsal fin origin over or only slightly behind pelvic fin origin; smaller, more terminal mouth, 10–14 (usually 11–12) predorsal scales. To 2½ in. (6.2 cm).
Range: Lower Caney Fork system and nearby tributaries of cen. Cumberland R. drainage, TN. Common. **Habitat:** Bedrock pools of headwaters, creeks, and small rivers; usually near vegetation.
Similar species: See Blacknose Shiner (Pl. 12).   **Map 171**

WHITEMOUTH SHINER *Notropis alborus*   **Pl. 12**
Identification: Body divided into straw yellow upper and white lower halves by *silver-black jagged-edged stripe* along side ending at *black wedge* on caudal fin base. *Black bridle* around blunt snout; no black on lips (Fig. 34). Scales on back outlined in black; *no dark stripe* along back. Body compressed, deepest at dorsal fin origin (over or slightly in front of pelvic fin origin) and strongly tapering to thin caudal peduncle. Nearly horizontal mouth. Usually complete lateral line. 31–35 lateral scales, 7 anal rays; pharyngeal teeth 0,4–4,0. To 2¼ in. (6 cm).
Range: Atlantic Slope drainages from Chowan R., VA, to Santee R., SC. Mostly restricted to Piedmont, where fairly common. **Habitat:** Sandy and rocky pools and runs of headwaters, creeks, and small rivers.
Similar species: (1) Swallowtail and (2) Cape Fear Shiners (both, Pl. 13) have black stripe on side but *not front* of snout, some black on lips, thin dark stripe along back, more slender body that is less highly arched at dorsal fin origin.   **Map 171**

PUGNOSE SHINER *Notropis anogenus*   **Pl. 12**
Identification: Small shiner with a very *small sharply upturned mouth* (Fig. 34) and *black peritoneum.* Dark stripe along side and around snout (on chin, lower lip, side of upper lip). *Black wedge* on caudal fin base. Fairly compressed body; dorsal fin origin over pelvic fin origin. Olive above, thin dark line along back; scales darkly out-

lined except above dark stripe along side; silver-white below. Breeding male has yellow body and fins. Usually complete lateral line; 34–38 lateral scales; 8 (often 7) anal rays; pharyngeal teeth 0,4–4,0. To 2¼ in. (5.8 cm).

Range: From Lake Ontario drainage of e. ON and w. NY to se. ND and cen. IL (where now extirpated). Mostly restricted to Great Lakes and Mississippi R. basins but also in Red. R. drainage (Hudson Bay basin) of MN and SD. Rare and becoming even less common over most of range. **Habitat:** Clear vegetated lakes; vegetated pools and runs of creeks and rivers. Usually over sand and mud.

Similar species: (1) Pugnose Minnow (Pl. 10) also has strongly upturned mouth but has dark areas on dorsal fin (except in parts of FL), cross-hatched pattern on upper side, *silvery-white peritoneum*, 9 dorsal rays (Pugnose Shiner has 8); pharyngeal teeth 0,5–5,0. (2) Bridle Shiner (Pl. 12) has black stripe around snout and *less upturned mouth* (Fig. 34), incomplete lateral line, usually 7 anal rays.

Map 162

BRIDLE SHINER *Notropis bifrenatus*　　　　　　　　**Pl. 12**

Identification: *Black spot* at base of caudal fin usually joined to *brown-black stripe* along side and *around snout* (narrower on snout, mostly confined to upper lip — Fig. 34). Light stripe above dark stripe. Scales on back darkly outlined; often a dusky stripe along midline of back; silver side. Body slightly compressed, deepest at dorsal fin origin which is slightly behind pelvic fin origin. Moderately blunt snout; small oblique mouth. Incomplete lateral line except in large (2 in.) individuals. 33–36 lateral scales; usually 7 anal rays; pharyngeal teeth 0,4–4,0. To 2½ in. (6.5 cm).

Range: St. Lawrence–Lake Ontario drainage, s. QU, e. ON, and NY; Atlantic Slope drainages from s. ME to Roanoke R. system, s. VA; isolated population in lower Neuse R. drainage, e. NC. Fairly common but decreasing in some areas. **Habitat:** Ponds, lakes, and sluggish mud-bottomed pools of creeks and small to medium rivers; often in vegetation.

Similar species: See Pl. 12. (1) Pugnose Shiner has extremely small, upturned mouth; dark stripe *absent* from snout, confined to lips; complete lateral line. (2) Whitemouth Shiner has more horizontal mouth; stripe around snout as wide in *front* as on side of snout, absent on exposed part of upper lip; no dark stripe along midline of back; usually complete lateral line.　　　　　　**Map 167**

TAILLIGHT SHINER *Notropis maculatus*　　　　　　**Pl. 20**

Identification: *Large black spot* at center, small black spots on upper and lower edge, of caudal fin base; *red* between spots. *Cross-hatched pattern* on back and side. Large black *blotch* (darkest on male) along front of dorsal fin. Male has *black bands* near edges of dorsal, caudal, anal, and pelvic fins. Slender, compressed body; fairly long, rounded snout; subterminal mouth; large, pointed fins; dorsal fin origin behind pelvic fin origin. Light olive above, thin dusky stripe along back; dusky stripe along silver side and around snout; snout usually

faint red. Breeding male has *bright red body and head, red-black edge on fins.* Incomplete lateral line, 8–10 pores; 34–39 lateral scales; 8 anal rays, 8 dorsal rays; pharyngeal teeth 0,4–4,0. To 3 in. (7.6 cm).
Range: Below Fall Line in Atlantic, Gulf, and Mississippi R. basins from Cape Fear R., NC, to Sabine R., TX; north in Former Mississippi Embayment to s. IL; throughout FL except extreme s. tip. Locally common in se. U.S.; uncommon in Mississippi basin. **Habitat:** Swamps, ponds, backwaters and pools of small to large rivers; usually near vegetation.
Similar species: Pugnose Minnow (Pl. 10) *lacks* large black spot on caudal fin base; has nearly vertical mouth, 9 dorsal rays, pharyngeal teeth 0,5–5,0 or 0,5–4,0; large male lacks red on body, has bright white anal and pelvic fins. **Map 170**

SPOTTAIL SHINER *Notropis hudsonius* Pl. 12
Identification: *Large eye;* short rounded snout; nearly horizontal, subterminal mouth. *Large black caudal spot* (inconspicuous in s. Atlantic drainages and often on large individuals elsewhere). Fairly slender, compressed body; dorsal fin origin over or slightly in front of pelvic fin origin. Olive-gray above, dusky stripe along back, dark-edged scales often form wavy lines on back and upper side; punctate (often faint) lateral line at front, dusky stripe along rear of silver side. 36–42 lateral scales; 8 anal rays; pharyngeal teeth usually 2,4–4,2 (1,4–4,1 or 0,4–4,0 on Atlantic Slope). To 5¾ in. (15 cm).
Range: Atlantic and Gulf Slope drainages from St. Lawrence R., QU, to Altamaha and upper Chattahoochee R., GA; Hudson Bay, Great Lakes, and Mississippi R. basins from ON to Mackenzie R. drainage (Arctic basin), NT and AB, and south to n. OH, s. IL, and ne. MT. Common; locally abundant. **Habitat:** Sandy and rocky pools and runs of small to large rivers; sandy and rocky shores of lakes; creeks on Atlantic Slope.
Similar species: Silver Chub (Pl. 8) has *no* black spot on caudal fin base, eye higher on head, barbel at corner of mouth. **Map 172**

BLACKSPOT SHINER *Notropis atrocaudalis* Pl. 12
Identification: *Narrow black stripe* along side and around snout (including on upper lip); *horizontally oblong black caudal spot, separated* from dark stripe along side and often streaking to end of caudal fin. *Stocky body,* slightly compressed; dorsal fin origin in front of pelvic fin origin. Small eye; rounded snout; nearly horizontal, subterminal mouth. Olive above, scales darkly outlined; dusky lines on back and upper side converging at rear; wide dusky stripe along back. Silver side, black specks above and below lateral-line pores. Usually complete lateral line, 35–40 lateral scales, 7 anal rays; pharyngeal teeth 0,4–4,0. To 3 in. (7.6 cm).
Range: Red (Mississippi R. basin) and Calcasieu R. (Gulf Slope) drainages to Brazos R. drainage, sw. AR, se. OK, w. LA, and e. TX. Fairly common in southern part of range; uncommon in north. **Habitat:** Sandy and rocky runs and pools of creeks and small to medium rivers; usually in shallow (to 50 cm) water.

Similar species: Topeka Shiner (Pl. 19) has black *wedge* on caudal base, *lacks* black stripe around snout, has red-orange fins on large male.   **Map 173**

TOPEKA SHINER *Notropis tristis*   **Pl. 19**
Identification: *Stocky,* compressed body; *small eye. Black wedge* on caudal fin base. Dusky to dark stripe along side, not extending around snout. Dorsal fin origin over pelvic fin origin, closer to tip of snout than to caudal fin base. Round snout; small, nearly terminal mouth. Olive above, large dark stripe along back in front of dorsal fin (often thin stripe behind dorsal fin); scales outlined in black. Silver-white below. Breeding male is *orange* below and on side of head, has *red-orange fins.* Complete lateral line. 32–37 lateral scales; 7 anal rays; pharyngeal teeth 0,4–4,0. To 3 in. (7.6 cm).
Range: Mississippi R. basin from s. MN and se. SD south to cen. MO and s. KS (Arkansas R. drainage); once more common in w. KS but now nearly extirpated. Generally uncommon. **Habitat:** Quiet gravel- and sand-bottomed pools of headwaters and creeks.   **Map 173**

• *HYBOPSIS*

Genus characteristics: Shinerlike minnows living on or close to the stream bottom. *Upwardly directed, horizontally elliptical eyes;* long snout overhanging *subterminal mouth.* All but the Pallid Shiner usually have *barbel at corner of mouth* (Fig. 21). Several species that this guide places in other genera (e.g., *Erimystax* and *Macrhybopsis*) are often listed by other sources as members of *Hybopsis.*

BIGEYE CHUB *Hybopsis amblops*   **Pl. 9**
Identification: *Black stripe* (faded in turbid water) along side and onto (often around) snout. *Large eye,* about equal to length of snout; small mouth; snout projecting well beyond upper lip. Slender, slightly compressed body; dorsal fin origin over or slightly behind pelvic fin origin. Light yellow above; dark streak along back in front of dorsal fin; scales dark-edged, producing wavy lines; silver side, often with a yellow streak above black stripe; sometimes a black caudal spot. Breeding male has many small tubercles scattered over head (Fig. 37). Complete lateral line; 33–38 lateral scales; 8 anal rays; pharyngeal teeth 1,4–4,1. To 3½ in. (9 cm).
Range: Lake Erie drainage, NY, PA, OH, and MI; Ohio R. basin from NY to e. IL, and south to Tennessee R. drainage, GA and AL; Ozarks of s. MO, n. AR, and ne. OK (absent in Missouri R. drainage). **Habitat:** Rocky pools with current, usually near riffles and vegetation. Common to abundant in s. part of range, but disappearing from much of north, especially agricultural areas.
Similar species: (1) See Rosyface Chub. (2) Pallid Shiner (Pl. 9) and (3) Clear Chub have arched, more strongly compressed body; fewer, larger tubercles on head of breeding male.   **Map 174**

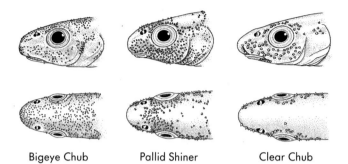

Bigeye Chub   Pallid Shiner   Clear Chub

Fig. 37 Bigeye Chub, Pallid Shiner, and Clear Chub — head tubercles on breeding male

ROSYFACE CHUB *Hybopsis rubrifrons*   **Not shown**
Identification: Similar to Bigeye Chub but has smaller eye (less than snout length) and during (spring) breeding season develops red on front ⅓ of body (snout usually brightest); 35–39 lateral scales. To 3¼ in. (8.4 cm).
Range: Saluda, Savannah, and Altamaha R. drainages, SC and GA. Mostly above Fall Line where common; locally abundant. **Habitat:** Sand and gravel pools and runs of creeks and small rivers.
Similar species: See Bigeye Chub (Pl. 9).   **Map 174**

LINED CHUB *Hybopsis lineapunctata*   **Pl. 9**
Identification: Black stripe along side and around snout, *broad and diffuse at midbody, narrow and black on caudal peduncle; clear stripe* above black stripe; *large black spot* on caudal fin base. Slender, slightly compressed body; small mouth; snout projecting well beyond upper lip. Dorsal fin origin over or in front of pelvic fin origin. Golden yellow above, scales black-edged, producing wavy lines; dark streak along back in front of dorsal fin; silver side; thin dark bar behind head. Breeding male has many small tubercles scattered over head. Complete lateral line; 34–38 lateral scales; 8 anal rays (often 7 in Tallapoosa R. system); pharyngeal teeth 1,4–4,1. To 3 in. (7.9 cm).
Range: Above Fall Line in Coosa and Tallapoosa R. systems (Mobile Bay drainage), se. TN, GA, and AL. Fairly common. **Habitat:** Rocky pools, often near riffles and vegetation.
Similar species: Other *Hybopsis* species *lack* strongly demarcated clear stripe along side.   **Map 174**

PALLID SHINER *Hybopsis amnis*   **Pl. 9**
Identification: *Back arched* at dorsal fin origin. *Large eye,* about equal to length of snout; small mouth; snout projecting well beyond upper lip. Straw yellow above; scales usually dark-edged; black stripe along silver side and around snout (stripe darkest at rear, absent in turbid

water); sometimes a black caudal spot. Fairly compressed body; dorsal fin origin over or in front of pelvic fin origin. Rarely a barbel at corner of mouth. Breeding male has tubercles concentrated on lower half of head (Fig. 37). Complete lateral line; 33–38 lateral scales; 8 anal rays; pharyngeal teeth 1,4–4,1. To 3¼ in. (8.4 cm).
Range: Mississippi R. basin from WI and MN south to LA, mostly in lowland areas but extending up Cumberland R. to s.-cen. KY, and in Arkansas and Red R. drainages to e. OK; Gulf drainages from Amite R., LA, to Guadalupe R., TX. Fairly common in s. half of range; rare in north. **Habitat:** Sandy and silty pools of medium to large rivers; often found in small rivers in e. TX.
Similar species: (1) See Clear Chub. (2) Bigeye Chub (Pl. 9) has less arched, less compressed body; barbel at corner of mouth; more, smaller tubercles on head of breeding male. (3) Blacknose Shiner (Pl. 12) has *round* (not elliptical) eye, black crescents in dark stripe along side; pharyngeal teeth 0,4–4,0.   **Map 175**

CLEAR CHUB *Hybopsis winchelli*   **Not shown**
Identification: Similar to Pallid Shiner but (almost always) has *barbel* at corner of mouth; *flatter, longer head*; black caudal spot; fewer, larger tubercles on head of breeding male (Fig. 37). Large adult has light orange caudal fin. 33–39 lateral scales. To 3¼ in. (8.4 cm).
Range: Gulf drainages from Ocklockonee R., FL, and Apalachicola R., GA and FL, to lower Mississippi R., MS and LA. Common. **Habitat:** Sand- and silt-bottomed pools, often near riffles, in creeks and small to medium rivers.
Similar species: See Pallid Shiner (Pl. 9).   **Map 174**

THICKLIP CHUB *Hybopsis labrosa*   **Pl. 9**
Identification: *Small dark brown blotches* and cross-hatching on back and side. Compressed body, *flattened below*, deepest under nape; dorsal fin origin over or slightly behind pelvic fin origin. *Long snout* overhanging mouth; large barbels; eyes directed upwardly. Large, horizontal pectoral fins. Straw yellow above; dark stripe (darkest at rear) along silver side; punctate lateral line, black spot on caudal fin base, black stripe from eye to snout. Breeding male is dark gray, has black membranes in yellow fins. Complete lateral line; 37–40 lateral scales; 8 anal rays; pharyngeal teeth 1,4–4,1. To 2¾ in. (6.7 cm).
Range: Upper Peedee and Santee R. drainages, VA, NC, and SC. Locally common, especially in mountain and upper Piedmont streams. **Habitat:** Rocky riffles and runs of creeks and small rivers.
Similar species: Santee Chub (Pl. 9) *lacks* dark mottling, is more slender.   **Map 116**

SANTEE CHUB *Hybopsis zanema*   **Pl. 9**
Identification: *Dark cross-hatching on back and side.* Slender, compressed body, *flattened below*, deepest under nape; dorsal fin origin behind pelvic fin origin. *Long snout* overhanging mouth; large barbels; eyes directed upwardly. Large, horizontal pectoral fins. Yellow above and on side; dark stripe (darkest at rear) along silver side,

black spot on caudal fin base, black stripe from eye to snout. Breeding male is silver with dark yellow fins, black streaks on dorsal and caudal fins. Complete lateral line; 38–42 lateral scales; 8 anal rays; pharyngeal teeth 1,4–4,1. To 3 in. (7.5 cm).
Range: Atlantic Slope from Cape Fear R. drainage, NC, to upper Santee R. drainage, NC and SC. Locally common in upper Piedmont streams of Santee drainage. **Habitat:** Sandy and rocky runs and current-swept pools of creeks and small rivers.
Similar species: Thicklip Chub (Pl. 9) has dark blotches on back and side, is deeper bodied. **Map 117**

HIGHBACK CHUB *Hybopsis hypsinotus* Pl. 19
Identification: Large dorsal fin on *strongly arched back*. Dark olive above, scales darkly outlined; dull purple stripe along side and around snout; *red fins*. Barely compressed body, deepest at dorsal fin origin; head flattened above and below; dorsal fin origin in front of pelvic fin origin. Complete lateral line; 35–40 lateral scales; 8 anal rays; pharyngeal teeth 1,4–4,1. To 2¾ in. (7.2 cm).
Range: Above Fall Line in Peedee and Santee R. drainages, VA, NC, and SC. Common; somewhat localized. **Habitat:** Sandy and rocky runs and pools of creeks and small to medium rivers.
Similar species: Yellowfin Shiner (Pl. 19) *lacks* barbel at corner of *terminal* mouth, has dorsal fin origin behind pelvic fin origin. **Map 175**

SILVERJAW MINNOW *Ericymba buccata* Pl. 9
Identification: Large *"pearl organs"* (silver-white chambers) on cheek and *flattened* underside of head; *upwardly* directed eyes high on head. Slightly compressed body deepest at nape; long snout, subterminal mouth; dorsal fin origin over pelvic fin origin. Light tan to olive-yellow above, dark streak along back, darkest in front of dorsal fin; scales may be darkly outlined; silver side, rarely with a dusky stripe. Complete lateral line; 31–36 lateral scales; 8 anal rays; pharyngeal teeth 1,4–4,1 or 0,4–4,0. To 3¾ in. (9.8 cm).
Range: 2 disjunct areas: Atlantic, lower Great Lakes, and Mississippi R. drainages from NY, PA, and MD, to e. MO; Gulf drainages from Apalachicola R., GA and FL, to Mississippi R., MS and LA. Absent from Tennessee R. drainage and most of Cumberland R. drainage below Cumberland Falls. **Habitat:** Shallow sandy riffles and raceways of creeks and small to medium rivers. Generally common but becoming less so.
Similar species: Other minnows lack "pearl organs." **Map 176**

■ SUCKERS: Family Catostomidae (63)

Sixty-three species of suckers are found in North America north of Mexico. The Longnose Sucker (*Catostomus catostomus*) lives in both North America and Siberia, and the Asiatic Sucker

(*Myxocyprinus asiaticus*) lives in China. Suckers have *large thick lips*, protrusible premaxillae (except in the Harelip Sucker), soft rays in the fins, no teeth on the jaws, numerous *comblike* or *molarlike teeth in a single row* on each pharyngeal arch, *1 dorsal fin, 9 or more dorsal rays*, abdominal pelvic fins, anal fin far back on body, cycloid scales on the body, and no scales on the head. The small sucker mouth with large lips is used in most species to "vacuum" and ingest invertebrates from stream and lake beds. Because of the abundance and large size reached by many suckers, suckers often account for the largest biomass in streams and lakes.

● *ICTIOBUS*

Genus characteristics: *Long, falcate dorsal fin*; 24–31 rays. *Gray or dark olive* (not silver) *body*; *semicircular subopercle*, broadest at middle (Fig. 38); dusky gray pelvic fin. Complete lateral line; sum of pelvic and anal rays 18 or more. 2-chambered gas bladder.

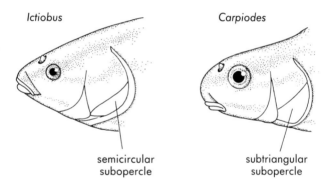

Ictiobus   *Carpiodes*

semicircular subopercle   subtriangular subopercle

Fig. 38 *Ictiobus* and *Carpiodes*

BIGMOUTH BUFFALO *Ictiobus cyprinellus*   **Pl. 21**
Identification: *Robust body; large ovoid head. Sharply oblique,* terminal *mouth*; front of upper lip *nearly level* with lower edge of eye. Upper jaw length *about equal* to snout length. *Faint grooves on thin upper lip.* Gray to olive-bronze above, green and copper reflections; black to olive-yellow side; white to pale yellow below; brown or black fins. Usually 35–36 lateral scales, 10–11 pelvic rays, 8–9 anal rays. To 40 in. (100 cm).
Range: Hudson Bay (Nelson R. drainage), lower Great Lakes, and Mississippi R. basins from ON to SA and MT, and south to LA. Introduced in lakes and impoundments in AZ and CA. Fairly common.
Habitat: Main channels, pools, and backwaters of small to large rivers; lakes and impoundments.

Similar species: (1) Smallmouth and (2) Black Buffalos (both, Pl. 21) have more *conical head*; more *horizontal mouth; distinct grooves* on *thick upper lip.* **Map 177**

SMALLMOUTH BUFFALO *Ictiobus bubalus* **Pl. 21**
Identification: Deep body; *small conical head. Fairly small, horizontal subterminal mouth*; front of upper lip well *below* lower edge of eye. Upper jaw length *much less* than snout length. Large eye. *Distinct grooves on thick upper lip.* Adult has strongly keeled nape. Gray, olive, or bronze above, dark blue and olive reflections; black to olive-yellow side; white to yellow below; olive to black fins. Usually 36–37 lateral scales, 10 pelvic rays, 9 anal rays. To 31 in. (78 cm).
Range: Lake Michigan drainage and Mississippi R. basin from PA and MI to MT and south to Gulf; Gulf Slope drainages from Mobile Bay, AL, to Rio Grande, TX and NM. Also in Mexico. Introduced in AZ impoundments. Common. **Habitat:** Pools, backwaters, and main channels of small to large rivers; impoundments; lakes.
Similar species: (1) See Black Buffalo (Pl. 21). (2) Bigmouth Buffalo (Pl. 21) has *ovoid head; sharply oblique, terminal mouth; faint grooves on thin upper lip.* **Map 178**

BLACK BUFFALO *Ictiobus niger* **Pl. 21**
Identification: Similar to Smallmouth Buffalo but has larger, *more conical head*; nearly terminal, *slightly oblique mouth*; wider, somewhat shallower body, smaller eye; adult has *rounded or only weakly keeled nape.* Usually 37–39 lateral scales. To 37 in. (93 cm).
Range: Lower Great Lakes and Mississippi R. basins from MI and OH to SD and south to LA; on Gulf Slope in Sabine Lake, Brazos R., and Rio Grande drainages, LA, TX, NM, and Mexico. Uncommon. **Habitat:** Pools and backwaters of small to large rivers; impoundments; lakes. Introduced in AZ impoundments.
Similar species: See Smallmouth Buffalo (Pl. 21). **Map 179**

• *CARPIODES*

Genus characteristics: *Long, falcate dorsal fin*; 23–30 rays. *Silver body; subtriangular subopercle,* broadest below middle (Fig. 38); white to orange pelvic fin (*not* densely covered with black specks). Complete lateral line. 2-chambered gas bladder.

QUILLBACK *Carpiodes cyprinus* **Pl. 21**
Identification: Deep body; adult body depth about 3 times into standard length; small conical head. *Long 1st dorsal ray* usually *not reaching* rear of dorsal fin base. *No nipple* on lower lip (Fig. 39). *Long snout,* about equal to distance from back of eye to upper end of gill opening. Upper jaw *does not* extend behind front of eye. Olive to gray above, silver or blue-green reflections; silver side; dusky gray median fins; white to orange paired fins. Usually 36–37 lateral scales. 9–10 pelvic rays, 8–9 anal rays; sum of anal and pelvic rays 18 or more. To 26 in. (66 cm).

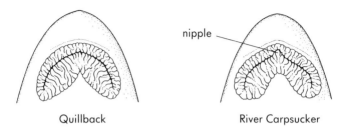

Quillback   River Carpsucker

Fig. 39 Quillback and River Carpsucker — lips

Range: Great Lakes–St. Lawrence R., Hudson Bay, and Mississippi R. basins from QU to AB and south to LA; Atlantic Slope drainages from Delaware R., NY, to Altamaha R., SC (except apparently absent from Rappahannock and York drainages, VA, and Tar and Neuse drainages, NC); Gulf Slope drainages from Apalachicola R., FL and GA, to Pearl R., LA. **Common. Habitat:** Pools, backwaters, and main channels of creeks and small to large rivers; lakes.
Similar species: (1) River and (2) Highfin Carpsuckers (both, Pl. 21) have *nipple* on lower lip (Fig. 39), *shorter snout*, upper jaw extending *behind* front of eye, usually 33–36 lateral scales.   **Map 180**

RIVER CARPSUCKER *Carpiodes carpio*   **Pl. 21**
Identification: Deep body; adult body depth about 2½ times into standard length; small conical head. *Fairly short 1st dorsal ray*, usually not reaching much beyond middle of fin. *Nipple* at middle of lower lip (Fig. 39). *Short (often bullet-shaped) snout*; length less than distance from back of eye to upper end of gill opening. Upper jaw extends *behind* front of eye. Olive green to bronze above, silver reflections; silver side; white or yellow below; dusky gray median fins; white or pink-orange paired fins. Usually *33–36* lateral scales, 9 pelvic rays, 8 anal rays; sum of anal and pelvic rays 17 or fewer. To 25 in. (64 cm).
Range: Mississippi R. basin from PA to MT and south to LA; Gulf Slope drainages from Calcasieu R., LA, to Rio Grande, TX and NM. Also in Mexico. Introduced into w. Lake Erie drainage, OH. Common. **Habitat:** Pools and backwaters of creeks and small to large rivers; lakes.
Similar species: (1) See Highfin Carpsucker (Pl. 21). (2) Quillback (Pl. 21) *lacks* nipple at middle of lower lip; has *longer snout*, upper jaw *not* extending behind front of eye, usually 36–37 lateral scales.
   Map 181

HIGHFIN CARPSUCKER *Carpiodes velifer*   **Pl. 21**
Identification: Similar to River Carpsucker but has *long 1st dorsal ray reaching to or beyond rear of dorsal fin*. Usually 9–10 pelvic rays, 8–9 anal rays; sum of anal and pelvic rays usually 18 or more. To 19½ in. (50 cm).

Range: Lake Michigan drainage and Mississippi R. basin from PA to MN and se. SD, and south to LA; Atlantic Slope in Cape Fear and Santee R. drainages, NC; Gulf Slope drainages from Choctawhatchee R., AL and FL, to Pearl R., MS and LA. Uncommon. **Habitat:** Pools and backwaters of creeks and small to large rivers.
Similar species: See River Carpsucker (Pl. 21). **Map 182**

BLUE SUCKER *Cycleptus elongatus* **Pl. 23**
Identification: Long, somewhat compressed body; *small head* (length 5 or more times into standard length). *Long falcate dorsal fin;* 28–37 rays. Blunt snout overhangs small horizontal mouth; many *blunt papillae on lips.* Long caudal peduncle; deeply forked caudal fin. Olive-blue or gray above; blue-white below; dark blue-gray fins. Large male is *blue-black;* minute white tubercles cover head, body, and fins of breeding male. Large female is tan to light blue, has fewer tubercles. 51–59 lateral scales, 7 anal rays. To 36 in. (93 cm).
Range: Mississippi R. basin from PA to cen. MT, and south to LA; Gulf Slope drainages from Mobile Bay, AL, to Rio Grande, TX, NM, and Mexico. Locally common but becoming less common over much of range. **Habitat:** Strong current in deep (1–2.5 m) chutes and main channels of medium to large rivers over bedrock, sand, and gravel.
Map 183

● *CHASMISTES*

Genus characteristics: *Large, robust body;* large head; distinct hump on snout. Large, *terminal or subterminal,* fairly to strongly *oblique mouth; thin, usually plicate* (sometimes sparsely papillose) *lips;* widely separated lower lip lobes (Fig. 40). Complete lateral line, 55–79 scales; 10–12 dorsal rays; 7 anal rays; *37–53 thin, branched or fimbriate (i.e., branched like broccoli) gill rakers,* flat and paddlelike on top; 2-chambered gas bladder.

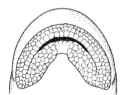

Fig. 40 *Chasmistes* — lips

JUNE SUCKER *Chasmistes liorus* **Pl. 21**
Identification: Large, terminal, *oblique* mouth. Thin, smooth or plicate lips (rarely with sparse papillae). Dark gray, bronze, or copper above and on side; white to dark gray fins. Large male may have rosy stripe along side. 55–70 lateral scales, 29–35 predorsal scales, 52–61

scales around body at dorsal fin origin, 19–20 scales around caudal peduncle. To 20 in. (52 cm).

Range: Utah Lake and its tributaries, UT. Original form of the June Sucker, recognized by the U.S. government as an *endangered species*, probably is extinct (see Remarks). **Habitat:** Formerly abundant in deep waters of Utah Lake; used tributaries of lake for spawning.

Remarks: 2 subspecies: *C. l. liorus*, formerly confined to Utah Lake, had 55–64 lateral scales, 45–53 gill rakers. *C. l. mictus*, with 60–70 lateral scales, 37–47 gill rakers, larger lip papillae, less oblique mouth, shorter, more slender head, and smaller eye, may have arisen as a hybrid between *C. l. liorus* and Utah Sucker and replaced original form of June Sucker in Utah Lake. The Snake River Sucker, *Chasmistes muriei*, a species known only from one specimen collected in Snake R. below Jackson Dam, WY (Map 184), and presumably extinct, was similar to the June Sucker but had a *subterminal mouth, papillose lips, and smaller scales* (72 lateral, 40 predorsal).

Similar species: (1) See Cui-ui and (2) Shortnose Sucker (both, Pl. 21).

Map 184

CUI-UI *Chasmistes cujus*   **Pl. 21**

Identification: Similar to June Sucker but has *larger, broader, blunter head;* less oblique mouth; 22–26 scales around caudal peduncle; more than 64 scales around body at dorsal fin origin. Blue-gray, brown, or black above and on side, copper or brassy reflections; white to dark gray fins. Breeding male has black and metallic red stripes on side, is silver or brassy below, has slate blue fins. Breeding female may have pink stripe along side. 59–68 lateral scales. To 26½ in. (67 cm).

Range: Pyramid and Winnemucca lakes, NV. Winnemucca Lake is dry. Cui-Ui is declining in Pyramid Lake and is protected as an *endangered species.* **Habitat:** Deep water; formerly made spectacular spawning runs up Truckee R. but now spawns only around margin of Pyramid Lake.

Remarks: Highly prized as food by the Northern Paiute Indians.

Similar species: (1) See June Sucker (Pl. 21). (2) Shortnose Sucker (Pl. 21) has a more oblique mouth; smaller (65–79 lateral) scales.

Map 184

SHORTNOSE SUCKER *Chasmistes brevirostris*   **Pl. 21**

Identification: Similar to June Sucker but has *shorter head, smaller eye,* few or no papillae on lips, 21–25 scales around caudal peduncle. Slate gray, brown, or black above; white to dark gray fins. Large adult may have red cast to scales. 65–79 lateral scales. To 25 in. (64 cm).

Range: Upper Klamath Lake and its tributaries, OR and CA. Rare and nearing extinction; recognized as an *endangered species.* **Habitat:** usually near vegetation around lake margin. Spawns in lake tributaries.

Remarks: Apparently no "pure" Shortnose Suckers persist. Recently captured individuals apparently represent hybrids with either the Klamath Largescale Sucker or the Klamath Smallscale Sucker.

Similar species: (1) See June Sucker (Pl. 21). (2) Cui-ui (Pl. 21) has *broader, blunter head;* more oblique mouth; 59–68 lateral scales.
Map 184

● *CATOSTOMUS*

Genus characteristics: Nearly *cylindrical body.* Large, *horizontal mouth; thick, strongly papillose lips* (Fig. 41); rounded snout. Shallow to deeply divided lower lip *joined at middle,* with or without notches (Fig. 41) at juncture of upper and lower lips. Complete lateral line, *54–124 scales;* 7–17 dorsal rays; usually 7 anal rays; 20–44 short to long, thin, unbranched gill rakers; 2-chambered gas bladder. Young of many species have *3 dark gray blotches* along side. *Catostomus* species readily hybridize with one another. Hybrids are especially common in streams where a non-native species has been introduced or where habitats have been altered.

Next 16 species: Outer edge of lips continuous, no deep indentations separating upper and lower lips (Fig. 41).

WHITE SUCKER *Catostomus commersoni* **Pl. 21**
Identification: Deep median lower lip notch; 0–3 rows of papillae at middle of lower lip; 2–6 rows of papillae on upper lip, lower lip about *twice as thick* as upper lip (Fig. 41). Caudal peduncle depth *more than half* dorsal fin base. No membrane connecting pelvic fin to body. Olive-brown to black above, often dusky-edged scales; clear to dusky fins. Breeding male is gold above, has scarlet stripe along side in most populations; cream to black stripe in some Canadian populations. Pale to lightly speckled peritoneum. Usually 10–12 dorsal rays, 53–74 lateral scales, 8–11 scale rows above lateral line. To 25 in. (64 cm).
Range: Atlantic, Arctic, Great Lakes, and Mississippi R. basins from NF to Mackenzie R., NT, south to Tennessee R. drainage, n. AL, and Arkansas R. drainage, NM; south on Atlantic Slope to Santee R. drainage, SC; upper Rio Grande drainage, NM; Skeena and Fraser R. drainages (Pacific Slope), BC. Introduced into Colorado R. drainage, WY, CO, and UT. Common. **Habitat:** Wide range of habitats from rocky pools and riffles of headwaters to large lakes. Usually in small, clear, cool creeks and small to medium rivers.
Similar species: (1) See Sonora Sucker (Pl. 22). (2) Utah Sucker (Pl. 22) has dorsal fin membranes densely speckled to edge; 9–14, usually 12, scale rows above lateral line. **Map 185**

SONORA SUCKER *Catostomus insignis* **Pl. 22**
Identification: Nearly identical to White Sucker but usually has dark spots on scales on upper side forming *faint dashed lines,* lower lip about *3 times as thick* as upper lip. Sometimes *sharply bicolored,* olive-brown above, deep yellow below; white or yellow to dusky fins.

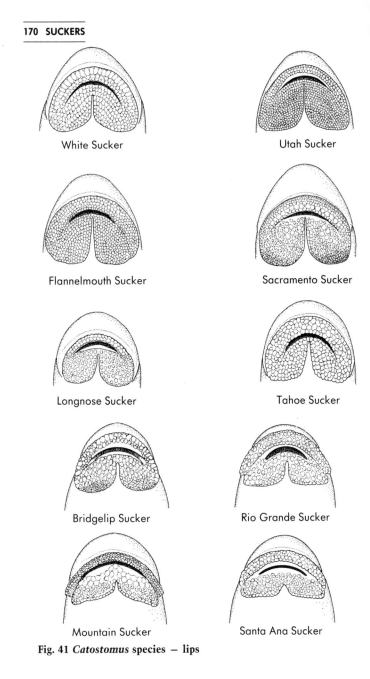

White Sucker

Utah Sucker

Flannelmouth Sucker

Sacramento Sucker

Longnose Sucker

Tahoe Sucker

Bridgelip Sucker

Rio Grande Sucker

Mountain Sucker

Santa Ana Sucker

Fig. 41 *Catostomus* species — lips

Usually 10–11 (rarely 12) dorsal rays; 54–67, usually fewer than 60, lateral scales. To 31½ in. (80 cm).
Range: Gila and Bill Williams R. systems (Colorado R. drainage), NM, AZ, and n. Sonora, Mexico. Common, but diminishing in southern half of range. **Habitat:** Rocky pools of creeks and small to medium rivers; large individuals in rocky riffles and runs at night.
Remarks: Some large individuals develop a massive, fleshy lower lip like that of Flannelmouth Sucker.
Similar species: (1) See White (Pl. 21) and (2) Yaqui Suckers. **Map 186**

YAQUI SUCKER *Catostomus bernardini*   **Not shown**
Identification: Nearly identical to Sonora Sucker but has usually *12 dorsal rays*; 62–80, usually *more than 65*, lateral scales; usually *lacks* sharp bicoloration. Dark olive-brown above; white or yellow below; dusky dorsal and caudal fins, white or yellow anal and paired fins. Large male has enlarged lower fins. To 15¾ in. (40 cm).
Range: Rio Yaqui basin, extreme se. AZ and nw. Mexico. Common in Mexico; extirpated in U.S. **Habitat:** Small mountain and desert creeks; deep pools, runs, and rapids of medium rivers.
Similar species: See Sonora Sucker (Pl. 22).   **Map 186**

UTAH SUCKER *Catostomus ardens*   **Pl. 22**
Identification: Very deep median lower lip notch; 0–1 row of papillae at middle of lower lip; 3–8 rows of papillae on upper lip (Fig. 41). Short, deep caudal peduncle (in some adults). Dorsal fin membranes *densely speckled to edge*. Dark olive to copper above; dusky fins. Breeding male usually has red stripe along side. 60–79 lateral scales; usually 12 scale rows above lateral line, 12 dorsal rays; 28–36 predorsal scales. To 25½ in. (65 cm).
Range: Snake R. system (Columbia R. drainage) above Shoshone Falls and adjacent endorheic drainages, WY, ID, and UT, and south through Lake Bonneville basin, ID and UT. Common. **Habitat:** Lakes, impoundments, and streams over silt, sand, gravel, or rocks; often near vegetation.
Similar species: See (1) Largescale Sucker (Pl. 22). (2) White Sucker (Pl. 21) has dorsal fin membranes densely speckled on *bottom* ⅓ of fin only, 2–6 rows of papillae on upper lip, usually 8–11 scale rows above lateral line.   **Map 187**

LARGESCALE SUCKER *Catostomus macrocheilus*   **Pl. 22**
Identification: Similar to Utah Sucker but has *lightly speckled* dorsal fin membranes, usually *13–15 dorsal rays, membrane connecting pelvic fin to body*, caudal peduncle depth less than ½ dorsal fin base, usually 36–52 predorsal scales. Olive to blue-gray above; white or yellow below; white to dusky fins. Breeding individual has iridescent olive green stripe above lateral line; dark bronze or *black stripe* along side; yellow stripe between black stripe and belly. To 24 in. (61 cm).
Range: Arctic basin from Peace R. drainage, BC, to Smokey R. drainage, AB; Pacific Slope from Nass R., BC, to Snake R. drainage (below Shoshone Falls), ID and NV, and Coquille R., OR. Common. **Habitat:**

Pools and runs of medium to large rivers; lakes.
Similar species: See Utah Sucker (Pl. 22). **Map 187**

FLANNELMOUTH SUCKER *Catostomus latipinnis* **Pl. 22**
Identification: *Narrow, pencil-shaped caudal peduncle* (in most populations). Very deep median lower lip notch; 0–1 row of papillae at middle of lower lip; 5–6 rows of papillae on upper lip (Fig. 41). Large adult has *large, fleshy lobes on lower lip. Large dorsal and caudal fins;* falcate dorsal fin. Green to blue-gray above, dusky scale edges; yellow to orange-red on lower side; white to dusky fins. Young are lighter with silver reflections. *90–116 lateral scales;* usually 12–13 dorsal rays. To 22 in. (56 cm).
Range: Colorado R. drainage from sw. WY to s. AZ. Common. **Habitat:** Rocky pools, runs, and riffles of medium to large rivers; less often in creeks and small rivers.
Similar species: (1) See Little Colorado River Sucker. (2) Utah Sucker (Pl. 22) has *shorter, deeper caudal peduncle;* deeper body; *smaller lower lip; 60–79 lateral scales; smaller* dorsal and caudal fins.
Map 187

LITTLE COLORADO RIVER SUCKER *Catostomus* species **Not shown**
Identification: Similar to Flannelmouth Sucker, but has *thicker, deeper caudal peduncle; smaller lower lip, slightly falcate to straight-edged dorsal fin,* usually 11–12 dorsal rays; 73–97, usually *fewer than 90,* lateral scales. Sharply bicolored, dark gray to blue-black above, white to yellow below; dusky fins. Young similar in color to adult. To 19¾ in. (50 cm).
Range: Upper Little Colorado R. system, AZ. Introduced into Salt R., AZ. Common. **Habitat:** Rocky pools and riffles of creeks and small to medium rivers; impoundments.
Similar species: See Flannelmouth Sucker (Pl. 22). **Map 187**

SACRAMENTO SUCKER *Catostomus occidentalis* **Pl. 22**
Identification: Deep median lower lip notch; *1* row of papillae at middle of lower lip; *4–6 rows* of papillae on upper lip (Fig. 41). Fairly blunt snout. Distance from pelvic fin origin to caudal fin base less than or equal to distance from eye to pelvic fin origin. Olive green, steel gray, or brown above; white to dirty *yellow-gold below;* white to dusky fins. Young are gray; 3–4 dark blotches along side. Breeding male has dark red stripe along side. 22–24 rakers in young, 25–30 in adult, on 1st gill arch; 56–75 lateral scales; 10–17 scale rows above, 8–10 below, lateral line; 18–22 scales around caudal peduncle; usually 12–15 dorsal rays. Dusky peritoneum. To 23½ in. (60 cm).
Range: Pacific Slope from Mad R., n. CA, to Salinas R., cen. CA; throughout Sacramento–San Joaquin drainage, s. OR and CA; south in endorheic basins of cen. CA to Kern R. Common. **Habitat:** Most common in pools of clear, cool streams; lakes and impoundments.
Similar species: See Klamath Largescale Sucker (Pl. 22). **Map 186**

KLAMATH LARGESCALE SUCKER *Catostomus snyderi* **Pl. 22**
Identification: Similar to Sacramento Sucker but has distance from

pelvic fin origin to caudal fin base equal to or greater than distance from eye to pelvic fin origin; *silver peritoneum;* thicker caudal peduncle; 10–12 scale rows below lateral line; 25–28 rakers in young, 30–35 in adult, on 1st gill arch; usually 11 (occasionally 12) dorsal rays. 67–77 lateral scales. To 21¾ in. (55 cm).
Range: Klamath R. drainage, OR and CA. Common. **Habitat:** Rocky pools and runs of creeks and small rivers; lakes; impoundments.
Similar species: See Sacramento Sucker (Pl. 22). **Map 186**

LONGNOSE SUCKER *Catostomus catostomus* **Pl. 21**
Identification: *Long snout. Very deep* median lower lip notch; *0–1* row of papillae at middle of lower lip; *2* rows of papillae on upper lip (Fig. 41). Dark olive or gray with brassy reflections or dark gray irregular blotches above; white or cream below. Breeding male is nearly black; large female is green-gold to copper-brown fading to white, yellow, orange, or pink below; both have red stripe along side, dusky median fins (sometimes with pale red edges); amber-pink paired fins. Usually 9–11 dorsal rays; usually *95–120 lateral scales;* 26–34 scales around caudal peduncle; 16–18 pectoral rays. Silver to black peritoneum. To 25 in. (64 cm); some populations dwarfed.
Range: Most widespread sucker of n. North America. Atlantic, Arctic, and Pacific basins throughout most of Canada and AK; Atlantic Slope south to Delaware R. drainage, NY; Great Lakes basin; upper Monongahela R. drainage, MD and WV; Missouri R. drainage south to NE and cen. CO. Introduced in upper Colorado R. drainage, WY and CO. Also in Arctic basin of e. Siberia. Common in northern cold waters; uncommon and sporadic in south. **Habitat:** Usually in clear, cold, deep water of lakes and tributary streams; occasionally in brackish water in Arctic. To depth of 600 ft. (183 m) in Great Lakes.
Similar species: (1) See Salish Sucker. (2) Sacramento Sucker (Pl. 22) has 4–6 rows of papillae on upper lip; shorter snout; *56–75 lateral scales;* usually 12–15 dorsal rays. (3) Tahoe Sucker (Pl. 22) has usually *82–95 lateral scales,* 14–16 pectoral rays. **Map 188**

SALISH SUCKER *Catostomus species* **Not shown**
Identification: Nearly identical to Longnose Sucker but has *shorter snout;* deeper head; smaller mouth; *usually 81–88 lateral scales, 21–25 scales* around caudal peduncle; reaches about 8 in. (20 cm).
Range: Puget Sound drainage, WA, and sw. lower Fraser Valley, BC. Protected in Canada as an *endangered species.* Rare. **Habitat:** Pools and runs of small cool headwaters and creeks; lakes.
Similar species: See Longnose Sucker (Pl. 21). **Map 188**

TAHOE SUCKER *Catostomus tahoensis* **Pl. 22**
Identification: *Large head; long snout; usually thick caudal peduncle. Deep median lower lip notch;* usually 1 row of papillae at middle of lower lip; 2–4 rows of papillae on upper lip (Fig. 41). Dark olive above sharply contrasting with yellow or white below; dusky fins. Breeding male has bright red stripe along brassy side. Usually *82–95 lateral scales;* 16–19 scale rows above, *12–15 below,* lateral line; 40–50

predorsal scales; usually 9–11 dorsal rays; *14–16 pectoral rays.* Black peritoneum. *Open frontoparietal fontanelle.* To 24 in. (61 cm).
Range: Native to Lahontan basin, se. OR, NV, and ne. CA. Recently established naturally or by way of introduction into upper Sacramento R. system, CA. Common. **Habitat:** Variable but most common in large lakes such as Lake Tahoe and Pyramid Lake, NV; also in pools along lower reaches of streams.
Similar species: See (1) Owens, (2) Warner, (3) Klamath Smallscale (Pl. 22), and (4) Modoc Suckers (Pl. 22). **Map 189**

OWENS SUCKER *Catostomus fumeiventris* **Not shown**
Identification: Similar to Tahoe Sucker but has usually *75–78 lateral scales; 13–16 scale rows above, 9–11 below,* lateral line; 16–19 pectoral rays. Breeding male *lacks* red stripe along side. Slate above; pale blue reflections on side; *dusky below* (especially large male); dull olive paired fins; dull amber median fins. To 19½ in. (50 cm).
Range: Owens R. drainage, CA. Introduced into June Lake and Santa Clara R. system, CA. Common. **Habitat:** Silty to rocky pools and runs of creeks.
Similar species: See Pl. 22. (1) See Tahoe Sucker. (2) Modoc Sucker has usually *80–89 lateral scales;* is *white or yellow below.* (3) Warner Sucker has usually *14–16 scale rows below* lateral line, 2–3 rows of papillae at middle of lower lip; is white or yellow below. **Map 189**

WARNER SUCKER *Catostomus warnerensis* **Not shown**
Identification: Similar to Tahoe Sucker but has moderately deep median lower lip notch, *2–3 rows* of papillae at middle of lower lip; usually *73–79 lateral scales, 14–16 scales below* lateral line. Light to dusky peritoneum. Olive green or gray above; white or yellow below; white to dusky fins. 24–26 scales around caudal peduncle. To 13¾ in. (35 cm).
Range: Restricted to endorheic Warner Lake basin, s. OR. Rare; protected as a *threatened species.* **Habitat:** Lakes; pools and runs of streams and large irrigation canals.
Similar species: See Pl. 22. (1) See Tahoe Sucker. (2) Sacramento Sucker has deep median lower lip notch, blunter snout, usually *1 row* of papillae at middle of lower lip, usually *12–15 dorsal rays, 18–22* scales around caudal peduncle. **Map 189**

KLAMATH SMALLSCALE SUCKER *Catostomus rimiculus* **Pl. 22**
Identification: Similar to Tahoe Sucker but has moderately deep median lower lip notch; *2 or more rows* of papillae at middle of lower lip; *5–6 rows* of papillae on upper lip. Dusky olive-brown above and on side, white to yellow below; fins similar in color to surrounding body parts. 81–93 lateral scales; 16–18 pectoral rays. *Closed frontoparietal fontanelle.* To 19¾ in. (50 cm).
Range: Rogue R. drainage, sw. OR, south to Trinity R. drainage, nw. CA. Common. **Habitat:** Silt- to rock-bottomed pools and runs of small to medium rivers; occasionally impoundments.

Similar species: (1) See Tahoe Sucker (Pl. 22). (2) Modoc Sucker (Pl. 22) has usually *1 row of papillae* at middle of lower lip, *2 rows of papillae* on upper lip. **Map 189**

MODOC SUCKER *Catostomus microps* Pl. 22

Identification: Similar to Tahoe Sucker but has shorter head, smaller eye, *small or closed frontoparietal fontanelle;* 9–13 scale rows below lateral line. Gray to olive-brown above fading to white or yellow below. Breeding male has red stripe along side, orange fins. 80–89 lateral scales. To 13¼ in. (34 cm).

Range: Ash, Turner, and Willow creeks (Pit R. system), n. CA. Common in small area; protected as an *endangered species.* **Habitat:** Shallow mud-bottomed pools of cool creeks.

Similar species: (1) See Tahoe Sucker (Pl. 22). (2) Owens Sucker has dusky belly, usually 75–78 lateral scales, 16–19 pectoral rays. (3) Sacramento Sucker (Pl. 22) has usually 12–15 dorsal rays, 5–6 rows of papillae on upper lip; 56–75 lateral scales; reaches 23½ in. (60 cm). **Map 189**

BRIDGELIP SUCKER *Catostomus columbianus* Pl. 22

Identification: *Weak or no* indentations separate upper and lower lips; *front of upper lip often papillose;* fairly deep median lower lip notch; 2–3 rows of papillae at middle of lower lip (Fig. 41). Truncate lower jaw. Usually 11–12 dorsal rays. Dusky caudal fin membranes. Olive green, mottled brown, or blue-black above; white to yellow below; dusky olive or blue-black fins. Breeding male has orange stripe along side. Black peritoneum. Pelvic axillary process absent or a simple fold. 43–75, usually more than 50, predorsal scales. Usually more than 29 rakers on 1st gill arch (see Remarks). To 12 in. (30 cm).

Range: Pacific Slope from Fraser R. drainage, BC, south through Columbia R. drainage, BC, ID, WA, OR, and NV (only below Shoshone Falls on Snake R.), and Harney R. basin, e. OR. Common. **Habitat:** Lake margins; backwaters, rocky riffles, and sand/silt runs of creeks and small to medium rivers.

Remarks: 3 subspecies. *C. c. hubbsi* in Wood R. system, ID, has usually 11 dorsal rays, relatively small lips with large papillae, 24–31 rakers on 1st gill arch. *C. c. palouseanus,* in Palouse R., w. ID and e. WA, and Crooked Cr., OR, has usually 11 dorsal rays, 30–39 rakers on 1st gill arch. *C. c. columbianus,* in rest of range, has usually 11–12 dorsal rays, relatively large lips with small papillae, 30–42 rakers on 1st gill arch.

Similar species: (1) Rio Grande Sucker (Pl. 22) has rounded lower jaw, fewer than 27 gill rakers, silver peritoneum, usually fewer than 50 predorsal scales, usually 9 dorsal rays; clear caudal fin membranes. (2) Mountain Sucker (Pl. 22) usually *lacks* papillae on front of upper lip, has *deep indentations* separating upper and lower lips, clear caudal fin membranes, usually 10 dorsal rays. **Map 190**

Next 5 species: Upper lip separated from lower lip by moderate to deep indentations (Fig. 41).

RIO GRANDE SUCKER *Catostomus plebeius* **Pl. 22**
Identification: *Small papillose lips.* Moderate indentations separate upper and lower lips; deep median lower lip notch; 2–3 rows of papillae at middle of lower lip (Fig. 41). Rounded lower jaw. Often sharply bicolored, olive-green to dusky brown above, white to yellow below; usually clear caudal fin. Breeding male has *red stripe* along side. Usually 9 dorsal rays; 32–55 (usually 40–50) predorsal scale rows; 20–27 rakers on 1st gill arch. No pelvic axillary process. Silver peritoneum. To about 7¾ in. (20 cm).
Range: Upper Rio Grande drainage, s. CO and NM, south through small, endorheic basins and headwaters of Pacific Slope drainages to Durango and Zacatecas, Mexico. Introduced into Gila R. system, NM and AZ. Common. **Habitat:** Rocky pools, runs, and riffles of small to medium rivers.
Similar species: (1) Bridgelip Sucker (Pl. 22) has *less papillose* front of upper lip, truncate lower jaw, usually more than 29 gill rakers (except *C. c. hubbsi*), black peritoneum, usually more than 50 predorsal scales, usually 11–12 dorsal rays, dusky caudal fin membranes. (2) Mountain Sucker (Pl. 22) usually *lacks* papillae on front of upper lip; has truncate lower jaw, pelvic axillary process, usually 10 dorsal rays, more than 26 gill rakers; black peritoneum. **Map 191**

MOUNTAIN SUCKER *Catostomus platyrhynchus* **Pl. 22**
Identification: Papillae on front of lower lip in a *half-rosette pattern with blank areas* on either side. *Deep indentations* separate upper and lower lips; few or no papillae on front of upper lip; shallow median lower lip notch; 3–4 rows of papillae at middle of lower lip (Fig. 41). Truncate lower jaw. Dusky gray to olive above, sometimes with dark stripe along side and 5 blotches on back; white to yellow below; clear or pale red fins. Breeding male has moss green back, bright *red stripe* along side above green-black stripe. Usually 10 dorsal rays; 23–37 rakers on 1st gill arch. *Pelvic axillary process.* Dusky or black peritoneum. To 9¾ in. (25 cm).
Range: W. Canada and U.S. from Saskatchewan R. system (Hudson Bay basin), SA and AB, and Fraser R. drainage, BC, south through upper Missouri and Colorado R. drainages to s. CO and UT, and through Columbia R. drainage, OR; Lahontan basin, OR, NV, and CA; upper Sacramento R. system, ne. CA. Common in center of range. **Habitat:** Variable; most common in rocky riffles and runs of clear mountain creeks and small to medium rivers.
Similar species: (1) Rio Grande Sucker (Pl. 22) has small, *papillose lips* (no blank areas), rounded lower jaw, *no* pelvic axillary process, usually 9 dorsal rays, silver peritoneum. (2) Bridgelip Sucker (Pl. 22) has *weak or no indentations* separating upper and lower lips, papillae on front of upper lip, dusky caudal fin, usually 11–12 dorsal rays. **Map 191**

SANTA ANA SUCKER *Catostomus santaanae* **Pl. 22**
Identification: *Deep indentations* separate upper and lower lips; shallow median lower lip notch; 3–4 rows of papillae at middle of lower

lip; front of upper lip often papillose (Fig. 41). Truncate lower jaw. Olive to dark gray above, dark blotches or faint dark stripes; silver below; dusky caudal fin membranes; other fins clear to dusky. 27–41 predorsal scales; 9–11 dorsal rays; 21–28 rakers on 1st gill arch; 67–86 lateral scales. Foldlike (poorly developed) pelvic axillary process. Black peritoneum. To 9¾ in. (25 cm).
Range: Native to Los Angeles, San Gabriel, and Santa Ana R. drainages, s. CA. Introduced into Santa Clara R. system, s. CA. Common. **Habitat:** Clear, cool rocky pools and runs of creeks and small to medium rivers.
Similar species: (1) See Desert Sucker (Pl. 22). (2) Bluehead Sucker (Pl. 22) has blue head (on adult), more than 43 predorsal scales, usually 86 or more lateral scales.   **Map 190**

DESERT SUCKER *Catostomus clarki*   **Pl. 22**
Identification: Similar to Santa Ana Sucker but *lacks* papillae on front of upper lip; has *4–7 rows* of papillae at middle of lower lip, *27–43 gill rakers*, 13–52 predorsal scales, usually 10–11 dorsal rays. Silver-tan to dark green above, silver to yellow below. To 13 in. (33 cm).
Range: Lower Colorado R. drainage (downstream of Grand Canyon), including Pluvial White R. and Meadow Valley Wash, NV; Virgin R., UT, AZ, and NV; Bill Williams R., AZ; and Gila R., NM, AZ, and n. Sonora, Mexico. Common. **Habitat:** Small to medium rivers; small individuals in riffles; adults in pools during day and riffles at night.
Similar species: See (1) Santa Ana and (2) Bluehead Suckers (both, Pl. 22).   **Map 190**

BLUEHEAD SUCKER *Catostomus discobolus*   **Pl. 22**
Identification: Similar to Desert Sucker but has slender caudal peduncle; *usually 50 or more predorsal scales*; 78–122 lateral scales; *blue head* — darkest on adult (blue absent in Little Colorado R., AZ, population). To 16 in. (41 cm).
Range: Snake R. system (Columbia R. drainage), WY and ID; Lake Bonneville basin, ID, WY, and UT; south through upper Colorado R. drainage (Grand Canyon and above), WY, CO, UT, NM, and AZ. Common. **Habitat:** Rocky riffles and runs of small to large rivers.
Remarks: 2 subspecies. *C. d. yarrowi,* in upper Zuni R., NM, has usually 42 or fewer vertebrae, 9–10 dorsal rays, fewer than 100 lateral scales, caudal peduncle depth usually more than 8% of standard length. *C. d. discobolus,* throughout rest of range, has usually 42 or more vertebrae, 10–11 dorsal rays, more than 100 lateral scales, caudal peduncle depth usually less than 8% of standard length.
Similar species: See Desert Sucker (Pl. 22).   **Map 190**

RAZORBACK SUCKER *Xyrauchen texanus*   **Pl. 21**
Identification: *Sharp keel* ("humpback") on nape (absent on small young). Long head and body; deep caudal peduncle. Horizontal mouth; few papillae on lips; *lower lip widely separated into 2 lobes* by deep median groove. Olive to brown-black above; brown or pink side; white to yellow below; olive to yellow dorsal fin; white to yellow-orange anal and paired fins. Breeding male is black or brown

above, *yellow to bright orange below*; sometimes has rosy fins. 68–87 lateral scales; 13–16 dorsal rays; 7 anal rays. To about 36 in. (91 cm).
Range: Formerly throughout medium to large rivers of Colorado R. basin from WY and CO to Baja California. Presently known only above Grand Canyon and in Lakes Mead, Mohave, and Havasu on lower Colorado R. Rare. **Habitat:** Silt- to rock-bottomed backwaters near strong current and deep pools in medium to large rivers; impoundments.
Remarks: Until nuchal hump develops, young are difficult to distinguish from young *Catostomus* species.
Similar species: No other sucker has large keel on nape.   **Map 192**

LOST RIVER SUCKER *Deltistes luxatus*   **Pl. 21**
Identification: *Distinct hump on snout.* Large robust body; long head; subterminal mouth. *Thin, moderately papillose lips;* moderately deep lower lip notch; no deep indentations separate upper and lower lips. Eye on rear half of head. Dark olive above; white or yellow below; fins similar in color to adjacent body. *82–88 lateral scales;* 11–12 dorsal rays; 7–8 anal rays. Usually 24–28 branched, triangular rakers on 1st gill arch. To 34 in. (86 cm).
Range: Lost R. system (upper Klamath R. basin), OR and CA. Rare; protected as an *endangered species.* **Habitat:** Lakes; impoundments; deep pools of small to medium rivers.
Similar species: (1) *Chasmistes* species (Pl. 21) have oblique mouth; thin, usually plicate, lips; 55–79 lateral scales; 38–53 gill rakers. (2) *Catostomus* species (Pls. 21 & 22) have thick, strongly papillose lips; long, slender body.   **Map 192**

SPOTTED SUCKER *Minytrema melanops*   **Pl. 23**
Identification: *Long, redhorselike body. 8–12 parallel rows of dark spots* (at scale bases) on back and side. Dusky to black, straight or concave, dorsal fin edge. *No lateral line* (rarely developed on a few scales). Small horizontal mouth; thin plicate lips, U-shaped lower lip edge. *Black edge* on lower caudal fin lobe. Dark green or olive-brown above; yellow to brown side; light yellow-orange to slate-olive median fins, usually white to dusky paired fins. Young has pink median fins. Breeding male has narrow pink stripe above brown to black stripe along side; above this is another stripe of dark lavender. Usually *42–47* lateral scales; 12 dorsal rays; 7 anal rays. To 19½ in. (50 cm).
Range: Lower Great Lakes and Mississippi R. basins from PA to MN and south to Gulf; Atlantic and Gulf Slope drainages from Cape Fear R., NC, to Colorado R., TX (absent from most of peninsular FL). Frequently encountered but rarely in large numbers. **Habitat:** Long deep pools of small to medium rivers over clay, sand, or gravel; occasionally creeks, large rivers, and impoundments.
Similar species: (1) *Moxostoma* species (Pls. 23 & 24) *lack* distinct rows of dark spots; have thicker lips, *lateral line.* (2) Chubsuckers (Pl. 23) have *deeper body,* more oblique mouth, rounded or sharply

pointed dorsal fin; snout extends only slightly beyond upper lip (versus far beyond in Spotted Sucker). **Map 193**

CREEK CHUBSUCKER *Erimyzon oblongus* **Pl. 23**
Identification: Chubby body. *Small, slightly oblique, nearly terminal mouth; plicate lips;* 2 halves of lower lip meet at nearly a right angle. *No lateral line. Rounded edge* on dorsal fin; usually 10–12 rays. Narrow caudal peduncle. Olive to brown above, dark-edged scales, *5–8 confluent dark blotches;* white to yellow below; yellow-orange to olive-gray fins. Young has broad yellow stripe above broad black stripe along side from snout tip to caudal fin base; amber or red caudal fin. Breeding male is dark brown above, pink-yellow below; has orange paired fins, yellow median fins, 3 large tubercles on each side of snout, *bilobed anal fin.* Usually 40–45 lateral scales, 7 anal rays. To 8½ in. (22 cm) in Mississippi R. Basin; to 14 in. (36 cm) on Atlantic and Gulf slopes.
Range: Atlantic Slope drainages from s. ME to Altamaha R., GA; Lake Ontario drainage, NY; Gulf Slope drainages from Chattahoochee R., AL (one record), to San Jacinto R., TX; lower Great Lakes and Mississippi R. basins from s. MI and se. WI south to Gulf. Common. **Habitat:** Sand- and gravel-bottomed pools of clear headwaters, creeks, and small rivers; often near vegetation. Occasionally in lakes.
Remarks: 2 subspecies: *E. o. oblongus,* on Atlantic Slope, has usually 12 dorsal rays; *E. o. claviformis,* throughout rest of range, has usually 10 dorsal rays. Intergrades occur in Altamaha R. system, GA.
Similar species: See (1) Lake and (2) Sharpfin Chubsuckers (both, Pl. 23). **Map 194**

LAKE CHUBSUCKER *Erimyzon sucetta* **Pl. 23**
Identification: Similar to Creek Chubsucker but has *deeper body,* usually *34–39 lateral scales; lacks* dark blotches along side (often dusky stripe). Breeding male is dark overall. To 16 in. (41 cm).
Range: Great Lakes and Mississippi R. basin lowlands from s. ON to WI and south to Gulf; Atlantic Slope from s. VA to s. FL; Gulf Slope drainages from Charlotte Harbor, FL, to Guadalupe R., TX. Sporadic in north; common on lower Coastal Plain. **Habitat:** Lakes, swamps, ponds, sloughs, and impoundments over silt, sand, or debris. Rarely in streams.
Similar species: See (1) Creek Chubsucker and (2) Sharpfin Chubsucker (both, Pl. 23). **Map 195**

SHARPFIN CHUBSUCKER *Erimyzon tenuis* **Pl. 23**
Identification: Similar to Creek and Lake Chubsuckers but has *sharply pointed dorsal fin,* longer head, larger eye. Breeding male has *4 large tubercles* on each side of snout; *lacks* bilobed anal fin. Dark stripe along side (becomes less defined with age); sometimes a black edge on light amber or olive dorsal and anal fins; yellow or olive caudal and paired fins. Young similar to Creek and Lake Chubsuckers, except black stripe along side is edged above by a *narrow yellow stripe.* Usually 40–44 lateral scales. To 13 in. (33 cm).

Range: Gulf Slope from Yellow R. system, AL and FL, to Amite R. system, MS and LA. Common; rare above Fall Line. **Habitat:** Pools and backwaters of creeks and small rivers over sand or silt; often near vegetation.

Similar species: See (1) Creek and (2) Lake Chubsuckers (both, Pl. 23).

Map 196

NORTHERN HOG SUCKER *Hypentelium nigricans*   **Pl. 23**

Identification: *Large, rectangular head, broadly flat* (in young) or *concave* (in adult) *between eyes.* Body wide in front, abruptly tapering behind dorsal fin. *3–6 dusky or brown saddles* (1 on nape) extend obliquely forward on upper side. Long, blunt snout; large fleshy lips on horizontal mouth; many large papillae on lips; 2 halves of lower lip broadly joined at middle (Fig. 42). Large, fanlike pectoral fins. Dark olive or bronze to red-brown above; often light stripes along scale rows on side; pale yellow or white below; blue-black snout; olive to light orange fins; often black edge on dorsal and caudal fins. Large individual has black-tipped dorsal fin. Complete lateral line, 44–54 scales; usually 11 dorsal rays, 32–38 total (both sides) pectoral rays. To 24 in. (61 cm).

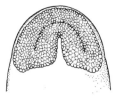

Northern   Roanoke

Fig. 42 Northern and Roanoke Hog Suckers — lips

Range: Great Lakes, Hudson Bay (Red R.), and Mississippi R. basins from NY and s. ON to MN, and south to n. AL, s. AR, and e. LA; Atlantic Slope drainages from Mohawk-Hudson R., NY, to Altamaha R., n. GA; Gulf Slope drainages from Pascagoula R., MS, to Comite R., LA. Recently reported from upper Mobile Bay drainage, AL, and upper Chattahoochee R. drainage, GA. Common; generally avoids lowlands (e.g., n. MO, Coastal Plain). **Habitat:** Rocky riffles, runs, and pools of clear creeks and small rivers; occasionally large rivers, impoundments.

Similar species: See (1) Alabama and (2) Roanoke Hog Suckers (Pl. 23).

Map 197

ALABAMA HOG SUCKER *Hypentelium etowanum*   **Not shown**

Identification: Nearly identical to Northern Hog Sucker but has usu-

ally *10 dorsal rays*, head *only slightly concave* between eyes, light stripes on upper side usually more prominent, *red-orange anal and paired fins, orange snout and lips*; reaches 9 in. (23 cm).
Range: Chattahoochee R. and Mobile Bay drainages, GA, AL, MS, and se. TN; recently discovered in Baker Cr. (Tennessee R. drainage), Polk Co., TN. Common; mostly found above Fall Line. **Habitat:** Rocky riffles and runs of clear fast creeks and small rivers.
Similar species: See Northern Hog Sucker (Pl. 23). **Map 198**

ROANOKE HOG SUCKER *Hypentelium roanokense* **Pl. 23**
Identification: Similar to Northern and Alabama Hog Suckers, but has *plicate lips* (papillose on outer surfaces) (Fig. 42); usually *lacks* or has *vague dark saddle* on nape; has usually *39–44 lateral scales, 28–32 total pectoral rays*; more prominent light stripes on back and side. Copper to brown above, usually 4 black saddles; clear to light orange fins. Usually 11 dorsal rays. To 6½ in. (16 cm).
Range: Roanoke R. drainage, VA and NC. Common. **Habitat:** Rocky riffles, runs, and pools of creeks and small rivers; often over sand in slow current.
Similar species: See (1) Northern (Pl. 23) and (2) Alabama Hog Suckers. **Map 198**

● *MOXOSTOMA* SPECIES

Genus characteristics: Robust to long and slender body. Large, *horizontal mouth; thick, papillose or plicate lips*; groove between upper lip and snout. Complete lateral line, 37–51 scales; 9–17 dorsal rays; 7 anal rays; 16–37 long, thin, flattened gill rakers; 3-chambered gas

Fig. 43 Harelip Sucker — lips

bladder. Young has usually 3 or 4 dark saddles and 4 dark blotches on side. The Harelip Sucker, *Moxostoma lacerum*, formerly in the Maumee (Lake Erie drainage), Ohio, and White R. drainages from OH and VA to AR and south to GA and AL (Map 199), but now extinct, had a highly unusual mouth with *upper lip bound to snout* (no groove between lip and snout) and *lower lip halves separate* (Fig. 43).

GREATER REDHORSE *Moxostoma valenciennesi* **Pl. 23**
Identification: Stout body; *large head* (about 25% of standard length in individual over 10 in. [25 cm]). *Red caudal fin. Thick plicate lips;*

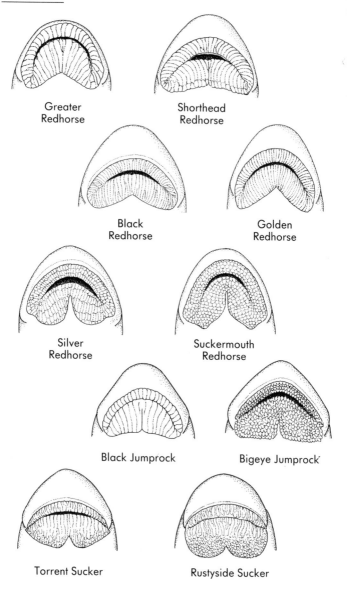

Greater
Redhorse

Shorthead
Redhorse

Black
Redhorse

Golden
Redhorse

Silver
Redhorse

Suckermouth
Redhorse

Black Jumprock

Bigeye Jumprock

Torrent Sucker

Rustyside Sucker

Fig. 44 Redhorses and related suckers — lips

V-shaped rear edge on lower lip (Fig. 44). Usually convex dorsal fin edge. Pointed lobes on large, forked caudal fin. Bronze or coppery above, dark spots on scales on back and side; silver-yellow or white below; yellow to red fins. Usually 42–45 lateral scales, 13–14 dorsal rays, 15–16 scales around caudal peduncle, 12–13 scales over back (in front of dorsal fin) from lateral line to lateral line (excluding lateral-line scales). Bladelike teeth on slender pharyngeal arch. To 31½ in. (80 cm).
Range: Great Lakes–St. Lawrence R., Hudson Bay (Red. R.), and Mississippi R. basins from QU and VT to s. ON and n. MN, and south to Ohio R., KY. Uncommon to rare; disappearing from southern parts of range. **Habitat:** Sandy to rocky pools and runs of medium to large rivers; lakes.
Similar species: (1) Copper Redhorse (Pl. 23) has shorter head, highly arched back, 15 or 16 scales over back in front of dorsal fin, molarlike teeth on pharyngeal arch. (2) River Redhorse (Pl. 23) has usually concave dorsal fin edge, 12–13 scales around caudal peduncle, molarlike teeth on pharyngeal arch.   **Map 200**

COPPER REDHORSE *Moxostoma hubbsi*   **Pl. 23**
Identification: Stout, *deep body. Highly arched back* behind *short head* (about 20% of standard length in individual over 10 in. [25 cm]). *Red caudal fin.* Plicate lips; slightly V-shaped rear edge on lower lip. Usually convex dorsal fin edge. Pointed lobes on large, forked caudal fin. Gold to olive, often a coppery sheen above; dark spots on scales on back and side; yellow to red fins. Usually 44–47 lateral scales, 12–13 dorsal rays, 16 scales around caudal peduncle, 15 or 16 scales over back (in front of dorsal fin) from lateral line to lateral line. 4–6 molarlike teeth on stout pharyngeal arch. To 28 in. (72 cm).
Range: St. Lawrence R. drainage, QU. Rare; protected as a *threatened species.* **Habitat:** Rocky pools, backwaters, and swift runs of medium to large rivers.
Similar species: (1) Greater Redhorse (Pl. 23) has *more elongate body; longer head,* thicker lips, usually 12–13 scales across back in front of dorsal fin, bladelike teeth on pharyngeal arch. (2) River Redhorse (Pl. 23) has usually concave dorsal fin edge; usually 12-13 caudal peduncle scales, 42–44 lateral scales.   **Map 201**

RIVER REDHORSE *Moxostoma carinatum*   **Pl. 23**
Identification: *Stout body; large head* (about 25% of standard length in individual over 10 in. [25 cm]). *Large plicate lips;* slightly V-shaped rear edge on lower lip. *Red caudal fin.* Usually concave dorsal fin. Large, forked caudal fin; pointed upper lobe usually longer than rounded lower lobe. Olive-bronze above, gold reflections; crescent-shaped *dark spots on scales* on back and side; deep yellow or orange anal and paired fins; red dorsal fin. Breeding male has dark stripe along side. Usually 42–44 lateral scales, 12–13 scales around caudal peduncle, 12–13 dorsal rays. 6–8 molarlike teeth on stout pharyngeal arch. To 30 in. (77 cm).
Range: St. Lawrence R.–Great Lakes and Mississippi R. basins from s.

QU to cen. MN and w. IA, and south to n. AL and e. OK; Gulf Slope from Escambia R., FL, to Pearl R., LA and MS. Locally common; disappearing from n. and w. parts of range. **Habitat:** Rocky pools and swift runs of small to large rivers; impoundments.
Similar species: See Pl. 23. (1) Shorthead Redhorse has *short head, papillae* on lower lip, straight rear edge on lower lip, bladelike teeth on pharyngeal arch. (2) Greater Redhorse has thicker lips, usually 15–16 scales around caudal peduncle, bladelike teeth on pharyngeal arch.
Map 202

SHORTHEAD REDHORSE *Moxostoma macrolepidotum*   **Pl. 23**
Identification: Fairly stout body; *short head* (about 20% of standard length in individual over 7½ in. [19 cm]). *Red caudal fin.* Plicate lips; large papillae on lower lip; *nearly straight rear edge* on lower lip (Fig. 44). Moderately *concave to falcate* dorsal fin. Large, moderately forked caudal fin; upper lobe usually distinctly longer than lower lobe (see Remarks). Olive or tan above; copper or silver cast on olive-yellow side; crescent-shaped dark spots on scales on back and side; white or yellow below; yellow to red fins. Usually 42–44 lateral scales, 12–13 scales around caudal peduncle, 12–13 dorsal rays. Bladelike teeth on slender pharyngeal arch. To 29½ in. (75 cm).
Range: Great Lakes–St. Lawrence R., Hudson Bay, and Mississippi R. basins from QU to AB and south to n. AL and OK (isolated population in Red R., s. OK); Atlantic Slope drainages from Hudson R., NY, to Santee R., SC. Locally common. **Habitat:** Rocky pools, runs, and riffles in small to large rivers; lakes.
Remarks: Three subspecies. *M. m. pisolabrum,* in Ozark Uplands (Arkansas and Red R. drainages), has usually a pea-shaped swelling at middle of upper lip; intergrades with *M. m. macrolepidotum* in lower Missouri R. drainage, MO, Mississippi R. tributaries, ne. MO; and Kaskaskia R., IL. *M. m. breviceps,* in Ohio R. basin, has usually 12 dorsal rays (vs. 13 in other subspecies), 10 pelvic rays (vs. 9), smaller lips, longer upper caudal lobe, and falcate dorsal fin; intergrades with *M. m. macrolepidotum* in Wabash R. drainage, IN and IL. *M. m. macrolepidotum,* throughout rest of range, has usually larger lips, equal caudal lobes, and straight to slightly falcate dorsal fin edge.
Similar species: (1) River Redhorse (Pl. 23) has *larger head,* thicker lips, slightly *V-shaped rear edge* on lower lip, molarlike teeth on pharyngeal arch. (2) Greater Redhorse (Pl. 23) has *larger head,* thicker lips; *V-shaped rear edge* on lower lip; usually 15–16 scales around caudal peduncle.
Map 203

BLACKTAIL REDHORSE *Moxostoma poecilurum*   **Pl. 23**
Identification: *Long, cylindrical body. Red caudal and lower fins; black stripe* on lower caudal fin lobe; dark and light stripes on side moderately developed. Plicate lips; slightly U-shaped rear edge on lower lip. Usually concave dorsal fin edge. Large, moderately forked caudal fin, lower lobe usually longer than upper lobe. Gold to bronze above, silver-green iridescence; silver-yellow or white below; dusky gray on lower half, red on outer half, of dorsal fin; white to red on

other fins. Bladelike teeth on slender pharyngeal arch. Usually 41–44 lateral scales, 12 scales around caudal peduncle, 12–13 dorsal rays. To 20 in. (51 cm).
Range: Mississippi R. tributaries on Former Mississippi Embayment from s. KY and s. AR south to LA; Gulf Slope drainages from Choctawhatchee R., AL and FL, to Galveston Bay, TX. Locally common; rare in KY and TN. **Habitat:** Sandy and rocky pools, runs, and riffles of small to medium rivers; impoundments.
Similar species: See Grayfin Redhorse. **Map 204**

GRAYFIN REDHORSE *Moxostoma* species **Not shown**
Identification: Similar to Blacktail Redhorse but has *dusky gray* caudal fin; darker *stripes on side; lacks* red on caudal and lower fins. To 20½ in. (52 cm).
Range: Apalachicola R. drainage, GA, AL, and FL. Locally common.
Habitat: Mud- to rock-bottomed pools, sandy to rocky runs and riffles of small to large rivers; impoundments.
Similar species: See Blacktail Redhorse (Pl. 23). **Map 204**

BLACK REDHORSE *Moxostoma duquesnei* **Pl. 24**
Identification: Long slender body; long *slender caudal peduncle. Gray caudal fin* (rarely pale red). Plicate lips; broadly V-shaped rear edge on lower lip (Fig. 44). Usually concave dorsal fin. Large, moderately forked caudal fin has usually equal, pointed lobes. Dusky olive above; gold to brassy side, green iridescence; white or yellow below; orange anal and paired fins; dusky or slate dorsal fin (sometimes redtinged). Breeding male has pink-orange stripe along side, pink-orange anal and paired fins, small tubercles on snout. Usually *44–47 lateral scales,* 12–14 scales around caudal peduncle, 12–14 dorsal rays, *10* pelvic rays (vs. 9 in other redhorses). Many bladelike teeth on slender pharyngeal arch. To 20 in. (51 cm).
Range: Lower Great Lakes and Mississippi R. basins from s. ON and NY and south to n. AL and e. OK (absent on Former Mississippi Embayment); upper and middle Mobile Bay drainage (absent in Tombigbee R. system), GA, AL, and se. TN. Generally common; protected in Canada as a *threatened species.* **Habitat:** Sand- to rockbottomed pools and runs of creeks and small to medium rivers; impoundments.
Similar species: (1) Golden Redhorse (Pl. 24) has *shorter, deeper caudal peduncle;* usually 40–42 lateral scales, *9 pelvic rays;* large male has large snout tubercles. (2) Silver Redhorse (Pl. 24) has papillose lips, acutely V-shaped rear edge on lower lip, usually convex or straight dorsal fin edge, usually 14–16 dorsal rays. **Map 201**

GOLDEN REDHORSE *Moxostoma erythrurum* **Pl. 24**
Identification: Moderately stout body; fairly *stout caudal peduncle. Gray caudal fin* (pale orange in young). Plicate lips; V- or U-shaped rear edge on lower lip (Fig. 44). Usually concave dorsal fin. Large, moderately forked caudal fin has equal, pointed lobes. Olive to brassbrown above; dark-edged scales on back and front half of side; yellow

to brass side, pale green reflections; yellow or white below; yellow to orange anal and paired fins; gray dorsal fin. Breeding male has dark stripe along side, bright salmon lower fins, large tubercles on snout. Usually *40–42 lateral scales,* 12 scales around caudal peduncle, 12–14 dorsal rays, 9 pelvic rays. Many *bladelike teeth* on slender pharyngeal arch. To 30½ in. (78 cm).

Range: Great Lakes, Hudson Bay (Red R.), and Mississippi R. basins from NY and s. ON to ND, and south to n. AL and s. OK; isolated population in sw. MS; Atlantic Slope from Potomac R., MD, to Roanoke R., NC (absent in Rappahannock and York R. drainages); Mobile Bay drainage, GA, AL, and se. TN. Common. **Habitat:** Mud- to rock-bottomed pools, runs and riffles of creeks and small to large rivers; occasionally lakes.

Similar species: See Pl. 24. (1) Black Redhorse has *longer, more slender caudal peduncle;* usually 44–47 lateral scales, 10 pelvic rays; large male has small tubercles on snout. (2) Silver Redhorse has papillose lips, acutely V-shaped rear edge on lower lip; usually convex or straight dorsal fin edge, usually 14–16 dorsal rays. (3) Suckermouth Redhorse has papillose lips, strongly V-shaped rear edge on lower lip.

Map 205

SILVER REDHORSE *Moxostoma anisurum* **Pl. 24**

Identification: Stout body; *straight or slightly convex dorsal fin. Acutely V-shaped* rear edge on *deeply divided lower lip; many small papillae* on upper and lower lips (Fig. 44). *Slate gray dorsal and caudal fins.* Large, moderately forked caudal fin; equal, usually pointed lobes. Iridescent blue-green to brown above; pale yellow-silver to brassy side, no dark spots on scale bases; pale yellow to red anal and paired fins. Usually 40–42 lateral scales, 12 scales around caudal peduncle, *14-16 dorsal rays.* To 28 in. (71 cm).

Range: Great Lakes–St. Lawrence R., Hudson Bay (Nelson and Red R. drainages), and Mississippi R. basins from QU to AB, and south to n. AL and n. AR; Atlantic Slope from Roanoke R. drainage, VA, to Altamaha R. drainage, GA. Uncommon. **Habitat:** Mud- to rock-bottomed pools and runs of small to large rivers; occasionally lakes.

Similar species: See Pl. 24. (1) Black and (2) Golden Redhorses have *plicate lips,* usually *concave dorsal fin, 12–14 dorsal rays.* (3) Suckermouth Redhorse has more slender body, *concave to falcate dorsal fin,* usually *12–13 dorsal rays.* **Map 206**

SUCKERMOUTH REDHORSE *Moxostoma pappillosum* **Pl. 24**

Identification: *Long slender body. Papillose lips; acutely V-shaped* rear edge on *deeply divided lower lip* (Fig. 44). Moderately *concave to falcate dorsal fin.* Equal, pointed lobes on large, moderately forked caudal fin. Olive-tan above; brassy to yellow side, silver-green iridescence; gray to salmon-orange fins. Usually 42–44 lateral scales, 12 scales around caudal peduncle, 12–13 dorsal rays. To 17¾ in. (45 cm).

Range: Atlantic Slope from Roanoke R. drainage, VA, to Santee R. drainage, SC. Uncommon; rare in Peedee and Santee R. drainages. **Habitat:** Rocky runs and mud- to rock-bottomed pools of small rivers; impoundments.

Similar species: (1) Silver Redhorse (Pl. 24) has *stouter body*, usually *straight or convex dorsal fin*, usually 14–16 dorsal rays. (2) Golden Redhorse (Pl. 24) has *plicate lips*. **Map 207**

GRAY REDHORSE *Moxostoma congestum*   **Pl. 24**
Identification: *Broad, U-shaped* (from above) *head.* Plicate lips; straight to rounded edge on lower lip. Long pectoral fin (length greater than head depth at rear). Straight to slightly concave dorsal fin. Moderately large, shallowly forked caudal fin; pointed upper lobe, rounded lower lobe. Olive to yellow-gray above, gray dorsal and caudal fins, yellow anal and paired fins. Breeding male is brassy gold, has *yellow to light orange fins.* Usually 42–46 lateral scales, 16 scales around caudal peduncle, 32–36 scales around body (at front of dorsal fin), 16–17 pectoral rays, 11–12 dorsal rays. To 25½ in. (65 cm).
Range: Brazos R. drainage to Rio Grande drainage, TX and s. NM. Also in Mexico (south to Rio Soto la Marina drainage). Locally common. **Habitat:** Deep runs and pools of small to medium rivers; lakes.
Similar species: (1) See West Mexican Redhorse. (2) Smallfin Redhorse (Pl. 24) has usually 45–48 lateral scales; young has dark stripes on back. **Map 208**

WEST MEXICAN REDHORSE *Moxostoma austrinum*   **Not shown**
Identification: Similar to Gray Redhorse but has usually 36–41 scales around body (at dorsal fin origin), dark crescents on upper body scales. To 19 in. (49 cm).
Range: Known only from Alamito Cr., Big Bend, TX; Mexico. Rare (possibly extirpated) in U.S.; uncommon in Mexico. **Habitat:** Rocky runs and riffles of creeks and small to medium rivers; often near boulders in swift water.
Similar species: See Gray Redhorse (Pl. 24). **Map 208**

SMALLFIN REDHORSE *Moxostoma robustum*   **Pl. 24**
Identification: *Moderate to deep head,* distinctly convex between eyes; *rounded snout* (viewed from above). Fairly deep caudal peduncle. Plicate lips; nearly straight lower lip edge. Small fins. Straight to slightly concave dorsal fin. Pointed upper lobe, rounded lower lobe, on moderately large, shallowly forked caudal fin. Gold-brown above and on side, dark-edged scales; dusky dorsal fin; olive caudal fin; orange to red on other fins. Young has dark stripes on back and side narrower than pale interspaces; 4–5 dark blotches along side may connect to 4 saddles. Usually 45–48 lateral scales, 34–37 scales around body at dorsal fin origin, 16 scales around caudal peduncle, 11–12 dorsal rays, 16–18 pectoral rays. To 16½ in. (42 cm).
Range: Atlantic Slope from Peedee R. drainage, VA, and Cape Fear R. drainage, NC, to Oconee R. system (Altamaha R. drainage), GA. Uncommon in mountain and Piedmont streams; absent on Coastal Plain. **Habitat:** Silty to rocky pools and slow runs of small to medium rivers; impoundments.
Similar species: See Pl. 24. (1) Striped Jumprock has more *slender body,* head *wider* than deep, usually 10–11 dorsal rays, plicate to semipapillose lips. (2) Black Jumprock has black or dusky tips on dor-

sal and caudal fins; usually 40–44 lateral scales, 30–34 scales around body, 11 dorsal rays. (3) Greater Jumprock has more *slender body, longer head*, blunt snout, usually 30–34 scales around body.

Map 202

STRIPED JUMPROCK *Moxostoma rupiscartes*   **Pl. 24**
Identification: Cylindrical body; nearly straight upper and lower profiles; fairly deep caudal peduncle. Head flat or slightly convex between eyes; *wider than deep*. Plicate (plicae divided at rear) to semipapillose lower lip; *nearly straight lower lip edge.* Straight to slightly concave dorsal fin. *Dusky edge* on dorsal and caudal fins (in some populations). Pointed to rounded lobes on moderately large, slightly forked caudal fin. Yellow-olive to brown above; *prominent dark stripes* on back and side wider than or equal to pale interspaces; dusky olive to orange fins. Breeding male has faint yellow-brown stripe along side. Young have 4–5 blotches along side, yellow caudal fin. Usually 45–48 lateral scales, 32–37 scales around body at dorsal fin origin, 16 scales around caudal peduncle, 10–11 dorsal rays, 16–18 pectoral rays. To 11 in. (28 cm).
Range: Atlantic Slope from Santee R. drainage, NC, to Altamaha R. drainage, GA; Gulf Slope in upper Chattahoochee R. drainage, GA. Recently discovered (possibly introduced) in extreme upper Peedee R. drainage, NC. Common in mountain and Piedmont streams; absent on Coastal Plain. **Habitat:** Sandy to rocky riffles and runs of small to medium rivers.
Similar species: See Pl. 24. (1) Smallfin Redhorse has plicate lips, moderate to deep head; usually 11–12 dorsal rays. (2) Black Jumprock has usually 40–44 lateral scales, 30–34 scales around body. (3) Greater Jumprock has *long narrow head*, U-shaped lower lip edge, usually 12 dorsal rays.

Map 209

BLACK JUMPROCK *Moxostoma cervinum*   **Pl. 24**
Identification: Long, cylindrical body. *Black or dusky tips* on dorsal, caudal, and often anal fins. Light stripes on back and upper side. *Plicate lips*; straight lower lip edge (Fig. 44). Head slightly convex between eyes. Pointed to rounded lobes on small, slightly forked caudal fin. Olive to brown above, white on lower side; olive-yellow to orange fins. Young has about 6 dark blotches along side. Breeding male has brassy lower side, sometimes a light yellow stripe along side, red-orange caudal and paired fins. Usually 40–44 lateral scales, 30–34 scales around body at dorsal fin origin, 14–16 scales around caudal peduncle, 11 dorsal rays, 15 pectoral rays. To 7½ in. (19 cm).
Range: Atlantic Slope drainages from James R., VA, to Neuse R., NC. Apparently introduced into New R. drainage, VA. Common. **Habitat:** Rocky riffles and runs of creeks and small rivers.
Similar species: See Pl. 24. (1) Greater Jumprock *lacks* black tips on fins; has longer, more narrow head; broadly U-shaped lower lip edge; usually 45–46 lateral scales, 12 dorsal rays; large male has blue-gray anal and caudal fins. (2) Striped Jumprock *lacks* black tips on fins; has usually 45–48 lateral scales, 16–18 pectoral rays. (3) Smallfin

Redhorse *lacks* black tips on fins; has usually 45–48 lateral scales, 11–12 dorsal rays, 34–37 scales around body. **Map 210**

GREATER JUMPROCK *Moxostoma lachneri* **Pl. 24**

Identification: Long, cylindrical body; *slender caudal peduncle. Long, narrow head* (deeper than wide); straight lower profile; blunt snout. Concave dorsal fin. *Plicate* lips; *broadly U-shaped lower lip edge. White lower ray* on caudal fin. *Pointed* upper lobe, rounded lower lobe on *large,* slightly forked caudal fin. Dark olive above (some individuals sharply bicolored: dark above, white below); about 8 dark stripes on back and upper side (obscure on large male); slate gray fins. Breeding male is iridescent silver-black above; has blue-gray anal and caudal fins; other fins slate gray with some orange (especially pelvic fins). Light and dark stripes on back and side, about 5 dark blotches along side of young. Usually 45–46 lateral scales, 30–34 scales around body at dorsal fin origin, 16 scales around caudal peduncle, 12 dorsal rays, 17 pectoral rays. To 17½ in. (44 cm).
Range: Apalachicola R. drainage, GA and AL. Uncommon. **Habitat:** Rocky riffles and runs of clear small to medium rivers.
Similar species: See Pl. 24. (1) Black Jumprock has black or dusky dorsal and caudal fin tips; *straight lower lip edge;* usually 40–44 lateral scales, 11 dorsal rays; red-orange caudal and paired fins. (2) Striped Jumprock has *nearly straight lower lip edge, head wider than deep,* usually 10–11 dorsal rays. (3) Smallfin Redhorse has rounded snout (viewed from above), usually 34–37 scales around body. **Map 210**

BIGEYE JUMPROCK *Moxostoma ariommum* **Pl. 24**

Identification: Long cylindrical body flattened in front, compressed behind. *Very large eye.* Head flat or *slightly concave* between eyes. Flat, *flaring papillose lips* (Fig. 44). Straight to slightly concave dorsal fin. Slightly forked caudal fin. Olive to brown above (often with violet hue), vague light stripes (often absent) on back and upper side; sometimes an iridescent green streak on opercle and front of upper side; dusky to orange-red fins. Young has dark blotches along side. Usually 43–46 lateral scales, 15–16 scales around caudal peduncle, 11 dorsal rays. To 8½ in. (22 cm).
Range: Upper Roanoke R. drainage, VA and NC. Uncommon. **Habitat:** Deep rocky runs and pools of small to medium rivers; usually among large rubble and boulders, rarely in riffles.
Similar species: No other *Moxostoma* species has a large eye, slightly concave head, and flaring papillose lips. **Map 209**

TORRENT SUCKER *Thoburnia rhothoeca* **Pl. 24**

Identification: Cylindrical body; *2 large pale (sometimes dusky) areas* on caudal fin base highlighted by black streaks on adjacent caudal rays. Slightly concave or straight-edged dorsal fin. Small mouth; each half of lower lip edge nearly triangular (Fig. 44); *fewer papillae than plicae on lower lip.* Rounded lobes on small, slightly forked caudal fin. Dark olive-brown above; 5–6 vague to dark brown blotches along side, sometimes connected to 4 dark saddles; white to pale orange fins; dusky streaks on caudal and pectoral fins. Breeding male has

rusty red stripe along side, bright yellow fins. 43–51 lateral scales; usually 16–18 scales around caudal peduncle, 10 dorsal rays. Black peritoneum. To 7¼ in. (18 cm).
Range: Atlantic Slope from upper Potomac R. drainage, VA and WV, to Roanoke R. drainage, n.-cen. VA and adjacent WV (absent in York R. system); upper New R. drainage, VA (apparently extirpated). Introduced into upper Rappahannock R. drainage, VA. Common. **Habitat:** Rocky riffles and runs of moderate to swift creeks and small rivers; young in rocky runs and pools.
Similar species: (1) See Rustyside Sucker. (2) Blackfin Sucker (Pl. 24) *lacks* pale areas on caudal fin base; has jet black blotch on dorsal fin, 7–9 bold black stripes on back and upper side. (3) Black Jumprock (Pl. 24) has pronounced black or dusky dorsal and caudal fin tips, *plicate lips*, usually 11 dorsal rays.   **Map 211**

RUSTYSIDE SUCKER *Thoburnia hamiltoni*   **Not shown**
Identification: Nearly identical to Torrent Sucker but has *larger lower lip*, each half *square or broadly rounded*; *more papillae than plicae* on lower lip (Fig. 44). To 7 in. (18 cm).
Range: Upper Dan R. system (Roanoke R. drainage), VA and NC. Locally common in small range. **Habitat:** Rocky riffles and runs of swift mountain creeks and small rivers; young in flowing pools.
Similar species: See Torrent Sucker (Pl. 24).   **Map 211**

BLACKFIN SUCKER *Thoburnia atripinnis*   **Pl. 24**
Identification: Cylindrical body. *Large jet black blotch* on tip of white or light yellow dorsal fin; straight dorsal fin edge. *7–9 bold black stripes on back and upper side.* Small mouth; plicate lips; straight lower lip edge. Small, slightly forked caudal fin. Olive-gold stripes between black stripes on back and upper side; 2 dark saddles (often vague); shiny white below; pale yellow or olive anal and pelvic fins; pink-olive pectoral fin; pink-orange caudal fin. Young has 4–5 black blotches along side. 46–50 lateral scales; usually 16 scales around caudal peduncle, 10 dorsal rays. To 6½ in. (17 cm).
Range: Upper Barren R. system (Green R. drainage), KY and TN. Locally common in small range. **Habitat:** Rocky pools and adjacent riffles of creeks and small rivers; hides in bedrock crevices, near boulders, or under shoreline brush.
Similar species: (1) Torrent (Pl. 24) and (2) Rustyside Suckers *lack* jet black blotch on dorsal fin, bold black stripes on back and upper side; have 2 large pale areas on caudal fin base, more *papillose* lower lip.
Map 211

LOACHES: Family Cobitidae (1)

Loaches, popular aquarium fishes, are native to the fresh waters of Eurasia, Morocco, and Ethiopia. At least 175 species are known, and one, the Oriental Weatherfish, was introduced into the U.S. in the 1930s.

Loaches (see endpapers) have a *wormlike to fusiform body shape*, subterminal mouth, *3–6 pairs of barbels*, tiny or no scales, 1 row of pharyngeal teeth, and a rounded to deeply forked caudal fin; some have an adipose fin.

ORIENTAL WEATHERFISH *Misgurnus anguillicaudatus* **Not shown**
Identification: *Long, cylindrical body; 10-12 barbels around mouth*; rounded caudal fin. *Stout spine* on pectoral fin. Dorsal fin origin above pelvic fin origin. Tiny scales. Faint dusky blotches on light olive or tan side; usually dark spots on dorsal and caudal fins; usually a small black spot at upper edge of caudal fin base. 9 dorsal rays, 6–7 pelvic rays, 7–8 anal rays. To 10 in. (25 cm).
Range: Native to eastern Asia. Established in headwaters of Shiawassee R., Oakland Co., MI; Harton Davis Canal, Ada Co., ID; and flood control canals in Huntington Beach and Westminster, Orange Co., CA. Common. **Habitat:** Mud-bottomed pools or runs, where it burrows into the bottom; survives in poorly oxygenated water.

■ BULLHEAD CATFISHES: Family Ictaluridae (40)

The bullhead catfish family is the largest family of freshwater fishes endemic to North America north of Mexico. In addition to the 40 species found in the U.S. and Canada, at least five species are known from Mexico and Guatemala. Elsewhere in the world are 30 other families of catfishes containing over 2200 species.

Bullhead catfishes have *4 pairs of barbels* ("whiskers") around the mouth, *no scales, an adipose fin, stout spines* at the dorsal and pectoral fin origins, and abdominal pelvic fins. Members of this family are active mainly at night. Glandular cells in the skin surrounding the fin spines of madtoms are venomous; reaction to the "sting" received from mishandling a madtom varies with the individual but is generally considered equivalent to a bee sting.

The Flathead and Blue Catfishes, the giants of the family at about 132 lb. (60 kg) and 5 ft. (1.5 m), and several other large species, especially the widely marketed channel catfish, are of major commercial, angling, and aquacultural value.

● *ICTALURUS* SPECIES

Genus characteristics: *Moderately to deeply forked caudal fin*; short base on *small adipose fin*, its rear edge free from back and far from caudal fin; anal fin moderately long, with 23–35 rays; upper jaw projects beyond lower jaw; no backward projections on premaxillary tooth patch; eyes fairly large, on side of head.

CHANNEL CATFISH *Ictalurus punctatus* **Pl. 25**
Identification: Scattered *dark spots* on light back and side (except in

small young and large adult); *rounded anal fin, 24–29 rays.* Gently sloping, slightly rounded predorsal profile. Pale blue to olive back and side; white below; fins similar in color to adjacent body; white to dusky chin barbels. Small young lacks spots, has black-tipped fins. Large individual has blue-black back; often lacks dark spots. Air bladder without a distinct constriction. To 50 in. (127 cm).
Range: Native to St. Lawrence–Great Lakes, Hudson Bay (Red R. drainage), and Missouri–Mississippi R. basins from s. QU to s. MB and MT south to Gulf. Possibly also native on Atlantic and Gulf Slopes from Susquehanna R. to Neuse R., and from Savannah R. to Lake Okeechobee, FL, and west to n. Mexico and e. NM. Introduced throughout most of U.S. Common. **Habitat:** Deep pools and runs over sand or rocks in small to large rivers; lakes. Avoids upland streams.
Similar species: (1) See Headwater Catfish. (2) Yaqui Catfish has a shorter pectoral spine, dorsal spine, and anal fin base and occurs only in the Yaqui River drainage. (3) Blue Catfish (Pl. 25) *lacks* dark spots on body, has *straight-edged anal fin* with *30–35 rays*, steeply sloping, straight predorsal profile. **Map 212**

HEADWATER CATFISH *Ictalurus lupus* Not shown
Identification: Nearly identical to Channel Catfish but has a deeper caudal peduncle; broader head, mouth, and snout. To 19 in. (48 cm).
Range: Restricted in U.S. to Rio Grande drainage, including Pecos R. system, se. NM, and Devils R., s. TX; perhaps formerly in Nueces, Colorado, and San Antonio Bay drainages, TX. Also in ne. Mexico. Locally common. **Habitat:** Sandy and rocky riffles, runs, and pools of clear creeks and small rivers; springs.
Remarks: The Headwater and Yaqui Catfishes are considered to be genetically distinct species but cannot be separated reliably from the Channel Catfish by means of external morphology.
Similar species: (1) See Channel Catfish (Pl. 25). (2) Yaqui Catfish has shorter anal fin base; is darker. **Map 213**

YAQUI CATFISH *Ictalurus pricei* Not shown
Identification: Similar to Channel Catfish but has shorter pectoral spine (3–4 times into predorsal length; 2–3 times in Channel Catfish) and shorter dorsal spine (2.6–4 times into predorsal length; 2.1–2.6 times in Channel Catfish). Numerous round dark spots scattered on dark gray to black (large males) back and side; white to gray below. To 22¼ in. (57 cm).
Range: Rio Yaqui and Rio Casas Grandes drainages, nw. Mexico and (presumably) extreme se. AZ. Rare; protected in U.S. as a *threatened species.* **Habitat:** Quiet water over sand–rock bottom in small to medium rivers.
Similar species: See (1) Channel (Pl. 25) and (2) Headwater Catfishes. **Map 212**

BLUE CATFISH *Ictalurus furcatus* Pl. 25
Identification: *Long, straight-edged anal fin,* tapered like a barber's comb, *30–35 rays. No dark spots* on body except in Rio Grande.

Steeply sloping and straight predorsal profile. Pale blue to olive above and on side; white below; clear or white fins, except black or dusky borders on dorsal and caudal fins; white chin barbels. Large individual is blue-black above; silver-blue below. Air bladder with a definite constriction. To 65 in. (165 cm).

Range: Mississippi R. basin from w. PA to s. SD and Platte R., sw. NE, south to Gulf; Gulf Slope from Mobile Bay drainage, AL, to Rio Grande drainage, TX and NM. Also in Atlantic Slope of Mexico. Introduced outside native range in Atlantic Slope drainages, western states, and MN. Fairly common. **Habitat:** Deep water of impoundments and main channels and backwaters of medium to large rivers, over mud, sand and gravel.

Similar species: Channel Catfish (Pl. 25) has dark spots on body, rounded anal fin with 24–29 rays.   **Map 214**

• *AMEIURUS* SPECIES

Genus characteristics: All but White Catfish have rear edge of caudal fin *rounded, straight,* or slightly *notched.* Short base on *small adipose fin,* its rear edge free from back and far from caudal fin; anal fin base usually shorter than in species of *Ictalurus,* with 17–27 rays. Upper jaw projecting beyond lower jaw or jaws nearly equal; eyes relatively small, on side of head; no backward projections on premaxillary tooth patch.

WHITE CATFISH *Ameiurus catus*   **Pl. 25**
Identification: *Moderately forked caudal fin.* Relatively short *anal fin base,* rounded in outline, *22–25 rays.* 11–15 moderately large *sawlike teeth* on rear of pectoral spine. Gray to blue-black above; white to light yellow below; dusky to black adipose fin; white or yellow chin barbels. No dark blotch at dorsal fin base. Large individual is blue-black on head and lips; dusky blue above; white or blue below. 18–21 rakers on 1st gill arch. To 24¼ in. (62 cm).
Range: Atlantic and Gulf Slope drainages from lower Hudson R., NY, to Pascagoula R., MS; south in peninsular FL to Peace R. drainage. Introduced widely outside native range. Common. **Habitat:** Sluggish, mud-bottomed pools, open channels, and backwaters of small to large rivers; lakes and impoundments.
Similar species: (1) Channel, (2) Headwater, (3) Yaqui, and (4) Blue Catfishes (Pl. 25) have a *more deeply forked caudal fin* and either a *straight-edged anal fin* (Blue Catfish) or scattered dark spots on a lighter body (Channel, Headwater, and Yaqui Catfishes).   **Map 213**

YELLOW BULLHEAD *Ameiurus natalis*   **Pl. 25**
Identification: *White or yellow chin barbels.* Moderately long *anal fin,* nearly straight in outline, *24–27 rays;* rays at front only slightly longer than rear rays. 5–8 large *sawlike teeth* on rear of pectoral spine. Rear edge of caudal fin rounded or nearly straight. Yellow-olive to slate-black above; lighter, often yellow-olive on side; bright

yellow to white below; dusky fins; often a dark stripe in middle of anal fin. No dark blotch at dorsal fin base. 13–15 rakers on 1st gill arch. To 18¼ in. (47 cm).

Range: Native to Atlantic and Gulf Slope drainages from NY to n. Mexico, and St. Lawrence–Great Lakes and Mississippi R. basins from s. QU west to cen. ND, and south to Gulf. Widely introduced outside native range. Common in center of range. **Habitat:** Pools, backwaters, and sluggish current over soft substrate in creeks and small to large rivers; oxbows, ponds, and impoundments.

Similar species: See Pl. 25. (1) Black and (2) Brown Bullheads have dusky or black chin barbels. **Map 215**

BLACK BULLHEAD *Ameiurus melas* Pl. 25

Identification: *Dusky or black chin barbels.* Relatively short *anal fin*, rounded in outline, *19–23 rays*; rays at front distinctly longer than rear rays. Usually *no strong sawlike teeth* on rear of pectoral spine (Fig. 45). Rear edge of caudal fin slightly notched. Dark olive, yellow-brown, or slate-olive above; lighter, often shiny green-gold side; bright yellow to white below; dusky to black fins. Pale rays, black membranes on caudal and anal fins. No mottling on body; no dark blotch at dorsal fin base. *15–21 rakers* on 1st gill arch. To 24¼ in. (62 cm).

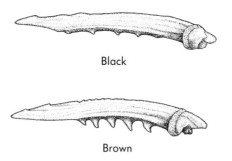

Black

Brown

Fig. 45 Black and Brown Bullheads — pectoral spine

Range: Native to Great Lakes, Hudson Bay, and Mississippi R. basins from NY to s. SA and MT, south to Gulf; Gulf Slope drainages from Mobile Bay, GA and AL, to n. Mexico. Apparently not native to Atlantic Slope. Introduced widely elsewhere in U.S. Common in center of range. **Habitat:** Pools, backwaters, and sluggish current over soft substrates in creeks and small to large rivers; impoundments, oxbows, and ponds.

Similar species: See Pl. 25. (1) See Brown Bullhead. (2) Yellow Bullhead has *white or yellow chin barbels, 24–27 anal rays.* **Map 216**

BROWN BULLHEAD *Ameiurus nebulosus* **Pl. 25**
Identification: Similar to Black Bullhead but has *5–8 large sawlike teeth on rear of pectoral spine* (sometimes eroded in large individual) (Fig. 45), *brown or black mottling or spots* on body, and *no* black membranes contrasting with pale rays on caudal and anal fins. *11–15 rakers* on 1st gill arch. To 21 in. (50 cm).
Range: Native to Atlantic and Gulf Slope drainages from NS and NB to Mobile Bay, AL, and St. Lawrence–Great Lakes, Hudson Bay, and Mississippi R. basins from QU west to se. SA, and south to LA. Widely introduced outside native range. Common in northeastern parts of range and on Atlantic and Gulf slopes; sporadic elsewhere.
Habitat: Pools and sluggish runs over soft substrates in creeks and small to large rivers; impoundments, lakes, and ponds.
Similar species: See Black Bullhead (Pl. 25). **Map 217**

Next 3 species: large dark blotch at dorsal fin base.

SPOTTED BULLHEAD *Ameiurus serracanthus* **Pl. 25**
Identification: Many small *round gray-white spots* on *dark body*. Narrow *black edge* on fins. 15–20 *large sawlike teeth* on rear of pectoral spine. Gray or blue-black above; gray to white below; gold-yellow cast to body and fins. Relatively short anal fin, rounded in outline, 20–23 rays. 12–14 rakers on 1st gill arch. To 10¾ in. (28 cm).
Range: Gulf Coastal Plain in Suwannee, St. Marks, Ochlockonee, Apalachicola, and St. Andrews Bay drainages of n. FL, s. GA, and se. AL. Uncommon. **Habitat:** Deep rock- or sand-bottomed pools of small to medium swift rivers; impoundments.
Similar species: No other catfish has light round spots on otherwise dark body. **Map 218**

SNAIL BULLHEAD *Ameiurus brunneus* **Pl. 25**
Identification: Flat head, *decurved snout profile*. Short anal fin, rounded in outline, *17–20 rays*. Large dark blotch at dorsal fin base. No large sawlike teeth on rear of pectoral spine. Yellow-green or olive above; gold to dusky yellow on side; blue-white to white below; narrow black edge (except pectoral) on dusky olive-brown fins. Some populations (e.g., St. Johns R., FL) strongly mottled. *14–17 rakers* on 1st gill arch. To 11½ in. (29 cm).
Range: Atlantic Slope from Dan R. system (where possibly introduced), s. VA, south to Altamaha R. drainage, GA, and middle St. Johns R. drainage, FL; Gulf Slope in Apalachicola R. drainage, GA, AL, and FL. Recently reported from upper Coosa R. system, n. GA. Common. **Habitat:** Rocky riffles, runs, and flowing pools of swift streams; rarely in backwaters.
Similar species: See Pl. 25. (1) Spotted Bullhead has light round spots on dark body, black edge on pectoral fin, and large sawlike teeth on rear of pectoral spine. (2) Flat Bullhead has *longer anal fin* with *21–24 rays*, *11–13 gill rakers*, a relatively *straight snout profile*, mottling on side. **Map 219**

FLAT BULLHEAD *Ameiurus platycephalus* **Pl. 25**
Identification: Flat head, *relatively straight snout profile. Relatively short anal fin,* rounded in outline, *21–24 rays.* Large dark blotch at dorsal fin base. No large sawlike teeth on rear of pectoral spine. Gold-yellow to dark brown above; *dark mottling* on side; dull cream below; dusky fins, narrow black edge on median fins; 11–13 rakers on 1st gill arch. To 11¼ in. (29 cm).
Range: Atlantic Piedmont and Coastal Plain from Roanoke R. drainage, VA, to Altamaha R. drainage, GA. Uncommon. **Habitat:** Mud-, sand-, or rock-bottomed pools of small to large rivers; lakes, impoundments, and ponds.
Similar species: See Pl. 25. (1) Snail Bullhead has *decurved snout profile, short anal fin* with *17–20 rays, 14–17 gill rakers,* no or little mottling on side. (2) Spotted Bullhead has light round spots on dark body, black edge on pectoral fin, large sawlike teeth on back of pectoral spine. **Map 218**

FLATHEAD CATFISH *Pylodictis olivaris* **Pl. 25**
Identification: *White tip on upper lobe of caudal fin* (except in large adult). Wide, *flat head; lower jaw* projecting *beyond upper jaw* (except in small young). Slender, somewhat compressed body; small eyes on top of head. Short, high adipose fin with rear end free from back and far from caudal fin. Yellow to dark purple-brown with *black or brown mottling* above; white to yellow below; white to yellow chin barbels; mottled fins. Short anal fin, rounded in outline, 14-17 rays. Rear edge of caudal fin rounded or slightly notched. Backward projections on each side of premaxillary tooth patch. To 61 in. (155 cm).
Range: Lower Great Lakes and Mississippi R. basins from w. PA to White–Little Missouri R. system, ND, and south to LA; Gulf Slope from Mobile Bay drainage, GA and AL, to Mexico. Introduced elsewhere in U.S. Usually common. **Habitat:** Pools with logs and other debris in low- to moderate-gradient, small to large rivers; lakes; impoundments. Young in rocky and sandy runs and riffles.
Similar species: Other large catfishes (Pl. 25) *lack* white tip on upper lobe of caudal fin. **Map 220**

WIDEMOUTH BLINDCAT *Satan eurystomus* **Pl. 25**
Identification: *No eyes;* white or pink (from blood pigments). *Jaw teeth well developed;* lips at corner of mouth thick; lower jaw normal in shape, slightly shorter than upper jaw. Separate gill membranes with strong fold between them. Broad, flat head and snout. Long, high adipose fin. Relatively short anal fin, rounded in outline, 19–20 rays. Rear edge of caudal fin straight or slightly notched. Lateral-line canals and pores on head well developed. To 5¼ in. (13.7 cm).
Range: Known from 5 artesian wells penetrating San Antonio Pool of Edwards Aquifer in and near San Antonio, Bexar Co., TX. Apparently abundant. **Habitat:** Subterranean waters at depths of 976–1862 ft. (305-582 m).

Similar species: Toothless Blindcat (Pl. 25) *lacks* jaw teeth; has lower jaw curved into mouth, fused gill membranes. **Map 221**

TOOTHLESS BLINDCAT *Trogloglanis pattersoni* **Pl. 25**
Identification: *No eyes;* white or pink body; red mouth (from blood pigments). *No jaw teeth;* lips at corner of mouth thin; *short lower jaw curved upward and into mouth;* snout overhangs mouth. Fused gill membranes with barely visible fold between them. Rounded head and snout profile. Long, high adipose fin joined to caudal fin. Short anal fin, rounded in outline, 16–17 rays. Rear edge of caudal fin straight or slightly notched. Lateral-line canals and pores on head well developed. No air bladder. To 4 in. (10.4 cm).
Range and Habitat: Same as Widemouth Blindcat.
Similar species: Widemouth Blindcat (Pl. 25) has *jaw teeth,* lower jaw *normal in shape,* separate gill membranes, 19–20 anal rays.
Map 221

• *NOTURUS* SPECIES

Large genus (26 named, 1 unnamed species). *Small,* less than 12¼ in. (31 cm); most species less than 4 in. (10 cm). *Long and low adipose fin* joined to, or slightly separated from, caudal fin.

Three subgenera are recognized: *Noturus, Schilbeodes,* and *Rabida.* The following accounts cover species of *Noturus* (Stonecat), then *Schilbeodes* (Tadpole Madtom to Orangefin Madtom) and *Rabida* (Least Madtom to Yellowfin Madtom). *Noturus* (1 species): narrow backward extension from each side of rectangular-shaped premaxillary tooth patch (Fig. 46). *Schilbeodes* (10 species): nearly

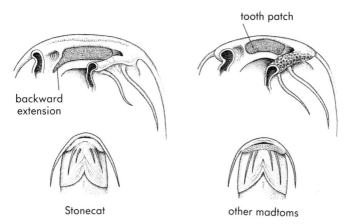

Fig. 46 *Noturus* species — premaxillary tooth patch

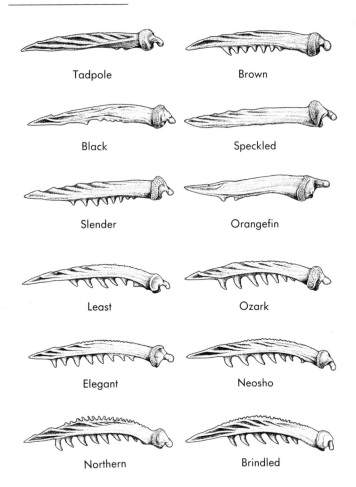

Tadpole

Brown

Black

Speckled

Slender

Orangefin

Least

Ozark

Elegant

Neosho

Northern

Brindled

Fig. 47 Madtoms — left pectoral spine

straight to slightly curved pectoral spine *lacking* well-developed sawlike teeth on front edge, usually straight teeth on rear edge (Fig. 47); somber or nearly uniform dark color pattern *lacking* dark blotches or saddles on back; rectangular premaxillary tooth patch. *Rabida* (15 species): curved or scimitarlike pectoral spine with *sawlike teeth* on front and rear edges, rear teeth curved (Fig. 47); color pattern usually of *dark blotches or saddles* on back against light background; rectangular premaxillary tooth patch.

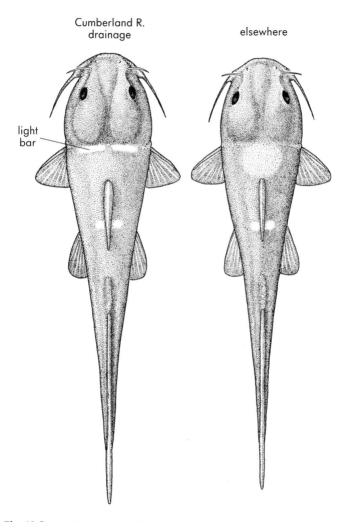

Cumberland R.
drainage

elsewhere

light
bar

Fig. 48 Stonecat — nape pattern

STONECAT *Noturus flavus*   **Pl. 26**
Identification: Long, somewhat slender body. *Light blotch on nape;
cream-white spot* at rear of dorsal fin base (Fig. 48). *Backward extension from each side of premaxillary tooth patch* (Fig. 46). *Cream-
white blotch* on upper edge of gray caudal fin. No or few weak

sawlike teeth on rear of pectoral spine. Rear edge of caudal fin straight or with slightly rounded corners. Yellow, slate, or olive above; gray pelvic and anal fins; pectoral, dorsal, and adipose fins dark at base, pale or white at edge. 15–18 anal rays. To 12¼ in. (31 cm). Larger in Lake Erie than in Mississippi R. basin.

Range: St. Lawrence–Great Lakes, Hudson Bay (Red R.) and Mississippi R. basins from QU to AB, and south to n. AL, n. MS, and ne. OK; Hudson R. drainage, NY. Common. **Habitat:** Rubble and boulder riffles and runs of creeks and small to large rivers; gravel shoals of lakes.

Remarks: Undescribed form in Cumberland R. drainage has unique pigment pattern on nape (Fig. 48). Individuals in main channel of Missouri and lower Mississippi rivers are distinctly small-eyed.

Similar species: No other madtom has backward extension from each side of premaxillary tooth patch or exceeds 7 in. (18 cm).   **Map 222**

TADPOLE MADTOM *Noturus gyrinus*   **Pl. 26**
Identification: Chubby body. Terminal mouth with *equal jaws. No sawlike teeth* on rear of pectoral spine (Fig. 47). Nearly uniform light tan or brown body; *dark gray veinlike line* along side. Rear edge of caudal fin rounded (more pointed on young). Gold-yellow to chocolate brown above; light below; uniform gray or brown fins. 13–18 anal rays. To 5 in. (13 cm).

Range: Atlantic and Gulf Slope drainages from NH to Nueces R., TX; St. Lawrence–Great Lakes, Hudson Bay (Red R.), and Mississippi R. basins from s. QU to s. SA, and south to Gulf. Absent from Appalachian and Ozark Highlands. Introduced into Snake R., ID and OR; presumably introduced into MA and NH. Usually common. **Habitat:** Rock-, mud-, or detritus-bottomed pools and backwaters of lowland creeks and small to large rivers; lakes.

Similar species: See Pl. 26. (1) See Ouachita Madtom. (2) Broadtail Madtom has *upper jaw projecting beyond lower jaw.* (3) Speckled Madtom has dark specks scattered over body and fins; rear edge of caudal fin straight.   **Map 223**

OUACHITA MADTOM *Noturus lachneri*   **Pl. 26**
Identification: Similar to Tadpole Madtom but has *shorter, flatter head; more slender body.* Uniform tan, dark gray or brown above; light below; uniform light tan or gray fins sometimes with dark borders (especially median fins). 16–19 anal rays. To 4 in. (10 cm).

Range: Upper Saline R. system and small unnamed tributary of Ouachita R., cen. AR. Rare to uncommon. **Habitat:** Rocky pools, backwaters, and runs of clear swift creeks and small rivers.

Similar species: See Tadpole Madtom (Pl. 26).   **Map 224**

SPECKLED MADTOM *Noturus leptacanthus*   **Pl. 26**
Identification: Slender body. *Black specks on body and fins. Short pectoral spine, no sawlike teeth* on rear edge (as in Tadpole Madtom — Fig. 47). Upper jaw projects beyond lower jaw. Rear edge of caudal fin straight. Red- or yellow-brown above; cream-white be-

low with dark specks; light anal and dorsal fins with dark specks; dark blotch at base of pectoral fin; caudal, anal, and adipose fins darkly blotched, with light edges. 14–19 anal rays. To 3½ in. (9.4 cm).
Range: Atlantic and Gulf Slope drainages from Edisto R., SC, to Amite-Comite R., LA; south in peninsular FL to St. John's R. drainage. Common. **Habitat:** Gravel–sand runs and rocky riffles of creeks and small to medium rivers; near vegetation.
Similar species: (1) See Broadtail Madtom (Pl. 26). (2) No other small, slender madtom has scattered dark specks on body and fins, rear edge of caudal fin straight. **Map 224**

BROADTAIL MADTOM *Noturus* species   **Pl. 26**
Identification: Similar to Speckled Madtom, but has *chubby body, rounded rear edge* on caudal fin, *no dark specks on body,* larger eye, dark blotch on caudal fin base. Tan to red-brown above; white or yellow below; all fins (except caudal) pale, dark at base; clear or pale border on light brown caudal fin. 12–16 anal rays. To 2¼ in. (6 cm).
Range: Coastal Plain of NC and SC in South (Cape Fear drainage), Waccamaw, Lumber, and Lynches R. systems (Peedee R. drainage). Locally common. **Habitat:** Sand and gravel shoals, debris-laden pools, and main channels of medium rivers. In Lake Waccamaw at 3–6 ft. (1–2 m) over sand.
Similar species: (1) See Speckled Madtom (Pl. 26). (2) Tadpole Madtom (Pl. 26) has *equal jaws,* reaches 5 in. (13 cm). **Map 224**

BROWN MADTOM *Noturus phaeus*   **Pl. 26**
Identification: *Robust. Many brown specks* on underside of head and *belly. Long anal fin, 20–22 rays;* narrow space between anal fin base and caudal fin. Upper jaw projects beyond lower jaw. About 6 distinct *sawlike teeth* on rear of pectoral spine (Fig. 47). Rear edge of caudal fin straight or slightly rounded. Uniform light to dark brown above; brown fins; sometimes light edge on median fins. To 5¾ in. (15 cm).
Range: Mississippi R. tributaries in sw. KY, w. TN, n. MS, and nw. AL; and in s. AR, LA, and sw. MS; Tennessee R. tributaries in w. TN and nw. AL; on Gulf Slope in Sabine R. and Bayou Teche drainages, LA. Locally common. **Habitat:** Sand–gravel riffles and runs among debris, rocks, and undercut banks of springs, creeks, and small rivers.
Similar species: See (1) Black and (2) Freckled Madtoms (both, Pl. 26).
Map 225

BLACK MADTOM *Noturus funebris*   **Pl. 26**
Identification: Similar to Brown Madtom but has *no* or *few* weak *sawlike teeth* on rear of pectoral spine (Fig. 47), a *longer anal fin* with *21–27 rays,* black or steel blue above; pale belly; sometimes a diffuse black edge on median fins. To 5¾ in. (15 cm).
Range: Gulf Slope drainages from Enconfina Cr., FL, to Pearl R., MS and LA. Locally common. **Habitat:** Near vegetation in moderate to fast clear water over gravel and sand in permanent springs, creeks, and small rivers.
Similar species: See Brown Madtom (Pl. 26). **Map 225**

FRECKLED MADTOM *Noturus nocturnus* Pl. 26

Identification: Similar to Brown and Black Madtoms but *belly mostly without dark specks; shorter anal fin,* usually *16–18 rays; 2-3 weak sawlike teeth* on rear of pectoral spine; *dusky black edge on anal fin.* Uniformly dark brown or gray above; yellow or white below; dark fin bases, lighter toward edge. To 5¾ in. (15 cm).

Range: Mississippi R. basin from n. IL to LA, and from e. KY to cen. KS and OK; Gulf Slope drainages from Mobile Bay, AL, to Guadalupe R., TX. Locally common. **Habitat:** Sand–gravel riffles and runs near debris and among tree roots along undercut banks in creeks to large rivers.

Similar species: See (1) Black and (2) Brown Madtoms (both, Pl. 26).
Map 226

SLENDER MADTOM *Noturus exilis* Pl. 26

Identification: Long, slender body; flat head. *Black border* on median fins. Terminal mouth with *equal jaws.* About 6 strong *sawlike teeth* on rear edge of pectoral spine (Fig. 47). Large *light yellow spot* on nape; smaller spot at rear of dorsal fin base. Rear edge of caudal fin straight or with slightly rounded corners. Yellow-brown to gray-black above; light yellow below; pale or light yellow fins. 17–22 anal rays. To 5¾ in. (15 cm).

Range: 2 disjunct areas: Green, Cumberland, and Tennessee R. drainages, cen. KY to n. AL; upper Mississippi R. basin from s. WI and s. MN to Ozark and Ouachita Highlands of AR, KS, and OK. Common. **Habitat:** Rocky riffles, runs, and flowing pools of clear creeks and small rivers; rarely in springs. Rarely along wave-swept margins of large impoundments.

Remarks: Slender and Margined Madtoms from cool clear streams are more slender and have more boldly edged fins than individuals from warm, turbid waters. Some individuals lack dark fin borders.

Similar species: See Margined Madtom (Pl. 26). **Map 227**

MARGINED MADTOM *Noturus insignis* Pl. 26

Identification: Similar to Slender Madtom, except *upper jaw projects beyond lower jaw,* longer caudal fin, *no light spot on nape or at rear end of dorsal fin base.* Yellow to slate gray above; white or light below; yellow or light gray fins; black edge on median fins variable. 15–21 anal rays. To 6 in. (15 cm).

Range: Atlantic Slope from St. Lawrence R. and se. Lake Ontario drainages, NY, to upper Altamaha R. drainage, GA; upper Kanawha (New) R. system, VA and NC; upper Monongahela R. system, PA and MD. Introduced into Merrimack R., NH, and upper Tennessee R. drainage, VA and TN. Common in U.S.; protected in Canada as a *threatened species.* **Habitat:** Rocky riffles and runs of clear, fast creeks and small to medium rivers.

Remarks: Individuals from Dan R. gorge, VA, have profusely spotted body and fins.

Similar species: See Slender Madtom (Pl. 26). **Map 227**

ORANGEFIN MADTOM *Noturus gilberti*   **Pl. 26**
Identification: Long, slender body; flat head. *White to orange triangle* (widest at rear) on upper edge of dusky to dark caudal fin. Short dorsal and pectoral spines; irregular, sometimes large sawlike teeth on rear edge of pectoral spine (Fig. 47). *Short anal fin; 14–16 rays.* Upper jaw projects beyond lower jaw. Straight or slightly rounded corners on rear edge of caudal fin. Olive or brown above; pale yellow or white below; light yellow or white edge on dark fins. To 3¾ in. (10 cm).
Range: Upper Roanoke R. (including Dan R.) drainage, VA and NC. Possibly introduced into upper James R., VA. Rare to uncommon.
Habitat: Rocky riffles and runs of clear, swift, small rivers.
Similar species: Stonecat (Pl. 26) has cream-white spot at rear of dorsal fin base, backward projections on premaxillary tooth patch.
Map 222

LEAST MADTOM *Noturus hildebrandi*   **Pl. 27**
Identification: Slender body; flat head. *White or clear adipose fin* (except dark blotch extends into base of fin in individuals from s. MS). *Short pectoral spine* with 4–5 large sawlike teeth on rear edge, *small teeth on front edge* (Fig. 47). Rear edge of caudal fin straight or with slightly rounded corners. Adipose and caudal fins broadly joined with a tiny notch between. Geographically variable in color (see Remarks); caudal fin dusky or has irregularly defined bars and clear edge. 12–17 anal rays. To 2½ in. (6.9 cm).
Range: Tributaries of Mississippi R. from North Fork Obion R., sw. KY, to Homochitto R., s. MS. Common. **Habitat:** Mixed rock and sand riffles and runs of clear lowland creeks and small rivers; often near debris.
Remarks: Two subspecies: *N. h. hildebrandi*, in Homochitto R. and Bayou Pierre, s. MS, has longer head; prominently blotched color pattern above and almost to belly. *N. h. lautus*, in Obion, Forked Deer, and Hatchie rivers, w. KY and TN, has shorter head, 4 white or light yellow oval areas on uniform red-brown to black back; is strongly bicolored, with brown to black upper side, white or yellow below. Intergrades occur in sw. TN and n. MS.
Similar species: (1) See Pygmy Madtom. (2) Smoky Madtom (Pl. 27) has more uniform olive-brown body, including well pigmented lower side; 3 small pale yellow saddles. **Map 228**

PYGMY MADTOM *Noturus stanauli*   **Not shown**
Identification: Similar to Least Madtom but has *white snout* (in front of nostrils); *3 dark spots* on caudal fin base. Dark gray or brown-black above; olive-brown or pale yellow on upper side; white on lower side; moderately light areas on back of head, back of dorsal fin base, and front and rear of adipose fin; mostly white or pale yellow fins, except dark band or dusky blotches in middle of caudal fin. 14–17 anal rays. To 1½ in. (4.2 cm).
Range: Tennessee R. drainage, TN; known only from Clinch R. at Frost Ford and Brooks Island, Hancock Co., and Duck R. just above

mouth of Hurricane Cr., Humphreys Co. Uncommon in Clinch R., rare in Duck R. **Habitat:** Moderate to swift gravel runs of clear medium-sized rivers.
Similar species: See Least Madtom (Pl. 27). **Map 228**

SMOKY MADTOM *Noturus baileyi* **Pl. 27**
Identification: Relatively slender body, deepest beneath dorsal fin. *Nearly uniform olive-brown above and on side;* usually *4 pale yellow saddles:* on nape, at rear of dorsal fin base, and at front and rear of adipose fin. Dusky band in adipose fin *extends nearly to fin edge.* Short pectoral spine with 4–5 sawlike teeth on rear edge, small teeth on front edge (as in Least Madtom — Fig. 47). Rear edge of caudal fin straight. Adipose fin joined to caudal fin, but with notch between. White to yellow below; white to light brown fins. 12–14 anal rays. To 2¾ in. (7.3 cm).
Range: Citico Cr. (Little Tennessee R. system), Monroe Co., TN. Formerly known but now considered extirpated from Abrams Cr. (Little Tennessee R. system), Blount Co., TN. Rare; protected as an *endangered species.* **Habitat:** Clear, cool, rocky riffles, runs, and flowing pools of creeks.
Similar species: (1) Least Madtom (Pl. 27) has *clear adipose fin* and white lower side (*N. h. lautus*), or is prominently *blotched above and on side (N. h. hildebrandi).* (2) Pygmy Madtom has white-tipped snout, *white lower side,* 14–17 anal rays. **Map 228**

OZARK MADTOM *Noturus albater* **Pl. 27**
Identification: Stout body; small head. *White* upper edge on *caudal fin.* Rounded upper edge on high adipose fin. Distinct notch between adipose fin and caudal fin; dark blotch beneath adipose fin usually extends into lower half of fin (sometimes to edge). Usually a diffuse dark bar on caudal fin base. Rear edge of caudal fin straight or with slightly rounded corners. 6–10 sawlike teeth on rear, small teeth on front, of pectoral spine (Fig. 47). Yellow-brown to light brown above; faint to prominent dark mottling or blotching. 4 dusky saddles; pale yellow to cream-white below; indistinct blotches on yellow or white fins; irregular dark bands on caudal fin. 13–16 anal rays. To 4¾ in. (12 cm).
Range: Ozark Uplands of MO and AR in upper White (including Red R.) and St. Francis R. drainages. Locally common. **Habitat:** Clear, cool, swift rocky riffles and pools of creeks and small to medium rivers.
Remarks: Two forms: a mottled, stout-bodied form in St. Francis R. drainage, and a boldly patterned, more slender form in upper White R. drainage.
Similar species: Least Madtom (Pl. 27) is more slender; has clear adipose fin and white lower side (*N. h. lautus*) or is prominently blotched above and on side and lacking white area on upper caudal fin base (*N. h. hildebrandi*). **Map 229**

ELEGANT MADTOM *Noturus elegans* **Pl. 27**
Identification: *Brown blotch on dorsal fin base extends up front edge*

of fin; no black on tips of 1st 2–4 dorsal fin rays. *Long slender body, 4 yellow saddles* on dark back (see Remarks). Small eye. Low adipose fin broadly joined to caudal fin but with notch between fins. Short pectoral spine with 5–9 sawlike teeth on rear edge, numerous small granular teeth on front edge (Fig. 47). Rear edge of caudal fin straight or with slightly rounded corners. Yellow-gray to dark brown above; usually 2 (or 3) dark bands on caudal fin, 1 in middle, 1 (or 2) near edge. To 3½ in. (8.9 cm).
Range: Green R. drainage, KY and TN; Tennessee R. drainage from Paint Rock R., AL, to Duck R., TN. Locally common. **Habitat:** Gravel riffles and runs of clear creeks and small rivers.
Remarks: Three distinct forms. Individuals from Green R. drainage have subdued color; lack black blotch at caudal fin base; no or diffuse black bands on dorsal, adipose, and anal fins; 14–18 anal rays. Individuals from Duck R. drainage have *4* pale yellow dorsal saddles contrasting sharply with dark brown to black back; black blotch at caudal fin base; black band in adipose fin; in adults, often submarginal black bands on dorsal fin and rear half of anal fin; 15–20 anal rays. Individuals from n. AL have a subdued color pattern similar to those from the Green R. drainage but have a more robust body; 16–17 anal rays.
Similar species: (1) Caddo Madtom (Pl. 27) has black-tipped dorsal fin; larger teeth on front of pectoral spine; larger eye; 13–16 anal rays. (2) Scioto Madtom has *clear adipose and dorsal fins; 13–16 anal rays.*
Map 229

CADDO MADTOM *Noturus taylori*   Pl. 27
Identification: Long, slender body. Adipose fin broadly joined, with small notch, to caudal fin. *Black tips* on 1st 2–4 dorsal fin rays. *Short pectoral spine* with 5–9 sawlike teeth on rear edge, *many small teeth* on front edge (as in Elegant Madtom − Fig. 47). Rear edge of caudal fin straight or with rounded corners. Brown band extends into upper half of adipose fin. Yellow to dark brown above; 4 dark brown saddles alternate with light yellow or cream ellipses; dark bands (often absent) near clear edge of anal and pectoral fins (in adult); 2 (or 3) vague brown crescent-shaped bands on caudal fin: 1 in middle of fin, 1 (or 2) near clear edge. 13–16 anal rays. To 3 in. (7.7 cm).
Range: Caddo, Ouachita, and Little Missouri rivers, sw. AR. Locally common. **Habitat:** Rocky riffles, pools, and shoals near shorelines of small to medium rivers.
Similar species: (1) Elegant Madtom (Pl. 27) *lacks* black tips on 1st 2–4 dorsal fin rays, has *smaller* teeth on front of pectoral spine; smaller eye. (2) Scioto Madtom has *clear adipose fin;* small teeth on front of pectoral spine.
Map 229

SCIOTO MADTOM *Noturus trautmani*   Not shown
Identification: Long, slender body. Low adipose fin broadly joined, with small notch between, to caudal fin. *Clear adipose fin. Short pectoral spine* with 5–7 sawlike teeth on rear edge; *small, often obscure, teeth* on front edge (as in Elegant Madtom − Fig. 47). Rear edge of caudal fin straight or with slightly rounded corners. Gray mottling

on dusky olive-brown above; 4 saddles; white below; 2 white areas on lower caudal peduncle between anal and caudal fins; *clear or yellow dorsal, pelvic, and anal fins*; 2 vague brown crescent-shaped bands on caudal fin: 1 in middle of fin, 1 near clear edge. 13–16 anal rays. To 2¼ in. (6.1 cm).

Range: Big Darby Cr. (Scioto R. system), s. OH. Rare; last seen in 1957. Protected as an *endangered species.* **Habitat:** Known mainly from downstream end of 60-ft. sand–gravel riffle.

Similar species: (1) Elegant Madtom (Pl. 27) has *dark band* on adipose fin; is more boldly patterned. (2) Caddo Madtom (Pl. 27) has larger teeth on front of pectoral spine, *dark band* on adipose fin, *black-tipped dorsal fin.* **Map 229**

NEOSHO MADTOM *Noturus placidus* Pl. 27

Identification: *White lower caudal rays.* Robust body, deepest beneath dorsal fin; relatively *deep caudal peduncle.* Faint to prominent blotches and saddles; no (or faint) pair of light spots in front of dorsal fin. Large pectoral spine with 6–10 prominent sawlike teeth on rear edge, *small teeth on front edge* (Fig. 47). Adipose fin joined to caudal fin. Dark crescent-shaped band in middle of caudal fin, another near white edge; dusky or gray band confined to lower half of adipose fin; usually no dark specks on belly. Rear edge of caudal fin straight or with slightly rounded corners. Light yellow-pink mottled with brown above; usually white to yellow below; blotched fins, usually white edges. 13–16 anal rays. To 3¼ in. (8.7 cm).

Range: Arkansas R. drainage: Spring R., sw. MO and se. KS; Cottonwood and Neosho rivers, e. KS and ne. OK; lower few miles of Illinois R., e.-cen. OK. Locally common; probably extirpated from lower Illinois R. **Habitat:** Gravel riffles and runs of small to medium rivers.

Similar species: See Pl. 27. (1) Northern Madtom has dark band extending into upper half of adipose fin, 2 large light spots in front of dorsal fin, *lacks* lower white caudal rays. (2) Frecklebelly Madtom has rear edge of adipose fin nearly free from caudal fin, *large teeth* on front of pectoral spine; dark band on adipose fin to fin edge; *4 prominent saddles* on back; dark specks on belly. (3) Mountain Madtom has dark brown bar at base of caudal peduncle; no dark crescent-shaped band in middle of caudal fin; rear edge of adipose fin nearly free from caudal fin; *large teeth* on front of pectoral spine. **Map 230**

NORTHERN MADTOM *Noturus stigmosus* Pl. 27

Identification: Robust body, deepest beneath dorsal fin; deep caudal peduncle. *Brown or black band extends into upper half of adipose fin,* but not to edge. Front edge of 1st saddle irregular, usually enclosing *2 large light spots* in front of dorsal fin. Dark crescent-shaped band in middle of caudal fin usually *extends forward* across upper and lower caudal rays *to caudal peduncle;* another band near clear edge. Large pectoral spine with 5–10 prominent sawlike teeth on rear edge; large teeth on front edge (Fig. 47). Rear edge of high adipose fin nearly free from caudal fin. Rear edge of caudal fin straight or with slightly rounded corners. Yellow or medium tan above, brown or

black mottling; 4 saddles; white to yellow below; blotched or banded fins; dark band near clear edge of dorsal fin. 13–16 anal rays. To 5 in. (13 cm).
Range: Lake Erie and Ohio R. basins from w. PA, s. MI, and e. KY, to Ohio R., w. KY; tributaries of Mississippi R. in w. TN and n. MS. Sporadic and uncommon; disappearing on edges of range; rare in main channels of Mississippi and Ohio rivers. **Habitat:** Mixed sand and rock riffles and runs with debris in small to large, often swift rivers.
Similar species: See Pl. 27. (1) Neosho Madtom has dark band restricted to *lower half* of adipose fin, *no (or faint) light spots* in front of dorsal fin, white lower front caudal rays. (2) Frecklebelly Madtom has more slender caudal peduncle, black band *to adipose fin edge.* (3) Mountain Madtom *lacks* 2 light spots in front of dorsal fin, broad dark band near dorsal fin edge, dark crescent-shaped band in middle of caudal fin; has dark brown bar at caudal fin base.   **Map 230**

FRECKLEBELLY MADTOM *Noturus munitus*   **Pl. 27**
Identification: Robust body, deepest beneath or in front of dorsal fin; slender caudal peduncle. Dark brown or black band to adipose fin *edge.* Usually *dark specks* on belly. Large pectoral spine with 5–10 prominent sawlike teeth on rear edge, large teeth on front edge (as in Northern Madtom — Fig. 47). Rear edge of high adipose fin nearly free from caudal fin. Rear edge of caudal fin straight to slightly rounded. Yellow to dark brown above with dark mottling; 4 distinct saddles; large light spots in front of dorsal fin often incompletely enclosed by dark pigment; blotched or mottled fins; broad dark band near clear edge of dorsal fin; 2 dark crescent-shaped bands on caudal fin, 1 in middle of fin, 1 near clear edge. 12–15 anal rays. To 3¾ in. (9.5 cm).
Range: Gulf Slope drainages: disjunct populations in Conasauga R., se. TN; Etowah R., n. GA; Cahaba R., cen. AL; Tombigbee R., w. AL and e. MS; and Pearl R., s. MS and e. LA. Locally common, but declining in Mobile Bay drainage. **Habitat:** Rocky riffles and runs of medium to large rivers. Often near vegetation.
Similar species: See Pl. 27. (1) Northern Madtom has black band *only into upper half* of adipose fin, dark band in middle of caudal fin usually forward to caudal peduncle, 2 light spots in front of dorsal fin usually enclosed by darker pigment. (2) Neosho Madtom lacks prominent saddles, specks on belly; has small teeth on front of pectoral spine, white lower front caudal rays, dusky band *confined to lower half* of adipose fin.   **Map 230**

CAROLINA MADTOM *Noturus furiosus*   **Pl. 27**
Identification: Robust body, deepest beneath dorsal fin; deep caudal peduncle. *No dark specks* on belly. *Brown or black band* extends nearly to *adipose* fin edge. Large pectoral spine with 5–12 prominent sawlike teeth on rear edge, large teeth on front edge (as in Northern Madtom — Fig. 47). Rear edge of high adipose fin nearly free from caudal fin. Rear edge of caudal fin straight or slightly rounded. Yel-

low to dark brown above, dark mottling; 4 distinct saddles; usually no pair of light spots in front of dorsal fin; white to yellow below; blotched fins; 2 distinct crescent-shaped bands in caudal fin, 1 in middle of fin, 1 near clear edge. 14–17 anal rays. To 4¾ in. (12 cm).
Range: On Piedmont and Coastal Plain in Neuse and Tar R. drainages, NC. Locally common, but disappearing from upstream localities. **Habitat:** Sand-, gravel-, and detritus-bottomed riffles and runs of small to medium rivers.
Similar species: See Pl. 27. (1) Northern Madtom has usually 2 large light spots in front of dorsal fin enclosed by dark pigment; black band extends *only into upper half* of adipose fin; dark band in middle of caudal fin usually extends forward to caudal peduncle. (2) Mountain Madtom lacks dark crescent-shaped band in middle of caudal fin; has dark brown band at base of caudal peduncle; usually is more mottled.
Map 230

MOUNTAIN MADTOM *Noturus eleutherus*   **Pl. 27**
Identification: Robust body; fairly deep caudal peduncle. *Dark brown bar* on caudal fin base. Front edge of 1st saddle at dorsal spine. Long pectoral spine with 6–10 prominent sawlike teeth on rear edge, large teeth on front edge (as in Northern Madtom − Fig. 47). Rear edge of high adipose fin nearly free from caudal fin. Dark *band on adipose fin irregular in outline,* usually *confined to lower half of fin.* Rear edge of caudal fin straight. Brown or gray above, usually dark mottling; usually 4 vague saddles; light below, usually no dark specks on belly; dark bands or mottling on other fins; dark band near clear edge of caudal fin. 12–16 anal rays. To 5 in. (13 cm).
Range: Ohio R. basin from nw. PA to e. IL, and south to TN and n. GA; White and St. Francis R. drainages, MO and AR; Mississippi R., w. TN; Ouachita R. drainage, AR; and Red R. drainage, AR and OK. Locally common. Rare in main channels of Mississippi and Ohio rivers. **Habitat:** Clean rocky riffles, shoals, and runs of small to large rivers; often near vegetation.
Similar species: See Pl. 27. (1) Most often confused with Northern Madtom, which usually has dark specks on belly, broad dark band near dorsal fin edge, dark crescent-shaped band in middle of caudal fin, 2 large light spots in front of dorsal fin. (2) Neosho Madtom has weak teeth on front of pectoral spine; white lower front caudal rays; dark crescent-shaped band in middle of caudal fin. (3) Frecklebelly and (4) Carolina Madtoms have distinct saddles; dark crescent-shaped band in middle of caudal fin; dark band extends *to or nearly to adipose fin edge.*   **Map 231**

CHECKERED MADTOM *Noturus flavater*   **Pl. 27**
Identification: Robust body, deepest in front of dorsal fin. *Broad black bar* on caudal fin base; *black blotch* on outer ⅓ of dorsal fin (across all fin rays except last 1–3). Black saddle under adipose fin extends up to fin edge. Rear edge of adipose fin free from caudal fin. Rear edge of caudal fin straight or with slightly rounded corners. About 10 prominent sawlike teeth on rear of pectoral spine (as in Brindled Madtom

PLATES

The plates portray fishes as they look when alive, and the fish shown usually is an "average" adult. However, the plates emphasize traits that are most useful in separating species, and often these traits are found only on certain individuals (often large males). For example, many sunfishes have similar color patterns as young and females, but large males develop unique color patterns; to emphasize differences among sunfishes, Plate 37 shows large males. The plate legends call attention to sexual and other potentially confusing variations. For some strongly sexually dimorphic species, both a female and breeding male are shown. Black and white plates depict fishes that lack bright colors or that show little variation in color among the species shown on the plate.

How to Use the Plates: (See also How to Use This Guide, p. 1.) Locate the plate with fishes that look most like the one you wish to identify and read the short descriptions of distinguishing features on the legend page opposite the plate. Arrows or other marks highlight these features. (Be sure to note characteristics that apply to more than one species — *those in italics*.) When you have found what you believe to be the correct species go to the longer text description (page number given on legend page) and compare the traits of the fish with those in the species account and, if necessary, in the generic and family accounts. A quick look at a map (map number given on legend page) will tell you if your identification is reasonable.

PLATE 1

LAMPREYS, EEL, STURGEONS

First 3 species are representative lampreys. See Fig. 5 for additional species. Suckerlike mouth; no paired fins; 7 porelike gill openings.

SEA LAMPREY *Petromyzon marinus*   **M1, p. 14**
2 dorsal fins. Expanded oral disc as wide as or wider than head. Prominent black mottling on back, side, and fins. To 47 in. (120 cm).

CHESTNUT LAMPREY *Ichthyomyzon castaneus*   **M4, p. 16**
1 slightly notched dorsal fin. Expanded oral disc as wide as or wider than head. Usually 51–56 trunk myomeres. To 15 in. (38 cm).

AMERICAN BROOK LAMPREY *Lampetra appendix*   **M12, p. 22**
2 dorsal fins. Expanded oral disc narrower than head. Usually blunt disc teeth. Usually 67–73 trunk myomeres. To 8½ in. (22 cm).

AMERICAN EEL *Anguilla rostrata*   **M25, p. 32**
Snakelike body. Long dorsal fin continuous with caudal and anal fins. No pelvic fins. To 60 in. (152 cm).

Next 7 species (sturgeons) have shovel-shaped snout, barbels, large bony scutes, heterocercal tail.

SHORTNOSE STURGEON *Acipenser brevirostrum*   **M14, p. 25**
Short snout. Anal fin origin beneath dorsal fin origin. To 43 in. (109 cm).

LAKE STURGEON *Acipenser fulvescens*   **M14, p. 26**
Anal fin origin behind dorsal fin origin. Scutes on back and along side same color as skin. To 9 ft. (275 cm).

GREEN STURGEON *Acipenser medirostris*   **M15, p. 26**
Barbels usually closer to mouth than to snout tip. Scutes along side paler than skin. To 7 ft. (213 cm).

WHITE STURGEON *Acipenser transmontanus*   **M16, p. 27**
Barbels closer to snout tip than to mouth. No obvious scutes behind dorsal and anal fins. To 20 ft. (6.1 m).

ATLANTIC STURGEON *Acipenser oxyrhynchus*   **M17, p. 27**
Long, sharply V-shaped snout. 4 small scutes, usually as 2 pairs, between anal fin and caudal fulcrum. To 14 ft. (4.3 m).

Next 2 species have long slender caudal peduncle.

SHOVELNOSE STURGEON *Scaphirhynchus platorynchus*   **M18, p. 27**
Bases of outer barbels in line with or ahead of inner barbels (Fig. 6). To 34 in. (86 cm).

PALLID STURGEON *Scaphirhynchus albus*   **M17, p. 28**
No scalelike scutes on belly. Bases of outer barbels usually behind bases of inner barbels (Fig. 6). To 66 in. (168 cm).

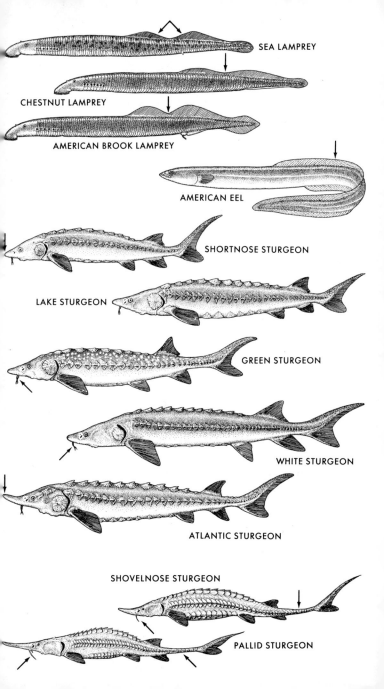

SEA LAMPREY

CHESTNUT LAMPREY

AMERICAN BROOK LAMPREY

AMERICAN EEL

SHORTNOSE STURGEON

LAKE STURGEON

GREEN STURGEON

WHITE STURGEON

ATLANTIC STURGEON

SHOVELNOSE STURGEON

PALLID STURGEON

PLATE 2
PADDLEFISH, GARS, BOWFIN, CISCO, WHITEFISHES

PADDLEFISH *Polyodon spathula* **M19, p. 29**
Long snout shaped like canoe paddle. Large, fleshy, pointed flap on rear edge of gill cover. To 87 in. (221 cm).

Next 5 species (gars) have long, sharply toothed jaws; diamond-shaped scales; dorsal and anal fins far back on body.

ALLIGATOR GAR *Atractosteus spatula* **M20, p. 29**
Giant of the gars. Short broad snout. 2 rows of teeth on upper jaw. To nearly 10 ft. (3 m).

SHORTNOSE GAR *Lepisosteus platostomus* **M21, p. 30**
Short broad snout. Paired fins usually lack spots. To 33 in. (83 cm).

LONGNOSE GAR *Lepisosteus osseus* **M22, p. 30**
Long, narrow snout. To 72 in. (183 cm).

SPOTTED GAR *Lepisosteus oculatus* **M23, p. 30**
Many dark spots on body, head, and fins. Bony plates on underside of isthmus. To 44 in. (112 cm).

FLORIDA GAR *Lepisosteus platyrhincus* **M23, p. 31**
Similar to Spotted Gar but lacks bony plates on underside of isthmus. To 52 in. (133 cm).

Alligator   Shortnose   Spotted   Longnose

Gar heads

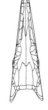

BOWFIN *Amia calva* **M24, p. 31**
Long, nearly cylindrical body. Long dorsal fin. Tubular nostrils. Large, bony gular plate. To 43 in. (109 cm).

Next 4 species are representative whitefishes. See Figs. 11-13 for additional species. Silvery; adipose fin; no fin spines.

CISCO or LAKE HERRING *Coregonus artedi* **M39, p. 41**
Terminal mouth. 38–64 long rakers on 1st gill arch. To 22½ in. (57cm).

LAKE WHITEFISH *Coregonus clupeaformis* **M36, p. 40**
Concavity between snout and humped nape. Subterminal mouth. 24–33 long rakers on 1st gill arch. To 31 in. (80 cm).

ROUND WHITEFISH *Prosopium cylindraceum* **M44, p. 47**
Subterminal mouth. 14–21 short rakers on 1st gill arch. 76–89 lateral scales. To 22 in. (56 cm).

PYGMY WHITEFISH *Prosopium coulteri* **M43, p. 45**
Large eye. Subterminal mouth. 13–20 short rakers on 1st gill arch. 54–70 lateral scales. To 11 in. (28 cm).

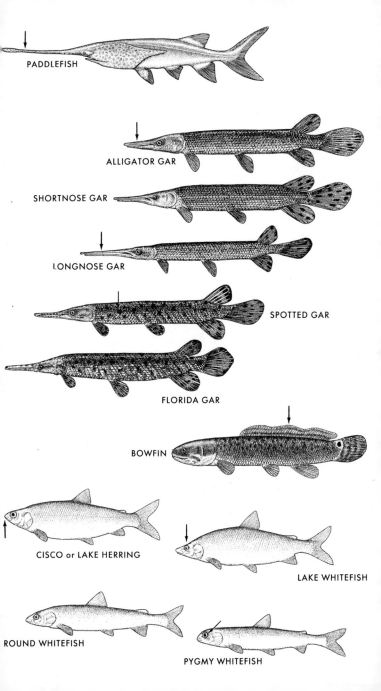

PADDLEFISH

ALLIGATOR GAR

SHORTNOSE GAR

LONGNOSE GAR

SPOTTED GAR

FLORIDA GAR

BOWFIN

CISCO or LAKE HERRING

LAKE WHITEFISH

ROUND WHITEFISH

PYGMY WHITEFISH

PLATE 3
MOONEYE, GOLDEYE, HERRINGS, SHADS, AND SMELT

All are silver, strongly compressed fishes.

MOONEYE *Hiodon tergisus* **M34, p. 37**
Large eye. Dorsal fin origin in front of anal fin origin. Untoothed keel along belly extends from pelvic fin base to anal fin. To 18¾ in. (47 cm).

GOLDEYE *Hiodon alosoides* **M33, p. 36**
Large eye. Dorsal fin origin over or behind anal fin origin. Untoothed keel along belly extends from pectoral fin base to anal fin. To 20 in. (51 cm).

Next 8 species (herrings and shads) lack lateral line; have jagged (sawtooth) belly.

BLUEBACK HERRING *Alosa aestivalis* **M26, p. 33**
Strongly oblique mouth. Blue above. Thin dark stripes on upper side. Usually 1 small dark spot behind opercle. Usually 44–50 rakers on lower limb of 1st gill arch. To 15¾ in. (40 cm).

ALEWIFE *Alosa pseudoharengus* **M27, p. 33**
Similar to Blueback Herring but is green above; has larger eye, usually 39–41 rakers on lower limb of 1st gill arch. To 15 in. (38 cm).

HICKORY SHAD *Alosa mediocris* **M28, p. 34**
Lower jaw projects beyond tip of snout. Dark spot behind opercle followed by dusky spots. Gray-green above shading to silver side. To 23¾ in. (60 cm).

SKIPJACK HERRING *Alosa chrysochloris* **M27, p. 34**
No dark spot behind opercle. Blue-green above ends abruptly on silver side. To 21 in. (53 cm).

AMERICAN SHAD *Alosa sapidissima* **M29, p. 34**
Adult lacks jaw teeth. Cheek deeper than long (Fig. 8). Dark spot behind opercle, usually followed by smaller spots. 59–73 rakers on lower limb of 1st gill arch of adult. To 30 in. (75 cm).

ALABAMA SHAD *Alosa alabamae* **M30, p. 35**
Similar to American Shad but adult has 42–48 rakers on lower limb of 1st gill arch. To 20¼ in. (51 cm).

GIZZARD SHAD *Dorosoma cepedianum* **M31, p. 35**
Long, whiplike last dorsal ray. Blunt snout. Subterminal mouth. Purple-blue shoulder spot. 52–70 lateral scales. To 20½ in. (52 cm).

THREADFIN SHAD *Dorosoma petenense* **M32, p. 36**
Similar to Gizzard Shad but has terminal mouth, yellow fins, 40–48 lateral scales. To 9 in. (22 cm).

RAINBOW SMELT *Osmerus mordax* **M61, p. 56**
Adipose fin. Large mouth. 2 large canine teeth. Usually a conspicuous silver stripe along side. To 13 in. (33 cm). See other smelts.

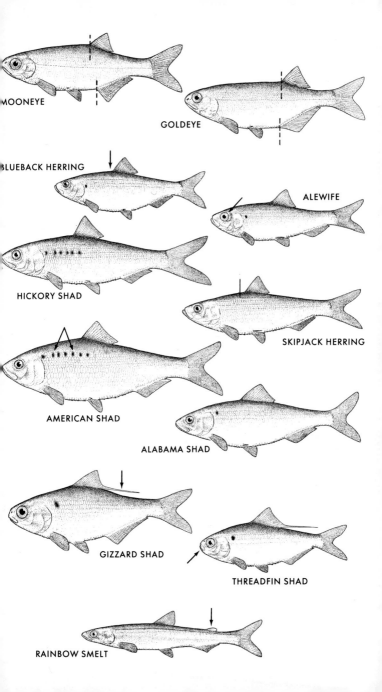

MOONEYE

GOLDEYE

BLUEBACK HERRING

ALEWIFE

HICKORY SHAD

SKIPJACK HERRING

AMERICAN SHAD

ALABAMA SHAD

GIZZARD SHAD

THREADFIN SHAD

RAINBOW SMELT

PLATE 4

TROUTS

One dorsal fin; adipose fin; abdominal pelvic fins. Young trout and char are shown in Fig. 9, p. 38.

ARCTIC GRAYLING *Thymallus arcticus* **M46, p. 47**
Huge purple to black dorsal fin. Small mouth. Forked caudal fin. To 30 in. (76 cm).

Next 4 species (Salvelinus) have light (pink, red, or cream) spots on body, minute scales, white leading edge on lower fins.

LAKE TROUT *Salvelinus namaycush* **M47, p. 48**
Deeply forked caudal fin. Many cream or yellow spots on dark head, body, and dorsal and caudal fins. To 49½ in. (126 cm).

BROOK TROUT *Salvelinus fontinalis* **M48, p. 48**
Blue halos around pink or red spots on side. Light green or cream wavy lines or blotches on back and dorsal fin. Slightly forked caudal fin. To 27½ in. (70 cm).

ARCTIC CHAR *Salvelinus alpinus* **M49, p. 49**
Pink to red spots (largest usually larger than pupil of eye) on back and side. Slightly forked caudal fin. 23–32 rakers on 1st gill arch; 35–75 pyloric caeca. To 38 in. (96 cm).

DOLLY VARDEN *Salvelinus malma* **M50, p. 49**
Similar to Arctic Char but has 14–21 rakers on 1st gill arch, usually 21–29 pyloric caeca. Largest spots on side usually smaller than pupil of eye. To 25 in. (63 cm). See also Bull Trout and Angayukaksurak Char.

BROWN TROUT *Salmo trutta* **p. 51**
Red and black spots on head and body; many spots on gill cover. Upper jaw reaches to or beyond eye. To 40½ in. (103 cm).

Next 4 species (Oncorhynchus — see also Pl. 5) have black spots on body, caudal fin, or both; no white leading edge on lower fins.

CUTTHROAT TROUT *Oncorhynchus clarki* **M57, p. 53**
Red "cutthroat" mark under lower jaw. Many black spots on body. No or faint red stripe on side. Coastal form is green above, has silver-blue to olive side. To 39 in. (99 cm).

GILA TROUT *Oncorhynchus gilae* **M58, p. 54**
Yellow "cutthroat" mark under lower jaw. Many small irregular black spots on side, head, and dorsal and caudal fins. Rose stripe along side of adult. To 12½ in. (32 cm). See also Apache Trout.

RAINBOW TROUT (STEELHEAD) *Oncorhynchus mykiss* **M59, p. 54**
Small, irregular black spots on back and most fins. Radiating rows of black spots on caudal fin. Pink to red stripe on side. Sea-run individual (Steelhead) is silvery. To 45 in. (114 cm).

GOLDEN TROUT *Oncorhynchus aguabonita* **M58, p. 55**
Similar to Rainbow Trout but has usually 10 parr marks on adult (as well as young), red belly and cheek, gold lower side, large black spots on dorsal and caudal fins. To 28 in. (71 cm).

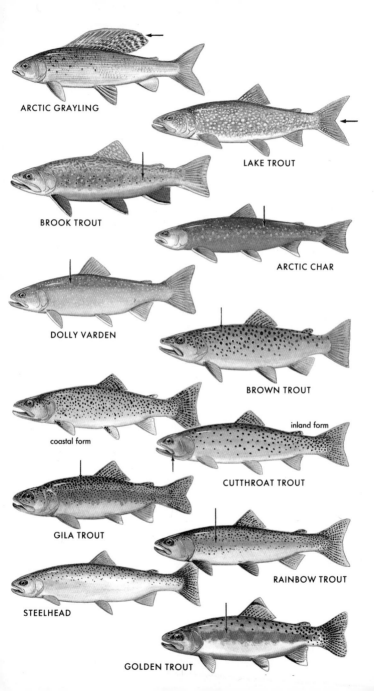

ARCTIC GRAYLING

LAKE TROUT

BROOK TROUT

ARCTIC CHAR

DOLLY VARDEN

BROWN TROUT

coastal form

inland form

CUTTHROAT TROUT

GILA TROUT

RAINBOW TROUT

STEELHEAD

GOLDEN TROUT

PLATE 5

SALMONS

One dorsal fin; adipose fin; abdominal pelvic fins. Young salmon are shown in Fig. 9. Metallic blue and silver at sea.

PINK SALMON *Oncorhynchus gorbuscha* **M56, p. 53**
Large, mostly oval black spots on back and both lobes of caudal fin. Breeding individual has brown to pink stripe along side. Male develops humped back. To 30 in. (76 cm).

SOCKEYE (RED) SALMON *Oncorhynchus nerka* **M52, p. 52**
Breeding individual has green head, brilliant red body. No large black spots on back or caudal fin (black specks present). 28–40 rakers on 1st gill arch. To 33 in. (84 cm).

COHO (SILVER) SALMON *Oncorhynchus kisutch* **M55, p. 53**
Breeding individual has pink (female) to red side (male). Black spots on back and upper lobe of caudal fin. Gums white at base of teeth. To 38½ in. (98 cm).

CHUM SALMON *Oncorhynchus keta* **M53, p. 52**
Red or dusky bars or fused blotches along green side. No large black spots on back or caudal fin (black specks present). White tips on anal and pelvic fins (brightest on male). To 40 in. (102 cm).

CHINOOK (KING) SALMON *Oncorhynchus tshawytscha* **M54, p. 52**
Largest salmon; salmon over 30 lb. (40 kg) are almost always this species. Black spots on back, adipose, and both lobes of caudal fin. Gums black at base of teeth. Large male may have dull red side. To 58 in. (147 cm).

ATLANTIC SALMON *Salmo salar* **M46, p. 50**
Black spots on head and body; 2–3 large spots on gill cover. Usually no spots on caudal fin. Silver at sea (oceanic form); bronze-brown in fresh water. To 55 in. (140 cm).

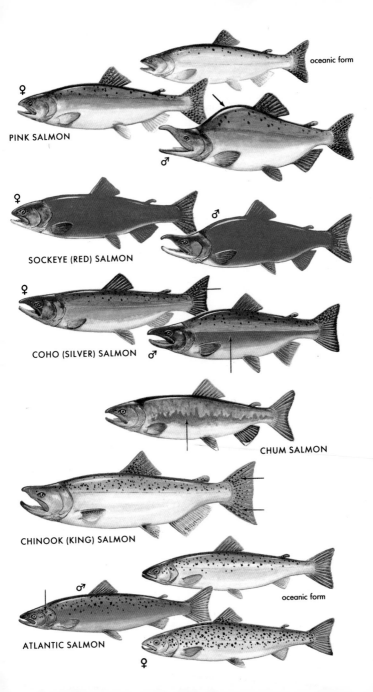

PINK SALMON
♀
♂
oceanic form

SOCKEYE (RED) SALMON
♀
♂

COHO (SILVER) SALMON
♀
♂

CHUM SALMON

CHINOOK (KING) SALMON

ATLANTIC SALMON
♂
♀
oceanic form

PLATE 6
PIRATE PERCH, TROUT-PERCH, SAND ROLLER, MUDMINNOWS, PICKERELS, PIKES

One dorsal fin.

PIRATE PERCH *Aphredoderus sayanus*   **M234, p. 212**
Large head. Large mouth. Anus on throat. Large individual has purple sheen. To 5½ in. (14 cm).

TROUT-PERCH *Percopsis omiscomaycus*   **M233, p. 211**
Rows of 7–12 black spots along back and side. Adipose fin. Large head. Pearl organs on lower jaw and cheek. To 7¾ in. (20 cm).

SAND ROLLER *Percopsis transmontana*   **M233, p. 212**
Similar to Trout-Perch but is dark blue-green above; has more arched back, incomplete lateral line. To 3¾ in. (9.6 cm).

Next 4 species (mudminnows) have dorsal fin far back on body, rounded or straight-edged caudal fin.

ALASKA BLACKFISH *Dallia pectoralis*   **M64, p. 59**
Black mottling and blotches on body and fins. Tiny pelvic fins, with 2–3 rays. To 13 in. (33 cm).

EASTERN MUDMINNOW *Umbra pygmaea*   **M65, p. 59**
Similar to Central Mudminnow but has 10–14 dark brown stripes on back and side. To 4½ in. (11 cm).

CENTRAL MUDMINNOW *Umbra limi*   **M65, p. 59**
Black bar on caudal fin base. Dorsal fin origin far in front of anal fin origin. To 5½ in. (14 cm).

OLYMPIC MUDMINNOW *Novumbra hubbsi*   **M63, p. 58**
10–15 cream to yellow, narrow interrupted bars on side. Dorsal fin origin above or only slightly in front of anal fin origin. To 3 in. (8 cm).

Next 4 species (pikes) have dorsal fin far back on body, duckbill-like snout, forked caudal fin. See also Fig. 14.

GRASS PICKEREL *Esox americanus vermiculatus*   **M66, p. 60**
Fully scaled cheek and opercle (Fig. 14). Black suborbital bar slanted toward rear. 11–13 branchiostegal rays. To 15 in. (38 cm).

REDFIN PICKEREL *Esox americanus americanus*   **M66, p. 60**
Subspecies of Grass Pickerel with red fins.

CHAIN PICKEREL *Exos niger*   **M67, p. 60**
Fully scaled cheek and opercle (Fig. 14). Chainlike pattern on side (adult). Vertical black suborbital bar. 14–17 branchiostegal rays. To 39 in. (99 cm).

NORTHERN PIKE *Esox lucius*   **M68, p. 61**
Partly scaled opercle; fully scaled cheek (Fig. 14). Rows of yellow bean-shaped spots (on adult). To 53 in. (133 cm).

MUSKELLUNGE *Esox masquinongy* (plus young)   **M69, p. 62**
Partly scaled cheek and opercle (Fig. 14). Dark spots, blotches, or bars on light yellow-green back and side. To 72 in. (183 cm).

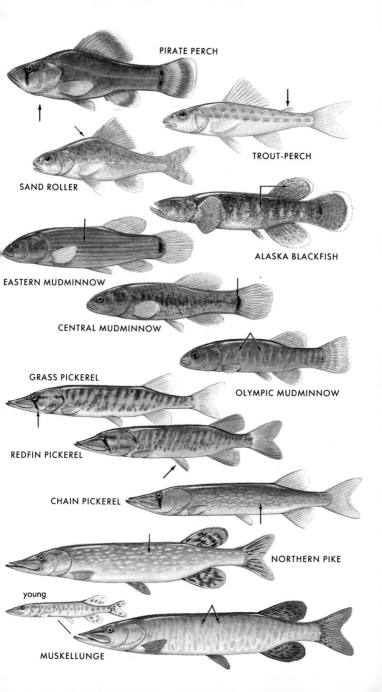

PIRATE PERCH

TROUT-PERCH

SAND ROLLER

ALASKA BLACKFISH

EASTERN MUDMINNOW

CENTRAL MUDMINNOW

GRASS PICKEREL

OLYMPIC MUDMINNOW

REDFIN PICKEREL

CHAIN PICKEREL

NORTHERN PIKE

young

MUSKELLUNGE

PLATE 7

MINNOWS (1)

All minnows have one dorsal fin; abdominal pelvic fins.

GRASS CARP *Ctenopharyngodon idella* **p. 63**
Wide head; terminal mouth. Large dark-edged scales. Slender, compressed body. To 49 in. (125 cm).

TENCH *Tinca tinca* **p. 66**
Small scales. Thick, leatherlike skin. Deep caudal peduncle. Long barbel at corner of mouth. To 33 in. (84 cm).

GOLDEN SHINER *Notemigonus crysoleucas* **M71, p. 66**
Extremely compressed body. Strongly decurved lateral line. Scaleless keel along belly (Fig. 16). Small, upturned mouth. Herringbone lines on young. To 12 in. (30 cm). See also Rudd (Fig. 15).

HITCH *Lavinia exilicauda* **M72, p. 67**
Deep, compressed body tapering to narrow caudal peduncle. Large caudal fin. Strongly decurved lateral line. To 14 in. (36 cm).

SPLITTAIL *Pogonichthys macrolepidotus* **M73, p. 67**
Upper lobe of large caudal fin longer than lower lobe. Barbel at corner of slightly subterminal mouth. To 17½ in. (44 cm). See also Clear Lake Splittail.

Next 3 species (squawfishes) have large terminal mouth extending to or past front of eye. Squawfishes are distinguished from one another by scale and fin ray counts.

COLORADO SQUAWFISH *Ptychocheilus lucius* **M74, p. 68**
76–97 lateral scales. Usually 9 dorsal rays, 9 anal rays. To 6 ft. (180 cm).

SACRAMENTO SQUAWFISH *Ptychocheilus grandis* **M74, p. 68**
65–78 lateral scales. Usually 8 dorsal rays, 8 anal rays. To 4½ ft. (140 cm).

NORTHERN SQUAWFISH *Ptychocheilus oregonensis* **M74, p. 69**
64–79 lateral scales. Usually 9 dorsal rays, 8 anal rays. To 25 in. (63 cm). See also Umpqua Squawfish.

HARDHEAD *Mylopharodon conocephalus* **M75, p. 69**
Premaxillary frenum. Long snout. Large terminal mouth reaches front of eye. To 39½ in. (1 m).

SACRAMENTO BLACKFISH *Orthodon microlepidotus* **M76, p. 69**
Small (90–105 lateral) scales. Wide head, flat above. Narrow caudal peduncle. To 21½ in. (55 cm).

CHISELMOUTH *Acrocheilus alutaceus* **M77, p. 70**
Large forked caudal fin. Wide head. Subterminal mouth; hard plate on lower jaw (Fig. 17). To 12 in. (30 cm).

ARROYO CHUB *Gila orcutti* **M79, p. 75**
Deep caudal peduncle. Short rounded snout. Large eye. To 16 in. (40 cm). See also Yaqui Chub.

ALVORD CHUB *Gila alvordensis* **M84, p. 77**
High nape. Short pointed head. Deep caudal peduncle. To 5¼ in. (14 cm). See also Borax Lake Chub.

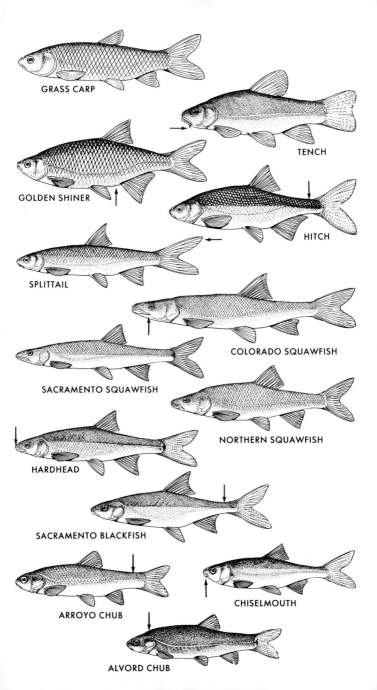

GRASS CARP

TENCH

GOLDEN SHINER

HITCH

SPLITTAIL

COLORADO SQUAWFISH

SACRAMENTO SQUAWFISH

NORTHERN SQUAWFISH

HARDHEAD

SACRAMENTO BLACKFISH

ARROYO CHUB

CHISELMOUTH

ALVORD CHUB

PLATE 8

MINNOWS (2)

MOAPA DACE *Moapa coriacea* **M87, p. 79**
Leatherlike skin (resulting from many small embedded scales). Large black spot on caudal fin base. To 3½ in. (9 cm).

RELICT DACE *Relictus solitarius* **M87, p. 80**
Chubby, soft-bodied. Incomplete lateral line, rarely reaching below dorsal fin. Large terminal mouth. To 5 in. (13 cm).

DESERT DACE *Eremichthys acros* **M87, p. 80**
Deep chubby body. Hard sheath on jaws. Small mouth. To 3 in. (7.7 cm)

LEAST CHUB *Iotichthys phlegethontis* **M83, p. 80**
Upturned mouth. Large eye. Large scales. Short rounded snout. To 2½ in. (6.4 cm).

*Next 5 species (*Phenacobius*) have long cylindrical body, large fleshy lips on subterminal mouth (Fig. 24).*

SUCKERMOUTH MINNOW *Phenacobius mirabilis* **M105, p. 96**
Bicolored body. Intense black spot on caudal fin base. (See also Fig. 24). To 4¾ in. (12 cm).

KANAWHA MINNOW *Phenacobius teretulus* **M106, p. 97**
Many small bumps on very fleshy lips (Fig. 24). Small black blotches on body. To 4 in. (10 cm).

FATLIPS MINNOW *Phenacobius crassilabrum* **M105, p. 97**
Pelvic fins reach to or past anus. To 4¼ in. (11 cm).

RIFFLE MINNOW *Phenacobius catostomus* **M106, p. 98**
Very long cylindrical body. Eyes high on head, directed upwardly. To 4½ in. (12 cm).

STARGAZING MINNOW *Phenacobius uranops* **M106, p. 98**
Similar to Riffle Minnow but has more elongated body, longer snout, more elliptical eye. To 4½ in. (12 cm).

CUTLIPS MINNOW *Exoglossum maxillingua* **M107, p. 99**
Fleshy lobe to either side of central bony plate on lower jaw (Fig. 25). Chubby body. Deep caudal peduncle. To 6¼ in. (16 cm). See also Tonguetied Minnow.

Next 4 species have black lower lobe on caudal fin, barbel in corner of mouth.

FLATHEAD CHUB *Platygobio gracilis* **M112, p. 103**
Broad flat head tapering to pointed snout. Large pointed dorsal and pectoral fins. To 12½ in. (32 cm).

SICKLEFIN CHUB *Macrhybopsis meeki* **M113, p. 103**
Large, sharply pointed, sickle-shaped fins. Deep head. Rounded snout. To 4¼ in. (11 cm).

STURGEON CHUB *Macrhybopsis gelida* **M114, p. 104**
Similar to Sicklefin Chub but has straight-edged fins. Keeled scales on back and side. Large papillae on underside of head. To 3¼ in. (8.4 cm).

SILVER CHUB *Macrhybopsis storeriana* **M103, p. 104**
Large eye on upper half of head. Bright silver-white side. Short rounded snout. To 9 in. (23 cm).

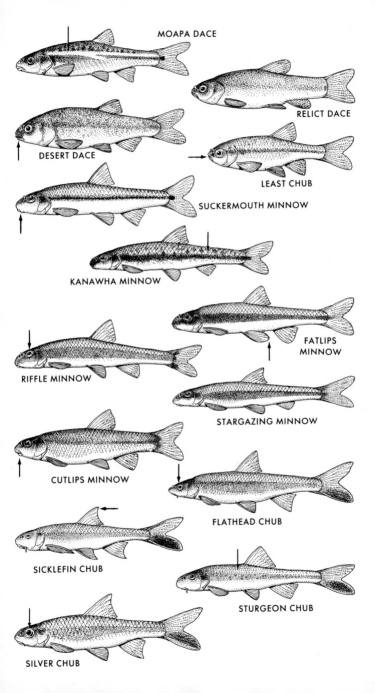

MOAPA DACE

RELICT DACE

DESERT DACE

LEAST CHUB

SUCKERMOUTH MINNOW

KANAWHA MINNOW

FATLIPS MINNOW

RIFFLE MINNOW

STARGAZING MINNOW

CUTLIPS MINNOW

FLATHEAD CHUB

SICKLEFIN CHUB

STURGEON CHUB

SILVER CHUB

PLATE 9

MINNOWS (3)

Subterminal mouth. All but Pallid Shiner and Silverjaw Minnow have barbel at corner of mouth (Fig. 21).

First 4 species have long slender body deepest at nape, flattened below.

STREAMLINE CHUB *Erimystax dissimilis*   **M114, p. 105**
7–15 horizontally oblong or round dark blotches along side. White to gold spot at front and back of dorsal fin. To 5½ in. (14 cm).

BLOTCHED CHUB *Erimystax insignis*   **M115, p. 105**
7–9 large vertical dark blotches along side. To 3½ in. (9.2 cm).

GRAVEL CHUB *Erimystax x-punctatus*   **M115, p. 105**
Many dark Xs on back and upper side. To 4¼ in. (11 cm).

SLENDER CHUB *Erimystax cahni*   **M116, p. 106**
Large dark <'s along rear half of side, darkest and largest on caudal peduncle. To 3½ in. (9 cm).

SPECKLED CHUB *Extrarius aestivalis*   **M118, p. 106**
Long bulbous snout overhangs mouth. Usually many small black spots on back and side. To 3 in. (7.6 cm).

Next 6 species have upwardly directed, horizontally elliptical eyes.

THICKLIP CHUB *Hybopsis labrosa*   **M116, p. 162**
Small dark brown blotches and cross-hatching on back and side. Long snout. Breeding male has yellow-black fins. To 2¾ in. (6.7 cm).

SANTEE CHUB *Hybopsis zanema*   **M117, p. 162**
Dark cross-hatching on back and side. Long snout. Breeding male has black streaks on dark yellow dorsal and caudal fins. To 3 in. (7.5 cm).

BIGEYE CHUB *Hybopsis amblops*   **M174, p. 160**
Black stripe (faded in turbid water) along side and onto snout. Large eye, about equal to snout length. To 3½ in. (9 cm). See also Rosyface Chub.

LINED CHUB *Hybopsis lineapunctata*   **M174, p. 161**
Clear stripe above black stripe (broad and diffuse at midbody) along side and around snout. Black spot on caudal fin base. To 3 in. (7.9 cm).

PALLID SHINER *Hybopsis amnis*   **M175, p. 161**
Body arched at dorsal fin origin. Large eye, about equal to snout length. To 3¼ in. (8.4 cm). See also Clear Chub.

SILVERJAW MINNOW *Ericymba buccata*   **M176, p. 163**
Large "pearl organs" (silver-white chambers) on cheek and flattened underside of head. To 3¾ in. (9.8 cm).

OREGON CHUB *Oregonichthys crameri*   **M84, p. 83**
Narrow caudal peduncle. Clusters of brown-black spots on back and silver side. To 2¾ in. (7 cm).

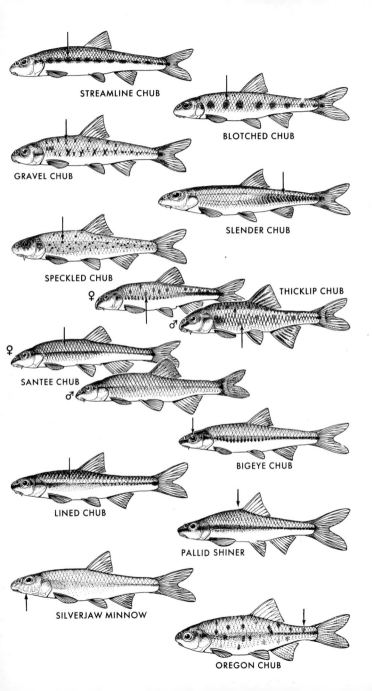

STREAMLINE CHUB

BLOTCHED CHUB

GRAVEL CHUB

SLENDER CHUB

SPECKLED CHUB

THICKLIP CHUB

♀

♂

SANTEE CHUB

♀

♂

BIGEYE CHUB

LINED CHUB

PALLID SHINER

SILVERJAW MINNOW

OREGON CHUB

PLATE 10

MINNOWS (4)

*First 3 species (*Hybognathus*) have long coiled intestine, black peritoneum, small slightly subterminal mouth (not reaching to eye). See also Fig. 26.*

MISSISSIPPI SILVERY MINNOW *Hybognathus nuchalis* **M119, p. 107**
Pointed dorsal fin. Silver side. To 7 in. (18 cm). See also Eastern Silvery, Western Silvery, and Plains Minnows.

BRASSY MINNOW *Hybognathus hankinsoni* **M122, p. 109**
Rounded dorsal fin. Stout brassy yellow body. To 3¾ in. (9.7 cm).

CYPRESS MINNOW *Hybognathus hayi* **M122, p. 109**
Scales on back and upper side darkly outlined, appear diamond shaped. Pointed dorsal fin. To 4½ in. (12 cm).

PUGNOSE MINNOW *Opsopoeodus emiliae* **M141, p. 129**
Cross-hatched pattern on back and side. Small strongly upturned mouth. Small scales on front half of nape. To 2½ in. (6.4 cm).

*Next 3 species (*Pimephales*) have scales on nape much smaller than elsewhere on body; short, stout 2d dorsal ray.*

FATHEAD MINNOW *Pimephales promelas* **M142, p. 129**
Deep body. Short head flat on top. Herringbone lines on upper side. Blunt snout. Breeding male has black head, 2 broad white or gold bars on side. To 4 in. (10 cm).

BLUNTNOSE MINNOW *Pimephales notatus* **M143, p. 130**
Blunt snout. Small subterminal mouth. Slender body. Black spot on caudal fin base. Breeding male is black with silver bar behind opercle, has about 16 tubercles in 3 rows on snout. To 4¼ in. (11 cm).

BULLHEAD MINNOW *Pimephales vigilax* **M144, p. 130**
Similar to Bluntnose Minnow but has larger eye directed more upwardly, body less slender, bluish sheen on side of body. Breeding male has 5–9 tubercles in 1–2 rows on snout. To 3½ in. (8.9 cm). See also Slim Minnow.

RIVER SHINER *Notropis blennius* **M154, p. 138**
Slender, fairly compressed body. Mouth extends to beneath front of eye. Dorsal fin origin over or slightly behind pelvic fin origin. To 5¼ in. (13 cm).

FLUVIAL SHINER *Notropis edwardraneyi* **M154, p. 139**
Large round eye, somewhat directed upwardly. Pallid. Dorsal fin origin in front of pelvic fin origin. To 3¼ in. (8 cm).

CHUB SHINER *Notropis potteri* **M153, p. 139**
Head flat above and below. Eye high on head, somewhat directed upwardly. To 4¼ in. (11 cm).

RED RIVER SHINER *Notropis bairdi* **M155, p. 140**
Broad flat head. Black specks concentrated in large patch on side of body. To 3¼ in. (8 cm). See also Smalleye and Arkansas River Shiners.

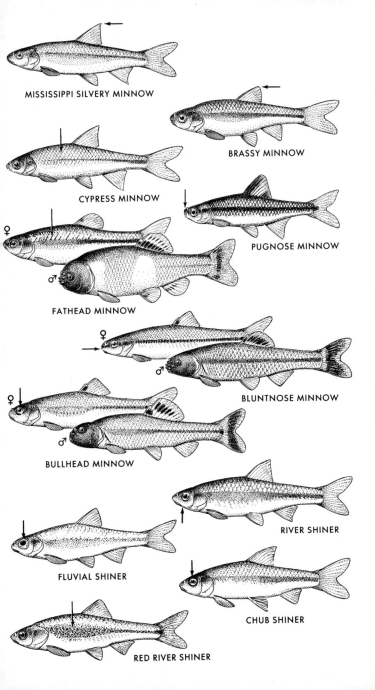

MISSISSIPPI SILVERY MINNOW

BRASSY MINNOW

CYPRESS MINNOW

PUGNOSE MINNOW

♀
♂
FATHEAD MINNOW

♀
♂
BLUNTNOSE MINNOW

♀
♂
BULLHEAD MINNOW

RIVER SHINER

FLUVIAL SHINER

CHUB SHINER

RED RIVER SHINER

PLATE 11
MINNOWS (5)

EMERALD SHINER *Notropis atherinoides*　　　　**M145, p. 132**
10–12 anal rays. Slender compressed body. Dorsal fin origin behind pelvic fin origin. To 5 in. (13 cm).

COMELY SHINER *Notropis amoenus*　　　　**M146, p. 132**
Nearly identical to Emerald Shiner but has smaller eye, rarely has T- or Y-shaped gill rakers (present in about 50% of Emerald Shiners). To 4¼ in. (11 cm).

RIO GRANDE SHINER *Notropis jemezanus*　　　　**M145, p. 132**
Similar to Emerald Shiner but has larger, less oblique mouth, deeper snout. To 3 in. (7.5 cm).

SHARPNOSE SHINER *Notropis oxyrhynchus*　　　　**M145, p. 132**
Sharply pointed snout. To 2½ in. (6.5 cm).

SILVER SHINER *Notropis photogenis*　　　　**M146, p. 133**
Slender compressed body. 2 black crescents (Fig. 32) between nostrils. To 5½ in. (14 cm).

SILVERBAND SHINER *Notropis shumardi*　　　　**M152, p. 137**
Tall pointed dorsal fin; origin over pelvic fin origin. To 4 in. (10 cm). See also Silverside Shiner.

SILVERSTRIPE SHINER *Notropis stilbius*　　　　**M148, p. 134**
Horizontally oval black spot on caudal fin base. Large eye. To 3½ in. (9 cm).

SANDBAR SHINER *Notropis scepticus*　　　　**M149, p. 134**
Large round eye. Darkly outlined scales on back and side. Punctate lateral line. To 3½ in. (9 cm).

POPEYE SHINER *Notropis ariommus*　　　　**M148, p. 136**
Huge eye. Darkly outlined scales on back and upper side. To 3¾ in. (9.5 cm).

TELESCOPE SHINER *Notropis telescopus*　　　　**M151, p. 136**
Dark wavy lines on back and upper side meet those of other side on caudal peduncle. Large eye. Punctate lateral line. To 3¾ in. (9.4 cm).

TEXAS SHINER *Notropis amabilis*　　　　**M150, p. 136**
Large eye. Black lips. Clear stripe above dark stripe (darkest at rear) along side. To 2½ in. (6.2 cm).

ROUGHHEAD SHINER *Notropis semperasper*　　　　**M151, p. 137**
Black stripe (darkest at rear) along side. Slender body. Large eye. To 3½ in. (9 cm).

KIAMICHI SHINER *Notropis ortenburgeri*　　　　**M162, p. 149**
Pale stripe above silver-black stripe along side. Dark-edged scales on back. Strongly upturned mouth. To 2¼ in. (5.5 cm). See also Blackmouth Shiner.

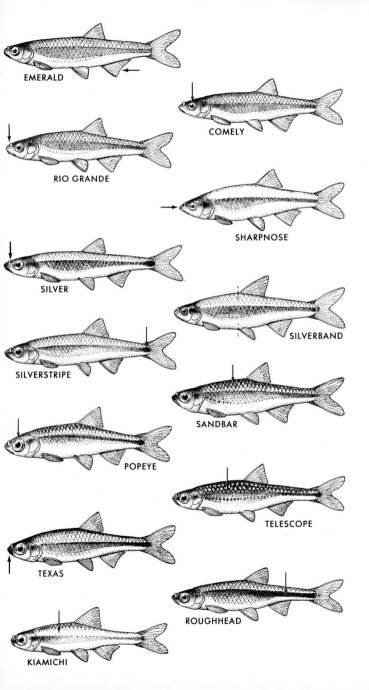

EMERALD

COMELY

RIO GRANDE

SHARPNOSE

SILVER

SILVERBAND

SILVERSTRIPE

SANDBAR

POPEYE

TELESCOPE

TEXAS

ROUGHHEAD

KIAMICHI

PLATE 12

MINNOWS (6)

PEPPERED SHINER *Notropis perpallidus*   **M150, p. 149**
Many black spots. Slender compressed body. To 2 in. (5 cm).

CHIHUAHUA SHINER *Notropis chihuahua*   **M168, p. 153**
Many black spots. Black wedge on caudal fin base. Stout body. To 3¼ in. (8 cm).

BLUNTNOSE SHINER *Notropis simus*   **M152, p. 138**
Blunt snout. Deep, wide head. Small eye. Small black specks on pallid body. To 4 in. (10 cm). See also Phantom Shiner.

TAMAULIPAS SHINER *Notropis braytoni*   **M169, p. 153**
Dusky stripe along side followed by clear area, then small black wedge on caudal fin base. To 2¾ in. (6.9 cm).

SPOTTAIL SHINER *Notropis hudsonius*   **M172, p. 159**
Large eye. Short rounded snout. Nearly horizontal subterminal mouth. Large black caudal spot (inconspicuous in s. Atlantic drainages and often on large individuals elsewhere). To 5¾ in. (15 cm).

BLACKSPOT SHINER *Notropis atrocaudalis*   **M173, p. 159**
Narrow black stripe along side. Black rectangle on caudal fin base. Stocky body. Subterminal mouth. To 3 in. (7.6 cm).

BLACKNOSE SHINER *Notropis heterolepis*   **M171, p. 156**
Black crescents within black stripe along side and around snout (absent on chin). Slender body. Dorsal fin origin behind pelvic fin origin. (See also Fig. 34.) To 3¾ in. (9.8 cm).

BEDROCK SHINER *Notropis rupestris*   **M171, p. 157**
Similar to Blacknose Shiner but has more arched back, complete lateral line, dorsal fin origin over pelvic fin origin. To 2½ in. (6.2 cm).

WHITEMOUTH SHINER *Notropis alborus*   **M171, p. 157**
Jagged-edged stripe along side. Black wedge on caudal fin base. No dark stripe along back. Black bridle around snout; no black on lips (Fig. 34). To 2¼ in. (6 cm).

PUGNOSE SHINER *Notropis anogenus*   **M162, p. 157**
Small upturned mouth (Fig. 34). Black peritoneum. Black stripe along side. Black wedge on caudal fin base. To 2¼ in. (5.8 cm).

BRIDLE SHINER *Notropis bifrenatus*   **M167, p. 158**
Black spot on caudal fin base usually joined to black stripe along side and around snout (where mostly confined to upper lip — Fig. 34). To 2½ in. (6.5 cm).

NEW RIVER SHINER *Notropis scabriceps*   **M149, p. 135**
Broad snout. Large upwardly directed eye. Darkly outlined scales. Punctate lateral line. To 3¼ in. (8.4 cm).

WEDGESPOT SHINER *Notropis greenei*   **M150, p. 135**
Black wedge on caudal fin base. Large upwardly directed eye. To 3 in. (7.5 cm).

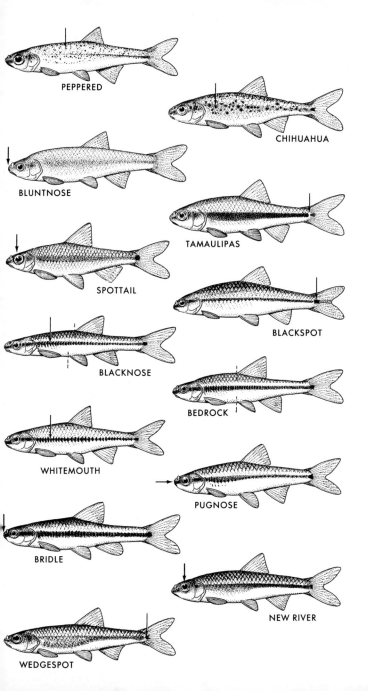

PEPPERED

CHIHUAHUA

BLUNTNOSE

TAMAULIPAS

SPOTTAIL

BLACKSPOT

BLACKNOSE

BEDROCK

WHITEMOUTH

PUGNOSE

BRIDLE

NEW RIVER

WEDGESPOT

PLATE 13
MINNOWS (7)

First 4 species have clear to yellow stripe above black stripe along side.

BLACKCHIN SHINER *Notropis heterodon* **M159, p. 145**
Black stripe extends around short pointed snout (Fig. 34.) Black stripe often has zigzag appearance on side. To 2¾ in. (7.1 cm).

BIGEYE SHINER *Notropis boops* **M159, p. 146**
Large eye. Punctate lateral line. To 3½ in. (9 cm).

COOSA SHINER *Notropis xaenocephalus* **M159, p. 146**
Large black spot on caudal fin base. Darkly outlined scales. Large eye. To 3 in. (7.9 cm).

BURRHEAD SHINER *Notropis asperifrons* **M160, p. 147**
Long rounded snout. Black spot on caudal fin base. To 3 in. (7.5 cm).

BIGMOUTH SHINER *Notropis dorsalis* **M158, p. 144**
Upwardly directed eye. Head flattened below. Strongly arched body. To 3¼ in. (8 cm).

SKYGAZER SHINER *Notropis uranoscopus* **M131, p. 147**
Large elliptical eye high on head. Small black wedge on caudal fin base. To 2¾ in. (7.1 cm).

HIGHSCALE SHINER *Notropis hypsilepis* **M160, p. 147**
Blunt snout. Small black wedge on caudal fin base. Eye high on head. To 2½ in. (6.4 cm).

WEED SHINER *Notropis texanus* **M161. p. 148**
Black stripe along side and around snout; some black-edged scales below stripe. Last 3–4 anal rays lined with black in Gulf Coast drainages. To 3½ in. (8.6 cm).

COASTAL SHINER *Notropis petersoni* **M160, p. 148**
Similar to Weed Shiner but lacks black-edged scales below stripe; has all anal rays lined with black, black wedge on caudal fin base. To 3¼ in. (8.2 cm).

GHOST SHINER *Notropis buchanani* **M168, p. 153**
Translucent milky white (some populations have black specks — see text). Body deep at dorsal fin origin, tapering to thin caudal peduncle. To 2½ in. (6.4 cm).

MIMIC SHINER *Notropis volucellus* **M169, p. 154**
Broad rounded snout. Scales along back in front of dorsal fin wider than adjacent scales. Scales along side on front half of body much deeper than wide (Fig. 35). To 3 in. (7.6 cm). See also Cahaba Shiner.

SAND SHINER *Notropis ludibundus* **M166, p. 151**
Punctate lateral line. Dusky stripe along back expanded into dark wedge at dorsal fin origin. To 3¼ in. (8.1 cm).

SWALLOWTAIL SHINER *Notropis procne* **M166, p. 152**
Similar to Sand Shiner but has longer snout, darker stripe (often black) along side, yellow body and fins on breeding male. To 2¾ in. (7.2 cm). See also Palezone Shiner.

CAPE FEAR SHINER *Notropis mekistocholas* **M167, p. 152**
Long coiled dark gut visible through belly wall. Black stripe along side of body and snout. To 3 in. (7.7 cm).

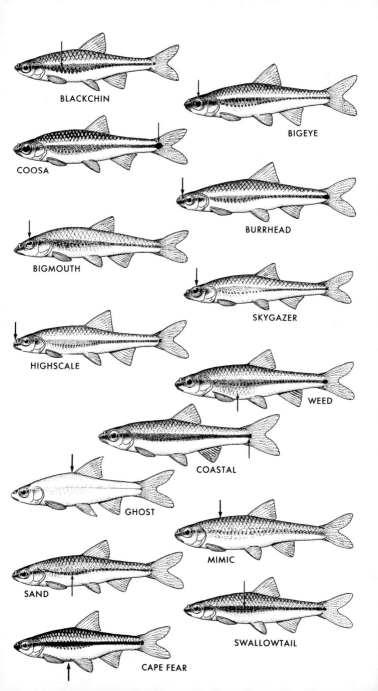

BLACKCHIN

BIGEYE

COOSA

BURRHEAD

BIGMOUTH

SKYGAZER

HIGHSCALE

WEED

COASTAL

GHOST

MIMIC

SAND

SWALLOWTAIL

CAPE FEAR

PLATE 14

MINNOWS (8)

GOLDFISH *Carassius auratus*   **p. 64**
Large scales. Long dorsal fin, 15–21 rays. Terminal mouth. To 16 in. (41 cm).

COMMON CARP *Cyprinus carpio*   **p. 64**
2 barbels on each side of upper jaw. Long dorsal fin, 17–21 rays. To 48 in. (122 cm).

PEAMOUTH *Mylocheilus caurinus*   **M75, p. 70**
2 dark stripes on side; lower one ends before anal fin. Large male (shown) has red on side and head. To 14 in. (36 cm).

REDSIDE SHINER *Richardsonius balteatus*   **M78, p. 71**
Narrow caudal peduncle. Dorsal fin origin far behind pelvic fin origin. Red above pectoral fin. To 7 in. (18 cm).

LAHONTAN REDSIDE *Richardsonius egregius*   **M78, p. 71**
Similar to Redside Shiner but has longer snout, more slender body. To 6½ in. (17 cm).

CALIFORNIA ROACH *Hesperoleucus symmetricus*   **M77, p. 72**
Slightly subterminal mouth. Deep body tapering to narrow caudal peduncle. To 4¼ in. (11 cm).

ROUNDTAIL CHUB *Gila robusta*   **M79, p. 72**
Slender caudal peduncle. Angle along anal fin base continues into middle of caudal fin (Fig. 18). To 17 in. (43 cm).

HUMPBACK CHUB *Gila cypha*   **M80, p. 74**
Long, extremely slender caudal peduncle. Large individual has hump behind small depressed head. Angle along anal fin base continues along upper edge of caudal fin (Fig. 18). To 15 in. (38 cm).

BONYTAIL *Gila elegans*   **M81, p. 74**
Similar to Humpback Chub but has terminal mouth, angle along anal fin base continues well above caudal fin (Fig. 18). To 24½ in. (62 cm).

CHIHUAHUA CHUB *Gila nigrescens*   **M82, p. 74**
Terminal mouth on rounded snout. Large individual has red-orange mouth and anal and paired fin bases. To 9½ in. (24 cm).

RIO GRANDE CHUB *Gila pandora*   **M82, p. 75**
2 dusky stripes along side (darkest on large individual). To 7 in. (18 cm). See also Sonora Chub.

BLUE CHUB *Gila coerulea*   **M84, p. 76**
Pointed snout. Terminal mouth extends to front of eye. Breeding male has blue snout, orange side and fins. To 16 in. (41 cm).

LEATHERSIDE CHUB *Gila copei*   **M81, p. 76**
Leatherlike appearance (created by small scales). Large male has red anal and paired fin bases. To 6 in. (15 cm).

UTAH CHUB *Gila atraria*   **M85, p. 76**
Yellow to brassy side. Short snout. To 22 in. (56 cm).

TUI CHUB *Gila bicolor*   **M80, p. 77**
Small rounded fins. Small mouth does not extend to eye. To 17¾ in. (45 cm).

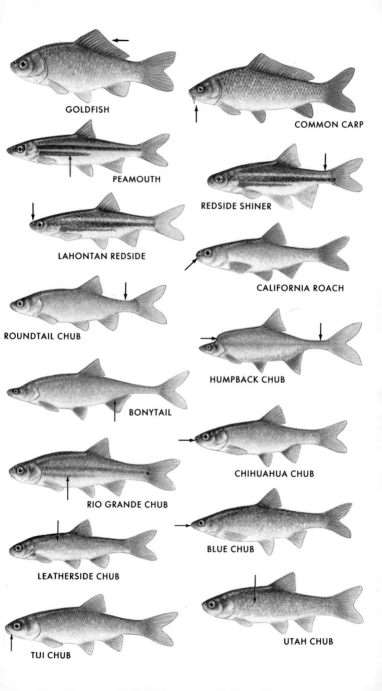

GOLDFISH

COMMON CARP

PEAMOUTH

REDSIDE SHINER

LAHONTAN REDSIDE

CALIFORNIA ROACH

ROUNDTAIL CHUB

HUMPBACK CHUB

BONYTAIL

RIO GRANDE CHUB

CHIHUAHUA CHUB

LEATHERSIDE CHUB

BLUE CHUB

TUI CHUB

UTAH CHUB

PLATE 15

MINNOWS (9)

ROSYSIDE DACE *Clinostomus funduloides*   **M86, p. 78**
Large oblique mouth; long pointed snout. Breeding male (shown) has bright red lower side. 43–57 lateral scales. To 4½ in. (11 cm).

REDSIDE DACE *Clinostomus elongatus*   **M86, p. 78**
Similar to Rosyside Dace but has more pointed snout, more slender body. 59–75 lateral scales. To 4½ in. (12 cm).

LONGFIN DACE *Agosia chrysogaster*   **M76, p. 79**
Small barbel at corner of mouth. Small scales. Large female (shown) has elongated lower lobe on anal fin. To 4 in. (10 cm).

Next 3 species have 2 large spines in dorsal fin, bright silver side.

VIRGIN SPINEDACE *Lepidomeda mollispinis*   **M88, p. 81**
Large, gray-black blotches on side, compressed body. To 5¾ in. (15 cm). See also Little Colorado, White River, and Pahranagat Spinedaces.

SPIKEDACE *Meda fulgida*   **M87, p. 82**
No scales. Slender body; subterminal mouth. To 3½ in. (9.1 cm).

WOUNDFIN *Plagopterus argentissimus*   **M83, p. 83**
No scales. Long snout; barbel at mouth corner. To 3½ in. (9 cm).

*Next 5 species (*Phoxinus*) have scales so small they appear absent; red side, yellow fins (brightest on large males — shown).*

FINESCALE DACE *Phoxinus neogaeus*   **M89, p. 84**
Dark "cape" on back. Many black specks on body. To 4¼ in. (11 cm).

SOUTHERN REDBELLY DACE *Phoxinus erythrogaster*   **M90, p. 84**
2 black stripes along side. Small black spots on upper side. To 3½ in. (9.1 cm). See also Northern Redbelly Dace.

MOUNTAIN REDBELLY DACE *Phoxinus oreas*   **M90, p. 85**
Black stripe along side broken under dorsal fin. Large black spots on back and upper side. To 2¾ in. (7.2 cm).

TENNESSEE DACE *Phoxinus tennesseensis*   **M90, p. 85**
Similar to Mountain Redbelly Dace but has smaller spots, thin black stripe along side. To 2¾ in. (7.2 cm).

BLACKSIDE DACE *Phoxinus cumberlandensis*   **M92, p. 86**
Two dusky stripes along side converge on caudal peduncle, coalesce into wide black stripe on breeding male (shown). To 2¾ in. (7.2 cm).

FLAME CHUB *Hemitremia flammea*   **M92, p. 86**
Chubby body. Deep caudal peduncle. Short snout. Large individual is scarlet red below (brightest on male). To 2¾ in. (7.2 cm).

*Next 3 species (*Semotilus*) have thick body, broad head, small barbel in groove above corner of large mouth (Fig. 21).*

CREEK CHUB *Semotilus atromaculatus*   **M93, p. 87**
Large black spot at dorsal fin origin. Breeding male has pink body, orange fins. To 12 in. (30 cm). See also Sandhills Chub.

DIXIE CHUB *Semotilus thoreauianus*   **M95, p. 88**
Similar to Creek Chub but has larger scales, more diffuse stripe along side. Breeding male (shown) has yellow fins. To 6 in. (15 cm).

FALLFISH *Semotilus corporalis*   **M94, p. 88**
Large (43–50 lateral), darkly outlined scales. To 20¼ in. (51 cm).

PEARL DACE *Margariscus margarita*   **M95, p. 89**
Small scales. Short head. Barbel (often absent) as in Creek Chub (Fig. 21). Breeding male (shown) is bright red-orange. To 6½ in. (16 cm).

LAKE CHUB *Couesius plumbeus*   **M96, p. 89**
Large eye. Barbel at corner of mouth. To 9 in. (23 cm).

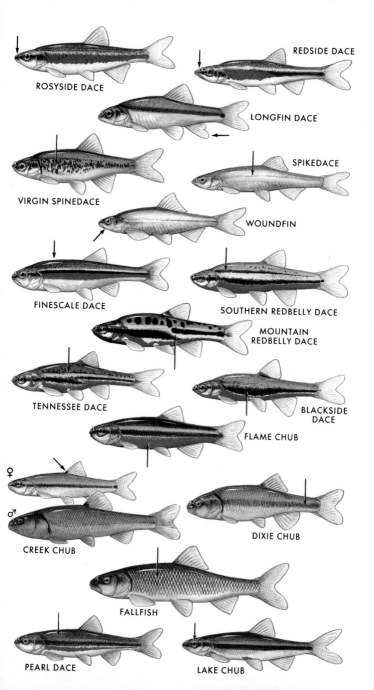

ROSYSIDE DACE

REDSIDE DACE

LONGFIN DACE

VIRGIN SPINEDACE

SPIKEDACE

WOUNDFIN

FINESCALE DACE

SOUTHERN REDBELLY DACE

MOUNTAIN REDBELLY DACE

TENNESSEE DACE

BLACKSIDE DACE

FLAME CHUB

♀
♂

CREEK CHUB

DIXIE CHUB

FALLFISH

PEARL DACE

LAKE CHUB

PLATE 16

MINNOWS (10)

*First 4 species (*Nocomis*) have stout body, large scales.*

HORNYHEAD CHUB *Nocomis biguttatus* **M97, p. 90**
Bright red (on male) or brassy (female) spot behind eye. To 10¼ in. (26 cm). See also Redspot Chub.

REDTAIL CHUB *Nocomis effusus* **M97, p. 91**
Similar to Hornyhead Chub but has brighter red-orange fins (especially on young — shown). To 9 in. (23 cm).

RIVER CHUB *Nocomis micropogon* **M98, p. 91**
Long snout. Small eye high on head. Breeding male (shown) has hump on head. To 12½ in. (32 cm). See also Bull Chub.

BLUEHEAD CHUB *Nocomis leptocephalus* **M100, p. 92**
Large loop on intestine (visible through body wall on young). Short snout. Breeding male (shown) has hump on blue head. To 10 in. (26 cm).

*Next 4 species (*Campostoma*) have cartilaginous ridge on lower jaw (Fig. 22), dark blotches on back and side of large individual.*

CENTRAL STONEROLLER *Campostoma anomalum* **M101, p. 93**
Breeding male (shown) has black band on orange dorsal and anal fins, 1–3 large tubercles on inner edge of nostril (Fig. 23). Usually 46–55 lateral scales, 36–46 scales around body at dorsal fin origin. To 8½ in. (22 cm).

BLUEFIN STONEROLLER *Campostoma pauciradii* **M92, p. 94**
Similar to Central Stoneroller but has 11–17 (vs. 21–23) rakers on 1st gill arch, usually 33–38 scales around body, blue-green dorsal and anal fins on large male. To 6¼ in. (16 cm).

LARGESCALE STONEROLLER *Campostoma oligolepis* **M102, p. 95**
Similar to Central Stoneroller but has usually 31–36 scales around body, 43–47 lateral scales; no black band on anal fin or large tubercles on inner edge of nostril of breeding male (Fig. 23). To 8½ in. (22 cm).

MEXICAN STONEROLLER *Campostoma ornatum* **M101, p. 95**
Similar to Central Stoneroller but has usually 58–77 lateral scales, no tubercles on nape of breeding male (shown). To 6¼ in. (16 cm).

ROUNDNOSE MINNOW *Dionda episcopa* **M103, p. 95**
Bicolored. Black stripe along side, zigzagged at front. To 3 in. (7.7 cm).

DEVILS RIVER MINNOW *Dionda diaboli* **M104, p. 96**
Black wedge on caudal fin base. Black stripe on side. To 2½ in. (6.4 cm).

*Next 5 species (*Rhinichthys*) have small scales; streamlined body, flattened below; usually many black specks on body.*

BLACKNOSE DACE *Rhinichthys atratulus* **M108, p. 100**
Many dark specks. Deep caudal peduncle. To 4 in. (10 cm). Breeding male (shown) of *R. a. atratulus* has gold-yellow below red-black stripe, of *R. a. meleagris* has red below black stripe.

SPECKLED DACE *Rhinichthys osculus* **M109, p. 100**
Usually many dark specks. Red-orange lips and fin bases on large individual. To 4¼ in. (11 cm). See also Las Vegas Dace.

LEOPARD DACE *Rhinichthys falcatus* **M110, p. 101**
Similar to Speckled Dace but has falcate dorsal fin, larger dark blotches on side and fins. To 5 in. (12 cm). See also Umatilla Dace.

LONGNOSE DACE *Rhinichthys cataractae* **M111, p. 101**
Long fleshy snout extends well in front of mouth. Deep caudal peduncle. To 6¼ in. (16 cm). See also Cheat Minnow and Umpqua Dace.

LOACH MINNOW *Rhinichthys cobitis* **M111, p. 103**
Upwardly directed eye. White bar on caudal fin base. To 2¼ in. (6 cm).

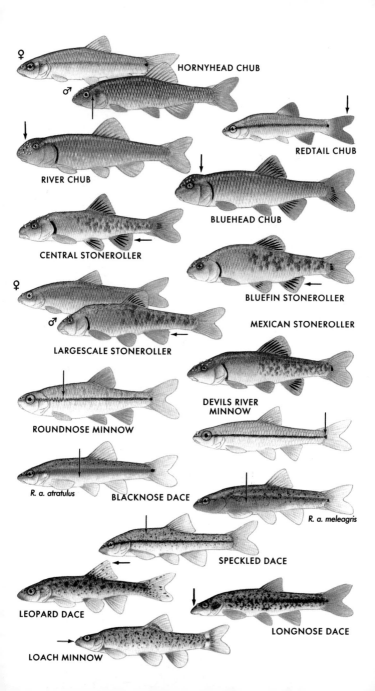

♀ HORNYHEAD CHUB
♂

REDTAIL CHUB

RIVER CHUB

BLUEHEAD CHUB

CENTRAL STONEROLLER

BLUEFIN STONEROLLER

♀
♂
LARGESCALE STONEROLLER

MEXICAN STONEROLLER

ROUNDNOSE MINNOW

DEVILS RIVER MINNOW

R. a. atratulus
BLACKNOSE DACE

R. a. meleagris

SPECKLED DACE

LEOPARD DACE

LONGNOSE DACE

LOACH MINNOW

PLATE 17

MINNOWS (11)

First 6 species (Lythrurus) have very small scales on nape, dorsal fin origin behind pelvic fin origin, usually 10–12 anal rays.

REDFIN SHINER *Lythrurus umbratilis* **M126, p. 113**
Dark blotch at dorsal fin origin. Deep body. Breeding male (shown) has red fins, blue body. To 3½ in. (8.5 cm).

ROSEFIN SHINER *Lythrurus ardens* **M127, p. 114**
Black blotch at dorsal fin origin. Dusky bars over back. Breeding male (shown) has red fins, blue body. To 3½ in. (8.5 cm).

PINEWOODS SHINER *Lythrurus matutinus* **M127, p. 115**
Similar to Rosefin Shiner but is more slender. Breeding male (shown) has bright red head, silver body. To 3½ in. (8.6 cm).

RIBBON SHINER *Lythrurus fumeus* **M128, p. 115**
Scales on nape outlined in black. Fairly slender body. Dusky lips and chin (Fig. 28). To 2¾ in. (7 cm). See also Ouachita Mountain Shiner.

MOUNTAIN SHINER *Lythrurus lirus* **M126, p. 116**
Slender body. Silver-black stripe along side. Black lips, white chin (Fig. 28). To 3 in. (7.5 cm).

CHERRYFIN SHINER *Lythrurus roseipinnis* **M129, p. 116**
Black spots on dorsal and anal fins (Fig. 29). Breeding male (shown) has red fins. To 3 in. (7.5 cm). See also Pretty and Blacktip Shiners.

Next 9 species (Luxilus) have scales on front half of body deeper than wide, deep body, usually 9 anal rays.

STRIPED SHINER *Luxilus chrysocephalus* **M123, p. 110**
Dark stripes on upper side meet those of other side to form large Vs (Fig. 27). Breeding male has pink or red body and fins. To 7¼ in. (18 cm).

COMMON SHINER *Luxilus cornutus* **M124, p. 110**
Similar to Striped Shiner but stripes on upper side are parallel to stripe along back (Fig. 27). To 7 in. (17.5 cm).

WHITE SHINER *Luxilus albeolus* **M124, p. 110**
Nearly identical to Common Shiner but is more silvery; has usually 26–30 scales around body at dorsal fin origin (Common Shiner has 30–35). To 5¼ in. (13 cm).

CRESCENT SHINER *Luxilus cerasinus* **M123, p. 111**
Large black crescents on side. Breeding male (shown) has red head, body, and fins. To 4½ in. (11 cm).

BLEEDING SHINER *Luxilus zonatus* **M125, p. 112**
Large black bar behind gill cover. Narrow black stripe along side, constricted behind head. Large individual has red head and fins. To 5 in. (13 cm).

CARDINAL SHINER *Luxilus cardinalis* **M125, p. 112**
Broad black stripe along side extends below lateral line. Large individual has red head, lower body, and fins. To 4¼ in. (11 cm).

DUSKYSTRIPE SHINER *Luxilus pilsbryi* **M125, p. 112**
Black stripe along body not constricted behind head, extends to (not below) lateral line. Large individual has red head and fins. To 5 in. (13 cm).

BANDFIN SHINER *Luxilus zonistius* **M125, p. 113**
Black band on dorsal fin. Large black spot on caudal fin base. Breeding male (shown) has red bar on caudal fin. To 4 in. (10 cm).

WARPAINT SHINER *Luxilus coccogenis* **M125, p. 113**
Black band on dorsal and caudal fins. Red bar on opercle. Breeding male (shown) has pink side, red snout. To 5½ in. (14 cm).

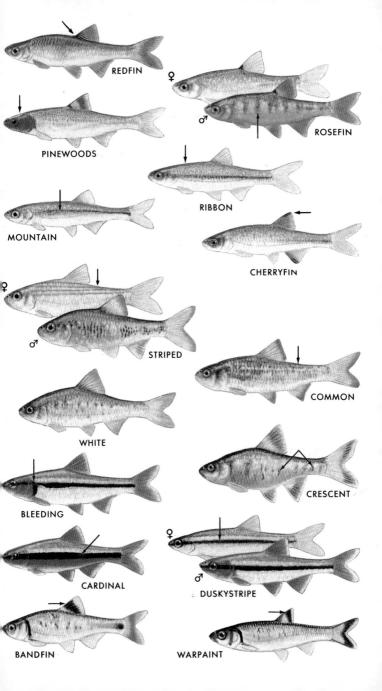

REDFIN

PINEWOODS

MOUNTAIN

♀
♂ ROSEFIN

RIBBON

CHERRYFIN

♀
♂ STRIPED

COMMON

WHITE

CRESCENT

BLEEDING

CARDINAL

♀
♂ DUSKYSTRIPE

BANDFIN

WARPAINT

PLATE 18

MINNOWS (12)

Species of Cyprinella *have scales that appear diamond-shaped, dusky to black bar (often faint) on chin.*

STEELCOLOR SHINER *Cyprinella whipplei* **M134, p. 120**
Black blotch on rear half, black specks on all membranes of dorsal fin (Fig. 30). Breeding male (shown) is blue; has red snout, yellow fins, enlarged dorsal fin. To 6½ in. (16 cm). See also Satinfin and Greenfin Shiners.

SPOTFIN SHINER *Cyprinella spiloptera* **M133, p. 120**
Black blotch on rear half of dorsal fin, little or no black on membranes of front half (Fig. 30). Breeding male is blue; has yellow fins, dusky dorsal fin. To 4¾ in. (12 cm).

BLUNTFACE SHINER *Cyprinella camura* **M136, p. 122**
Clear to white bar (sometimes absent) on caudal fin base. Breeding male (shown) has pale orange or red fins and snout, enlarged dorsal fin. To 4¼ in. (11 cm).

BLACKTAIL SHINER *Cyprinella venusta* **M135, p. 122**
Large black spot on caudal fin base. Breeding male is blue; has yellow or (in TX) red-orange fins, dusky dorsal fin. To 7½ in. (19 cm).

RED SHINER *Cyprinella lutrensis* **M137, p. 123**
Deep body. Blue triangular bar behind head on side. Breeding male has blue body, red fins. To 3½ in. (9 cm). See also Beautiful and Edwards Plateau Shiners.

PROSERPINE SHINER *Cyprinella proserpina* **M136, p. 124**
Subterminal mouth. Black stripe on chin and throat. Yellow fins. Breeding male (shown) is blue, has orange fins. To 3 in. (7.5 cm).

WHITETAIL SHINER *Cyprinella galactura* **M138, p. 124**
2 large white areas on caudal fin base. Slender body. To 6 in. (15 cm).

ALABAMA SHINER *Cyprinella callistia* **M139, p. 124**
Large black spot on caudal fin base. Pink to red dorsal and caudal fins. To 3¾ in. (9.5 cm).

TRICOLOR SHINER *Cyprinella trichroistia* **M138, p. 125**
Large black spot on caudal fin base fusing into black stripe on side. Yellow to red-orange fins. To 4 in. (10 cm). See also Tallapoosa Shiner.

BLUE SHINER *Cyprinella caerulea* **M140, p. 126**
Blue-black stripe along side, expanded on caudal fin base. Fairly slender body. Pointed snout. To 3½ in. (9 cm).

FIERYBLACK SHINER *Cyprinella pyrrhomelas* **M140, p. 126**
Black edge on caudal fin (of adult). Black bar behind head on side. Breeding male is blue; has bright red snout, red band after white band on caudal fin. To 4¼ in. (11 cm).

ALTAMAHA SHINER *Cyprinella xaenura* **M140, p. 126**
Pointed snout. Black stripe along rear half of side expanded into spot on caudal fin base. Breeding male has blue side, orange dorsal and anal fins. To 4½ in. (11 cm).

OCMULGEE SHINER *Cyprinella callisema* **M139, p. 127**
Deep blue stripe along side. Small black blotch at front of dorsal fin. Subterminal mouth. To 3½ in. (9 cm). See also Bluestripe Shiner.

WHITEFIN SHINER *Cyprinella nivea* **M139, p. 127**
Dark blue to black stripe along side. Black blotch on rear half of dorsal fin. Subterminal mouth. To 3½ in. (8.5 cm).

BANNERFIN SHINER *Cyprinella leedsi* **M140, p. 128**
Small black blotch at front of dorsal fin. Subterminal mouth. Breeding male (shown) has greatly enlarged black dorsal fin. To 4 in. (10 cm).

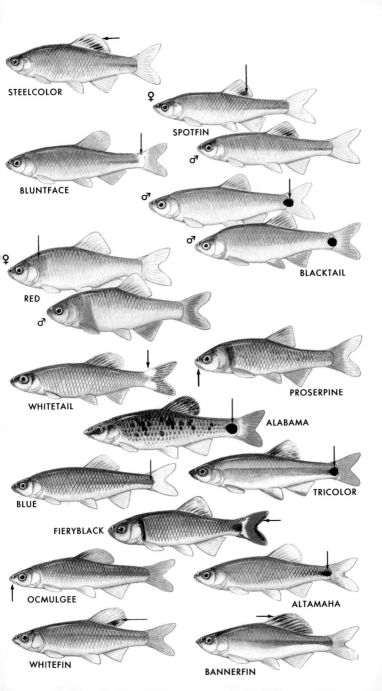

STEELCOLOR

SPOTFIN ♀

♂

BLUNTFACE

♂

BLACKTAIL ♂

RED ♀

♂

WHITETAIL

PROSERPINE

ALABAMA

BLUE

TRICOLOR

FIERYBLACK

OCMULGEE

ALTAMAHA

WHITEFIN

BANNERFIN

PLATE 19

MINNOWS (13)

LONGNOSE SHINER *Notropis longirostris*   **M158, p. 143**
Upwardly directed eye. Long rounded snout. Subterminal mouth. Yellow fins. To 2½ in. (6.5 cm).

ORANGEFIN SHINER *Notropis ammophilus*   **M158, p. 144**
Similar to Longnose Shiner but has dorsal fin origin over pelvic fin origin, orange snout and fins. To 2¼ in. (6 cm).

SABINE SHINER *Notropis sabinae*   **M158, p. 144**
Strongly arched body, flattened below. Subterminal mouth. Small eye slightly directed upwardly. To 2¼ in. (5.7 cm).

SPOTFIN CHUB *Cyprinella monacha*   **M117, p. 128**
Slender, arched body; flattened below. Long snout overhangs mouth. Silver side. Black blotch on dorsal fin. Breeding male (shown) has 2 white bars on blue side. To 4¼ in. (11 cm).

HIGHBACK CHUB *Hybopsis hypsinotus*   **M175, p. 163**
Large dorsal fin on arched back. Red fins. Barbel at corner of subterminal mouth. To 2¾ in. (7.2 cm).

ROUGH SHINER *Notropis baileyi*   **M156, p. 140**
Red-brown above; brown-black stripe along side uniformly dark from snout to caudal fin base. Black caudal spot. Yellow fins. To 3½ in. (9 cm).

YELLOWFIN SHINER *Notropis lutipinnis*   **M156, p. 141**
Similar to Rough Shiner but lacks caudal spot, has dorsal fin origin behind pelvic fin origin. Breeding male has yellow to red fins. To 3 in. (7.5 cm).

GREENHEAD SHINER *Notropis chlorocephalus*   **M156, p. 141**
Similar to Yellowfin Shiner but breeding male (shown) is red, has bright white fins. To 2¾ in. (7.2 cm).

REDLIP SHINER *Notropis chiliticus*   **M156, p. 141**
Bright red lips. Scattered black blotches on side. Breeding male has scarlet red body and eye, yellow fins. To 2¾ in. (7.2 cm).

SAFFRON SHINER *Notropis rubricroceus*   **M156, p. 142**
Similar to Redlip Shiner but has clear spot at rear of dorsal fin, black stripe along body begins at head. To 3¼ in. (8.4 cm).

RAINBOW SHINER *Notropis chrosomus*   **M157, p. 142**
Clear to red-purple stripe above silver-black stripe along side. Iridescent blue and pink head and body (most vivid on large male — shown). To 3¼ in. (8.1 cm).

TENNESSEE SHINER *Notropis leuciodus*   **M157, p. 142**
Dark wavy stripes on back and upper side. Black rectangle on caudal fin base. Punctate lateral line. Breeding male is red. To 3¼ in. (8.2 cm).

ROSYFACE SHINER *Notropis rubellus*   **M147, p. 133**
Sharply pointed snout longer than eye diameter. Dorsal fin origin well behind pelvic fin origin. Breeding male (shown) has orange to red head and fin bases. To 3½ in. (9 cm).

OZARK MINNOW *Notropis nubilus*   **M157, p. 143**
Bicolored; olive-brown above, white to yellow-orange below. Black stripe along side. Black lining of body cavity often visible through belly. To 3¾ in. (9.3 cm).

TOPEKA SHINER *Notropis tristis*   **M173, p. 160**
Stocky, compressed body. Small eye. Black wedge on caudal fin base. Breeding male (shown) has red-orange fins. To 3 in. (7.6 cm).

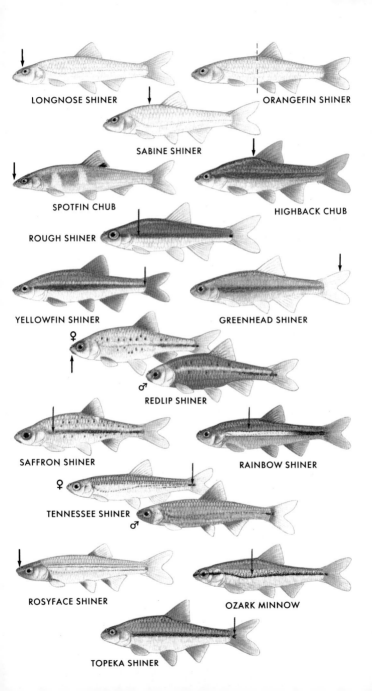

LONGNOSE SHINER

ORANGEFIN SHINER

SABINE SHINER

SPOTFIN CHUB

HIGHBACK CHUB

ROUGH SHINER

YELLOWFIN SHINER

GREENHEAD SHINER

♀

♂

REDLIP SHINER

SAFFRON SHINER

RAINBOW SHINER

♀

TENNESSEE SHINER

♂

ROSYFACE SHINER

OZARK MINNOW

TOPEKA SHINER

PLATE 20

MINNOWS (14)

IRONCOLOR SHINER *Notropis chalybaeus*   **M163, p. 149**
Well-defined black stripe from spot on caudal fin base along side and around snout covering both lips and chin (Fig. 34). Black inside mouth. To 2½ in. (6.5 cm).

DUSKY SHINER *Notropis cummingsae*   **M164, p. 150**
Wide black stripe along side, streaking onto caudal fin. To 2¾ in. (7.2 cm).

REDEYE CHUB *Notropis harperi*   **M165, p. 150**
Pink-tan above. Red eye. Yellow arc on snout. To 2¼ in. (6 cm).

HIGHFIN SHINER *Notropis altipinnis*   **M165, p. 151**
Boldly outlined scales on back separated from silver-black stripe along side by clear yellow stripe. To 2½ in. (6.1 cm).

Next 3 species have very broad blue-black stripe along side of deep body, 10–11 anal rays.

FLAGFIN SHINER *Pteronotropis signipinnis*   **M130, p. 118**
Red-orange edge on yellow dorsal, caudal, anal, and pelvic fins. To 2¾ in. (7 cm).

SAILFIN SHINER *Pteronotropis hypselopterus*   **M131, p. 118**
Red spots on caudal fin base. Large, nearly triangular dorsal and anal fins. To 2½ in. (6.5 cm).

BROADSTRIPE SHINER *Pteronotropis euryzonus*   **M130, p. 119**
Nearly identical to Sailfin Shiner but has rectangular dorsal fin. To 2¾ in. (7 cm).

BLUEHEAD SHINER *Pteronotropis hubbsi*   **M132, p. 119**
Black stripe along side. Deep body. Breeding male has bright blue on top of head, caudal fin, and huge dorsal fin. To 2½ in. (6 cm).

BLUENOSE SHINER *Pteronotropis welaka*   **M132, p. 119**
Black stripe along slender body. Breeding male has bright blue snout, huge dorsal fin. To 2½ in. (6.5 cm).

TAILLIGHT SHINER *Notropis maculatus*   **M170, p. 158**
Red above and below large black spot on caudal fin base. Cross-hatching on back and side. Large black blotch along front of dorsal fin. Breeding male (shown) has bright red body, red-black edge on fins. To 3 in. (7.6 cm).

Next 3 species have slender, usually arched, body; small subterminal mouth.

MIRROR SHINER *Notropis spectrunculus*   **M170, p. 155**
No, or small and crowded, scales on front half of nape. Upwardly directed eye. Large male has orange fins. To 3 in. (7.5 cm).

SAWFIN SHINER *Notropis* species   **M170, p. 156**
Similar to Mirror Shiner but has black specks (and orange on large male) confined to front half (not all) of dorsal fin. To 2½ in. (6.6 cm).

OZARK SHINER *Notropis ozarcanus*   **M170, p. 143**
Black spot at dorsal fin origin. To 3 in. (7.5 cm).

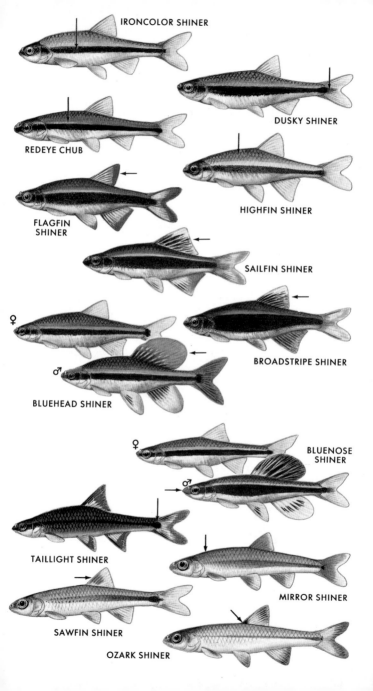

IRONCOLOR SHINER

DUSKY SHINER

REDEYE CHUB

HIGHFIN SHINER

FLAGFIN SHINER

SAILFIN SHINER

BROADSTRIPE SHINER

♀

BLUEHEAD SHINER

♂

BLUENOSE SHINER

♂

TAILLIGHT SHINER

MIRROR SHINER

SAWFIN SHINER

OZARK SHINER

PLATE 21

SUCKERS (1)

All suckers have one dorsal fin, more than 10 rays; large thick lips. First 6 species have long falcate dorsal fin.

*First 3 species (*Ictiobus*) have dark body, semicircular subopercle (Fig. 38).*

BIGMOUTH BUFFALO *Ictiobus cyprinellus*   **M177, p. 164**
Terminal, sharply oblique mouth. Large ovoid head. To 40 in. (100 cm).

SMALLMOUTH BUFFALO *Ictiobus bubalus*   **M178, p. 165**
Horizontal, subterminal mouth. Small conical head. Strongly keeled nape (on adult). To 31 in. (78 cm).

BLACK BUFFALO *Ictiobus niger*   **M179, p. 165**
Oblique, nearly terminal mouth. Large conical head. Rounded or weakly keeled nape (on adult). To 37 in. (93 cm).

*Next 3 species (*Carpiodes*) have silver body, subtriangular subopercle (Fig. 38).*

QUILLBACK *Carpiodes cyprinus*   **M180, p. 165**
Long 1st dorsal ray usually not reaching rear of dorsal fin base. No nipple on lower lip (Fig. 39). To 26 in. (66 cm).

RIVER CARPSUCKER *Carpiodes carpio*   **M181, p. 166**
Nipple at middle of lower lip (Fig. 39). To 25 in. (64 cm).

HIGHFIN CARPSUCKER *Carpiodes velifer*   **M182, p. 166**
Long 1st dorsal ray reaches to or beyond rear of dorsal fin base. Nipple at middle of lower lip (Fig. 39). To 19½ in. (50 cm).

*Next 3 species (*Chasmistes*) have thin (relative to other suckers), usually plicate lips (Fig. 40); branched gill rakers.*

JUNE SUCKER *Chasmistes liorus*   **M184, p. 167**
Large, terminal, oblique mouth. 19–20 scales around caudal peduncle. To 20 in. (52 cm). See also Snake River Sucker.

CUI-UI *Chasmistes cujus*   **M184, p. 168**
Similar to June Sucker but has larger, broader head; less oblique mouth. To 26½ in. (67 cm).

SHORTNOSE SUCKER *Chasmistes brevirostris*   **M184, p. 168**
Similar to June Sucker but has shorter head, smaller eye, 21–25 scales around caudal peduncle. To 25 in. (64 cm).

RAZORBACK SUCKER *Xyrauchen texanus*   **M192, p. 177**
Sharp keel on nape. To 36 in. (91 cm).

LOST RIVER SUCKER *Deltistes luxatus*   **M192, p. 178**
Distinct hump on snout. Thin, moderately papillose lips. To 34 in. (86 cm).

Catostomus *species (see also Pl. 22) have thick papillose lips (Fig. 41).*

LONGNOSE SUCKER *Catostomus catostomus*   **M188, p. 173**
Long snout. 95–120 lateral scales. See also Fig. 41. To 25 in. (64 cm). See also Salish Sucker.

WHITE SUCKER *Catostomus commersoni*   **M185, p. 169**
Lower lip about twice as thick as upper lip (Fig. 41). 53–74 lateral scales. To 25 in. (64 cm).

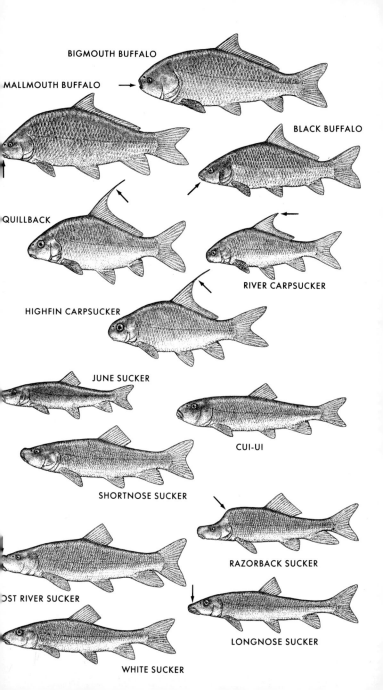

BIGMOUTH BUFFALO

SMALLMOUTH BUFFALO

BLACK BUFFALO

QUILLBACK

RIVER CARPSUCKER

HIGHFIN CARPSUCKER

JUNE SUCKER

CUI-UI

SHORTNOSE SUCKER

RAZORBACK SUCKER

LOST RIVER SUCKER

LONGNOSE SUCKER

WHITE SUCKER

PLATE 22

SUCKERS (2)

See also Fig. 41.

SONORA SUCKER *Catostomus insignis*   **M186, p. 169**
Dark spots on upper side form dashed lines. Sometimes sharply bicolored (as shown). To 31½ in. (80 cm). See also Yaqui Sucker.

UTAH SUCKER *Catostomus ardens*   **M187, p. 171**
Dorsal fin membranes densely speckled to edge. See also Fig. 41. To 25½ in. (65 cm).

LARGESCALE SUCKER *Catostomus macrocheilus*   **M187, p. 171**
Similar to Utah Sucker but has lightly speckled dorsal fin, membrane connecting pelvic fin to body. To 24 in. (61 cm).

FLANNELMOUTH SUCKER *Catostomus latipinnis*   **M187, p. 172**
Narrow caudal peduncle. Large fleshy lobes on lower lip (Fig. 41). To 22 in. (56 cm). See also Little Colorado River Sucker.

SACRAMENTO SUCKER *Catostomus occidentalis*   **M186, p. 172**
Yellow-gold below. 12–15 dorsal rays. See also Fig. 41. To 23½ in. (60 cm).

KLAMATH LARGESCALE SUCKER *Catostomus snyderi*   **M186, p. 172**
Similar to Sacramento Sucker but has usually 11 dorsal rays, distance from pelvic fin origin to caudal fin base equal to or greater than distance from eye to pelvic fin origin. To 21¾ in. (55 cm).

TAHOE SUCKER *Catostomus tahoensis*   **M189, p. 173**
Large head; long snout. Usually thick caudal peduncle. 12–15 scale rows below lateral line. See also Fig. 41. To 24 in. (61 cm). See also Owens and Warner Suckers.

KLAMATH SMALLSCALE SUCKER *Catostomus rimiculus*   **M189, p. 172**
Similar to Tahoe Sucker but has 2 or more rows of papillae at middle of lower lip, 5–6 rows of papillae on upper lip – see Fig. 41. To 19¾ in.

MODOC SUCKER *Catostomus microps*   **M189, p. 175**
Similar to Tahoe Sucker but has shorter head, smaller eye, 9–13 scale rows below lateral line. To 13¼ in. (34 cm).

BRIDGELIP SUCKER *Catostomus columbianus*   **M190, p. 175**
Green to blue-black above, white to yellow below. Weak or no indentations separate upper and lower lips (Fig. 41). To 12 in. (30 cm).

RIO GRANDE SUCKER *Catostomus plebeius*   **M191, p. 176**
Often sharply bicolored. Breeding male (shown) has red stripe along side. Small papillose lips (Fig. 41). To 7¾ in. (20 cm).

SANTA ANA SUCKER *Catostomus santaanae*   **M190, p. 176**
Dark blotches or stripes on side. Deep indentations separate upper and lower lips (Fig. 41). To 9¾ in. (25 cm).

MOUNTAIN SUCKER *Catostomus platyrhynchus*   **M191, p. 176**
Gray above, often with dark stripe (bright red on breeding male – shown) along side. Papillae on lower lip in half-rosette pattern with blank areas on either side (Fig. 41). To 9¾ in. (25 cm).

DESERT SUCKER *Catostomus clarki*   **M190, p. 177**
Similar to Santa Ana Sucker but lacks papillae on front of upper lip; has 4–7 rows of papillae at middle of lower lip; see Fig. 41. To 13 in. (33 cm).

BLUEHEAD SUCKER *Catostomus discobolus*   **M190, p. 177**
Blue head (darkest on adult). 50 or more predorsal scales. To 16 in. (41 cm).

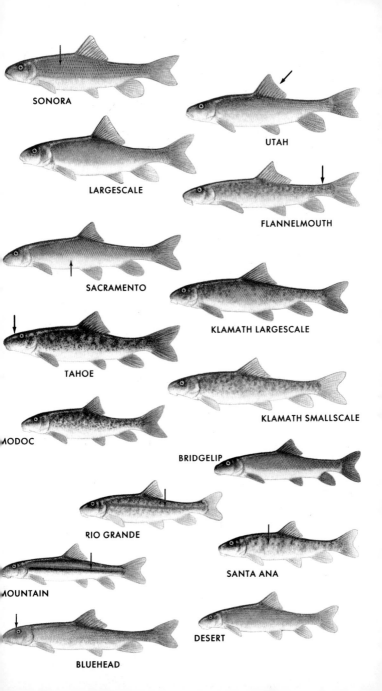

SONORA

UTAH

LARGESCALE

FLANNELMOUTH

SACRAMENTO

KLAMATH LARGESCALE

TAHOE

KLAMATH SMALLSCALE

MODOC

BRIDGELIP

RIO GRANDE

SANTA ANA

MOUNTAIN

DESERT

BLUEHEAD

PLATE 23
SUCKERS (3)

BLUE SUCKER *Cycleptus elongatus* **M183, p. 167**
Blue (brightest on large individual). Small head. Long falcate dorsal fin. To 36 in. (93 cm).

SPOTTED SUCKER *Minytrema melanops* **M193, p. 178**
Parallel rows of dark spots on back and side. Black edge on dorsal fin, lower lobe of caudal fin. To 19½ in. (50 cm).

*Next 3 species (*Erimyzon*) have small, oblique, nearly terminal mouth; no lateral line. Young has black stripe along side.*

CREEK CHUBSUCKER *Erimyzon oblongus* **M194, p. 179**
5–8 dark blotches along side; 40–45 lateral scales. Rounded dorsal fin. To 14 in. (36 cm).

LAKE CHUBSUCKER *Erimyzon sucetta* **M195, p. 179**
No dark blotches along side; 34–39 lateral scales. Rounded dorsal fin. To 16 in. (41 cm).

SHARPFIN CHUBSUCKER *Erimyzon tenuis* **M196, p. 179**
Sharply pointed dorsal fin. To 13 in. (33 cm).

NORTHERN HOG SUCKER *Hypentelium nigricans* **M197, p. 180**
Large rectangular head, broadly concave between eyes. 3–6 dark saddles (1 on nape). Papillose lips − see Fig. 42. To 24 in. (61 cm). See also Alabama Hog Sucker.

ROANOKE HOG SUCKER *Hypentelium roanokense* **M198, p. 181**
Similar to Northern Hog Sucker but has no or vague saddle on nape, plicate lips (Fig. 42), 39–44 lateral scales. To 6½ in. (16 cm).

Next 5 species have red caudal fin; large, thick lips.

GREATER REDHORSE *Moxostoma valenciennesi* **M200, p. 181**
Large head. Thick plicate lips; V-shaped lower edge on lower lip (Fig. 44). Usually 16 scales around caudal peduncle. To 31½ in. (80 cm).

COPPER REDHORSE *Moxostoma hubbsi* **M201, p. 183**
Deep body. Highly arched back. Short head. To 28 in. (72 cm).

SHORTHEAD REDHORSE *Moxostoma macrolepidotum* **M203, p. 184**
Short head. Straight rear edge on lower lip (Fig. 44). To 29½ in. (75 cm).

RIVER REDHORSE *Moxostoma carinatum* **M202, p. 183**
Large head. Thick plicate lips. Usually 12–13 scales around caudal peduncle. To 30 in. (77 cm).

BLACKTAIL REDHORSE *Moxostoma poecilurum* **M204, p. 184**
Black stripe on lower caudal fin lobe. Cylindrical body. To 20 in. (51 cm). See also Grayfin Redhorse.

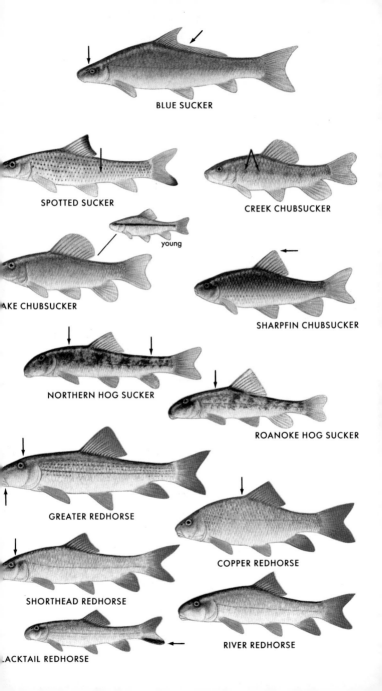

BLUE SUCKER

SPOTTED SUCKER

CREEK CHUBSUCKER

young

AKE CHUBSUCKER

SHARPFIN CHUBSUCKER

NORTHERN HOG SUCKER

ROANOKE HOG SUCKER

GREATER REDHORSE

COPPER REDHORSE

SHORTHEAD REDHORSE

RIVER REDHORSE

LACKTAIL REDHORSE

PLATE 24

SUCKERS (4)

Gray to light orange (never bright red) fins.

BLACK REDHORSE *Moxostoma duquesnei*   **M201, p. 185**
Long, slender caudal peduncle. Plicate lips; broadly V-shaped rear edge on lower lip (Fig. 44). 44–47 lateral scales. To 20 in. (51 cm).

GOLDEN REDHORSE *Moxostoma erythrurum*   **M205, p. 185**
Stout caudal peduncle. V- or U-shaped rear edge on lower lip (Fig. 44). 40–42 lateral scales. To 30½ in. (78 cm).

SILVER REDHORSE *Moxostoma anisurum*   **M206, p. 186**
Straight or convex dorsal fin, 14–16 dorsal rays. V-shaped rear edge on deeply divided lower lip (Fig. 44). To 28 in. (71 cm).

SUCKERMOUTH REDHORSE *Moxostoma pappillosum*   **M207, p. 186**
Long slender body. Concave to falcate dorsal fin. V-shaped rear edge on deeply divided lower lip (Fig. 44). To 17¾ in. (45 cm).

GRAY REDHORSE *Moxostoma congestum*   **M208, p. 187**
Broad, U-shaped head (viewed from above). Yellow to light orange fins. To 25½ in. (65 cm). See also West Mexican Redhorse.

SMALLFIN REDHORSE *Moxostoma robustum*   **M202, p. 187**
Rounded snout (viewed from above), deep head, dark stripes on back and side narrower than pale interspaces. To 16½ in. (42 cm).

STRIPED JUMPROCK *Moxostoma rupiscartes*   **M209, p. 188**
Similar to Smallfin Redhorse but has head wider than deep, dark stripes on back and side wider than or equal to pale interspaces, dusky edge on dorsal and caudal fins (in some populations). To 11 in. (28 cm).

BLACK JUMPROCK *Moxostoma cervinum*   **M210, p. 188**
Black tips on dorsal and caudal fins. Stripes on back and upper side. Plicate lips; straight lower lip edge (Fig. 44). To 7½ in. (19 cm).

GREATER JUMPROCK *Moxostoma lachneri*   **M210, p. 189**
Long slender head and body; slender caudal peduncle. White lower ray on gray caudal fin. To 17½ in. (44 cm).

BIGEYE JUMPROCK *Moxostoma ariommum*   **M208, p. 189**
Large eye. Flat, flaring papillose lips (Fig. 44). To 8½ in. (22 cm).

TORRENT SUCKER *Thoburnia rhothoeca*   **M211, p. 189**
2 large pale (or dusky) areas on caudal fin base. Red stripe along side of breeding male (shown). Small mouth; each half of lower lip edge nearly triangular (Fig. 44). To 7¼ in. (18 cm). See also Rustyside Sucker.

BLACKFIN SUCKER *Thoburnia atripinnis*   **M211, p. 190**
Large, jet black blotch on tip of dorsal fin. Black stripes on back and upper side. To 6½ in. (17 cm).

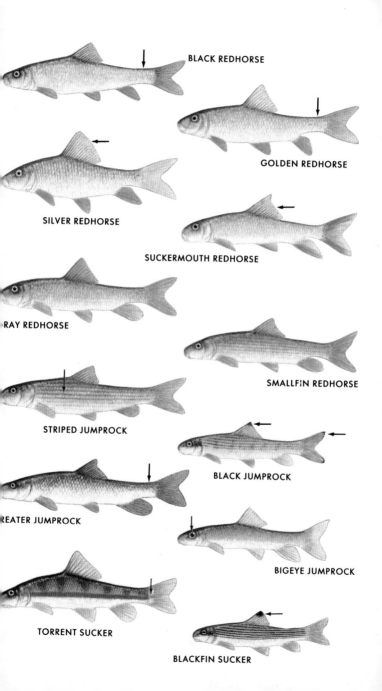

BLACK REDHORSE

GOLDEN REDHORSE

SILVER REDHORSE

SUCKERMOUTH REDHORSE

RAY REDHORSE

SMALLFIN REDHORSE

STRIPED JUMPROCK

BLACK JUMPROCK

REATER JUMPROCK

BIGEYE JUMPROCK

TORRENT SUCKER

BLACKFIN SUCKER

PLATE 25

BULLHEAD CATFISHES

Four pairs of barbels; no scales; short base on small adipose fin, its rear edge free from body (except for blindcats); stout spines on dorsal and pectoral fins.

First 3 species have forked caudal fin.

CHANNEL CATFISH *Ictalurus punctatus* **M212, p. 191**
Scattered dark spots on light back and side (except in small young and large adult); rounded anal fin, 24–29 rays. To 50 in. (127 cm). See also Headwater and Yaqui Catfishes.

BLUE CATFISH *Ictalurus furcatus* **M214, p. 192**
Long, straight-edged anal fin, tapered like a barber's comb, 30–35 rays. No dark spots on body. To 65 in. (165 cm).

WHITE CATFISH *Ameiurus catus* **M213, p. 193**
Relatively short anal fin base, rounded in outline, 22–25 rays. Large, sawlike teeth on rear of pectoral spine. To 24¼ in. (62 cm).

Next 9 species have straight or slightly notched caudal fin.

YELLOW BULLHEAD *Ameiurus natalis* **M215, p. 193**
White or yellow chin barbels. Moderately long anal fin, 24–27 rays. Large sawlike teeth on rear of pectoral spine. To 18¼ in. (47 cm).

BLACK BULLHEAD *Ameiurus melas* **M216, p. 194**
Dusky or black chin barbels. Relatively short anal fin, rounded in outline, 19–23 rays. Usually no large sawlike teeth on rear of pectoral spine (Fig. 45). To 24¼ in. (62 cm).

BROWN BULLHEAD *Ameiurus nebulosus* **M217, p. 195**
Similar to Black Bullhead but has brown or black mottling or spots on body, large sawlike teeth on rear of pectoral spine (Fig. 45). To 21 in. (50 cm).

Next 3 species have large dark blotch at dorsal fin base.

SPOTTED BULLHEAD *Ameiurus serracanthus* **M218, p. 195**
Many small round gray-white spots on dark body. Narrow black edge on fins. To 10¾ in. (28 cm).

SNAIL BULLHEAD *Ameiurus brunneus* **M219, p. 195**
Flat head, decurved snout profile. Black edge on fins. To 11½ in. (29 cm).

FLAT BULLHEAD *Ameiurus platycephalus* **M218, p. 196**
Dark mottling on side. Flat head; relatively straight snout profile. To 11¼ in. (29 cm).

FLATHEAD CATFISH *Pylodictis olivaris* **M220, p. 196**
White tip on upper lobe of caudal fin (except on large individual). Wide, flat head; projecting lower jaw. Black mottling on back and side. To 61 in. (155 cm).

WIDEMOUTH BLINDCAT *Satan eurystomus* **M221, p. 196**
No eyes. Jaw teeth well developed. Lower jaw normal in shape, slightly shorter than upper jaw. Separate gill membranes with strong fold between them. To 5¼ in. (13.7 cm).

TOOTHLESS BLINDCAT *Trogloglanis pattersoni* **M221, p. 197**
No jaw teeth. Short lower jaw curved upward and into mouth. Fused gill membranes. To 4 in. (10.4 cm).

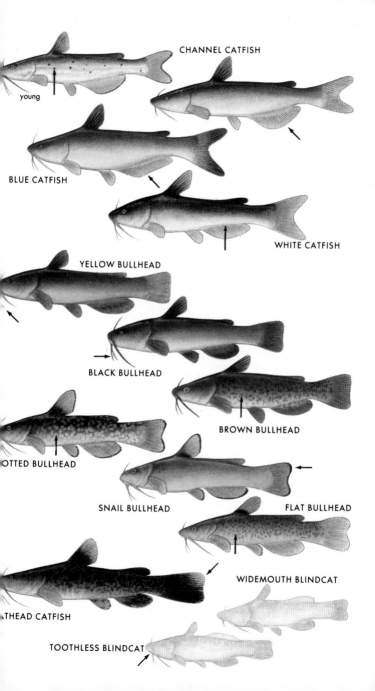

CHANNEL CATFISH

young

BLUE CATFISH

WHITE CATFISH

YELLOW BULLHEAD

BLACK BULLHEAD

BROWN BULLHEAD

OTTED BULLHEAD

SNAIL BULLHEAD

FLAT BULLHEAD

THEAD CATFISH

WIDEMOUTH BLINDCAT

TOOTHLESS BLINDCAT

PLATE 26

MADTOMS (1)

Madtoms have four pairs of barbels; no scales; long, low adipose fin joined to, or slightly separated from, caudal fin; stout spines on dorsal and pectoral fins.

STONECAT *Noturus flavus* **M222, p. 199**
Light blotch on nape. Cream-white spot at rear of dorsal fin base and on upper edge of gray caudal fin. Backward projections from premaxillary tooth patch (Fig. 46). To 12¼ in. (31 cm).

Species below have somber color; no dark blotches or saddles; no large teeth on front edge, usually straight teeth on rear edge, of pectoral spine (Fig. 47).

TADPOLE MADTOM *Noturus gyrinus* **M223, p. 200**
Chubby body. Terminal mouth with equal jaws. Dark veinlike line along side. To 5 in. (13 cm).

OUACHITA MADTOM *Noturus lachneri* **M224, p. 200**
Similar to Tadpole Madtom but has shorter, flatter head, more slender body. To 4 in. (10 cm).

SPECKLED MADTOM *Noturus leptacanthus* **M224, p. 200**
Black specks on body and fins. No sawlike teeth on rear edge of short pectoral spine (Fig. 47). To 3½ in. (9.4 cm).

BROADTAIL MADTOM *Noturus* species **M224, p. 201**
Chubby body. Dark blotch on caudal fin base. Rounded rear edge on caudal fin. To 2¼ in. (6 cm).

BROWN MADTOM *Noturus phaeus* **M225, p. 201**
Robust. Many brown specks on underside of head and belly. Long anal fin, 20–22 rays. About 6 sawlike teeth on rear of pectoral spine (Fig. 47). To 5¾ in. (15 cm).

BLACK MADTOM *Noturus funebris* **M225, p. 201**
Similar to Brown Madtom but has no or few weak sawlike teeth on rear of pectoral spine (Fig. 47), longer anal fin with 21–27 rays. To 5¾ in (15 cm).

FRECKLED MADTOM *Noturus nocturnus* **M226, p. 202**
No dark specks on mostly white belly. Dusky black edge on anal fin. Usually 16–18 anal rays. 2–3 weak sawlike teeth on rear of pectoral spine. To 5¾ in. (15 cm).

SLENDER MADTOM *Noturus exilis* **M227, p. 202**
Black border on median fins. Terminal mouth with equal jaws. To 5¾ in. (15 cm).

MARGINED MADTOM *Noturus insignis* **M227, p. 202**
Similar to Slender Madtom, but upper jaw projects beyond lower jaw. To 6 in. (15 cm).

ORANGEFIN MADTOM *Noturus gilberti* **M222, p. 203**
White to orange triangle on upper edge of caudal fin. Short anal fin; 14–16 rays. To 3¾ in. (10 cm).

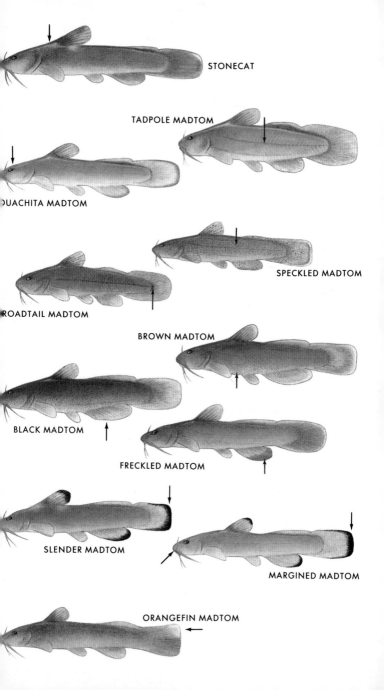

STONECAT

TADPOLE MADTOM

OUACHITA MADTOM

SPECKLED MADTOM

BROADTAIL MADTOM

BROWN MADTOM

BLACK MADTOM

FRECKLED MADTOM

SLENDER MADTOM

MARGINED MADTOM

ORANGEFIN MADTOM

PLATE 27

MADTOMS (2)

Sawlike teeth on front and rear edges of curved pectoral spine (Fig. 47); dark blotches or saddles.

LEAST MADTOM *Noturus hildebrandi*   **M228, p. 203**
White or clear adipose fin (except dark blotch extends onto fin on individuals from s. MS). Small teeth on front edge of short pectoral spine. *N. h. lautus* is strongly bicolored; has shorter head. *N. h. hildebrandi* is blotched on lower side; has longer head. To 2½ in. (6.9 cm). See also Pygmy Madtom.

SMOKY MADTOM *Noturus baileyi*   **M228, p. 204**
Four pale yellow saddles. Dusky band on adipose fin extends nearly to fin edge. To 2¾ in. (7.3 cm).

OZARK MADTOM *Noturus albater*   **M229, p. 204**
White upper edge on caudal fin. To 4¾ in. (12 cm).

ELEGANT MADTOM *Noturus elegans* (2 forms)   **M229, p. 204**
Brown blotch extends up front of dorsal fin. Green R. form has no or diffuse black bands on dorsal, adipose, and anal fins; has subdued color. Duck R. form has bold pattern, black band on adipose fin. To 3½ in. (8.9 cm). See also Scioto Madtom.

CADDO MADTOM *Noturus taylori*   **M229, p. 205**
Black tip on dorsal fin. Many small teeth on front edge of short pectoral spine — see Fig. 47. To 3 in. (7.7 cm).

NEOSHO MADTOM *Noturus placidus*   **M230, p. 206**
White lower caudal rays. Deep caudal peduncle. To 3¼ in. (8.7 cm).

FRECKLEBELLY MADTOM *Noturus munitus*   **M230, p. 207**
Dark brown or black band to adipose fin edge. Usually dark specks on belly. To 3¾ in. (9.5 cm).

NORTHERN MADTOM *Noturus stigmosus*   **M230, p. 206**
Front edge of 1st saddle irregular, usually enclosing 2 large light spots in front of dorsal fin. Dark band extends into upper half of adipose fin. Dark crescentic band in middle of caudal fin usually extends forward across upper and lower caudal rays to caudal peduncle. To 5 in. (13 cm).

CAROLINA MADTOM *Noturus furiosus*   **M230, p. 207**
No dark specks on belly. Brown or black band extends nearly to adipose fin edge. To 4¾ in. (12 cm).

MOUNTAIN MADTOM *Noturus eleutherus*   **M231, p. 208**
Dark brown bar on caudal fin base. Dark band on adipose fin usually confined to lower half of fin. To 5 in. (13 cm).

CHECKERED MADTOM *Noturus flavater*   **M232, p. 208**
Broad black bar on caudal fin base; black border on caudal fin; black blotch on dorsal fin. To 7 in. (18 cm).

BRINDLED MADTOM *Noturus miurus*   **M232, p. 209**
Black blotch on outer ⅓ of dorsal fin extends across first 3–5 rays. Dark band to edge of adipose fin. Rounded rear edge on caudal fin. To 5 in. (13 cm).

YELLOWFIN MADTOM *Noturus flavipinnis*   **M232, p. 209**
Pale edge on caudal fin; 2 light spots in front of dorsal fin. To 6 in. (15 cm).

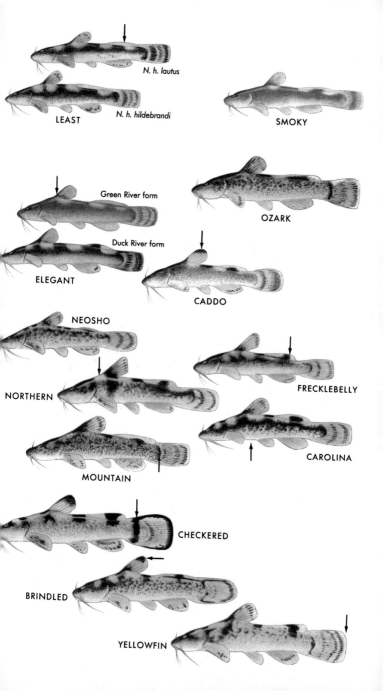

N. h. lautus

N. h. hildebrandi

LEAST

SMOKY

Green River form

Duck River form

ELEGANT

OZARK

CADDO

NEOSHO

NORTHERN

FRECKLEBELLY

MOUNTAIN

CAROLINA

CHECKERED

BRINDLED

YELLOWFIN

PLATE 28

TOPMINNOWS AND KILLIFISHES (1)

One dorsal fin far back on body; flattened head and back; upturned mouth; no lateral line.

SEMINOLE KILLIFISH *Fundulus seminolis* **M239, p. 216**
Metallic green side; interrupted rows of many small black spots; 15–20 dark green bars (often faint) on female. To 6½ in. (16 cm).

BANDED KILLIFISH *Fundulus diaphanus* **M240, p. 216**
10–20 green-brown bars along siver side. Long, slender body. To 5 in. (13 cm). See also Waccamaw Killifish.

NORTHERN STUDFISH *Fundulus catenatus* **M241, p. 217**
Rows of small brown (female and young) or red-brown spots (male) on side. Large male has bright blue side. To 7 in. (18 cm).

STIPPLED STUDFISH *Fundulus bifax* **M241, p. 217**
Similar to Northern Studfish but has short interrupted rows of red or brown spots on side. To 4¾ in. (12 cm).

SOUTHERN STUDFISH *Fundulus stellifer* **M241, p. 217**
Many brown or red spots scattered over side (rarely in irregular rows on upper side). Black edge on dorsal and caudal fins of some large males. To 4¾ in. (12 cm).

BARRENS TOPMINNOW *Fundulus julisia* **M239, p. 218**
Many scattered brown (female and young) or red-orange spots (male) on head and body. Yellow-orange fins. Iridescent white-gold stripe along back to dorsal fin. To 3¾ in. (9 cm). See also Whiteline Topminnow.

SPECKLED KILLIFISH *Fundulus rathbuni* **M241, p. 218**
Black line (absent on juvenile) from mouth to eye. Many dark brown spots on back and side of juvenile and female. To 3¾ in. (9.6 cm).

PLAINS TOPMINNOW *Fundulus sciadicus* **M242, p. 219**
Bronze flecks and dark cross-hatching on blue-green back and side. Narrow gold stripe in front of dorsal fin. To 2¾ in. (7 cm).

GOLDEN TOPMINNOW *Fundulus chrysotus* **M242, p. 219**
Gold flecks on side; usually 8–11 green bars (often faint) on side of large male. Breeding male has bright red to red-brown spots on rear half of body. To 3 in. (7.5 cm).

BANDED TOPMINNOW *Fundulus cingulatus* **M243, p. 219**
Rows of small brown to red spots on side. 12–15 green bars along side. Clear to light red fins. To 3 in. (7.8 cm).

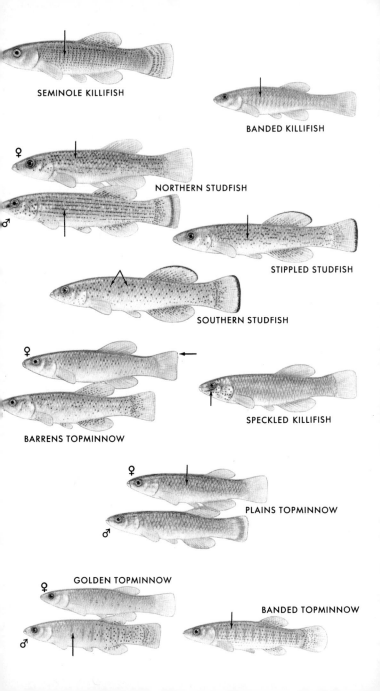

SEMINOLE KILLIFISH

BANDED KILLIFISH

♀ **NORTHERN STUDFISH**

♂

STIPPLED STUDFISH

SOUTHERN STUDFISH

♀ **BARRENS TOPMINNOW**

SPECKLED KILLIFISH

♀ **PLAINS TOPMINNOW**

♂

GOLDEN TOPMINNOW

♀ **BANDED TOPMINNOW**

♂

PLATE 29
TOPMINNOWS AND KILLIFISHES (2)

PLAINS KILLIFISH *Fundulus zebrinus*   **M244, p. 220**
12–26 gray-green bars (fewer, wider bars on male) on silver-white side. Breeding male (shown) has bright orange to red dorsal, anal and paired fins. To 4 in. (10 cm)

Next 5 species (starhead topminnows) have large, blue-black bar under eye, 6–8 brown to red-brown stripes (young and female) or rows of dots (male) along side, a large gold spot on top of head, small gold spot at dorsal fin origin. Male has dark green bars along side (except Western Starhead Topminnow). See also Fig. 49.

LINED TOPMINNOW *Fundulus lineolatus*   **M245, p. 222**
11–15 dark green bars along side of male thickest at middle. 6–8 black stripes on side of female. To 3¼ in. (8.4 cm).

SOUTHERN STARHEAD TOPMINNOW *Fundulus notti*   **M246, p. 222**
9–15 dark bars on side of male extend forward to pectoral fin base. Dark specks between stripes on female. To 3 in. (7.8 cm).

EASTERN STARHEAD TOPMINNOW *Fundulus escambiae*   **M246, p. 222**
Nearly identical to Southern Starhead Topminnow but lacks dark specks between stripes on female; has 0–14 dark bars on side of male extending forward only to between paired fins. To 3 in. (7.8 cm).

WESTERN STARHEAD TOPMINNOW *Fundulus blairae*   **M247, p. 223**
No dark bars on side of body. Many dark specks between 7–9 dark stripes on side of female. To 3 in. (7.8 cm).

NORTHERN STARHEAD TOPMINNOW *Fundulus dispar*   **M247, p. 222**
No or few dark specks between 6–8 thin dark stripes on side of female. 3–13 dark bars on side of male. To 3 in. (7.8 cm).

BLACKSTRIPE TOPMINNOW *Fundulus notatus*   **M248, p. 223**
Wide blue-black stripe along side, around snout, and onto caudal fin. Silver-white spot on top of head. To 3 in. (7.4 cm).

BLACKSPOTTED TOPMINNOW *Fundulus olivaceus*   **M245, p. 223**
Similar to Blackstripe Topminnow but has few to many (male has more) discrete black spots on light tan upper side. To 3¾ in. (9.7 cm).

BROADSTRIPE TOPMINNOW *Fundulus euryzonus*   **M239, p. 224**
Similar to Blackstripe and Blackspotted Topminnows but has extremely wide purple-brown stripe along side. No crossbars on stripe along side of male. To 3¼ in (8.3 cm).

RAINWATER KILLIFISH *Lucania parva*   **M249, p. 224**
Large, dark-edged scales on back and side. Large male has black spot at front of dusky orange dorsal fin. To 2¾ in. (7 cm).

BLUEFIN KILLIFISH *Lucania goodei*   **M250, p. 224**
Wide, zigzag, black stripe from tip of snout to black spot on caudal fin base. Bright iridescent blue dorsal and anal fins on large male. To 2 in. (5 cm).

PYGMY KILLIFISH *Leptolucania ommata*   **M251, p. 225**
Cream-yellow halo around large black spot on caudal peduncle. Male has 5–7 faint bars on rear half of side. Female has dusky stripe along side, black spot on midside. To 1¼ in. (2.9 cm).

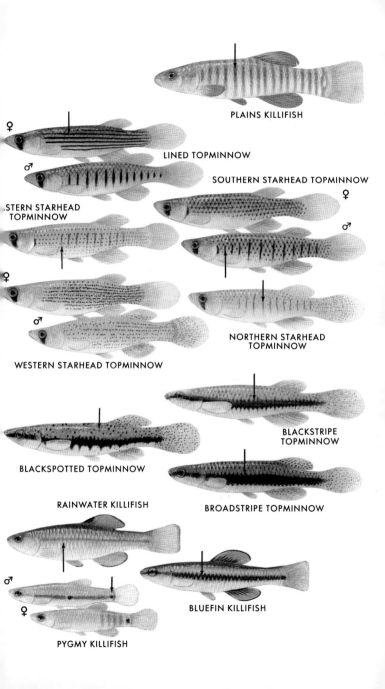

PLAINS KILLIFISH

♀ **LINED TOPMINNOW**
♂

SOUTHERN STARHEAD TOPMINNOW

_STERN STARHEAD TOPMINNOW

♀

♂

NORTHERN STARHEAD TOPMINNOW

♀

♂

WESTERN STARHEAD TOPMINNOW

BLACKSTRIPE TOPMINNOW

BLACKSPOTTED TOPMINNOW

RAINWATER KILLIFISH

BROADSTRIPE TOPMINNOW

♂

♀

BLUEFIN KILLIFISH

PYGMY KILLIFISH

PLATE 30

PUPFISHES AND SPRINGFISHES

Upturned mouth; deep body; no lateral line.

SHEEPSHEAD MINNOW *Cyprinodon variegatus* **p. 226**
5–8 triangular-shaped dark gray-brown bars (wide at top) along silver-olive side. To 3 in. (7.5 cm).

RED RIVER PUPFISH *Cyprinodon rubrofluviatilis* **M252, p. 226**
Unscaled belly. 5–8 large triangular brown blotches along silver side. No dark blotches on lower side. To 2¼ in. (5.8 cm).

PECOS PUPFISH *Cyprinodon pecosensis* **M252, p. 227**
Similar to Red River Pupfish but has partly scaled belly; lacks blue nape. To 2¼ in. (6 cm).

LEON SPRINGS PUPFISH *Cyprinodon bovinus* **M252, p. 227**
Dark brown blotches along silver side; many small brown blotches on lower side of female (rarely on male). To 2¼ in. (5.6 cm).

WHITE SANDS PUPFISH *Cyprinodon tularosa* **M253, p. 227**
Similar to Leon Springs Pupfish but has dark bars on females connected at bottom, orange dorsal fin on large male. To 2 in. (5 cm).

COMANCHE SPRINGS PUPFISH *Cyprinodon elegans* **M253, p. 227**
Slender caudal pecuncle. Black specks on silver side. Blue-black blotches form "stripe" (often faint on male) along silver side. To 2½ in. (6.2 cm).

DESERT PUPFISH *Cyprinodon macularius* **M254, p. 228**
Breeding male (shown) has blue body, lemon yellow to orange caudal peduncle and fin. To 2¾ in. (7.2 cm).

OWENS PUPFISH *Cyprinodon radiosus* **M254, p. 228**
Breeding male (shown) has deep blue body, orange edge on blue dorsal and anal fins. To 2¾ in. (7.2 cm).

AMARGOSA PUPFISH *Cyprinodon nevadensis* **M254, p. 228**
Dorsal fin origin nearer to caudal fin base than to tip of snout. To 3 in. (7.8 cm).

SALT CREEK PUPFISH *Cyprinodon salinus* **M254, p. 229**
Slender body. Dorsal fin far back on body. Scales on nape small and crowded. To 3 in. (7.8 cm).

DEVILS HOLE PUPFISH *Cyprinodon diabolis* **M255, p. 230**
No pelvic fins. To 1¼ in. (3.4 cm).

CONCHOS PUPFISH *Cyprinodon eximius* **M253, p. 230**
Faint brown blotches on silver side; rows of small brown spots on upper side. Breeding male (shown) has orange dorsal fin. To 2 in. (5 cm).

FLAGFISH *Jordanella floridae* **M256, p. 230**
Large black spot on midside. Alternating thin black and red-orange lines, gold flecks, on side. To 2½ in. (6.5 cm).

Next 3 species lack pelvic fins; have dorsal and anal fins far back on body.

WHITE RIVER SPRINGFISH *Crenichthys baileyi* **M255, p. 231**
Row of black spots (or black stripe) along side; 2d row of black spots along lower side from midbody to caudal fin. To 3½ in. (9 cm).

RAILROAD VALLEY SPRINGFISH *Crenichthys nevadae* **M255, p. 231**
Similar to White River Springfish but has 1 row of dark spots along side. To 2¼ in. (6 cm).

PAHRUMP KILLIFISH *Empetrichthys latos* **M255, p. 231**
Black mottling on silver side. Wide mouth. To 2¼ in. (6 cm). See also Ash Meadows Killifish.

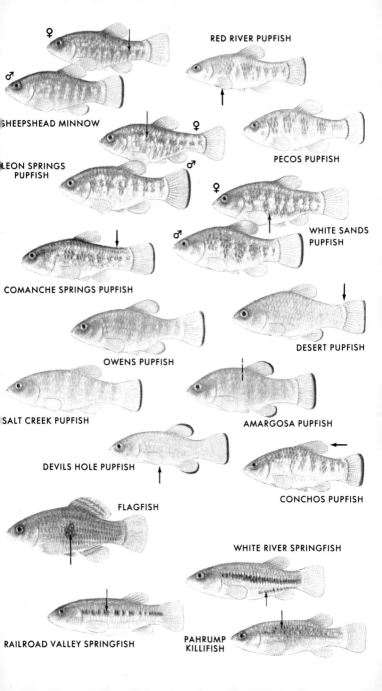

RED RIVER PUPFISH

♀
♂
SHEEPSHEAD MINNOW

PECOS PUPFISH

LEON SPRINGS
PUPFISH

♀
♂

WHITE SANDS
PUPFISH

♀
♂

COMANCHE SPRINGS PUPFISH

DESERT PUPFISH

OWENS PUPFISH

SALT CREEK PUPFISH

AMARGOSA PUPFISH

DEVILS HOLE PUPFISH

CONCHOS PUPFISH

FLAGFISH

WHITE RIVER SPRINGFISH

RAILROAD VALLEY SPRINGFISH

PAHRUMP
KILLIFISH

PLATE 31
LIVEBEARERS

Front rays of anal fin of male elongated and modified into a gonopodium to accomplish internal fertilization (Fig. 50). Flattened head; upturned mouth; no lateral line. See pp. 233–240 for introduced livebearers.

AMAZON MOLLY *Poecilia formosa* **M257, p. 233**
All-female species. Similar to Sailfin Molly (female) but lacks rows of brown spots on side. 10–12 dorsal rays. To 3¾ in. (9.6 cm).

SAILFIN MOLLY *Peocilia latipinna* **M257, p. 232**
Large male has huge, sail-like dorsal fin. About 5 rows of dark brown spots, iridescent yellow flecks on olive side. 13–16 dorsal rays. To 6 in. (15 cm). See also Shortfin Molly.

MOSQUITOFISH *Gambusia affinis* **M258, p. 235**
1–3 rows of black spots on dorsal and caudal fins. Large dusky to black teardrop. To 2½ in. (6.5 cm).

PECOS GAMBUSIA *Gambusia nobilis* **M259, p. 237**
Dusky edges on dorsal and caudal fins, anal fin of female. Darkly outlined scales on back and upper ⅔ of side. To 2 in. (4.8 cm).

BLOTCHED GAMBUSIA *Gambusia senilis* **M260, p. 237**
Dusky stripe (about 1 scale deep) along side. Black spots (often poorly developed on male) on lower side. To 2¼ in. (5.5 cm).

BIG BEND GAMBUSIA *Gambusia gaigei* **M260, p. 238**
Prominent black spots, crescents on upper side (absent on belly). Dark stripe along side. To 2¼ in. (5.4 cm).

AMISTAD GAMBUSIA *Gambusia amistadensis* **M260, p. 238**
Extinct. Similar to Big Bend Gambusia but was more slender; had more terminal mouth. To 2¼ in. (5.8 cm).

LARGESPRING GAMBUSIA *Gambusia geiseri* **M260, p. 238**
Distinct row of black spots on middle of dorsal and caudal fins (indistinct on juvenile). Scattered black spots on side. To 1¾ in. (4.4 cm).

CLEAR CREEK GAMBUSIA *Gambusia heterochir* **M260, p. 238**
Distinct notch at top of pectoral fin of male. No dark stripe along back. To 2¼ in. (5.4 cm).

SAN MARCOS GAMBUSIA *Gambusia georgei* **M260, p. 235**
Presumed extinct. Lemon yellow median fins. Dark edges (best developed on large individual) on dorsal and caudal fins. To 2 in. (4.8 cm).

LEAST KILLIFISH *Heterandria formosa* **M261, p. 239**
Red around black spot on front of dorsal fin. Series of black bars along side; black spot on caudal fin base. To 1½ in. (3.6 cm).

GILA TOPMINNOW *Peociliopsis occidentalis* **M259, p. 239**
Dark to dusky stripe along side. Large male is black. Extremely long gonopodium, more than ⅓ body length. To 2¼ in. (6 cm). See also Porthole Livebearer.

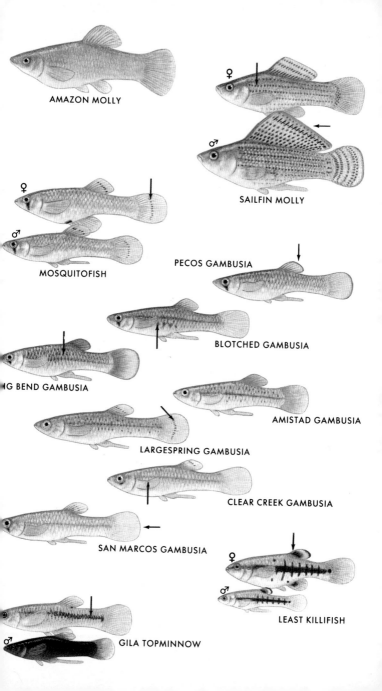

AMAZON MOLLY

♀

♂

SAILFIN MOLLY

♀

♂

MOSQUITOFISH

PECOS GAMBUSIA

BLOTCHED GAMBUSIA

G BEND GAMBUSIA

AMISTAD GAMBUSIA

LARGESPRING GAMBUSIA

CLEAR CREEK GAMBUSIA

SAN MARCOS GAMBUSIA

♀

♂

LEAST KILLIFISH

♂

GILA TOPMINNOW

PLATE 32

TETRA, CAVEFISHES, BURBOT, SILVERSIDES, STICKLEBACKS, DRUM

MEXICAN TETRA *Astyanax mexicanus* **M70, p. 62**
Adipose fin. Jaw teeth. Black stripe on caudal peduncle and fin. Large individual (shown) has yellow fins, red on caudal and anal fins. To 4¾ in. (12 cm).

Next 5 species (cavefishes) have no pelvic fins (Northern Cavefish has very small pelvic fins), small or rudimentary eyes.

SWAMPFISH *Chologaster cornuta* **M235, p. 213**
Strongly bicolored. Stripe on lower side wide at front, narrow at rear. To 2¾ in. (6.8 cm).

SPRING CAVEFISH *Forbesichthys agassizi* **M235, p. 213**
Long, slender salamanderlike body. 3 axial stripes along side. To 3¼ in. (8.4 cm).

SOUTHERN CAVEFISH *Typhlichthys subterraneus* **M236, p. 213**
Pink-white. No eyes. To 3½ in. (8.6 cm).

NORTHERN CAVEFISH *Amblyopsis spelaea* **M237, p. 213**
Pink-white. No eyes. Very small pelvic fins. To 4¼ in. (11 cm). See also Ozark Cavefish.

ALABAMA CAVEFISH *Speoplatyrhinus poulsoni* **M237, p. 214**
Pink-white. No eyes. Long flat head constricted behind snout. To 2¾ in. (7.2 cm).

BURBOT *Lota lota* **M238, p. 214**
Long slender body. Long barbel at tip of chin. 2 dorsal fins; 1st short, 2d very long. To 33 in. (84 cm).

BROOK SILVERSIDE *Labidesthes sicculus* **M262, p. 240**
Long beaklike snout. 2 widely separated dorsal fins; origin of 1st above anal fin origin. To 5 in. (13 cm).

INLAND SILVERSIDE *Menidia beryllina* **M263, p. 241**
2 widely separated dorsal fins; origin of 1st in front of anal fin origin. To 6 in. (15 cm). See also Waccamaw Silverside.

THREESPINE STICKLEBACK *Gasterosteus aculeatus* **M267, p. 243**
3 dorsal spines, last very short. Keel on caudal peduncle. To 4 in. (10 cm). See also Fourspine Stickleback.

BROOK STICKLEBACK *Culaea inconstans* **M265, p. 242**
4–6 short dorsal spines. No keel on short peduncle. To 3½ in. (8.7 cm).

NINESPINE STICKLEBACK *Pungitius pungitius* **M264, p. 242**
7–12, usually 9, short dorsal spines. Usually a keel on caudal peduncle. To 3½ in. (9 cm).

FRESHWATER DRUM *Aplodinotus grunniens* **M375, p. 326**
Strongly arched, silver body. Short 1st dorsal fin; long 2d dorsal fin. Long pelvic fin ray. Lateral line to end of caudal fin. To 35 in. (89 cm). See also Bairdiella and Orangemouth Corvina.

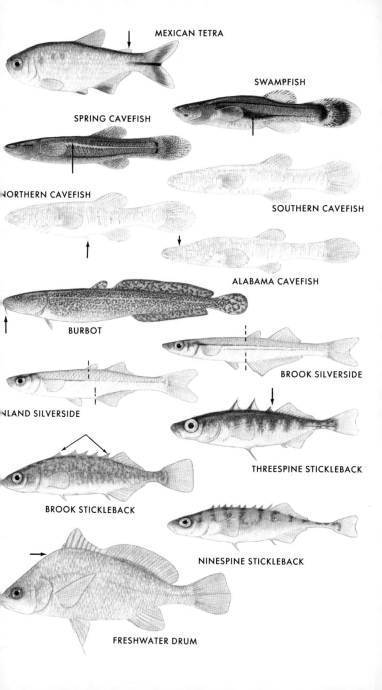

MEXICAN TETRA

SWAMPFISH

SPRING CAVEFISH

NORTHERN CAVEFISH

SOUTHERN CAVEFISH

ALABAMA CAVEFISH

BURBOT

BROOK SILVERSIDE

INLAND SILVERSIDE

THREESPINE STICKLEBACK

BROOK STICKLEBACK

NINESPINE STICKLEBACK

FRESHWATER DRUM

PLATE 33

SCULPINS (1)

Sculpins have large, fanlike pectoral fins; large mouth; no scales.

DEEPWATER SCULPIN *Myoxocephalus thompsoni* **M268, p. 244**
Large gap between dorsal fins. Extremely wide, flat head. To 9 in. (23 cm).
See also Fourhorn Sculpin.

SPOONHEAD SCULPIN *Cottus ricei* **M269, p. 245**
Wide, flat head. Extremely slender caudal peduncle. Prickles on most of
body. To 5 in. (13 cm).

TORRENT SCULPIN *Cottus rhotheus* **M269, p. 245**
"Pinched" caudal peduncle. 2 broad dark bars under 2d dorsal fin. To 6 in.
(15.5 cm).

BANDED SCULPIN *Cottus carolinae* **M270, p. 246**
4–5 brown-black saddles, last 3 extend down side as dark bars. Usually
complete lateral line. To 7¼ in. (18 cm).

POTOMAC SCULPIN *Cottus girardi* **M270, p. 246**
Similar to Banded Sculpin but has incomplete lateral line, less regularly
bordered bars on side. To 5¼ in. (14 cm).

COASTRANGE SCULPIN *Cottus aleuticus* **M271, p. 247**
Long pelvic fin reaches to anus. Long, tubular posterior nostril. To 6½ in.
(17 cm).

PRICKLY SCULPIN *Cottus asper* **M272, p. 247**
Long anal (usually 16–19 rays) and dorsal fins (19–23 rays). Large dark
brown blotches on upper side. Usually many prickles. To 12 in. (30 cm).

KLAMATH LAKE SCULPIN *Cottus princeps* **M273, p. 248**
Broadly joined dorsal fins. Large pores on flat head. Long fins. Many prickles. To 2¾ in. (7 cm).

SHOSHONE SCULPIN *Cottus greenei* **M272, p. 248**
Deep body. Deep caudal peduncle. To 3½ in. (9 cm).

SLENDER SCULPIN *Cottus tenuis* **M271, p. 248**
Strongly bicolored; brown above, white to brassy below. 1 or more
branched pelvic rays. To 3½ in. (9 cm). See also Rough Sculpin.

UTAH LAKE SCULPIN *Cottus echinatus* **M274, p. 249**
Presumed extinct. Many prickles on long slender body. No bold saddles or
bars. To 4¼ in. (11 cm).

BEAR LAKE SCULPIN *Cottus extensus* **M274, p. 249**
Similar to Utah Lake Sculpin but lacks prickles on breast and belly, has
smaller head. To 5¼ in. (13 cm).

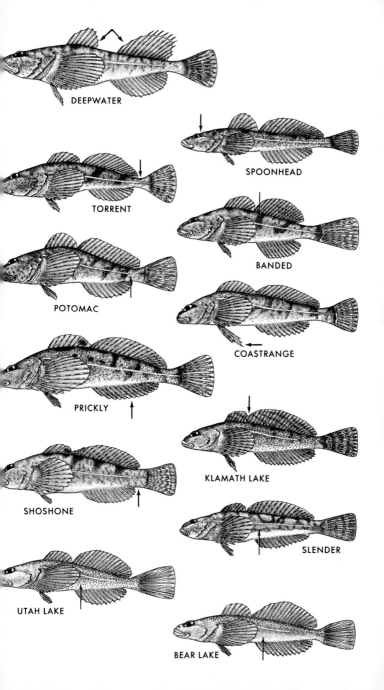

DEEPWATER

SPOONHEAD

TORRENT

BANDED

POTOMAC

COASTRANGE

PRICKLY

KLAMATH LAKE

SHOSHONE

SLENDER

UTAH LAKE

BEAR LAKE

PLATE 34

SCULPINS (2)

SLIMY SCULPIN *Cottus cognatus*   **M275, p. 249**
  3 pelvic rays. Long slender body. To 4½ in. (12 cm).

Next 4 species have 2 large black spots on 1st dorsal fin, incomplete lateral line.

MOTTLED SCULPIN *Cottus bairdi*   **M276, p. 250**
  Robust body. Dorsal fins joined at base. To 6 in. (15 cm).

SHORTHEAD SCULPIN *Cottus confusus*   **M274, p. 251**
  Slender body. Dorsal fins separate to base. Prickles on body behind pectoral fin. To 5¾ in. (15 cm).

OZARK SCULPIN *Cottus hypselurus*   **M277, p. 250**
  Wide, wavy black bands on dorsal and caudal fins. To 5½ in. (14 cm).

BLACK SCULPIN *Cottus baileyi*   **M277, p. 250**
  Nearly identical to Mottled Sculpin but smaller; usually lacks palatine teeth. To 3¼ in. (8.4 cm).

PYGMY SCULPIN *Cottus pygmaeus*   **M277, p. 252**
  Boldly patterned: black head, white nape, black saddles. To 1¾ in. (4.5 cm).

PAIUTE SCULPIN *Cottus beldingi*   **M278, p. 251**
  Dorsal fins separate to base. No prickles. 2 black spots on dorsal fin. To 5¼ in. (13 cm).

MARGINED SCULPIN *Cottus marginatus*   **M273, p. 252**
  Similar to Paiute Sculpin but has dorsal fins joined at base, usually 3 pelvic rays. To 5 in. (13 cm).

WOOD RIVER SCULPIN *Cottus leiopomus*   **M273, p. 252**
  Short head, about 3 times into slender body. Incomplete lateral line. To 4¼ in. (11 cm).

Next 3 species have large black spot at rear (only) of 1st dorsal fin.

RIFFLE SCULPIN *Cottus gulosus*   **M279, p. 252**
  Deep compressed caudal peduncle. To 4¼ in. (11 cm). See also Reticulate Sculpin.

PIT SCULPIN *Cottus pitensis*   **M274, p. 253**
  Dark vermiculations and small blotches on side. To 5 in. (13 cm).

MARBLED SCULPIN *Cottus klamathensis*   **M278, p. 253**
  Deep body. Marbled pattern on fins. To 3½ in. (9 cm).

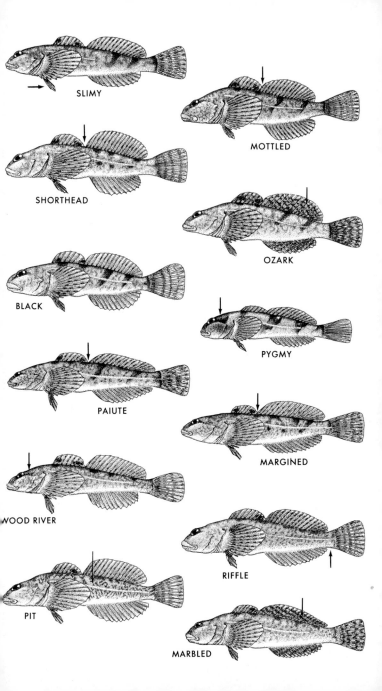

SLIMY

MOTTLED

SHORTHEAD

OZARK

BLACK

PYGMY

PAIUTE

MARGINED

WOOD RIVER

PIT

RIFFLE

MARBLED

PLATE 35

BASSES (1)

*First 4 species (*Morone*) have 2 dorsal fins, 1st tall and with usually 9 spines; spine on gill cover flap; small gill on underside of gill cover.*

WHITE PERCH *Morone americana*   **M281, p. 255**
No dark stripes along side (of adult). Body deepest under 1st dorsal fin. To 22¾ in. (58 cm).

WHITE BASS *Morone chrysops*   **M280, p. 255**
4–7 dark gray-brown stripes on silver-white side. Body deepest between dorsal fins. To 17¾ in. (45 cm).

YELLOW BASS *Morone mississippiensis*   **M281, p. 255**
5–7 black stripes on silver-yellow side broken and offset on lower side. To 18 in. (46 cm).

STRIPED BASS *Morone saxatilis*   **p. 254**
6–9 dark gray stripes (on adult) on silver-white side. To 79 in. (2 m).

*Next 7 species (*Micropterus*) have large mouth reaching to or beyond eye, elongate body, black spot at rear of gill cover, 3 anal spines.*

Next 6 species have confluent dorsal fins.

REDEYE BASS *Micropterus coosae*   **M296, p. 264**
White upper and lower outer edges on orange caudal fin. Rows of dark spots on lower side. 2d dorsal, caudal, and front of anal fin brick red on young. To 18½ in. (47 cm).

SPOTTED BASS *Micropterus punctulatus*   **M297, p. 264**
Rows of small black spots on lower side. Young has 3-colored (yellow, black, white edge) caudal fin. To 24 in. (61 cm).

GUADALUPE BASS *Micropterus treculi*   **M298, p. 264**
Similar to Spotted Bass but has 10–12 dark bars along side (darkest in young). To 15¾ in. (40 cm).

SHOAL BASS *Micropterus* species   **M296, p. 265**
Similar to Redeye Bass but lacks white outer edges on orange caudal fin, patch of teeth on tongue. To 15¼ in. (39 cm).

SUWANNEE BASS *Micropterus notius*   **M296, p. 263**
Color as in Largemouth Bass, except large male (shown) has bright turquoise cheek, breast, and belly. To 14¼ in. (36 cm).

SMALLMOUTH BASS *Micropterus dolomieu*   **M299, p. 265**
Dark brown; bronze specks, often coalesced into 8–16 bars, on yellow-green side. Young has 3-colored (yellow, black, white edge) caudal fin. To 27¼ in. (69 cm).

LARGEMOUTH BASS *Micropterus salmoides*   **M295, p. 263**
1st dorsal fin highest at middle, low at rear; 1st (spinous) and 2d (soft) dorsal fins nearly separate. Large mouth extends past eye. Broad black stripe (often broken into series of blotches) along side. To 38 in. (97 cm).

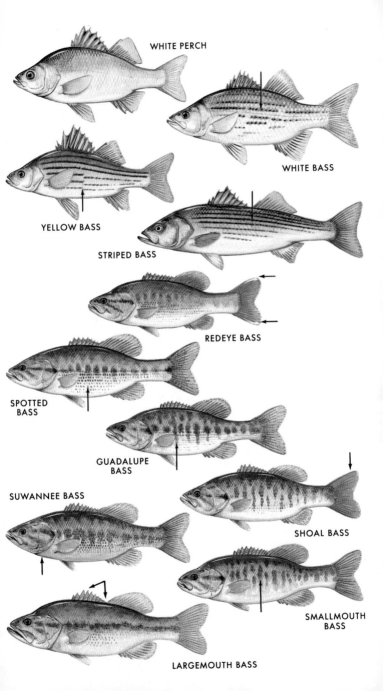

WHITE PERCH

WHITE BASS

YELLOW BASS

STRIPED BASS

REDEYE BASS

SPOTTED BASS

GUADALUPE BASS

SUWANNEE BASS

SHOAL BASS

LARGEMOUTH BASS

SMALLMOUTH BASS

PLATE 36
BASSES (2), CRAPPIES

SACRAMENTO PERCH *Archoplites interruptus*   **M285, p. 258**
6–7 anal spines, 12–13 dorsal spines. Dorsal fin base about twice anal fin base. To 28¾ in. (73 cm).

*Next 4 species (*Ambloplites*) have usually 6 anal spines, red eye.*

SHADOW BASS *Ambloplites ariommus*   **M289, p. 261**
Irregular marbling of brown or gray on light green or brown side. Large eye. To 8¾ in. (22 cm).

ROANOKE BASS *Ambloplites cavifrons*   **M289, p. 260**
Unscaled or partly scaled cheek. Many iridescent gold to white spots on upper side and head. To 14½ in. (36 cm).

OZARK BASS *Ambloplites constellatus*   **M290, p. 261**
Similar to Rock Bass but with freckled pattern (scattered dark brown spots) on side of body and head. To 7½ in. (19 cm).

ROCK BASS *Ambloplites rupestris*   **M290, p. 260**
Adult has rows of brown-black spots along side, largest and darkest below lateral line. Young has brown marbling on gray side. To 17 in. (43 cm).

WARMOUTH *Lepomis gulosus*   **M300, p. 266**
Dark red-brown lines (absent on young) radiating from back of red eye. Large mouth. Thick body. Patch of teeth on tongue (detect by feeling with finger). To 12 in. (31 cm).

FLIER *Centrarchus macropterus*   **M286, p. 259**
Large black teardrop. Interrupted rows of black spots along side. 7–8 anal spines. Red-orange around black spot near rear of 2d dorsal fin on young (absent on adult — shown). To 7½ in. (19 cm).

WHITE CRAPPIE *Pomoxis annularis*   **M288, p. 259**
Very long predorsal region arched with sharp dip over eye; dorsal fin base shorter than distance from eye to dorsal fin origin. 6 dorsal spines, 1st much shorter than last. To 21 in. (53 cm).

BLACK CRAPPIE *Pomoxis nigromaculatus*   **M287, p. 259**
Long predorsal region arched with sharp dip over eye; dorsal fin base about as long as distance from eye to dorsal fin origin. 7–8 dorsal spines, 1st much shorter than last. To 19¼ in. (49 cm).

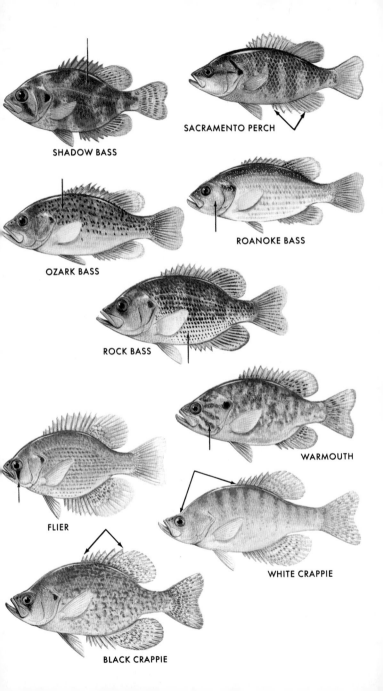

SHADOW BASS

SACRAMENTO PERCH

OZARK BASS

ROANOKE BASS

ROCK BASS

WARMOUTH

FLIER

WHITE CRAPPIE

BLACK CRAPPIE

PLATE 37

SUNFISHES (1)

Deep, strongly compressed body; 3 anal spines.

BANTAM SUNFISH *Lepomis symmetricus*   **M291, p. 268**
Lacks bright colors of other sunfishes. Usually interrupted, incomplete lateral line. Black spot at rear of dorsal fin on young. To 3½ in. (9 cm).

GREEN SUNFISH *Lepomis cyanellus*   **M301, p. 267**
Large mouth; upper jaw extends beneath eye pupil. Adult has large black spot at rear of 2d dorsal and anal fin bases; yellow or orange margins on 2d dorsal, caudal and anal fins. To 12 in. (31 cm).

BLUEGILL *Lepomis macrochirus*   **M303, p. 269**
Large black spot at rear of dorsal fin (faint on young). Dark bars (absent in turbid water; thin and chainlike on young) on deep, extremely compressed body. Long pointed pectoral fin usually extends far past eye when bent forward. To 16¼ in. (41 cm).

SPOTTED SUNFISH *Lepomis punctatus*   **M302, p. 268**
L. p. miniatus has rows of red (on male) or yellow-brown spots (female) on side. *L.p. punctatus* has black specks on side. To 8 in. (20 cm).

REDEAR SUNFISH *Lepomis microlophus*   **M304, p. 269**
Bright red or orange spot, light-colored margin on black ear flap (best developed on large adult). Long pointed pectoral fin usually extends far past eye when bent forward. To 10 in. (25 cm).

PUMPKINSEED *Lepomis gibbosus*   **M305, p. 270**
Bright red or orange spot, light-colored margin on black ear flap. Many bold dark brown wavy lines or orange spots on 2d dorsal, caudal, and anal fins. Wavy blue lines on cheek and opercle of adult. To 16 in. (40 cm).

LONGEAR SUNFISH *Lepomis megalotis*   **M306, p. 270**
Long ear flap (especially on adult male), horizontal on adult, slanted upward on young. Wavy blue lines on cheek and opercle. Adult is dark red above, bright orange below, marbled and spotted with blue. Usually 13–14 pectoral rays. To 9½ in. (24 cm).

DOLLAR SUNFISH *Lepomis marginatus*   **M307, p. 271**
Similar to Longear Sunfish but has shorter upwardly slanted ear flap, red streak along lateral line, usually 12 pectoral rays. To 4¾ in. (12 cm).

REDBREAST SUNFISH *Lepomis auritus*   **M308, p. 272**
Very long, narrow (no wider than eye) ear flap, black to edge. Wavy blue lines on cheek and opercle. Large male has bright orange breast and belly. To 9½ in. (24 cm).

ORANGESPOTTED SUNFISH *Lepomis humilis*   **M309, p. 272**
Bright orange (on large male) or red-brown (female) spots on silver-green side. Wide white margin on long black ear flap. Greatly elongated pores along preopercle margin. To 6 in. (15 cm).

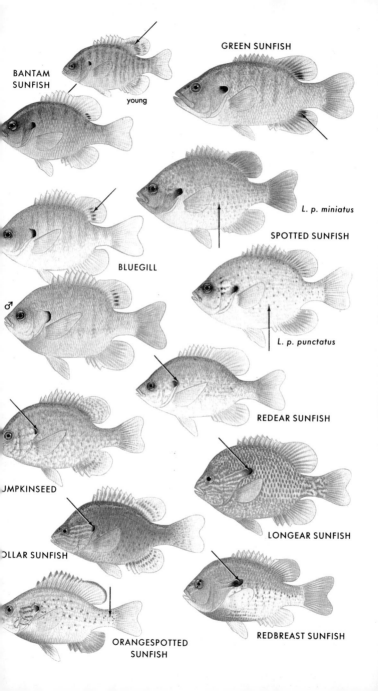

BANTAM
SUNFISH

young

GREEN SUNFISH

BLUEGILL

♂

L. p. miniatus

SPOTTED SUNFISH

L. p. punctatus

REDEAR SUNFISH

JMPKINSEED

LONGEAR SUNFISH

OLLAR SUNFISH

ORANGESPOTTED
SUNFISH

REDBREAST SUNFISH

PLATE 38
SUNFISHES (2), YELLOW PERCH, SAUGER, WALLEYE

First 10 species have rounded caudal fin.

MUD SUNFISH *Acantharchus pomotis*   **M291, p. 261**
Rounded caudal fin. 3–4 parallel black stripes across face and along side of body. To 8¼ in. (21 cm).

BLUESPOTTED SUNFISH *Enneacanthus gloriosus*   **M293, p. 262**
Rows of blue or silver spots along side of large young and adult (bars on side of small young). Slender caudal peduncle. To 3¾ in. (9.5 cm).

BANDED SUNFISH *Enneacanthus obesus*   **M292, p. 262**
Dark bars on side (darkest on large individual). Rows of purple-gold spots along side. To 3¾ in. (9.5 cm).

BLACKBANDED SUNFISH *Enneacanthus chaetodon*   **M294, p. 262**
6 black bars on side, 1st through eye, 6th (often faint) on caudal peduncle. 1st 2–3 membranes of dorsal fin black. Pink to red and black on pelvic fin. To 3¼ in. (8 cm).

*Next 6 species (*Elassoma*) have no lateral line, no notch in dorsal fin.*

BANDED PYGMY SUNFISH *Elassoma zonatum*   **M282, p. 256**
1–2 large black spots (rarely absent) on upper side. 7–12 dark green to black bars on side. To 1¾ in. (4.7 cm).

EVERGLADES PYGMY SUNFISH *Elassoma evergladei*   **M283, p. 256**
Scales on top of head. Usually light streaks along side. Dark-colored lips. Breeding male shown. To 1¼ in. (3.4 cm).

BLUEBARRED PYGMY SUNFISH *Elassoma okatie*   **M284, p. 257**
8–14 wide black bars along side, about 3 times as wide as interspaces. Breeding male shown. To 1¼ in. (3.4 cm).

SPRING PYGMY SUNFISH *Elassoma species*   **M282, p. 258**
6–8 thin gold bars along side. Clear window at rear of 2d dorsal and anal fin bases. To 1¼ in. (3 cm).

OKEFENOKEE PYGMY SUNFISH *Elassoma okefenokee*   **M284, p. 257**
Brown bars (darkest at rear, often broken into vertically aligned blotches) on side of female. Front of lips light colored (dark at sides) except in large male. Breeding male (shown) is black with iridescent blue bars. To 1¼ in. (3.4 cm).

CAROLINA PYGMY SUNFISH *Elassoma boehlkei*   **M284, p. 257**
10–16 narrow black bars along side, about as wide as interspaces. Breeding male shown. To 1¼ in. (3.2 cm).

YELLOW PERCH *Perca flavescens*   **M312, p. 275**
Fairly deep, compressed body. 6–9 green-brown saddles extend down side (often as triangular bars). Black blotch at rear of dorsal fin. To 16 in. (40 cm). See also Ruffe.

SAUGER *Stizostedion canadense*   **M311, p. 274**
Similar to Walleye but has many black half-moons on 1st dorsal fin; 3–4 dusky brown saddles extending down side as broad bars; no white tips on fins. To 30 in. (76 cm).

WALLEYE *Stizostedion vitreum*   **M310, p. 273**
Long slender body. Huge mouth extends beyond middle of eye; large canine teeth. Opaque, silver eye. Large black spot (absent on young) on rear of 1st dorsal fin. 5–12 dusky saddles. White tips on anal fin, lower lobe of caudal fin. To 36 in. (91 cm).

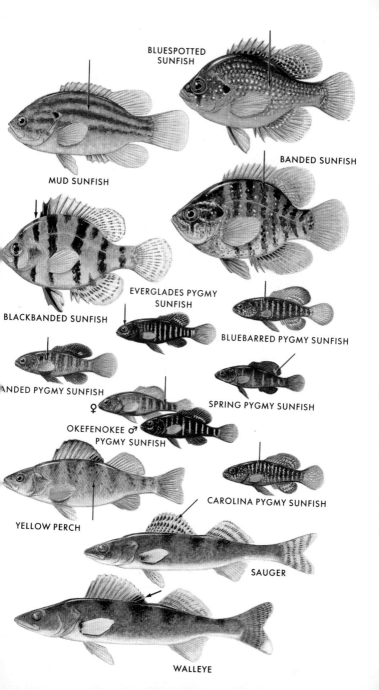

BLUESPOTTED
SUNFISH

MUD SUNFISH

BANDED SUNFISH

BLACKBANDED SUNFISH

EVERGLADES PYGMY
SUNFISH

BLUEBARRED PYGMY SUNFISH

BANDED PYGMY SUNFISH

SPRING PYGMY SUNFISH

OKEFENOKEE ♂
PYGMY SUNFISH

♀

CAROLINA PYGMY SUNFISH

YELLOW PERCH

SAUGER

WALLEYE

PLATE 39

DARTERS (1)

Scutes on breast (except on Bluestripe Darter) and along belly of male (Fig. 56).

LEOPARD DARTER *Percina pantherina*　　　　　**M315, p. 278**
10–14 round black spots along side. Black or dusky spots on upper side and back. To 3½ in. (9.2 cm).

LONGHEAD DARTER *Percina macrocephala*　　　**M314, p. 277**
Long snout. Sickle-shaped teardrop curved down onto underside of head. Dark bar below medial black caudal spot. To 4¾ in. (12 cm).

MUSCADINE DARTER *Percina* species　　　　　**M314, p. 280**
8–12 black blotches along side, fused into black stripe on adult. Black blotch on caudal fin base centered below black stripe. To 2½ in. (6.5 cm).

BLACKSIDE DARTER *Percina maculata*　　　　　**M316, p. 278**
Discrete medial black caudal spot. 6–9 large oval black blotches along side. To 4¼ in. (11 cm).

SHIELD DARTER *Percina peltata*　　　　　　　**M314, p. 279**
Black bar on chin, row of black crescents on 1st dorsal fin (Fig. 58). 6–7 horizontally rectangular black blotches along side. To 3½ in. (9 cm). See also Appalachia Darter.

STRIPEBACK DARTER *Percina notogramma*　　　**M317, p. 278**
Pale yellow stripe along upper side. 1st dorsal fin dusky, darkest at front. 6–8 horizontally oval black blotches along side. To 3½ in. (8.4 cm).

BLUESTRIPE DARTER *Percina cymatotaenia*　　　**M313, p. 276**
Broad, scallop-edged black stripe along side. Wedge-shaped black spot on caudal fin base. To 3½ in. (9 cm). See also Frecklebelly Darter.

Next 5 species have no or narrow premaxillary frenum (Fig. 55).

CHANNEL DARTER *Percina copelandi*　　　　　**M321, p. 282**
Blunt snout. 9–10 horizontally oblong black blotches along side. Black Xs and Ws on upper side. Medial black caudal spot. To 2¾ in. (7.2 cm).

Next 4 species have anal fin extending to caudal fin on large male.

RIVER DARTER *Percina shumardi*　　　　　　　**M322, p. 282**
Small black spot at front, large black spot near rear of 1st dorsal fin. 8–15 black bars along side. To 3 in. (7.8 cm).

SNAIL DARTER *Percina tanasi*　　　　　　　　**M323, p. 283**
Similar to Stargazing Darter but has gray edge and base on 1st dorsal fin. To 3½ in. (9 cm).

STARGAZING DARTER *Percina uranidea*　　　　**M323, p. 283**
Red-brown above; 4 dark brown saddles (1st under 1st dorsal fin) extend down side to lateral line. Blunt snout. To 3 in. (7.8 cm).

SADDLEBACK DARTER *Percina ouachitae*　　　　**M324, p. 283**
5 dark brown saddles; 1st under 1st dorsal fin. Small black spot on caudal fin base. To 3 in. (7.8 cm).

Next 4 species have 3 dark brown spots on caudal fin base.

BLACKBANDED DARTER *Percina nigrofasciata*　　**M319, p. 281**
12–15 dark bars along side. To 4½ in. (11 cm).

DUSKY DARTER *Percina sciera*　　　　　　　　**M318, p. 281**
8–12 oval dark blotches along side. To 5 in. (13 cm).

GOLDLINE DARTER *Percina aurolineata*　　　　**M318, p. 281**
Similar to Dusky Darter but has thin amber or brown stripe on upper side. To 3½ in. (9 cm).

FRECKLED DARTER *Percina lenticula*　　　　　**M320, p. 281**
Large black spot at front of 2d dorsal fin. To 8 in. (20 cm).

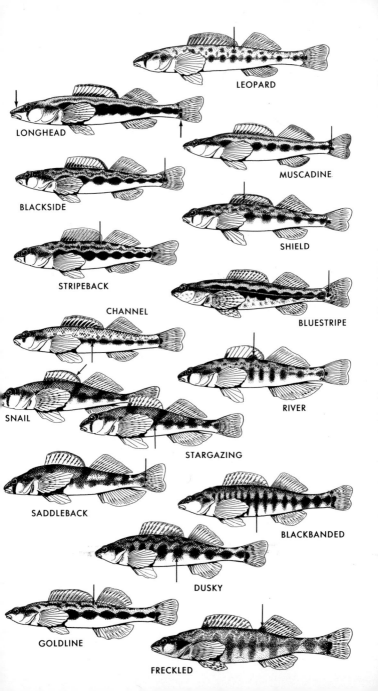

LEOPARD

LONGHEAD

MUSCADINE

BLACKSIDE

SHIELD

STRIPEBACK

CHANNEL

BLUESTRIPE

SNAIL

RIVER

STARGAZING

SADDLEBACK

BLACKBANDED

DUSKY

GOLDLINE

FRECKLED

PLATE 40

DARTERS (2)

No scutes on breast or belly (Fig. 56).

CRYSTAL DARTER *Crystallaria asprella*   **M328, p. 288**
Very slender body. Wide flat head. 4 dark saddles on back and upper side.
To 6¼ in. (16 cm).

NAKED SAND DARTER *Etheostoma beani*   **M330, p. 289**
Middle black band, most prominent near front, on each dorsal fin (Fig. 59).
To 2¾ in. (7.2 cm). See also Florida Sand Darter.

EASTERN SAND DARTER *Etheostoma pellucidum*   **M331, p. 290**
10–19 horizontal dark green blotches along side. To 3¼ in. (8.4 cm). See
also Southern Sand Darter.

WESTERN SAND DARTER *Etheostoma clarum*   **M329, p. 289**
Spine on opercle. To 2¾ in. (7.1 cm).

SCALY SAND DARTER *Etheostoma vivax*   **M331, p. 290**
Vertical dark green blotches along side. Black edge and middle black band
on each dorsal fin. To 2¾ in. (7.3 cm).

GLASSY DARTER *Etheostoma vitreum*   **M331, p. 291**
Translucent body. Many brown specks and black spots on back and side.
Dark dashes along lateral line. To 2½ in. (6.6 cm).

JOHNNY DARTER *Etheostoma nigrum*   **M332, p. 291**
Dark brown Xs and Ws on side. Blunt snout. No premaxillary frenum.
Black eye stripe extends onto upper lip (Fig. 60). Breeding male has black
head and lower fins, black spot on 1st dorsal fin. To 2¾ in. (7.2 cm).

TESSELLATED DARTER *Etheostoma olmstedi*   **M333, p. 292**
Similar to Johnny Darter but has uninterrupted infraorbital and
supratemporal canals (Fig. 53), enlarged 2d dorsal fin on breeding male
(shown). To 4½ in. (11 cm).

WACCAMAW DARTER *Etheostoma perlongum*   **M332, p. 292**
Nearly identical to Tessellated Darter but is more slender. To 3½ in. (9
cm).

BLUNTNOSE DARTER *Etheostoma chlorosomum*   **M334, p. 292**
Black bridle around extremely blunt snout (Fig. 60). Horizontal dark
blotches, Xs, and Ws along side. To 2½ in. (6 cm). See also
Choctawhatchee Darter.

OKALOOSA DARTER *Etheostoma okaloosae*   **M355, p. 309**
5–8 rows of small dark brown spots on side. Black spots on lower half of
head and breast. To 2 in. (5.3 cm).

TUSCUMBIA DARTER *Etheostoma tuscumbia*   **M359, p. 311**
Scales on top of head and often on branchiostegal membranes. Gold
specks on back, head, and upper side. To 2½ in. (6.1 cm).

MARYLAND DARTER *Etheostoma sellare*   **M337, p. 294**
Asymmetrical caudal fin base (upper half extends more to rear). Wide, flat
head. 4 large dark brown saddles. To 3¼ in. (8.4 cm).

GOLDSTRIPE DARTER *Etheostoma parvipinne*   **M359, p. 311**
Short blunt snout. Small upturned mouth. Yellow lateral line. Often
short wide bars on side. To 2¾ in. (6.7 cm).

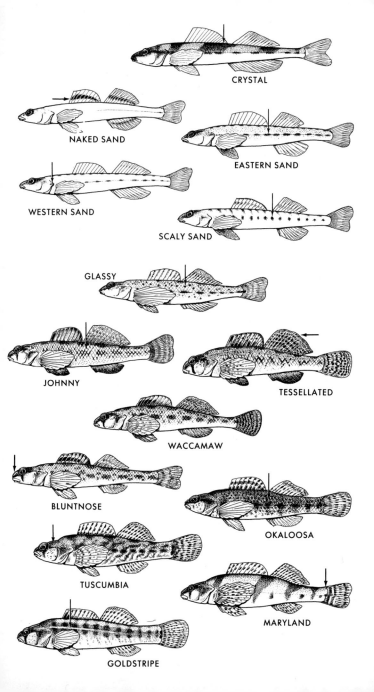

CRYSTAL

NAKED SAND

EASTERN SAND

WESTERN SAND

SCALY SAND

GLASSY

JOHNNY

TESSELLATED

WACCAMAW

BLUNTNOSE

OKALOOSA

TUSCUMBIA

MARYLAND

GOLDSTRIPE

PLATE 41

DARTERS (3)

Scutes on breast and along belly of male (Fig. 56).

TANGERINE DARTER *Percina aurantiaca*   **M313, p. 284**
Black stripe along back breaks into spots at rear. Small dark brown spots on upper side. Breeding male is bright red-orange below. To 7¼ in. (18 cm).

AMBER DARTER *Percina antesella*   **M324, p. 283**
4 dark brown saddles (1st in front of 1st dorsal fin). Pointed snout; premaxillary frenum absent or narrow. Breeding male (shown) has anal fin extending to caudal fin. To 2¾ in. (7.2 cm).

GILT DARTER *Percina evides*   **M315, p. 284**
Wide dusky green bars (darkest on adult). Yellow to bright orange below. Ozark subspecies has orange 1st dorsal fin. Upper Tennessee R. subspecies has orange edge on 1st dorsal fin. To 3¾ in. (9.6 cm).

BRONZE DARTER *Percina palmaris*   **M315, p. 284**
8–10 brown saddles; 8–11 brown blotches along side. On large individual wide bars join blotches to saddles. To 3½ in. (9 cm).

PIEDMONT DARTER *Percina crassa*   **M317, p. 280**
7–9 oval black blotches along side. Black bar on chin. Row of black crescents (see Fig. 58) on 1st dorsal fin. To 3½ in. (9 cm).

ROANOKE DARTER *Percina roanoka*   **M317, p. 280**
8–14 black bars (on adult) or oval blotches (on young) along side. Bright blue side, orange belly, orange band on 1st dorsal fin of large male (shown). To 3 in. (7.8 cm).

Next 3 species have orange band on 1st dorsal fin, black spot on caudal fin base.

LONGNOSE DARTER *Percina nasuta*   **M319, p. 286**
Long pointed snout (extreme in some populations). 12–15 dark bars along side. Unscaled or partly scaled breast. To 4½ in. (11 cm).

SLENDERHEAD DARTER *Percina phoxocephala*   **M325, p. 285**
Moderately long pointed snout. 10–16 round dark blotches along side. Unscaled or partly scaled breast. To 3¾ in. (9.6 cm).

OLIVE DARTER *Percina squamata*   **M325, p. 285**
Long, pointed snout. 10–12 dark rectangles along side. Fully scaled breast. To 5¼ in. (13 cm). See also Sharpnose Darter.

Next 5 species (logperches) have long bulbous snout, wide flat head.

BIGSCALE LOGPERCH *Percina macrolepida*   **M327, p. 288**
Similar to Logperch but has scales on top of small head. To 4½ in. (11 cm).

TEXAS LOGPERCH *Percina carbonaria*   **M326, p. 287**
Long dark bars along side constricted near middle. Large male (shown) has black breast; orange band on 1st dorsal fin. To 5¼ in. (13 cm).

LOGPERCH *Percina caprodes*   **M326, p. 286**
Many alternating long and short bars along side extend over back and join those of other side. *P. c. semifasciata* has unscaled nape. *P. c. caprodes* has fully scaled nape, no middle orange band on 1st dorsal fin. *P. c. fulvitaenia* has middle orange band on 1st dorsal fin. To 7¼ in. (18 cm). See also Conasauga Logperch.

BLOTCHSIDE LOGPERCH *Percina burtoni*   **M320, p. 286**
No scales on nape. 8–10 round blotches along side. Large black blotch at rear, orange edge on 1st dorsal fin. To 6½ in. (16 cm).

ROANOKE LOGPERCH *Percina rex*   **M320, p. 287**
10–12 short black bars along side, not joined over back with those of other side. Orange band on 1st dorsal fin. To 6 in. (15 cm).

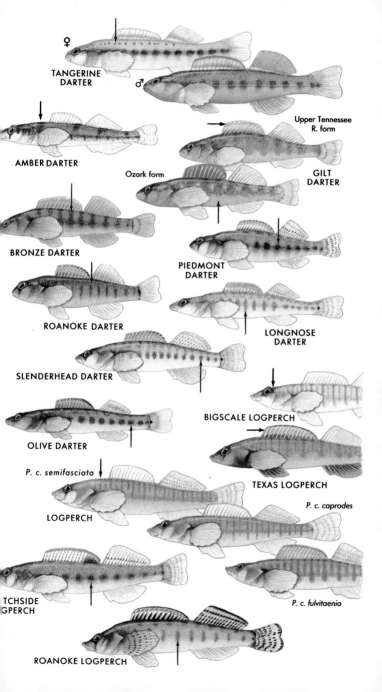

♀ TANGERINE DARTER

♂

AMBER DARTER

Upper Tennessee R. form

GILT DARTER

Ozark form

BRONZE DARTER

PIEDMONT DARTER

ROANOKE DARTER

LONGNOSE DARTER

SLENDERHEAD DARTER

OLIVE DARTER

BIGSCALE LOGPERCH

TEXAS LOGPERCH

P. c. semifasciata

LOGPERCH

P. c. caprodes

TCHSIDE GPERCH

ROANOKE LOGPERCH

P. c. fulvitaenia

PLATE 42

DARTERS (4)

Blunt snout; no scutes on breast or belly (Fig. 56).

GREENSIDE DARTER *Etheostoma blennioides*   **M338, p. 294**
5–8 green Ws, Us, or bars (on large male) on side. Brown to dark red spots on upper side. Skin on rear of upper lip fused to skin of snout. To 6½ in. (17 cm).

ROCK DARTER *Etheostoma rupestre*   **M338, p. 295**
Similar to Greenside Darter but lacks scales on cheek, fusion of skin at rear of upper lip to skin of snout. To 3¼ in. (8.3 cm).

ELLIJAY DARTER *Etheostoma* species   **M345, p. 302**
1st dorsal fin has red spot at front, blue edge. Breeding male (shown) has red between green bars along side. To 2½ in. (6.2 cm).

EMERALD DARTER *Etheostoma baileyi*   **M342, p. 299**
Extremely blunt snout. Red edge on 1st dorsal fin. 7–11 small emerald-green squares along side (expanded into bars on breeding male — shown). To 2¼ in. (5.6 cm).

BANDED DARTER *Etheostoma zonale*   **M341, p. 298**
9–13 large dark green bars on side extend onto belly and under caudal peduncle to join those of other side. To 3 in. (7.8 cm).

BRIGHTEYE DARTER *Etheostoma lynceum*   **M341, p. 298**
Similar to Banded Darter but interspaces about as wide as bars on side. To 2½ in. (6.4 cm).

LONGFIN DARTER *Etheostoma longimanum*   **M335, p. 293**
9–14 dark squares (or Ws) along side. Breeding male has orange and black fins. Broadly joined branchiostegal membranes. To 3½ in. (8.9 cm). See also Riverweed Darter.

HARLEQUIN DARTER *Etheostoma histrio*   **M339, p. 295**
2 large dark brown to green caudal spots. Many dark brown or black specks on yellow belly and underside of head. To 3 in. (7.7 cm).

SEAGREEN DARTER *Etheostoma thalassinum*   **M340, p. 295**
7 small dark brown blotches (often Ws) along side. Red edge, dusky black base on 1st dorsal fin. To 3¼ in. (8 cm). See Turquoise Darter.

SWANNANOA DARTER *Etheostoma swannanoa*   **M340, p. 296**
Rows of small red spots on side. 8–9 black blotches on side — vertically oval at front, round at rear. To 3½ in. (9 cm).

BLENNY DARTER *Etheostoma blennius*   **M340, p. 296**
Body thick at front, strongly tapering to narrow caudal peduncle. 4 large dark saddles extend down side. To 3¼ in. (8.3 cm).

FINESCALE SADDLED DARTER *Etheostoma osburni*   **M335, p. 297**
5 large dark saddles. 9–11 green bars alternate with orange interspaces (much brighter on male) on side. 58–70 lateral scales. To 4 in. (10 cm).

KANAWHA DARTER *Etheostoma kanawhae*   **M337, p. 297**
Nearly identical to Finescale Saddled Darter but has 48–58 lateral scales. To 3½ in. (8.6 cm).

VARIEGATE DARTER *Etheostoma variatum*   **M337, p. 297**
4 large saddles angle down and forward to lateral line. Green and orange bars on side. Breeding male is blue and orange. To 4½ in. (11 cm).

MISSOURI SADDLED DARTER *Etheostoma tetrazonum*   **M337, p. 297**
Nearly identical to Variegate Darter but has smaller eye, darker saddles. To 3½ in. (9 cm).

ARKANSAS SADDLED DARTER *Etheostoma euzonum*   **M337, p. 298**
4 large saddles angle down and forward to lateral line. Large head and eye. Green and orange spots on upper side. To 4¾ in. (12 cm).

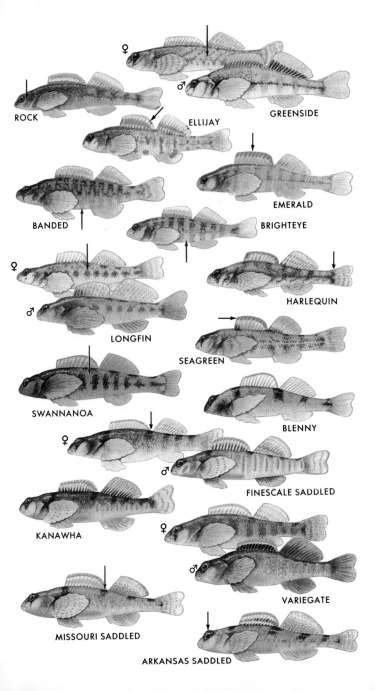

ROCK

GREENSIDE

ELLIJAY

EMERALD

BANDED

BRIGHTEYE

LONGFIN

HARLEQUIN

SWANNANOA

SEAGREEN

BLENNY

KANAWHA

FINESCALE SADDLED

VARIEGATE

MISSOURI SADDLED

ARKANSAS SADDLED

PLATE 43

DARTERS (5)

Blunt snout; broadly joined branchiostegal membranes (Fig. 54); no or narrow premaxillary frenum (Fig. 55); no scutes on breast or belly (Fig. 56).

TENNESSEE SNUBNOSE DARTER *Etheostoma simoterum* **M343, p. 299**
Many small red spots on upper side; 1st dorsal fin has red spot at front, red edge, wavy black lines. To 3 in. (7.7 cm).

BLACKSIDE SNUBNOSE DARTER *Etheostoma duryi* **M344, p. 300**
Dark blotches along side fused into stripe. 1st dorsal fin has red spot at front, red edge, wavy red and black lines. To 2¾ in. (7.2 cm). See also Saffron Darter.

CHERRY DARTER *Etheostoma etnieri* **M344, p. 301**
Dark lines along upper side. 1st dorsal fin has small red spot at front, thin black bands. To 3 in. (7.7 cm).

KENTUCKY SNUBNOSE DARTER *Etheostoma rafinesquei* **M342, p. 300**
Cross-hatching (created by dark scale edges) and 7–10 short dark bars on side. To 2½ in. (6.5 cm).

SPLENDID DARTER *Etheostoma barrenense* **M342, p. 300**
7–10 black blotches on side fused into stripe. Breeding male is red above and below stripe. Narrow premaxillary frenum. To 2½ in. (6.4 cm).

Next 7 species have thin brown stripe above lateral line interrupted by 7–10 black or brown blotches (front blotches often fused into stripe).

BANDFIN DARTER *Etheostoma zonistium* **M342, p. 301**
1st dorsal fin has red spot at front, 2 red bands through middle. Breeding male has bright red body. To 2¾ in. (7.1 cm).

YAZOO DARTER *Etheostoma* species **M345, p. 302**
Nearly identical to Coastal Plain Darter but has 8–10 narrow red-brown rectangles along side just above lateral line. To 2¼ in. (6 cm).

FIREBELLY DARTER *Etheostoma pyrrhogaster* **M345, p. 301**
1st dorsal fin has red spot at front, red band (wide on male). Breeding male has bright red body. To 2¾ in. (7 cm).

WARRIOR DARTER *Etheostoma* species **M346, p. 303**
1st dorsal fin has red spot at front, red edge. Red lower side on breeding male. To 2¾ in. (7.2 cm).

COOSA DARTER *Etheostoma coosae* **M342, p. 303**
1st dorsal fin has bright red spot at front, 1–2 red bands, blue-green edge (faint on female). 8–10 blue-brown bars along side of large male. To 2¾ in. (7.2 cm).

TALLAPOOSA DARTER *Etheostoma* species **M346, p. 304**
Similar to Coastal Plain Darter but has larger blacker blotches on side; large male has low 1st dorsal fin with blue edge, red throughout. To 2½ in. (6.6 cm).

COASTAL PLAIN DARTER *Etheostoma* species **M346, p. 302**
1st dorsal fin has blue edge, no red spot at front. Breeding male has high 1st dorsal fin with blue edge, red band; orange side. To 2½ in. (6.6 cm).

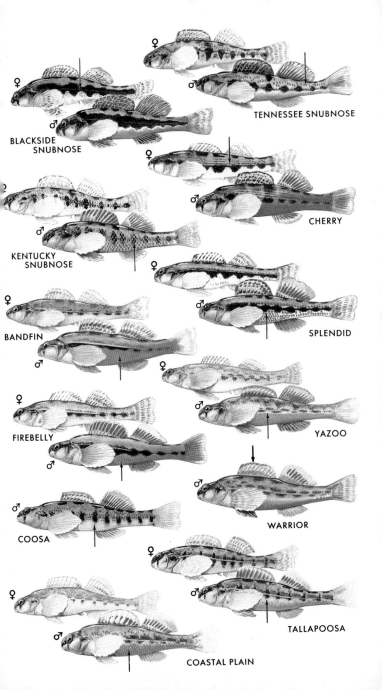

BLACKSIDE
SNUBNOSE

♀
♂

TENNESSEE SNUBNOSE
♀
♂

KENTUCKY
SNUBNOSE
♂

CHERRY
♀
♂

BANDFIN
♀
♂

SPLENDID
♀
♂

FIREBELLY
♀
♂

YAZOO
♀
♂

WARRIOR
♂

COOSA
♂

TALLAPOOSA
♀
♂

COASTAL PLAIN
♀
♂

PLATE 44

DARTERS (6)

Alternating dark and light lines (except on Tippecanoe Darter) on side of deep compressed body; no scutes on breast or belly (Fig. 56). All live in fast, rocky riffles.

GREENBREAST DARTER *Etheostoma jordani* **M347, p. 304**
No teardrop. Small dark blotches along side just below lateral line. Male is blue below, has small red spots on side. To 3 in. (7.9 cm).

Next 7 species have many black spots on fins of females.

REDLINE DARTER *Etheostoma rufilineatum* **M348, p. 304**
Black dashes on cheek and opercle. Red spots on side of male. Cream-colored caudal fin base. To 3½ in. (8.4 cm).

YELLOWCHEEK DARTER *Etheostoma moorei* **M349, p. 304**
Green base, middle red band on 1st dorsal fin of male. Black teardrop on dusky cheek. To 2¾ in. (7.2 cm).

BAYOU DARTER *Etheostoma rubrum* **M349, p. 305**
Cream-colored caudal fin base followed by 2 large black spots. Red spots on side of male. Large black teardrop on white cheek. To 2¼ in. (5.5 cm).

Next 4 species have black halos around red spots on side.

SMALLSCALE DARTER *Etheostoma microlepidum* **M350, p. 305**
Black edge on 2d dorsal, caudal, and anal fins. Large male has bright green and orange median fins. To 2¾ in. (7.2 cm)

SPOTTED DARTER *Etheostoma maculatum* **M351, p. 305**
Compressed body. Narrow pointed snout. No red on fins. To 3½ in. (9 cm). See also Bloodfin Darter.

WOUNDED DARTER *Etheostoma vulneratum* **M351, p. 306**
Black edge on median fins. 2 red spots at front, 1 at rear, of 1st dorsal fin. Red 2d dorsal and caudal fins. To 3¼ in. (8 cm). See also Boulder Darter.

COPPERCHEEK DARTER *Etheostoma aquali* **M351, p. 306**
Wavy copper lines on cheek and opercle. No teardrop. 2 red spots at front, 1 at rear, of 1st dorsal fin. Red fins. To 3¼ in. (8 cm).

SHARPHEAD DARTER *Etheostoma acuticeps* **M347, p. 307**
Compressed body. Extremely pointed snout. Dusky bars on side. Female is yellow-brown. Male is olive to blue, has turquoise fins. To 3¼ in. (8.4 cm).

TIPPECANOE DARTER *Etheostoma tippecanoe* **M347, p. 308**
Small — to 1¾ in. (4.3 cm). Blue-black bars on side, darkest at rear; last bar large, encircling caudal peduncle, followed by 2 white (female) or orange (male) caudal spots.

BLUEBREAST DARTER *Etheostoma camurum* **M352, p. 306**
Male has bright red spots (not surrounded by black halos) on side; red fins, blue breast. Female has brown spots on side. To 3¼ in. (8.4 cm).

ORANGEFIN DARTER *Etheostoma bellum* **M350, p. 307**
Large black teardrop (obscure on large male). Male has blue breast, red spots on side, orange fins. To 3½ in. (9 cm).

GREENFIN DARTER *Etheostoma chlorobranchium* **M350, p. 307**
Large male is deep green with green fins except pink pectoral fins. Female similar to Bluebreast Darter. To 4 in. (10 cm).

YOKE DARTER *Etheostoma juliae* **M349, p. 307**
Large black saddle ("yoke") on nape and down side to pectoral fin. Orange fins. To 3 in. (7.8 cm).

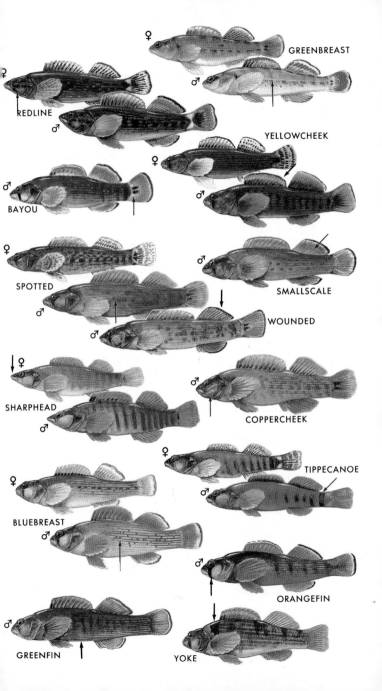

GREENBREAST

REDLINE

YELLOWCHEEK

BAYOU

SPOTTED

SMALLSCALE

WOUNDED

SHARPHEAD

COPPERCHEEK

BLUEBREAST

TIPPECANOE

ORANGEFIN

GREENFIN

YOKE

PLATE 45

DARTERS (7)

No scutes on breast or belly (Fig. 56).

ARROW DARTER *Etheostoma sagitta*   **M353, p. 308**
  2 black caudal spots fused into short bar. Long pointed snout. 7–9 green Us alternate with orange bars (brightest on breeding male — shown) along side. 52–69 lateral scales. To 4¾ in. (12 cm).

NIANGUA DARTER *Etheostoma nianguae*   **M353, p. 308**
  Similar to Arrow Darter but has 2 (unfused) jet black caudal spots, 72–82 lateral scales. To 5¼ in. (13 cm).

PINEWOODS DARTER *Etheostoma mariae*   **M354, p. 308**
  1st dorsal fin with bright red edge, black spot at front. Black spots on lower half of head and breast. To 3 in. (7.6 cm).

SAVANNAH DARTER *Etheostoma fricksium*   **M354, p. 309**
  Similar to Pinewoods Darter but is green below, with bright orange bars on belly of male (shown). To 3 in. (7.4 cm).

ORANGEBELLY DARTER *Etheostoma radiosum*   **M360, p. 312**
  Short dark bars (rear ones long) along side, cut into upper and lower halves by yellow lateral line. Orange branchiostegal membranes, blue pelvic fins on large male (shown). To 3½ in. (8.5 cm).

REDFIN DARTER *Etheostoma whipplei*   **M360, p. 312**
  Many small bright red (on male) or yellow (female) spots on side. Slender, relatively uniform body depth from head to caudal peduncle. To 3½ in. (9 cm).

RIO GRANDE DARTER *Etheostoma grahami*   **M361, p. 312**
  Deep bodied. Many small red (on male) or black (female) spots on side. Red 1st dorsal fin (faint on female). To 2¼ in. (6 cm).

Next 5 species have bright orange on head and body of breeding male.

STIPPLED DARTER *Etheostoma punctulatum*   **M356, p. 309**
  Dark brown mottling, specks on head and body. White to orange below. Large black teardrop. Pointed snout. To 4 in. (10 cm). See also Sunburst Darter.

SLACKWATER DARTER *Etheostoma boschungi*   **M357, p. 310**
  Many black specks on back and side. Large black teardrop. Blunt snout. To 3 in. (7.8 cm).

ARKANSAS DARTER *Etheostoma cragini*   **M358, p. 310**
  Strongly bicolored body — upper half dark brown, lower half white to orange. Black specks on body and fins. To 2¼ in. (6 cm).

PALEBACK DARTER *Etheostoma pallididorsum*   **M358, p. 310**
  Nearly identical to Arkansas Darter but is more slender; has wide, pale olive stripe along back. To 2¼ in. (6 cm).

TRISPOT DARTER *Etheostoma trisella*   **M357, p. 311**
  3 dark brown saddles. Complete lateral line; 1 anal spine. To 2¼ in. (5.9 cm).

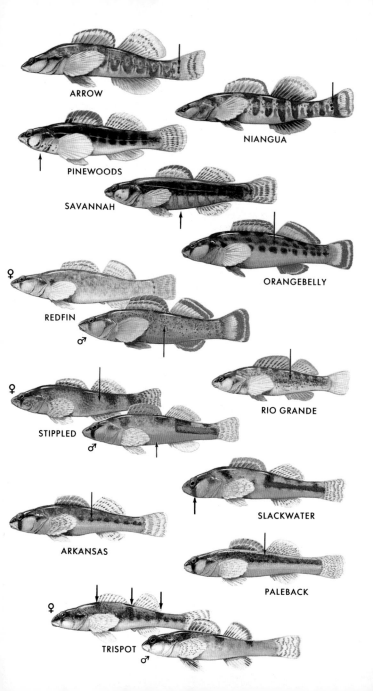

ARROW

NIANGUA

PINEWOODS

SAVANNAH

ORANGEBELLY

♀ REDFIN

♂

♀ STIPPLED

♂

RIO GRANDE

ARKANSAS

SLACKWATER

PALEBACK

♀ TRISPOT

♂

PLATE 46

DARTERS (8)

No scutes on breast or belly (Fig. 56).

RAINBOW DARTER *Etheostoma caeruleum* **M362, p. 313**
Deep bodied. Dark bars on side (blue between red on male; dark brown between yellow-white on female). Anal fin red with blue edge (faint on female). In some populations, males have red spots on side; in others, they do not (both forms shown). To 3 in. (7.7 cm).

ORANGETHROAT DARTER *Etheostoma spectabile* **M363, p. 314**
Arched body, deepest at front of 1st dorsal fin. Dark bars (blue between orange on male, brown between yellow-white on female) on side. *E. s. spectabile* has thin dark stripes on side. *E. s. squamosum* has mostly orange 1st dorsal fin. *E. s. fragi* has wide turquoise bars on side. To 2¾ in. (7.2 cm).

MUD DARTER *Etheostoma asprigene* **M357, p. 313**
Large black blotch at rear of 1st dorsal fin (faint on female). Dark bars on side darkest at rear. Fully scaled cheek. To 2¾ in. (7.1 cm).

REDBAND DARTER *Etheostoma luteovinctum* **M353, p. 314**
Body deepest at front of 1st dorsal fin, strongly tapering to narrow caudal peduncle. 7–9 dark squares just below lateral line. To 2¾ in. (6.8 cm).

GULF DARTER *Etheostoma swaini* **M356, p. 315**
Dark bars on side (often obscured by dark mottling on female). Thin dark lines on upper side, white to orange (large male) below. 35–50, usually 38–45, lateral scales. To 3 in. (7.8 cm).

CREOLE DARTER *Etheostoma collettei* **M356, p. 315**
Similar to Gulf Darter but has 44–60, usually 46–55, lateral scales; large male is more blue. To 3 in. (7.4 cm).

WATERCRESS DARTER *Etheostoma nuchale* **M355, p. 316**
Similar to Gulf Darter but is smaller, more compressed; has shorter (12–24 pored scales) lateral line. To 2¼ in. (5.4 cm).

COLDWATER DARTER *Etheostoma ditrema* **M355, p. 316**
Dark mottling on back and side, orange belly on male. 3 black caudal spots. To 2¼ in. (5.4 cm).

GREENTHROAT DARTER *Etheostoma lepidum* **M361, p. 316**
Red-orange specks or spots between long green bars on side of male; yellow between short brown-black bars on female. To 2½ in. (6.6 cm).

CHRISTMAS DARTER *Etheostoma hopkinsi* **M355, p. 316**
10–12 dark green bars on side, separated by brick red on male, yellow on female. To 2½ in. (6.6 cm)

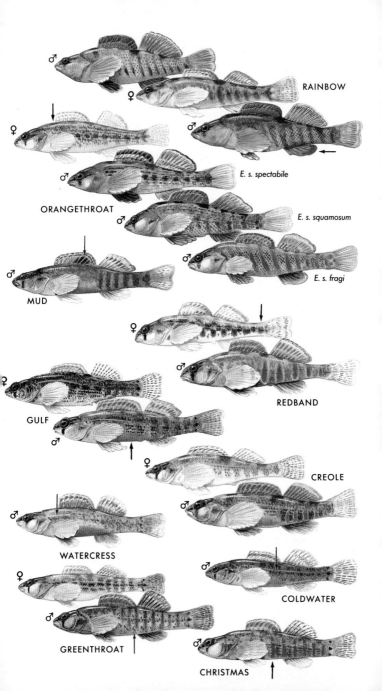

RAINBOW

♀

♂

E. s. spectabile

ORANGETHROAT
♂

♂ E. s. squamosum

♂ E. s. fragi

MUD

♀

REDBAND
♂

GULF
♀

♂

CREOLE
♀

♂

WATERCRESS
♂

COLDWATER
♂

GREENTHROAT
♂

CHRISTMAS
♂

PLATE 47
DARTERS (9)

No scutes on breast or belly (Fig. 56). Large male shown unless female indicated.

First 5 species have iridescent bar on cheek. Breeding male has red dorsal, caudal, and anal fins; blue-black edge on anal and caudal fins.

STRIPED DARTER *Etheostoma virgatum* **M369, p. 321**
Dark brown stripes on side. To 3 in. (7.8 cm).

BARCHEEK DARTER *Etheostoma obeyense* **M370, p. 321**
Dark brown blotches, no stripes or rows of dark spots, on side. To 3¼ in. (8.4 cm).

TEARDROP DARTER *Etheostoma barbouri* **M364, p. 322**
Large black teardrop. Rows of small dark brown spots and blotches on side. To 2¼ in. (6 cm).

SLABROCK DARTER *Etheostoma smithi* **M370, p. 322**
Similar to Barcheek Darter but is smaller; has more darkly outlined scales. To 2½ in. (6.2 cm).

STRIATED DARTER *Etheostoma striatulum* **M369, p. 322**
Similar to Teardrop Darter but has narrow bar on cheek, darker rows of spots on side. To 2¼ in. (5.6 cm).

Next 6 species have black bands on 2nd dorsal, caudal, and (often) pectoral fins.

STRIPETAIL DARTER *Etheostoma kennicotti* **M367, p. 320**
Gold knobs on tips of dorsal spines. Dark blotches along side. To 3¼ in. (8.3 cm).

FANTAIL DARTER *Etheostoma flabellare* **M368, p. 320**
Gold knobs on tips of dorsal spines — large on male, small on female. Broadly joined branchiostegal membranes. 19–23 dorsal spines and rays. *E.f. brevispina* has dark bars along side. *E.f. flabellare* has protruding lower jaw, often thin dark stripes on side. To 3¼ in. (8.4 cm).

DUSKYTAIL DARTER *Etheostoma species* **M366, p. 321**
Similar to Fantail Darter but has 10–15 long bars along side, 17–20 dorsal spines and rays. To 2½ in. (6.4 cm).

DIRTY DARTER *Etheostoma olivaceum* **M364, p. 317**
Thin stripes, black mottling, sometimes black bars on side. Long sharp snout. Large male is black. To 3¼ in. (8 cm).

Next 2 species (and 3 similar species — see Fig. 61) have 3 black spots on caudal fin base, dark brown mottling on back and side (obscure on large male); are distinguishable only as breeding males.

LOLLYPOP DARTER *Etheostoma neopterum* **M364, p. 319**
Breeding male has large yellow knobs on tips of 2nd dorsal fin rays (Fig. 61). To 3½ in. (8.9 cm).

FRINGED DARTER *Etheostoma crossopterum* **M366, p. 318**
Breeding male has white edge on 2d dorsal fin (Fig. 61). To 4 in. (10 cm). See also Spottail, Blackfin, and Crown Darters.

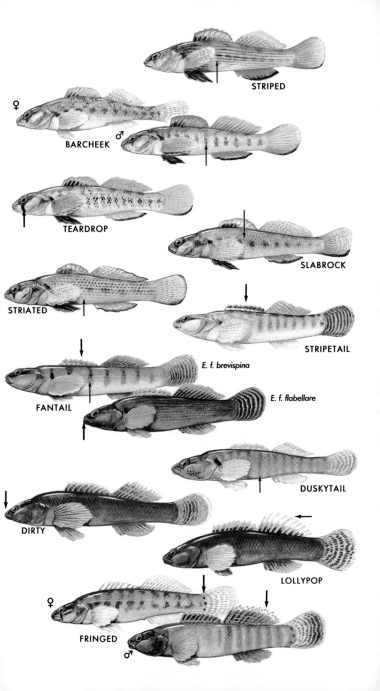

STRIPED

♀ BARCHEEK ♂

TEARDROP

SLABROCK

STRIATED

STRIPETAIL

E. f. brevispina

FANTAIL

E. f. flabellare

DUSKYTAIL

DIRTY

LOLLYPOP

♀ FRINGED ♂

PLATE 48

DARTERS (10)

No scutes on breast or belly (Fig. 56).

ASHY DARTER *Etheostoma cinereum*   **M339, p. 303**
Longitudinal rows of small brown spots on upper side. Row of small black rectangles along side. Breeding male has huge 2d dorsal fin. To 4¾ in. (12 cm).

SPECKLED DARTER *Etheostoma stigmaeum*   **M336, p. 293**
7–11 dark brown squares (Ws if examined closely) along side just below lateral line on female and juvenile; 7-11 turquoise bars on large male. To 2½ in. (6.1 cm).

BLUESIDE DARTER *Etheostoma jessiae*   **M336, p. 294**
Similar to Speckled Darter but has pointed snout, narrow premaxillary frenum, deep blue bars on body and fins of male. To 2¾ in. (6.8 cm).

Next 3 species are small (to 2 in. [5 cm]); have very short lateral line (fewer than 10 pores), large flap on pelvic fin of male.

LEAST DARTER *Etheostoma microperca*   **M371, p. 322**
Deep, compressed body. Extremely short (0–3 pores) lateral line. Large teardrop. Orange anal and pelvic fins on large male. To 1¾ in. (4.4 cm).

CYPRESS DARTER *Etheostoma proeliare*   **M372, p. 323**
Short (0–9 pores) lateral line. Black or brown dashes along side, spots on upper and lower side. To 2 in. (4.8 cm).

FOUNTAIN DARTER *Etheostoma fonticola*   **M372, p. 323**
Short (0–6 pores) lateral line. 1 anal spine. Cross-hatching on upper and lower side. Smallest darter − to 1¾ in. (4.3 cm).

Next 8 species have incomplete lateral line strongly arched near front (often only slightly arched in Iowa Darter).

SWAMP DARTER *Etheostoma fusiforme*   **M343, p. 324**
Slender, compressed body. Many dark specks below. To 2¼ in. (5.9 cm).

SAWCHEEK DARTER *Etheostoma serrifer*   **M348, p. 323**
Red around 2 black caudal spots. Yellow lateral line, usually 28–38 pores. To 2¾ in. (6.8 cm).

BACKWATER DARTER *Etheostoma zonifer*   **M373, p. 325**
Nearly identical to Slough Darter but has interrupted infraorbital canal, usually with 6 pores (Fig. 53). To 1¾ in. (4.4 cm).

SLOUGH DARTER *Etheostoma gracile*   **M373, p. 324**
Bright green bars on side of male, green squares or mottling on female. Middle red band on 1st dorsal fin (faint on female). To 2¼ in. (6 cm).

SALUDA DARTER *Etheostoma saludae*   **M371, p. 325**
Nearly identical to Carolina Darter but has interorbital pores (Fig. 53), usually 2 anal spines. To 2 in. (5.3 cm).

CAROLINA DARTER *Etheostoma collis*   **M371, p. 325**
Many small dark brown spots on side; brown blotches along side. To 2¼ in. (6 cm).

IOWA DARTER *Etheostoma exile*   **M374, p. 325**
Slender body; long, narrow caudal peduncle. Incomplete lateral line, often arched near front. Alternating blue and brick-red bars on side of large male. To 2¾ in. (7.2 cm).

BROWN DARTER *Etheostoma edwini*   **M354, p. 326**
Incomplete yellow lateral line, arched at front. Bright red spots on body and fins of male (sometimes of female). To 2 in. (5.3 cm).

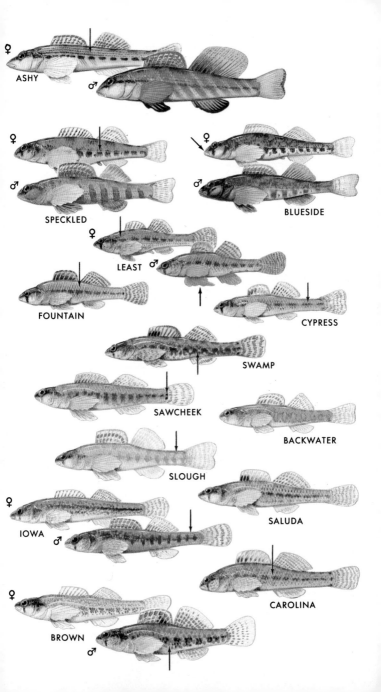

♀
ASHY
♂

♀
SPECKLED
♂

♀
BLUESIDE
♂

♀
LEAST
♂

FOUNTAIN

CYPRESS

SWAMP

SAWCHEEK

BACKWATER

SLOUGH

SALUDA

♀
IOWA
♂

CAROLINA

♀
BROWN
♂

— Fig. 47). Dusky mottling on yellow back; 4 prominent black saddles; white to yellow below; prominent *black border on caudal fin*; black bands and blotches on other fins. 14–17 anal rays. To 7 in. (18 cm).

Range: Upper White R. drainage (excluding Black R. system), MO and AR. Uncommon. **Habitat:** Pools and backwaters of clear small to medium rivers with moderate to high gradients.

Similar species: (1) Brindled Madtom (Pl. 27) *lacks* broad black bar at caudal fin base, prominent saddles; has adipose fin *broadly joined* to caudal fin, rounded caudal fin. (2) Yellowfin Madtom (Pl. 27) *lacks* black blotch on dorsal fin; has more mottled body, more confluent adipose and caudal fins.   **Map 232**

BRINDLED MADTOM *Noturus miurus*   **Pl. 27**
Identification: Robust body, deepest in front of dorsal fin; head rounded above, only slightly flattened. *Black blotch* on outer ⅓ of dorsal fin *extends across first 3–5 rays;* dark saddle under adipose fin extends to fin edge. *Rounded rear edge on caudal fin.* Adipose and caudal fins broadly joined. Usually 5–9 prominent sawlike teeth on rear of pectoral spine (Fig. 47). Light yellow or brown above, dark mottling; 4 vague saddles; white to yellow below; brown or black border on caudal fin; brown or black mottling on other fins. 13–17 anal rays. To 5 in. (13 cm).

Range: Lower Great Lakes drainages, ON and NY, southwest through most of Ohio R. basin and lower Mississippi R. basin (west to e. KS and OK); Mohawk R., NY; Pearl R. and Lake Pontchartrain drainages on central Gulf Slope, MS and LA. Common. **Habitat:** Riffles, pools below riffles, and runs over gravel and sand mixed with sticks and leaves in creeks and small rivers; lakes.

Similar species: (1) Checkered Madtom (Pl. 27) has broad black bar at caudal fin base, adipose fin free from caudal fin, straight rear edge on caudal fin, prominent saddles. (2) Yellowfin Madtom (Pl. 27) *lacks* dark blotch on dorsal fin; has straight rear edge on caudal fin, usually 2 light spots in front of dorsal fin.   **Map 232**

YELLOWFIN MADTOM *Noturus flavipinnis*   **Pl. 27**
Identification: Robust body, deepest in front of dorsal fin; flat head. *Pale edge* on caudal fin; brown saddle usually *encloses 2 light spots in front of dorsal fin;* dark saddle under adipose fin extends to fin edge (in adult). Rear edge of caudal fin straight or with slightly rounded corners. Rear edge of adipose fin free from caudal fin. 4–10 prominent sawlike teeth on rear of pectoral spine (as in Brindled Madtom — Fig. 47). Yellow above, dark mottling and specks; 4 saddles; yellow to white below; yellow fins with dark bands or mottling at middle and near edge. 14–16 anal rays. To 6 in. (15 cm).

Range: Upper Tennessee R. drainage, VA, TN, and GA. Populations extant in Copper Cr. (Clinch R. system), VA, Powell R., TN, and Citico Cr. (Little Tennessee R. system), TN; apparently extirpated from North Fork Holston R., VA, Chickamauga Cr., n. GA, and Hines Cr., e. TN. Uncommon to rare; protected as a *threatened spe-*

cies. **Habitat:** Pools and backwaters around slab rocks, bedrock ledges, and tree roots in clear creeks and small rivers.
Similar species: (1) Brindled and (2) Checkered Madtoms (both, Pl. 27) have black blotch on dorsal fin, *black border* on caudal fin.

Map 232

■ LABYRINTH CATFISHES: Family Clariidae (1)

A large family of catfishes with *long dorsal fin,* usually with no spines and more than 30 rays; a rounded caudal fin, long anal fin base, adipose fin frequently absent, no scales, 4 pairs of barbels, wide gill openings. An unusual feature is the air-breathing ("labyrinth") organ made of modified gill filaments. These filaments are supported by a cartilaginous treelike structure so they do not collapse when exposed to air.

Labyrinth catfishes are native to Africa, Syria, and southwestern Asia (Philippines to Java). About 100 species; one was introduced in the late 1960s into Florida, where it is thriving despite periodic die-offs caused by cold weather.

WALKING CATFISH *Clarias batrachus*   **Not shown**
Identification: Long body, broad in front, narrow in back. *60–75 dorsal rays; 45–58 anal rays.* Dorsal and anal fins not joined to caudal fin. *No adipose fin.* Olive, dark brown, or purple-black above; blue-green on side; white below; white specks on rear side; gray-green fins, some yellow on dorsal fin; red borders on median fins. Albino (white to pink; red eyes) populations rare. To 24 in. (61 cm). Rarely over 14 in. (36 cm) in U.S.
Range: Native to Sri Lanka through e. India to Malay Archipelago. Established in peninsular FL. Collected in MA, GA, NV, and CA. Abundant in s. and cen. FL. **Habitat:** Slow creeks and small rivers, canals, lakes, swamps, and ponds with mud bottom and vegetation.
Remarks: The Walking Catfish walks, including over land on rainy nights, using the tips of its stout pectoral spines as pivots as it shoves itself along by flexing its body.

■ SUCKERMOUTH CATFISHES: Family Loricariidae (4)

Suckermouth catfishes are native to Costa Rica, Panama, and South America and occur in a variety of habitats ranging from marshes to mountain streams to large rivers. Because of their interest to aquarists, many species have been imported into North America; at least 4 species have been introduced into North American waters and are reproducing. The taxonomy of the 450 or so species in this family is relatively primitive, and accurate identification of the 3 introduced *Hypostomus* species is not possible. Suckermouth catfishes are characterized by usually having *bony plates* covering the body; *1 pair of barbels* on subterminal, *papillose, sucking lips; spine* at front of adipose fin (when present). Body shape varies tremendously, but most species are *flattened below.*

SUCKERMOUTH CATFISHES *Hypostomus* species (3)   **Not shown**
Identification: At least 3 morphologically distinct but unidentified species established in U.S. waters. *Large bony plates above;* no or small plates below; no granular edge on snout; stout spine at front of dorsal, pectoral, and pelvic fins. Usually black or brown spots or stripes on olive-brown body and fins. Dorsal fin has usually 1 spine, *7 rays;* no membrane between last dorsal ray and following scute. To 18 in. (46 cm).
Range: Native to Middle and South America from Costa Rica south to Rio de la Plata drainage. 1 species established in Six Mile Cr. near Eureka Springs, Hillsborough Co., FL; 2d species in Indian Spring, Clark Co., NV; 3d species in San Antonio R., Bexar Co., TX. Abundant. **Habitat:** Adult in rocky pools and runs; young near vegetation.
Similar species: See Radiated Ptero.

RADIATED PTERO *Pterygoplichthys multiradiatus*   **Not shown**
Identification: Similar to *Hypostomus* species but has longer dorsal fin with 1 spine, *10–12 rays;* granular edge on snout; last dorsal ray *connected* at base to following bony plate by small membrane. To 27½ in. (70 cm).
Range: Native to Bolivia, Paraguay, Brazil, and Peru. Established in Dade, Broward, and Palm Beach cos., FL. Common. **Habitat:** Weedy, mud-bottomed canals.
Similar species: See Suckermouth Catfishes.

■ TROUT-PERCHES: Family Percopsidae (2)

Trout-perches have a *large unscaled head*, both cycloid and ctenoid scales, subthoracic pelvic fins, 1 large dorsal fin and an *adipose fin*, and *spines* in the dorsal, anal, and pelvic fins.

TROUT-PERCH *Percopsis omiscomaycus*   **Pl. 6**
Identification: Transparent yellow-olive with silver flecks above; *rows of 7–12 dusky spots* along back, upper side, and side. Large head, flattened below; large "pearl organs" (silver-white chambers) on lower jaw and edge of cheek. Fairly deep body, slender caudal peduncle; large eye high on head; large forked caudal fin. Complete lateral line; no or small spines on preopercle. To 7¾ in. (20 cm).
Range: Atlantic and Arctic basins throughout most of Canada from QU to YU and BC, and south to Potomac R. drainage, VA; Yukon R. drainage, YU and AK; Great Lakes and Mississippi R. basins south to WV, e. KY, s. IL, cen. MO, ND, and n. MT. Locally common in lakes; uncommon throughout most of range. **Habitat:** Lakes; deep flowing pools of creeks and small to large rivers; usually over sand.
Similar species: (1) See Sand Roller (Pl. 6).   **Map 233**

SAND ROLLER *Percopsis transmontana* **Pl. 6**
Identification: Similar to Trout-Perch but is *darker blue-green* above; has *more arched back*, incomplete lateral line, few large spines on preopercle. To 3¾ in. (9.6 cm).
Range: Columbia R. drainage, w. ID, s. WA, and n. and w. OR. Uncommon. **Habitat:** Quiet backwaters and pool margins of small to large rivers. Usually near vegetation over sand.
Similar species: See Trout-Perch (Pl. 6). **Map 233**

■ **PIRATE PERCH: Family Aphredoderidae (1)**

The Pirate Perch is the only living member of its family. It has a *large mouth, ctenoid scales* on the head and body, *1 dorsal fin* with both spines and rays, thoracic pelvic fins, and the *anus and urogenital openings between the gill membranes.* The anus and urogenital openings are positioned normally, i.e., just in front of the anal fin, in the juvenile, but migrate forward during development to rest on the throat in the adult.

PIRATE PERCH *Aphredoderus sayanus* **Pl. 6**
Identification: Short, deep body; *large head; large mouth,* lower jaw protruding; square, barely notched, caudal fin. *Gray to black above,* often speckled with black; yellow-white below; black teardrop; black bar on caudal fin base; dusky to black fins. Large individual has *purple sheen.* No or incomplete lateral line. To 5½ in. (14 cm).
Range: Atlantic and Gulf Slopes from Long Island, NY, to Colorado R. drainage, TX; Great Lakes and Mississippi R. basins from MI, WI, and s. MN to Gulf. Isolated population in Lakes Ontario and Erie drainages, NY. Common; primarily restricted to Coastal Plain and other lowland regions. **Habitat:** Swamps, vegetated sloughs, ponds, lakes, backwaters, and quiet pools of creeks and small to large rivers. Usually over mud. **Map 234**

■ **CAVEFISHES: Family Amblyopsidae (6)**

Amblyopsids are small cave-, spring-, and swamp-inhabiting fishes with *no or very tiny pelvic fins, small or rudimentary eyes,* strongly protruding lower jaw, flattened head, tubular anterior nostrils, the anus and urogenital openings located between the gill membranes, small and embedded cycloid scales, 1 dorsal fin, 0–2 spines in the dorsal and anal fins, and sensory papillae in rows on the head, body, and caudal fin. Although cave-adapted fishes in other families occur elsewhere in the world, the 6 members of this family occur only in the unglaciated portion of the eastern United States. The evolutionary transition from surface to spring to cave living is apparent among living amblyopsids, and this fact makes them an especially interesting group.

The numerous and large sensory papillae scattered over the head, body, and caudal fin of cavefishes are sensitive to touch and compensate for their lack of sight.

SWAMPFISH *Chologaster cornuta*   **Pl. 32**
Identification: *Strongly bicolored; dark brown above, white to yellow below. Small eyes. No pelvic fins.* 3 narrow black stripes on side; one on lower side *wide at front, narrow at rear.* 2 black streaks along back before dorsal fin separate to encircle dorsal fin; pink gills visible. Caudal fin clear near base, often black in center; dusky black band in dorsal fin. 0–2 rows of papillae on caudal fin. 9–12 (usually 11) dorsal rays; 9–10 anal rays; 9–11 branched caudal rays. To 2¾ in. (6.8 cm).
Range: Atlantic Coastal Plain from Roanoke R. drainage, VA, to Altamaha R. drainage, GA. Common. **Habitat:** Vegetation and debris in swamps, sloughs, and quiet pools and backwaters of streams.
Similar species: Spring Cavefish (Pl. 32) *lacks* strong bicoloration, wide black stripe on lower side; has 11–16 branched caudal rays.
Map 235

SPRING CAVEFISH *Forbesichthys agassizi*   **Pl. 32**
Identification: *Small eyes. Extremely long, slender* (salamanderlike) *body. No pelvic fins.* Dark brown above; 2 black streaks along back before dorsal fin separate to encircle dorsal fin; 3 thin axial stripes along side; pink gills visible; white to yellow-brown below; black bar at base of dusky black caudal fin; other fins clear. 0–2 rows of papillae on caudal fin. 9–11 dorsal rays; 9–11 anal rays; 11–16 branched caudal rays. To 3¼ in. (8.4 cm).
Range: Cen. and w. KY (west to Tennessee R.) to s.-cen. TN; west across s. IL to se. MO. Common in a few localities; uncommon to rare elsewhere. **Habitat:** Springs and caves (but almost always near surface). Lives underground but emerges above ground in springs.
Similar species: Swampfish (Pl. 32) is bicolored with bold black stripes on side, less slender; has 9–11 branched caudal rays.   **Map 235**

SOUTHERN CAVEFISH *Typhlichthys subterraneus*   **Pl. 32**
Identification: *Pink-white. No eyes* (vestigial eye tissues under skin). *No pelvic fins.* Large, broad head. 0–2 rows of papillae on caudal fin. 7–10 (usually 8–9) dorsal rays; 7–10 anal rays; 10–15 branched caudal rays. To 3½ in. (8.6 cm).
Range: Disjunct. East of Mississippi R. in Cumberland and Interior Low plateaus from extreme s. IN to nw. GA and n. AL (to Coosa R. system); west of Mississippi R. in Ozark Plateau of s. MO and ne. AR. Uncommon. **Habitat:** Subterranean water.
Similar species: See Pl. 32. (1) Northern, (2) Ozark, and (3) Alabama Cavefishes have 4–6 rows of papillae on caudal fin.   **Map 236**

NORTHERN CAVEFISH *Amblyopsis spelaea*   **Pl. 32**
Identification: *Pink-white. No eyes* (vestigial eye tissues under skin). *Extremely small pelvic fins* (rarely absent). Large, broad head. 4–6 rows of papillae on caudal fin. 9–11 dorsal rays; 8–11 (usually 9–10) anal rays; 11–13 branched caudal rays. To 4¼ in. (11 cm).

Range: S.-cen. IN to Mammoth Cave area, cen. KY. Rare. **Habitat:** Subterranean water.
Similar species: (1) See Ozark Cavefish. (2) Southern Cavefish (Pl. 32) *lacks* pelvic fins, has 0–2 rows of papillae on caudal fin. **Map 237**

OZARK CAVEFISH *Amblyopsis rosae* **Not shown**
Identification: Similar to Northern Cavefish but *lacks pelvic fins*, has 7–8 dorsal rays, usually 8 anal rays, 9–11 branched caudal rays. To 2½ in. (6.2 cm).
Range: Springfield Plateau, sw. MO, ne. OK, and nw. AR (Arkansas and upper White R. drainages). Rare; protected as a *threatened species.* **Habitat:** Subterranean water.
Similar species: See Northern Cavefish (Pl. 32). **Map 237**

ALABAMA CAVEFISH *Speoplatyrhinus poulsoni* **Pl. 32**
Identification: *Long flat head constricted* behind snout. *White. No eyes.* No pelvic fins. No branched fin rays; incised fin membranes. 4 rows of papillae on caudal fin. 9–10 dorsal rays; 8–9 anal rays; 21–22 caudal rays (all unbranched). To 2¾ in. (7.2 cm).
Range: Known only from Key Cave, Lauderdale Co., AL (Tennessee R. drainage). Rare; protected as an *endangered species.* **Habitat:** Subterranean water.
Similar species: Other cavefishes (Pl. 32) have *shorter, less flattened head lacking constriction* behind snout; branched fin rays. **Map 237**

■ CODS: Family Gadidae (2)

All members of this family (about 60 species) are marine except for the Burbot, which occurs in the fresh waters of both North America and Eurasia. Another species, the Atlantic Tomcod, is established in a few freshwater lakes.

Important food fishes, cods are recognized by an *elongate body* with small cycloid scales, large head, *long barbel at tip of chin*, spineless fins, and thoracic or jugular pelvic fins.

BURBOT *Lota lota* **Pl. 32**
Identification: Two dorsal fins, *1st short* with 8–16 rays, *2d very long*, with 60–80 rays. Long thin *barbel at tip of chin*. Large, wide head; small eye. Long, slender body, strongly compressed posteriorly. Long anal fin; small pelvic fin located in front of pectoral fin. Scales very small and embedded. Light brown to yellow with dark brown to black mottling on back and side. 2d dorsal and anal fins may have dark edge. To 33 in. (84 cm).
Range: Throughout Canada, AK, and n. U.S. (south to PA, KY, MO, WY, and OR). Also in n. Eurasia. **Habitat:** Deep water, to 300 ft. (90 m), of large rivers and lakes.
Similar species: See Atlantic Tomcod. **Map 238**

ATLANTIC TOMCOD *Microgadus tomcod* **Not shown**
Identification: Similar to Burbot but with *three* dorsal fins of nearly equal length, *two* anal fins, 2d ray of pelvic fin almost *twice* the length of other rays. 1st dorsal fin has 11–15 rays, 2d has 15–19, 3d has 16–21; 1st anal fin has 12–21 rays, 2nd has 16–20. Brown with yellow or green sheen above; black blotches on back, side, and fins; white lateral line; white to yellow below. To 15 in. (38 cm).
Range: Marine species that frequently enters Atlantic drainages from s. Labrador to VA. More common in n. part of range where some populations have become permanent residents of freshwater lakes.
Similar species: See Burbot (Pl. 32).

■RIVULINES: Family Rivulidae (1)

Rivulines are found in southern Florida, the West Indies, Middle America, and South America south to Uruguay. Most species occupy fresh, brackish, or, rarely, coastal marine waters. Over 60 species are recognized; many are popular aquarium fishes.

Rivulines are characterized by having a *killifish body shape;* *tubular nostrils;* opercular and branchiostegal membranes *united* and often covered with scales. Some have *rounded fins.* Males of many species are brilliantly colored. Length is usually less than 4 in. (10 cm).

RIVULUS *Rivulus marmoratus* **Not shown**
Identification: Brown to maroon above and on side; many small *black spots* on side; *cream-colored ring* around *large black spot* on upper half of caudal fin base; dusky to marbled median fins. Large male (males are exceedingly rare in wild FL populations) has orange body and fins, obscure caudal spot. To 2¼ in. (6 cm).
Range: Atlantic and Gulf coasts, s. FL; West Indies. Rare in FL. **Habitat:** Shallow, mud-bottomed ditches, bays, salt marshes, and other brackish-water environments; crab burrows.
Similar species: Topminnows and killifishes *lack* tubular nostrils.

■TOPMINNOWS AND KILLIFISHES: Family Fundulidae (24)

As their name implies, many topminnow species spend most of their time swimming at or near the surface of water. They are one of the easiest groups of fishes to observe without getting in the water yourself or removing the fishes from the water. Several species have bright gold or silver marks on top of the head and body.

Topminnows and killifishes are small, often brightly colored fishes with *flattened head and back, upturned mouth, large eyes,* spineless fins, *1 dorsal fin located far back* on the body, no lateral line, and abdominal pelvic fins. The 40 species in this family are found in fresh, brackish, and salt water of North and Middle America south to Yucatan, and in Bermuda and Cuba.

SEMINOLE KILLIFISH *Fundulus seminolis* **Pl. 28**

Identification: *Metallic green side;* interrupted rows of *many small black spots,* dusky cross-hatching on large male; fewer spots, *15–20 dark green bars* (often faint) on female. Dark green above; white below; clear to dusky orange fins. Breeding male has bright pink to red anal fin, dark brown wavy lines in dorsal and caudal fins, black border on anal and pelvic fins. Long, fairly slender body; dorsal fin origin in front of anal fin origin. 50–55 lateral scales; 16–17 dorsal rays; 13 anal rays. To 6½ in. (16 cm).

Range: Peninsular FL from St. Johns (Atlantic) and New (Gulf) R. drainages south to just below Lake Okeechobee. Common. **Habitat:** Open areas of lakes and quiet stream pools. Young usually in schools near vegetation.

Similar species: (1) Banded (Pl. 28) and (2) Waccamaw Killifishes *lack* rows of small black spots, have more distinct bars on side, more slender caudal peduncle. (3) Banded Topminnow (Pl. 28) *lacks* metallic green side, dark brown wavy lines in fins; is smaller; has red fins on adult, 6–8 dorsal rays, 9–10 anal rays, 28–32 lateral scales. **Map 239**

BANDED KILLIFISH *Fundulus diaphanus* **Pl. 28**

Identification: *10–20 green-brown bars* along silver side; bars more numerous and wider in male. *Long, slender body;* dorsal fin origin in front of anal fin origin. Color variable — see Remarks. Dark olive to tan above, brown stripe along back; white to yellow below; clear to dusky olive-yellow fins. Breeding male has wide green bars along side, yellow throat and fins. 35–50, usually 40–49, lateral scales; 13–15 dorsal rays, 10–12 anal rays. To 5 in. (13 cm).

Range: Atlantic Slope drainages from NF to Peedee R., SC; St. Lawrence–Great Lakes and Mississippi R. basins from QU to MB, and south to s. PA, n. IL, and ne. NE. Common; locally abundant. Enters brackish water. **Habitat:** Shallow, quiet margins of lakes, ponds, and sluggish streams; usually over sand or mud; often near vegetation. Swims in schools a few inches below surface of water.

Remarks: Two subspecies, with intergrades in St. Lawrence and Lake Erie drainages: *F. d. diaphanus*, on Atlantic Slope, lacks brown spots on back and upper side, dark stripe along caudal peduncle; has dusky cross-hatching on back and side, more (usually 45–49 lateral) scales and fin (usually 16–17 pectoral) rays. *F. d. menona*, occupying the rest of species' range, has many brown spots on back and upper side, bars on caudal peduncle partially fused at middle into dark stripe, no cross-hatching, usually 40–44 lateral scales, 14–15 pectoral rays.

Similar species: See Waccamaw Killifish. **Map 240**

WACCAMAW KILLIFISH *Fundulus waccamensis* **Not shown**

Identification: Nearly identical to Banded Killifish but is more slender, has usually 54–64 lateral scales. To 4 in. (10 cm).

Range: Lake Waccamaw, Columbus Co., NC. Common. Recently found in Phelps Lake, Washington Co., NC, where probably introduced through its use as fishing bait. **Habitat:** Over sand in lakes, near and away from shoreline; often near vegetation. Swims a few inches below surface.

Similar species: See Banded Killifish (Pl. 28).   **Map 240**

Next 7 species (studfishes and close relatives) are robust, brightly colored topminnows. Other topminnows differ from these species by having dark bars on side of body, a dark stripe along side of body, or a large black teardrop.

NORTHERN STUDFISH *Fundulus catenatus*   Pl. 28
Identification: Light yellow-brown above, short *gold stripe* in front of dorsal fin; silver-blue side, *rows of small brown* (female and young) or *red-brown spots* (male) on side. Adult has rows of small brown spots on dorsal and caudal fins. Breeding male (color extremely variable geographically) has *bright blue side,* red spots on head and fins; usually yellow paired fins; orange edge, often a submarginal black band on caudal fin. Dorsal fin origin over or slightly in front of anal fin origin. Breeding male has tubercles on side of head, body, and caudal peduncle, and on dorsal, anal, and paired fins. Usually 19 scales around caudal peduncle; 12–17 dorsal rays, 13–18 anal rays, 30–52 (usually 41–50) lateral scales; peglike pharyngeal teeth in adult. To 7 in. (18 cm).
Range: Upper East Fork White R. system, IN; upper Salt and Kentucky R. drainages, KY; upper Green, middle and lower Cumberland, and Tennessee R. drainages, VA, KY, TN, and AL; west of Mississippi R. (primarily Ozark and Ouachita Uplands) in cen. and s. MO, se. KS, e. OK, and s. AR; sw. MS in Mississippi (Coles Cr., Homochitto R., and Buffalo Bayou) and Gulf Slope drainages (Amite R. and Pearl R.). Introduced into Licking R. drainage, KY. Common.
Habitat: Margins, pools, and backwaters of creeks and small to medium rivers; most common in shallow sandy backwaters of clean rocky creeks.
Similar species: See Pl. 28. See (1) Stippled and (2) Southern Studfishes. (3) Barrens Topminnow *lacks* interrupted rows of spots on side, black band on caudal fin; has yellow-orange fins, 9–12 dorsal rays, 10–12 anal rays, usually 36–41 lateral scales.   **Map 241**

STIPPLED STUDFISH *Fundulus bifax*   Pl. 28
Identification: Similar to Northern Studfish but has *short interrupted rows* of red or brown spots on side. No black band on dorsal or caudal fins. 13–14 dorsal rays, 13–15 anal rays, 42–52 lateral scales. To 4¾ in. (12 cm).
Range: Tallapoosa R. system, GA and AL; Sofkahatchee Cr. (lower Coosa R. system), AL. Locally common. **Habitat:** Same as Northern Studfish.
Similar species: (1) See Northern Studfish (Pl. 28). (2) Southern Studfish (Pl. 28) *lacks* rows of brown or red spots on side, often has black edge on caudal fin.   **Map 241**

SOUTHERN STUDFISH *Fundulus stellifer*   Pl. 28
Identification: Similar to Stippled and Northern Studfishes but has few to many brown or red spots *scattered* over side (rarely in irregular rows on upper side); *black edge* on dorsal and caudal fins of some large males (about 60%); usually 21–22 scales around caudal

peduncle, molariform pharyngeal teeth in adult. 12–16 dorsal rays, 13–17 anal rays, 38–53 (usually 41–50) lateral scales. To 4¾ in. (12 cm).

Range: Alabama (except Tallapoosa R. system) and upper Chattahoochee R. drainages, GA, AL, and se. TN. One record for Chickamauga Cr., Tennessee R. drainage, nw. GA. Fairly common. **Habitat:** Same as Northern Studfish.

Similar species: See (1) Stippled and (2) Northern Studfishes (both, Pl. 28).   **Map 241**

BARRENS TOPMINNOW *Fundulus julisia*   **Pl. 28**

Identification: Many *scattered brown* (female and young) or *red-orange spots* (male) on side of head and body; *yellow-orange fins*, yellow eye on large male. Olive above, *iridescent white-gold stripe* along back to dorsal fin; brown-gray side; white below. Breeding male has red-orange spots on iridescent blue-yellow side; small orange spots on yellow anal and paired fins; yellow edge, orange spots on dusky dorsal and caudal fins. Breeding male has tubercles on cheek and opercle. Dorsal fin origin over anal fin origin. 9–12 dorsal rays, 10–12 anal rays, 35–43 lateral scales. To 3¾ in. (9.4 cm).

Range: Upper Caney Fork (Cumberland R. drainage) and upper Duck R. (Tennessee R. drainage) systems, cen. TN. Rare. **Habitat:** Vegetated pools and margins of springs and spring-fed headwaters and creeks.

Remarks: Whiteline Topminnow, *Fundulus albolineatus*, known only from Big Spring, Madison Co., AL (Map 239), and presumed extinct, was nearly identical to the Barrens Topminnow but had interrupted white streaks on rear half of side of large male. Big Spring was impounded, lined with concrete, and stocked with carp and goldfish.

Similar species: Northern Studfish (Pl. 28) has rows of spots on side, black band on caudal fin of large male, usually 12–14 dorsal rays, 13–16 anal rays, 41–50 lateral scales; *lacks* orange spots on yellow fins of large male.   **Map 239**

SPECKLED KILLIFISH *Fundulus rathbuni*   **Pl. 28**

Identification: *Black line* (absent on juvenile) from mouth to bottom of eye. Yellow-brown above and on side, *many dark brown spots* on back and side of juvenile and female; silver cheek, opercle, and throat; white to yellow below; clear to yellow fins. Breeding male is gold-brown with black spots on side of iridescent gold head; has dusky fins, yellow edge on caudal fin. Dorsal fin origin in front of anal fin origin. 10–12 dorsal rays, 10–12 anal rays; 34–40 (usually 35–37) lateral scales. To 3¾ in. (9.6 cm).

Range: Dan (Roanoke), Neuse, Cape Fear, Peedee, and Catawba (Santee) R. drainages, VA and NC. Primarily on Piedmont and upper Coastal Plain. Common but somewhat localized. **Habitat:** Backwaters and pools of creeks and small to medium rivers. Usually over sand or mud.

Similar species: Other topminnows (Pls. 28 & 29) *lack* black line on side of head, yellow-brown to gold head and body.   **Map 241**

PLAINS TOPMINNOW *Fundulus sciadicus* **Pl. 28**

Identification: Bronze flecks and dark cross-hatching on *blue-green back and upper side;* narrow *gold stripe* in front of dorsal fin; silver-blue dashes on side of head; white below; clear to yellow-orange fins. Breeding male has red-orange band on dusky caudal fin, red-orange edges on dorsal and anal fins. Dorsal fin origin behind anal fin origin; deep caudal peduncle. 9–11 dorsal rays, 12–15 anal rays, 33–37 lateral scales. To 2¾ in. (7 cm).

Range: Disjunct distribution: Missouri R. basin from w. IA to e. WY; Missouri R. drainage, cen. MO; and Neosho R. system, sw. MO, se. KS, and ne. OK. Common but somewhat localized. **Habitat:** Springs and their effluents; quiet to flowing pools and backwaters of creeks and small to medium rivers; usually near vegetation.

Similar species: (1) Golden Topminnow (Pl. 28) has dark bars, red spots on body and fins of large male; 7–9 dorsal rays, 9–11 anal rays, 30–34 lateral scales; *lacks* dark cross-hatching on blue-green back and upper side. (2) Northern Studfish (Pl. 28) has rows of small brown or red-brown spots on side, dorsal fin origin above or in front of anal fin origin. **Map 242**

GOLDEN TOPMINNOW *Fundulus chrysotus* **Pl. 28**

Identification: *Gold flecks* on side; usually *8–11 green bars* (often faint) on side of large male. Yellow-green above; white below; clear to yellow fins. Breeding male has *bright red to red-brown spots* on rear half of body and on dorsal, caudal, and anal fins; red caudal fin. Dorsal fin origin behind anal fin origin; large eye. 7–9 dorsal rays; 9–11 anal rays; 30–34 lateral scales. To 3 in. (7.5 cm).

Range: Atlantic and Gulf Coastal Plain from Santee R. drainage, SC, to Trinity R. drainage, TX; Former Mississippi Embayment north to KY and MO. East of Mississippi R. mostly restricted to lower Coastal Plain. Common in FL; localized and uncommon elsewhere. **Habitat:** Swamps, sloughs, vegetated pools, and backwaters of sluggish creeks and small to medium rivers.

Similar species: (1) Banded Topminnow (Pl. 28) *lacks* gold flecks on side; has 12–15 bars along side of male and female, smaller eye, dorsal fin origin in front of anal fin origin. (2) Plains Topminnow (Pl. 28) *lacks* dark bars on side, red spots on body and fins; has dark cross-hatching on blue-green back and upper side, 9–11 dorsal rays, 12–15 anal rays, 33–37 lateral scales. **Map 242**

BANDED TOPMINNOW *Fundulus cingulatus* **Pl. 28**

Identification: Olive above, *rows of small brown to red spots* on side; white to orange below; clear to light *red-orange fins.* Large male has red-orange fins, *12–15 green bars* along side. Dorsal fin origin in front of anal fin origin; moderate eye. 6–8 dorsal rays; 9–10 anal rays; 28–32 lateral scales. To 3 in. (7.8 cm).

Range: Lower Coastal Plain from Satilla R. drainage, e. GA, to lower Mobile Bay drainage, AL; south in FL to Tamiami Canal. Fairly common. **Habitat:** Swamps, sloughs, pools, and backwaters of sluggish creeks and small to medium rivers; usually near vegetation.

Similar species: (1) Golden Topminnow (Pl. 28) has gold flecks on side, dorsal fin origin behind anal fin origin, usually *fewer than 11 dark bars* along side of male, *no* bars on female, larger eye. (2) Lined and (3) Eastern Starhead Topminnows (both, Pl. 29) have large blue-black bar under eye, large gold spots on top of head and at dorsal fin origin; *lack red fins.* **Map 243**

PLAINS KILLIFISH *Fundulus zebrinus* **Pl. 29**

Identification: *12–26 gray-green bars* (fewer, wider bars on male) on silver-white side. Breeding male has *bright orange to red dorsal, anal, and paired fins* (see Remarks). Tan-olive above, white to yellow below; clear to dusky fins, yellow pectoral fins. Deep caudal peduncle; dorsal fin origin in front of anal fin origin. 41–68 lateral scales; 13–16 dorsal rays; 13–14 anal rays. To 4 in. (10 cm).

Range: Native to Mississippi R. and Gulf Slope basins from n.-cen. MO to cen. WY, and south to Colorado R., Brazos R., Galveston Bay, and Rio Grande (primarily Pecos R.) drainages, TX. Mostly on Great Plains. Also present, and thought to be introduced, in upper Missouri R. basin, SD, MT, and WY. Introduced into upper Rio Grande, NM, Colorado R. drainage, UT and AZ, and possibly other western drainages. Common; locally abundant. **Habitat:** Shallow sandy runs, pools, and backwaters of headwaters, creeks, and small to medium rivers. Tolerant of extremely alkaline and saline streams, and often found where few other fishes can survive.

Remarks: Sometimes placed in monotypic genus, *Plancterus.* Two subspecies. *F. z. zebrinus,* in Trinity R., Brazos R., Colorado R., and Rio Grande drainages, TX and NM, has bright red fins on large male, 41–49 lateral scales. *F. z. kansae,* Mississippi R. basin, has yellow-orange fins on large male, 52–68 lateral scales. Plains Killifish bury headfirst in sand and orient themselves so that only their mouths and eyes are visible. Burying may protect killifish from the intense sunlight of the Great Plains (thus avoiding overheating in shallow sandy streams), or it may help them avoid predators, detection by potential prey, or stream desiccation.

Similar species: (1) Banded Killifish (Pl. 28) is more slender (especially caudal peduncle), *lacks* bright orange to red fins, has many brown spots on back and upper side (within range of Plains Killifish); has 35–50, usually 40–49, lateral scales, 10–12 anal rays. (2) Plains Topminnow (Pl. 28) *lacks* bars on side; is smaller; has dorsal fin origin behind anal fin origin, 33–37 lateral scales, 9–11 dorsal rays. **Map 244**

Starhead topminnows: The next five species have a *large blue-black bar* under eye, *6–8 thin brown to red-brown stripes (on female and juvenile) or rows of dots (on male)* along the side of the body, a *large iridescent gold spot* on top of head, and a *small iridescent gold spot* at dorsal fin origin. Olive above; green, red, and blue flecks on silver-yellow side; white below. *Dark green bars* (usually absent on Western Starhead Topminnow) along side of male (faint bars, usually restricted to rear half of side, may be present on female); small red-

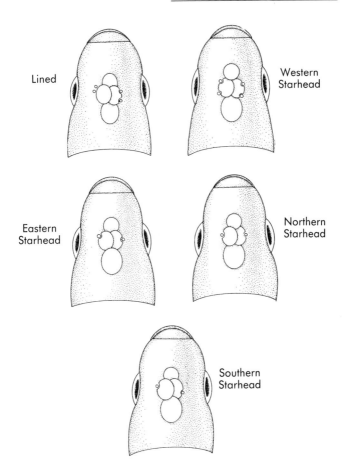

Fig. 49 Starhead Topminnows — scale and supraorbital pattern

brown spots in dorsal, caudal, and anal fin of male. Dorsal fin origin behind anal fin origin; 6–8 dorsal rays; 8–11 anal rays; 30–36 lateral scales.

Starhead topminnows differ from one another primarily in color pattern, arrangement of scales on top of the head, and configuration of supraorbital canal pores (Fig. 49).

To escape predators, these fishes may jump on land, wait there a few minutes, and then jump back into the water.

LINED TOPMINNOW *Fundulus lineolatus* **Pl. 29**
Identification: 11–15 dark green bars on side of male *thickest at middle;* no or few dark dashes and specks between *6–8 black stripes* on side of female. Head red from eye to opercle. Black blotch on pectoral fin base. 16–19, usually 16, scales around caudal peduncle. To 3¼ in. (8.4 cm).
Range: Atlantic and Gulf Coastal Plains from s. VA to Ocklockonee R. drainage, GA and FL; south in FL to Lake Okeechobee. Common.
Habitat: Swamps and other vegetated standing water bodies; quiet pools and backwaters of streams.
Similar species: Other starhead topminnows (Pl. 29) have dark bars along side of male *uniform in width* or *lack* them, have usually 17–20 scales around caudal peduncle. **Map 245**

SOUTHERN STARHEAD TOPMINNOW *Fundulus notti* **Pl. 29**
Identification: 9–15 dark bars of *nearly uniform width* on side of male extending forward to (or near) pectoral fin base and ventrally below lowest dark stripe; many dark dashes and specks between 6–8 dark stripes on side of female. 18–20 scales around caudal peduncle. To 3 in. (7.8 cm).
Range: Gulf Coastal Plain from Mobile Bay drainage, AL, to Lake Pontchartrain drainage, LA. Common. **Habitat:** Swamps, sloughs, and vegetated backwaters and pools of streams.
Similar species: See Pl. 29. (1) See Eastern Starhead Topminnow. (2) Lined Topminnow has bars along side of male *thickest at middle,* usually 16 scales around caudal peduncle. **Map 246**

EASTERN STARHEAD TOPMINNOW *Fundulus escambiae* **Pl. 29**
Identification: Nearly identical to Southern Starhead Topminnow but *lacks* many dark dashes and specks between dark stripes on side of female, has 0–14 dark bars on side of male extending *forward only to between paired fins* and below only as far as lowest dark stripe. To 3 in. (7.8 cm).
Range: Gulf Coastal Plain from Suwannee River drainage, FL, to Perdido R. drainage, AL. Common. **Habitat:** Same as that of the Western Starhead Topminnow.
Similar species: See Southern Starhead Topminnow (Pl. 29). **Map 246**

NORTHERN STARHEAD TOPMINNOW *Fundulus dispar* **Pl. 29**
Identification: *No or few dark dashes and specks* between 6–8 thin dark stripes on side of female; *3–13 dark bars* on side of male, those at front thin and restricted to midside. 16–20, usually 18–20, scales around caudal peduncle. To 3 in. (7.8 cm).
Range: Lake Michigan and Mississippi R. basins from s. MI and WI south to Ouachita R. drainage, AR and LA. Locally common but becoming less so as wetlands are drained. **Habitat:** Vegetated standing water bodies; quiet pools and backwaters of streams.
Similar species: See Pl. 29. (1) Western Starhead Topminnow *lacks* dark bars along side of body of male, has *many dark dashes and*

specks between dark stripes along side of female. (2) Southern Starhead, (3) Eastern Starhead, and (4) Lined Topminnows have *many dark dashes and specks* between dark stripes along side of female.
Map 247

WESTERN STARHEAD TOPMINNOW *Fundulus blairae*   **Pl. 29**
Identification: *No dark bars* (rarely present on large male) on side of body; *many dark dashes and specks* between 7–9 dark stripes on side of female. 16–20, usually 17–18, scales around caudal peduncle. To 3 in. (7.8 cm).
Range: Gulf Slope drainages from Escambia R., AL and FL, to Brazos R., TX; north in Red R. drainage to sw. AR and se. OK. Common west of Mississippi R.; rare east of Mississippi R. **Habitat:** Vegetated sloughs, swamps, and quiet pools and backwaters of streams.
Similar species: See Pl. 29. (1) Northern Starhead Topminnow has *dark bars* along side of body of male, *lacks* dark dashes and specks between dark stripes along side of female. (2) Southern Starhead, (3) Eastern Starhead, and (4) Lined Topminnows have *dark bars* along side of body of male.   **Map 247**

BLACKSTRIPE TOPMINNOW *Fundulus notatus*   **Pl. 29**
Identification: *Wide blue-black stripe* along side, around snout, and onto caudal fin. Olive-tan above, *silver-white spot* on top of head; usually few dusky to dark (rarely black) spots (often absent) on upper side; light blue along upper edge of stripe; yellow fins; dorsal, caudal, and anal fins amber at base and heavily spotted with black; white to light yellow below. Male has crossbars on stripe, larger dorsal and anal fins; is deeper bodied. To 3 in. (7.4 cm).
Range: Lake Erie, Lake Michigan, and Mississippi R. basins from s. ON, MI, WI, and n. IA south to Gulf (west to cen. KS and OK); Gulf Slope drainages from Mobile Bay, AL, to San Antonio Bay, TX. Common in lowlands, rare to absent in upland areas. **Habitat:** Quiet surface water, usually near margins of creeks and small rivers, ponds, and lakes.
Similar species: See (1) Blackspotted and (2) Broadstripe Topminnows (Pl. 29).   **Map 248**

BLACKSPOTTED TOPMINNOW *Fundulus olivaceus*   **Pl. 29**
Identification: Similar to Blackstripe Topminnow but has few to many (male has more) *discrete, intensely black spots* on light tan upper side, slightly longer snout. To 3¾ in. (9.7 cm).
Range: Mississippi R. basin from e. TN, w. KY, s. IL, and cen. MO south to Gulf (west to cen. OK); Gulf Slope drainages from Chattahoochee R., GA, to Galveston Bay, TX. Common, except in Appalachian uplands. **Habitat:** Near surface of quiet to flowing water, usually near margins of clear, sandy to gravelly headwaters, creeks, and small rivers.
Similar species: See (1) Blackstripe and (2) Broadstripe Topminnows (both, Pl. 29).   **Map 245**

BROADSTRIPE TOPMINNOW *Fundulus euryzonus* **Pl. 29**
Identification: Similar to Blackstripe and Blackspotted Topminnows but has *extremely wide, purple-brown stripe* along side, lower edge reaching to middle of pectoral fin base and to within 1 scale row of lower edge of caudal peduncle when viewed from side; *no crossbars* on stripe along side of male; usually 8 dorsal rays (Blackstripe and Blackspotted Topminnows have usually 9 and 10, respectively, within range of Broadstripe Topminnow). Spots on upper side like those of Blackstripe Topminnow. To 3¼ in. (8.3 cm).
Range: Tangipahoa and upper Amite R. systems (Lake Pontchartrain drainage), MS and LA. Uncommon. **Habitat:** Usually at surface near shoreline vegetation in quiet pools and backwaters of creeks and small rivers.
Similar species: See (1) Blackstripe and (2) Blackspotted Topminnows (Pl. 29). **Map 239**

RAINWATER KILLIFISH *Lucania parva* **Pl. 29**
Identification: *Large dark-edged scales* on back and side. Large male has *black spot* at front of dusky orange dorsal fin, thin *black edges* on all but pectoral fins. Deep compressed body; small upturned mouth. Dorsal fin origin in front of anal fin origin; light brown to olive above, dusky stripe along silver side; white below; orange-yellow anal and paired fins. 23–29 lateral scales; 9–13 dorsal rays; 5–6 branchiostegal rays. To 2¾ in. (7 cm).
Range: Marine but enters fresh water from MA to Mexico. Ascends Rio Grande and Pecos R., TX and NM. Introduced in OR, UT, NV, and CA. Common along coast and in St. Johns R., FL. **Habitat:** Vegetated quiet water; usually swims several inches below surface of water.
Similar species: (1) Bluefin Killifish (Pl. 29) has dark stripe along side, blue dorsal and anal fins on male. (2) Pygmy Killifish (Pl. 29) has large black spot on caudal peduncle and dark spot on midside or dark bars along rear half of side, 6–8 dorsal rays, 3 branchiostegal rays.

Map 249

BLUEFIN KILLIFISH *Lucania goodei* **Pl. 29**
Identification: *Wide zigzag black stripe* from tip of snout to *black spot* on caudal fin base. Dorsal and anal fins of large male *bright iridescent blue with black band on base*, thin black edge; caudal fin red-orange. Fairly slender, compressed body; small upturned mouth. Dorsal fin origin in front of anal fin origin. Dusky brown to olive back; light stripe along upper side; dark-edged scales on side; silver-white below. 29–32 lateral scales; 9–12 dorsal rays; 5–6 branchiostegal rays. To 2 in. (5 cm).
Range: Throughout FL, except in panhandle only as far west as Choctawhatchee R. drainage; sporadically along Atlantic Coast as far north as cen. SC (where possibly introduced); se. AL in Chipola R. drainage. Common. **Habitat:** Vegetated sloughs, ponds, lakes; pools and backwaters of streams; often common near springs; usually swims well below surface of water.

Similar species: (1) Rainwater Killifish (Pl. 29) *lacks* dark stripe along side, blue dorsal and anal fins; is deeper bodied. (2) Pygmy Killifish (Pl. 29) *lacks* dark stripe along side, blue dorsal and anal fins; has large black spot on caudal peduncle and dark spot on midside or dark bars along rear half of side; 6–8 dorsal rays, 3 branchiostegal rays.
Map 250

PYGMY KILLIFISH *Leptolucania ommata* **Pl. 29**
Identification: *Cream-yellow halo* around *large black spot* on caudal peduncle. Male has *5–7 faint bars* rear half of side; female has dusky brown stripe along side, *black spot* on midside. Slender body; small upturned mouth; large eye. Dorsal fin origin behind anal fin origin. Dusky green to straw yellow above; dusky stripe through eye and across lower jaw; yellow below. Large male has yellow-orange median and pelvic fins. 26–32 lateral scales; 6–8 dorsal rays; 9–10 anal rays; 3 branchiostegal rays. To 1¼ in. (2.9 cm).
Range: Atlantic and Gulf Slope drainages from Ogeechee R., GA, to Perdido R., AL; south to cen. FL. One record from Escatawpa R. drainage, se. MS. Common; locally abundant. **Habitat:** Surface waters of swamps, vegetated sloughs, and quiet water areas of creeks and small rivers.
Similar species: Least Killifish (Pl. 31) has red around black spot at front of dorsal fin, black spot at front of anal fin of female, gonopodium on male, 6–9 anal rays on female. **Map 251**

■PUPFISHES: Family Cyprinodontidae (13)

Like topminnows and killifishes, pupfishes are small and have *upturned mouths*, 1 dorsal fin, no lateral line, abdominal pelvic fins (if present), and cycloid scales. Unlike topminnows and killifishes, pupfishes are *deep bodied* and most species have a *deep, strongly compressed caudal peduncle.* The top of the head is flattened, but the back usually is *highly arched* (especially on the male). The family contains about 107 species in North America, South America, southern Eurasia, and Africa. Most of our pupfishes inhabit southwestern deserts, and some are among our most endangered fishes.

Pupfishes are able to survive extreme environmental conditions. They have been found to tolerate temperatures from 0°C to 45°C (113°F); salinity as high as 142 ppt (ocean water is typically 33 ppt), and oxygen concentrations as low as 0.13 mg/liter (the lowest known for any fishes restricted to gill breathing).

● *CYPRINODON*

Genus characteristics: Robust body, deep in male, more slender in female; arched back; 1 row of *tricuspid teeth* in each jaw; large scales (22–34 lateral scales); long, coiled intestine. Breeding male becomes brightly colored and develops contact organs on scales and a narrow to broad black edge on caudal fin. Only other freshwater fish in our area with tricuspid teeth is Flagfish.

SHEEPSHEAD MINNOW *Cyprinodon variegatus* **Pl. 30**
Identification: Extremely deep-bodied. *5–8 triangular shaped dark gray-brown bars* along silver-olive side, wide at top, narrow on lower side. Green to blue-gray above; large dark brown blotches on rear half of upper side; white below; clear to light orange fins. Breeding male is blue above and has wide dark gray bars along side (best developed at rear); brass-salmon cheek, breast, and belly; dusky orange fins; black edge on caudal fin. Fully scaled belly. 22–28 lateral scales; 10–12 dorsal rays; 9–11 anal rays; 6–8 pelvic rays; 18–22, usually 19–21, rakers on 1st gill arch. To 3 in. (7.5 cm).
Range: Coastal waters from MA to ne. Mexico. Also in West Indies. Common; locally abundant. Rarely occurring far inland except in peninsular FL. Introduced population in Pecos R., TX, is displacing native Pecos Pupfish. **Habitat:** Salt, brackish, and fresh water; usually near vegetation.
Remarks: Lake-inhabiting individuals of fishes are often more elongate than their counterparts in streams. Although populations of the Sheepshead Minnow in Lake Eustis and other headwater lakes of the Oklawaha R. in central FL have been recognized taxonomically (as the Lake Eustis Minnow, *Cyprinodon hubbsi* or *C. variegatus hubbsi*), most of the differences used to separate this form, mainly a more slender body and caudal peduncle, seem likely to be only developmental responses to the lake habitat.
Similar species: See Pl. 30. (1) Red River and (2) Pecos Pupfishes have unscaled or partly scaled belly and yellow paired fins, head, and belly on large male. (3) Leon Springs and (4) White Sands Pupfishes have many small dark blotches on lower side, yellow on dorsal and caudal fins of male.

RED RIVER PUPFISH *Cyprinodon rubrofluviatilis* **Pl. 30**
Identification: *Unscaled belly; 5–8 large triangular brown blotches* along silver side, *no dark blotches on lower side.* Green-brown above, dusky dorsal and caudal fins; white below. Breeding male has iridescent blue nape; wide black bars on side; yellow paired fins, head, and belly; narrow black edge on caudal fin; clear to white edges on black dorsal and anal fins. 25–29 lateral scales; 9–12 dorsal rays; 8–11 anal rays; usually 6–7 pelvic rays; usually 21–23 rakers on 1st gill arch; no (rarely 1 or 2) mandibular pores. To 2¼ in. (5.8 cm).
Range: Upper Red and Brazos R. drainages, OK and TX. Common. Introduced into Canadian R. and headwaters of Colorado R., TX. **Habitat:** Shallow, sandy pools and runs of headwaters, creeks, and small to medium rivers. Often in extremely shallow and hot (to 100°F [37°C]) water.
Similar species: See Pl. 30. (1) See Pecos Pupfish. (2) Leon Springs and (3) White Sands Pupfishes have *fully scaled belly, many small dark brown blotches* on lower side; yellow on dorsal and caudal fins. (4)

Sheepshead Minnow has *fully scaled belly*, orange fins on male; is deeper-bodied. **Map 252**

PECOS PUPFISH *Cyprinodon pecosensis* **Pl. 30**
Identification: Similar to Red River Pupfish but has *partly unscaled belly*, bars on side of female usually broken into blotches on lower side; has usually 2–3 mandibular pores; has less iridescent blue on nape, clear to pale yellow belly and pectoral fins on large male. To 2¼ in. (6 cm).
Range: Pecos R. system, TX and NM. Common but hybridizing with, and possibly being replaced by, introduced population of Sheepshead Minnow. **Habitat:** Springs, sinkholes, and pools of streams.
Similar species: (1) See Red River Pupfish (Pl. 30). (2) Leon Springs Pupfish (Pl. 30) has *fully scaled belly; many small brown blotches on lower side* of female; yellow in dorsal and caudal fins, wide black edge on caudal fin of male. **Map 252**

LEON SPRINGS PUPFISH *Cyprinodon bovinus* **Pl. 30**
Identification: *Dark brown* (rectangular or triangular) *blotches* along silver side, *many small brown blotches* on lower side of female (rarely on male). *Usually 25 or fewer lateral scales.* Fully scaled belly. Gray-brown above; white below; dusky dorsal and caudal fins; pale yellow bar on caudal fin base. Large male has yellow dorsal fin edge, wide jet black edge on yellow caudal fin. 23–26 lateral scales; 9–11 dorsal rays, 9–12 anal rays; usually 7 pelvic rays; 18–23, usually 19–21, rakers on 1st gill arch; 2 mandibular pores. To 2¼ in. (5.6 cm).
Range: Leon Cr. (Pecos R. system), Pecos Co., TX. Common in extremely small area; protected as an *endangered species*. **Habitat:** Margins of spring-fed marsh pools; most common away from vegetation.
Similar species: Other pupfishes in the Rio Grande drainage have *usually 26 or more lateral scales*. See Pl. 30. (1) See White Sands Pupfish. (2) Pecos Pupfish has mostly unscaled belly; *few dark blotches* on lower side of female; no yellow in dorsal and caudal fins, narrow black bar on caudal fin edge of male. (3) Red River Pupfish has unscaled belly; *no dark blotches on lower side*; yellow pectoral fins, head, and belly, narrow black bar on caudal fin edge, no yellow in dorsal and caudal fins of male. **Map 252**

WHITE SANDS PUPFISH *Cyprinodon tularosa* **Pl. 30**
Identification: Similar to Leon Springs Pupfish but has dark bars on side of female *joined at bottom*, yellow to orange *outer half* of dorsal fin on large male, *26–28 lateral scales*; usually 21–24 rakers on 1st gill arch, 6 pelvic rays; 0–5 mandibular pores. To 2 in. (5 cm).
Range: Tularosa Valley, NM. Abundant in small area. **Habitat:** Clear, shallow spring-fed marsh pools and saline creek.
Similar species: See Leon Springs Pupfish (Pl. 30). **Map 253**

COMANCHE SPRINGS PUPFISH *Cyprinodon elegans* **Pl. 30**
Identification: *Slender body* (relative to other pupfishes); *long slender*

caudal peduncle. Brown-black blotches form *"stripe"* (often faint on male) along silver side; additional blotches on upper and lower side of female. Gray-green above; pale yellow to white below; clear to light orange fins. Large male has *black specks on silver side,* black edge on caudal fin. Usually fully scaled belly. 25–28 lateral scales; 10–12 dorsal rays; 9–11 anal rays; usually 6–7 pelvic rays; 19–22 rakers on 1st gill arch. To 2½ in. (6.2 cm).
Range: Restricted to Toyah Cr. and the effluents (including irrigation canals) of San Solomon, Phantom Cave, and Griffin springs, Reeves Co., TX; formerly also in Comanche Springs, Pecos Co., TX. Common in small area but threatened by removal of water for irrigation for agriculture. Protected as an *endangered species.* **Habitat:** Springs, spring-fed canals, and ditches; usually over mud in current.
Similar species: Other pupfishes (Pl. 30) have less distinct black stripe along side, *lack* pattern of black specks on silver side.   **Map 253**

DESERT PUPFISH *Cyprinodon macularius*   **Pl. 30**
Identification: Breeding male has *light blue body, lemon yellow to orange caudal peduncle and fin,* black edge on median fins. Dark olive above; dark brown blotches or bars along silver side; smaller dark blotches on upper and lower sides; white below. Deep body; dorsal fin origin equidistant between tip of snout and caudal fin base. Usually 25–26 lateral scales, 7 pelvic rays. To 2¾ in. (7.2 cm).
Range: Lower Colorado R. drainage, including Gila R. system and south through s. AZ and CA (including Salton Sea) into n. Mexico. Uncommon; protected as an *endangered species.* **Habitat:** Springs, marshes, lakes, and pools of creeks; usually over mud or sand.
Remarks: Two subspecies: *C. m. eremus,* restricted to Organ Pipe Cactus National Monument, has a larger head and, on the female, a longer dorsal fin base than do populations of *C. m. macularius.*
Similar species: Other pupfishes *lack* yellow to orange caudal peduncle and fin on large male. See Pl. 30. (1) See Owens Pupfish. (2) Amargosa, (3) Salt Creek, and (4) Devils Hole Pupfishes have dorsal fin origin *nearer to caudal fin base than to tip of snout,* small or no pelvic fins.   **Map 254**

OWENS PUPFISH *Cyprinodon radiosus*   **Pl. 30**
Identification: Similar to Desert Pupfish, but breeding male has deep blue body, purple-gray bars along side, *orange edge on blue dorsal and anal fins.* Usually 26–27 lateral scales. To 2¾ in. (7.2 cm).
Range: Owens Valley, s. CA. Formerly common within small range, now restricted to small area near Bishop, CA. Protected as an *endangered species.* **Habitat:** Marshes, vegetated sloughs and backwaters of Owens R.
Similar species: See Desert Pupfish (Pl. 30).   **Map 254**

AMARGOSA PUPFISH *Cyprinodon nevadensis*   **Pl. 30**
Identification: Deep body; *dorsal fin origin nearer to caudal fin base than to tip of snout.* Dark olive above; teardrop-shaped blotches or bars (often faint) on yellow-brown to silver-blue side; smaller dark

blotches on upper and lower side; white below. Breeding male has gray bars on deep blue side, black edges on blue-gray median fins. Small pelvic fins (occasionally absent), usually 6 pelvic rays. Usually 25–26 lateral scales. To 3 in. (7.8 cm).
Range: Amargosa R. basin, NV and CA. **Habitat:** Springs, their effluents, and spring-fed ponds and lakes.
Remarks: Six subspecies, often distinguished from one another by only average differences. *C. n. nevadensis,* restricted to Saratoga Springs and adjoining lakes, Death Valley National Monument, CA, has a deep, broad body, intensely blue breeding male. *C. n. amargosae,* restricted to Amargosa R., CA, has small scales (usually 25 or more scales around body at dorsal fin origin; other subspecies have usually 25 or fewer). *C. n. calidae,* now extinct, occurred in outlets of North and South Tecopa Hot Springs, CA, and had large scales, a wide body, and a short caudal peduncle. *C. n. shoshone,* in the outlet of Shoshone Spring, CA, has a slender body, large scales. *C. n. mionectes* (protected as an *endangered subspecies*), in several large springs in Ash Meadows, NV, has low scale and fin ray counts; a short, deep body; silver-blue side and yellow nape on breeding male. *C. n. pectoralis* (protected as an *endangered subspecies*), in several small springs in hills around Devils Hole, Ash Meadows, NV, has usually 17 pectoral rays (other subspecies have usually 16), bright yellow nape on breeding male.
Similar species: See Pl. 30. (1) Salt Creek Pupfish has more slender body, usually 28–29 lateral scales, usually 24–27 predorsal scales (Amargosa Pupfish has usually 17–19 predorsal scales). (2) Devils Hole Pupfish lacks pelvic fins; has more slender body; yellow-gold dorsal, caudal, and anal fins on large male. (3) Desert and (4) Owens Pupfishes have dorsal fin *equidistant* between tip of snout and caudal fin base, usually 7 pelvic rays, yellow or orange on median fins of large male.   **Map 254**

SALT CREEK PUPFISH *Cyprinodon salinus*   **Pl. 30**
Identification: *Slender body; dorsal fin far back on body,* origin closer to caudal fin base than to tip of snout. *Scales on nape small and crowded;* 22–30, usually 24–27, predorsal scales. Olive-brown above; dark brown bars or blotches (largest at top) along silver-brown (female) to blue (male) side; smaller dark blotches on upper and lower sides; white below. Breeding male has gray bars along silver-turquoise side; gray dorsal fin; black edges on caudal, anal, and paired fins. Small pelvic fins (occasionally absent), usually 6 pelvic rays. Usually 28–29 lateral scales; 4–8, usually 6, preorbital pores. To 3 in. (7.8 cm).
Range: Salt Cr., Death Valley, CA. Extreme population fluctuations in harsh environment, but typically abundant in small natural range. **Habitat:** Vegetated spring-fed pools and marshes. Salt Cr., a spring-fed flowing stream of high salinity during most of the year, dries in summer to a series of marshes.
Remarks: The Cottonball Pupfish, sometimes considered a species (*Cyprinodon milleri*) and sometimes a subspecies (*C. salinus milleri*)

of the Salt Creek Pupfish, occupies Cottonball Marsh, adjacent to Salt Cr. in Death Valley, CA, and differs from the Salt Creek Pupfish by having a shorter and more slender caudal peduncle, more reduced pelvic fins (usually 3–5 pelvic rays); 0–7, usually 0 preorbital pores. **Similar species:** See Pl. 30. (1) Amargosa and (2) Devils Hole Pupfishes have usually 15–19 predorsal scales, 24–26 lateral scales. (3) Desert and (4) Owens Pupfish are *deeper bodied,* have dorsal fin origin equidistant between tip of snout and caudal fin base, usually 17–19 predorsal scales, 27 or fewer lateral scales. **Map 254**

DEVILS HOLE PUPFISH *Cyprinodon diabolis* **Pl. 30**
Identification: A *dwarf species;* rarely more than 1 in. long. *No pelvic fins.* Fairly slender body; large head and eye; dorsal fin *far back* on body, origin closer to caudal fin base than to tip of snout. Dark brown above; many black specks, no dark bars on silver side; white below. Breeding male has blue side, black edges on yellow-gold dorsal, caudal, and anal fins. Usually 24–25 lateral scales. To 1¼ in. (3.4 cm).
Range: Restricted to Devils Hole, Ash Meadows, Nye Co., NV. Rare; population endangered by lowering water table. Protected as an *endangered species.* **Habitat:** Deep limestone pool; entire population feeds and breeds in an area 20 meters square, a limestone ledge along one side of Devils Hole. This is smallest known range of any vertebrate animal.
Similar species: Other pupfishes (Pl. 30) are *larger; have* pelvic fins (rarely absent in Amargosa and Salt Creek Pupfishes), dark bars on side of female, smaller head and eye, deeper body, dorsal fin farther forward. **Map 255**

CONCHOS PUPFISH *Cyprinodon eximius* **Pl. 30**
Identification: *Faint brown blotches* on silver side, *rows of small brown spots* on upper side. Gray-brown above; white below; dusky median fins. Breeding male has *yellow-orange dorsal fin;* dark brown bars along side; *black spots, dashes* on front half, wide black edge on caudal fin. Usually 26–27 lateral scales; 12–18 gill rakers; 6–7 pelvic rays; 0 mandibular pores. To 2 in. (5 cm).
Range: Rio Grande drainage, TX, from Devils R. to mouth of Rio Conchos. Also in Rio Conchos system and endorheic Rio Sauz basin, Mexico. Localized and uncommon in U.S.; common in Mexico. **Habitat:** Sloughs, backwaters, and margins of small to medium rivers (avoids hot springs).
Similar species: Other pupfishes (Pl. 30) *lack* rows of small brown spots on upper side, black spots and dashes on caudal fin. **Map 253**

FLAGFISH *Jordanella floridae* **Pl. 30**
Identification: *Large black spot* on midside; often several smaller spots along side. *Alternating thin black and red-orange lines, gold flecks,* on side. Long dorsal fin, 14–18 rays. Gray-green above; silver white below; clear to dusky red fins. Large male is bright red-orange, has red wavy lines, white spots in dusky black dorsal fin; juveniles and females have white halo around small black spot at rear of dorsal fin. 25–27 lateral scales; 11–13 anal rays. To 2½ in. (6.5 cm).

Range: Peninsular FL north to St. Johns and Ochlockonee R. drainages. Common. **Habitat:** Vegetated sloughs, ponds, lakes, and sluggish streams; enters brackish water.   **Map 256**

■ SPRINGFISHES: Family Goodeidae (4)

Most of the 40 species of goodeids are found on the Mesa Central of Mexico. The Mexican species are live-bearing fishes in which the anterior rays of the anal fin of the male are shortened and slightly separated from the rest of the fin, possibly functioning as a primitive gonopodium. Species in the United States, which (unlike their Mexican relatives) lay eggs, are easily recognized by their *thick bodies, lack of pelvic fins,* absence of lateral line, and presence of dorsal and anal fins *far back* on the body.

Species of *Empetrichthys* feed on both plant and animal material and have a relatively short gut. Species of *Crenichthys* feed more heavily on plant matter and have a long, coiled intestine.

WHITE RIVER SPRINGFISH *Crenichthys baileyi*   **Pl. 30**
Identification: *Row of black spots* (or black stripe) along side; *2d row of black spots* along lower side from midbody to caudal fin. Dark olive above; silver-white below; bright silver cheek and opercle; clear to light olive fins, sometimes with dusky edges. Jaws about equal in length; bicuspid jaw teeth. To 3½ in. (9 cm).
Range: White R. system, NV. Common but threatened by human encroachment and introductions of non-native fishes. Protected as an *endangered species.* **Habitat:** Warm springs and their effluents.
Similar species: See Pl. 30. (1) See Railroad Valley Springfish. (2) Pahrump and (3) Ash Meadows Killifishes have distinctly *mottled side,* lower jaw projecting beyond upper jaw; conical jaw teeth.
Map 255

RAILROAD VALLEY SPRINGFISH *Crenichthys nevadae*   **Pl. 30**
Identification: Similar to White River Springfish but has *1 row of dark spots* along side. To 2¼ in. (6 cm).
Range: Native to springs in Railroad Valley, Nye Co., NV; introduced into spring in sw. Mineral Co., NV. Common in extremely small area; protected as a *threatened species.* **Habitat:** Warm (about 95°F [35°C]) springs.
Similar species: See White River Springfish (Pl. 30).   **Map 255**

PAHRUMP KILLIFISH *Empetrichthys latos*   **Pl. 30**
Identification: *Black mottling,* usually a black streak, on silver side. *Wide mouth,* sides of snout barely converging at front. Green-brown above; white to light yellow below. Breeding male has silver-blue side, orange eye, yellow-orange dorsal, caudal, and anal fins. Lower jaw projects beyond upper jaw. Conical jaw teeth. 29–33, usually 31–32, lateral scales. To 2¼ in. (6 cm).
Range: Native to three springs in Pahrump Valley, Nye Co., NV,

where it was the only native fish. Once common, but removal of water for irrigation eliminated species from native habitats. Species now exists only outside Pahrump Valley, where it was transplanted to prevent its extinction. Protected as an *endangered species*. **Habitat:** Warm (about 77°F [25°C]) springs; usually deep holes.

Remarks: Three subspecies, differing slightly in fin lengths and body proportions, sometimes recognized: *E. l. latos* (only surviving subspecies), *E. l. pahrump*, and *E. l. concavus*. The Ash Meadows Killifish, *Empetrichthys merriami*, formerly in Ash Meadows, NV (Map 255), but now extinct, was similar to Pahrump Killifish but had an *interrupted black stripe* along side, sides of snout *converging* at front to narrow mouth.   **Map 255**

■ LIVEBEARERS: Family Poeciliidae (19)

Male fishes of this family from North and South America have the front rays of anal fin *elongated and modified into an intromittent organ* (gonopodium) to accomplish internal fertilization. Poeciliids occur in both fresh and brackish water. Most of the 150 species are found in the tropics. The Mosquitofish has been introduced into many parts of the world to control mosquitoes; the Guppy and several other species have been introduced outside their native ranges through the aquarium trade.

Livebearers are similar in appearance to killifishes, with the top of the *head flattened*, the mouth strongly upturned, *no lateral line*, 1 dorsal fin, and abdominal pelvic fins. They differ in that the 3d anal fin ray is unbranched (branched in killifishes); the male has the anal fin modified into an intromittent organ; and they give birth to live young (except *Tomeurus gracilis*, which lives in South America).

Some populations consist only of females (see Amazon Molly). In some, but not all, of these populations, the female mates with a male of another species; the sperm stimulates egg development but does not contribute genetic material to the offspring.

SAILFIN MOLLY *Poecilia latipinna*   **Pl. 31**
Identification: Large male has *huge sail-like dorsal fin* with orange edge, black spots on outer half, black wavy lines on lower half. Small head; deep, compressed body; extremely deep caudal peduncle; dorsal fin origin over pelvic fin origin. About *5 rows of dark brown spots*, iridescent yellow flecks on olive side. Olive above; white to yellow below; brown spots on dorsal and caudal fins. Large male has iridescent blue back; orange on lower head and breast; black edge (often absent), orange spots on purple-blue caudal fin. 23–28 lateral scales; 13–16 dorsal rays. To 6 in. (15 cm).
Range: Atlantic and Gulf Coast drainages from Cape Fear drainage, NC, to Veracruz, Mexico. Restricted to coastal areas in most of range; found farther inland in FL, LA, and TX. Introduced into Colorado R. drainage, AZ, and elsewhere in w. U.S. and Canada. Abun-

dant in peninsular FL; less common elsewhere. **Habitat:** Ponds, lakes, sloughs, and quiet, often vegetated, backwaters and pools of streams; in fresh and brackish water.

Similar species: (1) See Amazon (Pl. 31), and (2) Shortfin Mollies.
Map 257

AMAZON MOLLY *Poecilia formosa*   Pl. 31

Identification: Similar to Sailfin Molly but *lacks* males (see Remarks); lacks rows of brown spots on side (may have rows of dusky black spots); has *10–12 dorsal rays.* To 3¾ in. (9.6 cm).

Range: Lower Nueces R. (where possibly introduced) and Rio Grande drainages, extreme s. TX; also in Mexico south to Veracruz. Introduced populations at San Antonio and San Marcos, TX. Common in lower Rio Grande Valley. **Habitat:** Backwaters and quiet pools of streams, sloughs, and ditches, usually over mud; fresh and brackish water.

Remarks: The Amazon Molly is an all-female species thought to have originated as a result of hybridization between Sailfin and Shortfin Mollies, and is intermediate between these two species in its characteristics. Eggs develop in Amazon Mollies following stimulation by sperm from either parental species.

Similar species: (1) See Sailfin Molly (Pl. 31). (2) Shortfin Molly *has males,* rows of orange spots on side, 8–11 dorsal rays.   **Map 257**

SHORTFIN MOLLY *Poecilia mexicana*   Not shown

Identification: Similar to Sailfin Molly, but dorsal fin origin *well behind* pelvic fin origin; large male *lacks* sail-like dorsal fin. Dark olive above; usually 5–6 rows of orange spots on side (see Remarks); white to pale orange below; orange anal and pelvic fins. Large male is dark green (rarely black); has orange edge, many black spots on base of dorsal fin; broad orange band, black edge on blue caudal fin. Usually 25–29 lateral scales, 8–11 dorsal rays. To about 4 in. (10 cm).

Range: Native to Atlantic Slope from Rio San Juan, Mexico, to Guatemala. Established in a drainage canal south of Mecca, Riverside Co., CA; Bruneau Hot Springs, Owyhee Co., ID; and in springs and the Moapa R., Clark and Lincoln cos., NV. Common at some localities. **Habitat:** Warm springs and their effluents, canals, weedy ditches, and stream pools.

Remarks: Two subspecies. *P. m. limantouri,* from Rio San Juan, Nuevo Leon, to Rio Tamesi-Panuco region, Tamaulipas, has a more slender body, slightly convex predorsal profile, short dorsal fin on male; cross-hatching on side. *P. m. mexicana,* from Rio Soto la Marina, Tamaulipas, to at least Rio San Carlos, Veracruz (southern end of range unknown), has a deeper body, straight predorsal profile, stripes on side; dorsal fin extends to caudal fin base on adult male. Intergrades occur in Rio Tamesi-Panuco basin.

Similar species: (1) See Sailfin Molly (Pl. 31). (2) Amazon Molly (Pl. 31) *lacks males,* lacks rows of orange spots on side; has 10–12 dorsal rays.

GUPPY *Poecilia reticulata* **Not shown**
Identification: Similar to Mosquitofish but *lacks* black teardrop, has usually *12 or more* dorsal rays; large male usually has *black spot(s)* on lower side. Gray body; lightly outlined scales. Large male has red or blue in fins, sometimes on body. To 2 in. (5.1 cm); males usually less than 1 in. (2.5 cm).
Range: Native to the West Indies and n. South America from w. Venezuela to Guyana. Established in AB, AZ, ID, NV, TX, and WY, and possibly CA. Generally uncommon. **Habitat:** Warm springs and their effluents, weedy ditches, and canals.
Similar species: See Mosquitofish (Pl. 31).

GREEN SWORDTAIL *Xiphophorus helleri* **Not shown**
Identification: Lower caudal fin rays elongated into a *black-edged "sword"* on large male. Green above; dark-edged scales on back and side; yellow below. Large male is usually red below; has *black stripe along side*, yellow-orange to red "sword"; *scythe-shaped claw* at tip of ray 5a (as large as ray 3 hook) on gonopodium; usually small, blunt serrae at tip of ray 4p. Usually 26–27 lateral scales, *12–14* dorsal rays; 1 row of jaw teeth. To 5 in. (13 cm).
Range: Native from Rio Nantla, Veracruz, Mexico, to nw. Honduras. Established in canals near Tampa, Hillsborough Co., FL; Warm Springs Cr., Clark Co., ID; Trudeau and Beaverhead Rock ponds, Madison Co., MT; Kelly Warm Spring, Teton Co., WY; and (as hybrid with Southern Platyfish) Indian Spring, Clark Co., NV. Abundant at some localities. **Habitat:** Warm springs and their effluents, weedy canals, and ponds.
Similar species: (1) Variable and (2) Southern Platyfishes *lack* "sword" tail on large male, have usually 9–12 dorsal rays.

VARIABLE PLATYFISH *Xiphophorus variatus* **Not shown**
Identification: Olive; *black spots or marbling* on side of caudal peduncle; often a green edge on caudal fin. Large male has dusky or black blotches on dorsal fin. No claw at tip of ray 5a; well-developed serrae at tip of ray 4p. Usually *24–25* lateral scales, *10–12* dorsal rays; 2 rows of jaw teeth. To 2¾ in. (7 cm).
Range: Native to Atlantic Slope of Mexico from s. Tamaulipas to n. Veracruz. Established in canals along e. shore of Tampa Bay, Hillsborough Co., FL; in Gainesville, Alachua Co., FL; and in springs in Beaverhead, Granite, and Madison cos., MT. Uncommon. **Habitat:** Warm springs; weedy canals and ditches.
Similar species: See Southern Platyfish.

SOUTHERN PLATYFISH *Xiphophorus maculatus* **Not shown**
Identification: Similar to Variable Platyfish but has usually *23–24 lateral scales, 9–10 dorsal rays.* Extremely variable in color: olive, yellow, orange, red, black, or combinations of those colors on body and fins. To 2¼ in. (6 cm).
Range: Native to Atlantic Slope from Ciudad Veracruz, Mexico, to n. Belize. Established in Alachua, Hillsborough, and Brevard cos., FL;

Beaverhead Rock Pond, Madison Co., WY. Uncommon. **Habitat:** Warm springs and their effluents; weedy canals. **Similar species:** See Variable Platyfish.

● *GAMBUSIA*

Genus characteristics: Upper 4–6 pectoral fin rays of male distinctly *thickened* and usually *curved upward* to form a bow or notch. Dark scale outlines (usually darkest on upper side) produce a cross-hatched appearance; white to light yellow below. Deep caudal peduncle; small dorsal fin, origin behind anal fin origin. Females much larger than males; large females usually pregnant and potbellied. Well-developed spines on 3d ray of gonopodium (Fig. 50). A dark spot (anal spot), thought to provide a target at which males can aim their gonopodia during copulation, is present near the urogenital opening on females of some species of *Gambusia*. The intensity of the spot varies with the female's reproductive condition. The eight freshwater species of *Gambusia* in North America north of Mexico are similar in appearance; however, only the Mosquitofish occurs outside Texas and New Mexico.

The San Marcos Gambusia, *Gambusia georgei*, (Pl. 31), known only from San Marcos Spring and River, TX (Map 260), and thought to be extinct, had *dark edges* on dorsal and caudal fins, distinctly cross-hatched side, *5–6 segments* fused in elbow on ray 4a of gonopodium (Fig. 50), and was the only *Gambusia* species with *lemon yellow median fins*.

MOSQUITOFISH *Gambusia affinis*   **Pl. 31**
Identification: *Large dusky to black teardrop* (often reduced). 1–3 rows of *black spots* on dorsal and caudal fins. No discrete dark spots or stripes on side (black specks may be present, and *black-blotched individuals* are common in FL). Light olive-gray to yellow-brown above, dark stripe along back to dorsal fin; yellow and blue iridescence on transparent silver-gray side. Black anal spot on pregnant female. 6–7 dorsal rays. Gonopodium has elbow on ray 4a composed of 2 or more segments; 8–11 short spines on ray 3 (Fig. 50). To 2½ in. (6.5 cm).
Range: Atlantic and Gulf Slope drainages from s. NJ to Mexico; Mississippi R. basin from cen. IN and IL south to Gulf. Widely transplanted elsewhere, including many western U.S. drainages. Common; locally abundant. **Habitat:** Standing to slow-flowing water; most common in vegetated ponds and lakes, backwaters and quiet pools of streams. Frequents brackish water.
Remarks: Two subspecies: *G. a. holbrooki*, in the Atlantic and Gulf Slope drainages as far west as s. AL, has usually 7 dorsal rays and a gonopodium with a series of prominent teeth on ray 3. *G. a. affinis*, throughout rest of range, has usually 6 dorsal rays and lacks prominent teeth on gonopodial ray 3. Intergrades occupy Mobile Bay basin. Introductions of this species, often for mosquito control, have caused or contributed to the elimination of many populations of fishes with

Mosquitofish

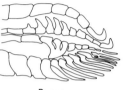

Pecos

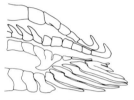

Blotched

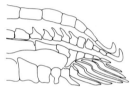

Big Bend

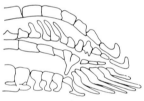

Amistad

Largespring

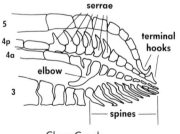

Clear Creek

San Marcos

Fig. 50 *Gambusia* species — gonopodium

similar ecological requirements. Introductions into western drainages have been especially deleterious to the survival of certain rare fishes.

Similar species: See Pl. 31. (1) Pecos Gambusia is deeper bodied; has dark edges on median fins, usually 8 dorsal rays; lacks row of black spots on middle of caudal fin. (2) Blotched, (3) Big Bend, and (4) Amistad Gambusia have black spots and crescents on side, dark stripe along side. (5) Largespring Gambusia has many black spots on side; *lacks* black to dusky teardrop, black anal spot on female. (6) Clear Creek Gambusia has distinct notch in pectoral fin of male, no dark stripe along back, *no* row of black spots on caudal fin, is deeper bodied. (7) San Marcos Gambusia has lemon yellow fins, *no* row of black spots on middle of caudal fin.   **Map 258**

PECOS GAMBUSIA *Gambusia nobilis*   **Pl. 31**

Identification: *Black scale outlines* on back and upper ⅔ of side. *Dusky edges* on dorsal and caudal fins, anal fin of female. Deep bodied. Olive above, dark stripe along back to dorsal fin; iridescent blue and yellow on silver side; large black teardrop. Black anal spot on female. Often a few dusky spots on middle of caudal fin. Usually 8 dorsal rays. Gonopodium has large elbow of 2–4 (usually 3) segments on ray 4a (Fig. 50). To 2 in. (4.8 cm).

Range: Pecos R. system, NM and TX. Uncommon and localized; protected as an *endangered species.* **Habitat:** Vegetated springs and effluents.

Similar species: See Pl. 31. (1) Blotched, (2) Big Bend, and (3) Amistad Gambusia have black spots and crescents on side, dark stripe along side. (4) Largespring Gambusia has row of discrete black spots on caudal fin. (5) Clear Creek Gambusia has distinct notch in pectoral fin, no dark stripe along back. (6) San Marcos Gambusia has lemon yellow fins. (7) Mosquitofish is more slender; *lacks* black edges on median fins; has less distinct scale outlines, usually 6–7 dorsal rays.
                Map 259

BLOTCHED GAMBUSIA *Gambusia senilis*   **Pl. 31**

Identification: *Dusky stripe* (about 1 scale deep) along side, dark scale outlines (often appearing as black crescents) and *black spots* (often poorly developed on male) on lower side. Usually a large black teardrop. Dusky olive above, dark stripe along back to dorsal fin; silver side; light yellow median fins, small dusky spots near base of dorsal fin. No dark anal spot; no spots on caudal fin. Individuals in some populations have scattered large, black spots on body. Usually 8 dorsal rays. Gonopodium has ray 4a much shorter than 4p; elbow on ray 4a of 2–4 segments (Fig. 50). To 2¼ in. (5.5 cm).

Range: Devils R. (Rio Grande drainage), TX. Extinct in U.S. Common in Rio Conchos drainage, Mexico. **Habitat:** Springs; vegetated quiet pools and backwaters.

Similar species: See Pl. 31. (1) Big Bend and (2) Amistad Gambusia *lack* prominent black marks on lower side; have dark anal spot on female.   **Map 260**

BIG BEND GAMBUSIA *Gambusia gaigei* **Pl. 31**
Identification: *Prominent black spots, crescents* on upper side (absent on belly), *dark stripe* along side. Dusky teardrop; dusky edge on dorsal fin. Golden olive above, dark stripe along back to dorsal fin; faint orange stripes on side. Dark anal spot on female; row of dusky spots on lower third of dorsal fin; dark specks on outer third of anal fin of female. Large male has orange snout; black edge, basal row of black spots on red-orange dorsal fin; dusky edge, orange base on caudal fin. Usually 8 dorsal rays; 6–15 teeth in anterior row on each jaw. Gonopodium has elbow of 1–2 segments on ray 4a; ray 4a much shorter than 4p (Fig. 50). To 2¼ in. (5.4 cm).
Range: Formerly Boquillas and Graham Ranch springs, Brewster Co., TX; now restricted to an artificial spring-fed pond in Big Bend National Park, TX. Protected as an *endangered species.* **Habitat:** Vegetated, spring-fed sloughs and ponds.
Remarks: The Amistad Gambusia, *Gambusia amistadensis* (Pl. 31), formerly in Goodenough Spring (Rio Grande drainage), TX (Map 260), but eliminated by the U.S. Boundary Commission during construction of Amistad Reservoir, was similar to Big Bend Gambusia but was *more slender;* had a *more terminal mouth* and longer serrae on ray 4p of gonopodium (Fig. 50).
Similar species: See Pl. 31. (1) Blotched Gambusia has black spots and crescents *on lower side;* lacks dark anal spot. (2) Other *Gambusia* species *lack* black spots and crescents, dark stripe on side. **Map 260**

LARGESPRING GAMBUSIA *Gambusia geiseri* **Pl. 31**
Identification: *Distinct row of black spots* on middle of dorsal and caudal fins (indistinct on juvenile); often additional faint rows. Dark scale outlines (some appearing as crescents) produce cross-hatching, scattered *black spots* on side. Olive above, dark stripe along back to dorsal fin; iridescent blue and yellow on silver side. No teardrop, no black anal spot. Gray edge, row of dusky spots on middle of anal fin of female. Usually 7 dorsal rays. Gonopodium has hook on ray 3, angular terminal hooks on rays 4p and 5 (Fig. 50). To 1¾ in. (4.4 cm).
Range: San Marcos and Guadalupe R. systems, TX. Introduced into Colorado and Rio Grande (including Pecos R.) drainages, TX. Highly localized and uncommon. **Habitat:** Large springs.
Similar species: See Pl. 31. (1) Mosquitofish and (2) Pecos Gambusia *lack* black spots on side; have black teardrop, black anal spot on female. (3) Other *Gambusia* species *lack* row of discrete black spots on caudal fin. **Map 260**

CLEAR CREEK GAMBUSIA *Gambusia heterochir* **Pl. 31**
Identification: *Deep notch* at top of pectoral fin of male. *No dark stripe* along back. Deep bodied. Dark anal spot on female. Dusky teardrop. Olive above; iridescent blue and yellow on silver side. Dusky to clear fins; row of faint spots on middle of dorsal fin. Usually 7–8 dorsal rays. Gonopodium has long elbow on ray 4a (Fig. 50). To 2¼ in. (5.4 cm).
Range: Headwater springs of Clear Creek (San Saba R. system), Menard Co., TX. Rare; headwater springs of Clear Cr. are now im-

pounded, and Clear Creek Gambusia is threatened with extinction. Recognized as an *endangered species*. **Habitat:** Vegetated springs. **Similar species:** Other species of *Gambusia* (Pl. 31) *lack* deep notch in pectoral fin; have *dark or dusky stripe* along back, shorter elbow on gonopodium (Fig. 50).   **Map 260**

PIKE KILLIFISH *Belonesox belizanus*   Not shown
Identification: *Giant* of the livebearer family; females reach about 6 in. (15 cm), males about 4½ in. (11 cm). Long jaws form *pointed beak; large teeth*. Dorsal fin origin well *behind* anal fin origin. Dark olive above fading to white below; *several rows of black spots on side; black spot* at base of caudal fin. Small (usually 52–63 lateral) scales; usually 8–9 dorsal rays.
Range: Native from Laguna San Julian, ne. of Ciudad Veracruz, Mexico, to Costa Rica. Established in canals in s. Dade and Monroe cos., FL. Common. **Habitat:** Weedy canals; tolerates poorly oxygenated waters and salinity to 40 ppt.
Remarks: Two subspecies: *B. b. maxillosus*, from the Yucatan Peninsula, has a robust body and jaws; *B. b. belizanus*, occupying the remainder of the range, is more slender and has smaller jaws. FL population is *B. b. maxillosus*.

LEAST KILLIFISH *Heterandria formosa*   Pl. 31
Identification: *Red around black spot* on front of dorsal fin. *Black spot* at front of anal fin of female. Olive above; black to dusky stripe, series of *black bars* along side; *black spot* on caudal fin base; silver white to light yellow below. Deep, chubby body; large eye. Long gonopodium, more than ⅓ standard length. 24–30 lateral scales; 6–9 anal rays (in female). To 1½ in. (3.6 cm).
Range: Lower Coastal Plain from Cape Fear R. drainage, NC, to s. LA. Common; abundant throughout peninsular FL. **Habitat:** Heavily vegetated standing to slow-flowing fresh and brackish water.
Similar species: Pygmy Killifish (Pl. 29) *lacks* black spots at front of dorsal and anal fins, gonopodium; has large black spot on side of female, 9–10 anal rays.   **Map 261**

GILA TOPMINNOW *Poeciliopsis occidentalis*   Pl. 31
Identification: *Extremely long gonopodium*, more than ⅓ body length. *Dark to dusky stripe* along side; small black spot at rear of dorsal fin. Light olive-tan above; large, darkly outlined scales on back and upper side, black specks (often absent) on lower side; white to yellow below. Large male is *black*; has orange at base of gonopodium, sometimes at base of dorsal and caudal fins. Slender body; small eye. To 2¼ in. (6 cm).
Range: Gila R. system, NM and AZ, and streams south into w. Mexico. Once considered the most abundant "low desert" fish in U.S. (still common in Mexico); now extirpated in NM, rare in AZ. Protected as an *endangered species*. **Habitat:** Vegetated springs and margins, pools and backwaters of creeks and small to medium rivers. Usually found in shallow, warm water.
Remarks: Two subspecies in U.S. *P. o. occidentalis*, in the Gila R. ba-

sin, has a short snout, nearly terminal mouth, dark stripe along side extending forward to opercle. *P. o. sonoriensis*, in the Rio Yaqui system, has longer snout (longer than diameter of eye), more upturned mouth, dark stripe usually extending forward only to above pelvic fin.

Similar species: (1) See Porthole Livebearer. (2) Species of *Gambusia* (Pl. 31) are deeper bodied; have larger eye, gonopodium usually much *less* than ⅓ body length, often a black anal spot on female, upper pectoral fin rays of male thickened and curved upward; black males (usually blotched rather than black overall) occur only in Mosquitofish. **Map 259**

PORTHOLE LIVEBEARER *Poeciliopsis gracilis* **Not shown**
Identification: Similar to Gila Topminnow but has 3–6 black spots along side (no dark to dusky stripe). To 2 in. (5.1 cm).
Range: Native from s. Mexico to Honduras on Atlantic and Pacific slopes. Established south of Mecca, Riverside Co., CA. Common.
Habitat: Irrigation canals.
Similar species: See Gila Topminnow (Pl. 31).

■ SILVERSIDES: Family Atherinidae (3)

Small, silvery, translucent, strongly compressed fishes with scales on the head, large eyes, terminal mouth, *long snout, no lateral line*, long sickle-shaped anal fin, abdominal pelvic fins, and *2 widely separated dorsal fins, the 1st small* and with spines.

Atherinids swim, often in large schools, near the surface of the water and correspondingly have the top of the head flattened, an upturned mouth, and pectoral fins located high on the body. They often leave the water and glide through the air for short distances when spawning or disturbed. The family is worldwide in distribution; most of the species are marine. Of the 160 species, only 3 occur in the fresh waters of North America.

BROOK SILVERSIDE *Labidesthes sicculus* **Pl. 32**
Identification: *Long beak-like snout*, length about 1½ times eye diameter. *2 widely separated dorsal fins*, the 1st *small* and with spines. 1st dorsal fin origin *above* anal fin origin. Long sickle-shaped anal fin. Pale green above, scales faintly outlined; bright silver stripe along side. In se. U.S., breeding male has red snout, bright yellow-green body. Usually 74–87 lateral scales, 22–25 anal rays. To 5 in. (13 cm).
Range: St. Lawrence–Great Lakes (except Lake Superior) and Mississippi R. basins from s. QU to e. MN and south to LA; Atlantic and Gulf slopes from Santee R. drainage, SC, to Galveston Bay drainage, TX. Introduced elsewhere, usually into impoundments as forage for sport fishes. Common; locally abundant. **Habitat:** Near surface of lakes, ponds, and quiet pools of creeks and small to large rivers. Usually in open water.

Remarks: Two subspecies, *L. s. vanhyningi* in se. U.S. and *L. s. sicculus* elsewhere, are probably recognizable but in need of study.
Similar species: (1) Inland (Pl. 32) and (2) Waccamaw Silversides *lack* beaklike snout (have length equal to or less than diameter of eye); have 1st dorsal fin origin *in front of* anal fin origin, 36–46 lateral scales, 14–21 anal rays.   **Map 262**

INLAND SILVERSIDE *Menidia beryllina*   **Pl. 32**
Identification: *2 widely separated dorsal fins,* the 1st *small* and with spines. 1st dorsal fin origin *in front of* anal fin origin. Long snout, length about equal to eye diameter. Long sickle-shaped anal fin. Pale yellow-green above, scales faintly outlined; bright silver stripe along side. 36–44 lateral scales, usually 16–18 anal rays. To 6 in. (15 cm).
Range: Atlantic and Gulf slopes (mostly near coast) from MA to Rio Grande drainage, TX and se. NM; north in Mississippi R. and major tributaries (mainly Arkansas and Red rivers) to s. IL and e. OK. Also in Mexico. Common. **Habitat:** A marine species that ascends rivers. In fresh water, usually found at surface of clear, quiet water over sand or gravel. Some landlocked populations, many of which have been established in impoundments as forage for sport fishes, reproduce in fresh water.
Similar species: (1) See Waccamaw Silverside. (2) Brook Silverside (Pl. 32) has long beaklike snout, 1st dorsal fin origin *over* anal fin origin, usually 74–87 lateral scales, 22–25 anal rays.   **Map 263**

WACCAMAW SILVERSIDE *Menidia extensa*   **Not shown**
Identification: Similar to Inland Silverside but with *much more slender body* (depth about 1½ times width), *darkly outlined* scales on back, usually 44–50 lateral scales, 19–20 (often 18) anal rays. To 3 in. (8 cm).
Range: Lake Waccamaw, NC. Common; usually in large schools. Protected as a *threatened species* because of extremely small range. **Habitat:** Near surface in open water.
Similar species: See Inland Silverside (Pl. 32).   **Map 263**

■ STICKLEBACKS: Family Gasterosteidae (4)

Sticklebacks are highly distinctive, small, *scaleless* fishes with *3–16 isolated dorsal spines* along the back, followed by a normal dorsal fin with 14–16 rays, and an *extremely narrow caudal peduncle.* The thoracic or subthoracic pelvic fin is small, with 1 spine and 1–2 rays. Some populations have *large bony plates* along the side. Presently recognized in the family are only 7 species, but numerous taxonomic problems remain (see Threespine Stickleback). Sticklebacks inhabit both marine and fresh waters of North America and Eurasia.

   Sticklebacks are well known for their complex mating behavior and nest-building activities. The male builds an oblong nest of plant material held together with a sticky kidney secretion and with an opening on one side. Through complex courting maneuvers of the male, the female is enticed to enter the nest and deposit eggs. She then leaves the nest, and the male enters and fertilizes the eggs. The male remains to guard the eggs and young.

NINESPINE STICKLEBACK *Pungitius pungitius* **Pl. 32**

Identification: 7–12, *usually 9, short dorsal spines* angled alternately to left and right. *Slender, compressed body;* usually a well-developed *keel* on caudal peduncle. No large bony plates on side (except in some Atlantic Coast populations); 0–8 small plates on lateral-line pores on front half of body. Gill membranes joined to one another but free from isthmus. Pelvic fin with 1 spine and 1 ray. Gray to olive above, dark mottling on back and side; silver below. Breeding male may develop black belly and white pelvic fins, sometimes red on head. To 3½ in. (9 cm).

Range: Arctic and Atlantic drainages across Canada and AK, and as far south as NJ; Pacific Coast of AK; Great Lakes basin. Also in Eurasia. Common. **Habitat:** Usually in shallow vegetated areas of lakes, ponds, and pools of sluggish streams; sometimes in open water over sand. Marine populations live near shore and move into fresh water to spawn.

Remarks: Two North American forms recognizable but not described as subspecies. Coastal form, ranging from AK to NJ, has more lateral plates and dorsal spines, fewer gill rakers than does the inland form. **Similar species:** Other North American sticklebacks (Pl. 32) have *fewer* than 6 dorsal spines, are *deeper bodied.* **Map 264**

BROOK STICKLEBACK *Culaea inconstans* **Pl. 32**

Identification: *4–6 short dorsal spines. Deep, compressed body;* no large bony plates on side (small plates on lateral-line pores). No keel on *short caudal peduncle.* Gill membranes joined to one another but free of isthmus. Pelvic fin (absent in AB and SA) with 1 spine and 1 ray. Olive above with pale green flecks, dark green mottling; often a pale stripe along side; silver-white to light green below. Breeding male is dark green to black, sometimes with red on pelvic fins. To 3½ in. (8.7 cm).

Range: Atlantic and Arctic drainages from NS to NT; Great Lakes-Mississippi R. basins south to s. OH and NB, and west to MT and e. BC. Isolated population in Canadian R. system, ne. NM. Introduced elsewhere. Common; abundant in cen. part of range. **Habitat:** Vegetated lakes and ponds; vegetated, usually mud-bottomed, quiet to flowing pools and backwaters of headwaters, creeks, and small rivers; usually over sand or mud. Rarely in brackish water.

Similar species: (1) Fourspine Stickleback (Atlantic Guide Pl. 20) usually has 1st and 2d dorsal spines *longer* than 3d and 4th; *long,* slender caudal peduncle. (2) Threespine Stickleback (Pl. 32) has usually *3 dorsal spines,* gill membranes broadly united to isthmus, keel on caudal peduncle. **Map 265**

FOURSPINE STICKLEBACK *Apeltes quadracus* **Not shown**

Identification: *4* (range is *3–5) dorsal spines,* of *various lengths* and angled alternately right and left; 1st and 2d *longer* than 3d and 4th; a

wide gap before last spine. No bony plates on side. No keel on *long, slender caudal peduncle.* Gill membranes broadly united to isthmus. Pelvic fin with 1 spine and 2 rays. Olive-brown above, dark brown mottling on side; silver-white below. Large male is black; breeding male has red pelvic fin. To 2½ in. (6.4 cm).
Range: Atlantic Slope from Gulf of St. Lawrence to Trent R. system, NC. Mostly a nearshore marine species, but far inland populations occur in lakes in NS, and in Hudson, Delaware, and Susquehanna R. drainages. Common. **Habitat:** Vegetated, quiet water areas.
Similar species: Threespine Stickleback (Pl. 32) has *3 dorsal spines, short caudal peduncle.*   **Map 266**

THREESPINE STICKLEBACK *Gasterosteus aculeatus*   **Pl. 32**
Identification: *3* (rarely 2 or 4) *dorsal spines, last very short.* 0–30 bony plates on side (fewer in freshwater populations). *Bony keel* along side of caudal peduncle. Gill membranes broadly united to isthmus. Pelvic fin with 1 spine and *1 ray;* spine with *1 cusp* at base. Silver-green to brown above; silver side, often with dark mottling. Large male is black, often with red on fins; breeding male has blue side, bright red belly and lower side, bright blue eye. Large female has pink throat and belly. To 4 in. (10 cm).
Range: Marine and fresh water. Arctic and Atlantic drainages from Baffin Island and w. side of Hudson Bay to Chesapeake Bay, VA; Pacific drainages from AK to Baja California. Eastern freshwater populations found far inland, including Lake Ontario. Also in Europe, Iceland, Greenland, and Pacific Coast of Asia. Common; locally abundant. **Habitat:** Shallow vegetated areas, usually over mud or sand.
Remarks: "Threespine Stickleback" may refer to more than 1 species. Although hybridization occurs when the fully plated marine (anadromous) form and the partially plated freshwater form come together, the zone of hybridization is usually very narrow and suggests reproductive isolation. Subspecies have been proposed (*G. a. williamsoni* is s. CA plateless form protected as an *endangered subspecies*) but ranges are poorly demarcated.
Similar species: Other sticklebacks (Pl. 32) have 4 or more dorsal spines.   **Map 267**

■ SCULPINS: Family Cottidae (27)

Most of the more than 300 species of sculpins are marine, but several inhabit the fresh waters of North America and northern Eurasia. Sculpins have a *suborbital stay* (a bony connection under the cheek that connects bones under the eye with the front of the gill cover); *large mouth; large fanlike pectoral fins, 1–4 preopercular spines* (at front of gill cover — Fig. 51), thoracic pelvic fins with 1 hidden spine (i.e., a fleshy sheath covers the small spine and 1st much larger ray) and 3–4 rays; and *no or few* (ctenoid) *scales.* There are 2 dorsal fins, the 1st with spines and the 2d longer and with rays. The anal fin is

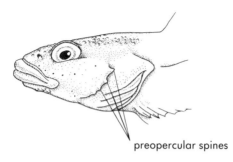

preopercular spines

Fig. 51 Sculpin

long and lacks spines. The body is wide at front, then tapers to a slender, compressed caudal peduncle, and often has small spines or prickles.

Sculpins are among the most difficult North American freshwater fishes to identify. Most are relatively drab and variably mottled, and color pattern is of less use than in other speciose groups. The development of prickles and preopercular spines, useful characteristics in identifying some species, unfortunately varies within species depending on habitat. Populations from small cold streams tend to have poorly developed prickles and spines; those from lakes and other quiet water tend to have large prickles and spines. Other useful (often necessary) traits, such as the presence or absence of palatine teeth, require close, often microscopic, examination. And finally, some forms recognized as species appear to grade into one another, and other "species" appear to contain several recognizable, reproductively isolated populations each of which may warrant recognition as a species.

DEEPWATER SCULPIN *Myoxocephalus thompsoni*   **Pl. 33**
Identification: *Large gap* between dorsal fins. *Bony plates* along lateral line. *Extremely wide, flat head;* huge mouth extends to beneath eye. Large disklike scales (often absent on juveniles) on back and side above lateral line. Long body, wide at front, tapered to extremely slender caudal peduncle. Large male has huge 2d dorsal, pectoral fins. Complete or nearly complete (in eastern populations) lateral line. 4 preopercular spines; upper 2 large, directed upward, appearing as 1 divided spine; lower 2 small, directed downward. Dark brown to green mottling, often 4–7 green saddles, on gray-brown back and side; white below; dark bars on fins except pelvics. 3 (rarely 4) pelvic rays. To 9 in. (23 cm).
Range: St. Lawrence–Great Lakes and Arctic basins from w. QU and NY west to AB and north to NT. Extremely localized; common in some lakes (e.g., Lake Michigan). Protected in Canada as a *threat-*

ened species. **Habitat:** Bottoms of deep (to 1200 ft. [366 m]), cold lakes.
Similar species: See Fourhorn Sculpin.   **Map 268**

FOURHORN SCULPIN *Myoxocephalus quadricornis*   **Not shown**
   Identification: Nearly identical to Deepwater Sculpin but has *4 large horns* on top of head (2 between eyes, 2 at rear of head); large disklike scales *below*, as well as above, lateral line. To 14¾ in. (37 cm).
   Range: Arctic drainages of North America and Eurasia. Common.
   Habitat: Near shore (to 60 ft. [20 m]) in brackish water. Enters coastal rivers and may occur as much as 120 miles inland.
   Similar species: See Deepwater Sculpin (Pl. 33).

● *COTTUS*

   Genus characteristics: *Joined or narrowly separated dorsal fins.* No bony plates along lateral line; no cirri; upper preopercular spine not branched. Usually many thin dark brown bands on 2d dorsal, caudal, and pectoral fins.

SPOONHEAD SCULPIN *Cottus ricei*   **Pl. 33**
   Identification: *Very wide flat head; extremely slender caudal peduncle. Prickles* on most of body. Dorsal fins separate to base. Complete lateral line; 33–36 pores. Light to dark brown above, dark brown specks and mottling on back and side, often 4 dark saddles on back. No large black spots on dorsal fins. 3 preopercular spines, uppermost spine long, curved inward. 4 pelvic rays, 7–10 dorsal spines, 16–18 dorsal rays, 12–15 anal rays, 14–16 pectoral rays, 1 pore at tip of chin. No palatine teeth. To 5 in. (13 cm).
   Range: St. Lawrence–Great Lakes and Arctic basins from s. QU to the Mackenzie R. drainage, NT, YU, and ne. BC, and south to n. OH and n. MT. Common. **Habitat:** Variable. Rocky areas of swift creeks and small to medium rivers; shores and deep water of lakes. To 450 ft. (137 m) depth.
   Similar species: Other *Cottus* species (Pls. 33 & 34) have *narrower, deeper head; deeper caudal peduncle.*   **Map 269**

TORRENT SCULPIN *Cottus rhotheus*   **Pl. 33**
   Identification: *"Pinched" caudal peduncle* (extremely slender just behind dorsal and anal fins). Robust body; large head (about ⅓ body length); with or without prickles. Dorsal fins separate to base. Complete lateral line; 23–27 pores. Brown to black above, dark mottling on back and side of some individuals; 2 broad dark bars under 2d dorsal fin (slanted forward); white below. No large black spots on dorsal fins. Large male has orange edge on 1st dorsal fin. 3–4 preopercular spines (upper one large, others small), 4 pelvic rays, 7–9 dorsal spines, 15–17 dorsal rays, 11–13 anal rays, 15–17 pectoral rays, 2 pores at tip of chin. Palatine teeth. To 6 in. (15 cm).

Range: Pacific Slope drainages from upper Fraser R. drainage, BC, to Nehalem R., OR (including Columbia R. drainage of BC, WA, ID, MT, and OR). Common. **Habitat:** Rubble and gravel riffles of small to large rivers; rocky lake shores.

Similar species: Other *Cottus* species (Pls. 33 & 34) *lack* pinched caudal peduncle; peduncle is slender in Coastrange Sculpin (Pl. 33) which has pelvic fins reaching anus, tubular posterior nostril, 1 preopercular spine. **Map 269**

BANDED SCULPIN *Cottus carolinae* **Pl. 33**
Identification: Olive, tan, or red-brown above; 4–5 brown-black saddles, last 3 extending onto side as *sharply defined bars* (often vague in upper Tennessee R. drainage); mottled chin (see Remarks). No large black spots on dorsal fins. No prickles, or prickles only in patch behind pectoral fin base. Dorsal fins separate to base. Complete lateral line (except *C. c. zopherus* and Kanawha R. population; see Remarks); usually 29–34 pores. 3 preopercular spines (see Remarks), 4 pelvic rays, 6–9 dorsal spines, 15–18 dorsal rays, 11–14 anal rays, 15–17 pectoral rays, 2 pores at tip of chin. Palatine teeth. To 7¼ in. (18 cm).
Range: Upland streams in Mississippi R. basin from New (upper Kanawha) R. drainage, WV and VA, across cen. KY, s. IN, and s. and sw. IL to Ozark Mountain drainages, s. MO, se. KS, n. AR, and ne. OK; south to upland and lowland streams in Mobile Bay drainage, GA, TN, and AL. Common. **Habitat:** Gravel and rubble riffles of headwaters, creeks, and small rivers; springs and their effluents.
Remarks: Three subspecies recognized, but populations in Mobile Bay basin are highly variable and in need of study. *C. c. infernatus*, in the Mobile Bay basin below the Fall Line, and above the Fall Line in the Cahaba R. system, has a complete and uninterrupted lateral line (29–34 pores), a uniformly speckled chin, 2 preopercular spines (and sometimes a 3d knob), usually 15 pectoral rays and broad dark bars on the body. *C. c. zopherus*, above the Fall Line in the Mobile Bay basin (Coosa, Tallapoosa, Cahaba, and Black Warrior R. systems), has a usually incomplete and interrupted lateral line (22–34 pores), mottled chin, 3 preopercular spines, usually 15 pectoral rays and narrow dark bars on the body. *C. c. carolinae*, throughout rest of species' range, has usually a complete lateral line (28–34 pores), strongly mottled chin, 3 (rarely 4) preopercular spines, usually 16–17 pectoral rays and narrow dark bars on the body. The population in Kanawha R. system, WV and VA, has an incomplete lateral line with 24–33 pores, has usually 17 pectoral rays and a relatively uniformly speckled chin, and may warrant taxonomic recognition.
Similar species: (1) See Potomac Sculpin (Pl. 33). (2) Often in same streams as Mottled Sculpin (Pl. 34), which has black spots on 1st dorsal fin; black base, orange edge on 1st dorsal fin of large male; dorsal fins joined at base; *less distinct bars* on side. **Map 270**

POTOMAC SCULPIN *Cottus girardi* **Pl. 33**
Identification: Similar to Banded Sculpin but has *incomplete lateral line* (17–25 pores), *1 pore* at tip of chin, *irregularly bordered bars* on

side; large male is dark overall, has narrow orange edge on 1st dorsal fin. In contrast to the geographically proximal Kanawha R. Banded Sculpin (see Banded Sculpin, Remarks), the Potomac Sculpin has usually 15 pectoral rays and a strongly mottled chin. To 5¼ in. (14 cm).

Range: Mountain and Piedmont streams in upper Potomac R. drainage, PA, MD, VA, and WV; Cowpasture R. (James R. drainage), VA. Common. **Habitat:** Rocky runs and pools of creeks and small to medium rivers; often near vegetation.

Similar species: See Banded Sculpin (Pl. 33).   **Map 270**

COASTRANGE SCULPIN *Cottus aleuticus*   **Pl. 33**

Identification: *Long pelvic fin reaches to anus. Long, tubular posterior nostril.* Fairly slender body; slender caudal peduncle. Prickles restricted to patch behind pectoral fin. Dorsal fins joined at base. Complete lateral line, 32–44 pores. Brown to gray above, dark brown mottling on back; 2–3 dark bars below 2d dorsal fin. No large black spots on dorsal fins. Large male has black base, orange edge, on 1st dorsal fin. 1 large preopercular spine (often 2d small spine), 4 pelvic rays, 8–10 dorsal spines, 17–20 dorsal rays, 12–15 anal rays, 13–15 pectoral rays, 1 pore at tip of chin. No palatine teeth. To 6½ in. (17 cm).

Range: Pacific Slope drainages from Bristol Bay and Aleutian Islands, AK, to n. CA; isolated population in lower Kobuk R., AK. Most populations near coast. Common; locally abundant. **Habitat:** Gravel and rubble riffles of medium to large rivers; rocky shores of lakes. Occasionally enters estuaries.

Similar species: (1) Klamath Lake Sculpin (Pl. 33) has broadly joined dorsal fins; large pores on flat head; many prickles on body; *short posterior nostril;* incomplete lateral line, 15–25 lateral-line pores; 5–8 dorsal spines, 20–25 dorsal rays; 15–19 anal rays. (2) Other *Cottus* species (Pls. 33 & 34) have pelvic fins *too short* to reach anus, *short posterior nostril.*   **Map 271**

PRICKLY SCULPIN *Cottus asper*   **Pl. 33**

Identification: *Long anal* (usually *16–19 rays*) and *dorsal fins (19–23 rays).* Often *many prickles* on body (greatly reduced in some populations). Dorsal fins joined at base. Complete lateral line, 28–43 pores. Red-brown to brown above, large *dark brown blotches,* mottling on back and upper side, 5 small black saddles on back, often 3 black bars under 2d dorsal fin; large black spot at rear (only) of 1st dorsal fin; white to yellow below. Orange edge on 1st dorsal fin of large individual. Large male is dark brown overall. 2–3 preopercular spines (1 large, 1–2 small); 4 pelvic rays, 7–10 dorsal spines, 15–18 pectoral rays, 1 pore at tip of chin. Large palatine teeth. To 12 in. (30 cm).

Range: Pacific Slope drainages from Seward, AK, to Ventura R., CA; east of Continental Divide in upper Peace R. (Arctic basin), BC. Common; locally abundant. **Habitat:** Usually over sand in pools and quiet runs of small to medium rivers; sandy and rocky shores of lakes. Enters brackish tidepools and estuaries.

Similar species: (1) Klamath Lake Sculpin (Pl. 33) has broadly joined dorsal fins; long, slender body; flatter, wider head; no black spot in

1st dorsal fin. (2) Other *Cottus* species (Pls. 33 & 34) have usually *fewer* than 16 anal rays, 19 dorsal rays.   **Map 272**

KLAMATH LAKE SCULPIN *Cottus princeps*   **Pl. 33**
Identification: *Long, slender body; long fins* (pelvic fins reach anus on adult). *Broadly joined dorsal fins. Large pores* on flat head. *Many prickles* on body. Incomplete lateral line ends under 2d dorsal fin; 15–25 lateral-line pores. Olive to purple above, 6–7 dark brown saddles (4 under 2d dorsal fin); dark blotches on side; white to gray below. 0–1 preopercular spines, 4 pelvic rays, 5–8 dorsal spines, 20–25 dorsal rays; 15–19 anal rays, 14–16 pectoral rays, 1 pore at tip of chin. No palatine teeth. To 2¾ in. (7 cm).
Range: Upper Klamath and Agency lakes, OR. Abundant. Formerly in Lost R., OR, but now extirpated. **Habitat:** Rocky and sandy shores of lakes.
Similar species: (1) Spoonhead Sculpin (Pl. 33) has separate dorsal fins; wider, flatter head; complete lateral line. (2) Other *Cottus* species (Pls. 33 & 34) are *deeper bodied,* have deeper heads, *separate to narrowly joined dorsal fins, smaller pores* on head.   **Map 273**

SHOSHONE SCULPIN *Cottus greenei*   **Pl. 33**
Identification: *Deep body; deep caudal peduncle.* Prickles absent or only behind pectoral fin base. Dorsal fins joined at base. Incomplete lateral line, 20–28 pores. Brown to gray above; 4–5 black saddles (darkest on juveniles), 3 under 2d dorsal fin; large black spot at rear (only) of 1st dorsal fin. 2 preopercular spines (upper large, lower small), 3 pelvic rays, usually 6 dorsal spines, 18–19 dorsal rays, 12–13 anal rays, 14–15 pectoral rays, 2 pores at tip of chin. Palatine teeth. To 3½ in. (9 cm).
Range: Hagerman Valley (Snake R. system), ID. Uncommon in extremely small area. **Habitat:** Rocky springs and their effluents.
Similar species: Other *Cottus* species (Pls. 33 & 34) have *more slender caudal peduncle.*   **Map 272**

SLENDER SCULPIN *Cottus tenuis*   **Pl. 33**
Identification: *Strongly bicolored;* chestnut brown above, silver-white to brassy below. 1 or more *branched pelvic rays* (except in young). 3 *large preopercular spines.* Prickles on upper side of body (best developed on individuals from lakes; often absent on stream-living individuals). Dorsal fins separate to base. Incomplete lateral line extends to end of 2d dorsal fin; 23–32 pores. Fairly long, slender body. No large black spots on dorsal fins; 4–5 dark brown blotches on side. 3 pelvic rays, 5–7 dorsal spines, 17–19 dorsal rays, 13–17 anal rays, 12–16 pectoral rays, 2 pores at tip of chin. Usually no palatine teeth. To 3½ in. (9 cm).
Range: Upper Klamath R. drainage (Upper Klamath Lake and upstream), OR. Uncommon. **Habitat:** Over mud, sand, and gravel on lake shores; riffles, runs, and pools of creeks and small to medium rivers.
Similar species: (1) See Rough Sculpin. (2) Other *Cottus* species (Pls. 33 & 34) are *less* bicolored, *lack* branched pelvic rays.   **Map 271**

ROUGH SCULPIN *Cottus asperrimus* **Not shown**
Identification: Similar to Slender Sculpin but has only *1–2 large preopercular spines* (and often a 2d or 3d blunt knob), lateral line usually extending only to *middle* of 2d dorsal fin, *many black specks* on underside. To 3¾ in. (9.6 cm).
Range: Pit R. system, Shasta and Lassen cos., CA. Abundant in small range. **Habitat:** Vegetated runs and riffles of creeks and small to medium rivers; usually over mud in clear, fairly deep water (3–6 ft. [1–2 m]).
Similar species: See Slender Sculpin (Pl. 33). **Map 271**

BEAR LAKE SCULPIN *Cottus extensus* **Pl. 33**
Identification: *Many prickles* on *long, slender body* (none on breast and belly); usually *3 preopercular spines*. Light brown above; dark mottling on side but *no bold saddles or bars*; black band on 1st dorsal fin of large male. Dorsal fins separate to base. Incomplete lateral line, 26–29 pores. 4 pelvic rays, 7–8 dorsal spines, 16–19 dorsal rays, 13–15 anal rays, 15–18 pectoral rays, 2 pores at tip of chin. Palatine teeth. To 5¼ in. (13 cm).
Range: Bear Lake, ID and UT. Common. **Habitat:** Rocky bottom from near shore to deep (at least 175 ft. [53 m]) water.
Remarks: The Utah Lake Sculpin, *Cottus echinatus* (Pl. 33), formerly endemic to Utah Lake, UT (Map 274) but presumably extinct, was similar to Bear Lake Sculpin but had prickles on breast and belly, larger head, slightly less slender body, usually 4 preopercular spines. **Map 274**

SLIMY SCULPIN *Cottus cognatus* **Pl. 34**
Identification: Usually *3* (if 4, 4th is greatly reduced) *pelvic rays*. Long, fairly slender body. Prickles often on head and behind pectoral fin base. Dorsal fins separate to base. Usually incomplete lateral line (to 2d dorsal fin); 12–26 pores. Dark brown, green, or gray above; dark gray mottling on back and upper side, often 2 dark saddles under 2d dorsal fin; large black spots at front and rear of 1st dorsal fin (often joined into black bar). Breeding male is dark gray to black overall, has orange edge on 1st dorsal fin. 2–3 preopercular spines (uppermost large), 7–9 (rarely 10) dorsal spines, 14–19 dorsal rays, 10–13 (usually 10–11) anal rays, 12–15 pectoral rays, 2 pores at tip of chin. No palatine teeth. To 4½ in (12 cm).
Range: Atlantic, Arctic, and Pacific basins throughout most of mainland Canada (except NS, much of s. SA and s. AB, and the lower Pacific coast of BC) and Alaska; Atlantic Slope drainages south to Potomac R., VA (see Remarks); St. Lawrence–Great Lakes basin; upper Mississippi R. basin in w. WI, e. MN, and ne. IA; upper Columbia R. drainage, BC, MT, ID, and WA. Also in e. Siberia. Common. **Habitat:** Rocky riffles of cold streams; rocky areas of lakes (commonly at a depth of 300–350 ft. [90–106 m]); springs and their effluents.
Remarks: Potomac R. population has usually 1 pore at tip of chin and palatine teeth.
Similar species: (1) Mottled Sculpin (Pl. 34) has *4 pelvic rays*, deeper body, darker saddles and bars, dorsal fins joined at base, palatine

teeth, 12–14 anal rays. (2) Shorthead Sculpin (Pl. 34) has 3 saddles under 2d dorsal fin, palatine teeth, *4 pelvic rays*, 12–14 anal rays.
Map 275

Mottled Sculpin look-alikes: The next 6 species are so similar in appearance that it often is necessary to rely on microscopic examination of specimens and geography to identify them. All have *2 large black spots* (largest and blackest in large males) on 1st dorsal fin and an *incomplete lateral line.*

MOTTLED SCULPIN *Cottus bairdi*   **Pl. 34**

Identification: *Robust body;* large head; incomplete lateral line, usually 18–36 pores. Dorsal fins *joined* at base. Light to dark brown above, dark brown to black mottling on back and side; 2–3 dark brown to black bars on body under 2d dorsal fin; uniformly speckled chin. Large black spots at front and rear of 1st dorsal fin. Large male has black band, orange edge on 1st dorsal fin. *3 preopercular spines*, 4 pelvic rays, 6–9 dorsal spines, 15–18 dorsal rays, 12–14 anal rays, 14–16 pectoral rays, usually 2 pores at tip of chin. *Palatine teeth* usually present. To 6 in. (15 cm).
Range: Widespread with highly disjunct eastern and western distributions. In e. North America in Arctic, Atlantic, and Mississippi R. basins from Labrador and n. QU west to w. MB, and south to Roanoke R. drainage, VA, and Tennessee R. drainage, n. GA and AL; isolated populations in extreme upper Santee (NC), Savannah (SC and GA), Chattahoochee (GA), Coosa (GA), and Osage (MO) R. systems. In w. North America in upper Missouri R. basin, AB, MT, and WY; Columbia R. drainage from BC south to OR and east to WY; upper Colorado R. drainage, NM, CO, and WY; isolated populations in endorheic basins in UT and NV. Common. **Habitat:** Rubble and gravel riffles, less often sand–gravel runs, of headwaters, creeks, and small rivers; springs and their effluents; rocky shores of lakes.
Similar species: See Pl. 34. See (1) Black and (2) Ozark Sculpins. (3) Shorthead Sculpin is more *slender*, has dorsal fins *separate* to base, 11–15 (usually 14) pectoral rays, *2 preopercular spines.* (4) Paiute Sculpin has dorsal fins *separate* to base, *no* palatine teeth, *1–2 preopercular spines.* (5) Margined Sculpin has 3 pelvic rays, 1 pore at tip of chin, *no* palatine teeth, 14–16 anal rays.   **Map 276**

BLACK SCULPIN *Cottus baileyi*   **Pl. 34**

Identification: Nearly identical to Mottled Sculpin but is *smaller*, usually *lacks* palatine teeth. To 3¼ in. (8.4 cm).
Range: Extreme upper Clinch and Holston R. systems (Tennessee R. drainage), VA and TN. Common within small range. **Habitat:** Rocky riffles of headwaters and creeks; springs.
Similar species: See Mottled Sculpin (Pl. 34).   **Map 277**

OZARK SCULPIN *Cottus hypselurus*   **Pl. 34**

Identification: Similar to Mottled Scuplin but has *wide, wavy black bands* on dorsal and caudal fins (within the range of the Ozark

Sculpin, the Mottled Sculpin lacks mottling on the median fins); sharper snout; deeper body (width under 2d dorsal fin enters depth 2 or more times). 17–26 lateral-line pores. To 5½ in. (14 cm).
Range: Meramec, Missouri, and White (including Black) R. drainages in Ozark Uplands of MO and AR. Abundant. **Habitat:** Gravel riffles of creeks and small to medium rivers; often near vegetation in springs and their effluents.
Similar species: (1) See Mottled Sculpin (Pl. 34) — Ozark and Mottled Sculpins occur together only in the Osage R. system, MO. (2) Banded Sculpin (Pl. 33) has complete lateral line, *no* large black spots or wide bands in dorsal fin, 29 or more lateral-line pores, darkly mottled chin, broad dark band on caudal fin base. **Map 277**

SHORTHEAD SCULPIN *Cottus confusus* Pl. 34
Identification: *Long, slender body;* short head. Prickles restricted to area behind pectoral fin. Dorsal fins *separate* to base. Usually incomplete lateral line, usually 22–37 pores. Light yellow-brown above, dark mottling on back and side; often 5–6 black saddles, 3 under 2d dorsal fin. Black band (or spots at front and rear), orange edge, on 1st dorsal fin of large male. *2 preopercular spines,* 4 pelvic rays, 7–9 dorsal spines, 15–19 dorsal rays, 12–14 anal rays, 11–15 (usually 13–14) pectoral rays, 2 pores at tip of chin. *Palatine teeth* usually present. To 5¾ in. (15 cm).
Range: Columbia R. drainage, BC, MT, ID, WA, and OR; Puget Sound drainage, WA. Common in parts of range; protected in Canada as a *threatened species.* **Habitat:** Fast, rocky riffles of cold headwaters, creeks, and small to large rivers.
Similar species: See Pl. 34. (1) Mottled Sculpin is *deeper bodied,* has dorsal fins *joined* at base, 14–16 (usually 15) pectoral rays, *3* preopercular spines. (2) Paiute Sculpin is *deeper bodied;* usually *lacks* palatine teeth, patch of prickles behind pectoral fin. (3) Margined Sculpin *lacks* palatine teeth, patch of prickles behind pectoral fin; has 14–16 anal rays, 3 pelvic rays. **Map 274**

PAIUTE SCULPIN *Cottus beldingi* Pl. 34
Identification: No prickles. Dorsal fins *separate* to base. Complete or incomplete lateral line; 23–35 pores. Brown to gray above, dark mottling on back and side; 5–7 black saddles often extending onto side as dark bars. Black spots at front and rear of 1st dorsal fin, often joined into black bar. Orange edge on 1st dorsal fin. 1–2 (upper large) preopercular spines, 3–4 pelvic rays, 7–8 dorsal spines, 15–16 dorsal rays, 11–13 anal rays, 14–15 pectoral rays, usually 2 pores at tip of chin. No or small palatine teeth. To 5¼ in. (13 cm).
Range: Columbia R. drainage from ID, w. WY, and ne. NV to w. WA and OR; western endorheic basins, including Lake Tahoe, NV and CA, Humboldt R., NV, and Bear R., UT. Common; abundant in Lake Tahoe. **Habitat:** Rubble and gravel riffles of cold creeks and small to medium rivers; rocky shores of lakes.
Similar species: See Pl. 34. (1) See Margined Sculpin. (2) Mottled Sculpin has dorsal fins *joined* at base, 3 preopercular spines, palatine

teeth. (3) Shorthead Sculpin is more slender; has patch of prickles behind pectoral fin, palatine teeth. **Map 278**

MARGINED SCULPIN *Cottus marginatus* **Pl. 34**
Identification: Similar to Paiute Sculpin but has dorsal fins *joined* at base; usually *3 pelvic rays,* 1 pore at tip of chin; 14–16 anal rays. To 5 in. (13 cm).
Range: Columbia R. drainage from the Walla Walla R. system, WA, to the Umatilla R. system, OR. Fairly common in small range. **Habitat:** Rubble and gravel riffles.
Similar species: See Pl. 34. (1) See Paiute Sculpin. (2) Mottled Sculpin has 2 pores at tip of chin, palatine teeth, 4 pelvic rays, 12–14 anal rays. (3) Shorthead Sculpin has dorsal fins *separate* to base, 2 pores at tip of chin, palatine teeth, 12–14 anal rays, *4 pelvic rays,* usually no prickles behind pectoral fin. **Map 273**

PYGMY SCULPIN *Cottus pygmaeus* **Pl. 34**
Identification: *Small;* to 1¾ in. (4.5 cm). *Boldly patterned* (especially juvenile) with black head, white nape, black saddle under 1st dorsal fin, 2 black saddles under 2d dorsal fin extending onto side as wide bars, wide black bar at caudal fin base. With or without prickles. Dorsal fins joined at base. Incomplete lateral line, 20–24 pores. First dorsal fin of large male has large black spots at front and rear, orange edge. 1–2 preopercular spines, *3 pelvic rays,* 7–8 dorsal spines, 14–16 dorsal rays, 11–13 anal rays, 13–15 pectoral rays, 2 pores at tip of chin. No palatine teeth.
Range: Known only from Coldwater Spring (Coosa R. system), Calhoun Co., AL. Common within extremely small range; protected as a *threatened species.* **Habitat:** Rocky spring runs.
Similar species: Mottled Sculpin (Pl. 34) is *larger* (to 6 in.), *less boldly patterned;* has *4 pelvic rays,* 3 preopercular spines, usually palatine teeth. **Map 277**

WOOD RIVER SCULPIN *Cottus leiopomus* **Pl. 34**
Identification: *Short head,* about 3 times into *long, slender body.* No prickles. Dorsal fins separate at base. Incomplete lateral line; 30–36 pores. Gray-olive above, 4 black saddles (3 under 2d dorsal fin); mottled with dark brown or black. Dark spots at front and rear of 1st dorsal fin. 1 preopercular spine, 4 pelvic rays, 6–8 dorsal spines, 17–19 dorsal rays, 12–14 anal rays, 12–14 pectoral rays, 2 pores at tip of chin. No or small palatine teeth. To 4¼ in. (11 cm).
Range: Little and Big Wood R. systems (Snake R. system), ID. Fairly common in small area. **Habitat:** Rubble and gravel riffles of creeks and small rivers.
Similar species: (1) Slimy Sculpin (Pl. 34) has 12–26 lateral-line pores, usually 3 pelvic rays, 2 saddles under 2d dorsal fin. (2) Other slender sculpins (Pl. 34) lack black spots in 1st dorsal fin. **Map 273**

RIFFLE SCULPIN *Cottus gulosus* **Pl. 34**
Identification: *Deep compressed caudal peduncle.* Large mouth (width more than body width just behind pectoral fins). Large black

spot at rear (only) of 1st dorsal fin; none at front (often some black but no distinct spot). Prickles confined to area behind pectoral fin base. Dorsal fins joined at base. Complete or incomplete lateral line, 21–38 (usually 22–36) pores. Brown above, dark brown mottling on back and upper side, 5–6 small black saddles on back, no black bars under 2d dorsal fin; white to yellow below. Black band, orange edge, on 1st dorsal fin of large individual. Breeding male is dark brown overall. 2–3 preopercular spines, 4 pelvic rays, 8–9 dorsal spines, 16–19 dorsal rays, 12–17 anal rays, 15–16 pectoral rays, usually 1 pore at tip of chin. Palatine teeth. To 4¼ in. (11 cm).
Range: Pacific Slope drainages from lower Columbia R. drainage, WA, to Morro Bay, CA (including Sacramento-San Joaquin R. drainage except upper Pit R.); absent in Rogue and Klamath R. drainages, s. OR and n. CA. Common. **Habitat:** Sand and gravel riffles of headwaters and creeks; sand-gravel runs and backwaters of small to large rivers.
Similar species: See (1) Reticulate and (2) Pit Sculpins (Pl. 34). (3) Marbled Sculpin (Pl. 34) has dark marbled pattern on fins, 14–22 lateral-line pores, 5–8 dorsal spines. **Map 279**

RETICULATE SCULPIN *Cottus perplexus* Not shown
Identification: Nearly identical to Riffle Sculpin but has mouth *narrower* than body just behind pectoral fins, *no* palatine teeth. 1–2 pores at tip of chin. To 4 in. (10 cm).
Range: Pacific Slope drainages from Snohomish R. and Puget Sound, WA, to Rogue R. system, OR and CA. Abundant. **Habitat:** Rubble- and gravel-bottomed pools and riffles of headwaters, creeks, and small rivers. See Remarks.
Remarks: Although fishes usually show a distinct preference for a particular habitat, many are able to shift to other habitats in response to certain environmental conditions, such as the presence of other closely related species. Where the Torrent and Coastrange Sculpins do not occur, the Reticulate Sculpin occupies riffles; at localities where all occur together, the Reticulate Sculpin shifts to pools.
Similar species: See Riffle Sculpin (Pl. 34). **Map 273**

PIT SCULPIN *Cottus pitensis* Pl. 34
Identification: Similar to Riffle Sculpin but has dark vermiculations and *small blotches* on back and side, dorsal fins separate to base, *no* palatine teeth, usually *complete lateral line* with 31–39 (usually 33–37) pores, usually 2 pores at tip of chin. To 5 in. (13 cm).
Range: Pit and upper Sacramento R. (above mouth of Pit R.) systems, OR and CA. Common. **Habitat:** Rocky riffles of headwaters, creeks, and small rivers.
Similar species: (1) See Riffle Sculpin (Pl. 34). (2) Reticulate Sculpin has 22–32 lateral-line pores, dorsal fins joined at base. **Map 274**

MARBLED SCULPIN *Cottus klamathensis* Pl. 34
Identification: *Deep body. Black spot* at rear (only) of 1st dorsal fin. Prickles on small individuals (to 2½ in. [6.5 cm]) only. Dorsal fins joined at base. Usually incomplete lateral line, 14–22 pores. Brown

above, black-brown mottling on back and upper side, 5–6 small black saddles on back; white to yellow below; *marbled pattern* of alternating dark and light spots on fin rays. Breeding male is dark brown overall. 1 large preopercular spine (1–2 blunt spines also may be present), 4 pelvic rays, 5–8 dorsal spines, 18–20 dorsal rays, 13–15 anal rays, 14–16 pectoral rays, 1–2 pores at tip of chin. No palatine teeth. To 3½ in. (9 cm).

Range: Klamath R. drainage, OR and CA; Pit R. system from Fall R. to Hat Cr., CA. Abundant in Klamath R. drainage; locally common in Pit R. system. **Habitat:** Soft-bottomed runs of clear, cold creeks and small to medium rivers.

Remarks: Marbled Sculpins in Klamath R. system have strongly contrasting, marbled appearance and black-banded fins; those in Pit R. system are much darker overall, lack marbled appearance.

Similar species: (1) Riffle and (2) Pit Sculpins (both, Pl. 34) lack prominent marbling on fins, have more than 22 lateral-line pores, 8–9 dorsal spines.

Map 278

■ TEMPERATE BASSES: Family Moronidae (4)

Temperate basses are compressed, deep-bodied fishes with 2 dorsal fins, the first with usually 9 spines and the 2d with 1 spine and 11–14 rays; 3 anal spines; large mouth; ctenoid scales; thoracic pelvic fins; complete lateral line; a large spine on the gill cover; a *small gill* (pseudobranch) on the underside of the gill cover; and a strongly sawtoothed preopercle. Until recently, temperate basses were considered members of the family Percichthyidae. Now they are placed in Moronidae, with species in North America, Europe, and northern Africa. Temperate basses are moderate-to-large, active fishes that are among the most popular sport fishes.

STRIPED BASS *Morone saxatilis* **Pl. 35**

Identification: *6–9 dark gray stripes* (on adult) on silver-white side. Smoothly arched dorsal profile; body deepest between dorsal fins. Dark olive to blue-gray above; silver-white side, often with brassy specks; clear to gray-green fins. Large adult has white pelvic fin, white edge on anal fin. Young lacks dark stripes, has dusky bars, on side. 2d anal spine distinctly shorter than 3d; 9–13 (usually 11) anal rays. 1–2 patches of teeth on rear of tongue. To 79 in. (2 m).

Range: Atlantic and Gulf Slope drainages from St. Lawrence R., NB, to Lake Pontchartrain, LA; south in FL to St. Johns and Suwannee R. drainages. Widely introduced in U.S. including Pacific Coast drainages and freshwater impoundments far inland. Fairly common, but less so than formerly because of pollution of major spawning areas. **Habitat:** Marine; ascends large rivers far upstream to spawn. Channels of medium to large rivers during spring spawning runs; lakes, impoundments, and connecting rivers.

Remarks: Hybrids of White and Striped Bass are common in areas where "stripers" have been introduced.
Similar species: (1) White Bass (Pl. 35) has a deeper body, strongly arched behind head; reaches only 17¾ in. (45 cm). (2) White Perch (Pl. 35) *lacks* dark stripes on side, has body deepest under 1st dorsal fin, 2d anal spine about as long as 3d, usually 9–10 anal rays, no teeth on tongue.

WHITE BASS *Morone chrysops*   **Pl. 35**

Identification: *4–7 dark gray-brown stripes* on silver-white side. Deep body, strongly arched behind head; deepest between dorsal fins. Blue-gray above; silver-white side; yellow eye; clear to gray dorsal and caudal fins, clear to white paired fins. 2d anal spine distinctly shorter than 3d; 11–13 anal rays. 1–2 patches of teeth on rear of tongue. To 17¾ in. (45 cm).
Range: St. Lawrence–Great Lakes, Hudson Bay (Red R.), and Mississippi R. basins from QU to MB and south to LA; Gulf Slope drainages from Mississippi R., LA, to Rio Grande, TX and NM. Introduced into several Atlantic, e. Gulf Coast, and w. U.S. drainages. Common.
Habitat: Lakes, ponds, and pools of small to large rivers.
Similar species: See Pl. 35. (1) Striped Bass is more slender, not strongly arched behind head; reaches 79 in. (2 m). (2) White Perch *lacks* dark stripes on side; has body deepest under 1st dorsal fin, 2d anal spine about as long as 3d, usually 9–10 anal rays, no teeth on tongue. (3) Yellow Bass has broken and offset stripes on yellow side, 2d anal spine about as long as 3d, usually 9 anal rays, no teeth on tongue.   **Map 280**

YELLOW BASS *Morone mississippiensis*   **Pl. 35**

Identification: *5–7 black stripes* on side; *broken and offset on lower side.* Olive-gray above; silver-*yellow side,* often with green cast; clear to blue-gray fins. Body deepest between dorsal fins. 2d anal spine about as long as 3d; usually 9 anal rays. No teeth on tongue. To 18 in. (46 cm).
Range: Lake Michigan and Mississippi R. basins from WI and MN south to Gulf; east to w. IN and e. TN, and west to w. IA and e. OK. On Gulf Slope in lower Mobile Bay drainage, AL, and from Pearl R. drainage, LA, to Galveston Bay drainage, TX. Introduced elsewhere in U.S. Fairly common; mostly restricted to lowland areas. **Habitat:** Pools and backwaters of small to large rivers; ponds and lakes.
Similar species: Other temperate basses (Pl. 35) *lack* broken stripes on side; have *silver-white side.*   **Map 281**

WHITE PERCH *Morone americana*   **Pl. 35**

Identification: *No dark stripes* along side (of adult). Body deepest *under 1st dorsal fin.* Olive to dark green-brown above; silver-green, often brassy, side; white below; dusky fins. Young have interrupted dark lines, bars on sides. Large adult has blue cast on head. 2d anal spine about as long as 3d; usually 9–10 anal rays. *No teeth* on tongue. To 22¾ in. (58 cm).

Range: Atlantic Slope drainages from St. Lawrence–Lake Ontario drainage, QU, south to Peedee R., SC. Populations in Lake Ontario drainage may have become established following construction of the Erie Canal. One recent record for Lake Erie drainage, PA. **Habitat:** Primarily brackish water but common in pools and other quiet water areas of medium to large rivers; usually over mud.

Similar species: (1) White and (2) Striped Basses (both, Pl. 35) have *dark stripes* on side, body deepest *between* dorsal fins, 2d anal spine distinctly shorter than 3d, usually 11–12 anal rays, *1–2 patches of teeth* on rear of tongue. **Map 281**

■PYGMY SUNFISHES: Family Elassomatidae (6)

Often treated as members of the family Centrarchidae, but pygmy sunfishes have *no lateral line*, no lateralis canal on the mandible, and a *round caudal fin* (most sunfishes have a forked fin), and they are much *smaller* (to 1¾ in. [4.7 cm]).

• *ELASSOMA*

Genus characteristics: *Cycloid scales*; 3–5 dorsal spines, usually 3 anal spines. Large eye; upturned mouth with distinctly protruding lower jaw. Dark olive to light brown, *many black specks* on head and body; *2 large cream-colored spots* on caudal fin base; rows of black spots on median fins.

BANDED PYGMY SUNFISH *Elassoma zonatum* **Pl. 38**
Identification: *1–2 large black spots* (rarely absent) on upper side below dorsal fin origin; *7–12 dark green to blue-black bars* on side. *No scales* on top of head. Breeding male is black with green-gold flecks, alternating gold and black bars on side; black fins, gold-green bar under eye. 28–45 lateral scales. 4–5 dorsal spines, 9–10 rays; 5–6 anal rays. To 1¾ in. (4.7 cm).
Range: Atlantic and Gulf Coastal Plain from Roanoke R., NC, to n. FL, and west to Brazos R., TX; north in Former Mississippi Embayment to s. IL. Rarely found above Fall Line. Common. **Habitat:** Swamps, heavily vegetated sloughs, and small sluggish streams; usually over mud.
Similar species: Other pygmy sunfishes (Pl. 38) *lack* large black spot(s) on side, have 3–4 dorsal spines. **Map 282**

EVERGLADES PYGMY SUNFISH *Elassoma evergladei* **Pl. 38**
Identification: *Scales* on top of head. Usually *light streaks* along side; breeding male is shiny black with bright iridescent blue bars on side and below eye. *Dark-colored lips. No large black spots* on upper side. Usually 4 dorsal spines, 8–10 rays; 4–6 anal rays; 13–15 pectoral rays; 23–32 lateral scales. To 1¼ in. (3.4 cm).

Range: Atlantic and Gulf Coastal Plain drainages from Cape Fear R., NC, to Mobile Bay, AL; south in FL to n. edge of Everglades. Common. **Habitat:** Swamps; heavily vegetated sloughs and small sluggish streams; usually over mud.

Similar species: Other pygmy sunfishes (Pl. 38) *lack* scales on top of head.   **Map 283**

OKEFENOKEE PYGMY SUNFISH *Elassoma okefenokee*   **Pl. 38**
Identification: *Brown bars* (darkest at rear, often broken into vertically aligned blotches) on side of female; breeding male is shiny black with bright iridescent blue bars on side and below eye. *No scales* on top of head. Front of lips *light-colored* (dark at sides) except in large male. *No large black spots* on upper side. Usually 4 dorsal spines. 10–13 dorsal rays; 6–8 anal rays; 14–17 pectoral rays; 31–34 lateral scales. To 1¼ in. (3.4 cm).
Range: Coastal Plain from Altamaha R. drainage, GA, to Choctawhatchee R. drainage, FL; south in FL to Hillsborough R. drainage (cen. FL). Common. **Habitat:** Swamps; heavily vegetated sloughs and small sluggish streams; usually over mud.
Similar species: (1) Everglades Pygmy Sunfish (Pl. 38) has *light streaks* along side, *scales* on top of head, dark-colored mouth; usually 9 dorsal, 5 anal, and 14 pectoral rays. (2) Banded Pygmy Sunfish (Pl. 38) has 1–2 large black spots on side, 5 dorsal spines.   **Map 284**

CAROLINA PYGMY SUNFISH *Elassoma boehlkei*   **Pl. 38**
Identification: 10–16 (usually 12–13) *narrow black bars* along side, about same width as light interspaces. *No large black spots* on upper side. *No scales* on top of head. Breeding male is black with blue-green flecks, alternating blue-green and black bars on side. Usually 4 dorsal spines. 8–12 dorsal rays; 4–8 anal rays; 14–17 pectoral rays; 24–30 lateral scales. To 1¼ in. (3.2 cm).
Range: Waccamaw and Santee R. drainages, NC and SC. Localized and uncommon. **Habitat:** Heavily vegetated creeks, sloughs, and roadside ditches.
Similar species: See Pl. 38. (1) Bluebarred Pygmy Sunfish has usually *10–11 wide bars* along side, usually 5 dorsal spines. (2) Okefenokee Pygmy Sunfish has 31–34 lateral scales. (3) Everglades Pygmy Sunfish has scales on top of head.   **Map 284**

BLUEBARRED PYGMY SUNFISH *Elassoma okatie*   **Pl. 38**
Identification: 8–14 (usually 10–11) *wide black bars* along side, about 3 times as wide as light interspaces. *No large black spots* on upper side. *No scales* on top of head. Breeding male is black with blue-green flecks and alternating blue-green and black bars on side. Usually 5 (often 4) dorsal spines. 8–12 dorsal rays; 4–8 anal rays; 14–17 pectoral rays; 24–30 lateral scales. To 1¼ in. (3.4 cm).
Range: Lower Edisto, New, and Savannah R. drainages, SC. Localized and uncommon. **Habitat:** Heavily vegetated creeks, sloughs, and roadside ditches.
Similar species: See Pl. 38. (1) Carolina Pygmy Sunfish has usually

12–13 narrow bars along side, usually 4 dorsal spines. (2) Okefenokee Pygmy Sunfish has 31–34 lateral scales, usually 4 dorsal spines. (3) Everglades Pygmy Sunfish has scales on top of head.   **Map 284**

SPRING PYGMY SUNFISH *Elassoma* species   **Pl. 38**
Identification: *6–8 thin gold bars* along dark brown to black side. *Clear "window"* at rear of 2d dorsal and anal fins of large male. No large black spots on upper side. No scales on head. Usually 3 dorsal spines. 10–12 dorsal rays; 6–7 anal rays; 15–17 pectoral rays; 28–30 lateral scales. To 1¼ in. (3 cm).
Range: Springs and spring runs in Tennessee R. drainage in Lauderdale and Limestone cos., AL. Uncommon within restricted habitat; several populations extirpated within historic times. **Habitat:** Vegetated, spring-fed pools.
Similar species: See Pl. 38. Other pygmy sunfishes *lack* 6–8 thin gold bars along side, clear window at rear of 2d dorsal and anal fins.
Map 282

■ SUNFISHES AND BASSES: Family Centrarchidae (30)

The 30 species of sunfishes and basses occur naturally only in the fresh waters of North America. They have been introduced into parts of North America where they did not occur naturally, and into Europe and Africa. Included in this family are some of the most popular sport fishes, such as crappies, basses, and Bluegill.

Sunfishes and basses are laterally compressed fishes with 2 dorsal fins, the 1st with spines, the 2d with rays, so *broadly joined* that they appear as 1 fin. These fishes have 3–8 anal spines, thoracic pelvic fins, no sharp spine near the back of the gill cover, and ctenoid scales (except Mud Sunfish).

Except for the Sacramento Perch, sunfishes and basses build nests and guard their young. The male constructs a circular pit of gravel or vegetation by vigorously fanning his fins. After spawning, the male remains to guard the eggs and young.

SACRAMENTO PERCH *Archoplites interruptus*   **Pl. 36**
Identification: *12–13 dorsal spines, 6–7 anal spines.* Dorsal fin base about *twice* as long as anal fin base. Deep, fairly compressed body; large mouth, upper jaw extending under eye pupil. Olive-brown above; 6–7 irregular dark bars on upper side down to lateral line; silver-green to purple sheen on mottled black and white side; white below; black spot on ear flap. 38–48 lateral scales; 10–11 anal rays. To 28¾ in. (73 cm).
Range: Native to Sacramento–San Joaquin, Pajaro, and Salinas R. drainages, CA; widely introduced elsewhere in w. U.S. Uncommon, declining in native range; seemingly unable to compete with other sunfishes introduced into its range. **Habitat:** Originally vegetated sloughs, pools of sluggish rivers, and lakes; now most common in ponds and impoundments.

Similar species: (1) White and (2) Black Crappies (both, Pl. 36) have anal fin base about as long as dorsal fin base, 6–8 dorsal spines.
Map 285

FLIER *Centrarchus macropterus* **Pl. 36**
Identification: *Large black teardrop. Interrupted rows of black spots* along side. *7–8 anal spines.* Deep, extremely compressed body; small mouth. *Red-orange* around black spot near rear of 2d dorsal fin on young. Dorsal fin base about as long as anal fin base. Dusky gray back; silver side, many green and bronze flecks; brown-black spots, often in wavy bands, on dorsal, caudal, and anal fins; black edge on front half of anal fin. 4 broad dark brown bars, widest at top, on side of young. 36–44 lateral scales; 11–13 dorsal spines, 12–15 rays; 13–17 anal rays. To 7½ in. (19 cm).
Range: Coastal Plain from Potomac R. drainage, MD, to cen. FL, and west to Trinity R., TX; north in Former Mississippi Embayment to s. IL and s. IN; above Fall Line in s. IN, s. IL, rarely elsewhere. **Habitat:** Swamps; vegetated lakes, ponds, sloughs, and backwaters and pools of creeks and small rivers; usually over mud.
Similar species: (1) Black and (2) White Crappies (both, Pl. 36) *lack* bold black teardrop, rows of black spots on side; have 6–8 dorsal spines.
Map 286

BLACK CRAPPIE *Pomoxis nigromaculatus* **Pl. 36**
Identification: *Long predorsal region* arched with *sharp dip* over eye; dorsal fin base about as long as distance from eye to dorsal fin origin, about as long as anal fin base. *7–8 dorsal spines,* 1st much shorter than last. Large mouth; upper jaw extends under eye. Deep, extremely compressed body. Gray-green above; wavy black lines, blotches, green flecks on silver-blue side; white below; many wavy black bands, spots on dorsal, caudal, and anal fins. 15–16 dorsal rays; 6 anal spines, 17–19 rays. To 19¼ in. (49 cm).
Range: So widely introduced throughout U.S. that native range is difficult to determine; presumably Atlantic Slope from VA to FL, Gulf Slope west to TX, St. Lawrence–Great Lakes and Mississippi R. basins from QU to MB south to Gulf. Common in lowlands; rare in uplands. **Habitat:** Lakes, ponds, sloughs, and backwaters and pools of streams. Usually among vegetation over mud or sand; most common in clear water.
Similar species: White Crappie (Pl. 36) has 6 dorsal spines, dark bars on side, dorsal fin base less than distance from eye to dorsal fin origin.
Map 287

WHITE CRAPPIE *Pomoxis annularis* **Pl. 36**
Identification: *Very long predorsal region* arched with *sharp dip* over eye; dorsal fin base shorter than distance from eye to dorsal fin origin, about as long as anal fin base. *6 dorsal spines,* 1st much shorter than last. Large mouth; upper jaw extends under eye. Deep, extremely compressed body. Gray-green above; silver side with 6–9 dusky chainlike bars on side (widest at top), black blotches, green flecks; white below; wavy black bands, spots on dorsal, caudal, and

anal fins. 14–15 dorsal rays; 6 anal spines, 17–19 rays. To 21 in. (53 cm).

Range: Native to Great Lakes, Hudson Bay (Red R.), and Mississippi R. basins from NY and s. ON west to MN and SD, and south to Gulf; Gulf drainages from Mobile Bay, GA and AL, to Nueces R., TX. Widely introduced elsewhere in U.S. Common. **Habitat:** Sand- and mud-bottomed pools and backwaters of creeks and small to large rivers; lakes, ponds. Often in turbid water.

Similar species: Black Crappie (Pl. 36) has 7–8 dorsal spines, *no dark bars* on side, dorsal fin base about same length as distance from eye to dorsal fin origin; is deeper bodied.   **Map 288**

• *AMBLOPLITES*

Genus characteristics: Usually 6 (range is 5–7) *anal spines. Red eye.* Dusky spots, brown wavy lines on dorsal, caudal, and anal fins; white edge on ear flap; dusky to black teardrop. Compressed as young; thicker bodied as adult. Large mouth, upper jaw extending under eye pupil. Short, rounded pectoral fin. Fairly long, fairly slender rakers on 1st gill arch. Complete lateral line.

ROANOKE BASS *Ambloplites cavifrons*   **Pl. 36**
Identification: *Unscaled or partly scaled cheek.* Many *iridescent gold to white spots* on upper side and head. Olive to tan above; dark and light marbling on side, often with rows of black spots; white to bronze breast and belly. 39–49 lateral scales, 11 anal rays, 27–35 scale rows across breast (pectoral fin to pectoral fin). To 14½ in. (36 cm).
Range: Chowan, Roanoke, Tar, and Neuse R. drainages, VA and NC. Uncommon and localized; reduced populations at least in part due to competition with introduced Rock Bass. **Habitat:** Rocky and sandy pools of creeks and small to medium rivers; most common in clear streams above Fall Line.
Similar species: Other *Ambloplites* species (Pl. 36) have fully scaled cheek, *lack* gold to white spots; Rock Bass has black edges on median fins of adult.   **Map 289**

ROCK BASS *Ambloplites rupestris*   **Pl. 36**
Identification: Adult has rows of *brown-black spots* along side, largest and darkest below lateral line. Young has *brown marbling* on gray side. Light green above, brassy yellow flecks on back and down to midside; about 5 wide dark saddles over back and down to midside; white to bronze breast and belly; black edges on dorsal, caudal, and anal fins of adult. 36–47 lateral scales; usually 7–8 scales above lateral line, 21–25 scale rows across breast from pectoral fin to pectoral fin; usually 11–13 dorsal spines, 10–11 anal rays. To 17 in. (43 cm).
Range: Native to St. Lawrence R.–Great Lakes, Hudson Bay (Red R.), and Mississippi R. basins, from QU to SD, and south to n. GA, n. AL, and MO (native in MO only to Meramec R.). Introduced in Atlantic drainages as far south as Roanoke R., VA, in Missouri and Arkansas

R. drainages, MO, AR, se. KS, and ne. OK, and in some western states. Common. **Habitat:** Vegetated and brushy stream margins and pools of creeks and small to medium rivers; rocky and vegetated margins of lakes. Most common in clear, silt-free rocky streams.
Similar species: See Pl. 36. See (1) Ozark and (2) Shadow Basses. (3) Roanoke Bass has unscaled or partly scaled cheek, iridescent gold to white spots on upper side and head. (4) Warmouth has only 3 anal spines, dark lines radiating from eye. **Map 290**

OZARK BASS *Ambloplites constellatus* Pl. 36
Identification: Similar to Rock Bass but with *freckled pattern* (scattered dark brown spots) on side of body and head, more slender body, no black edge on anal fin of large male, usually 41–46 lateral scales (range is 38–48), 8–9 scale rows above lateral line. To 7½ in. (19 cm).
Range: Native to White R. drainage, MO and AR; introduced in other streams in MO and AR, but no evidence of establishment. **Habitat:** Clear rocky pools of creeks and small to medium rivers; usually found near stream bank, large boulders, or brush.
Similar species: See Pl. 36. (1) See Rock Bass. (2) Shadow and (3) Roanoke Basses *lack* freckled pattern. **Map 290**

SHADOW BASS *Ambloplites ariommus* Pl. 36
Identification: Similar to young Rock Bass with *irregular marbling* of brown or gray on light green or brown side, *large eye* and compressed body, but with usually 15–18 scale rows across breast (pectoral fin to pectoral fin). To 8¾ in. (22 cm).
Range: Gulf Slope from Apalachicola R. drainage, GA, to lower Mississippi R. basin, LA; St. Francis, Black, Arkansas, Red, and upper Ouachita R. drainages, MO and AR. Common. **Habitat:** Brushy and vegetated, gravel-, sand-, and mud-bottomed pools of creeks and small to medium rivers.
Similar species: (1) Rock Bass (Pl. 36) has rows of dark spots along side of adult, smaller eye, usually 21–25 scale rows across breast. (2) Ozark Bass (Pl. 36) has freckled pattern on side, smaller eye, 20–26 scale rows across breast. **Map 289**

MUD SUNFISH *Acantharchus pomotis* Pl. 38
Identification: *Rounded caudal fin. Oblong*, compressed body. *3–4 parallel black stripes* across face (above eye, through eye, along upper jaw) and along side of body. Large eye; short snout; large mouth, upper jaw extending under eye. Light to dark green body; 4–5 dark brown stripes (often faint) along side; black spot, orange edge (on large individual) on ear flap; clear to dusky olive fins, black edge on anal fin. *Cycloid scales.* 32–45 lateral scales; 20–30 (usually 24–28) scales around caudal peduncle; 10–12 dorsal spines, 9–13 rays; usually 5 (4–6) anal spines, 9–11 rays. To 8¼ in. (21 cm).
Range: Atlantic Coastal Plain and lower Piedmont drainages from Hudson R., NY, to St. Johns R., FL; Gulf Coastal Plain drainages of n. FL and s. GA from Suwannee R. to St. Marks R. Widely distributed but uncommon. **Habitat:** Vegetated sloughs, lakes; pools and back-

waters of creeks and small to medium rivers; usually over mud and detritus.
Similar species: All other sunfishes have *ctenoid scales*; only the Green Sunfish (Pl. 37) has 23 or more scales around caudal peduncle.
Map 291

BANDED SUNFISH *Enneacanthus obesus*   **Pl. 38**
Identification: *Round caudal fin; dark bars* on side (darkest on large individual). Dusky olive above; rows of *purple-gold spots* along side; light olive below; black teardrop; median fins dark with rows of pale spots. Dark spot on ear flap larger than eye pupil. Deep, compressed body. Usually 19–22 scales around caudal peduncle. 29–35 lateral scales; 8–9 (rarely 10) dorsal spines, 10–13 rays; 3 anal spines, 9–12 rays. To 3¾ in. (9.5 cm).
Range: Below Fall Line in Atlantic and Gulf Slope drainages from s. NH to Perdido R., FL; south to cen. FL. Common. **Habitat:** Heavily vegetated lakes, ponds, sluggish sand- or mud-bottomed pools and backwaters of creeks and small to large rivers.
Similar species: (1) See Bluespotted Sunfish (Pl. 38). (2) Blackbanded Sunfish (Pl. 38) has black blotch at front of dorsal fin, red/pink and black pelvic fin; usually 10 dorsal spines, 12–13 anal rays. **Map 292**

BLUESPOTTED SUNFISH *Enneacanthus gloriosus*   **Pl. 38**
Identification: Similar to Banded Sunfish but with usually *16–18 scales* around more slender caudal peduncle; rows of *blue or silver spots* along side of large young and adult; dark spot on ear flap about ⅔ as large as eye pupil, bars on side *indistinct* in adult. 28–33 lateral scales. To 3¾ in. (9.5 cm).
Range: In Atlantic and Gulf Slope drainages below Fall Line from s. NY to lower Tombigbee R., AL; south to s. FL; above Fall Line in NY and PA. Common. **Habitat:** Vegetated lakes, ponds, sluggish sand- and mud-bottomed pools and backwaters of creeks and small to large rivers.
Similar species: See Banded Sunfish (Pl. 38).   **Map 293**

BLACKBANDED SUNFISH *Enneacanthus chaetodon*   **Pl. 38**
Identification: *6 black bars* on side, 1st through eye, 6th (often faint) on caudal peduncle. *1st 2–3 membranes* of dorsal fin black; middle spines longest. *Pink to red* (spine and 1st membrane), then black, on pelvic fin. Deep, extremely compressed body; small mouth. Dusky yellow-gray above, light below; yellow flecks on side; black spot on ear flap; dorsal, anal, and caudal fins with black mottling. Usually 19–21 scales around caudal peduncle. 26–30 lateral scales; usually 10 dorsal spines, 11–12 rays; 3 anal spines, 11–14 (usually 12–13) rays. To 3¼ in. (8 cm).
Range: Below Fall Line in Atlantic and Gulf Slope drainages from NJ to cen. FL, west to Flint R., GA. Locally common but absent from some drainages within range. **Habitat:** Vegetated lakes, ponds, quiet sand- and mud-bottomed pools and backwaters of creeks and small to medium rivers.

Similar species: (1) Banded and (2) Bluespotted Sunfishes (both, Pl. 38) *lack* black at front of dorsal fin, red/pink and black pelvic fin; have usually 8–9 dorsal spines, 9–11 anal rays.   **Map 294**

● *MICROPTERUS*

Genus characteristics: *Large* (all species reach at least 14 in. [36 cm]), feisty fishes that are among the most popular sport fishes in the world. Moderately compressed, *elongate body*, becoming deeper with age. *Large mouth*, extends under or past eye. Anal fin base less than half dorsal fin base; shallowly forked caudal fin; smooth (not serrated) opercle edge. Black spot at rear of gill cover (no long flap); dark brown lines radiating from snout and back of eye to edge of opercle; clear to yellow-olive fins, dusky spots on median fins. *3 anal spines; 55 or more lateral scales; 9–11 dorsal spines.*

LARGEMOUTH BASS *Micropterus salmoides*   **Pl. 35**
Identification: 1st dorsal fin *highest at middle*, low at rear; 1st (spinous) and 2d (soft) dorsal fins *nearly separate. Very large mouth*, upper jaw extending well past eye (except in young). Silver to brassy green (brown in dark water) above, dark olive mottling; *broad black stripe* (often broken into series of blotches) along side and onto snout; brown eye; scattered black specks on lower side; white below. Usually no patch of teeth on tongue. Forked pyloric caeca. Usually 60–72 lateral scales, 13–14 dorsal rays, 14–15 pectoral rays, 11–12 anal rays. To 38 in. (97 cm).
Range: Native to St. Lawrence–Great Lakes, Hudson Bay (Red R.), and Mississippi R. basins from s. QU to MN and south to Gulf; Atlantic drainages from NC to FL; Gulf drainages from s. FL into n. Mexico. Now introduced over most of U.S. and extreme s. Canada. Common. **Habitat:** Clear, vegetated lakes, ponds, swamps, and backwaters and pools of creeks and small to large rivers; usually over mud or sand. Common in impoundments.
Remarks: Two subspecies. *M. s. floridanus*, in peninsular FL, attains a larger size, has usually 69–76 lateral scales, 28–31 scales around caudal peduncle. *M. s. salmoides*, throughout rest of range except for broad area of subspecific intergradation in se. U.S., has usually 59–66 lateral scales, 26–28 scales around caudal peduncle.
Similar species: Other species of *Micropterus* (Pl. 35) have more *confluent* dorsal fins, upper jaw to or barely past eye, unforked pyloric caeca.   **Map 295**

SUWANNEE BASS *Micropterus notius*   **Pl. 35**
Identification: Large mouth, upper jaw extending under eye. Color as in Largemouth Bass except usually brown overall; large male has bright *turquoise* cheek, breast, and belly. Usually a patch of teeth on tongue. Unforked pyloric caeca. Usually 59–64 lateral scales, 16 pectoral rays, 5 rakers on 1st gill arch; 12–13 dorsal rays; 10–11 anal rays. To 14¼ in. (36 cm).

Range: Suwannee R. drainage, FL (fairly common), and Ochlockonee R. drainage, FL and GA (uncommon). **Habitat:** Rocky riffles, runs, and pools; large springs and spring runs.
Similar species: Largemouth Bass (Pl. 35) has deep notch between 1st and 2d dorsal fin; usually 14–15 pectoral rays, 8 rakers on 1st gill arch; forked pyloric caeca. **Map 296**

SPOTTED BASS *Micropterus punctulatus* **Pl. 35**
Identification: *Rows of small black spots* on lower side; black stripe (or series of partly joined blotches) along side; black caudal spot (darkest on young). Light gold-green above, dark olive mottling; yellow-white below. Young has *3-colored* (yellow, black, white edge) caudal fin. Large mouth, upper jaw extending under rear half of eye. Patch of teeth on tongue. Unforked pyloric caeca. Usually 61–73 lateral scales, 23–26 scales around caudal peduncle, 12–13 dorsal rays, 9–11 anal rays, 15–16 pectoral rays. To 24 in. (61 cm).
Range: Mississippi R. basin from s. OH and WV to se. KS, and south to Gulf; Gulf drainages from Chattahoochee (where possibly introduced), GA, to Guadalupe R., TX. Introduced onto Atlantic Slope in VA and NC, in lower Pecos R., NM, and Consumnes and Feather rivers, CA. **Habitat:** Clear, gravelly flowing pools and runs of creeks and small to medium rivers; occupies impoundments in s. part of range.
Remarks: Three subspecies. *M. p. henshalli*, an elongate form in the upper Mobile Bay basin, GA, AL, and MS, with usually 68–75 lateral scales, 27–28 scales around caudal peduncle and 12 dorsal rays, intergrades with *M. p. punctulatus* in Mobile Bay basin below Fall Line, AL. *M. p. wichitae*, confined to Cache Cr. (Red R. system) in Wichita Mountains, sw. OK, has usually 13 dorsal rays, often lacks rows of black spots along lower side. *M. p. punctulatus*, in rest of range, has usually 60–68 lateral scales, 23–26 scales around caudal peduncle, 12 dorsal rays.
Similar species: See Pl. 35. (1) See Guadalupe Bass. (2) Redeye and (3) Shoal Basses have dark bars along side, usually 26 or more scales around caudal peduncle; Redeye has white or orange upper and lower outer edges on caudal fin lobes, red fins on young; Shoal has no patch of teeth on tongue. (4) Largemouth Bass *lacks* rows of black spots, has deep notch between dorsal fins; has *2-colored* (white, black edge) caudal fin on young. **Map 297**

GUADALUPE BASS *Micropterus treculi* **Pl. 35**
Identification: Similar to Spotted Bass but has *10–12 dark bars* along side (darkest in young), usually 16 pectoral rays, 26–27 scales around caudal peduncle. To 15¾ in. (40 cm).
Range: On Edwards Plateau in Brazos, Colorado, Guadalupe, San Antonio, and upper Nueces (where introduced) R. drainages, TX. Common. **Habitat:** Gravel riffles, runs, and flowing pools of creeks and small to medium rivers.
Similar species: See Spotted Bass (Pl. 35). **Map 298**

REDEYE BASS *Micropterus coosae* **Pl. 35**
Identification: *White upper and lower outer edges* on orange caudal fin. *Rows of dark spots* on lower side; *dark bars* (often absent) along

side, diamond shaped and with *light centers* on caudal peduncle. 2d dorsal, caudal, and front of anal fin *brick red* on young. Bronze-olive above, dark olive mottling; yellow-white to blue below; dusky spot on caudal fin base (darkest on young). Large mouth, upper jaw extending under rear half of eye. Usually a patch of teeth on tongue. Unforked pyloric caeca. Usually 64–73 lateral scales, 26–30 scales around caudal peduncle, 13–18 scales below lateral line, 12 dorsal rays, 10 anal rays. To 18½ in. (47 cm).
Range: Above Fall Line in Savannah, Chattahoochee, and Mobile Bay basins, NC, SC, GA, TN, and AL. Introduced elsewhere, including Altamaha R., GA; Sisquoc R., CA; and upper Cumberland R. drainage (Martins Fork), KY. Common, especially in upper Alabama R. system. **Habitat:** Rocky runs and pools of creeks and small to medium rivers.
Similar species: (1) See Shoal Bass (Pl. 35). (2) Spotted Bass (Pl. 35) *lacks* white or orange upper and lower outer edges on caudal fin lobes, red fins; has *black stripe* along side, black caudal spot, usually 23–26 scales around caudal peduncle.   **Map 296**

SHOAL BASS *Micropterus* species   **Pl. 35**
Identification: Similar to Redeye Bass but *lacks* white outer edges on caudal fin; has *smaller scales* (usually 29–34 around caudal peduncle, 70–79 lateral scales, 18–21 scales below lateral line), *no* patch of teeth on tongue. Usually 12–13 dorsal rays, 10–11 anal rays. To 15¼ in. (39 cm).
Range: Apalachicola R. system, GA and AL. Uncommon. **Habitat:** Rocky riffles and runs of creeks and small to large rivers.
Similar species: See Redeye Bass (Pl. 35).   **Map 296**

SMALLMOUTH BASS *Micropterus dolomieu*   **Pl. 35**
Identification: *Dark brown; bronze specks*, often coalesced into *8–16 bars*, on yellow-green side. Olive-brown above, dark mottling on back and side; red eye; yellow-white below. Young has *3-colored* (yellow, black, white edge) caudal fin. Large male is green-brown to bronze with black mottling on back, bars on side. Large mouth; upper jaw extends under eye. Usually no patch of teeth on tongue. Unforked pyloric caeca. Usually 69–77 lateral scales, 29–32 scales around caudal peduncle, 13–14 dorsal rays, 11 anal rays. To 27¼ in. (69 cm).
Range: Native to St. Lawrence-Great Lakes, Hudson Bay (Red R.), and Mississippi R. basins from s. QU to ND and south to n. AL and e. OK. Now widely introduced throughout s. Canada and U.S. except in Atlantic and Gulf Slope drainages, where rare south of VA and east of cen. TX. Fairly common. **Habitat:** Clear, gravel-bottom runs and flowing pools of small to large rivers; shallow rocky areas of lakes.
Remarks: Two subspecies often recognized. *M. d. velox*, in the Arkansas R. drainage, se. MO, se. KS, nw. AR, and ne. OK, is slender, has protruding lower jaw (teeth visible from above), usually 13 dorsal rays. Intergrades (usually 14 dorsal rays) occupy rest of s. Ozark and Ouachita uplands. *M. d. dolomieu*, in rest of range, is more robust, has less protruding lower jaw, usually 14 dorsal rays.

Similar species: See Pl. 35. (1) Spotted Bass has rows of black spots along lower side, black stripe (*no bars*) along side, usually 60–68 lateral scales. (2) Redeye Bass has rows of black spots along lower side, white or orange upper and lower outer edges on caudal fin lobes. (3) Largemouth Bass has black stripe (*no bars*) along side, larger mouth, deep notch between 1st and 2d dorsal fin, usually 60–72 lateral scales.   **Map 299**

• *LEPOMIS*

Genus characteristics: Deep, *strongly compressed body* ("pan fish"); *3 anal spines;* shallowly forked caudal fin; smooth (not serrated) opercle edge; fewer than 55 lateral scales. Adult male sunfishes are among the most brightly colored fishes in North America. Colors of adults are some of the best characteristics to distinguish species. Other characters include the size and shape of the rakers on the 1st gill arch (Fig. 52), which may be viewed when the gill cover is lifted; the "ear flap," a fleshy extension at the rear of the gill cover; and the gill cover itself, which may be stiff to its edge or which may have a thin and flexible edge. *Lepomis* species readily hybridize with one another. Hybrids are especially characteristic of turbid or polluted waters, where fishes are forced to spawn under conditions that hinder accurate species recognition. Spawning behavior in some species (e.g., Bluegill) involves individuals that have been referred to as "sneakers" and "satellites." A small male, unable to command a good territory himself, may successfully spawn within the territory of a larger male by "sneaking" in and fertilizing eggs when the larger male is paying attention only to a female, or by mimicking a female (i.e., as a "satellite") and being allowed by the territorial male to join in.

WARMOUTH *Lepomis gulosus*   **Pl. 36**
Identification: *Dark red-brown lines* (absent on young) radiating from back of *red eye. Large mouth,* upper jaw extending under or beyond eye pupil. Fairly slender, *thick body. Patch of teeth* on tongue (detect by feeling with finger). Short, rounded pectoral fin, usually not reaching past eye when bent forward. Short ear flap; stiff rear edge on gill cover (excluding ear flap). Olive-brown above, often with purple sheen overall; dark brown mottling on back and upper side; often 6–11 chainlike dark brown bars on side; red spot (on adult) on yellow edge of ear flap; cream to bright yellow below; dark brown spots (absent on young) and wavy bands on fins. Breeding male has bold pattern on body and fins, bright red-orange spot at base of 2d dorsal fin, black pelvic fins. Complete lateral line; 36–44 lateral scales; usually 14 pectoral rays, 9–10 anal rays. Long, thin rakers on 1st gill arch. To 12 in. (31 cm).
Range: Native to Great Lakes and Mississippi R. basins from w. PA to MN, and south to Gulf; Atlantic and Gulf drainages from

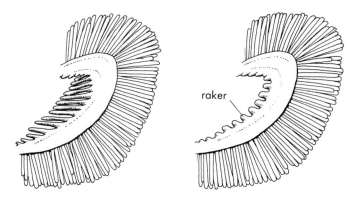

Fig. 52 Long and short gill rakers of sunfishes (*Lepomis*)

Rappahannock R., VA, to Rio Grande, TX and NM. Introduced else-where in U.S., including lower Colorado R. drainage, where com-mon. Common in lowland areas; uncommon in uplands. **Habitat:** Vegetated lakes, ponds, swamps and quiet water areas of streams; usually over mud.
Similar species: (1) Green sunfish (Pl. 37) *lacks* dark lines behind eye, patch of teeth on tongue; has large black spot at rear base of 2d dorsal and anal fins; yellow or orange edges on median fins. (2) Rock Bass (Pl. 36) has 6 anal spines, *no* dark lines behind eye.   **Map 300**

GREEN SUNFISH *Lepomis cyanellus*   **Pl. 37**
Identification: Fairly long snout, *large mouth,* upper jaw extending be-neath eye pupil. Fairly *slender, thick body.* Adult has *large black spot* at rear of 2d dorsal and anal fin bases; *yellow or orange edges* on 2d dorsal, caudal, and anal fins. Blue-green back and side; often yellow–metallic green flecks, sometimes dusky bars on side; green wavy lines on cheek and opercle; white to yellow edge (some red on young) on black ear flap; white to yellow belly. Short, rounded pec-toral fin, usually not reaching past front of eye when bent forward. Short ear flap; stiff rear edge of gill cover (excluding ear flap). Com-plete lateral line; 41–53 lateral scales; usually 13–14 pectoral rays, 9 anal rays. Long, slender rakers on 1st gill arch. To 12 in. (31 cm).
Range: Native to Great Lakes, Hudson Bay, and Mississippi R. basins from NY and ON to MN and SD, and south to Gulf; Gulf Slope drain-ages from Escambia R., FL, and Mobile Bay, GA and AL, to Rio Grande, TX. Also n. Mexico. Introduced over much of U.S., including Pacific drainages in CA and OR. Common to abundant; one of the most frequently encountered North American fishes. **Habitat:** Quiet pools and backwaters of sluggish streams; lakes and ponds. Often near vegetation.

Similar species: (1) Other sunfishes (Pl. 37) *lack* yellow-orange edges on fins and black spot at rear base of anal fin (except Bluegill); and have *smaller mouth* (except Warmouth). (2) Warmouth (Pl. 36) has dark brown lines radiating from eye, mottling on side, teeth on tongue. **Map 301**

BANTAM SUNFISH *Lepomis symmetricus* **Pl. 37**
Identification: *Black spot* at rear of dorsal fin on young (spot diminishes as fish grows, is absent in large adult). *Lacks* bright coloration of other sunfishes. *Chubby body* (less compressed). *Usually interrupted, incomplete lateral line.* Short, rounded pectoral fin, usually not reaching past eye when bent forward. Fairly large mouth; upper jaw extending under eye pupil. Short ear flap; stiff rear edge on gill cover (excluding ear flap). Dusky green back and side; yellow flecks and scattered small dark brown spots on side of adult, chainlike bars on side of young; white edge on black ear flap; yellow-brown below; red dorsal and anal fins on young, clear to dusky fins on adult. 30–40 lateral scales; usually 12–13 pectoral rays, 10 anal rays. Long, thin rakers on 1st gill arch. To 3½ in. (9 cm).
Range: Former Mississippi Embayment from s. IL to Gulf; Gulf Coastal Plain drainages from Bay St. Louis, MS, to Colorado R., TX. Isolated populations occurred historically above Fall Line in Illinois R. and Wabash R. drainages, IL. Common in s.-cen. (especially LA) part of range. **Habitat:** Swamps; mud-bottomed and heavily vegetated ponds, lakes, and sloughs.
Similar species: (1) Other sunfishes except Green Sunfish and Bluegill *lack* black spot at rear of dorsal fin. (2) Green Sunfish (Pl. 37) is more slender, has larger mouth, yellow-orange edges on fins. (3) Bluegill (Pl. 37) has long pectoral fin and dark edge on ear flap, is more compressed. **Map 291**

SPOTTED SUNFISH *Lepomis punctatus* **Pl. 37**
Identification: *Many black specks or rows of red-orange* (in male) *or yellow-brown spots* (female) along side (see Remarks). Short, rounded pectoral fin, usually not reaching past eye when bent forward. Short ear flap; stiff rear edge of gill cover (excluding ear flap). Dark olive above; white to yellow edge on black ear flap; white, yellow, or red-orange below; clear to dusky fins. Complete lateral line; 34–45 lateral scales; usually 13–14 pectoral rays, 10 anal rays. Moderately long, slender rakers on 1st gill arch. To 8 in. (20 cm).
Range: Atlantic and Gulf Slope drainages from Cape Fear R., NC, to Nueces R., TX; north in Mississippi R. basin to cen. IL. Introduced into Devils R. (Rio Grande drainage), TX. Common; locally abundant in s. part of range. **Habitat:** Heavily vegetated ponds, lakes, pools of creeks and small to medium rivers; swamps. Usually over mud or sand.
Remarks: Two subspecies. *L. p. punctatus*, in the Atlantic drainages and throughout most of FL, has many *black specks* on body and head, *no* rows of red/yellow spots on side, smaller scales (usually 38–44 lateral scales). *L. p. miniatus*, throughout rest of the range, has pale to

bright red-orange patch on side just above ear flap, rows of *red/yellow spots* on side, *no* black specks on body, larger scales (usually 35–41 lateral scales). Intergrades occur in the FL panhandle, w. GA, and se. AL.

Similar species: See Pl. 37. (1) Bantam Sunfish *lacks* black specks on head, rows of red or yellow spots, red patch near ear flap; has black spot at rear of 2d dorsal fin, interrupted lateral line. (2) Longear, (3) Dollar, and (4) Redbreast Sunfishes have wavy blue lines on cheek and opercle, longer ear flap, and short gill rakers and *lack* black specks on head, red patch near ear flap; Longear and Dollar Sunfishes *lack* many black specks or rows of red spots.   **Map 302**

BLUEGILL *Lepomis macrochirus*   **Pl. 37**
Identification: *Large black spot* at rear of dorsal fin (faint on young); often a dusky spot at rear of anal fin. *Dark bars* (absent in turbid water; thin and chainlike on young) on deep, *extremely compressed body. Long pointed pectoral fin*; usually extends far past eye when bent forward. Ear flap black to edge, fairly long in adult; thin, flexible rear edge on gill cover. Small mouth, upper jaw not extending under eye pupil. Olive back and side with yellow and green flecks; adult with blue sheen overall, 2 blue streaks from chin to edge of gill cover; white to yellow below; clear to dusky fins. Breeding male has blue head, back; bright red-orange breast and belly; black pelvic fins. Complete lateral line; 38–48 lateral scales; usually 13 pectoral rays, 11 anal rays. Long, thin rakers on 1st gill arch. To 16¼ in. (41 cm).
Range: Native to St. Lawrence–Great Lakes and Mississippi R. basins from QU and NY to MN and south to Gulf; Atlantic and Gulf Slope drainages from Cape Fear R., VA, to Rio Grande, TX and NM. Also in n. Mexico. Now introduced over most of the U.S. Common. Often abundant in impoundments. **Habitat:** Vegetated lakes, ponds, swamps, and pools of creeks and small to large rivers.
Remarks: Three subspecies generally recognized, but ranges uncertain. *L. m. purpurescens*, on the Atlantic Slope and peninsular FL, has usually 12 anal rays, redder fins and broader bars in the young, a cream-colored bar on nape of adult, and a larger size than other subspecies. *L. m. speciosus*, in w. TX and Mexico, with usually 10 anal rays, intergrades with *L. m. macrochirus* in the Arkansas and Red R. drainages, AR, OK, and TX. *L. m. macrochirus*, throughout rest of range, has usually 11 anal rays, numerous narrow dark bars on side. Stocking programs have mixed populations, and subspecies may no longer be recognizable.
Similar species: Redear Sunfish (Pl. 37) *lacks* large spot in 2d dorsal fin; has red edge on ear flap, short gill rakers.   **Map 303**

REDEAR SUNFISH *Lepomis microlophus*   **Pl. 37**
Identification: *Bright red or orange spot,* light-colored edge on black ear flap (best developed on large adult). *Long, pointed pectoral fin;* usually extends far past eye when bent forward. Fairly pointed snout; small mouth, upper jaw not extending under eye pupil. Light gold-green above; dusky gray spots (on adult) or bars (on young) on side;

white to yellow below; mostly clear fins, some dark mottling in 2d dorsal of adult. Breeding male is brassy gold, has dusky pelvic fins. Short ear flap; thin, flexible rear edge on gill cover. Complete lateral line; 34–47 lateral scales; usually 13–14 pectoral rays, 10 anal rays. Short, thick rakers on 1st gill arch. To 10 in. (25 cm).
Range: Native to Atlantic and Gulf Slope drainages from about Savannah R., SC, to Nueces R., TX; north in Mississippi R. basin to s. IN and IL. Now widely introduced in e. U.S. as far north as PA and n. IL. Common. **Habitat:** Ponds, swamps, lakes; vegetated pools, usually with mud or sand bottoms, of small to medium rivers.
Remarks: Two unnamed subspecies. First, in FL, GA, and s. AL, has 40–47 lateral scales and 5–6 scale rows on cheek. Second, throughout rest of range, has 34–39 lateral scales and 3–4 scale rows on cheek. Although these subspecies were historically recognizable, they may no longer be separable because stocking programs have mixed populations.
Similar species: See Pl. 37. (1) Pumpkinseed has bold spots on 2d dorsal fin, wavy blue lines on cheek and opercle, stiff rear edge on gill cover. (2) Longear and (3) Dollar Sunfishes have short, rounded pectoral fins, wavy blue lines on cheek and opercle, long ear flap.

Map 304

PUMPKINSEED *Lepomis gibbosus* Pl. 37
Identification: *Bright red or orange spot,* light-colored edge on black ear flap. Many *bold dark brown wavy lines* or *orange spots* on 2nd dorsal, caudal, and anal fins. *Wavy blue lines* on cheek and opercle of adult. *Long, pointed pectoral fin;* usually extends far past eye when bent forward. Small mouth, upper jaw not extending under eye pupil. Olive back and side, many gold and yellow flecks; adult blue-green, spotted with orange; dusky chainlike bars on side of young and adult female; white to red-orange below. Short ear flap; stiff rear edge on gill cover (excluding ear flap). Complete lateral line; 35–47 lateral scales; usually 12–13 pectoral rays, 10 anal rays. Short, thick rakers on 1st gill arch. To 16 in. (40 cm).
Range: Native to Atlantic drainages from NB to Edisto R., SC; Great Lakes, Hudson Bay, and upper Mississippi basins from QU and NY west to se. MB and ND, and south to n. KY and MO. Introduced over much of s. Canada and U.S., including some Pacific drainages. Common. **Habitat:** Vegetated lakes and ponds; quiet vegetated pools of creeks and small rivers.
Similar species: (1) Redear Sunfish (Pl. 37) *lacks* bold spots on 2d dorsal fin, wavy blue lines on cheek, stiff rear edge on gill cover. (2) Longear Sunfish (Pl. 37) *lacks* bold spots on 2d dorsal fin; has short, rounded pectoral fin, flexible rear edge on gill cover. **Map 305**

LONGEAR SUNFISH *Lepomis megalotis* Pl. 37
Identification: *Long ear flap* (especially in adult male), usually bordered above and below by *blue line;* horizontal in adult, slanted upward in young. *Wavy blue lines* on cheek and opercle. Short and rounded pectoral fin, usually not reaching past eye when bent for-

ward. Fairly large mouth, upper jaw extending under eye pupil. Thin, flexible rear edge on gill cover. Young has olive back and side speckled with yellow flecks, often with chainlike bars on side, white below. Adult is dark red above, *bright orange* below, marbled and spotted with *blue;* white (rarely orange) edge on black ear flap (see Remarks); clear to orange and blue, unspotted fins. Breeding male is a brilliant contrast in orange and blue, has red eye, orange to red median fins, blue-black pelvic fins. Complete lateral line; 33–46 lateral scales; usually 13–14 pectoral rays, 9–10 anal rays, 5–7 scale rows on cheek (along imaginary line from eye to preopercle angle – Fig. 1). Very short, thick rakers on 1st gill arch. To 9½ in. (24 cm).

Range: Native to St. Lawrence–Great Lakes, Hudson Bay, Mississippi R., and Gulf Slope drainages west of Appalachian Mountains from s. QU west to w. ON and MN, and south to FL panhandle and s. TX; on Gulf Slope from Choctawhatchee R., FL, to Rio Grande, TX and NM. Also in ne. Mexico. Introduced sporadically elsewhere in U.S. Common; locally abundant in upland areas and in clear streams throughout range. **Habitat:** Rocky and sandy pools of headwaters, creeks, and small to medium rivers; usually near vegetation.

Remarks: Variable, with up to 6 subspecies, but ranges and variation poorly understood. The form generally known as the Northern Longear Sunfish, *L. m. peltastes,* occurring south to n. OH, IN, IL, and IA, is small (usually less than 5 in.), has a large *red spot* on an *upwardly slanted* ear flap, has 40 or fewer lateral scales, and may be a distinct species.

Similar species: (1) See Dollar Sunfish. (2) Redbreast Sunfish (Pl. 37) *lacks* blue spots on side; has rows of red-brown spots on upper side; longer, narrower ear flap black to its edge. (3) Pumpkinseed (Pl. 37) has bold spots on 2d dorsal and anal fins; long, pointed pectoral fin; stiff rear edge on gill cover. **Map 306**

DOLLAR SUNFISH *Lepomis marginatus* **Pl. 37**
Identification: Similar to Longear Sunfish but reaches only 4¾ in. (12 cm); has shorter, *upwardly slanted ear flap,* red streak along lateral line, usually *12 pectoral rays,* 4 scale rows on cheek. Breeding male is bright red, marbled and spotted with blue-green, and has *large silver-green specks* on ear flap. 34–44 lateral scales.

Range: Atlantic and Gulf Slope drainages (generally below Fall Line) from Tar R., NC, to Brazos R., TX; Former Mississippi Embayment from w. KY and e. AR south to Gulf. Common in se. U.S., especially FL; generally uncommon in w. part of range. **Habitat:** Sand- and mud-bottomed, usually brushy, pools of creeks and small to medium rivers; swamps.

Remarks: Difficult to distinguish from Longear Sunfish except when habitat is considered. A Longear-like sunfish found in a swamp or swamplike stream habitat is probably a Dollar Sunfish.

Similar species: (1) See Longear Sunfish (Pl. 37). (2) Redbreast Sunfish (Pl. 37) *lacks* blue spots on side; has rows of red-brown spots on upper side; longer, narrower ear flap black to its edge; usually 14 pectoral rays. **Map 307**

REDBREAST SUNFISH *Lepomis auritus* **Pl. 37**
Identification: *Very long, narrow* (no wider than eye) *ear flap,* black to edge, usually bordered above and below by *blue line; wavy blue lines* on cheek and opercle. Dark olive back and side, yellow flecks, rows of *red-brown to orange spots* on upper side, orange spots scattered on lower side; white to orange below; clear to dusky orange fins. Breeding male has bright orange breast and belly, orange fins. Short, rounded pectoral fin, usually not reaching past eye when bent forward. Fairly long snout; large mouth, upper jaw extending under eye pupil. Thin, flexible rear edge on gill cover. Complete lateral line; 39–54 lateral scales; usually 14 pectoral rays, 9–10 anal rays, 6–9 scale rows on cheek. Short, thick rakers on 1st gill arch. To 9½ in. (24 cm).
Range: Native to Atlantic and Gulf Slopes, from NB to cen. FL and west to Apalachicola and Choctawhatchee drainages, GA and FL. Introduced into Gulf drainages as far west as Rio Grande and in Mississippi R. basin as far north as KY and AR. Locally common. **Habitat:** Rocky and sandy pools of creeks and small to medium rivers; rocky and vegetated lake margins.
Similar species: (1) Longear and (2) Dollar Sunfishes (both, Pl. 37) have *shorter* ear flap with white or orange edge, blue marbling and spots on side of adult; *lack* distinct rows of red-brown spots. **Map 308**

ORANGESPOTTED SUNFISH *Lepomis humilis* **Pl. 37**
Identification: *Bright orange* (on large male) or *red-brown* (female) *spots* on silver-green side; young have vertical bars, not spots, on side. Long black ear flap in adult has *wide white edge. Greatly elongated pores* along preopercle edge; large sensory pits between eyes. Short, rounded pectoral fin, usually not reaching past eye when bent forward. Fairly long snout; large mouth, upper jaw extending under eye pupil. Thin, flexible rear edge on gill cover. Olive above, silver-blue flecks on side; white to orange below; orange (on male) or red-brown (female) wavy lines on cheek and opercle; unspotted fins. Young have chainlike dark bars on side. Breeding male is brilliantly colored, with bright red-orange spots on side; red eye, belly, and edges on anal and dorsal fins; black edge on white pelvic fins. Complete lateral line; 32–41 lateral scales; usually 14 pectoral rays, 9 anal rays. Fairly long, thin rakers on 1st gill arch. To 6 in. (15 cm).
Range: Lower Great Lakes (s. ends of Lakes Erie and Michigan), Hudson Bay (Red R.), and Mississippi R. basin from OH to s. ND, and south to LA; Gulf Slope drainages from Mobile Bay, AL, to Colorado R., TX. Common. Sporadically introduced elsewhere in U.S. **Habitat:** Quiet pools of creeks and small to large, often turbid, rivers; usually near brush.
Similar species: Other sunfishes (Pl. 37) with orange spots have dark (blue or olive-brown) side; lack *wide* white edge on ear flap, elongated pores on preopercle. **Map 309**

■ DARTERS, PERCHES, WALLEYE, AND SAUGER
Family Percidae (153)

With at least 153 species, Percidae is the second most diverse family (after Cyprinidae) of North American freshwater fishes. All but 3 species of North American percids are darters. Darters are small — most are less than 4 in. (10 cm) long — and found throughout the U.S. and Canada except in Pacific and Arctic drainages (1 species introduced to California). Most have lost the gas bladder and, as their name implies, dart about on the bottoms of streams and lakes and eat small crustaceans and insects. Some darters are drab, but many are extremely colorful, especially as breeding males. Other than darters, Percidae includes the Walleye, Sauger, Yellow Perch, and about 14 Eurasian species.

Percids have 2 dorsal fins, separate or slightly joined (broadly joined in some Eurasian species), 1st with spines, 2d with rays; thoracic pelvic fins with *1 spine and 5 rays;* ctenoid scales. Characteristics especially useful in the identification of some groups of darters include the shape and completeness of the lateral line and head canals (Fig. 53), the connection of the branchiostegal membranes (Fig. 54), the presence or absence of a premaxillary frenum (Fig. 55), and the number of anal spines. Unless stated otherwise, the lateral line is straight and complete, the branchiostegal membranes are separate or narrowly joined, and the number of anal spines is 2.

WALLEYE *Stizostedion vitreum* **Pl. 38**

Identification: *Huge mouth* extends beyond middle of eye; *large canine teeth. Opaque, silver eye. Large black spot* (absent on young) on rear of 1st dorsal fin. Long, slender body; long pointed snout; forked caudal fin. Yellow-olive to brown above, dark green vermiculations; brassy yellow–blue side; 5–12 dusky saddles extend onto side as short bars (faint on adult); wavy dark brown bands on yellow fins; white tips on anal fin, lower lobe of caudal fin. 77–104 lateral scales; usually 19–22 dorsal rays, 12–14 anal rays; 3 pyloric caeca. To 36 in. (91 cm).

Range: Native to St. Lawrence–Great Lakes, Arctic, and Mississippi R. basins from QU to NT, and south to AL and AR. Widely introduced elsewhere in U.S., including Atlantic, Gulf, and Pacific drainages. Uncommon; locally common. **Habitat:** Lakes; pools, backwaters, and runs of medium to large rivers. Usually in clear water, often near brush.

Remarks: Because of its fighting characteristics and large size, the Walleye is one of our most popular sport fishes. The color morph known as the Blue Pike, sometimes considered a subspecies (*S. v. glaucum*), formerly occurred in Lakes Erie and Ontario and the lower Niagara R., but it is probably extinct. The Blue Pike lacked the brassy yellow color of other Walleyes, was gray-blue with blue-white lower fins, and had a larger eye.

Similar species: (1) See Sauger (Pl. 38). (2) Yellow Perch (Pl. 38) is deeper bodied; *lacks* large canine teeth, opaque silver eye; has trian-

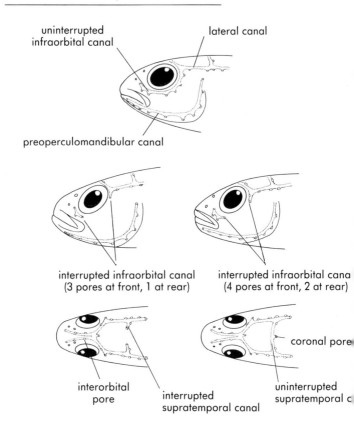

Fig. 53 Darters — head canals and pores

gular bars on side, 52–61 lateral scales, 12–14 dorsal rays, 6–8 anal rays. **Map 310**

SAUGER *Stizostedion canadense* **Pl. 38**
Identification: Similar to Walleye but has *many black half-moons on 1st dorsal fin of adult, 3–4 dusky brown saddles extending onto side as broad bars,* usually 17–19 dorsal rays, 11–12 anal rays, 5–8 pyloric caeca; *lacks* large black spot at rear of 1st dorsal fin, white tip on caudal fin. To 30 in. (76 cm).
Range: Native to St. Lawrence–Great Lakes, Hudson Bay, and Mississippi R. basins from QU to AB, and south to n. AL and LA. Introduced into Atlantic, Gulf, and southern Mississippi R. drainages. Un-

narrow   moderate   broad

Fig. 54 Darters — branchiostegal membrane connection

frenum

groove between
upper lip
and snout

Fig. 55 Darters — presence and absence of premaxillary frenum

common; locally common. **Habitat:** Sand and gravel runs, sandy and muddy pools and backwaters, of small to large rivers; less often in lakes and impoundments.

Remarks: The opaque silver color of Walleye and Sauger eyes is due to the *tapetum lucidum,* a special layer of light-gathering tissue that enables these fishes to be active in twilight and at night.

Similar species: See Walleye (Pl. 38). **Map 311**

YELLOW PERCH *Perca flavescens* **Pl. 38**
Identification: *Fairly deep, compressed body;* forked caudal fin. Green above, *6–9 green-brown saddles extend down yellow side* (often as triangular bars); *black blotch* at rear (and often another at front) of dusky 1st dorsal fin; yellow to red paired fins. Large mouth extends to middle of eye; no canine teeth. 52–61 lateral scales; 12–14 dorsal rays, 6–8 anal rays. To 16 in. (40 cm).
Range: Native to Atlantic, Arctic, Great Lakes, and Mississippi R. basins from NS and QU west to Great Slave Lake, NT, and south to OH, IL, and NE; south in Atlantic drainages to Santee R., SC. Widely introduced elsewhere in U.S. Common. **Habitat:** Lakes, ponds, and pools of creeks and small to large rivers. Most common in clear water near vegetation.
Similar species: (1) See Ruffe. (2) Walleye and (3) Sauger (both, Pl. 38)

are *more slender; lack* triangular bars on side; have large canine teeth, opaque silver eye, more than 80 lateral scales, 11–14 anal rays.

Map 312

RUFFE *Gymnocephalus cernuus*   **Not shown**
 Identification: Similar to Yellow Perch but has *broadly joined dorsal fins,* large (35–40 lateral) scales, and *many small black spots* on dorsal and caudal fins. Green-brown above; many small dark blotches on light brown side; yellow below; clear to pink pectoral fins. To 10 in. (25 cm).
 Range: Native to Eurasia. Recently established in Lakes Superior and Michigan. **Habitat:** Lakes; quiet pools and margins of streams.
 Similar species: See Yellow Perch (Pl. 38).

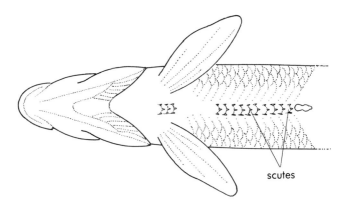

scutes

Fig. 56 *Percina* species — breast and belly

● *PERCINA*

 Genus characteristics: *Percina* contains the primitive darters, which are generally larger than other darters, retain a small gas bladder, and spend more time swimming off the stream bottom than do other darters. *Percina* species have 2 anal spines; a complete lateral line; no interruptions in head canals (Fig. 53); and *scutes* on the breast and, in all species except the Bluestripe and Frecklebelly Darters, in a row along the midline of the belly of the male (Fig. 56). Darters other than *Percina* species lack scutes.

BLUESTRIPE DARTER *Percina cymatotaenia*   **Pl. 39**
 Identification: Highly distinctive, with *broad, scallop-edged black stripe* along side, uninterrupted light stripe on upper side, 3 dark

brown stripes along back to 2d dorsal fin. Yellow below with *many black blotches. Black wedge* on caudal fin base. No scutes on belly; no teardrop; no large black bands on fins. Fully scaled breast. 62–78 lateral scales. "Bluestripe" refers to blue-green squares along side of large male. To 3½ in. (9 cm).
Range: Gasconade and Osage R. drainages, s.-cen. MO. Rare. **Habitat:** Quiet pools and backwaters with submerged or emergent vegetation, usually over mud or sand, in small to medium rivers. Swims in midwater.
Similar species: See Frecklebelly Darter. **Map 313**

FRECKLEBELLY DARTER *Percina* species **Not shown**
Identification: Similar to Bluestripe Darter but has *black teardrop.* Large male has *black bands* on 1st dorsal fin (Fig. 57), black bar on chin. To 3¼ in. (8.5 cm).

Fig. 57 Frecklebelly Darter — 1st dorsal fin

Range: Upper Kentucky and upper Green R. (including Barren R.) drainages, e. and cen. KY, and n.-cen. TN. Fairly common in Kentucky R. drainage; uncommon and localized in Green R. drainage. **Habitat:** Quiet water areas, especially vegetated marginal pools, of creeks and small to medium rivers.
Similar species: (1) See Bluestripe Darter (Pl. 39). (2) Longhead Darter (Pl. 39) *lacks* black chin bar and fully scaled breast, has midbelly row of scutes. **Map 313**

LONGHEAD DARTER *Percina macrocephala* **Pl. 39**
Identification: *Long snout. Sickle-shaped teardrop* curved back and down onto underside of head. *Black bar* below medial black caudal spot. Olive above, wavy black lines, 10–15 dark saddles; *9–15 fused black blotches* along side; light yellow below; black edge and base on 1st dorsal fin. Unscaled or partly scaled cheek and opercle; unscaled breast (except large scutes near pelvic fins). 70–90 lateral scales. To 4¾ in. (12 cm).
Range: Ohio R. basin from NY to NC, and west to w.-cen. KY and TN. Rare and highly localized. **Habitat:** Rocky flowing pools, usually above and below rubble riffles, of clear, small to medium rivers.
Remarks: Three races. One in Green R. system (KY and n. TN) has longest snout, usually a black stripe along side, 8–10 scales above lateral line. Race in upper Tennessee R. system (w. VA, w. NC, e. TN)

has shortest snout; usually a black stripe along side, 7–8 scales above lateral line. One in upper Ohio R. system (w. PA, w. NY, OH, WV, e. KY) is deeper bodied, has an intermediate snout, black blotches along side, usually 9–10 scales above lateral line.

Similar species: (1) Blackside Darter (Pl. 39) has *shorter snout, straight* (not curved) teardrop, *no* bar on caudal fin base, fully scaled opercle. (2) Muscadine Darter (Pl. 39) *lacks* teardrop, black bar on caudal fin base; has *shorter snout.* (3) Frecklebelly Darter has *straight teardrop, shorter snout,* black chin bar, fully scaled breast. **Map 314**

LEOPARD DARTER *Percina pantherina* **Pl. 39**
Identification: Named for *10–14 round black spots* along side, *black or dusky spots* on upper side and back. Black teardrop. Medial round or vertically oval black caudal spot. 1st dorsal fin dusky, black along base and at front. 81–96 lateral scales. To 3½ in. (9.2 cm).
Range: Little R. system (Red R. drainage) of sw. AR and se. OK. Rare; protected as a *threatened species.* **Habitat:** Gravel and rubble runs of clear, small to medium rivers.
Similar species: See Pl. 39: (1) Blackside Darter has *6–9 large blotches* along side, *no* round spots on upper side, fewer than 81 lateral scales. (2) Dusky and (3) Channel Darters, common within range of Leopard Darter, *lack* spotted pattern. **Map 315**

BLACKSIDE DARTER *Percina maculata* **Pl. 39**
Identification: *Discrete medial black caudal spot.* Prominent teardrop. Olive above, wavy black lines, 8–9 dark saddles. *6–9 large oval black blotches* along side. 1st dorsal fin dusky, black at front and along base. Fully scaled opercle. 56–81 lateral scales. To 4¼ in. (11 cm).
Range: Great Lakes, Hudson Bay, and Mississippi R. basins from s. ON and NY to se. SA and south to LA; Gulf drainages from Mobile Bay, AL, to Calcasieu R., LA. One of most common and widespread darters. **Habitat:** Pools of creeks and small to medium rivers, usually with moderate current and gravel or sand bottoms.
Similar species: See Pl. 39. Often confused with (1) Dusky Darter, which has vertical row of *3 diffuse dark brown caudal spots.* (2) Longhead Darter has longer snout, curved teardrop, black bar below caudal spot. (3) Leopard Darter has *10–14 round spots* along side, spots on upper side and back, 81–96 lateral scales. **Map 316**

STRIPEBACK DARTER *Percina notogramma* **Pl. 39**
Identification: *Pale yellow stripe* along upper side (on large individual). *1st dorsal fin dusky throughout,* darkest at front and along base; fin lacks yellow or orange band, black crescents or ovals. No black bar on chin. Light brown back, dark saddles joined by wavy lines to *6–8 horizontally oval black blotches* along side. Usually a discrete black caudal spot. Black teardrop. 49–67 lateral scales. To 3½ in. (8.4 cm).
Range: Patuxent, Potomac, Rappahannock, York, and James R. drainages (all tributaries of Chesapeake Bay) in MD, VA, and WV. Fairly

common. **Habitat:** Pools, usually with rock bottoms and near riffles, of creeks and small to medium rivers.

Remarks: Two subspecies. *P. n. montuosa*, endemic to upper James R. system, VA and WV, has higher scale counts (usually 59 or more lateral scales) than *P. n. notogramma* (usually 58 or fewer lateral scales), occupying rest of range.

Similar species: (1) Shield Darter (Pl. 39), only similar species within range, has black bar on chin, *black crescents* on 1st dorsal fin, no yellow stripe on upper side. (2) Blackside Darter (Pl. 39) *lacks* yellow stripe, has more discrete black caudal spot. **Map 317**

SHIELD DARTER *Percina peltata* **Pl. 39**

Identification: *Black or dusky bar on chin;* often a large black spot on breast; *row of black crescents* on 1st dorsal fin (Fig. 58). Olive to tan above; *6–7 horizontally rectangular black blotches* along side, usually joined by narrow black stripe. Wavy brown lines join 8–11 dark saddles on back to dark blotches along side. Large black teardrop. Large black blotch *below* center of caudal fin base. Unscaled or partly scaled opercle. 48–66 lateral scales. To 3½ in. (9 cm).

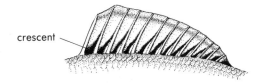

crescent

Fig. 58 Shield Darter — 1st dorsal fin

Range: Atlantic Slope drainages from Hudson and Susquehanna R., NY, to Neuse R., NC. Most widespread and common black-striped darter of Atlantic drainages. **Habitat:** Gravel and sand riffles and runs of creeks and small to medium rivers.

Similar species: (1) See Appalachia Darter. (2) Piedmont Darter (Pl. 41), only other darter with crescents on dorsal fin and black chin bar, is deeper bodied, usually has *7–9 vertically oval blotches* along side, bright yellow band on 1st dorsal fin of large male. **Map 314**

APPALACHIA DARTER *Percina gymnocephala* **Not shown**

Identification: Similar to Shield Darter but *lacks* black bar on chin, has *black ovals (not crescents)* on 1st dorsal fin. 56–72 lateral scales. To 3¾ in. (9.6 cm).

Range: New R. drainage above Kanawha Falls, WV, VA, and NC. Fairly common. **Habitat:** Gravel and rubble runs and riffles of small to medium rivers.

Similar species: (1) See Shield Darter (Pl. 39). (2) Blackside Darter (Pl. 39) has dusky 1st dorsal fin (*no* black ovals), fully scaled opercle. **Map 314**

PIEDMONT DARTER *Percina crassa*   **Pl. 41**
Identification: *Black bar* on chin. *Large black spot* on breast. *Row of black crescents* (as on Shield Darter — Fig. 58), yellow band (best developed on large male) on 1st dorsal fin. Olive to tan above. 7–9 vertically oval black blotches along side joined by wavy brown lines to 8–10 dark saddles. Large black teardrop. Black bar below medial black caudal spot. 44–58 lateral scales. To 3½ in. (9 cm).
Range: Cape Fear, Peedee, and Santee R. drainages, VA, NC, and SC. Common in Cape Fear R. and on Piedmont; uncommon on Coastal Plain. **Habitat:** Rocky riffles and runs of small to medium rivers.
Similar species: (1) Shield Darter (Pl. 39) *lacks* yellow band on 1st dorsal fin, is more slender, has 6–7 horizontally rectangular black blotches along side. (2) Roanoke Darter (Pl. 41) *lacks* black bar on chin and has *orange band* on 1st dorsal fin, 8–14 black bars along side; large male is bright blue and orange.   **Map 317**

ROANOKE DARTER *Percina roanoka*   **Pl. 41**
Identification: *Bright blue side, orange breast and belly, orange band on 1st dorsal fin* of large male. *8–14 black bars* (on adult) or oval blotches (on young) along side. Olive-brown above, wavy lines join 7–9 dark saddles on back to bars or blotches along side; white to orange below. Black bar on lower half of caudal fin base. 38–54 lateral scales. To 3 in. (7.8 cm).
Range: Roanoke, Neuse, and Tar R. drainages, VA and NC; extreme upper James R. drainage, VA; New R. drainage, WV and VA. James and New R. populations probably are recent introductions. Common; locally abundant. **Habitat:** Fast gravel and rubble riffles (adult), gravel-bottomed pools and runs near riffles (young) of small to medium rivers.
Similar species: Young Roanoke and Piedmont Darters are difficult to separate, but Roanoke Darter usually has 10–12 dorsal spines, 10–11 dorsal rays; Piedmont Darter usually has 11–12 dorsal spines and 12 dorsal rays. Adults easy to distinguish — see Piedmont Darter (Pl. 41).   **Map 317**

MUSCADINE DARTER *Percina* species   **Pl. 39**
Identification: 8-12 black blotches along side, fused into *black stripe* on adult, followed by rectangular *black blotch* on caudal fin base; caudal blotch centered *below* black stripe; *small black spot* at top, often another at bottom, of caudal fin base. Olive above, wavy brown lines, 8–9 dark brown saddles. No teardrop. Black edge and base on 1st dorsal fin of large adult. 56–77 lateral scales; no pored scales on caudal fin. To 3 in. (7.6 cm).
Range: Above Fall Line in Mobile Bay drainage, GA, AL, and se. TN. Uncommon. **Habitat:** Rocky flowing pools and runs of creeks and small to medium rivers.
Similar species: See Pl. 39. (1) Blackside Darter has 6–9 *separate* blotches (partially fused only on large male) along side, teardrop much more discrete, round black *spot* on caudal fin base. (2) Dusky Darter has *separate* blotches along side, serrated preopercle; often has pored scales on caudal fin.   **Map 314**

Next 4 species: vertical row of 3 *dark brown spots* on caudal fin base, lower 2 often *fused.*

DUSKY DARTER *Percina sciera* **Pl. 39**

Identification: Olive to dusky black above, 8–9 dark brown saddles on back; wavy dark brown lines on upper side; *8–12 oval black blotches* along side. Usually no teardrop. Fins mostly clear; often a dusky spot at rear of 1st dorsal fin. Serrated preopercle. 56–78 lateral scales. To 5 in. (13 cm).

Range: Mississippi R. basin from OH and WV to e. IL and south to LA; Gulf drainages from Black Warrior R., AL, to Guadalupe R., TX. Common; locally abundant. **Habitat:** Fast gravel runs, sometimes riffles, of creeks and small to medium rivers. Often near brush.

Remarks: Two subspecies: *P. s. apristis*, restricted to Guadalupe R. drainage, TX, has 0–1 (rarely 2–6) serrae on preopercle; *P. s. sciera* has 2–20 serrae.

Similar species: See Pl. 39. (1) See Goldline Darter. (2) Blackside Darter has *1 black caudal spot.* (3) Blackbanded Darter has *12–15 black bars* along side, usually no serrae on preopercle. (4) Freckled Darter has large dark spot at front of 2d dorsal fin, 77–93 lateral scales. **Map 318**

GOLDLINE DARTER *Percina aurolineata* **Pl. 39**

Identification: Similar to Dusky Darter but has *thin amber or brown stripe* (often interrupted) on upper side. 59–74 lateral scales. To 3½ in. (9 cm).

Range: Above Fall Line in Coosa and Cahaba R. systems (Mobile Bay drainage), GA and AL. Rare and localized. **Habitat:** Fast rocky runs of small to medium rivers.

Similar species: See Dusky Darter (Pl. 39). **Map 318**

BLACKBANDED DARTER *Percina nigrofasciata* **Pl. 39**

Identification: Olive to dusky black above, 6–8 dark saddles on back; dark wavy lines on upper side; *12–15 dusky to black bars* along side. Usually no serrae on preopercle. No or faint teardrop. Fins clear or with thin dark bands. 46–71 lateral scales. To 4½ in. (11 cm).

Range: Atlantic and Gulf Slope drainages from Edisto R., SC, south into s.–cen. FL (almost to Lake Okeechobee) and west to Mississippi R., LA. Most common darter throughout most of range, but absent in St. Marys and Satilla rivers in se. GA, and rare in Altamaha R., GA. **Habitat:** Headwaters to medium-sized rivers; usually over gravel or sand, often over mud on Coastal Plain.

Similar species: See Pl. 39. (1) Dusky, (2) Goldline, and (3) Freckled Darters have *fewer* (usually 8–10), *more oval blotches* along side, serrated edge on preopercle. **Map 319**

FRECKLED DARTER *Percina lenticula* **Pl. 39**

Identification: *Giant* of the darters — to 8 in. (20 cm). *Large black spot* at front of 2d dorsal fin; smaller spot at front of 1st dorsal fin. Olive to dusky overall, 8 dark brown saddles on back; brown wavy

lines on upper side, 8 black vertical blotches along side. Small (77–93 lateral) scales.
Range: Mobile Bay, Pascagoula R., and Pearl R. drainages, GA, AL, MS, and LA. Rare. **Habitat:** Fast, deep rocky riffles of small to medium rivers.
Similar species: See Pl. 39. (1) Dusky, (2) Blackbanded, and (3) Goldline Darters *lack* large black spot at front of 2d dorsal fin, have fewer than 76 lateral scales; none exceeds 4½ in. (11 cm).

Map 320

Next 6 species: premaxillary frenum *absent or narrow* (Fig. 55).

CHANNEL DARTER *Percina copelandi*   **Pl. 39**

Identification: *Blunt snout.* Olive above; 9–10 *horizontally oblong black blotches* along side; black Xs and Ws on back and upper side. *Medial black caudal spot.* Dusky teardrop often reduced to spot. Black along edge and base of 1st dorsal fin of male. *No premaxillary frenum* (Fig. 55). 43–61 lateral scales. To 2¾ in. (7.2 cm).
Range: Wide-ranging but highly localized in St. Lawrence–Great Lakes and Mississippi R. basins from s. QU and VT, south to n. LA; on Gulf Slope in Mobile Bay, Pascagoula, and Pearl R. drainages. Most common west of Mississippi R. in Red, Ouachita, and Arkansas R. drainages. **Habitat:** Pools and margins of riffles of small to medium rivers over sand or gravel bottoms; shores of lakes.
Similar species: (1) Johnny and (2) Tessellated Darters (both, Pl. 40) have *brown* (not black) marks, no black edge on 1st dorsal fin, no scutes (Fig. 56). (3) Blackside and (4) Dusky Darters (both, Pl. 39) have *larger, rounder black blotches* along side, *wide* premaxillary frenum.

Map 321

Next 5 species: anal fin extends to caudal fin on large male (see Pl. 39).

RIVER DARTER *Percina shumardi*   **Pl. 39**

Identification: *Small black spot at front, large black spot near rear* of 1st dorsal fin. Dusky olive above; 8–15 *black bars* along side; small black caudal spot; black teardrop. Moderately blunt snout. 46–62 lateral scales. To 3 in. (7.8 cm).
Range: Hudson Bay basin, ON, MB, and ND, and south in Great Lakes and Mississippi R. basins to LA; Gulf drainages from Mobile Bay, AL, to Neches R., TX; isolated population in San Antonio Bay drainage, TX. Locally common; most common darter in very large rivers, including the Mississippi. **Habitat:** Rocky riffles of small to large rivers. Adult usually in deep swift riffles; young in shallow riffles and runs.
Similar species: Similar darters *lack* black spots at front and rear of 1st dorsal fin. See Pl. 39. (1) Channel Darter has *horizontally* oriented blotches along side, *no* long anal fin on male. (2) Saddleback, (3) Stargazing, and (4) Snail Darters have 4–5 dark saddles, larger blotches (*not bars*) on side.

Map 322

STARGAZING DARTER *Percina uranidea*   **Pl. 39**
   Identification: *Red-brown above; 4 dark brown saddles (1st under 1st dorsal fin)* extend down side to lateral line; yellow below. Small black spot at front of 1st dorsal fin. 9–12 dark brown blotches along side. Large black teardrop. *Blunt snout;* robust body. 46–58 lateral scales. To 3 in. (7.8 cm).
   Range: St. Francis, White, and Ouachita R. drainages, MO, AR, and LA. Formerly in lower Wabash R., IN and IL. Localized and uncommon. **Habitat:** Fast gravel runs of clear, medium-sized rivers.
   Similar species: (1) See Snail Darter (Pl.39). (2) River Darter (Pl. 39) is dusky olive above; *lacks* bold dark saddles; has large black spot at rear of 1st dorsal fin, 8–15 black bars along side. (3) Saddleback Darter (Pl. 39) has 5 dark saddles.   **Map 323**

SNAIL DARTER *Percina tanasi*   **Pl. 39**
   Identification: Nearly identical to Stargazing Darter but has *gray edge and base on 1st dorsal fin.* 48–57 lateral scales. To 3½ in. (9 cm).
   Range: Upper Tennessee R. drainage of e. TN and n. GA. Localized and uncommon; protected as a *threatened species.* **Habitat:** Gravel and sand runs of medium-sized rivers.
   Remarks: Made famous by the 1970s conflict over the choice between completing Tellico Dam and saving the Little Tennessee R., then believed to support the only population of the Snail Darter.
   Similar species: See Stargazing Darter (Pl. 39).   **Map 323**

SADDLEBACK DARTER *Percina ouachitae*   **Pl. 39**
   Identification: *5 dark brown saddles; 1st under 1st dorsal fin;* 5th near front of caudal fin, small, and often indistinct. *Small black spot* on caudal fin base. Over sandy bottom, saddles fade and dark hatchmarks and wavy lines cover back. 8–10 rectangular blotches along side, often fused together but not joined to dorsal saddles. Dusky edge and base on 1st dorsal fin. Teardrop faint or absent. Fairly slender body; moderately pointed snout. 46–62 lateral scales. To 3 in. (7.8 cm).
   Range: Mississippi R. basin from sw. IN and se. MO to LA; Gulf Slope from Escambia R. drainage, AL and FL, to Mississippi R., LA. Mostly confined to Coastal Plain. Common but somewhat localized. **Habitat:** Sand and gravel runs of creeks and small to medium rivers; sometimes in very shallow water.
   Similar species: (1) River and (2) Channel Darters (both, Pl. 39) *lack* large dark saddles (but may have about 8 small dark blotches on back).   **Map 324**

AMBER DARTER *Percina antesella*   **Pl. 41**
   Identification: Yellow-brown above, *4 dark brown saddles (1st in front of 1st dorsal fin)* extending down side to lateral line; 8–12 small dark brown blotches along side; yellow to white below. Black along edge and base of 1st dorsal fin. Black teardrop. Slender body; *pointed snout.* Breeding male has semicircular *keel* below front part of caudal fin. 51–66 lateral scales. To 2¾ in. (7.2 cm).

Range: Conasauga and Etowah rivers (Coosa R. system) in se. TN and n. GA. Rare; may be extirpated in Etowah R., extremely localized in Conasauga R. Protected as an *endangered species.* **Habitat:** Swift gravel and sand riffles and runs of medium-sized rivers.
Similar species: Saddleback Darter (Pl. 39) has 5 dark saddles on back, *1st under* 1st dorsal fin. **Map 324**

BRONZE DARTER *Percina palmaris* Pl. 41

Identification: Yellow-brown above, *8–10 brown saddles;* 8–11 *brown blotches* along side. On large individual *wide dusky brown (bronze* on large male) *bars join* blotches along side to saddles. 2 large white to yellow areas on caudal fin base. Teardrop weak or absent. 1st dorsal fin of male has amber base and white edge, of female is mottled with brown. 57–73 lateral scales. To 3½ in. (9 cm).
Range: Above Fall Line in Coosa and Tallapoosa R. systems (Mobile Bay drainage) in GA, AL, and extreme se. TN. Locally common. **Habitat:** Swift riffles over gravel and rubble in small to medium rivers.
Similar species: (1) Gilt Darter (Pl. 41) has dusky *black bars* over back, *yellow to orange* breast and belly. (2) Blackbanded Darter (Pl. 39) has 12–15 *narrow* dark (more black than brown) bars on side, clear or mostly clear 1st dorsal fin. **Map 315**

GILT DARTER *Percina evides* Pl. 41

Identification: *Wide dusky green bars* (darkest on adult) *join* 6–8 dark saddles to dark blotches along side. *Yellow to bright orange belly, breast, and underside of head.* 1st dorsal fin often orange or amber at base; has orange band below edge. Black teardrop. 2 large white or yellow areas on caudal fin base. Breeding male has blue-green bars over back, bright orange breast and belly. 51–77 lateral scales. To 3¾ in. (9.6 cm).
Range: Mississippi R. basin from NY to MN and south to n. AL and n. AR; Maumee R. system (Lake Erie drainage), OH and IN. Locally common but extirpated from much of former range, including all of OH, IA, and IL. **Habitat:** Rocky riffles of small to medium rivers.
Remarks: Unnamed but geographically definable populations recognizable as subspecies. Subspecies west of Mississippi R. has partly scaled cheek; orange 1st dorsal fin and yellow belly on large male. Subspecies in part of upper Tennessee R. drainage (w. NC, n. GA, and e. TN) usually has unscaled cheek; orange edge on 1st dorsal fin and orange belly on large male. Subspecies in rest of range has partly scaled cheek, orange 1st dorsal fin and orange belly on large male.
Similar species: (1) Bronze Darter (Pl. 41) has *brown* marks on side and back; *lacks* orange breast. Probably most often confused with (2) Blackside and (3) Dusky Darters (both, Pl. 39), which *lack* bright colors, broad bands over back, large white or yellow spots on caudal fin base. **Map 315**

TANGERINE DARTER *Percina aurantiaca* Pl. 41

Identification: Large and colorful. *Thin black stripe* along back breaks into *spots* at rear. Broad black stripe of 8–12 fused blotches along side, longitudinal *row of small dark brown spots* on upper side. No

teardrop. Underside of young white, of large female yellow, of large male orange. Breeding male has bright red-orange belly, blue breast, orange edge on 1st dorsal fin, and red gill membranes. 84–99 lateral scales. To 7¼ in. (18 cm).
Range: Upper Tennessee R. drainage, VA, NC, TN, and GA. Fairly common locally. **Habitat:** Clear, fairly deep, rocky pools (usually below riffles) of creeks and small rivers. Large male often in rocky riffles. **Map 313**

Next 4 species: orange band on 1st dorsal fin, small but distinct *black spot* on caudal fin base.

OLIVE DARTER *Percina squamata* **Pl. 41**
Identification: *Long pointed snout.* Olive-brown above, 13–15 small dark brown saddles; dark wavy lines on upper side; *10–12 dark brown rectangles* along side; white or yellow below. Teardrop usually present. *Fully scaled breast.* 71–88 lateral scales. To 5¼ in. (13 cm).
Range: Middle Cumberland R. drainage (Big South Fork and Rockcastle R.), KY and TN; upper Tennessee R. drainage, NC, TN, and GA. Localized but relatively common in a few streams. **Habitat:** Moderately deep boulder riffles and runs of small to medium rivers.
Remarks: Snouts of this and related species (Sharpnose, Slenderhead, and Longnose Darters) become proportionally longer as fish grows.
Similar species: (1) See Sharpnose Darter. (2) Slenderhead Darter (Pl. 41) has shorter snout, 10–16 *round blotches* along side, *unscaled or partly scaled breast.* **Map 325**

SHARPNOSE DARTER *Percina oxyrhynchus* **Not shown**
Identification: Nearly identical to Olive Darter but has an *unscaled or only partly scaled breast.* 68–80 lateral scales. To 4½ in. (12 cm.).
Range: Southern tributaries of Ohio R. from Monongahela R., PA, to Kentucky R., KY; south in New R. drainage to NC. Locally common. **Habitat:** Fast boulder riffles and runs of small to medium rivers.
Similar species: See Olive Darter (Pl. 41). **Map 325**

SLENDERHEAD DARTER *Percina phoxocephala* **Pl. 41**
Identification: *Moderately long, pointed snout.* Yellow-brown above with dark brown wavy lines; *10–16 round brown-black blotches* along side; white to yellow below. Black teardrop. *Unscaled* (except large scutes near pelvic fins) or partly scaled breast. 58–80 lateral scales. To 3¾ in. (9.6 cm).
Range: Mississippi R. basin from OH to ne. SD and south to n. AL and s. OK; Lake Winnebago system (Lake Michigan drainage) in WI. Common in some parts of range. **Habitat:** Gravel runs and riffles of creeks and small to medium rivers.
Similar species: (1) Olive (Pl. 41) and (2) Sharpnose Darters have *longer* snout, 10–12 *rectangular blotches* along side; Olive Darter has *fully scaled* breast. (3) Longnose Darter (Pl. 41) has *longer* snout, *bars* along side. **Map 325**

LONGNOSE DARTER *Percina nasuta*   **Pl. 41**

Identification: *Long pointed snout* (extremely so in some populations). Yellow-brown above; dark brown wavy lines on upper side; *12–15 brown-black bars* along side; white to yellow below. No teardrop. *Unscaled* (except large scutes near pelvic fins) or partly scaled breast. To 4½ in. (11 cm).

Range: Ozark and Ouachita Uplands (St. Francis, White, Arkansas, and Ouachita R. drainages), MO, AR, and OK. Uncommon. **Habitat:** Gravel runs and riffles of small to medium clear rivers.

Similar species: Slenderhead Darter (Pl. 41) has 10–16 *round blotches* along side, *shorter snout.*   **Map 319**

Next 6 species, the logperches, are a distinctive group of darters with a *bulbous snout* extending well beyond the upper jaw (especially on large individual) and a *wide flat area* between the eyes. Logperches use the long snout to flip over stones and root in gravel to expose food organisms. *Black spot* on caudal fin base.

BLOTCHSIDE LOGPERCH *Percina burtoni*   **Pl. 41**

Identification: *No* (or few) *scales on nape. 8–10 dark green to black round or oval blotches* along side. Yellow-brown above, *dark blotches* and bars on back extending down upper side, yellow to white below. Black teardrop. Large black blotch at rear, *orange band* on 1st dorsal fin. 79–92 lateral scales. To 6½ in. (16 cm).

Range: Tennessee and Cumberland R. drainages, VA, NC, KY, and TN. Extremely rare in Tennessee R. drainage; probably extirpated in Cumberland R. drainage. **Habitat:** Gravel runs and riffles of clear, small to medium rivers.

Similar species: Other logperches (Pl. 41) have 10 or more *bars* along side, and all except northern populations of Logperch have *scaled nape.*   **Map 320**

LOGPERCH *Percina caprodes*   **Pl. 41**

Identification: Yellow-brown above; *many alternating long and short bars* along side extend over back and *join* those of other side; bars relatively uniform, not constricted at middle. Dusky teardrop. Nape usually scaled (unscaled only in northern populations). No orange band on 1st dorsal fin (except in Ozark subspecies). No scales on top of head, usually none on area in front of pectoral fin. 67–100 lateral scales. To 7¼ in. (18 cm).

Range: St. Lawrence–Great Lakes, Hudson Bay, and Mississippi R. basins from e. QU to SA and south to Gulf; Atlantic Slope drainages from Hudson R., NY, to Potomac R., MD; Gulf Slope drainages from Choctawhatchee R., AL and FL, to Mississippi R., LA (see Remarks). Generally common, but rare in Atlantic drainages. **Habitat:** Most common over gravel and sand in medium-sized rivers but can be found almost anywhere from small, fast-flowing rock-bottomed streams to vegetated lakes.

Remarks: Highly variable; 3 described subspecies (shown on Pl. 41). *P. c. semifasciata* (Canada and n. states) has no orange band on 1st dorsal fin, unscaled nape. *P. c. fulvitaenia*, in tributaries of Missouri and Arkansas rivers in MO, AR, KS, and OK, and in Blue R., OK, has orange band on 1st dorsal fin, fully scaled nape. *P. c. caprodes*, throughout rest of range, has no orange band, fully scaled nape. *Note:* As many as 3 undescribed species of logperches (all with orange band on 1st dorsal fin), presently referred to as *P. caprodes*, inhabit rivers draining into the Gulf of Mexico, FL to LA.

Similar species: See Pl. 41. See (1) Conasauga and (2) Texas Logperches. (3) Blotchside and (4) Roanoke Logperches *lack* long bars extending over back to join those of other side. (5) Bigscale Logperch has smaller head, scales on top of head. **Map 326**

CONASAUGA LOGPERCH *Percina jenkinsi* Not shown

Identification: Similar to Logperch but has *black spot* at pectoral fin origin, 9 long bars along side (usually 8 on Logperch), 32–38 transverse scales (rarely more than 30 in Logperch). To 5½ in. (14 cm).

Range: Conasauga R. (Alabama R. system), TN and GA. Uncommon in extremely small range; protected as an *endangered species.* **Habitat:** Rocky runs and flowing pools of Conasauga R., a small, fast-flowing river.

Similar species: See Logperch (Pl. 41). **Map 321**

TEXAS LOGPERCH *Percina carbonaria* Pl. 41

Identification: Similar to Logperch but has *black breast, gill membranes, and anal and pelvic fins* on large male; *orange band* on 1st dorsal fin (unlike Logperch except Ozark subspecies and Gulf Slope forms). Olive-brown above; 15–21 dark bars along side alternately long and short; long bars are constricted near middle, extend over back and *join* those of other side. Black teardrop. 80–93 lateral scales. To 5¼ in. (13 cm).

Range: Brazos, Colorado, Guadalupe, and San Antonio R. drainages, TX. Nearly confined to Edwards Plateau. Common. **Habitat:** Rocky riffles and runs of small to medium rivers.

Similar species: (1) See Logperch (Pl. 41). (2) Only other logperch within range is Bigscale Logperch (Pl. 41), which is much *lighter* in color; *lacks* orange band on 1st dorsal fin; has a relatively small head; has scales on top of head and on area in front of pectoral fin.

Map 326

ROANOKE LOGPERCH *Percina rex* Pl. 41

Identification: *10–12 short black bars* along side, *not* joined over back with those of other side. *Orange band* on 1st dorsal fin. Olive to yellow-brown above, wavy dark blotches on back. Black teardrop. Fully scaled nape. 83–89 lateral scales. To 6 in. (15 cm).

Range: Upper Roanoke, upper Dan, and upper Chowan R. systems (Roanoke R. drainage), VA. Uncommon; protected as an *endangered species.* **Habitat:** Gravel and boulder runs of small to medium rivers.

Similar species: (1) Blotchside Logperch (Pl. 41) has *oval blotches* along side. (2) Other logperches (Pl. 41) have long bars extending over back to *join* those of other side. **Map 320**

BIGSCALE LOGPERCH *Percina macrolepida* **Pl. 41**
Identification: *Light-colored* logperch with small head. *15–20 long dark bars* along side extend over back and *join* those of other side. Olive to yellow above; clear or yellow 1st dorsal fin, *no orange band.* Teardrop reduced to dusky spot. Scales on nape, on *top of head,* and in front of pectoral fin. 77–90 lateral scales. To 4½ in. (11 cm).
Range: From Sabine R., LA, and Red R., OK, to Rio Grande drainage, TX, NM, and Mexico. Introduced into Sacramento–San Joaquin R. drainage, CA. Locally common; localized and uncommon in Rio Grande drainage. **Habitat:** Gravel and sand runs and pools of small to medium rivers; impoundments.
Similar species: Other logperches (Pl. 41) *lack* scales on top of head, have larger head. **Map 327**

CRYSTAL DARTER *Crystallaria asprella* **Pl. 40**
Identification: Very *slender body; wide flat head,* closely set eyes. *Forked caudal fin;* large anal and dorsal fins. Brown mottling, *4 dark brown saddles* (1st 3 large) on back and upper side; dark brown oblong blotches along side. Black stripe around snout continuous from eye to eye. 12–15 anal fin rays; 81–93 lateral scales. To 6¼ in. (16 cm).
Range: Mississippi R. basin from OH to MN and south to s. MS, n. LA, and se. OK; on Gulf Slope in Escambia, Mobile Bay, and Pearl R. drainages. Now extirpated from OH, KY, IN, and IL. Localized and rare. **Habitat:** Clean sand and gravel runs of small to medium rivers. Usually in fairly fast water 2 ft. (60 cm) or more deep.
Remarks: A highly distinctive darter sharing some ecological and morphological characteristics with sand darters but only distantly related to them.
Similar species: Sand darters (Pl. 40) *lack* dark dorsal saddles, have a straight-edged or shallowly forked caudal fin. **Map 328**

• *ETHEOSTOMA*

Genus characteristics: *Etheostoma* is the largest genus of North American fishes. Included in *Etheostoma* are some of our rarest fishes (e.g., Maryland Darter), some of our most common fishes (e.g., Johnny and Greenside Darters), and some of our most spectacularly colorful fishes. Species of *Etheostoma lack* the scutes of *Percina* (Fig. 56).

Next 6 species, referred to as Sand Darters and until recently placed in genus *Ammocrypta,* are *long, slender glass-clear* darters that bury themselves in sandy streams with only their eyes and snout protruding. Adaptations for living in sand include transparent bodies (usually yellow tint above, iridescent green on back and side, silver-white below) to blend in with the sand, loss of scales and long slender shape to facilitate burying; and eyes near top of the head for viewing above while buried. Protruding snout, *no* premaxillary frenum, complete lateral line, *1 anal spine.*

WESTERN SAND DARTER *Etheostoma clarum* **Pl. 40**
Identification: *Spine* on opercle. No black on dorsal or pelvic fins, weakly developed dark green blotches along back and side. 63–84 lateral scales. Lateral line slants down at rear. To 2¾ in. (7.1 cm).
Range: Mssissippi R. basin from WI and MN south to VA, MS, and TX; Lake Michigan drainage, WI; Sabine and Neches R. drainages, TX. Generally sporadic and uncommon; common in a few rivers in n. and w. parts of range; extremely rare in KY, TN, VA, and MS. **Habitat:** Sandy runs of medium to large rivers.
Similar species: Other sand darters (Pl. 40) *lack* spine on opercle, have well-developed dark blotches along side or have black bands on dorsal fins. **Map 329**

NAKED SAND DARTER *Etheostoma beani* **Pl. 40**
Identification: *Middle black band* (most prominent near front) on each dorsal fin (Fig. 59). No spine on opercle. No black pigment on pelvic fin. "Naked" refers to lack of scales except along lateral line and on caudal peduncle. 57–77 lateral scales. Lateral line slants down at rear. To 2¾ in. (7.2 cm).

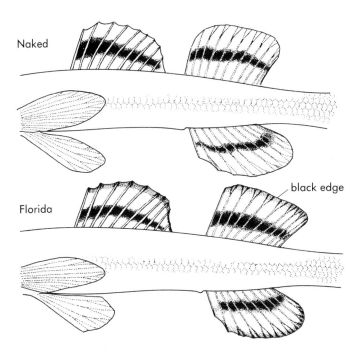

Naked

Florida

black edge

Fig. 59 Naked and Florida Sand Darters

Range: Mississippi R. and w. Gulf drainages in w. TN, AL, MS, and e. LA as far east as the Mobile Bay drainage. Common. **Habitat:** Sandy runs of creeks and small to medium rivers.

Similar species: (1) See Florida Sand Darter. (2) Scaly Sand Darter (Pl. 40) has *dark blotches* along side, black pigment on pelvic fin of male.

Map 330

FLORIDA SAND DARTER *Etheostoma bifascia* **Not shown**
Identification: Nearly identical to Naked Sand Darter (above) but has *2 black bands* on each dorsal fin (Fig. 59). 63–78 lateral scales. To 3 in. (7.7 cm).

Range: Gulf Slope drainages from Apalachicola R. to Perdido R., s. AL and FL panhandle. Common. **Habitat:** Sandy runs of small to medium rivers.

Similar species: See Naked Sand Darter (Pl. 40). **Map 330**

EASTERN SAND DARTER *Etheostoma pellucidum* **Pl. 40**
Identification: 12–17 small dark green blotches along back; 10–19 *horizontal dark green blotches* along side. No spine on opercle. No black bands on dorsal fins. Black pigment on pelvic fin of male. 62–84 lateral scales. To 3¼ in. (8.4 cm).

Range: St. Lawrence R. drainage, s. QU, VT, and NY; Great Lakes (Lake Erie, Lake St. Clair, and s. Lake Huron) and Ohio R. basins from w. NY to e. IL, and south to KY. Locally common but rapidly decreasing in abundance because of siltation and deteriorating water quality. **Habitat:** Sandy runs of small to medium rivers; usually.in water 2 ft. (60 cm) or more deep.

Similar species: (1) See Southern Sand Darter. (2) Other sand darters (Pl. 40), except Scaly Sand Darter, *lack* dark blotches on side; Scaly Sand Darter has *vertical* blotches. **Map 331**

SOUTHERN SAND DARTER *Etheostoma meridianum* **Not shown**
Identification: Similar to Eastern Sand Darter but has usually 14–16 transverse scales (versus 11–13 in Eastern Sand Darter). 63–79 lateral scales. To 2¾ in. (7 cm).

Range: Mobile Bay drainage, AL and MS. Common. **Habitat:** Sandy runs of small to medium rivers.

Similar species: See Eastern Sand Darter (Pl. 40). **Map 329**

SCALY SAND DARTER *Etheostoma vivax* **Pl. 40**
Identification: *Vertical dark green blotches* along side. *Dusky edge* and *middle band* on each dorsal fin. No spine on opercle. Black pigment on pelvic fin of male. 10–15 dark green blotches along back. 58–79 lateral scales. To 2¾ in. (7.3 cm).

Range: Mississippi R. basin from w. KY and se. MO, south to s. MS, and west to e. OK and TX; Gulf drainages from Pascagoula R., MS, to San Jacinto R., TX. Primarily on Coastal Plain. Locally common. **Habitat:** Sandy runs of creeks and small to medium rivers.

Similar species: Other sand darters (Pl. 40) have *horizontal* (not vertical) or *no* dark blotches along side. **Map 331**

GLASSY DARTER *Etheostoma vitreum* **Pl. 40**
Identification: *Translucent.* 7–8 dark brown saddles, many dark brown specks and *small black spots* on back and upper side; *dark brown dashes* along lateral line. No teardrop. Protruding snout, no premaxillary frenum, closely set eyes, 1–2 anal spines, narrowly joined branchiostegal membranes (Fig. 54). Fleshy villi around anus. Complete lateral line; 50–65 lateral scales. To 2½ in. (6.6 cm).
Range: Atlantic Slope drainages from Bush R., MD, to Neuse R., NC. Common. **Habitat:** Sandy runs of creeks and small to medium rivers.
Similar species: (1) Johnny and (2) Tessellated Darters (both, Pl. 40) are much more *opaque;* have blunter snout, Xs and Ws along side, teardrop, black spot on dorsal fin of male, no villi around anus.

Map 331

JOHNNY DARTER *Etheostoma nigrum* **Pl. 40**
Identification: Dark brown Xs and Ws along side, wavy brown lines on upper side. Light brown above, 6 dark brown saddles; black teardrop. Breeding male has black head and anal and pelvic fins; black spot at front of 1st dorsal fin; often has white knobs on tips of pelvic spine and rays. *1 anal spine, no premaxillary frenum,* interrupted infraorbital and supratemporal canals (Fig. 53), narrowly joined branchiostegal membranes (Fig. 54), moderately blunt snout, slender caudal peduncle. Complete lateral line; 35–56 lateral scales. To 2¾ in. (7.2 cm).
Range: St. Lawrence–Great Lakes, Hudson Bay, and Mississippi R. basins from Hudson Bay to s. MS, and from QU and VA to SA and CO; on Atlantic Slope in James, Roanoke, Tar, and Neuse R. drainages, VA and NC; on Gulf Slope in Mobile Bay drainage, AL and MS. Absent in White R. drainage (AR and MO), most of Arkansas R. drainage, upper Tennessee R. drainage, and middle Cumberland R. drainage. Recently introduced into Colorado R. drainage, CO. Common to abundant. **Habitat:** Sandy and muddy, sometimes rocky, pools of headwaters, creeks, and small to medium rivers; sandy shores of lakes.

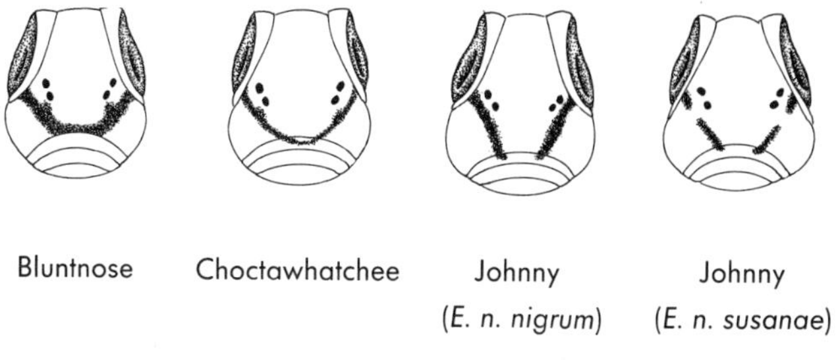

Bluntnose   Choctawhatchee   Johnny   Johnny
(*E. n. nigrum*)   (*E. n. susanae*)

Fig. 60 Bluntnose, Choctawhatchee, and Johnny (*Etheostoma nigrum*) Darters

Remarks: Two subspecies. *E. n. susanae*, endemic to Cumberland R. drainage above Cumberland Falls, KY and TN, is extremely rare and, unlike *E. n. nigrum*, has break in eye stripe (Fig. 60) and no scales on top of head, on opercle, or along midbelly. Intergrades occupy headwaters of Kentucky R., KY.

Similar species: (1) See Tessellated Darter (Pl. 40). (2) Speckled and (3) Blueside Darters (both, Pl. 48) have *2 anal spines*, row of dark squares just below lateral line (*no Xs and Ws along lateral line*), red and blue on body and fins of large male. (4) Longfin (Pl. 42) and (5) Riverweed Darters have deep caudal peduncle, broadly joined branchiostegal membranes, *2 anal spines*. (6) Bluntnose Darter (Pl. 40) has bridle (Fig. 60) around extremely blunt snout, horizontal black blotches along side. **Map 332**

TESSELLATED DARTER *Etheostoma olmstedi* **Pl. 40**
Identification: Similar to Johnny Darter but has *uninterrupted infraorbital and supratemporal canals* (Fig. 53), enlarged 2d dorsal fin on breeding male. 1 anal spine, except *E. o. maculaticeps* has 2. 34–64 (usually 36–56) lateral scales. To 4½ in. (11 cm).
Range: Atlantic drainages from St. Lawrence R., QU and ON (absent in ME) to Altamaha R., GA; St. Johns R. drainage, FL; Lake Ontario drainage, NY. Abundant in cen. part of range, generally common elsewhere; mostly restricted to Coastal Plain in VA. **Habitat:** Sandy and muddy pools of headwaters, creeks, and small to medium rivers; shores of lakes.
Remarks: Three subspecies. *E. o. maculaticeps*, from Cape Fear R., NC, to FL, has 2 anal spines. *E. o. vexillare*, in upper Rappahannock R. drainage, VA, has 1 anal spine, 42 or fewer lateral scales. *E. o. olmstedi*, in rest of range, has 1 anal spine, usually 43 or more lateral scales.
Similar species: See Pl. 40. (1) See Johnny and (2) Waccamaw Darters. (3) Glassy Darter is transparent and has protruding snout, many dark specks on back and side. **Map 333**

WACCAMAW DARTER *Etheostoma perlongum* **Pl. 40**
Identification: Nearly identical to Tessellated Darter but has *more slender body*, 58–66 (usually 60–62) lateral scales. To 3½ in. (9 cm).
Range: Lake Waccamaw, Columbus Co., NC. Moderately common. **Habitat:** Shallow, sandy areas of lake.
Similar species: See Tessellated Darter (Pl. 40). **Map 332**

BLUNTNOSE DARTER *Etheostoma chlorosomum* **Pl. 40**
Identification: *Black bridle* (Fig. 60) around extremely *blunt snout*, no premaxillary frenum, *1 anal spine*, slender body, scaled breast. Olive above, 6 dusky saddles; brown Xs and Ws on side and back; *horizontal dusky to black blotches* along side; black teardrop. Middle black band (darkest at front), dusky edge on 1st dorsal fin of breeding male. Incomplete lateral line; 49–60 lateral scales. To 2½ in. (6 cm).
Range: Mississippi R. basin from s. MN to LA; Gulf Slope from Mobile Bay drainage, AL, to San Antonio R. drainage, TX. Formerly Lake Michigan drainage, IL. Generally restricted to lowland areas. Com-

mon; locally abundant. **Habitat:** Muddy (sometimes sandy) pools and backwaters of creeks and small to medium rivers; weedy lakes and ponds; swamps.
Similar species: (1) See Choctawhatchee Darter. (2) Johnny (Pl. 40) and (3) Speckled Darters (Pl. 48) *lack* snout bridle and horizontal blotches along side, have more *pointed snout.*   **Map 334**

CHOCTAWHATCHEE DARTER *Etheostoma davisoni*   **Not shown**
Identification: Similar to Bluntnose Darter but *snout bridle faint at front* and mostly on upper lip (Fig. 60), *2 anal spines, unscaled breast.* 44–57 lateral scales. To 2½ in. (6.1 cm).
Range: Choctawhatchee and Pensacola Bay drainages, s. AL and FL panhandle. Fairly common. **Habitat:** Sandy and muddy pools of creeks and small rivers.
Similar species: See Bluntnose Darter (Pl. 40).   **Map 334**

LONGFIN DARTER *Etheostoma longimanum*   **Pl. 42**
Identification: *Deep caudal peduncle, broadly joined branchiostegal membranes* (Fig. 54), *2 anal spines.* Large pectoral and pelvic fins. No premaxillary frenum. Light brown above, 6 dark brown saddles; wavy lines on upper side; 9–14 dark squares (Ws when examined closely) along side. Small black teardrop often reduced to spot. Breeding male has enlarged 2d dorsal fin; orange belly and caudal and dorsal fins; black spot at front of 1st dorsal fin; blue-green head and lower fins. Breeding male may be almost black. Complete lateral line; 39–51 (usually 42–46) lateral scales. To 3½ in. (8.9 cm).
Range: Upper James R. drainage, VA and WV. Common. **Habitat:** Rocky riffles of creeks and small rivers.
Similar species: (1) See Riverweed Darter. (2) Johnny and (3) Tessellated Darters (both, Pl. 40) have *slender* caudal peduncle, *narrowly* joined branchiostegal membranes, *1* anal spine (except *E. o. maculaticeps*), no orange or blue-green on large male.   **Map 335**

RIVERWEED DARTER *Etheostoma podostemone*   **Not shown**
Identification: Nearly identical to Longfin Darter but has *rows of dark spots* on side (best developed on upper side) and on caudal peduncle; 35–41 (usually 37–40) lateral scales. To 3 in. (7.6 cm).
Range: Upper Roanoke R. drainage, VA and NC. Common. **Habitat:** Rocky riffles of creeks and small rivers.
Similar species: See Longfin Darter (Pl. 42).   **Map 335**

SPECKLED DARTER *Etheostoma stigmaeum*   **Pl. 48**
Identification: *7–11 dark brown squares* (Ws if examined closely) along side *just below lateral line* on female and young; *7–11 turquoise bars on large male.* Moderately blunt snout; no premaxillary frenum. Light brown above, 6 dark brown saddles. Dusky teardrop often reduced to spot. Middle orange band, light blue edge and base on 1st dorsal fin (bands faint on female); other fins mostly clear on female, blue and orange on breeding male. 2 anal spines. Incomplete lateral line; 39–67 lateral scales. To 2½ in. (6.1 cm).
Range: Mississippi R. basin from w. VA to se. KS, and south to LA;

Gulf Slope drainages from Mobile Bay and Pensacola Bay, GA, AL, and FL, to Sabine R., LA. In Clinch and Powell rivers, VA and TN, but absent in rest of middle and upper Tennessee R. drainage. Common; locally abundant. **Habitat:** Clear sandy and rocky pools of creeks and small to medium, usually fast, rivers.
Similar species: (1) See Blueside Darter (Pl. 48). (2) Johnny Darter (Pl. 40) has Xs and Ws (not squares) *along* lateral line, no red or blue on body or fins, 1 anal spine.   **Map 336**

BLUESIDE DARTER *Etheostoma jessiae*   **Pl. 48**
Identification: Similar to Speckled Darter but has *pointed snout, narrow premaxillary frenum, deep blue bars* on body and fins of male. 44–53 lateral scales. To 2¾ in. (6.8 cm).
Range: Middle and upper Tennessee R. drainage — Bear Cr., AL, and upstream, VA, NC, TN, GA, and AL. Generally common; rare in NC.
Habitat: Rocky pools and adjacent riffles of clear creeks and small fast rivers.
Similar species: See Speckled Darter (Pl. 48).   **Map 336**

MARYLAND DARTER *Etheostoma sellare*   **Pl. 40**
Identification: *Asymmetrical caudal fin base;* upper half extends farther back than lower half. *Wide, flat head,* closely set eyes; narrowly joined branchiostegal membranes (Fig. 54). Brown to olive above; 4 large dark brown saddles extend down side, often to below lateral line; 3–7 dark brown blotches on lower side; large dusky teardrop; small black caudal spot. Complete lateral line; 43–53 lateral scales. To 3¼ in. (8.4 cm).
Range: Tributaries of lower Susquehanna R., Harford Co., MD. Near extinction; protected as an *endangered species.* The Maryland Darter is known with certainty to exist in only one riffle. **Habitat:** Fast rocky riffles of creeks.
Similar species: No other darter has an asymmetrical caudal fin base.
                                                           Map 337

GREENSIDE DARTER *Etheostoma blennioides*   **Pl. 42**
Identification: *Skin on rear of upper lip fused to skin of snout.* Blunt snout; broadly joined branchiostegal membranes (Fig. 54); scales on cheek. Yellow-green; 6–7 square dark green saddles; brown to dark red spots on upper side; *5–8 green* Ws, Us, *or bars on side.* Dorsal fins red along base; green on male, clear to dusky on female. Dusky teardrop. Bright green fins and bars on side of breeding male. Complete lateral line; 50–86 lateral scales. Largest *Etheostoma* species — to 6½ in. (17 cm).
Range: Great Lakes and Mississippi R. basins from NY and MD to e. KS and OK, and from ON south to GA, AL, and AR; Atlantic Slope in Mohawk, Susquehanna, and Potomac drainages, NY to VA. Hiatus in range coincides with Former Mississippi Embayment and lowlands of sw. IN and IL. Usually common to abundant; along Atlantic, common only in Potomac R. **Habitat:** Rocky riffles of creeks and small to medium rivers; shores of large lakes.

Remarks: Four subspecies. *E. b. gutselli* (Little Tennessee and Pigeon R. systems, e. TN) is only subspecies with a premaxillary frenum, no scales on opercle. *E. b. pholidotum* (in Great Lakes, Mohawk, Maumee, Wabash, and Missouri R. drainages) has low scale counts (usually 55–65 lateral scales). *E. b. newmani* (Cumberland, Tennessee, St. Francis, White, Arkansas, and Ouachita R. drainages) has high scale counts (usually 66–78 lateral scales). *E. b. blennioides* (Ohio R. basin above confluence of Green R., KY; Potomac R. on Atlantic Slope; upper Genessee R. of Great Lakes basin) has intermediate scale counts (usually 63–70 lateral scales).

Similar species: Other darters *lack* fusion of skin on rear of lip to skin on snout. See Rock Darter (Pl. 42). **Map 338**

ROCK DARTER *Etheostoma rupestre* Pl. 42

Identification: Similar to Greenside Darter but smaller; *lacks* scales on cheek, fusion of skin at rear of upper lip to skin of snout. 46–65 lateral scales. To 3¼ in. (8.3 cm).

Range: Mobile Bay drainage, GA, AL, MS, and extreme se. TN. Common, especially near Fall Line where rapids prevail. **Habitat:** Fast rocky riffles of creeks and small to medium rivers.

Similar species: See Greenside Darter (Pl. 42). **Map 338**

HARLEQUIN DARTER *Etheostoma histrio* Pl. 42

Identification: *2 large dark brown to green caudal spots. Many dark brown or black specks* on yellow belly and underside of head. Yellow to green above, 6–7 dark brown saddles; 7–11 dark brown blotches along side. 1st dorsal fin clear with dark red edge; dusky green on large male. Black teardrop. Breeding male is emerald green with brown and black mottling. Broadly joined branchiostegal membranes (Fig. 54). Complete lateral line; 45–58 lateral scales. To 3 in. (7.7 cm).

Range: Mostly confined to Former Mississippi Embayment and Gulf Slope drainages from w. KY and se. MO to LA, and from Escambia R., AL and FL, to Neches R., TX. In Red and Arkansas drainages west to e. OK and TX, in isolated areas in Wabash R. drainage, IL and IN, and Green R. system, KY. Widely distributed but generally uncommon.

Habitat: Sand and gravel runs of small to medium rivers; usually near debris. **Map 339**

SEAGREEN DARTER *Etheostoma thalassinum* Pl. 42

Identification: Light brown, 7 dark brown saddles; *about 7 small dark brown blotches* (often Ws) along side. On large male, blue-green bars pass through blotches on side and encircle body near caudal fin. Brown mottling on upper side. *Red edge,* dusky black base on 1st dorsal fin. Blue anal and pelvic fins on breeding male. Black teardrop. *Broadly joined branchiostegal membranes* (Fig. 54). Usually 9–10 dorsal spines. Complete lateral line; 38–50 lateral scales. To 3¼ in. (8 cm).

Range: Santee R. drainage, NC and SC. Common. **Habitat:** Rocky riffles of creeks and small to medium rivers.

Similar species: (1) See Turquoise Darter. (2) Swannanoa Darter (Pl.

42) has *8–9 black, oval to round blotches* on side, usually 12 dorsal spines. **Map 340**

TURQUOISE DARTER *Etheostoma inscriptum*   **Not shown**
Identification: Nearly identical to Seagreen Darter but has *6 dark saddles; horizontal rows of small red spots* on side of large male. 39–61 lateral scales. To 3¼ in. (8 cm).
Range: Edisto, Savannah, and Altamaha R. drainages, NC, SC, and GA. Common. **Habitat:** Rocky riffles of creeks and small to medium rivers.
Similar species: See Seagreen Darter (Pl. 42).   **Map 340**

SWANNANOA DARTER *Etheostoma swannanoa*   **Pl. 42**
Identification: *Rows of small red spots* on side (more prominent on male). Light brown above, 6 black saddles; 8–9 black blotches on side *vertically oval* at front, round at rear. *Orange edge and base* on dusky 1st dorsal fin. Blue-green anal and pelvic fins on breeding male. Dusky to black teardrop. Broadly joined branchiostegal membranes (Fig. 54). Complete lateral line; 46–62 lateral scales; usually 12 dorsal spines. To 3½ in. (9 cm).
Range: Upper Tennessee R. drainage, VA, NC, and TN. Common locally, especially in French Broad and Little Pigeon R. systems. **Habitat:** Swift rubble riffles of small to medium rivers.
Similar species: See Pl. 42. (1) Blenny Darter has 4 large saddles, strongly tapering body. (2) Seagreen and (3) Turquoise Darters have small dark brown blotches (*not* vertically oval) or Ws along side, usually 9–10 dorsal spines. (4) Greenside Darter has Ws along side, *green edge* on 1st dorsal fin.   **Map 340**

BLENNY DARTER *Etheostoma blennius*   **Pl. 42**
Identification: Body *thick at front,* strongly tapering to *narrow caudal peduncle. 4 large* dark brown to black *saddles* extend down to meet dark blotches along side; white to yellow below. Red edge on 1st dorsal fin. Breeding male has red spots on upper side; bright blue lips; red-purple dorsal fins; blue-black breast and anal and pelvic fins. Teardrop usually prominent. Broadly joined branchiostegal membranes (Fig. 54). Complete lateral line; 40–51 lateral scales. To 3¼ in. (8.3 cm).
Range: West- and south-flowing tributaries of Tennessee R. in cen. TN and n. AL (east to Sequatchie R. system). Locally common. **Habitat:** Fast, rocky riffles of creeks and small to medium rivers.
Remarks: Two subspecies. *E. b. sequatchiense* (endemic to Sequatchie R.) has 40–44 lateral scales, dark lines on side of large adult; usually has scales on upper opercle. *E. b. blennius* has 42–51 lateral scales, unscaled opercle, and no dark lines on side; it occupies rest of range except Elk R., s.–cen. TN and n. AL, where intergrades occur.
Similar species: See Pl. 42. (1) Swannanoa Darter is similar to *E. b. sequatchiense* but has *6 saddles,* less tapering body. (2) Other darters with large dark saddles are not in Tennessee R. system.   **Map 340**

FINESCALE SADDLED DARTER *Etheostoma osburni* **Pl. 42**
Identification: Dark green above, *5 large dark brown saddles.* 9–11 *green bars* alternate with *orange interspaces* (much brighter on male) on side; yellow to orange below. Orange edge, middle green band on 1st dorsal fin. Bright green and orange breeding male may be most vivid freshwater fish in North America. Broadly joined branchiostegal membranes (Fig. 54). Unscaled breast. Complete lateral line; *58–70 lateral scales.* To 4 in. (10 cm).
Range: Kanawha R. drainage above Kanawha Falls, WV and VA. Fairly common. **Habitat:** Fast rubble riffles of small to medium rivers.
Similar species: (1) See Kanawha Darter (Pl. 42). (2) Variegate Darter (Pl. 42) has *4* saddles, *48–60* lateral scales, scaled breast. **Map 335**

KANAWHA DARTER *Etheostoma kanawhae* **Pl. 42**
Identification: Nearly identical to Finescale Saddled Darter but has *48–58 lateral scales,* is slightly less brilliantly colored. 5–6 large dark brown saddles. Large male has bright orange belly and gill membranes. To 3½ in. (8.6 cm).
Range: New R. drainage, VA and NC. Fairly common. **Habitat:** Fast gravel and rubble riffles of small to medium rivers.
Similar species: See Finescale Saddled Darter (Pl. 42). **Map 337**

VARIEGATE DARTER *Etheostoma variatum* **Pl. 42**
Identification: *4 large brown saddles* angle down and forward to lateral line. *Green and orange bars* on side. Red edge, middle blue band, brown base on 1st dorsal fin. Breeding male is deep blue with orange or red belly, orange spots on side and fins. Broadly joined branchiostegal membranes (Fig. 54). Scales on rear of breast. Large eye (about equal to snout length). Complete lateral line; 48–60 lateral scales; To 4½ in. (11 cm).
Range: Ohio R. basin from sw. NY to VA, e. KY, and s. IN. Only below Kanawha Falls in Kanawha R. system of WV. Common; sometimes abundant in clear streams. **Habitat:** Swift gravel and rubble riffles of small to medium rivers.
Similar species: See Pl. 42. (1) See Missouri Saddled Darter. (2) Finescale Saddled Darter and (3) Kanawha Darter (both restricted to Kanawha R. system) have *5–6* dark saddles, unscaled breast.
Map 337

MISSOURI SADDLED DARTER *Etheostoma tetrazonum* **Pl. 42**
Identification: Nearly identical to Variegate Darter but has smaller eye, darker saddles; breeding male is blue-green, has orange belly, orange bars on side, red-orange edge on 1st dorsal fin. 46–57 lateral scales. To 3½ in. (9 cm).
Range: Missouri Ozarks from Meramec R. (Mississippi R. tributary) to Osage and Moreau rivers (Missouri R. tributaries). Common. **Habitat:** Fast gravel and rubble riffles of small to medium rivers.
Similar species: (1) See Variegate Darter (Pl. 42). (2) Arkansas Saddled Darter (Pl. 42) *lacks* green bars on side, has 54–71 lateral scales.
Map 337

ARKANSAS SADDLED DARTER *Etheostoma euzonum*   **Pl. 42**
   Identification: Olive above; *4 large dark brown saddles* angle down
   and forward to lateral line; *green and orange spots* on upper side; yellow lower side. Red-orange edge, middle blue band, dusky green base
   on 1st dorsal fin. *Large head and eye.* Broadly joined branchiostegal
   membranes (Fig. 54). Complete lateral line; 54–71 lateral scales. To
   4¾ in. (12 cm).
   Range: White R. drainage (including Current and Black rivers), MO
   and AR. Generally uncommon. **Habitat:** Deep, fast gravel and rubble
   riffles of small to medium rivers.
   Remarks: Two subspecies. *E. e. erizonum,* Current R. system, has
   scales on cheek, long snout, and relatively small eye. *E. e. euzonum,*
   occupying rest of range except Black R. system where intergrades occur, lacks scales on cheek; has blunter snout and larger eye.
   Similar species: Only similar darter west of Mississippi R. is Missouri
   Saddled Darter (Pl. 42), which has green bars on side (most prominent
   at rear), 46–57 lateral scales.   **Map 337**

BANDED DARTER *Etheostoma zonale*   **Pl. 42**
   Identification: *9–13 large dark green bars on side* extend *onto belly*
   and under caudal peduncle to *join* those of other side. Yellow-green,
   6 dark saddles; 2 large yellow caudal spots. Narrow teardrop, often
   broken into 2 black spots. Green edge, red base on 1st dorsal fin (colors brighter on male). Wide premaxillary frenum, moderate snout,
   broadly joined branchiostegal membranes (Fig. 54), 5 (rarely 6)
   branchiostegal rays. Complete lateral line; 38–63 (usually 45 or
   more) lateral scales. To 3 in. (7.8 cm).
   Range: Lake Michigan and Mississippi R. basins from sw. NY to MN,
   and south to n. GA, n. AL, and s. AR (except absent from Former Mississippi Embayment; Wabash R. drainage of OH, IN, and IL; and
   streams of s. IL, s. IA, and n. MO). Introduced on Atlantic Slope into
   Susquehanna R., PA, and headwaters of Savannah R., SC. Common;
   locally abundant. **Habitat:** Rocky riffles of creeks and small to medium rivers.
   Similar species: See Pl. 42. (1) See Brighteye Darter. (2) Harlequin
   Darter has 2 large dark spots at front of caudal fin. In (3) Greenside,
   (4) Rock, and (5) Emerald Darters, green bars on side *rarely join* (except occasionally on large male) those of other side; Greenside and
   Rock Darters have *fewer* than 9 bars; Emerald Darter has a much
   blunter snout, usually 8 dark squares on back.   **Map 341**

BRIGHTEYE DARTER *Etheostoma lynceum*   **Pl. 42**
   Identification: Similar to Banded Darter, but green bars on side are
   darker, with interspaces about as wide as bars (interspaces narrower
   than bars in Banded Darter); has usually *fewer than 45 lateral scales.*
   To 2½ in. (6.4 cm).
   Range: Tributaries of the Mississippi R. on the Former Mississippi
   Embayment, w. KY, w. TN, MS, and LA. Gulf Coast drainages from
   the Escatawpa R., AL, to the Mississippi R., LA. Common. **Habitat:**

Rocky riffles of creeks, small rivers; near debris in sand and gravel runs.
Similar species: See Banded Darter (Pl. 42). **Map 341**

Next 15 species (Snubnose Darters): *Extremely blunt snout; broadly joined branchiostegal membranes* (Fig. 54); *no or narrow premaxillary frenum* (Fig. 55); *8–9 dark saddles.* Most have *bright red spot* at front of 1st dorsal fin. Complete lateral line; usually 10–12 dorsal spines, 10–12 dorsal rays, 6–8 anal rays, 14 pectoral rays; usually *5 branchiostegal rays* (except 6 in Coosa Darter), whereas most other darters have 6; usually *9 preoperculomandibular pores*, whereas most other darters have 10. Snubnose Darters are among the most colorful North American fishes. Unfortunately, about 6 species remain unnamed and unstudied.

Next 4 species: narrow premaxillary frenum, no vomerine teeth.

EMERALD DARTER *Etheostoma baileyi* **Pl. 42**
Identification: Olive above, 7–10 (usually 8) dark green saddles; *7–11 small emerald-green squares* along side (expanded into bars on breeding male); white to yellow below; bright red spot at front, *red edge* on 1st dorsal fin; dusky teardrop. Unscaled breast. 45–56 lateral scales. To 2¼ in. (5.6 cm).
Range: Upper Kentucky and upper Cumberland R. drainages, e. KY and ne. TN. Locally common. **Habitat:** Rocky pools, sometimes riffles, of creeks and small to medium rivers.
Similar species: (1) Banded Darter (Pl. 42) has 6 dorsal saddles, large dark green *bars* on side extending onto belly and joining those of other side, more pointed snout. (2) Tennessee Snubnose Darter (Pl. 43) has small red spots on upper side (often faint on female), wavy black lines on 1st dorsal fin, black blotches along side. **Map 342**

TENNESSEE SNUBNOSE DARTER *Etheostoma simoterum* **Pl. 43**
Identification: *Many small red spots* (brightest on large male) in short rows on upper side; 1st dorsal fin has red spot at front, *red edge, wavy black lines.* Light green or brown above, 8–9 dark green saddles; 8–9 black blotches along side; white to orange below; large black teardrop. Breeding male is bright orange below; has red dorsal fins, blue to blue-green snout, and anal and pelvic fins. Usually unscaled breast. 42–61 lateral scales. To 3 in. (7.7 cm).
Range: Cumberland and Tennessee R. drainages, VA, NC, KY, TN, GA, and AL. Locally common in middle Cumberland drainage, absent in upper (above Big South Fork) and lower drainage; common to abundant in most of Tennessee drainage, although rare in NC and absent in w. tributaries of Tennessee R. in w. TN. **Habitat:** Current-swept rocky pools and adjacent riffles of creeks and small to medium rivers.
Similar species: (1) Blackside Snubnose Darter (Pl. 43) *lacks* red spots on upper side; has dark blotches along side fused together, no premaxillary frenum. (2) Emerald Darter (Pl. 42) *lacks* red spots on upper side and wavy black lines on 1st dorsal fin, has green squares or bars along side. **Map 343**

KENTUCKY SNUBNOSE DARTER *Etheostoma rafinesquei* **Pl. 43**
Identification: *Cross-hatching* (created by dark scale edges), *7–10 (usually 8) short black bars* on side. 1st dorsal fin has red spot at front, red edge. Yellow-brown; 7–9 dark saddles, 1st saddle covering most of nape; dusky teardrop. Breeding male has bright red dorsal fins (green base on 1st dorsal fin deepest at front); blue-green head and anal and pelvic fins; orange breast and belly. Rear half of breast usually scaled. 37–43 lateral scales. To 2½ in. (6.5 cm).
Range: Upper Green and Gasper R. (Barren R. tributary) systems, KY. Locally common. **Habitat:** Rocky pools, runs, and adjacent riffles of creeks and small rivers.
Similar species: Splendid Darter (Pl. 43), only other snubnose darter in Green R. system, *lacks* cross-hatching, has black blotches along side fused into stripe, 1st dorsal saddle only on front half of nape, 42–49 lateral scales. **Map 342**

SPLENDID DARTER *Etheostoma barrenense* **Pl. 43**
Identification: *7–10 black blotches on side fused into stripe.* Yellow-brown above; 7–9 black saddles, 1st only on front half of nape; red spot at front of 1st dorsal fin; thin, dusky teardrop. Breeding male is *red above and below* black stripe along side; has green head, blue anal and pelvic fins, red edge and green base on 1st dorsal fin, red middle band in 2d dorsal fin. Unscaled breast. 42–49 lateral scales. To 2½ in. (6.4 cm).
Range: Barren R. system (except Gasper R.), s.-cen. KY and n.-cen. TN. Common. **Habitat:** Rocky pools and adjacent riffles of creeks and small rivers.
Similar species: (1) Blackside Snubnose (Pl. 43) and (2) Saffron Darters lack premaxillary frenum, have orange or yellow (not red) on side. (3) Kentucky Snubnose Darter (Pl. 43) has cross-hatching and dark bars on side, 37–43 lateral scales. **Map 342**

Next 11 species: usually vomerine teeth, no premaxillary frenum.

BLACKSIDE SNUBNOSE DARTER *Etheostoma duryi* **Pl. 43**
Identification: *9–10 black blotches along side fused into stripe.* 1st dorsal fin usually has red spot at front, red edge (faint on female), wavy red and black lines. Light olive-brown to orange above, usually 8 black saddles; green or gray lips; dusky teardrop. Breeding male has *orange upper and lower sides;* 2 red-orange spots on caudal fin base; red dorsal fins. Unscaled breast. 38–54 lateral scales. To 2¾ in. (7.2 cm).
Range: Tennessee R. drainage, TN, GA, and AL (absent in extreme upper Tennessee — occurs east to near Knoxville). Common. **Habitat:** Rocky pools and adjacent riffles of creeks and small rivers.
Similar species: (1) See Saffron Darter. (2) Tennessee Snubnose Darter (Pl. 43) has red spots on upper side, *little or no fusion* of dark blotches along side, premaxillary frenum. (3) Splendid Darter (Pl. 43) has *bright red side* on large male, premaxillary frenum. **Map 344**

SAFFRON DARTER *Etheostoma flavum* **Not shown**
Identification: Similar to Blackside Snubnose Darter but has *more discrete brown blotches* along side (less fused into stripe). Breeding male has *yellow-gold lips and upper and lower sides;* green caudal peduncle; yellow spots on caudal fin base; *no red on fins.* 42–59 lateral scales. To 2¾ in. (7 cm).
Range: Lower Cumberland and lower Tennessee R. drainages, KY and TN. Upstream in Cumberland R. drainage to Harpeth R.; upstream in Tennessee R. drainage (on east side of Tennessee R. only) to upper Duck R., upper Buffalo R., and Indian Cr. (Wayne Co., TN). Common; locally abundant. **Habitat:** Rocky pools and adjacent riffles of headwaters, creeks, and small rivers.
Similar species: See Blackside Snubnose Darter (Pl. 43). **Map 345**

CHERRY DARTER *Etheostoma etnieri* **Pl. 43**
Identification: *Black lines* along upper side of body. 1st dorsal fin has small red spot at front, thin black bands. Olive above, 7–9 black saddles; 8–10 black blotches along side; white to red below; thin black teardrop. Breeding male has green head and breast; bright red belly, side and 2d dorsal, anal, and caudal fins. Premaxillary frenum absent or narrow. Unscaled breast. 45–57 lateral scales. To 3 in. (7.7 cm).
Range: Upper Caney Fork (of Cumberland R.) system, cen. TN. Locally common. **Habitat:** Bedrock pools and rocky riffles of creeks and small rivers.
Similar species: Other snubnose darters (Pls. 42 & 43) *lack* black lines along upper side. **Map 344**

Next 8 species: thin brown stripe above lateral line *interrupted* by 7–10 black or brown blotches; front blotches sometimes fused into black or brown stripe.

FIREBELLY DARTER *Etheostoma pyrrhogaster* **Pl. 43**
Identification: Front blotches often fused into black stripe. 1st dorsal fin has red spot at front, *red band* near edge (faint on female). Light brown above, 8–9 black saddles; teardrop faint or absent. Breeding male has *wide red band* on each dorsal fin, anal fin; *bright red body;* green head; black blotches on front half of side fused into black stripe. Scales (partially embedded) on rear half of breast. 36–46 lateral scales. To 2¾ in. (7 cm).
Range: Obion and Forked Deer R. drainages (Mississippi R. basin), w. KY and w. TN. Uncommon. **Habitat:** Sand- and gravel-bottomed pools of headwaters, creeks, and small rivers.
Similar species: Bandfin Darter (Pl. 43) has *2 thin red bands* through middle of 1st and 2d dorsal fins. **Map 345**

BANDFIN DARTER *Etheostoma zonistium* **Pl. 43**
Identification: 1st dorsal fin has red spot at front, blue edge, *2 red bands* (faint on female) through middle. Yellow-brown above, 8 dark saddles; no or thin teardrop. Breeding male has blue edge, 2 bright red bands on 1st dorsal fin; 1–2 red bands on 2d dorsal fin; *bright red*

body; green head; blue anal and pelvic fins; black blotches on front half of side fused into black stripe. Scales (partly embedded) on rear half of breast. 40–52 lateral scales. To 2¾ in. (7.1 cm).
Range: Tributaries of lower Tennessee R. system, KY, TN, ne. MS, and nw. AL upstream to Bear Cr. system; confined to w. tributaries except in Land Between the Lakes, KY, and Hardin Co., TN. Spring Cr. (Hatchie R. drainage), w. TN; extreme upper Black Warrior R. system (Mobile Bay drainage), AL. Common. **Habitat:** Sand- and gravel-bottomed pools of headwaters, creeks, and small rivers.
Similar species: (1) Firebelly Darter (Pl. 43) has *1 red band* near edge of 1st dorsal fin on female, *1 wide red band* on male. (2) Coosa Darter (Pl. 43) has 8–10 blue-brown bars along side of large male, unscaled breast; *lacks* bright red body. **Map 342**

COASTAL PLAIN DARTER *Etheostoma* species **Pl. 43**
Identification: 1st dorsal fin has *blue edge* (faint on female), *no red spot* at front. Yellow-brown above, 8 dark brown saddles; 7–10 red-brown blotches along side; dusky teardrop. Breeding male has *high, arched 1st dorsal fin*; bright blue edge, bright red band on each dorsal fin; green head; blue anal, caudal, and pelvic fins; *orange upper and lower sides*. Unscaled breast. 41–47 lateral scales. To 2½ in. (6.6 cm).
Range: Gulf Coastal Plain from Pensacola Bay drainage, FL, to Mobile Bay drainage, AL and MS (to ne. Mississippi in Tombigbee R. system). Common. **Habitat:** Sand- and gravel-bottomed pools of headwaters, creeks, and small rivers.
Similar species: See (1) Yazoo and (2) Tallapoosa Darters (both, Pl. 43). **Map 346**

YAZOO DARTER *Etheostoma* species **Pl. 43**
Identification: Nearly identical to Coastal Plain Darter but has *8–10 narrow, red-brown horizontal rectangles* along side *just above* (sitting on) lateral line. To 2¼ in. (6 cm).
Range: Upper Yazoo R. drainage, MS. Uncommon. **Habitat:** Sandy pools of headwaters and creeks.
Similar species: Coastal Plain Darter (Pl. 43) has *larger* red-brown rectangles *well above* lateral line and extending as *bars* onto upper side on large male. **Map 345**

TALLAPOOSA DARTER *Etheostoma* species **Pl. 43**
Identification: Similar to Coastal Plain Darter but has larger, blacker blotches on side; smaller (48–55 lateral) scales; *red-brown throughout* (except blue edge) *low* (not arched) *1st dorsal fin* on breeding male. To 2½ in. (6.6 cm).
Range: Above Fall Line in Tallapoosa R. system, GA and AL. Locally common. **Habitat:** Bedrock pools and rocky riffles of creeks and small rivers.
Similar species: See Coastal Plain Darter (Pl. 43). **Map 346**

ELLIJAY DARTER *Etheostoma* species **Pl. 42**
Identification: Red-brown blotches (appearing as interrupted brown

stripe on juvenile) between *8–10 green bars* along side. 1st dorsal fin
has red spot at front, *blue edge* (faint on female). Yellow-green above,
8 dorsal saddles; black teardrop. Breeding male has bright *blue edge,*
red band on each dorsal fin; *short red-brown bars between wide
green bars* on side; green head; red-orange belly; blue pelvic fins; red
band on anal fin. Unscaled breast. 45–54 lateral scales. To 2½ in. (6.2
cm).
Range: Conasauga and Ellijay R. systems (upper Coosa R. system),
GA, AL, and se. TN. Uncommon. **Habitat:** Rocky runs and pools,
sometimes riffles, of creeks and small to medium rivers.
Similar species: Coosa Darter (Pl. 43) has *blue-brown bars* along side,
2 red bands on 1st dorsal fin.   **Map 345**

COOSA DARTER *Etheostoma coosae*   **Pl. 43**
Identification: 1st dorsal fin has bright red spot at front, *1–2 red
bands,* blue-green edge (faint on female). Light brown to olive above,
8–9 dark saddles; black teardrop. Breeding male has *8–10 dark blue-
brown bars* along side; bright blue edge, 2 red bands on 1st dorsal fin;
red 2d dorsal fin; green head; blue-black anal and pelvic fins. *6
branchiostegal rays;* unscaled breast. 42–59 lateral scales. To 2¾ in.
(7.2 cm).
Range: Coosa R. system, GA, AL, and se. TN. Fairly common. **Habitat:** Rocky pools and adjacent riffles of creeks and small to medium
rivers.
Similar species: Only other Snubnose Darter with 2 red bands in 1st
dorsal fin is Bandfin Darter (Pl. 43), which *lacks* dark bars on side;
has red body, green head on large male. Other Snubnose Darters have
5 branchiostegal rays.   **Map 344**

WARRIOR DARTER *Etheostoma* species   **Pl. 43**
Identification: 1st dorsal fin has red spot at front, *red edge* (faint on
female). Yellow-brown above, 8 dark brown saddles; dusky teardrop.
Breeding male has bright red edge on 1st dorsal fin; middle red band
on 2d dorsal fin; *red lower side;* blue-green head and anal, caudal, and
pelvic fins. Unscaled breast. 48–52 lateral scales. To 2¾ in. (7.2 cm).
Range: Above Fall Line in Black Warrior R. system, AL. Common but
localized. **Habitat:** Bedrock pools and rocky riffles of creeks and small
rivers.
Similar species: Other snubnose darters in Gulf drainages (Pl. 43) have
blue edge on 1st dorsal fin, orange (not red) lower side.   **Map 346**

ASHY DARTER *Etheostoma cinereum*   **Pl. 48**
Identification: *Longitudinal rows of small brown spots* on upper side.
Row of small black rectangles along side; oblique dusky bars extend
down from rectangles. *Red lips* (absent in Tennessee R. system); red
wavy lines and red-orange edge on 1st dorsal fin. Preorbital bars form
large black V on snout. Red dorsal and pectoral fins (*greatly enlarged
2d dorsal fin*), blue anal and pelvic fins on breeding male. Long, sharp
snout. Complete lateral line; 55–61 lateral scales. To 4¾ in. (12 cm).
Range: Cumberland and Tennessee R. drainages, VA, KY, TN, GA,

and AL. Rare over most of range; fairly common locally in a few streams. **Habitat:** Rocky pools with current in small to medium rivers; usually near vegetation. **Map 339**

Next 15 species: alternating *dark and light lines* (often faint on Greenbreast Darter) on side of *deep, compressed body.* All live in fast, rocky riffles.

GREENBREAST DARTER *Etheostoma jordani* **Pl. 44**
Identification: Large eye; *no teardrop.* Small *black blotches* along side just below lateral line; often small blotches on upper side. Black edge on 2d dorsal, caudal, and anal fins. Male is dark gray above, *blue below;* has small red spots on side; black spot at front, *red edge* on 1st dorsal fin; red band in 2d dorsal and caudal fins; other fins blue. Female is brown above, white to light blue below; has dusky yellow fins. 44–56 lateral scales. To 3 in. (7.9 cm).
Range: Alabama and Black Warrior R. systems (Mobile Bay drainage), GA, AL, and se. TN. Common. **Habitat:** Fast rocky riffles of creeks and small to medium rivers.
Similar species: No similar species in Mobile Bay drainage. **Map 347**

REDLINE DARTER *Etheostoma rufilineatum* **Pl. 44**
Identification: *Black dashes* on cheek and opercle. Teardrop broken into *2 black spots. Cream-colored caudal fin base.* Pointed snout. Dark gray above; dark blotches on side. Black edge on 2d dorsal, caudal, and anal fins. Male has red spots on side, orange belly, blue breast, red-orange band on fins; female has brown spots on side, white to dusky blue breast, black spots on fins. To 3½ in. (8.4 cm).
Range: Cumberland (below Big South Fork) and Tennessee R. drainages, VA, KY, NC, TN, GA, AL, and MS. Abundant. **Habitat:** Clear, fast rocky riffles of creeks and small to medium rivers.
Similar species: Similar darters (Pl. 44) *lack* black dashes on cheek and cream on caudal fin base. **Map 348**

YELLOWCHEEK DARTER *Etheostoma moorei* **Pl. 44**
Identification: Dark gray above; black mottling on side; light gray to white below; *blue breast. Green base, red band* on 1st dorsal fin of male; other fins red, black at base. *Black spots* on fins of female. Black edge on dorsal, caudal, and anal fins; black teardrop on dusky cheek. 51–60 lateral scales. To 2¾ in. (7.2 cm).
Range: Little Red R. system, n.-cen. AR. Uncommon. **Habitat:** Fast rocky riffles of small to medium rivers.
Similar species: No similar species west of Mississippi R. (1) Bayou Darter (Pl. 44) *lacks* green in fins, has white cheek, red spots on side. (2) Smallscale Darter (Pl. 44) has red spots on side of male. **Map 349**

Next 10 species: *discrete, small bright red spots* on side of large male, *small brown spots* on side of female.

BAYOU DARTER *Etheostoma rubrum*   **Pl. 44**
  Identification: Dark gray above; large black teardrop on *white cheek. Cream-colored caudal fin base* followed by *2 large black spots.* Black edge on dorsal, caudal, and anal fins. Blue breast. Fins red on male, black spot at front of 1st dorsal fin; black-spotted on female. 45–55 lateral scales. To 2¼ in. (5.5 cm).
  Range: Bayou Pierre system, sw. MS. Uncommon; protected as a *threatened species.* **Habitat:** Fast, rocky riffles of creeks and small to medium rivers.
  Similar species: No similar species within range; closely related Yellowcheek Darter (Pl. 44) *lacks* red spots on side; has dusky black cheek, green on 1st dorsal fin of male.   **Map 349**

SMALLSCALE DARTER *Etheostoma microlepidum*   **Pl. 44**
  Identification: Large male is gray, with bright *green and orange* dorsal, caudal, and anal fins; has *black halos* around red spots on side. Female is brown, with *black spots* on fins. Black edge on 2d dorsal, caudal, and anal fins; black teardrop. 55–71 lateral scales. To 2¾ in. (7.2 cm).
  Range: Lower Cumberland R. drainage, w. KY and n.-cen. TN. Localized and uncommon. **Habitat:** Clear, shallow gravel riffles of small rivers.
  Similar species: (1) Bloodfin Darter *lacks* black edge on fins, green on fins of large male. (2) Redline Darter (Pl. 44) has dark dashes on cheek and opercle; *lacks* green on fins.   **Map 350**

SPOTTED DARTER *Etheostoma maculatum*   **Pl. 44**
  Identification: *Extremely compressed body; narrow pointed snout;* round caudal fin. Gray body; male has *black halos* around red spots on side, blue breast, gray or blue fins. Female has black mottling on side, *black spots* on fins. Teardrop thin or absent. 53–68 lateral scales. To 3½ in. (9 cm).
  Range: Ohio R. basin from w. NY and PA to n. IN, and south to WV and KY. Extremely localized and uncommon. **Habitat:** Fast, rocky riffles of small to medium rivers.
  Similar species: See Pl. 44: (1) See Bloodfin Darter. (2) Wounded Darter has bright red spots on 1st dorsal fin; red 2d dorsal and caudal fins; black edge on 2d dorsal, caudal, and anal fins; straight-edged caudal fin. (3) Smallscale Darter has green on fins of male. (4) Bluebreast Darter, often found with Spotted Darter, is *less compressed,* has *blunter snout, lacks* black halos around red spots on side of male.   **Map 351**

BLOODFIN DARTER *Etheostoma sanguifluum*   **Not shown**
  Identification: Similar to Spotted Darter, but large male has *2 bright red spots* at front, usually 1 at rear, of 1st dorsal fin; red fin membranes. 51–66 lateral scales. To 3½ in. (9 cm).
  Range: Middle Cumberland R. drainage (Rockcastle R., KY, to Caney Fork, TN), KY and TN. Generally uncommon. **Habitat:** Fast rocky riffles of small to medium rivers.

Similar species: See Pl. 44. See (1) Spotted, (2) Coppercheek, and (3) Wounded Darters. **Map 351**

COPPERCHEEK DARTER *Etheostoma aquali* **Pl. 44**
Identification: Nearly identical to Bloodfin Darter but has wavy *copper lines* on cheek and opercle, no teardrop. 57–67 lateral scales. To 3¼ in. (8 cm).
Range: Duck R. system (Tennessee R. drainage), w.-cen. TN. Fairly common. **Habitat:** Clear, fast rocky riffles of small to medium rivers.
Similar species: See Bloodfin Darter. **Map 351**

WOUNDED DARTER *Etheostoma vulneratum* **Pl. 44**
Identification: *Extremely compressed body; narrow pointed snout;* straight-edged caudal fin. Gray body; *black edge* on 2d dorsal, caudal, and anal fins. Male has *black halos* around red spots on side; 2 bright red spots at front, usually 1 at rear, of 1st dorsal fin; red 2d dorsal and caudal fins; blue breast. No red on anal and pelvic fins. 51–66 lateral scales. To 3¼ in. (8 cm).
Range: Upper Tennessee R. drainage, VA, NC, and e. TN. Common. **Habitat:** Fast rocky riffles of small to medium rivers.
Similar species: (1) See Boulder Darter. (2) Coppercheek (Pl. 44), (3) Bloodfin, and (4) Spotted Darters (Pl. 44) *lack* black edge on 2d dorsal, caudal, and anal fins; have rounded caudal fin. **Map 351**

BOULDER DARTER *Etheostoma wapiti* **Not shown**
Identification: Nearly identical to Wounded Darter but *lacks* red on 1st dorsal fin; male has *no red* on body or fins. To 3¼ in. (8.5 cm).
Range: Elk R. and Shoal Cr. systems (Tennessee R. drainage), s. TN and n. AL. Rare in Elk R.; possibly extirpated in Shoal Cr. Protected as an *endangered species.* **Habitat:** Fast, rocky riffles of small to medium rivers.
Similar species: (1) See Wounded Darter (Pl. 44). (2) Spotted Darter (Pl. 44) *lacks* black edge on 2d dorsal, caudal, and anal fins; has rounded caudal fin. **Map 350**

BLUEBREAST DARTER *Etheostoma camurum* **Pl. 44**
Identification: Male has bright red spots *not* surrounded by black halos on side; red fins, *blue breast.* Female has *brown spots* on side, brown fins, white to light blue breast. Olive green to gray above; light green to white below; black edge on 2d dorsal, caudal, and anal fins. Dusky teardrop, unscaled nape, moderately blunt snout. 47–70 lateral scales. To 3¼ in. (8.4 cm).
Range: Ohio R. basin from w. NY to e. IL, and south to Tennessee R., NC and TN. Locally common but absent from many rivers within range. **Habitat:** Fast, rocky riffles of small to medium rivers.
Similar species: See Pl. 44. (1) Greenfin Darter has green fins, dark teardrop, more pointed snout. (2) Spotted, (3) Bloodfin, and (4) Wounded Darters have pointed snout, *black halos* around red spots on side. (4) Coppercheek and (5) Redline Darters have pointed snout, distinctive marks on cheek. **Map 352**

GREENFIN DARTER *Etheostoma chlorobranchium* **Pl. 44**
Identification: Large male is *deep green* with *green fins* except *pink pectoral fins.* Female and juvenile are brown above; have blue breast, yellow-brown fins (often with some green), small black and red-brown spots on side. Black edge on dorsal, caudal, and anal fins; black teardrop. Moderately pointed snout. 52–72 lateral scales. To 4 in. (10 cm).
Range: Upper Tennessee R. drainage from S.F. Holston R. to Hiwassee R. systems, VA, NC, TN, and GA. Common. **Habitat:** Very fast, rocky riffles of creeks and small to medium rivers.
Similar species: Bluebreast Darter (Pl. 44) *lacks* green; has blunter snout, less distinct teardrop. **Map 350**

ORANGEFIN DARTER *Etheostoma bellum* **Pl. 44**
Identification: *Large black teardrop* (sometimes obscure on large male); black blotches along side; black edge on dorsal, caudal, and anal fins. Male is brown to orange; has blue breast, *orange fins.* Female is brown above, yellow below; has yellow-brown fins. Scales on rear of nape; moderately pointed snout. 48–63 lateral scales. To 3½ in. (9 cm).
Range: Upper Green and Barren R. systems, KY and n.-cen. TN. Common. **Habitat:** Fast, rocky riffles of creeks and small to medium rivers.
Similar species: Only similar species in Green R. system is Spotted Darter (Pl. 44), which is more compressed and has long pointed snout, *small* teardrop, *no* orange on fins, black spots on fins of female. **Map 350**

SHARPHEAD DARTER *Etheostoma acuticeps* **Pl. 44**
Identification: *Compressed body; extremely pointed snout.* Long dusky bars on side. No red on body or fins; no black edge on fins. Female is yellow-brown; no spots on fins. Male is olive to *blue;* has *turquoise* fins, black spot at front of 1st dorsal fin. Teardrop absent or dusky. Unscaled opercle. Complete lateral line; 54–65 lateral scales. To 3¼ in. (8.4 cm).
Range: Holston and Nolichucky R. systems (Tennessee R. drainage), w. VA, w. NC, and e. TN. Rare. **Habitat:** Fast, deep rocky riffles in small to medium rivers.
Similar species: See Pl. 44. (1) Wounded, (2) Redline, (3) Bluebreast, and (4) Greenfin Darters have red spots on side of male; black edge on 2d dorsal, caudal, and anal fins; scales on opercle. **Map 347**

YOKE DARTER *Etheostoma juliae* **Pl. 44**
Identification: *Large black saddle* ("yoke") on nape and down side to pectoral fin; 3 smaller saddles. Brown above; light green below; large *metallic green humeral spot;* wide dusky bars on side; *orange fins;* large teardrop. Pointed snout. 50–65 lateral scales. To 3 in. (7.8 cm).
Range: White R. drainage (excluding Black R. system), s. MO and n. AR. Common; locally abundant. **Habitat:** Clear, fast, rocky riffles of creeks and small to medium rivers.

Similar species: Yellowcheek Darter (Pl. 44) *lacks yoke; is gray with red fins on male;* female has black-spotted fins. Other close relatives of Yoke Darter (Pl. 44) occur east of Mississippi R.   **Map 349**

TIPPECANOE DARTER *Etheostoma tippecanoe*   **Pl. 44**
Identification: *Small* — to 1¾ in. (4.3 cm). Blue-black bars on side, darkest at rear; *last bar large, encircles caudal peduncle,* followed by 2 yellow (female) or orange (male) spots on caudal fin base. Male is orange; has blue breast, dark orange fins. Female is dark brown above, yellow below; has black spots on fins. Moderately pointed snout. Incomplete lateral line; 40–65 lateral scales.
Range: Ohio R. basin from w. PA to IN, and south to Tennessee R. drainage, VA and TN. Extremely localized; locally common. **Habitat:** Shallow gravel riffles of medium-sized rivers.
Similar species: Similar Darters (Pl. 44) *lack* black bar on caudal peduncle.   **Map 347**

ARROW DARTER *Etheostoma sagitta*   **Pl. 45**
Identification: Long slender body; *long pointed snout. 2 black caudal spots* partially fused into short bar. Straw-colored to olive above, 6–9 brown saddles; *7–9 large green Us* alternate with orange bars (faint on female) along side; yellow below. Breeding male has bright orange bars on side, red-orange edge on 1st dorsal fin, bands of red-orange spots on 2d dorsal and caudal fins, blue-green anal and pelvic fins. Usually incomplete lateral line; 52–69 lateral scales. To 4¾ in. (12 cm).
Range: Upper Kentucky and upper Cumberland R. drainages, KY and TN. Generally uncommon and declining; coal-mine pollution has eliminated many populations. **Habitat:** Rocky riffles and pools of headwaters, creeks, and small rivers.
Remarks: Two subspecies. *E. s. sagitta,* in Cumberland R. drainage, has usually 60 or more lateral scales. *E. s. spilotum,* in Kentucky R. drainage, has usually 59 or fewer lateral scales.
Similar species: See Niangua Darter (Pl. 45).   **Map 353**

NIANGUA DARTER *Etheostoma nianguae*   **Pl. 45**
Identification: Similar to Arrow Darter but has *2 (unfused) jet black caudal spots,* 72–82 lateral scales. Breeding male has large bright orange and green bars along side, orange and green bands on dorsal and caudal fins. To 5¼ in. (13 cm).
Range: Osage R. drainage (Missouri R. basin), s.-cen MO. Rare; protected as a *threatened species.* **Habitat:** Rocky pools and runs of creeks and small to medium rivers.
Similar species: See Arrow Darter (Pl. 45).   **Map 353**

PINEWOODS DARTER *Etheostoma mariae*   **Pl. 45**
Identification: 1st dorsal fin with *bright red edge, black spot* at front. *Small black blotches* on lower half of head and breast; thin teardrop broken into spots. Light brown above; *broad dark brown to black stripe* (often broken into wide bars), *yellow lateral line* on side; white to yellow-green below. Dark spots on 2d dorsal, caudal, and anal fins.

Broadly joined branchiostegal membranes (Fig. 54,). 35–39 lateral scales. To 3 in. (7.6 cm).

Range: Little Peedee R. system near Fall Line, NC and SC. Common within small range. **Habitat:** Gravel riffles and current-swept vegetation in creeks.

Similar species: Savannah Darter (Pl. 45) has moderately joined branchiostegal membranes, bright green belly (interrupted by bright orange bars on male); *no* black spot at front of 1st dorsal fin.

Map 354

SAVANNAH DARTER *Etheostoma fricksium* **Pl. 45**

Identification: Light brown above, *green below*; bright *orange bars* on belly of male; *broad dark brown to black stripe* on side. Red-brown spots on fins, *red edge* on 1st dorsal fin. *Small black blotches* on lower half of head and breast. Black teardrop, 3–4 black caudal spots. Moderately joined branchiostegal membranes. Usually complete lateral line; 35–45 lateral scales. To 3 in. (7.4 cm).

Range: Below Fall Line in Edisto, Combahee, Broad, and Savannah R. drainages, SC and GA. Common. **Habitat:** Gravel riffles, gravel and sand runs of creeks and small rivers. Often in vegetation.

Similar species: (1) Pinewoods Darter (Pl. 45) has broadly joined branchiostegal membranes, black spot at front of 1st dorsal fin, no orange on belly. (2) Christmas Darter (Pl. 46) has *middle* red band, dusky green edge on 1st dorsal fin; *no* broad dark brown to black stripe on side. **Map 354**

OKALOOSA DARTER *Etheostoma okaloosae* **Pl. 40**

Identification: Brown above; *5–8 rows of small dark brown spots* on side, row of larger dark brown dashes just below yellow lateral line; white to yellow below. *Black spots* on lower half of head and breast. Dusky brown fins; thin middle red band on 1st dorsal fin. Pointed snout. Thin, broken teardrop. Lateral line not strongly arched near front; 32–37 lateral scales. To 2 in. (5.3 cm).

Range: Choctawhatchee Bay drainage, FL panhandle. Uncommon; protected as an *endangered species.* **Habitat:** Vegetated sand runs of clear creeks.

Similar species: (1) Gulf Darter (Pl. 46) has incomplete lateral line, blunter snout, bright blue and orange on male's body and fins. (2) Brown Darter (Pl. 48) has lateral line incomplete and arched at front, *no* rows of brown spots on side; bright red spots on body and fins of male. **Map 355**

STIPPLED DARTER *Etheostoma punctulatum* **Pl. 45**

Identification: Light brown above, 6–8 dark saddles; *dark brown mottling, specks on head and body,* white to *orange* below. *Large black teardrop.* Speckled fins; brown base and edge on 1st dorsal fin, orange band near edge on male. Breeding male has bright orange head and lower half of body (to caudal fin), *wide blue stripe* on rear half of side, orange and blue bands on 1st dorsal fin (clear along base). Pointed snout. Incomplete lateral line; 58–80 lateral scales; usually 31–33 scales around caudal peduncle, 8 infraorbital pores. To 4 in. (10 cm).

Range: Missouri and White R. drainages in Ozark Uplands of MO and AR. Isolated population in upper Castor R. (Mississippi R. tributary) of se. MO. Common. **Habitat:** Rocky pools of headwaters, creeks, and, less often, small rivers; near springs and debris.
Similar species: (1) See Sunburst Darter. (2) Arkansas and (3) Paleback Darters (both, Pl. 45) have strongly bicolored body (upper half brown, lower half white to orange), blunt snout, fewer than 58 lateral scales.

Map 356

SUNBURST DARTER *Etheostoma* species   **Not shown**
Identification: Similar to Stippled Darter but has *4 dark saddles; more heavily speckled,* more robust body; usually 28–29 scales around caudal peduncle, 9–10 infraorbital pores. Breeding male has orange *restricted to belly, no* blue stripe on side, dark band along 1st dorsal fin base. To 3 in. (7.7 cm).
Range: Arkansas R. drainage, sw. MO, se. KS, nw. AR, and ne. OK. Common. **Habitat:** Same as Stippled Darter.
Similar species: See Stippled Darter (Pl. 45).   **Map 356**

SLACKWATER DARTER *Etheostoma boschungi*   **Pl. 45**
Identification: Brown above, 3 black saddles; *many black specks on back and side,* black blotches on upper side; white to orange (large male) below. *Large black teardrop.* Dusky fins; wide orange edge, blue base on 1st dorsal fin. Large head; blunt snout. Incomplete lateral line (30–44 pores); 43–58 lateral scales. To 3 in. (7.8 cm).
Range: Middle Tennessee R. drainage, s.-cen. TN and n. AL. Rare. Protected as a *threatened species.* **Habitat:** Gravel-bottomed pools and runs of creeks and small rivers; usually found in debris. Spawns in headwaters.
Similar species: See Pl. 45. (1) Trispot Darter has *thin* teardrop, 1 anal spine, complete lateral line. (2) Arkansas and (3) Paleback Darters — both west of Mississippi R. — have fewer than 26 lateral-line pores.   **Map 357**

ARKANSAS DARTER *Etheostoma cragini*   **Pl. 45**
Identification: Strongly *bicolored* body — upper half dark brown, lower half white to *orange. Black specks* on body and fins; black blotches sometimes on upper side. Blue edge, orange middle band, blue base on 1st dorsal fin of breeding male. Large black teardrop. Large head; blunt snout. Incomplete lateral line (4–25 pores); 42–57 lateral scales. To 2¼ in. (6 cm).
Range: Arkansas R. drainage, sw. MO, nw. AR, KS, OK, and CO. Uncommon. **Habitat:** Spring-fed vegetated headwaters and creeks, usually over mud.
Similar species: (1) See Paleback Darter (Pl. 45). (2) Stippled (Pl. 45) and (3) Sunburst Darters *lack* bicolored body; have more than 57 lateral scales, longer snout.   **Map 358**

PALEBACK DARTER *Etheostoma pallididorsum*   **Pl. 45**
Identification: Nearly identical to Arkansas Darter but is more *slen-*

der; has *wide, pale olive stripe along back.* Incomplete lateral line (8–19 pores); 43–55 lateral scales. To 2¼ in. (6 cm).
Range: Caddo R. and Hallmans Cr. (upper Ouachita R. drainage), sw. AR. Fairly common in small range. **Habitat:** Shallow, rocky pools of headwaters and creeks; vegetated springs.
Similar species: See Arkansas Darter (Pl. 45).   **Map 358**

TRISPOT DARTER *Etheostoma trisella*   **Pl. 45**
  Identification: Brown above and on side; *3 dark brown saddles;* white to yellow below. *Complete lateral line; 1 anal spine.* Thin teardrop. Breeding male has bright *orange body,* dusky fins, middle red band on 1st dorsal fin. 42–52 lateral scales. To 2¼ in. (5.9 cm).
  Range: Coosa R. system, GA, AL, and se. TN. Rare. **Habitat:** Sand and gravel runs of creeks and small rivers. Spawns in headwaters.
  Similar species: Slackwater Darter (Pl. 45) has large black teardrop, *2* anal spines, *incomplete* lateral line.   **Map 357**

GOLDSTRIPE DARTER *Etheostoma parvipinne*   **Pl. 40**
  Identification: Yellow body, dark brown mottling (sometimes coalesced into short wide bars); red eye; usually incomplete "gold" (yellow) lateral line. *Very short, blunt snout;* small *upturned mouth.* Black teardrop. Large male has black spot at front of 1st dorsal fin, thin stripes on rear half of body. Usually 2 anal spines. 40–62 lateral scales. To 2¾ in. (6.7 cm).
  Range: Coastal Plain from Altamaha (Atlantic Slope) and Flint (Gulf Slope) R. systems, GA, to Navasota R. system (Brazos R. drainage), TX; north in Former Mississippi Embayment to w. KY and se. MO. Fairly common. **Habitat:** Clay- and sand-bottomed runs and pools of vegetated, spring-fed headwaters and creeks.
  Similar species: (1) Blackfin, (2) Fringed (Pl. 47) and (3) Lollypop Darters (Pl. 47) have much larger, nearly *horizontal* mouth, more pointed snout; no black spot at front of 1st dorsal fin, thin stripes on body. (4) Tuscumbia Darter (Pl. 40) has gold specks, scales on top of head, 1 anal spine, no black spot at front of dorsal fin, no thin stripes on side.
                                                                    Map 359

TUSCUMBIA DARTER *Etheostoma tuscumbia*   **Pl. 40**
  Identification: Olive-brown, *gold specks* on back, head, and upper side. 4–6 dark brown saddles; small, dark blotches along side; dark bar on caudal fin base. *Scales* on top of head and often on branchiostegal membranes. *1 anal spine.* Long and tubular genital papilla on male. Incomplete lateral line. 37–51 lateral scales. To 2½ in. (6.1 cm).
  Range: Springs along Tennessee R. in AL and, formerly, s.-cen. TN. Common in a few springs. **Habitat:** Large vegetated springs.
  Similar species: (1) Goldstripe (Pl. 40) and (2) Trispot Darters (Pl. 45) lack scales on top of head and on gill membranes, gold specks; Goldstripe Darter has 2 anal spines; Trispot Darter has complete lateral line.   **Map 359**

REDFIN DARTER *Etheostoma whipplei* **Pl. 45**

Identification: Many small *bright red* (on male) or *yellow* (female) spots on side; thin dark lines, many interrupted, on side. *Slender*, relatively *uniform body depth* from head to caudal peduncle. Mottled body; often dark bars on rear of body, sometimes cut into upper and lower halves by yellow lateral line. Olive above, 8–10 brown saddles; white to orange (on male) below. Faint to black teardrop. Blue edge, middle red band on dorsal, caudal, and anal fins of male and 1st dorsal fin of female (faint). Blue pelvic fins on large male. Incomplete lateral line; 46–76 (usually 50–70) lateral scales. To 3½ in. (9 cm).

Range: Gulf drainages from Mobile Bay, AL, to Neches R., TX; Mississippi R. basin from MS to se. KS, e. OK, and ne. TX. Primarily on Coastal Plain and Arkansas R. lowlands. Common. **Habitat:** Sandy and rocky pools, sometimes runs or riffles, of headwaters, creeks, and small rivers.

Remarks: Two subspecies. *E. w. whipplei*, above Fall Line in White and Arkansas R. systems, has high (usually 60–73 lateral, 28–34 around caudal peduncle) scale counts. *E. w. artesiae*, in rest of range, has usually 50–62 lateral scales, 22–29 around caudal peduncle.

Similar species: (1) Orangebelly Darter (Pl. 45) *lacks* red and yellow spots and thin dark lines on side, is *deeper bodied* (as adult). (2) Other similar darters (see Pl. 46) have more distinct dark bars on side, are *deeper bodied*, rarely have more than 50 (Creole and Orangethroat, 55) lateral scales. **Map 360**

ORANGEBELLY DARTER *Etheostoma radiosum* **Pl. 45**

Identification: *Short dark bars* (rear ones long) along side, *cut into upper and lower halves by yellow lateral line.* Olive to tan above, 8–10 dark saddles; white to orange below. Black teardrop. Blue edge, middle red band on dorsal, caudal, and anal fins (faint on female). Orange branchiostegal membranes, blue pelvic fins on large male. Incomplete lateral line; 47–66 (usually 52–61) lateral scales. To 3½ in. (8.5 cm).

Range: Ouachita and Red R. drainages above Fall Line, sw. AR and se. OK. Abundant. **Habitat:** Gravel and rubble riffles and runs of creeks and small to medium rivers.

Remarks: Three subspecies. *E. r. cyanorum* in Blue R., OK, has blunt snout, 39–60 lateral-line pores. *E. r. paludosum*, Clear Boggy, Kiamichi, and Washita rivers, OK, has row of blue spots on edge of 1st dorsal fin. *E. r. radiosum* occupies rest of range. Orangebelly and Orangethroat Darters hybridize freely in Blue R., OK, forming hybrid swarms.

Similar species: Redfin Darter (Pl. 45) is more slender (as adult); has many small red (on male) or yellow (female) spots, thin dark lines on side. **Map 360**

RIO GRANDE DARTER *Etheostoma grahami* **Pl. 45**

Identification: *Deep bodied. Many small red* (on male) *or black* (female) *spots* on side. *Red 1st dorsal fin* (faint on female). Male has red 2d dorsal, anal, and pelvic fins; yellow caudal and pectoral fins. Olive

above, 8–10 dark saddles; often dusky blotches along side; white to yellow below. Faint teardrop. Incomplete lateral line; 40–56 (usually 45–51) lateral scales; interrupted infraorbital and supratemporal canals (Fig. 53). To 2¼ in. (6 cm).
Range: Lower Rio Grande drainage, TX and Mexico. In TX only in Sycamore Cr., Devils R., and lower Pecos R. Common in Devils R.
Habitat: Gravel and rubble riffles of creeks and small rivers.
Similar species: (1) Greenthroat and (2) Orangethroat Darters (both, Pl. 46) have dark bars on side, blue edge on 1st dorsal fin; Orangethroat Darter *lacks* many small red or black spots on side. **Map 361**

RAINBOW DARTER *Etheostoma caeruleum* **Pl. 46**
Identification: *Deep body*, deepest under middle of 1st dorsal fin. *Dark bars* on side (blue between red on male; dark brown between yellow-white on female). Light brown above, 6–10 dark saddles − 2–3 prominent; yellow, green, or red below. Dorsal, caudal, and anal fins *red with blue edge* (faint on female). Large male has red pectoral fin, blue pelvic fin, orange branchiostegal membranes, blue cheek, and, in some populations, rows of red spots on side. Unscaled cheek and breast; uninterrupted infraorbital canal (Fig. 53); usually 13 pectoral rays; incomplete lateral line; 36–57 (usually 41–50) lateral scales. To 3 in. (7.7 cm).
Range: Great Lakes and Mississippi R. basins from s. ON and w. NY to MN, and south to n. AL and AR. Isolated populations in sw. MS and e. LA, and in upper Potomac R. drainage (Atlantic Slope), WV. Abundant. **Habitat:** Fast gravel and rubble riffles of creeks and small to medium rivers.
Similar species: See Pl. 46. (1) Orangethroat and (2) Redband Darters have body deepest at *nape or front of* 1st dorsal fin, no red in anal fin, infraorbital canal interrupted; Orangethroat Darter usually has 11–12 pectoral rays; Redband Darter has partly scaled cheek and breast, usually 52–59 lateral scales. (3) Mud Darter has fully scaled cheek, dark blotch at rear of 1st dorsal fin, no red on anal fin. (4) Gulf Darter has thin dark lines on upper side, scales on cheek. **Map 362**

MUD DARTER *Etheostoma asprigene* **Pl. 46**
Identification: *Dark bars* on side (darkest at rear), blue between dull orange on male. *Fully scaled cheek.* 1st dorsal fin has middle red band, blue edge and base, *large black blotch* at rear (faint on female). Body deepest under middle of 1st dorsal fin. Olive-brown above, 6–10 dark saddles; white to dull orange below. Large dusky teardrop. Middle red band on 2d dorsal fin of male. Incomplete lateral line; 44–54 (usually 48–51) lateral scales. To 2¾ in. (7.1 cm).
Range: Mississippi R. basin lowlands from WI and MN to LA and e. TX (Red R. drainage); on Gulf Slope in Sabine-Neches drainage, LA and TX. Fairly common. **Habitat:** Sluggish riffles over rocks or debris in small to large rivers; lowland lakes.
Similar species: See Pl. 46. (1) Orangethroat, (2) Rainbow, (3) Gulf, and (4) Creole Darters *lack* large blotch at rear of 1st dorsal fin, usually are more brightly colored. Body of Orangethroat Darter is deepest at

nape or front of 1st dorsal fin; Rainbow Darter has *unscaled cheek*, red in anal fin of male; Gulf Darter usually has 38–45 lateral scales; Creole Darter has *partly scaled cheek*. **Map 357**

ORANGETHROAT DARTER *Etheostoma spectabile*   **Pl. 46**
Identification: Most variable darter. *Arched body, deepest at nape or front of 1st dorsal fin.* Dark bars (blue between orange on male, brown between yellow-white on female) on side. Olive to light brown above, usually 7–10 dark saddles; white to orange below. Often thin dark stripes on side (see Remarks). Thin black or dusky teardrop. Blue edge, red on dorsal and caudal fins (faint on female). Large male has blue anal fin; blue or black pelvic fin; orange branchiostegal membranes (and often orange breast and belly); 2 orange spots on caudal fin base. Interrupted infraorbital canal; uninterrupted supratemporal canal (Fig. 53); incomplete lateral line; 17–20 scales around caudal peduncle; 32–61 (usually 40–53) lateral scales; usually 11–12 pectoral rays. To 2¾ in. (7.2 cm).
Range: Lake Erie and Mississippi R. basins from se. MI and OH to e. WY, and south to TN and n. TX; Gulf drainages (Trinity R. to San Antonio R.) of TX — mostly on Edwards Plateau. Abundant. **Habitat:** Shallow gravel riffles, sometimes rocky runs and pools, of headwaters, creeks, and small rivers.
Remarks: Five named subspecies. *E. s. uniporum*, in Black R., MO and AR, has mostly blue 1st dorsal fin, thin slanted bars on side; *E. s. fragi* (shown), in Strawberry R., AR, has wider,·more vertical bars (turquoise on male) on side. *E. s. pulchellum*, western subspecies from Platte R., NE, to Guadalupe R., TX, has mostly orange 1st dorsal fin, dark vertical bars on side. *E. s. squamosum* (shown), in Arkansas R. drainage of sw. MO, sw. KS, ne. OK, and nw. AR, has mostly orange 1st dorsal fin, vertical bars darkest on lower side. *E. s. spectabile* (shown), over rest of range with several races, has mostly blue 1st dorsal fin, usually thin dark stripes on side.
Similar species: (1) Redband Darter (Pl. 46) has dark stripe along, and dark squares below, lateral line; 21–26 scales around narrow caudal peduncle. (2) Rainbow Darter (Pl. 46) is deepest under *middle* of 1st dorsal fin; has *red* on anal fin of male, uninterrupted infraorbital canal; usually has 13 pectoral rays. (3) Greenthroat Darter (Pl. 46) is deepest under *middle* of 1st dorsal fin, has an interrupted supratemporal canal (Fig. 53), green branchiostegal membranes and breast. (4) Mud, (5) Gulf, and (6) Creole Darters (all, Pl. 46) are deepest under *middle* of 1st dorsal fin, have uninterrupted infraorbital canal, usually 13–14 pectoral rays. **Map 363**

REDBAND DARTER *Etheostoma luteovinctum*   **Pl. 46**
Identification: *Body deepest at front of 1st dorsal fin*, strongly tapering to *narrow caudal peduncle*. Tan above, 7–9 dark saddles; *light brown stripe* along lateral line, 7–9 *dark squares* just below lateral line; white to yellow below. Black teardrop. Blue edge, red base on dorsal fins (faint on female). Breeding male has bright blue bars be-

tween red-orange on side, black pelvic fin, blue anal fin. Partly scaled cheek and breast; 21–26 scales around caudal peduncle; incomplete lateral line; 50–61 (usually 52–59) lateral scales. To 2¾ in. (6.8 cm). **Range:** Stones, Collins (Cumberland R. drainage), and Duck R. (Tennessee R. drainage) systems, cen. TN. Fairly common in Duck R.; rare elsewhere. **Habitat:** Shallow rocky pools of headwaters, creeks, and small rivers.

Similar species: (1) Orangethroat Darter (Pl. 46) *lacks* dark stripe along, and dark squares below, lateral line; has deeper caudal peduncle, 17–20 scales around caudal peduncle, usually 40–53 lateral scales. (2) Rainbow Darter (Pl. 46) is deepest under *middle* of 1st dorsal fin; has unscaled cheek and breast, red in anal fin of male, usually 41–50 lateral scales. **Map 353**

GULF DARTER *Etheostoma swaini* **Pl. 46**
Identification: *Dark bars* on side (blue-brown between orange on male, brown between yellow-white on female), often obscured by dark mottling on female. Light brown above, about 7 dark saddles; *thin dark lines* (rows of small black spots) on upper side, white to *orange* (large male) below. 3 black caudal spots; dusky to dark teardrop. Blue edge, red base, middle red and blue bands on dorsal fins (faint on female). Blue anal and pelvic fins, blue and red-orange caudal fin on large male. Incomplete lateral line; 35–50 (usually 38–45) lateral scales. Fully to partly scaled cheek; body deepest under middle of 1st dorsal fin; uninterrupted infraorbital and (usually) supratemporal canals (Fig. 53). To 3 in. (7.8 cm).
Range: Gulf drainages from Ochlockonee R., GA and FL, to Mississippi R., LA, and north on Former Mississippi Embayment (e. of Mississippi R. only) to KY; Bear Cr. (Tennessee R. drainage), nw. AL and ne. MS. Mostly below Fall Line. Common. **Habitat:** Shallow rocky riffles, current-swept vegetation in headwaters, creeks, and small to medium rivers.
Similar species: See Pl. 46. See (1) Creole and (2) Watercress Darters. (3) Mud Darter has large black blotch at rear of 1st dorsal fin, usually 46 or more lateral scales; *lacks* dark lines on upper side. (4) Orangethroat Darter has body deepest at front of 1st dorsal fin, interrupted infraorbital canal. **Map 356**

CREOLE DARTER *Etheostoma collettei* **Pl. 46**
Identification: Similar to Gulf Darter but has *44–60, usually 46–55, lateral scales;* breeding male is more blue, has breeding tubercles on lower body scales (absent on Gulf Darter). 11–16 transverse scales. To 3 in. (7.4 cm).
Range: Ouachita, Red, Calcasieu, and Sabine R. drainages, AR and LA. Abundant in Ouachita; less common elsewhere. **Habitat:** Gravel riffles, current-swept vegetation and debris in creeks and small to medium rivers.
Similar species: (1) See Gulf Darter (Pl. 46). (2) Redfin and (3) Orangebelly Darters (both, Pl. 45) *lack* blue and orange bars on side; have red on anal fin of male, 16–23 transverse scales. **Map 356**

WATERCRESS DARTER *Etheostoma nuchale* **Pl. 46**
Identification: Similar to Gulf Darter but is *smaller, more compressed*; has *12–24 pored lateral line scales* (Gulf Darter has 28–43), interrupted infraorbital and supratemporal canals (Fig. 53). 35–42 lateral scales. To 2¼ in. (5.4 cm).
Range: Springs on Halls and Village creeks (Black Warrior R. system), Jefferson Co., AL. Rare; protected as an *endangered species.* **Habitat:** Vegetated springs.
Similar species: See Gulf Darter (Pl. 46). **Map 355**

COLDWATER DARTER *Etheostoma ditrema* **Pl. 46**
Identification: *Dark brown mottling* on yellow back and side; *orange belly* on male. *3 black caudal spots.* Black teardrop. Blue edge and middle red band on 1st dorsal fin of male, sometimes on 1st dorsal fin of female and 2d dorsal fin of male. Incomplete lateral line; 41–54 (usually 43–50) lateral scales. To 2¼ in. (5.4 cm).
Range: Coosa R. system, GA, AL, and se. TN. Rare and highly localized. **Habitat:** Vegetated springs and spring runs.
Similar species: (1) Gulf and (2) Watercress Darters (both, Pl. 46) have dark *bars* and thin dark *lines* on side; large males have blue and orange bars on side. **Map 355**

GREENTHROAT DARTER *Etheostoma lepidum* **Pl. 46**
Identification: *Red-orange specks or spots* between *long green bars* on side of male; yellow between short brown-black bars on female. Body deepest under middle of 1st dorsal fin. Olive above, dark saddles; white to orange below. 3 black caudal spots; thin black teardrop. Blue-green edge on red 1st dorsal fin; red spots on green 2d dorsal and caudal fins (faint on female). Large male with green branchiostegal membranes and breast; green anal and pelvic fins, sometimes with red bands. Interrupted infraorbital and supratemporal canals (Fig. 53). Incomplete lateral line; 43–67 (usually 48–55) lateral scales. To 2½ in. (6.6 cm).
Range: Colorado, Guadalupe, and Nueces R. drainages, TX; Pecos R. system, NM. Common on Edwards Plateau in TX; uncommon in NM. **Habitat:** Gravel and rubble riffles, especially spring-fed and vegetated riffles, of headwaters, creeks, and small rivers.
Similar species: (1) Orangethroat Darter (Pl. 46) is deepest at nape or front of 1st dorsal fin; has orange branchiostegal membranes and breast, uninterrupted supratemporal canal. (2) Geographically close Rio Grande Darter (Pl. 45) is deeper bodied; has many small red (on male) or black (female) spots on side of body, red edge on 1st dorsal fin. **Map 361**

CHRISTMAS DARTER *Etheostoma hopkinsi* **Pl. 46**
Identification: 10–12 *dark green bars* on side, separated by *brick red* on large male, yellow on female. Thin green edge, middle red band on 1st dorsal fin. Yellow to green above, 8 dark green saddles; yellow to green below. 3 black caudal spots. Black teardrop. Incomplete lateral line; 39–52 (usually 40–49) lateral scales. To 2½ in. (6.6 cm).

Range: Savannah, Ogeechee, and Altamaha R. drainages, SC and GA. Fairly common. **Habitat:** Rocky riffles of creeks and small to medium rivers.

Remarks: Two subspecies. *E. h. binotatum*, Savannah R. drainage, has an unscaled opercle, 2 dark squares on nape. *E. h. hopkinsi*, Ogeechee and Altamaha R. drainages, has fully scaled opercle, no or faint squares on nape.

Similar species: (1) Savannah Darter (Pl. 45) has broad dark brown stripe along side, red edge on 1st dorsal fin. (2) Gulf Darter (Pl. 46) is deeper bodied, has blue (on male) or brown (female) bars on side, orange belly on male, thin dark lines on upper side. **Map 355**

DIRTY DARTER *Etheostoma olivaceum* **Pl. 47**

Identification: *Dark brown to black bands* on 2d dorsal and caudal fins. *Thin black stripes*, black mottling, sometimes black bars, on side. Olive to gray above, white to light brown below. *Long sharp snout*, unscaled opercle, scaled nape, no teardrop. Breeding male is black with small white knobs on tips of dorsal spines; 2d dorsal fin has black margin; usually 12 rays; 3 branches per ray, 2d and 3rd branches equal in length; 3–4 white bars per ray (Fig. 61). Incomplete lateral line; 44–58 lateral scales. To 3¼ in. (8 cm).

Dirty

Blackfin

Crown

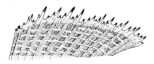
Fringed

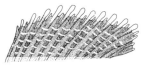
Spottail

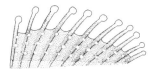
Lollypop

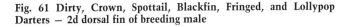

Fig. 61 Dirty, Crown, Spottail, Blackfin, Fringed, and Lollypop Darters — 2d dorsal fin of breeding male

Range: Lower Caney Fork system and nearby tributaries of Cumberland R., cen. TN. Common. **Habitat:** Rocky pools and nearby riffles of headwaters and creeks. Often in very shallow water — less than 1½ in. (4 cm).

Remarks: Dirty Darter and relatives (next 13 species — through Striated Darter) are one of two groups of darters (the other is the Johnny Darter and relatives) in which the eggs are laid in a single-layer cluster on the underside of a stone and guarded by a male. Females of both groups have a wide flat genital papilla; papillae of other darters usually are tubular.

Similar species: (1) Spottail, (2) Fringed (Pl. 47), (3) Blackfin, (4) Crown, and (5) Lollypop Darters (Pl. 47) have scaled opercle, teardrop, *no stripes* on side, *shorter snout.* **Map 364**

Next 5 species are closely related and easily distinguishable only as breeding males (Fig. 61). All have *bold dark brown bands* (alternating black and white bands on breeding male) on 2d dorsal and caudal fins, *3 vertically aligned black spots* on caudal fin base. Brown above, *dark brown mottling* on back and side; black teardrop. Scaled cheek and opercle; incomplete lateral line. Breeding male has black head, body, and fins (except pectoral) and during spawning develops wide black and white bars on side.

SPOTTAIL DARTER *Etheostoma squamiceps* **Not shown**
Identification: 2d dorsal fin of breeding male has *small white knobs* (3 branches per ray, 2d and 3d branches equal in length, adnate and tipped with small white knob — Fig. 61); usually 13 rays; 6–7 white bars per ray. Usually 9 dorsal spines. Interrupted infraorbital canal. To 3½ in. (8.8 cm).

Range: Lower Ohio R. basin (Green R. drainage, KY and TN, to Cache R. system, IL), including extreme lower Wabash R. drainage, IN and IL, and Red R. system (Cumberland R. drainage), KY and TN. Common; locally abundant. **Habitat:** Rocky pools and adjacent riffles of headwaters, creeks, and small rivers.

Similar species: (1) Fringed (Pl. 47), (2) Blackfin, (3) Crown, and (4) Dirty Darters (Pl. 47) *lack* knobs on 2d dorsal fin rays; (5) Lollypop Darter (Pl. 47) has *large yellow knobs,* 2 branches per dorsal ray. **Map 365**

FRINGED DARTER *Etheostoma crossopterum* **Pl. 47**
Identification: 2d dorsal fin of breeding male has *white edge* (small black tips on rays may be visible); 3 branches per ray, *3d branch much longer than 2d* (Fig. 61); 6–7 white bars per ray; usually 12–13 rays. 1st dorsal fin of large male has dull orange band. Usually 9 dorsal spines. Interrupted infraorbital canal. To 4 in. (10 cm).

Range: Lower Cumberland R. drainage (below Caney Fork), KY and TN; middle Duck R. system, TN, and Shoal Cr. system (Tennessee R. drainage), TN and AL; Reelfoot Lake tributaries, TN. Common; locally abundant. **Habitat:** Rocky pools and adjacent riffles of headwaters, creeks, and small rivers.

Similar species: (1) Spottail, (2) Blackfin, (3) Crown, (4) Lollypop (Pl. 47) and (5) Dirty Darters (Pl. 47) have 3d branch of each dorsal ray of breeding male *equal* to 2d ray.   **Map 366**

BLACKFIN DARTER *Etheostoma nigripinne*   **Not shown**
Identification: 2d dorsal fin of breeding male has *black margin* (Fig. 61); 3 branches per ray, 2d and 3d branches equal in length; 3–4 white bars per ray; usually 13 rays. 1st dorsal fin of large male has thin bright orange band. Usually 8 dorsal spines. Interrupted infraorbital canal. To 3½ in. (8.8 cm).
Range: Tennessee R. drainage from Paint Rock R. downstream to Duck R. system (in upper and lower Duck R. system), TN, AL, and MS; absent in Cypress and most of Shoal Cr. systems. Common; locally abundant. **Habitat:** Rocky pools and adjacent riffles of headwaters, creeks, and small rivers.
Similar species: (1) Spottail Darter has small white knobs on 2d dorsal fin of breeding male. (2) Fringed Darter (Pl. 47) has *white margin* (small black tips on rays may be visible) on 2d dorsal fin of breeding male, 3d branch much longer than 2d. (3) Crown Darter has bright yellow margin on 2d dorsal fin of breeding male. (4) Lollypop Darter (Pl. 47) has large knobs on 2d dorsal fin of breeding male. (5) Dirty Darter (Pl. 47) has unscaled opercle, uninterrupted infraorbital canal; usually 9 dorsal spines, 12 dorsal rays.   **Map 365**

CROWN DARTER *Etheostoma* species   **Not shown**
Identification: 2d dorsal fin of breeding male has *bright yellow margin*; 3 branches per ray, 2d and 3d branches equal in length; 6–7 white bars per ray (Fig. 61); usually 14 rays. Usually 9 dorsal spines. Interrupted infraorbital canal. To 3½ in. (9.2 cm).
Range: Cypress Cr. (Tennessee R. drainage), sw. TN and nw. AL. Common; locally abundant. **Habitat:** Rocky pools and adjacent riffles of headwaters, creeks, and small rivers.
Similar species: (1) Spottail, (2) Fringed (Pl. 47), (3) Blackfin, and (4) Dirty Darters (Pl. 47) *lack* yellow margin on 2d dorsal fin of breeding male. (5) Lollypop Darter (Pl. 47) has large knobs on 2d dorsal fin of breeding male.   **Map 365**

LOLLYPOP DARTER *Etheostoma neopterum*   **Pl. 47**
Identification: 2d dorsal fin of breeding male has *large yellow knobs* (Fig. 61); 2 branches per ray, equal in length; 3–4 white bars per ray; usually 11 rays. Usually 9 dorsal spines. Uninterrupted or interrupted infraorbital canal. 41–58 lateral scales. To 3½ in. (8.9 cm).
Range: Tennessee R. drainage: tributaries of Tennessee R. in w. KY and w. TN upstream to near Duck R.; lower Duck R. system, TN; Shoal Cr., sw. TN and nw. AL. Bayou du Chien (Mississippi R. tributary), w. KY. Common. **Habitat:** Rocky and sandy pools of headwaters and creeks.
Similar species: (1) Spottail, (2) Fringed (Pl. 47), (3) Blackfin, (4) Crown, and (5) Dirty Darters (Pl. 47) *lack* large yellow knobs on 2d dorsal fin of breeding male; have usually 12 or more dorsal rays.   **Map 364**

STRIPETAIL DARTER *Etheostoma kennicotti*   **Pl. 47**
Identification: *Black bands* on 2d dorsal, caudal, and often pectoral fins. *Gold knobs* on tips of dorsal spines of adult. Tan to yellow above, 6–7 brown saddles; dark brown blotches on upper side, *larger dark blotches* along side. Teardrop thin or absent; moderate snout; unscaled nape. Widely interrupted infraorbital canal (Fig. 53), 4 front pores, 1 rear pore. Incomplete lateral line; 38–53 lateral scales. Usually 7 dorsal spines, 11–12 dorsal rays, 7 anal rays. To 3¼ in. (8.3 cm).
Range: Tributaries of Ohio R. in s. IL and w. KY; Green R. drainage, KY; upper Cumberland R. drainage — Big South Fork and above, KY and TN; Tennessee R. drainage, KY, TN, GA, AL, and MS. Fairly common but localized. **Habitat:** Rocky pools of headwaters, creeks, and small rivers.
Similar species: See Pl. 47. (1) Fantail Darter has broadly joined branchiostegal membranes, protruding lower jaw, pointed snout, usually stripes or rows of black spots on side, 2 rear infraorbital canal pores. (2) Spottail and related darters have scaled nape, *no* gold knobs on dorsal spines, narrowly interrupted infraorbital canal. Small (3) Teardrop, (4) Slabrock, and (5) Striated Darters resemble small Stripetail Darters but usually have 8–9 dorsal spines, 13–14 dorsal rays, 9 anal rays.   **Map 367**

FANTAIL DARTER *Etheostoma flabellare*   **Pl. 47**
Identification: *Black bands* on 2d dorsal and caudal fins. *Gold knobs* on tips of dorsal spines of adult — large on male, small on female. *Broadly joined branchiostegal membranes* (Fig. 54); *protruding lower jaw* (over most of range; see Remarks); pointed snout, unscaled nape. Teardrop thin or absent. Infraorbital canal widely interrupted (Fig. 53), 4 front pores, 2 rear pores. Color pattern highly variable (Pl. 47): brown to olive above, yellow to white below. Western populations have thin black stripes on side. Eastern populations have black bars, mottling, or rows of black spots on side. Breeding male is bright yellow (in parts of KY and TN) to olive brown with black head and fins. Incomplete lateral line; 38–60 (usually 45–55) lateral scales. To 3¼ in. (8.4 cm).
Range: Atlantic, Great Lakes, and Mississippi R. basins from s. QU to MN, and south to SC (Santee R. system), n. AL, and ne. OK. Abundant. **Habitat:** Rocky riffles of creeks and small to medium rivers.
Remarks: Four subspecies. *E. f. brevispina* (shown), in the Catawba, Broad, and Peedee R. drainages, NC and SC, has a terminal mouth, large eye, black anal and pelvic fins on breeding male, usually 7 dark bars along side, 7 dorsal spines, and 12 pectoral rays. *E. f. humerale*, in Atlantic drainages from the lower Susquehanna R. to the Cape Fear R., has a terminal mouth, small eye, black anal and pelvic fins on breeding male, usually 10 dark bars along side, 7 dorsal spines, and 12 pectoral rays. *E. f.* subspecies in the upper Tennessee R. drainage (upstream of the Little Tennessee R.), New R., and headwaters of Shavers Fork Cheat R. (Monongahela R. system) has a terminal mouth, black anal and pelvic fins on breeding male, and usually 8–10 dark bars along side, 8 dorsal spines, and 13 pectoral rays. *E. f.*

flabellare (shown), throughout rest of range, has a protruding lower jaw, upturned mouth, and dusky white anal and pelvic fins on breeding male.
Similar species: See Pl. 47. See (1) Duskytail Darter. (2) Stripetail Darter has *narrowly* joined branchiostegal membranes, *less* protruding lower jaw; series of black blotches along side, no stripes or rows of small black spots, 1 rear infraorbital canal pore. **Map 368**

DUSKYTAIL DARTER *Etheostoma* species   **Pl. 47**
Identification: Similar to Fantail Darter but has *less broadly* joined branchiostegal membranes; 10–15 long bars on side; 38–48 (usually 40–45) lateral scales, 17–20 (usually 18–19) dorsal spines and rays (19–23 in Fantail Darter). To 2½ in. (6.4 cm).
Range: Big South Fork Cumberland R., TN, and upper Tennessee R. drainage, VA and TN. Rare; extremely localized. **Habitat:** Gravel and rubble pools and riffles of small to medium rivers.
Similar species: See Fantail Darter (Pl. 47). **Map 366**

Next 5 species: distinctive *iridescent bar* on cheek (Pl. 47). Yellow-brown above, 6–8 dark brown saddles; white to yellow below. *Brown bands* on fins; red edge, black spot near front of 1st dorsal fin. Breeding male has red dorsal, caudal, and anal fins; black pectoral and pelvic fins; blue-black edge on anal and caudal fins. Incomplete lateral line.

STRIPED DARTER *Etheostoma virgatum*   **Pl. 47**
Identification: *Dark brown stripes* on side. *Narrow iridescent bar* on cheek. Small dark blotches along side; regions in front of and behind teardrop dusky. Widely interrupted infraorbital canal (Fig. 53), 4 front pores, 2 rear pores. 38–58 lateral scales. To 3 in. (7.8 cm).
Range: Lower Cumberland R. drainage (Stones R. to Red R.), KY and TN; upper Caney Fork system, cen. TN; Rockcastle R. and nearby streams, e. KY. Common. **Habitat:** Rocky pools of headwaters, creeks, and small to medium rivers.
Similar species: See Pl. 47: (1) Barcheek, (2) Teardrop, (3) Slabrock, and (4) Striated Darters *lack dark stripes* on side; Teardrop, Slabrock, and Striated Darters have 3 front, 1 rear infraorbital canal pores.
Map 369

BARCHEEK DARTER *Etheostoma obeyense*   **Pl. 47**
Identification: *Narrow iridescent bar* on cheek, areas in front of and behind teardrop *dusky*. Dark brown blotches, sometimes bars, *no stripes or rows of dark spots* on side. Widely interrupted infraorbital canal (Fig. 53). 4 front pores, 2 rear pores. Incomplete lateral line (10–26 pores); 39–56 lateral scales. To 3¼ in. (8.4 cm).
Range: Middle Cumberland R. drainage from Big South Fork to Obey R., KY and TN. Fairly common. **Habitat:** Rocky pools of headwaters, creeks, and small rivers.
Similar species: See Pl. 47. (1) See Slabrock Darter. (2) Striped Darter has *dark stripes* on side. (3) Teardrop and (4) Striated Darters have 3

front and 1 rear infraorbital canal pores, rows of *small dark spots* on side; are smaller — to 2¼ in. (5.5 cm). **Map 370**

SLABROCK DARTER *Etheostoma smithi* **Pl. 47**
Identification: Similar to Barcheek Darter but is *smaller; has more darkly outlined scales, 3 front and 1 rear* infraorbital canal pores, fewer than 14 lateral-line pores. 41–54 lateral scales. To 2½ in. (6.2 cm).
Range: Lower Cumberland (below Caney Fork) and lower Tennessee R. (lower Duck R. and downstream) drainages, KY and TN. Fairly common. **Habitat:** Rocky pools of headwaters, creeks, and small rivers; rocky margins of medium-sized rivers, impoundments.
Similar species: See Barcheek Darter (Pl. 47). **Map 370**

TEARDROP DARTER *Etheostoma barbouri* **Pl. 47**
Identification: *Wide iridescent bar on cheek* (covers most of cheek). *White areas* in front of and behind *black teardrop.* Rows of *small dark brown spots* and blotches on side. Widely interrupted infraorbital canal (Fig. 53), 3 front pores, 1 rear pore. Usually 9 dorsal spines. Incomplete lateral line; 40–49 lateral scales. To 2¼ in. (6 cm).
Range: Middle and upper Green R. drainage, KY and TN. Fairly common. **Habitat:** Rocky pools of headwaters, creeks, and small rivers.
Similar species: See Pl. 47. (1) See Striated Darter. (2) Slabrock and (3) Barcheek Darters have a *narrow* iridescent bar on cheek, *dusky* areas in front of and behind teardrop, *no* rows of dark spots on side; Barcheek Darter has 4 front and 2 rear infraorbital canal pores. (4) Striped Darter has *dark stripes* on side; 4 front, 2 rear infraorbital canal pores. **Map 364**

STRIATED DARTER *Etheostoma striatulum* **Pl. 47**
Identification: Similar to Teardrop Darter but has *narrow* bar on cheek, *dusky* areas in front of and behind teardrop, darker rows of spots on side. Usually 8 dorsal spines. 38–50 lateral scales. To 2¼ in. (5.6 cm).
Range: Duck R. system, cen. TN. Rare. **Habitat:** Rocky pools of headwaters and creeks.
Similar species: See Teardrop Darter (Pl. 47). **Map 369**

Next 11 species: incomplete lateral line, strongly arched (if present) near front (see Pl. 48.) (Often only slightly arched in Iowa Darter.)

Next 3 species: small (to 2 in. [5 cm]); very *short* lateral line — fewer than 10 pores; large *lateral flap* (see Pl. 48) on pelvic fin of large male.

LEAST DARTER *Etheostoma microperca* **Pl. 48**
Identification: *Deep, compressed body. Extremely short (0–3 pores) lateral line.* Olive above, dark green saddles; green blotches along side, rows of dark green spots on upper and lower side; white to yellow below. *Large teardrop.* Black edge and base, middle red band on 1st dorsal fin of male. *Orange or red anal and pelvic fins* on breeding

male. Unscaled breast. Usually 2 anal spines; 2–3 infraorbital canal pores (Fig. 53); 30–36 lateral scales. To 1¾ in. (4.4 cm).

Range: Great Lakes and Mississippi R. basins from e. ON and MN south to s. OH, cen. IN, and cen. IL; (1 verified record in n. KY near Louisville); Ozark-Ouachita drainages of s. MO, se. KS, nw. AR, and e. OK. Common; sometimes abundant in spring-fed streams. **Habitat:** Quiet, vegetated lakes, headwaters, creeks, and small rivers. Usually over mud and sand.

Similar species: See Pl. 48. (1) Cypress, (2) Fountain, and (3) Iowa Darters are more *slender,* lack dark green on body, orange anal and pelvic fins on male; Cypress and Fountain Darters have 4 infraorbital canal pores, Iowa Darter has 8.   **Map 371**

CYPRESS DARTER *Etheostoma proeliare*   Pl. 48
Identification: *Short (0–9 pores) lateral line.* Olive above, 6–9 dark brown saddles; *black or brown dashes* along side, spots on upper and lower sides. Thin teardrop. Black edge and base, spot at front, middle red band on 1st dorsal fin of male. Black anal and pelvic fins on breeding male. Unscaled breast. 2 anal spines; 4 infraorbital canal pores (Fig. 53); 34–38 lateral scales. To 2 in. (4.8 cm).

Range: Mississippi R. basin from s. IL and e. OK to Gulf; Gulf Slope drainages from Choctawhatchee R., FL, to San Jacinto R., TX. Primarily on Coastal Plain. Common. **Habitat:** Standing or slow-flowing water, usually in vegetation over mud.

Similar species: See Pl. 48. (1) See Fountain Darter. (2) Least Darter has 2–3 infraorbital canal pores, orange anal and pelvic fins on male, large teardrop; is dark green, deeper bodied. (3) Slough Darter has green bars or squares on side, longer lateral line (13–27 pores), 8 infraorbital canal pores.   **Map 372**

FOUNTAIN DARTER *Etheostoma fonticola*   Pl. 48
Identification: Similar to Cypress Darter but has *dark brown cross-hatching* on upper and lower side, *1 anal spine.* 31–37 lateral scales. *Smallest* darter − to 1¾ in. (4.3 cm).

Range: San Marcos and Comal springs and their effluent rivers (Guadalupe R. system), s.-cen. TX. Common in San Marcos Spring; extirpated but reintroduced in Comal Spring and may be repopulating. **Habitat:** Vegetated springs, pools, and runs of effluent rivers.

Remarks: Common in San Marcos Spring, but protected, because of its restricted distribution, as an *endangered species.*

Similar species: See Cypress Darter (Pl. 48).   **Map 372**

SAWCHEEK DARTER *Etheostoma serrifer*   Pl. 48
Identification: *Red* around *2 black caudal spots.* Incomplete *yellow lateral line,* usually 28–38 pores. Tan above; dark brown mottling, often bars on side; green to white, often with black specks below. Teardrop absent or faint. Clear to dusky fins. 6 infraorbital canal pores (Fig. 53); 44–66 lateral scales. Serrated preopercle. To 2¾ in. (6.8 cm).

Range: Atlantic Coastal Plain from Dismal Swamp, s. VA, to Altamaha R. drainage, GA. Common in n. half of range, uncommon in s. half. **Habitat:** Swamps; lakes; sluggish headwaters, creeks, and small rivers; usually near vegetation.
Similar species: See Pl. 48. (1) Swamp, (2) Carolina, and (3) Saluda Darters *lack* 2 black spots at middle of caudal fin base, usually have fewer than 28 lateral-line pores.   **Map 348**

SWAMP DARTER *Etheostoma fusiforme*   **Pl. 48**
Identification: *Slender, compressed body.* Green to tan above, small dark saddles; dark green and brown mottling, 10–12 squares on side; white to yellow, *many black and brown specks* below. Thin teardrop; 3 dusky black caudal spots. Scaled breast. Widely interrupted infraorbital canal, 4–5 pores (Fig. 53). Incomplete lateral line, usually 28 or fewer pores; 40-63 (usually 46–56) lateral scales. To 2¼ in. (5.9 cm).
Range: Seaboard Lowlands, Atlantic and Gulf coastal plains from s. ME to LA (Sabine R.) and se. OK (Red R.); Former Mississippi Embayment north to KY and se. MO. Introduced into French Broad system in NC. Common to abundant in coastal streams; uncommon on Embayment. **Habitat:** Standing or slow-flowing water over mud, sometimes sand; often in vegetation.
Remarks: Two subspecies. *E. f. fusiforme* (ME to Waccamaw R., NC) has 2 rear infraorbital canal pores (Fig. 53), 0–4 interorbital scales. *E. f. barratti* (rest of range) usually has 1 rear infraorbital canal pore, 5 or more interorbital scales.
Similar species: See Pl. 48. (1) Slough and (2) Backwater Darters have bright green bars on side, red band on 1st dorsal fin, unscaled breast. (3) Carolina and (4) Saluda Darters have many small dark brown spots on side, black spot at front of 1st dorsal fin of male, usually 47 or fewer lateral scales.   **Map 343**

SLOUGH DARTER *Etheostoma gracile*   **Pl. 48**
Identification: Yellow above, green saddles and wavy lines on back; bright *green bars* on side of male, green squares or mottling on female; yellow to white below. Blue-gray edge and base, *middle red band* on 1st dorsal fin (faint on female). Thin teardrop. Unscaled breast. Uninterrupted infraorbital canal (Fig. 53) — usually 8 pores. Incomplete lateral line (13–27 pores); 40–55 lateral scales. To 2¼ in. (6 cm).
Range: Mississippi R. basin from cen. IL and ne. MO to LA; extends up Arkansas and Red. R. drainages to se. KS and e. OK. Gulf Slope drainages from Tombigbee R. (1 record), MS, to Nueces R., TX. Abundant, especially on Coastal Plain. **Habitat:** Standing or slow-flowing water over mud; often in vegetation.
Similar species: See Pl. 48. (1) See Backwater Darter. (2) Swamp Darter *lacks* bright green bars on side, red band on 1st dorsal fin; has scaled breast, 4–5 infraorbital canal pores. (3) Cypress Darter has brown or black dashes, no green, on side; 0–9 lateral-line pores; 4 infraorbital canal pores.   **Map 373**

BACKWATER DARTER *Etheostoma zonifer*   **Pl. 48**
Identification: Nearly identical to Slough Darter but has *interrupted* infraorbital canal (Fig. 53), usually *6 pores*. 41–53 lateral scales. To 1¾ in. (4.4 cm).
Range: Coastal Plain streams in Mobile Bay drainage, AL and MS. Localized and uncommon. **Habitat:** Mud-bottomed, often vegetated, pools of sluggish creeks and small rivers.
Similar species: See Slough Darter (Pl. 48).   **Map 373**

CAROLINA DARTER *Etheostoma collis*   **Pl. 48**
Identification: Light brown above; *many small dark brown spots* on side; *brown dashes or blotches* along side; white to yellow below. Black teardrop; black spot at front of 1st dorsal fin of male; 3 black caudal spots (top, middle, bottom). Incomplete lateral line, 5–30 pores; 35–49 lateral scales; 1 *anal spine*; usually no interorbital pores; 4–5 infraorbital canal pores (Fig. 53). To 2¼ in. (6 cm).
Range: Atlantic Piedmont from Roanoke R. drainage, VA, to Santee R. drainage, SC. Uncommon. **Habitat:** Muddy and rocky pools and backwaters of sluggish headwaters and creeks.
Remarks: Two subspecies. *E. c. lepidinion,* Roanoke and Neuse R. drainages, has partly scaled breast, fully scaled nape. *E. c. collis,* Peedee and Santee R. drainages, has unscaled breast, unscaled or partly scaled nape.
Similar species: See Pl. 48. (1) See Saluda Darter. (2) Sawcheek Darter has 2 black spots at middle of caudal fin base, 2 anal spines. (3) Swamp Darter is more slender; *lacks* small brown spots on side; has 2 anal spines.   **Map 371**

SALUDA DARTER *Etheostoma saludae*   **Pl. 48**
Identification: Nearly identical to Carolina Darter but has *interorbital pores* (Fig. 53), usually *2 anal spines.* 36–50 lateral scales. To 2 in. (5.3 cm).
Range: On Piedmont in Saluda and Broad R. systems (Santee R. drainage), SC. Uncommon. **Habitat:** Mud-, sand-, and rock-bottomed pools of sluggish headwaters and creeks.
Similar species: See Carolina Darter (Pl. 48).   **Map 371**

IOWA DARTER *Etheostoma exile*   **Pl. 48**
Identification: *Slender body; long, narrow caudal peduncle.* Tan above; dark brown mottling, often short bars on side. Black teardrop. Blue edge and base, middle red band on 1st dorsal fin (faint on female). Breeding male has orange belly, alternating *blue and brick-red bars* on side. 8 infraorbital canal pores (Fig. 53). Incomplete lateral line, 19–34 pores; often arched near front. 45–69 lateral scales. To 2¾ in. (7.2 cm).
Range: St. Lawrence–Great Lakes, Hudson Bay, and Mississippi R. basins from s. QU to n. AB, and south to OH, IL, and CO. Occurs farthest north and west of any darter. Common. **Habitat:** Vegetated lakes, pools of headwaters, creeks, and small to medium rivers.
Similar species: Least Darter (Pl. 48) is green, *deeper bodied;* has 0–3

lateral-line pores, 30–36 lateral scales, 2–3 infraorbital canal pores, pelvic-fin flaps on male. **Map 374**

BROWN DARTER *Etheostoma edwini* **Pl. 48**
Identification: *Bright red spots* on *deep, compressed body* and dorsal, caudal, and anal fins of male (sometimes of female). *Incomplete yellow lateral line.* Tan above, brown mottling on side, white to yellow below. Thin teardrop; often black spots on lower half of head. 34–42 lateral scales. To 2 in. (5.3 cm).
Range: St. Johns R. drainage, FL, to Perdido R. drainage, AL. Common in w. half of range, uncommon and localized in e. half. **Habitat:** Sandy runs, especially near vegetation, of creeks and small rivers.
Similar species: (1) Swamp Darter (Pl. 48) is much *more slender, lacks* red spots. (2) Okaloosa Darter (Pl. 40) has complete, *unarched* lateral line; rows of brown spots on side; *no* red spots. **Map 354**

■ DRUMS Family Sciaenidae (3)

Widely distributed family of about 210 species. Most drums occupy continental shelves of tropical and temperate oceans. One species is restricted to the fresh waters of North America, and two marine species are established in the Salton Sea, s. CA. The name drum (or croaker) refers to the fishes' ability to produce sounds using the gas bladder as a resonating chamber.

Drums have 2 dorsal fins, the *1st relatively short* and with spines, the *2d longer* and with rays; 1–2 anal spines; a lateral line that *extends to the end of the caudal fin;* thoracic pelvic fins; ctenoid scales; and the lateralis system on the head consisting of large cavernous canals and pores. In most species the body is deep and highly arched at the origin of the 1st dorsal fin.

FRESHWATER DRUM *Aplodinotus grunniens* **Pl. 32**
Identification: *Strongly arched body;* subterminal mouth. Silver above and on side; dusky fins (except white pelvic fin). *Pointed caudal fin.* Outer *pelvic ray a long filament.* 2d dorsal fin about twice as long as 1st dorsal fin; usually 10 spines, 29–32 rays. To 35 in. (89 cm).
Range: Greatest latitudinal range of any North American freshwater fish. East of Rocky Mountains in St. Lawrence–Great Lakes, Hudson Bay, and Mississippi R. basins from QU to n. MB and s. SA, and south to Gulf; Gulf Coast drainages from Mobile Bay, GA and AL, through e. Mexico to Rio Usumacinta system, Guatemala. Common. **Habitat:** Bottom of medium to large rivers and lakes.
Remarks: The Freshwater Drum is unique among freshwater North American fishes in producing an egg and larva that float at the water's surface. Sound production intensifies during spawning and presumably serves to aggregate ripe males and females in a spawning area. **Map 375**

BAIRDIELLA *Bairdiella icistia*   **Not shown**
Identification: *Large, terminal mouth*; rounded caudal fin. Gray above, silver below. Usually 24–28 dorsal rays, 7–8 anal rays. To 12 in. (30 cm).
Range: Pacific Coast of Mexico south from Almejas Bay, east of Isla Santa Margarita, Baja California. Established in Salton Sea, s. CA. Abundant. **Habitat:** 1 of 3 dominant fishes in the Salton Sea, a warm, relatively shallow, and highly saline lake.
Remarks: Introduced into Salton Sea as a game fish and as forage for the Orangemouth Corvina.

ORANGEMOUTH CORVINA *Cynoscion xanthulus*   **Not shown**
Identification: *Troutlike body. Lower jaw projects beyond* upper jaw; large mouth; large teeth. Blue-gray above; bright *yellow-orange* inside mouth, *yellow caudal fin*, rear edge of caudal fin somewhat pointed at middle. To 36 in. (90 cm).
Range: Pacific Coast from Gulf of California to Acapulco, Mexico. Established in Salton Sea, s. CA. Abundant. **Habitat:** 1 of 3 dominant fishes in the Salton Sea.
Remarks: Introduced as a game fish by the California Department of Fish and Game.

■ CICHLIDS: Family Cichlidae (19)

Cichlids, popular aquarium fishes, are native to Central and South America (1 species extends north into Texas), West Indies, Africa, Madagascar, Syria, and coastal India. Most species are freshwater; a few live in brackish water. About 680 species are recognized; 1 is native to our region, and 18 have been introduced into the U.S. from either the American tropics or Africa.

Some introductions into the U.S. have been (and continue to be) deliberate; others are presumed to have been accidental. Deliberate introductions, especially of the African cichlids, have been mainly for the purposes of aquatic vegetation control and aquaculture. Most accidental introductions were from fish farms or releases of aquarium pets.

Cichlids are easily distinguished by having only *1 nostril* on each side, a *2-part lateral line* with the front portion higher on the body than the rear portion, and exceedingly protractile premaxillaries. Most species do not exceed 12 in. (30 cm).

OSCAR *Astronotus ocellatus*   **Fig. 62**
Identification: White edge on *large, rounded* (fanlike) *2d dorsal, caudal, and anal fins.* Red around *large black spot* on upper caudal fin base; sometimes a similar spot at rear of 2d dorsal fin. Many small scales on 2d dorsal and anal fins. Olive blue-green body and fins; large black blotches on body and fins. Aquarium varieties are iridescent orange or red on gray or black body. Young has wavy white and

CICHLIDS

1 nostril on each side; 2-part lateral line, front part higher on body than rear part.

OSCAR *Astronotus ocellatus* **p. 327**
Large rounded 2d dorsal, caudal, and anal fins. Large black spot on upper caudal fin base. To 15¾ in. (40 cm).

PEACOCK CICHLID *Cichla ocellaris* **p. 330**
Elongate body. Large mouth; projecting lower jaw. Silver halo around large black spot on caudal fin. To 16 in. (41 cm).

REDSTRIPED EARTHEATER *Geophagus surinamensis* **p. 330**
Long snout; eye high on head. Black blotch on side. 3 anal spines. To 12 in. (30 cm).

JEWELFISH *Hemichromis bimaculatus* **p. 330**
Fairly long, slender body. Rounded caudal fin. Large black blotch on side. Large individual is bright red. To 8 in. (20 cm).

Next 7 species (Cichlasoma) have more than 3 anal spines, usually a black blotch on caudal fin base.

RIO GRANDE CICHLID *Cichlasoma cyanoguttatum* **M376, p. 330**
4–6 dark blotches along rear half of side. Many small white to blue spots on side. Breeding individual is white on front, black on rear half of body. To 12 in. (30 cm).

JACK DEMPSEY *Cichlasoma octofasciatum* **p. 331**
2 gray to black lines between eyes. Adult is deep blue, has many iridescent spots on head and body. To 10 in. (25 cm).

CONVICT CICHLID *Cichlasoma nigrofasciatum* **p. 331**
Usually 7 bars on side extend onto dorsal and anal fins. 1st bar Y-shaped. To 4¾ in. (12 cm).

MIDAS CICHLID *Cichlasoma citrinellum* **p. 332**
Color highly variable. Usually 6 dusky to black bars or large black blotch on side and smaller black spot on caudal fin base. Nuchal hump on breeding male (shown). To 9½ in. (24 cm).

BLACK ACARA *Cichlasoma bimaculatum* **p. 332**
Dark blotches along side extend as dark stripe onto opercle. Adult is dark green and yellow, has blue-gray fins. To 4¾ in. (12 cm).

FIREMOUTH *Cichlasoma meeki* **p. 333**
Large black blotch on lower half of gill cover. Bright red or orange underside of head (on adult). To 6¾ in. (17 cm).

BANDED CICHLID *Cichlasoma severum* **p. 333**
Deep, compressed body. Usually 5–7 dusky to black bars on side. Bar on caudal peduncle extends onto dorsal and anal fins. To 8 in. (20 cm).

Next 3 species have black spot on opercle. 3 anal spines.

MOZAMBIQUE TILAPIA *Oreochromis mossambicus* **p. 334**
Large oblique mouth reaches under front of eye or beyond. Large male has white underside of head, red edge on black fins. To 15¼ in. (39 cm).

BLACKCHIN TILAPIA *Sarotherodon melanotheron* **p. 334**
Small mouth. Orange or yellow back; pale blue below. Large male has black underside of head. To 10¼ in. (26 cm).

SPOTTED TILAPIA *Tilapia mariae* **p. 335**
6–9 black blotches or bars on side that continue onto dorsal fin. To 12 in. (31 cm).

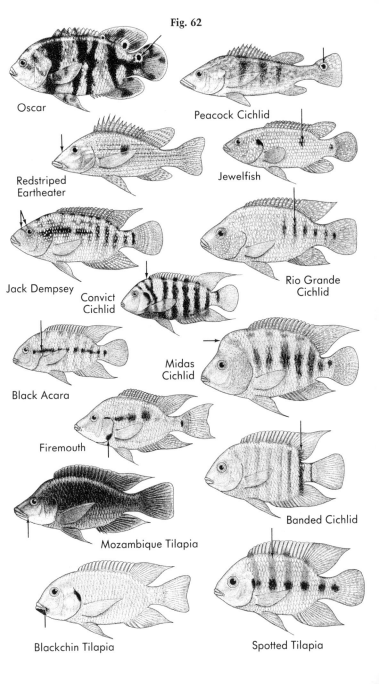

Fig. 62

Oscar

Peacock Cichlid

Redstriped Eartheater

Jewelfish

Jack Dempsey

Convict Cichlid

Rio Grande Cichlid

Black Acara

Midas Cichlid

Firemouth

Mozambique Tilapia

Banded Cichlid

Blackchin Tilapia

Spotted Tilapia

orange bars and spots on black head, body, and fins. 3 anal spines. To 15¾ in. (40 cm).
Range: Native to Orinoco, Amazon, and La Plata R. basins, South America. Established in Broward, Collier, Dade, Glades, Hendry, and Palm Beach cos., FL. Common. **Habitat:** Mud- and sand-bottomed canals and ponds.

PEACOCK CICHLID *Cichla ocellaris*   **Fig. 62**
Identification: Elongate body; *deeply notched dorsal fin. Scales on 2d dorsal and anal fins. Large mouth,* projecting lower jaw. Silver halo around *large black spot* on caudal fin. Olive green above; dark spots between *3 black bars* on side; yellow-white below; white spots on dark gray 2d dorsal fin, upper lobe of caudal fin; other fins gray or black. Large adult has yellow-orange stripe from mouth to caudal fin base; red on anal and pelvic fins, lower half of caudal fin; red iris. To 16 in. (41 cm).
Range: Native to the Amazon basin of the Guianas west of the Marowijne R. drainage. Established in Black Cr. and nearby canals, Dade Co., se. FL. **Habitat:** Drainage canals.

REDSTRIPED EARTHEATER *Geophagus surinamensis*   **Fig. 62**
Identification: *Long snout;* eye high on head; dip between eyes gives fish a "bug-eyed" look. *Black blotch* on side. Lateral line bifurcates on caudal peduncle; straight-edged caudal fin. Olive to green; many iridescent blue-green stripes on side; iridescent powder blue spots on fins (except pectoral). Large male may have rows of red spots on side, red fins (except pectoral), long 1st pelvic ray. *3 anal spines.* To about 12 in. (30 cm).
Range: Native to the Guianas and the Amazon basin, n. South America. Established in canals in Dade Co., FL. Uncommon. **Habitat:** Mud- and sand-bottomed canals.

JEWELFISH *Hemichromis bimaculatus*   **Fig. 62**
Identification: *Fairly long, slender body; rounded caudal fin.* Yellow-green to red-brown body and fins; *large black blotch* on side, smaller blotches on opercular tab and caudal fin base (blotches rarely connected into stripe). Large individual has iridescent blue spots on *brilliant red body.* 13–15 dorsal spines, *3 anal spines.* To 8 in. (20 cm).
Range: Native to rivers and lakes of w. Africa south of the Atlas Mountains, Morocco. Established in canals in Dade Co., FL. Common. **Habitat:** Mud- and sand-bottomed canals.

● *CICHLASOMA*

Genus characteristics: Always *more than 3 anal spines;* usually a black spot, blotch, or bar on caudal fin base.

RIO GRANDE CICHLID *Cichlasoma cyanoguttatum*   **Fig. 62**
Identification: Dusky to olive above; *4–6 dark blotches* (1st one most prominent) along rear half of side, usually confluent with dusky sad-

dles; black blotch on caudal fin base. *Many small white to blue spots* on blue-green or gray side. Adult has iridescent blue-green spots or wavy lines on head, body, and fins. Breeding individual has white head, front half of body; black rear half of body. Breeding male has nuchal hump. 15–17 dorsal spines, usually 10–12 dorsal rays; 5–7 anal spines, 9–10 anal rays. To about 12 in. (30 cm).
Range: Our only native cichlid. Originally restricted to the lower Rio Grande drainage, TX, and south to ne. Mexico. Introduced on Edwards Plateau of cen. TX and cen. peninsular FL. Common. **Habitat:** Pools and runs of small to large rivers; prefers warm water and vegetation.
Similar species: See Fig. 62. (1) Jack Dempsey has usually 2 dark lines on top of head between eyes, 8–9 anal spines, 17–19 dorsal spines. (2) Convict Cichlid has 9–11 anal spines, 7 intense black bars along side. (3) Midas Cichlid lacks iridescent spotting pattern.   **Map 376**

JACK DEMPSEY *Cichlasoma octofasciatum*   **Fig. 62**
Identification: *2 gray to black lines* between eyes. Olive, gray, or tan above; gray to black connected blotches along side (may form vague to intense bars); white to iridescent blue spots on median fins. Adult is usually *deep blue*; has dark bars, *many iridescent white, blue, or green spots* on head, body, and median fins; some varieties have purple or red below, red edge on dorsal fin. 17–19 dorsal spines, 9–10 dorsal rays, 8–9 anal spines, 7–8 anal rays. To about 10 in. (25 cm).
Range: Native to Atlantic Slope from Rio Chachalacas, Ciudad Veracruz, Mexico, to Rio Ulua, Honduras. Established in ditches and canals in Alachua, Brevard, Dade, and Hillsborough cos., FL. Uncommon. **Habitat:** Weedy, mud- and sand-bottomed canals and drainage ditches.
Remarks: This species is especially pugnacious and combative — hence the name.
Similar species: See Fig. 62. (1) Rio Grande Cichlid *lacks* 2 dark lines on top of head; has usually 5–7 anal spines, 15–17 dorsal spines. (2) Convict Cichlid has usually 9–11 anal spines, 7 intense black bars along side. (3) Midas Cichlid *lacks* 2 dark lines on top of head, has usually 6–8 anal spines.

CONVICT CICHLID *Cichlasoma nigrofasciatum*   **Fig. 62**
Identification: Usually 7 *black bars* (see Remarks) on side extend onto dorsal and anal fins (intensity of bars variable; sometimes 1st 3 appear as blotches); *1st bar* Y-*shaped*, crosses nape; 7th bar on caudal fin base. *Black spot* on upper half of opercle. Light blue or gray; clear or light blue-gray fins. Large male has intense black bars, black underside of head, long rays at rear of dorsal and anal fins; female has gold-yellow lower side. Female may be orange or red in some populations, have gold eye. 18–19 dorsal spines, 7–9 dorsal rays, 9–11 anal spines, 6–8 anal rays, 12–14 pectoral rays. To 4¾ in. (12 cm).
Range: Native to Pacific Slope of Guatemala, Atlantic and Pacific slopes of Costa Rica, and Atlantic Slope of Panama. Established in springs of Custer Co., ID (see Remarks), and Lincoln and Clark cos., NV. Common. **Habitat:** Warm pools of springs and their effluents.

Remarks: Aquarium-developed white form (lacks black pigment) established in ID.
Similar species: (1) Midas Cichlid (Fig. 62) lacks Y-shaped bar on nape; has usually 6–8 anal spines, 14–18 pectoral rays, 10–13 dorsal rays. (2) Black Acara (Fig. 62) *lacks* black bars on side; has usually 4 anal spines, 15–16 dorsal spines.

MIDAS CICHLID *Cichlasoma citrinellum* Fig. 62
Identification: *6 dusky to black bars* (darkest at middle) on side; *large black blotch* on midside, *smaller black spot* on caudal fin base (spots always prominent; bars vary in intensity). Color highly variable (see Remarks). Gray-brown; small white spots on gray fins (except clear pectoral). Large male has nuchal hump, long rays at rear of dorsal and anal fins. Red, orange, yellow, or white variants may be found; some have thick, fleshy lips. 15–18 dorsal spines, 10–13 dorsal rays, 6–8 anal spines, 5–10 anal rays, 14–18 pectoral rays. To 9½ in. (24 cm).
Range: Native to Atlantic Slope of Nicaragua and Costa Rica. Established in canals near Homestead, Dade Co., FL. Uncommon. **Habitat:** Box-cut canals with rocky vertical sides; crevices used for spawning and protection of young.
Remarks: Midas Cichlids begin life as normally colored (i.e., gray with black marks). A few individuals become brightly colored (gold, red, or white), usually gold. These brightly colored individuals are more aggressive, obtain more food, and grow faster, but also are more vulnerable to predation.
Similar species: (1) See Mayan Cichlid. (2) Convict Cichlid (Fig. 62) has Y-shaped black bar crossing nape, usually 7–9 dorsal rays, 9–11 anal spines, 12–14 pectoral rays. (3) Black Acara (Fig. 62) has black stripe on side usually extending onto opercle, 4 anal spines; reaches only 4¾ in. (12 cm).

MAYAN CICHLID *Cichlasoma urophthalmus* Not shown
Identification: Similar to Midas Cichlid but has 5–7 bold dark green to black bars on side; blue halo around *large black blotch* on upper caudal fin base (spot is about ½ depth of caudal peduncle). Olive green above and on side; red-edged dorsal and caudal fins; red on chin, throat, and breast. Yellow iris. 5–7 anal spines. To 12 in. (30 cm).
Range: Native to the Atlantic Slope from Rio Coatzcoalcos, Mexico, to the Rio Prinzapolka, Nicaragua. Established in Everglades National Park and just outside its boundaries, s. FL. **Habitat:** Freshwater marshes and mangrove swamps. Tolerates a wide variety of salinities; breeds in both fresh and salt water.
Similar species: See Midas Cichlid (Fig. 62).

BLACK ACARA *Cichlasoma bimaculatum* Fig. 62
Identification: Yellow, gray, or olive body and fins; light brown to black blotches along side usually extend as *dark stripe onto opercle*; often 6–7 olive to dark brown bars on side; black blotch on caudal fin base. Adult is dark green and yellow; has blue-gray fins, except yellow to light orange pectoral fin; has long rays at rear of dorsal and

anal fins. Usually 15–16 dorsal spines, 10–11 dorsal rays; 4 anal spines; usually 9–10 anal rays; 13–15 pectoral rays. To 4¾ in. (12 cm).
Range: Native to the Guianas and Venezuela. Established in Broward, Collier, Dade, Glades, Hendry, Monroe, and Palm Beach cos., FL. Common. **Habitat:** Canals and swamps; tolerates low oxygen.
Similar species: (1) Convict Cichlid (Fig. 62) has 7 intense black bars along side, usually 9–11 anal spines, 18–19 dorsal spines. (2) Midas Cichlid (Fig. 62) has 6–8 anal spines, usually no black stripe on opercle; reaches 9½ in. (24 cm).

FIREMOUTH *Cichlasoma meeki*   **Fig. 62**
Identification: *Large black blotch* on lower half of gill cover; *bright red or orange underside of head* (brightest on adult). Yellow-olive to gray head and body; 3–5 black blotches along side, 1 on caudal fin base; red edge, rows of blue spots or blotches on clear fins. Large male has long rays at rear of dorsal and anal fins and upper and lower edges of caudal fin; is dark green with iridescent blue spots on side, brilliant red underside of head, iridescent blue spots on red fins (except pectoral). 15–17 dorsal spines, 10–13 dorsal rays, 8–10 anal spines, 7–9 anal rays. To 6¾ in. (17 cm).
Range: Native to Atlantic Slope from Rio Tonala, Veracruz, Mexico, to s. Belize. Established in Dade Co., FL. Common. **Habitat:** Mud- and sand-bottomed canals and rocky ponds.

BANDED CICHLID *Cichlasoma severum*   **Fig. 62**
Identification: Deep, compressed body. Usually *5–7 dusky to black bars* on side; bar on caudal fin base extends *onto dorsal and anal fins.* Yellow-olive to dark green head and body. Adult is yellow below; has yellow lower fins. Young has many black spots on purple-tan body; lacks black bars. 15–17 dorsal spines, usually 11–13 dorsal rays; 6–8 anal spines; usually 11–12 anal rays. To about 8 in. (20 cm).
Range: Native to n. South America. Apparently established in Rogers Spring, Clark Co., NV. Uncommon. **Habitat:** Warm spring pools and their effluents.

JAGUAR GUAPOTE *Cichlasoma managuense*   **Not shown**
Identification: *Very large oblique mouth,* rear edge reaching below front of eye; *lower jaw projects* slightly beyond upper jaw. Distinctive lobe on rear edge of preopercle. Green above; purple tinge on yellow-gold side; *many purple-black spots and blotches on body and fins;* usually a row of black squares along side; yellow below. Red iris. 17–18 dorsal spines, 10–11 dorsal rays, 8–9 anal spines, 8–9 anal rays. To 24½ in. (63 cm).
Range: Native to the Atlantic Slope from Rio Uliua, Honduras, to Rio Matina, Costa Rica. Established in a warm spring pool and nearby pond near St. George, Washington Co., UT. Common. **Habitat:** Springs and ponds over detritus and sand bottom.

Next 6 species: 3 anal spines (rarely 4); usually a straight-edged or slightly forked caudal fin, a *black spot* on opercle; rarely a black spot or blotch on caudal fin base.

MOZAMBIQUE TILAPIA *Oreochromis mossambicus*   **Fig. 62**
Identification: *Large oblique mouth* reaches under front of eye or beyond. Gray to olive above; 3–4 black spots on dull yellow to gray-green side; yellow below. Large male has *thick blue upper lip,* blue or black body, *white underside of head, red edge* on black dorsal and caudal fins, red pectoral fin. Young has 6–8 black bars on silver side. 29–33 lateral scales, 15–17 (usually 16) dorsal spines, 10–12 dorsal rays, 9–10 anal rays, 14–20 rakers on lower limb of 1st gill arch. To 15¼ in. (39 cm).
Range: Native to Indian Slope of se. Africa. Established in agricultural drains and ponds near Yuma, AZ; in several counties in s. CA (now the most abundant fish in the Salton Sea); in canals, ponds, and streams in Brevard and Dade cos., s. FL; Barney Hot Spring, Custer Co., ID; and in reservoirs of Hays and Bexar cos., TX. Annually stocked in ponds and lakes in AL. Common. **Habitat:** Warm, weedy pools of sluggish streams; canals; and ponds.
Similar species: See (1) Wami and (2) Blue Tilapias. (3) Blackchin Tilapia (Fig. 62) has a *small mouth,* usually 27–29 lateral scales; large male has *black underside* of head, gold gill cover.

WAMI TILAPIA *Oreochromis urolepis*   **Not shown**
Identification: Nearly identical to Mozambique Tilapia but *lacks* white underside of head on large male; has 15–18, *usually 17, dorsal spines; 19–27 rakers* on lower limb of 1st gill arch. To 17 in. (43 cm).
Range: Native to Wami R. basin, Zanzibar. Established in irrigation canals, flood control channels, and associated drainages in s. CA. Common. **Habitat:** Warm weedy ditches and canals.
Similar species: See Mozambique Tilapia (Fig. 62).

BLUE TILAPIA *Oreochromis aureus*   **Not shown**
Identification: Similar to Mozambique Tilapia but has usually *12–15 dorsal rays, 18–26 rakers* on lower limb of 1st gill arch. Large male has bright metallic blue head, pale blue side, *blue-black chin and breast.* To 14½ in. (37 cm).
Range: Native to n. Africa. Established in lower Colorado R. drainage, sw. AZ and se. CA; in peninsular FL; in a cooling impoundment, Buncombe Co., NC; in North Canadian R. drainage, OK; and in several impoundments and the Rio Grande, sw. TX. Possibly established near Alamosa, San Luis Valley, CO, and in golf course ponds, Glynn Co., GA. Annually stocked in ponds in AL. Common. **Habitat:** Warm ponds and impoundments. Reproduces in both fresh and brackish water.
Similar species: See Mozambique Tilapia (Fig. 62).

BLACKCHIN TILAPIA *Sarotherodon melanotheron*   **Fig. 62**
Identification: *Small mouth;* rear edge does not reach front of eye. Orange or metallic gold-yellow on back and upper side, pale blue below. Large male has metallic gold gill cover, *black underside* of head,

black edge on median fins; often has dark bars on side. Usually 27–29 lateral scales; 15–16 dorsal spines, 10–12 dorsal rays, 8–10 anal rays, 12–19 rakers on lower limb of 1st gill arch. To 10¼ in. (26 cm).
Range: Native to river delta lagoons from middle Liberia to s. Cameroon, w. Africa. Established in FL from Lithia Springs, Hillsborough Co., to e. shore of Tampa Bay, Manatee Co., and in canals and rivers of Brevard Co. Common. **Habitat:** Lower reaches of streams; tolerant of high salinity.
Similar species: (1) Mozambique Tilapia (Fig. 62) has large mouth, usually 29–33 lateral scales; large male has *white underside* of head. (2) Blue Tilapia has *metallic blue head* on large male, 12–15 dorsal rays, 18–26 rakers on lower limb of 1st gill arch.

REDBELLY TILAPIA *Tilapia zilli*   Not shown
Identification: *Large, nearly horizontal mouth.* Head wider than body. Silver-gray to dark olive above; 6–7 faint dark bars on light olive to yellow-brown side (often with metallic green or red sheen); yellow to brown belly and fins. Black blotch on upper edge of opercle; many yellow spots around black spot on 2d dorsal fin. Adult has 6–8 black bars on side, *blood red underside* (brightest on male) of head, belly, and side of caudal peduncle; blue-green vermiculations on blue-black head. 14–16 dorsal spines, 10–13 dorsal rays, 7–10 anal rays. To about 12½ in. (32 cm).
Range: Native to n. and cen. Africa. Established in ponds and other waters in Maricopa Co., AZ; irrigation canals in Coachella, Imperial, and Palo Verde valleys, CA; and headwater springs of San Antonio R., Bexar Co., TX. Common. **Habitat:** Irrigation canals, ponds, and springs, where stocked for aquatic weed control or as a food fish.
Similar species: See Spotted Tilapia (Fig. 62).

SPOTTED TILAPIA *Tilapia mariae*   Fig. 62
Identification: Similar to Redbelly Tilapia but *lacks* blood red below; has usually 6–9 black blotches or bars on side that *continue onto dorsal fin.* 15–16 dorsal spines, 12–15 dorsal rays, 10–12 anal rays. To 12 in. (31 cm).
Range: Native to Atlantic Slope of w-cen. Africa. Established in canals of Broward and Dade cos., FL, and in Rogers Spring, Clark Co., NV. Common. **Habitat:** Mud- to sand-bottomed canals; warm springs.
Similar species: See Redbelly Tilapia.

◼ SURFPERCHES: Family Embiotocidae (1)

Most surfperches are marine and occur inshore, in the surf zone, in kelp, and in tidepools. One species, the Tule Perch, lives in fresh water in northern California. Two species of this family are found off Japan and Korea; the other 19 occur along the Pacific Coast of North America.
Surfperches have a compressed, elliptical to oblong perchlike body;

a continuous (unnotched) dorsal fin with usually 9–11 spines, 19–28 rays; a *scaled ridge* along the dorsal fin base; 3 anal spines; 15–35 anal rays; a forked caudal fin; and *cycloid scales.* Most are silver and barred or striped. All species are *livebearers.*

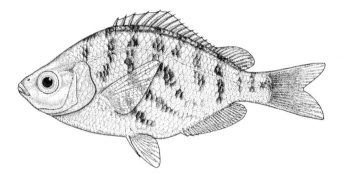

Fig. 63 Tule Perch *Hysterocarpus traski*

TULE PERCH *Hysterocarpus traski* **Fig. 63**
Identification: Deep body, terminal mouth, forked caudal fin. *Ridge of scales* at base of dorsal fin. Dark blue or purple above, white to yellow below. 3 color phases: wide dark bars, narrow dark bars, or no bars on side. Adult may have large hump on nape. 3 anal spines; 20–26 anal rays. To 5¾ in (15 cm).
Range: Clear Lake; Russian, Sacramento–San Joaquin, and Pajaro–Salinas R. drainages, CA. Common in north; severely decimated in Pajaro-Salinas and San Joaquin R. drainages. **Habitat:** Mud- to gravel-bottomed pools and runs of small to large, low-elevation rivers; lakes. Usually near emergent aquatic plants or overhanging banks. Rare in brackish water. **Map 377**

■GOURAMIES: Family Belontiidae (1)

Gouramies, popular among aquarists, are native to the fresh waters of India, southeast Asia, and the Malay Archipelago. One species, the Croaking Gourami, of 28 recognized in the family, apparently escaped from a fish farm and is established in southern Florida.

Gouramies have *no or a short lateral line, 10 or fewer dorsal rays,* and a protrusible upper jaw; many species have *long pelvic rays.* Most species are small (usually under 4 in. [10 cm]).

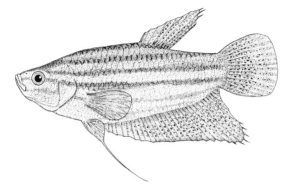

Fig. 64 Croaking Gourami *Trichopsis vittata*

CROAKING GOURAMI *Trichopsis vittata* **Fig. 64**
Identification: *Long 1st pelvic fin ray;* usually long rays at rear of dorsal and anal fins. Upturned mouth. Short lateral line. *Long anal fin* covers length of belly and lower peduncle. *Short dorsal fin.* Color highly variable; light green to dark purple body and fins; black or red spots on fins; sometimes has black stripes or rows of spots on side; thin iridescent blue edge on median fins; red eye. To 2¼ in. (6 cm).
Range: Native to se. Asia. Established in a drainage canal, Delray Beach, Palm Beach Co., FL. Uncommon. **Habitat:** Weedy canals.

GLOSSARY
ABBREVIATIONS
REFERENCES
RANGE MAPS
INDEX

GLOSSARY

Some of the terms below have broader or alternate meanings, but they are defined here as they apply to fishes in this guide. For anatomical features that are illustrated in this book, a figure citation is given after the definition.

Abdomen. Belly or lower surface of a fish, especially between the pelvic fins and the anus (Fig. 1).

Adipose eyelid. Translucent tissue that partially covers the eyeball in some fishes (Fig. 7).

Adipose fin. Small fleshy fin, without spines or rays, on the back between the dorsal fin and the caudal fin (e.g., see Pl. 25).

Adnate. Joined together congenitally.

Allopatric. Occurring in different geographic areas. See sympatric.

Ammocoete. Blind larva of a lamprey (Fig. 4).

Anadromous. Moving from the ocean into fresh water to spawn, as in salmons and shads.

Anal fin. Median fin located on the undersurface, usually just behind the anus (Fig. 1).

Axillary process. Fleshy flap (actually a modified scale), usually narrow and projecting to the rear, just above the pectoral or pelvic fins.

Backwater. Quiet pool on the side of a stream channel. See pool.

Band. Bar or stripe on a fin. See Bar, Stripe.

Bar. (1) Vertical band of color. See Band, Stripe. (2) Ridge of sand or gravel in a stream or along a shore, formed by water currents.

Barbel. Fleshy projection (sometimes whiskerlike) found on the head (usually near the mouth) (Fig. 21). Barbels are sensitive to touch and taste.

Basioccipital process. Extension of bone at lower rear edge of skull.

Benthic. Living on or near the bottom.

Blotch. Irregularly shaped color mark. See Speck, Spot.

Branchiostegal ray. Raylike bony support of the branchiostegal membranes.

Breast. Chest; area in front of the belly (Fig. 1).

Bridle. Color mark across the snout that suggests a bridle (Fig. 60).

Canine. Pointed, conical tooth that is usually larger than the surrounding teeth.

Carnivorous. Meat eating; feeding on animals.

Cartilage. Translucent material that makes up the skeleton of young fishes and which persists in adults of some species (notably sharks and rays) but is largely converted to bone in most fishes.

Catadromous. Moving from fresh water to the ocean to spawn, as in the American Eel.

Caudal fin. Median fin at the rear of the body; the "tail" (Fig. 1).

Caudal fulcrum. V-shaped, spinelike scale at front of caudal fin.

Caudal peduncle. Rear, usually slender, part of the body between the base of the last dorsal- and anal-fin rays and the caudal-fin base (Fig. 1).

Caudal spot. Spot at base (origin) of caudal fin.

Channel. Main course of a stream.

Cirrus (plural: cirri). Elongate, fleshy appendage or tab on the head or body.

Coastal Plain. Plain extending inland along the Atlantic (Atlantic Coastal Plain) and Gulf coasts; extends to s. IL along the Former Mississippi Embayment.

Compressed. Flattened from side to side.

Concave. Bowed or curved inward.

Convex. Bowed or curved outward.

Ctenoid. Type of scale with a toothed rear edge, making the scale rough to touch.

Cusp. Principal projecting point of a tooth.

Cycloid. Type of scale with a smooth rear edge, making the scale smooth to touch.

Deciduous. In reference to scales, loosely attached to the body and easily shed when the fish is handled.

Decurved. Curved downward.

Depressed. Flattened from top to bottom.

Disc. See Oral Disc.

Dorsal. Above; on top.

Dorsal fin. Median rayed fin on the back, often notched or subdivided; sometimes fully divided into 2 separate fins (Fig. 1).

Ear flap. Fleshy or bony extension on the rear edge of the opercle, as on sunfishes.

Embedded. Covered by skin (usually refers to scales).

Endemic. Restricted to a particular drainage, lake, etc.

Endorheic. In reference to a surface drainage not reaching the sea.

Extirpated. Removed completely; exterminated.

Falcate. Deeply indented or sickle-shaped, e.g., the edge of a fin.

Fall Line. Boundary between Coastal Plain and the Piedmont, typically marked by waterfalls on rivers.

Fin base. Part of a fin that is attached to the body.

Forked. In reference to the caudal fin; used when the rear edge is distinctly indented.

Former Mississippi Embayment. See Mississippi Embayment.

Frenum. Fleshy bridge or connection, as between the snout and upper lip (Fig. 55).

Fusiform. Cigar-shaped; tapering at both ends (usually refers to body shape).

Ganoid. Type of scale covered with hard enamel (e.g., on gars).

Gas bladder. Sac located between the spinal column and the gut cavity; also called the air or swim bladder.

Genital papilla. Small, fleshy projection at the genital pore (immediately behind the anus) in some fishes.

Genus (plural: genera). A taxonomic category including one or a closely related (i.e., of common phylogenetic origin) group of species.

Gill. Breathing organ in fishes, including the highly vascularized filaments that are used to extract oxygen from water.

Gill arch. Bony or cartilaginous support to which gill filaments and gill rakers are attached (Fig. 3).

Gill chamber. Cavity where the gills are located.

Gill cover. Bony flap covering the outside of the gill chamber (Fig. 1).

Gill opening. Opening at the rear of the head, from the gill chamber to the outside (most fishes have 1 on each side); called gill slits in sharks and rays.

Gill raker. Toothlike projection on the front edge of the gill arch; often used to trap food items between the gill arches (Fig. 3).

Gonopodium. Front rays of anal fin of male livebearers, modified to serve as a reproductive organ.

Gular plate. Bony plate on the throat.

Habitat. Place where a fish normally lives.

Halo. Circle of color around a spot of another color.

Head length. Distance from the tip of the snout, lip, or chin — whichever is farthest forward — to the rear edge of the gill cover (Fig. 1).

Herbivorous. Vegetarian; feeding on plants.

Hermaphrodite. Having both male and female organs in one individual.

Herringbone lines. Pattern of parallel slanting lines (e.g., ribs of a herring; blood vessels on the upper side of a minnow).

Heterocercal. Type of caudal fin in which the vertebral column extends into the upper lobe, which is usually longer (e.g., on sturgeons — Pl. 1).

Homocercal. Type of caudal fin in which all of the principal rays of the fin attach to the modified last vertebra (the hypural plate). This type of caudal fin is usually symmetrical (e.g., on shads — Pl. 3).

Humeral spot. Large spot at upper edge of pectoral fin base (often on "humeral scale").

Ichthyologist. One who studies fishes.

Infraorbital. Below the eye; e.g., infraorbital canal or pores (Fig. 53).

Intergrade. Individual with characteristics intermediate between those of two subspecies and found in "zone of intergradation."

Interorbital. Between the eyes (orbits).

Interpelvic width. Straight-line distance between the pelvic fin bases.

Invertebrate. Animal lacking a backbone (e.g., insect, crayfish, worm).

Isthmus. Triangular, frontmost part of the underside of the body; largely separated from the head, in most bony fishes, by the gill openings.

Jugular. In the throat area; usually refers to location of the pelvic fins.

Juvenile. Young of a species; usually a small version of the adult.

Keel. A shelflike fleshy or bony ridge.

Lacrimal. Bone between the eye and the nostril (Fig. 13).

Larva (plural: larvae). Newborn; the developmental stage of a fish before it becomes a juvenile.

Lateral. On the side.

Lateralis system. Sensory system consisting of a series of pores and canals on the head, body, and sometimes caudal fin of a fish; used to detect water movements.

Lateral line. Canal along the body, usually single and located roughly at midside, but sometimes branched and variously placed. This canal is a rearward extension of a sensory canal system (the lateralis system) on the head and contains sense organs which detect pressure changes (Fig. 1).

Lateral scales. Row of scales along the midside (usually along the lateral line) from rear edge of gill cover to base of caudal fin (Fig. 1). Often called lateral-line scales. See lateral scale count.

Lateral scale count. Number of scales along lateral line, if present and complete, or along midside if lateral line is absent or incomplete (Fig. 1).

Leptocephalus. Transparent, ribbonlike larva of eels, tarpons, and their allies.

Littoral. Occurring at or in the immediate vicinity of the shoreline.

Mandible. Lower jaw.

Maxilla. Rear bone of the two bones that form the upper jaw.

Medial. In the middle plane or axis of the body.

Median fins. Unpaired fins located on the median plane of the body; the dorsal, caudal, and anal fins.

Melanophore. Cell containing melanin, a dark brown or black pigment. When contracted, these cells appear as pepperlike dots; when expanded, large areas of the fish may become dark.

Midwater. In or near the middle water stratum, as opposed to at the surface or on the bottom (see Benthic).

Mississippi Embayment. Low plain, submerged under the sea through much of its history, now traversed by the lower Mississippi River. Also called Former Mississippi Embayment.

Monotypic. Used to describe a genus or family that contains only one species.

Nape. Part of the back immediately behind the head, or, in spiny-rayed fishes, the part between the head and the point where the 1st (spiny) dorsal fin begins (Fig. 1).

Neoteny. Retention of juvenile features in the adult.

Nipple. Small projection resembling a teat.

Nocturnal. Active at night.

Nostril. Nasal opening (fishes usually have 2 on each side).

Nuchal. Pertaining to the nape (e.g., a nuchal hump).

Ocellus (plural: ocelli). Eyelike spot; usually dark, bordered by a ring of light pigment.

Omnivorous. Feeding on both plants and animals.

Opercle. Uppermost and largest of the bones that form the gill cover (Fig. 1).

Oral disc. Fleshy circular structure surrounding mouth of lamprey (Fig. 4).

Orbital. Related to the eye.

Origin. Point where a fin begins — the point at which the most anterior ray is inserted.

Oxbow. Lake formed in the abandoned channel of a stream meander after the stream has cut through the land at a narrow point in the meander.

Papilla (plural: papillae). Small nipplelike projection of connective tissue.

Papillose. With papillae.

Paired fins. Collectively, the pectoral and pelvic fins (Fig. 1).

Palatine. One of a pair of bones on the roof of the mouth, one on each side, between the jaw and the midline.

Palatine teeth. Teeth on the palatine bones.

Parr marks. Dark bars on young fish that usually are absent on adult.

Pectoral fin. One of a pair of fins (one on each side) that are attached to the shoulder girdle, just behind the head (Fig. 1).

Peduncle. See Caudal Peduncle.

Pelagic. Living in open water away from the bottom.

Pelvic fin. One of a pair of fins on the lower part of the body (Fig. 1). The position of these fins ranges from on the belly just in front of the anal fin (abdominal), to under the pectoral fin (thoracic), to the isthmus (jugular).

Peritoneum. Lining of the abdominal cavity. May be pigmented and visible externally and thus an aid to identification.

Pharyngeal. Of, or near, the pharynx.

Piedmont. Hilly, upland region between the Atlantic-Gulf Coastal Plain and the Appalachian Mountains, stretching from se. NY to cen. AL.

Plankton. Small plants (called phytoplankton) and animals (zooplankton) that are mostly free-floating.

Plica (plural: plicae). Small fold of skin.

Plicate. With folds of skin.

Pool. Quiet, often relatively deep, segment of a stream. See Backwater, Riffle, Run.

Pore. Tiny opening in the skin; usually involved with sensory perception in fishes.

Pored scale. Scale with a pore; e.g., lateral-line scales.

Predorsal scales. Row of scales along middle of back between head and dorsal fin.

Premaxilla. Bone at the front of the upper jaw.

Premaxillary frenum. Bridge of flesh connecting the upper lip and snout (Fig. 55).

Preopercle. Bone at the rear end of the cheek and in front of the gill cover, often separated from the gill cover by a groove (Fig. 1).

Preopercular spine. Any of the spines along the rear or lower edges of the preopercle (Fig. 51).

Preoperculomandibular canal (or **pores**). Canal (or pores) extending along rear edge of preopercle and onto mandible (Fig. 53).

Preorbital. In front of the eye; e.g., preorbital bar.

Protrusible. In reference to a mouth whose upper lip is not attached to the snout, and which may be extended far forward to catch prey.

Punctate lateral line. Pattern of rows of black spots above and below lateral line (Fig. 33).

Pyloric caecum (plural: caeca). Fingerlike tubes at the junction of the stomach and intestine.

Ray. Flexible, segmented fin ray; often branched (Fig. 1). Also used to refer to any of the bony elements that support and spread the branchiostegal membrane. See Branchiostegal ray.

Redd. Depression, usually a pit or trough, dug in preparation for, or during, spawning. Eggs are laid in the redd.

Reticulate. Color markings in a chainlike pattern or network.

Riffle. Fast-flowing, shallow segment of a stream where the surface of the water is broken over rocks or debris. See Pool, Run.

Rudiment. A small, incompletely developed fin ray or gill raker (Figs. 2 and 3).

Run. Transitional segment of a stream between a riffle and a pool, with moderate current and depth. See Pool, Riffle.

Saddle. Color mark, more or less rectangular, on the back.

Scalation. Arrangement of scales; squamation.

Scute. Enlarged scale, often with one or more bony projections (Fig. 56).

Seaboard Lowlands. Low coastal border of New England.

Sea-run. Anadromous; moving from the ocean into fresh water to spawn.

Serrae. Sawlike notches along an edge.

Serrate. With serrae.

Shoal. Shallow, usually gravel-bottomed, area of a stream; often the submerged area of a bar.

Snout. Portion of the head in front of the eyes and above the mouth (Fig. 1).

Soft ray. See Ray.

Speck. Very small blotch. See Blotch, Spot.

Spine. (1) Bony projection, usually on the head. (2) Hard, unbranched ray in a fin — a spinous ray (Fig. 1).

Spiracle. Opening (behind the eye) of a separate duct or canal that leads to the gill chamber in sharks, rays, and certain primitive bony fishes. (Not the gill opening.)

Spiral valve. Fold of tissue twisting in spiral fashion along the walls of the intestine.

Spot. Circular color mark. See Blotch, Speck.

Squamation. Arrangement of scales.

Standard length. Straight-line distance from the tip of the snout, lip, or chin — whichever is farthest forward — to the rear end of the vertebral column (end of hypural plate — locate by lifting caudal fin and noting crease at caudal fin base). Used as a standard measure of the length of a fish (Fig. 1).

Stripe. Horizontal band of color. See Band, Bar.

Submandibular pores. Pores along the underside of the mandible (lower jaw).

Submarginal. In reference to fins, the area along, but not including, the edge of the fin.

Suborbital. Below the eye.

Subspecies. A geographically delimited, distinguishable population of a species. A subspecies name consists of three parts: genus, species, subspecies; e.g., *Percina caprodes fulvitaenia.*

Subterminal. In reference to the position of the mouth; used when the mouth opens below the foremost point of the head. See Terminal, Upturned.

Supratemporal canal (or **pores**). Canal (or pores) across the back of the head (Fig. 53).

Sympatric. Occurring in same geographic area. See Allopatric.

Symphyseal knob. Bony protuberance at junction of two bones (e.g., two halves of lower jaw).

Teardrop. Vertical color mark under eye.

Terminal. In reference to the position of the mouth; used when the mouth opens at the foremost point of the head, the upper and lower jaws being equally far forward. See Subterminal, Upturned.

Territorial. Defending a particular area.

Thoracic. On the breast (refers to pelvic fin location).

Transverse scales. Row of scales from anal fin origin to dorsal fin (or middle of back) (Fig. 1).

Truncate. Having a square or flattened end.

Trunk myomeres. Body segments. In lampreys, trunk myomeres extend from the 1st segment after the last gill pore to, and including, the segment before the anus.

Tubercle. Small, white, hard (keratinized) protuberances on the skin; usually seasonal in occurrence and usually only on breeding males (Fig. 31).

Tubercle spot. White area where tubercle will develop.

Upturned. In reference to the position of the mouth; used when the mouth opens above the foremost point of the head. See Subterminal, Terminal.

Ventral. Below; on the lower half of the head or body.

Vermiculations. Color pattern of short, wavy (wormlike) lines.

Vertebrate. Animal with a backbone (e.g., fish, frog, squirrel).

Vomerine. Pertaining to the vomer — a median bone in the front of the roof of the mouth; often used to describe location of teeth on this bone.

ABBREVIATIONS

United States

AL	Alabama	MT	Montana
AK	Alaska	NE	Nebraska
AZ	Arizona	NV	Nevada
AR	Arkansas	NH	New Hampshire
CA	California	NJ	New Jersey
CO	Colorado	NM	New Mexico
CT	Connecticut	NY	New York
DE	Delaware	NC	North Carolina
DC	District of Columbia	ND	North Dakota
FL	Florida	OH	Ohio
GA	Georgia	OK	Oklahoma
ID	Idaho	OR	Oregon
IL	Illinois	PA	Pennsylvania
IN	Indiana	RI	Rhode Island
IA	Iowa	SC	South Carolina
KS	Kansas	SD	South Dakota
KY	Kentucky	TN	Tennessee
LA	Louisiana	TX	Texas
ME	Maine	UT	Utah
MD	Maryland	VT	Vermont
MA	Massachusetts	VA	Virginia
MI	Michigan	WA	Washington
MN	Minnesota	WV	West Virginia
MS	Mississippi	WI	Wisconsin
MO	Missouri	WY	Wyoming

Canadian Provinces and Territories

AB	Alberta	NS	Nova Scotia
BC	British Columbia	ON	Ontario
MB	Manitoba	PE	Prince Edward Island
NB	New Brunswick	QU	Quebec
NF	Newfoundland	SA	Saskatchewan
NT	Northwest Territories	YU	Yukon Territory

Compass Directions

e.	east	se.	southeast
n.	north	sw.	southwest
s.	south	e.-cen.	east central
w.	west	n.-cen.	north central
ne.	northeast	s.-cen.	south central
nw.	northwest	w.-cen.	west central

Other Abbreviations

R.	River	lb.	pound
Cr.	Creek	cm	centimeter
Co.	County	m	meter
U.S.	United States	km	kilometer
in.	inch	kg	kilogram
ft.	foot	ppt	parts per thousand

REFERENCES

The information used to prepare a Field Guide like this one is drawn primarily from technical papers. They are not cited here because of established field guide practice and space limitations. Listed below are general books that provide additional information and serve as sources for technical literature. The *Atlas of North American Freshwater Fishes* and *Handbook of Darters* provide comprehensive lists of regional (mostly state and provincial) books on fishes.

Bond, Carl E. 1979. *The Biology of Fishes.* Philadelphia: W. B. Saunders Co.

Eschmeyer, William N., and Earl S. Herald. 1983. *A Field Guide to Pacific Coast Fishes of North America.* Boston: Houghton Mifflin Co.

Kuehne, Robert A., and Roger W. Barbour. 1983. *The American Darters.* Lexington: University Press of Kentucky.

Lagler, Karl F., John E. Bardach, Robert R. Miller, and Dora R. Passino. 1977. *Ichthyology.* 2d ed. New York: John Wiley & Sons.

Lee, David S., Carter R. Gilbert, Charles H. Hocutt, Robert E. Jenkins, Don E. McAllister, and Jay R. Stauffer, Jr., (eds.). 1980 et seq. *Atlas of North American Freshwater Fishes.* Raleigh: North Carolina State Museum of Natural History.

Moyle, Peter B., and Joseph J. Cech, Jr. 1988. *Fishes: An Introduction to Ichthyology.* 2d ed. New Jersey: Prentice-Hall, Inc.

Nelson, Joseph S. 1984. *Fishes of the World.* 2d ed. New York: John Wiley & Sons.

Norman, J. R., and P. H. Greenwood. 1963. *A History of Fishes.* 2d ed. New York: Hill and Wang.

Page, Lawrence M. 1983. *Handbook of Darters.* Neptune City, New Jersey: T.F.H. Publications, Inc.

Robins, C. Richard, et al. (eds). 1980. *A List of Common and Scientific Names of Fishes from the United States and Canada.* 4th ed. American Fisheries Society Special Publication 12.

Robins, C. Richard, and G. Carleton Ray. 1986. *A Field Guide to Atlantic Coast Fishes of North America.* Boston: Houghton Mifflin Co.

RANGE MAPS

The maps on the following pages show approximate ranges of species (see Maps, p. 7). Within these ranges, large gaps in distribution may occur in ecologically unsuitable areas. For example, the Rainbow Darter ranges over much of the eastern United States, but it is found only in rocky riffles and thus is absent from much of the area within its range. When a notation such as "Introduced elsewhere" appears on a map, the text should be consulted.

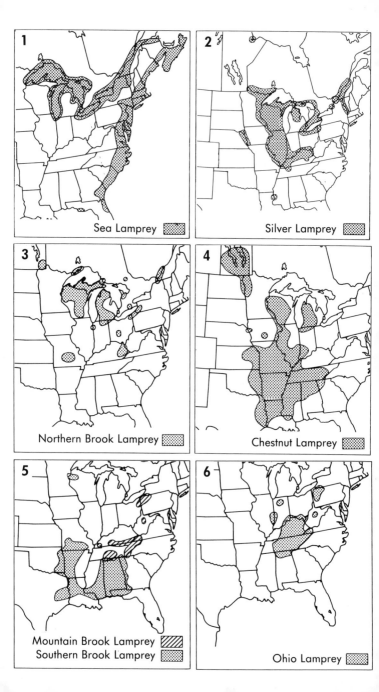

1. Sea Lamprey

2. Silver Lamprey

3. Northern Brook Lamprey

4. Chestnut Lamprey

5. Mountain Brook Lamprey
   Southern Brook Lamprey

6. Ohio Lamprey

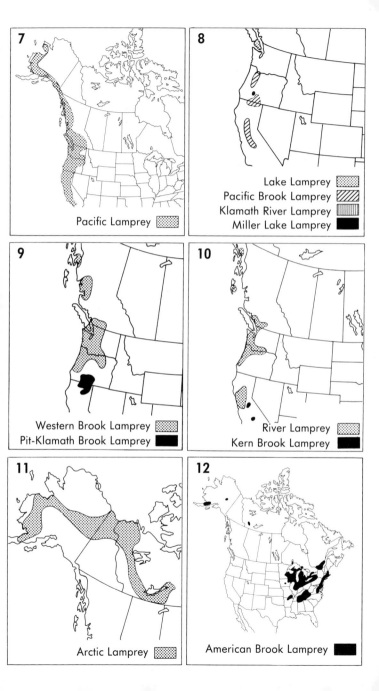

7 Pacific Lamprey

8
Lake Lamprey ▦
Pacific Brook Lamprey ▨
Klamath River Lamprey ▥
Miller Lake Lamprey ■

9
Western Brook Lamprey ▦
Pit-Klamath Brook Lamprey ■

10
River Lamprey ▦
Kern Brook Lamprey ■

11 Arctic Lamprey ▦

12 American Brook Lamprey ■

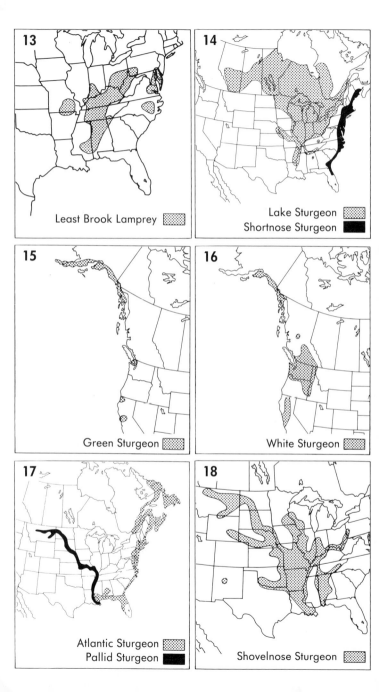

13 Least Brook Lamprey

14 Lake Sturgeon
Shortnose Sturgeon

15 Green Sturgeon

16 White Sturgeon

17 Atlantic Sturgeon
Pallid Sturgeon

18 Shovelnose Sturgeon

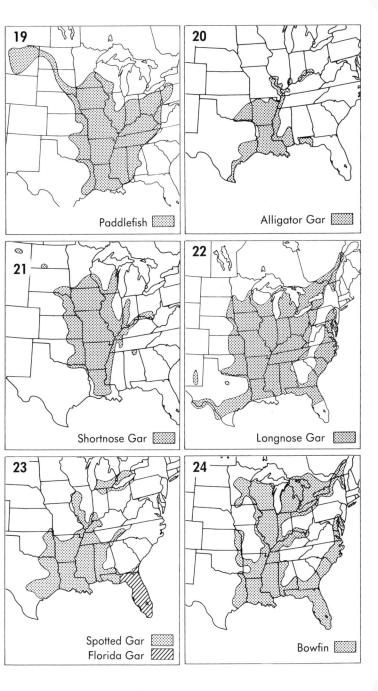

19 Paddlefish

20 Alligator Gar

21 Shortnose Gar

22 Longnose Gar

23 Spotted Gar / Florida Gar

24 Bowfin

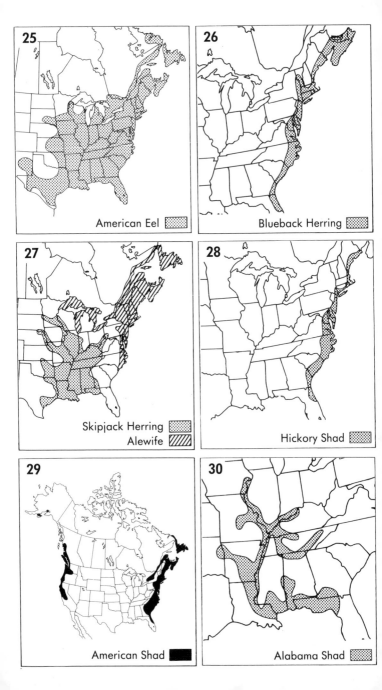

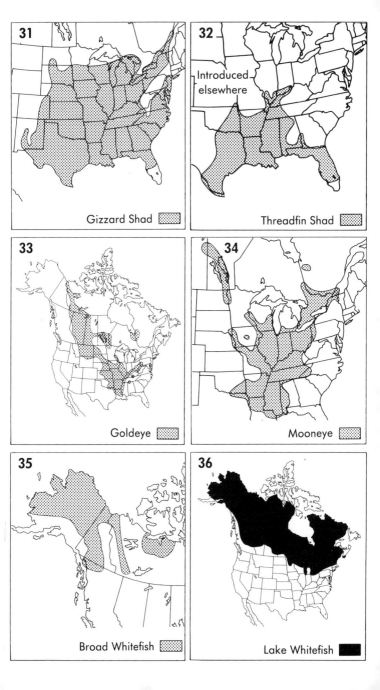

31 Gizzard Shad

32 Introduced elsewhere — Threadfin Shad

33 Goldeye

34 Mooneye

35 Broad Whitefish

36 Lake Whitefish

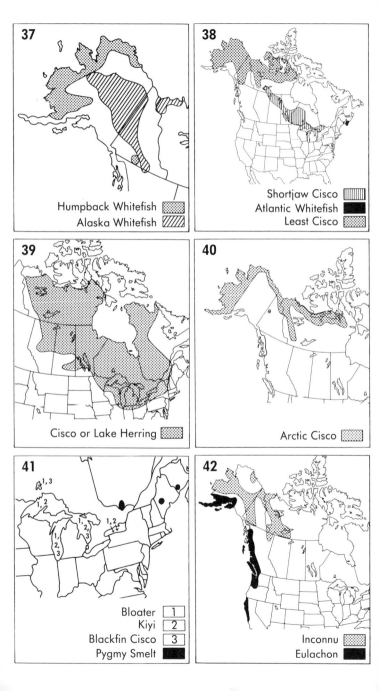

37
Humpback Whitefish
Alaska Whitefish

38
Shortjaw Cisco
Atlantic Whitefish
Least Cisco

39
Cisco or Lake Herring

40
Arctic Cisco

41
Bloater 1
Kiyi 2
Blackfin Cisco 3
Pygmy Smelt

42
Inconnu
Eulachon

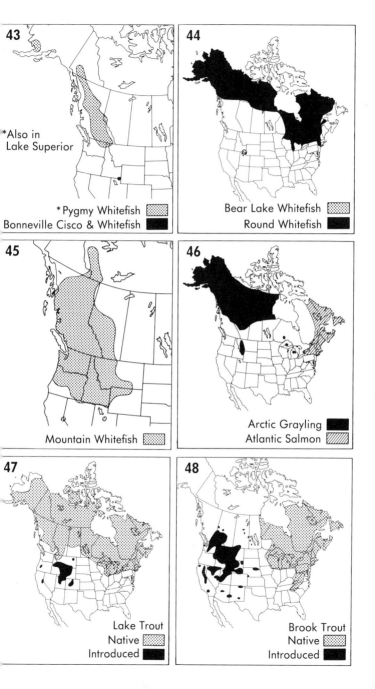

43

*Also in Lake Superior

*Pygmy Whitefish
Bonneville Cisco & Whitefish

44

Bear Lake Whitefish
Round Whitefish

45

Mountain Whitefish

46

Arctic Grayling
Atlantic Salmon

47

Lake Trout
Native
Introduced

48

Brook Trout
Native
Introduced

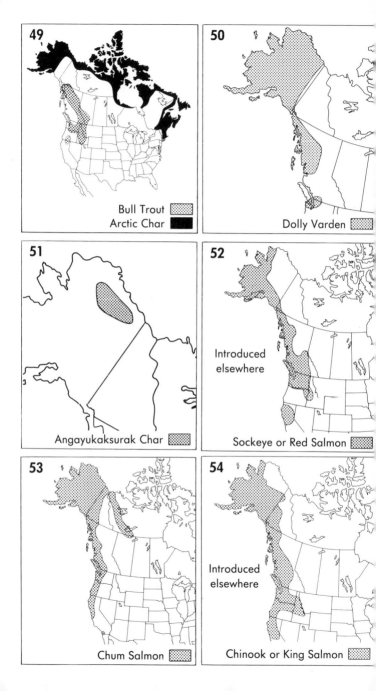

49 Bull Trout ▧ Arctic Char ■

50 Dolly Varden ▧

51 Angayukaksurak Char ▧

52 Introduced elsewhere Sockeye or Red Salmon ▧

53 Chum Salmon ▧

54 Introduced elsewhere Chinook or King Salmon ▧

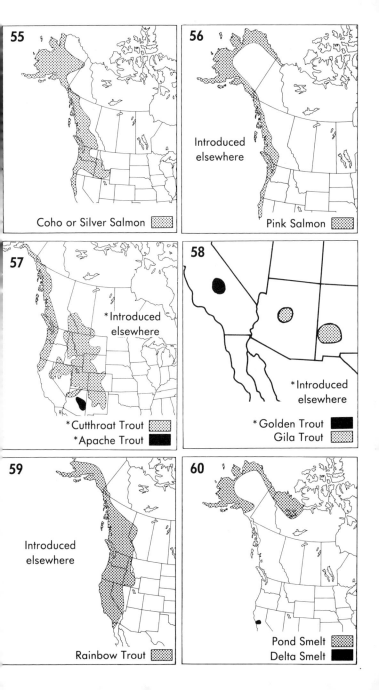

55 — Coho or Silver Salmon

56 — Pink Salmon
Introduced elsewhere

57 — *Cutthroat Trout / *Apache Trout
*Introduced elsewhere

58 — *Golden Trout / Gila Trout
*Introduced elsewhere

59 — Rainbow Trout
Introduced elsewhere

60 — Pond Smelt / Delta Smelt

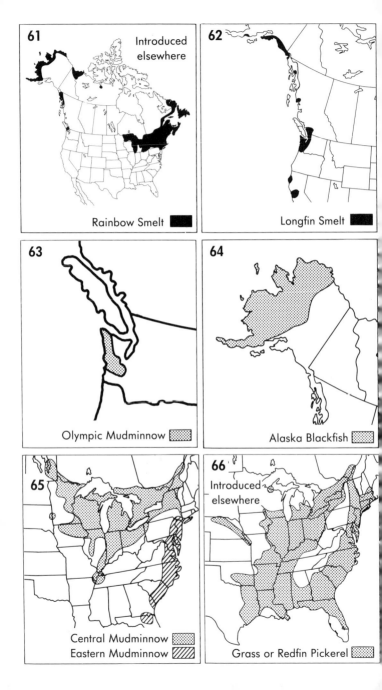

61 Introduced elsewhere — Rainbow Smelt ■

62 Longfin Smelt ■

63 Olympic Mudminnow ▨

64 Alaska Blackfish ▨

65 Central Mudminnow ▨
Eastern Mudminnow ▨

66 Introduced elsewhere — Grass or Redfin Pickerel ▨

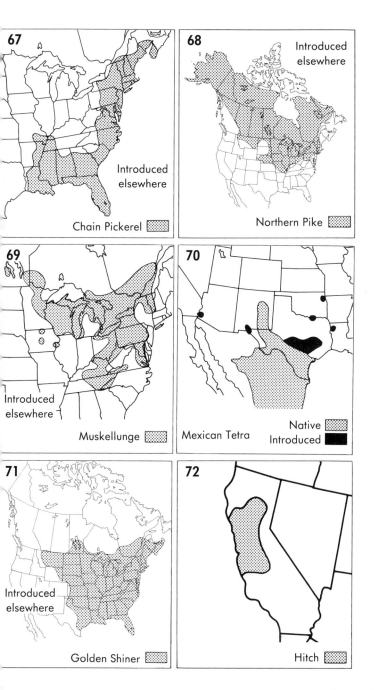

67 Chain Pickerel — Introduced elsewhere

68 Northern Pike — Introduced elsewhere

69 Muskellunge — Introduced elsewhere

70 Mexican Tetra — Native, Introduced

71 Golden Shiner — Introduced elsewhere

72 Hitch

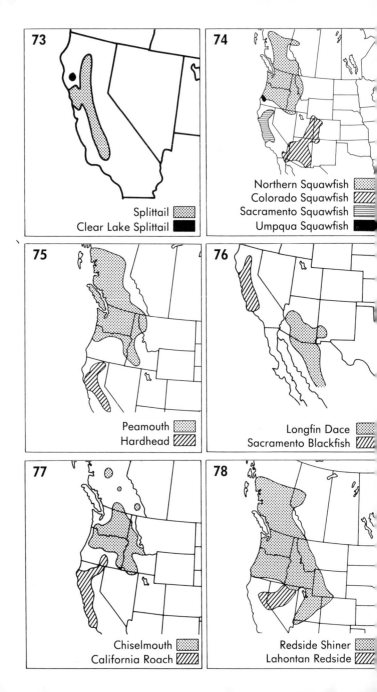

73
Splittail ⬚
Clear Lake Splittail ⬛

74
Northern Squawfish ⬚
Colorado Squawfish ⬚
Sacramento Squawfish ☰
Umpqua Squawfish ⬛

75
Peamouth ⬚
Hardhead ⬚

76
Longfin Dace ⬚
Sacramento Blackfish ⬚

77
Chiselmouth ⬚
California Roach ⬚

78
Redside Shiner ⬚
Lahontan Redside ⬚

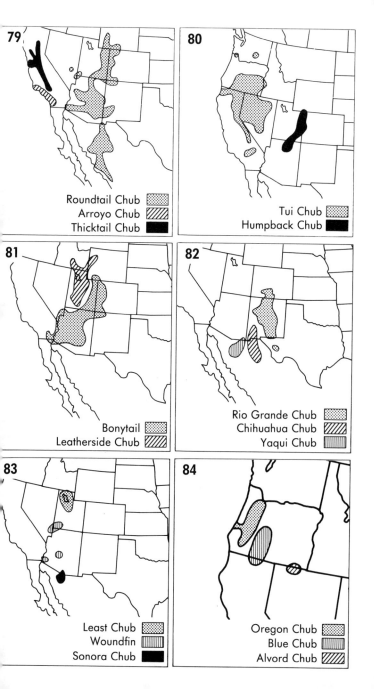

79
Roundtail Chub
Arroyo Chub
Thicktail Chub

80
Tui Chub
Humpback Chub

81
Bonytail
Leatherside Chub

82
Rio Grande Chub
Chihuahua Chub
Yaqui Chub

83
Least Chub
Woundfin
Sonora Chub

84
Oregon Chub
Blue Chub
Alvord Chub

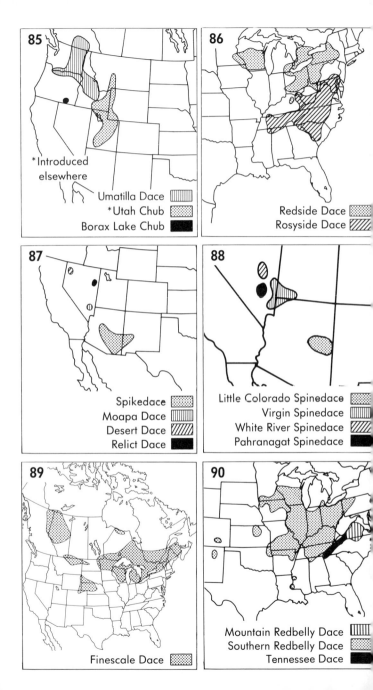

85

*Introduced
elsewhere

Umatilla Dace
*Utah Chub
Borax Lake Chub

86

Redside Dace
Rosyside Dace

87

Spikedace
Moapa Dace
Desert Dace
Relict Dace

88

Little Colorado Spinedace
Virgin Spinedace
White River Spinedace
Pahranagat Spinedace

89

Finescale Dace

90

Mountain Redbelly Dace
Southern Redbelly Dace
Tennessee Dace

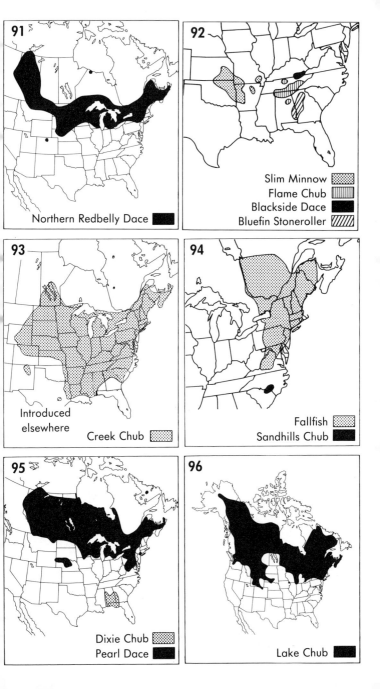

91 Northern Redbelly Dace ■

92
Slim Minnow ▨
Flame Chub ▥
Blackside Dace ■
Bluefin Stoneroller ▧

93 Introduced elsewhere
Creek Chub ▨

94
Fallfish ▨
Sandhills Chub ■

95
Dixie Chub ▨
Pearl Dace ■

96 Lake Chub ■

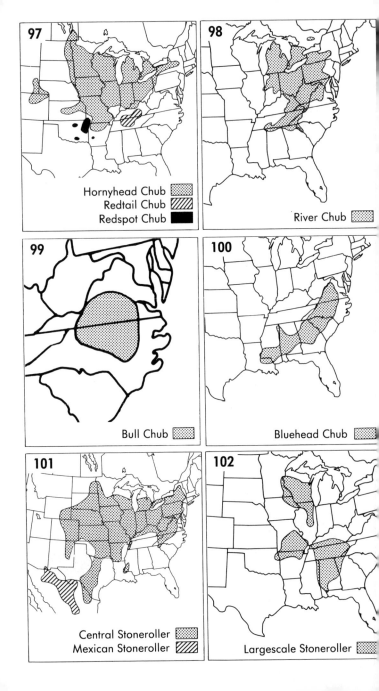

97
Hornyhead Chub
Redtail Chub
Redspot Chub

98
River Chub

99
Bull Chub

100
Bluehead Chub

101
Central Stoneroller
Mexican Stoneroller

102
Largescale Stoneroller

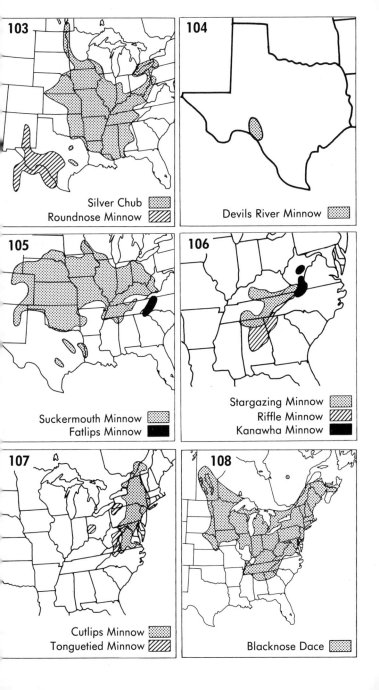

103
Silver Chub
Roundnose Minnow

104
Devils River Minnow

105
Suckermouth Minnow
Fatlips Minnow

106
Stargazing Minnow
Riffle Minnow
Kanawha Minnow

107
Cutlips Minnow
Tonguetied Minnow

108
Blacknose Dace

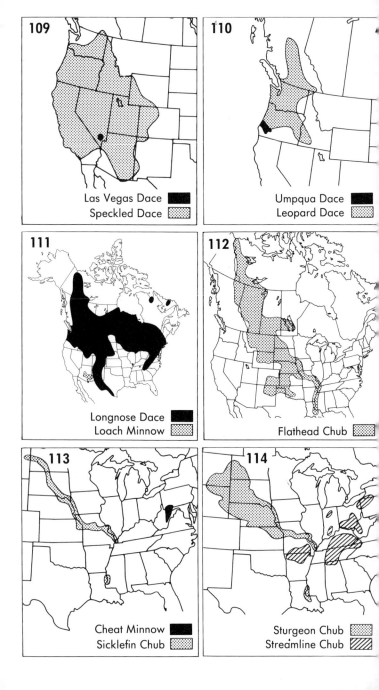

109
Las Vegas Dace ■
Speckled Dace ▨

110
Umpqua Dace ■
Leopard Dace ▨

111
Longnose Dace ■
Loach Minnow ▨

112
Flathead Chub ▨

113
Cheat Minnow ■
Sicklefin Chub ▨

114
Sturgeon Chub ▨
Streamline Chub ▧

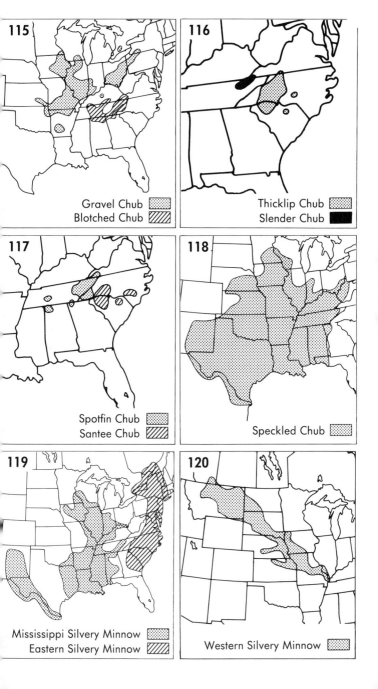

115
Gravel Chub 🔲
Blotched Chub ▨

116
Thicklip Chub 🔲
Slender Chub ■

117
Spotfin Chub 🔲
Santee Chub ▨

118
Speckled Chub 🔲

119
Mississippi Silvery Minnow 🔲
Eastern Silvery Minnow ▨

120
Western Silvery Minnow 🔲

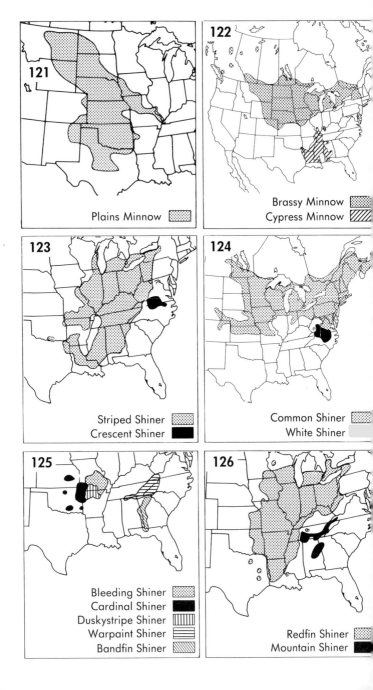

121 Plains Minnow

122 Brassy Minnow / Cypress Minnow

123 Striped Shiner / Crescent Shiner

124 Common Shiner / White Shiner

125 Bleeding Shiner / Cardinal Shiner / Duskystripe Shiner / Warpaint Shiner / Bandfin Shiner

126 Redfin Shiner / Mountain Shiner

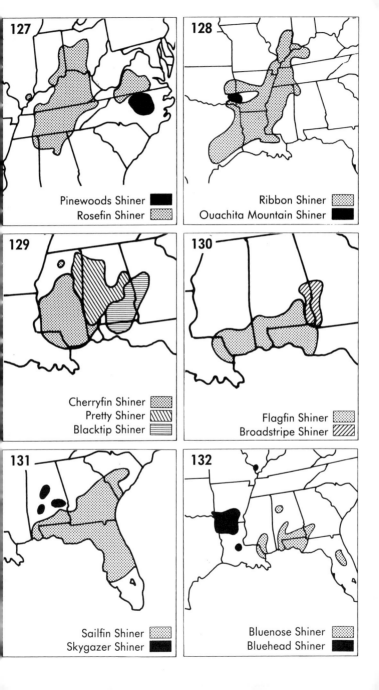

127
Pinewoods Shiner ■
Rosefin Shiner ▨

128
Ribbon Shiner ▨
Ouachita Mountain Shiner ■

129
Cherryfin Shiner ▨
Pretty Shiner ▨
Blacktip Shiner ▤

130
Flagfin Shiner ▨
Broadstripe Shiner ▨

131
Sailfin Shiner ▨
Skygazer Shiner ■

132
Bluenose Shiner ▨
Bluehead Shiner ■

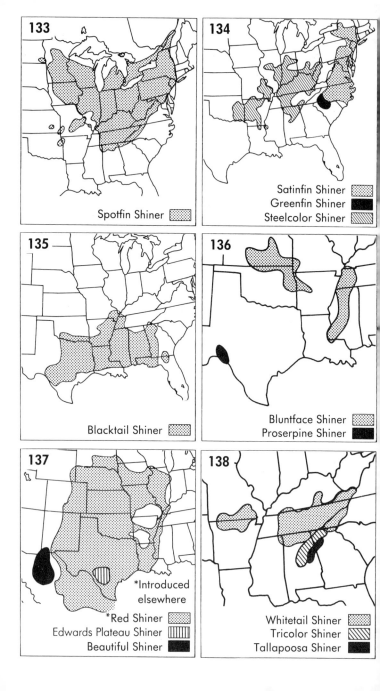

133

Spotfin Shiner

134

Satinfin Shiner
Greenfin Shiner
Steelcolor Shiner

135

Blacktail Shiner

136

Bluntface Shiner
Proserpine Shiner

137

*Introduced elsewhere

*Red Shiner
Edwards Plateau Shiner
Beautiful Shiner

138

Whitetail Shiner
Tricolor Shiner
Tallapoosa Shiner

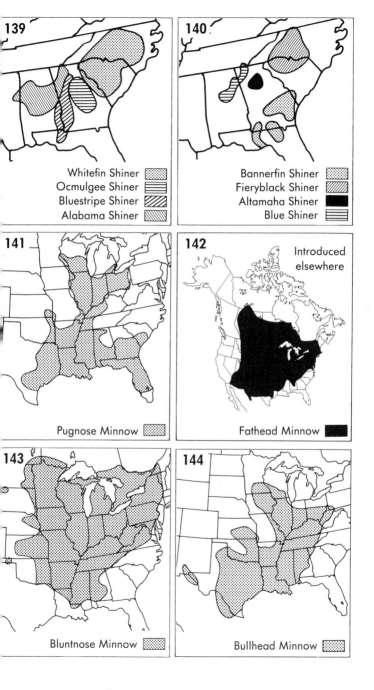

139
Whitefin Shiner
Ocmulgee Shiner
Bluestripe Shiner
Alabama Shiner

140
Bannerfin Shiner
Fieryblack Shiner
Altamaha Shiner
Blue Shiner

141
Pugnose Minnow

142
Introduced elsewhere
Fathead Minnow

143
Bluntnose Minnow

144
Bullhead Minnow

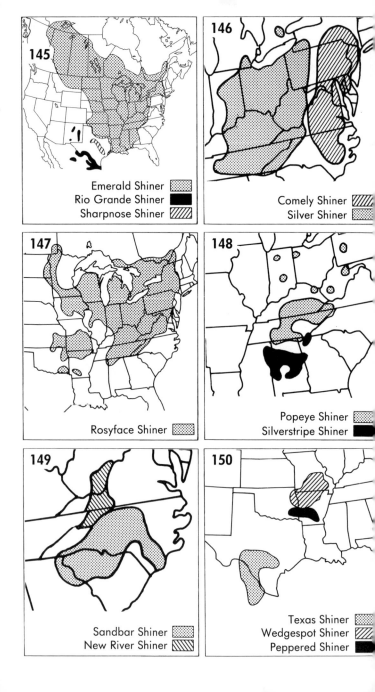

145
Emerald Shiner
Rio Grande Shiner
Sharpnose Shiner

146
Comely Shiner
Silver Shiner

147
Rosyface Shiner

148
Popeye Shiner
Silverstripe Shiner

149
Sandbar Shiner
New River Shiner

150
Texas Shiner
Wedgespot Shiner
Peppered Shiner

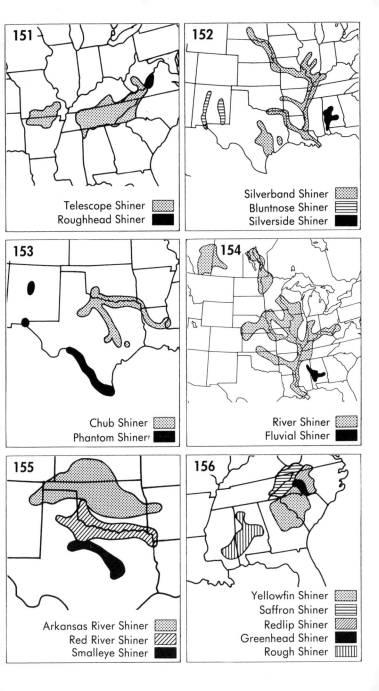

151
Telescope Shiner
Roughhead Shiner

152
Silverband Shiner
Bluntnose Shiner
Silverside Shiner

153
Chub Shiner
Phantom Shiner

154
River Shiner
Fluvial Shiner

155
Arkansas River Shiner
Red River Shiner
Smalleye Shiner

156
Yellowfin Shiner
Saffron Shiner
Redlip Shiner
Greenhead Shiner
Rough Shiner

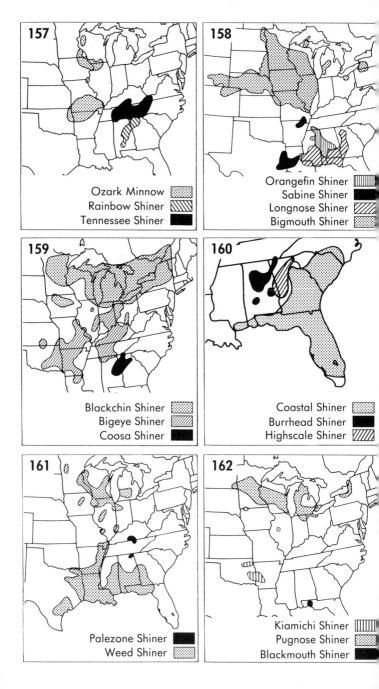

157
Ozark Minnow
Rainbow Shiner
Tennessee Shiner

158
Orangefin Shiner
Sabine Shiner
Longnose Shiner
Bigmouth Shiner

159
Blackchin Shiner
Bigeye Shiner
Coosa Shiner

160
Coastal Shiner
Burrhead Shiner
Highscale Shiner

161
Palezone Shiner
Weed Shiner

162
Kiamichi Shiner
Pugnose Shiner
Blackmouth Shiner

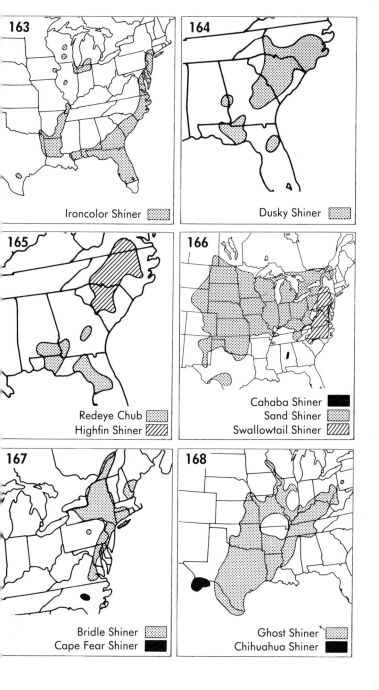

163 Ironcolor Shiner ▨

164 Dusky Shiner ▨

165 Redeye Chub ▨
Highfin Shiner ▧

166 Cahaba Shiner ■
Sand Shiner ▨
Swallowtail Shiner ▧

167 Bridle Shiner ▨
Cape Fear Shiner ■

168 Ghost Shiner ▨
Chihuahua Shiner ■

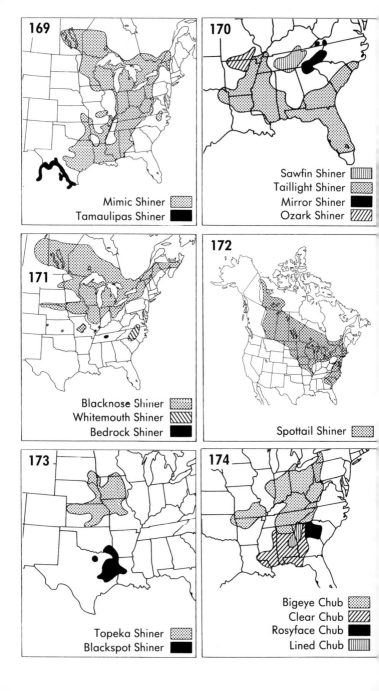

169
Mimic Shiner
Tamaulipas Shiner

170
Sawfin Shiner
Taillight Shiner
Mirror Shiner
Ozark Shiner

171
Blacknose Shiner
Whitemouth Shiner
Bedrock Shiner

172
Spottail Shiner

173
Topeka Shiner
Blackspot Shiner

174
Bigeye Chub
Clear Chub
Rosyface Chub
Lined Chub

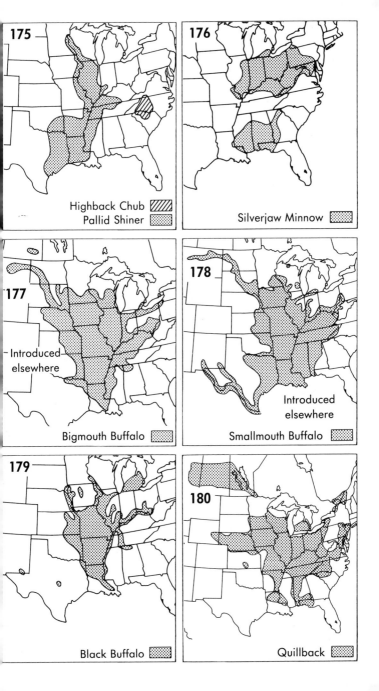

175 | Highback Chub / Pallid Shiner

176 | Silverjaw Minnow

177 | Introduced elsewhere | Bigmouth Buffalo

178 | Introduced elsewhere | Smallmouth Buffalo

179 | Black Buffalo

180 | Quillback

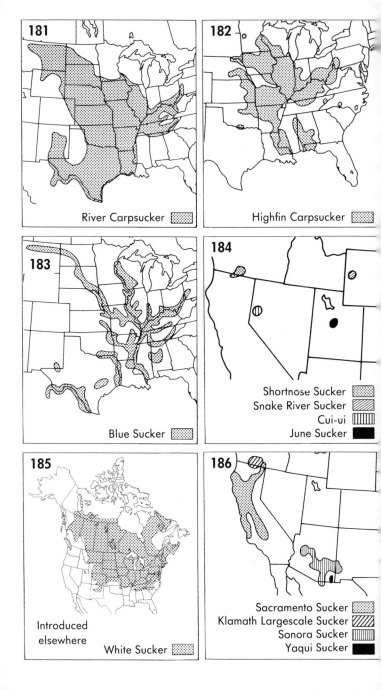

181 River Carpsucker

182 Highfin Carpsucker

183 Blue Sucker

184
Shortnose Sucker
Snake River Sucker
Cui-ui
June Sucker

185 Introduced elsewhere — White Sucker

186
Sacramento Sucker
Klamath Largescale Sucker
Sonora Sucker
Yaqui Sucker

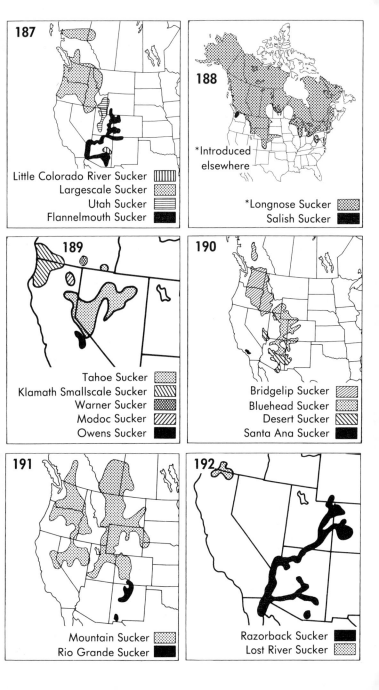

187

Little Colorado River Sucker ‖‖‖
Largescale Sucker ▦
Utah Sucker ☰
Flannelmouth Sucker ■

188

*Introduced elsewhere

*Longnose Sucker ▦
Salish Sucker ■

189

Tahoe Sucker ▦
Klamath Smallscale Sucker ◩
Warner Sucker ■
Modoc Sucker ◪
Owens Sucker ■

190

Bridgelip Sucker ◩
Bluehead Sucker ▦
Desert Sucker ◪
Santa Ana Sucker ■

191

Mountain Sucker ▦
Rio Grande Sucker ■

192

Razorback Sucker ■
Lost River Sucker ▦

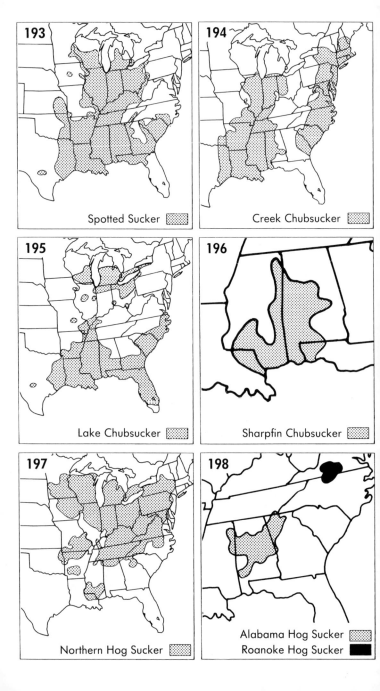

193 Spotted Sucker

194 Creek Chubsucker

195 Lake Chubsucker

196 Sharpfin Chubsucker

197 Northern Hog Sucker

198 Alabama Hog Sucker
Roanoke Hog Sucker

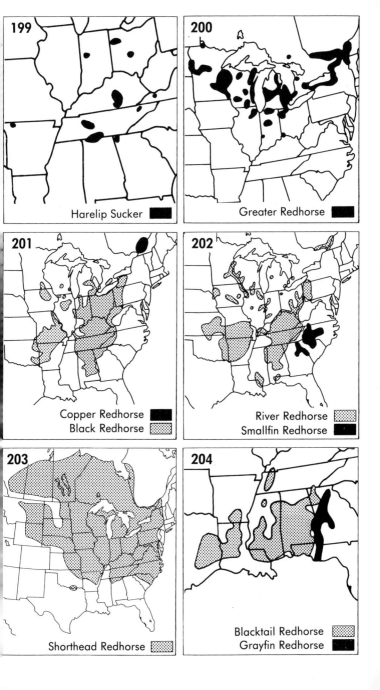

199 Harelip Sucker

200 Greater Redhorse

201 Copper Redhorse
Black Redhorse

202 River Redhorse
Smallfin Redhorse

203 Shorthead Redhorse

204 Blacktail Redhorse
Grayfin Redhorse

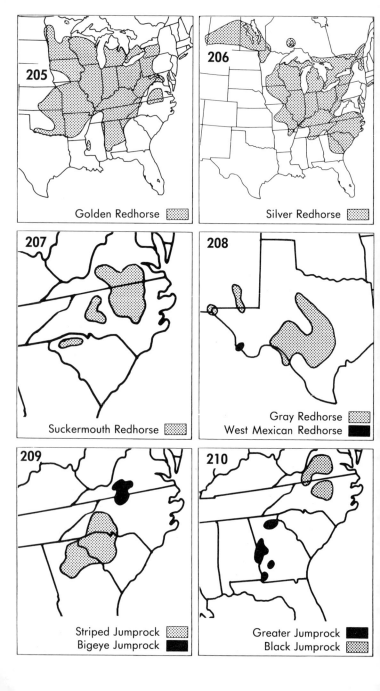

205 Golden Redhorse

206 Silver Redhorse

207 Suckermouth Redhorse

208 Gray Redhorse
West Mexican Redhorse

209 Striped Jumprock
Bigeye Jumprock

210 Greater Jumprock
Black Jumprock

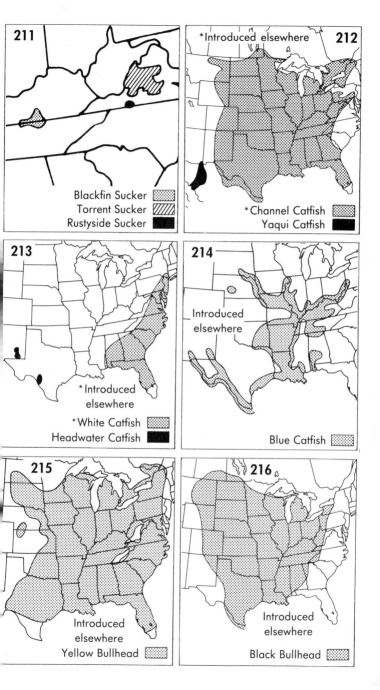

211
Blackfin Sucker
Torrent Sucker
Rustyside Sucker

212
*Introduced elsewhere
*Channel Catfish
Yaqui Catfish

213
*Introduced elsewhere
*White Catfish
Headwater Catfish

214
Introduced elsewhere
Blue Catfish

215
Introduced elsewhere
Yellow Bullhead

216
Introduced elsewhere
Black Bullhead

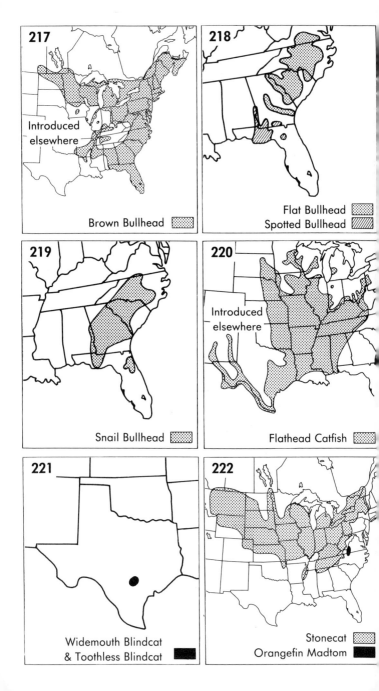

217
Introduced elsewhere

Brown Bullhead

218
Flat Bullhead
Spotted Bullhead

219
Snail Bullhead

220
Introduced elsewhere

Flathead Catfish

221
Widemouth Blindcat & Toothless Blindcat

222
Stonecat
Orangefin Madtom

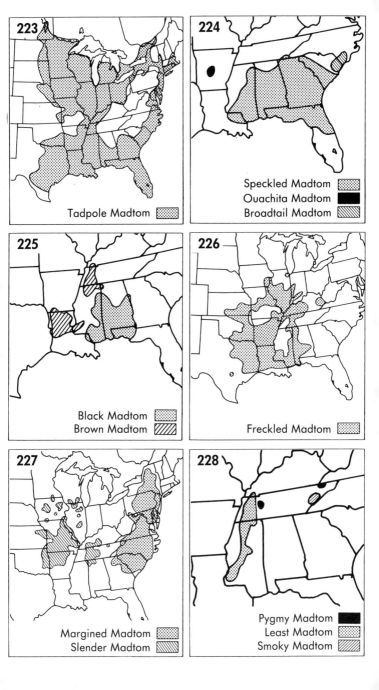

223 Tadpole Madtom

224
Speckled Madtom
Ouachita Madtom
Broadtail Madtom

225
Black Madtom
Brown Madtom

226 Freckled Madtom

227
Margined Madtom
Slender Madtom

228
Pygmy Madtom
Least Madtom
Smoky Madtom

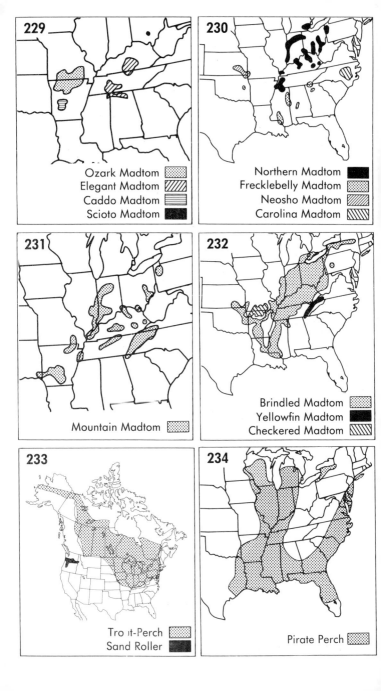

229

Ozark Madtom
Elegant Madtom
Caddo Madtom
Scioto Madtom

230

Northern Madtom
Frecklebelly Madtom
Neosho Madtom
Carolina Madtom

231

Mountain Madtom

232

Brindled Madtom
Yellowfin Madtom
Checkered Madtom

233

Trout-Perch
Sand Roller

234

Pirate Perch

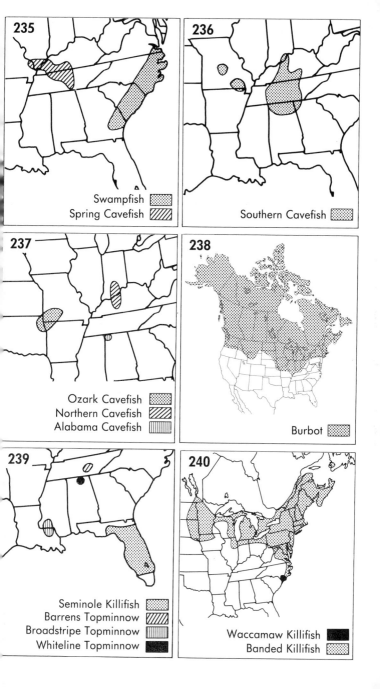

235
Swampfish
Spring Cavefish

236
Southern Cavefish

237
Ozark Cavefish
Northern Cavefish
Alabama Cavefish

238
Burbot

239
Seminole Killifish
Barrens Topminnow
Broadstripe Topminnow
Whiteline Topminnow

240
Waccamaw Killifish
Banded Killifish

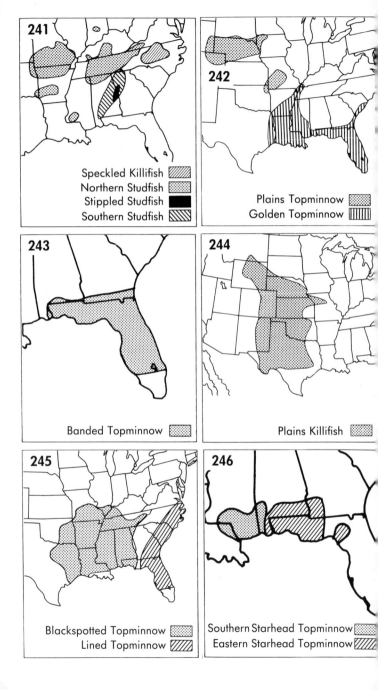

241

Speckled Killifish
Northern Studfish
Stippled Studfish
Southern Studfish

242

Plains Topminnow
Golden Topminnow

243

Banded Topminnow

244

Plains Killifish

245

Blackspotted Topminnow
Lined Topminnow

246

Southern Starhead Topminnow
Eastern Starhead Topminnow

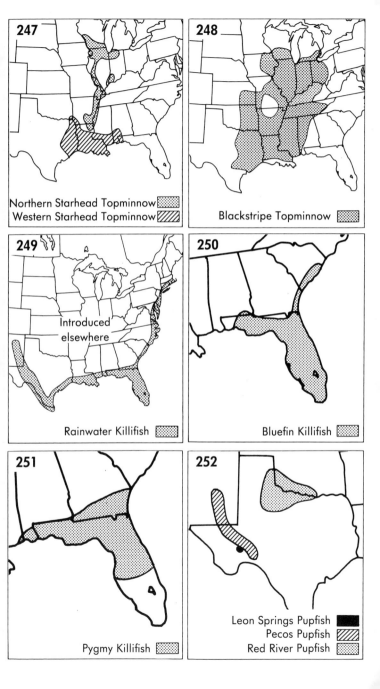

247
Northern Starhead Topminnow
Western Starhead Topminnow

248
Blackstripe Topminnow

249
Introduced elsewhere
Rainwater Killifish

250
Bluefin Killifish

251
Pygmy Killifish

252
Leon Springs Pupfish
Pecos Pupfish
Red River Pupfish

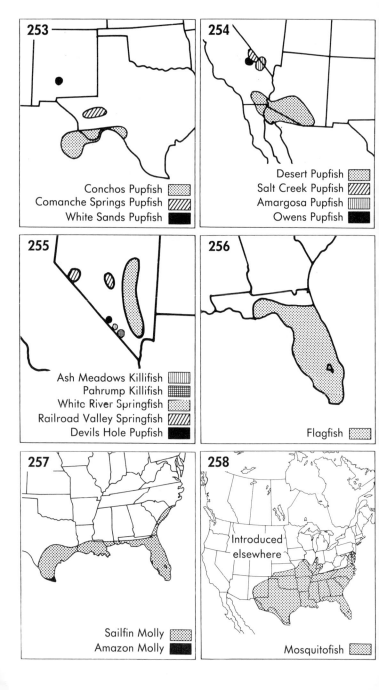

253
Conchos Pupfish ⬚
Comanche Springs Pupfish ▨
White Sands Pupfish ●

254
Desert Pupfish ⬚
Salt Creek Pupfish ▨
Amargosa Pupfish ▥
Owens Pupfish ●

255
Ash Meadows Killifish ▥
Pahrump Killifish ▦
White River Springfish ⬚
Railroad Valley Springfish ▨
Devils Hole Pupfish ●

256
Flagfish ⬚

257
Sailfin Molly ⬚
Amazon Molly ●

258
Introduced elsewhere
Mosquitofish ⬚

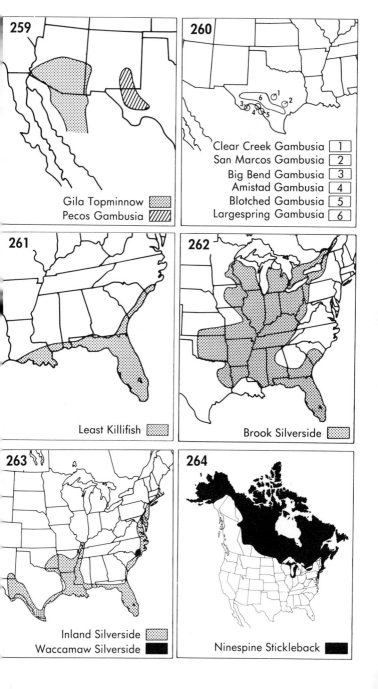

259

Gila Topminnow
Pecos Gambusia

260

Clear Creek Gambusia 1
San Marcos Gambusia 2
Big Bend Gambusia 3
Amistad Gambusia 4
Blotched Gambusia 5
Largespring Gambusia 6

261

Least Killifish

262

Brook Silverside

263

Inland Silverside
Waccamaw Silverside

264

Ninespine Stickleback

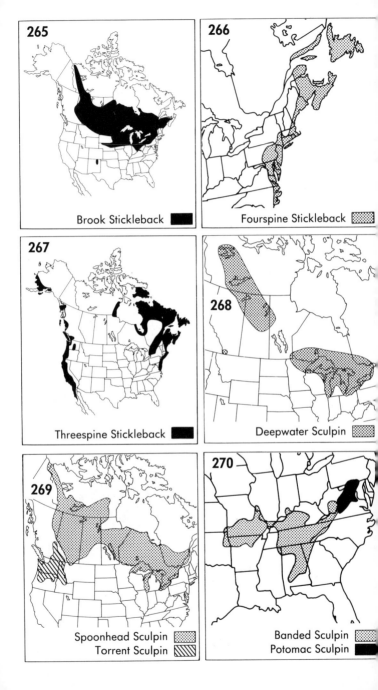

265 Brook Stickleback

266 Fourspine Stickleback

267 Threespine Stickleback

268 Deepwater Sculpin

269 Spoonhead Sculpin
Torrent Sculpin

270 Banded Sculpin
Potomac Sculpin

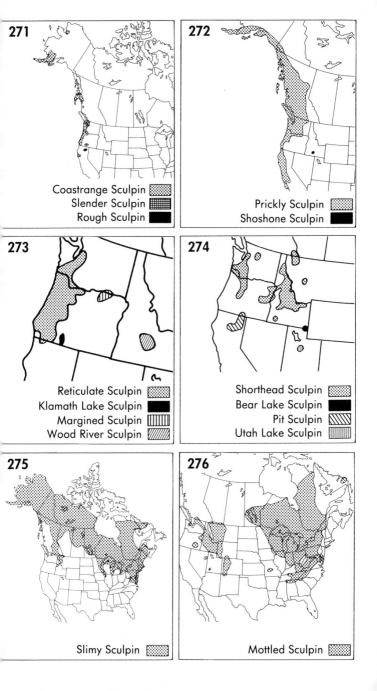

271
Coastrange Sculpin
Slender Sculpin
Rough Sculpin

272
Prickly Sculpin
Shoshone Sculpin

273
Reticulate Sculpin
Klamath Lake Sculpin
Margined Sculpin
Wood River Sculpin

274
Shorthead Sculpin
Bear Lake Sculpin
Pit Sculpin
Utah Lake Sculpin

275
Slimy Sculpin

276
Mottled Sculpin

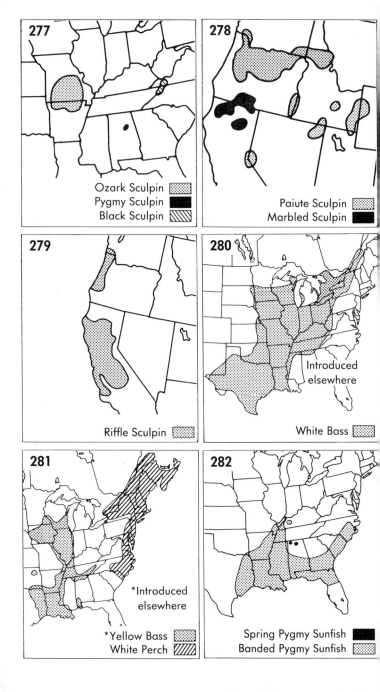

277
Ozark Sculpin
Pygmy Sculpin
Black Sculpin

278
Paiute Sculpin
Marbled Sculpin

279
Riffle Sculpin

280
Introduced elsewhere
White Bass

281
*Introduced elsewhere
*Yellow Bass
White Perch

282
Spring Pygmy Sunfish
Banded Pygmy Sunfish

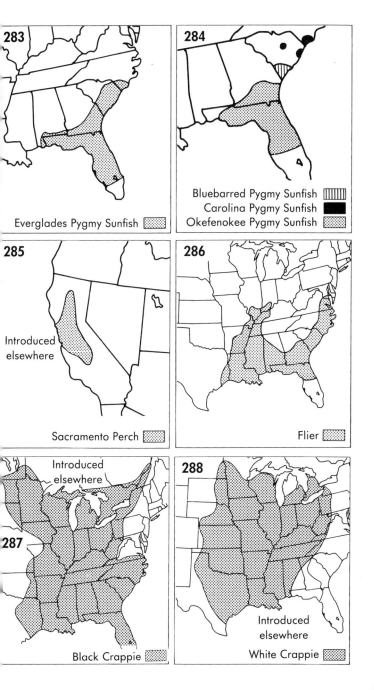

283 Everglades Pygmy Sunfish

284
Bluebarred Pygmy Sunfish
Carolina Pygmy Sunfish
Okefenokee Pygmy Sunfish

285 Introduced elsewhere — Sacramento Perch

286 Flier

287 Introduced elsewhere — Black Crappie

288 Introduced elsewhere — White Crappie

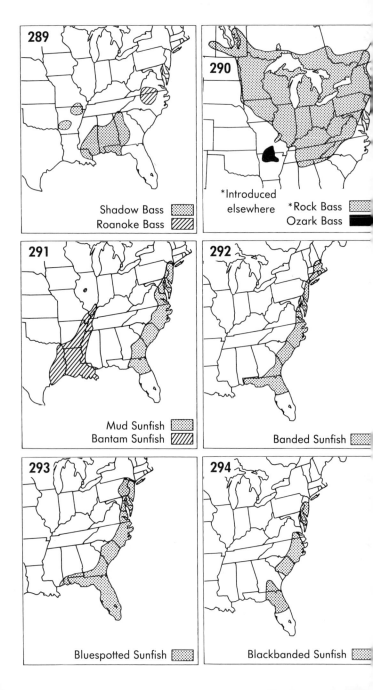

289

Shadow Bass ▓
Roanoke Bass ▨

290

*Introduced elsewhere   *Rock Bass ▓
                          Ozark Bass ■

291

Mud Sunfish ▓
Bantam Sunfish ▨

292

Banded Sunfish ▓

293

Bluespotted Sunfish ▓

294

Blackbanded Sunfish ▓

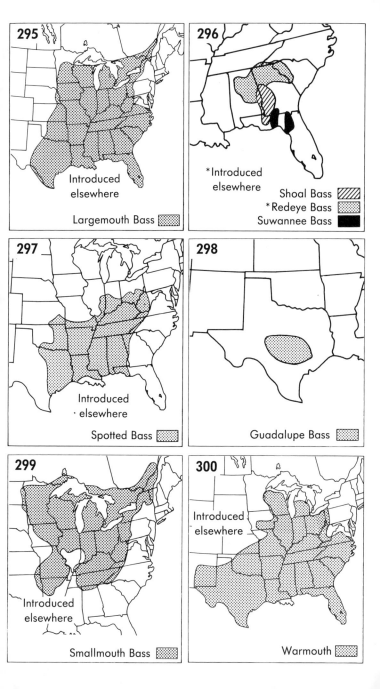

295

Introduced elsewhere

Largemouth Bass

296

*Introduced elsewhere

Shoal Bass
*Redeye Bass
Suwannee Bass

297

Introduced elsewhere

Spotted Bass

298

Guadalupe Bass

299

Introduced elsewhere

Smallmouth Bass

300

Introduced elsewhere

Warmouth

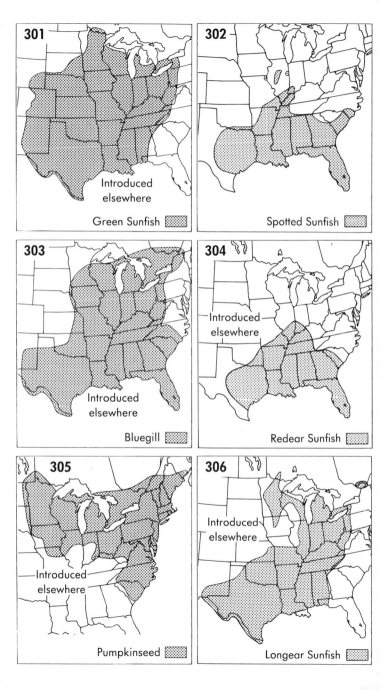

301 Green Sunfish — Introduced elsewhere

302 Spotted Sunfish

303 Bluegill — Introduced elsewhere

304 Redear Sunfish — Introduced elsewhere

305 Pumpkinseed — Introduced elsewhere

306 Longear Sunfish — Introduced elsewhere

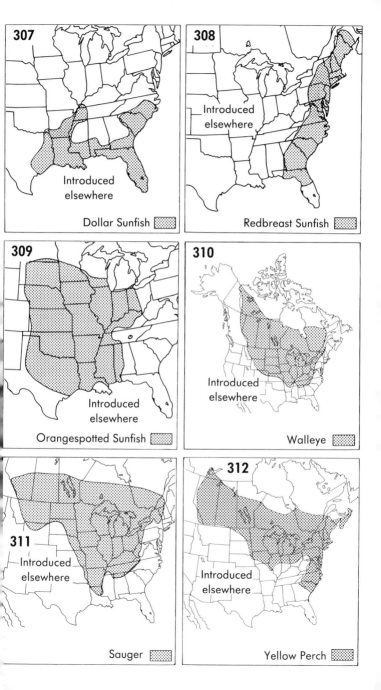

307 Dollar Sunfish
Introduced elsewhere

308 Redbreast Sunfish
Introduced elsewhere

309 Orangespotted Sunfish
Introduced elsewhere

310 Walleye
Introduced elsewhere

311 Sauger
Introduced elsewhere

312 Yellow Perch
Introduced elsewhere

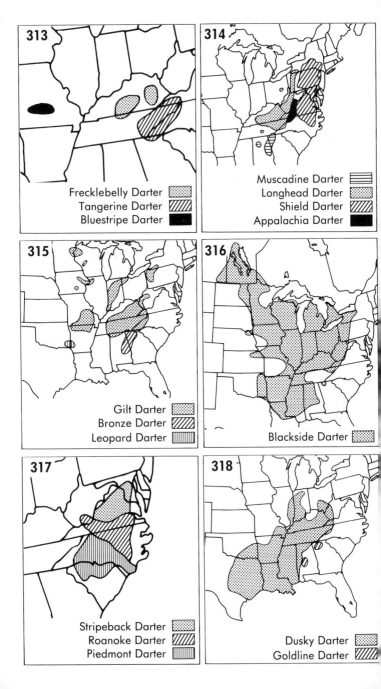

313

Frecklebelly Darter ▨
Tangerine Darter ▨
Bluestripe Darter ■

314

Muscadine Darter ▤
Longhead Darter ▨
Shield Darter ▨
Appalachia Darter ■

315

Gilt Darter ▨
Bronze Darter ▨
Leopard Darter ▥

316

Blackside Darter ▨

317

Stripeback Darter ▨
Roanoke Darter ▨
Piedmont Darter ▥

318

Dusky Darter ▨
Goldline Darter ▨

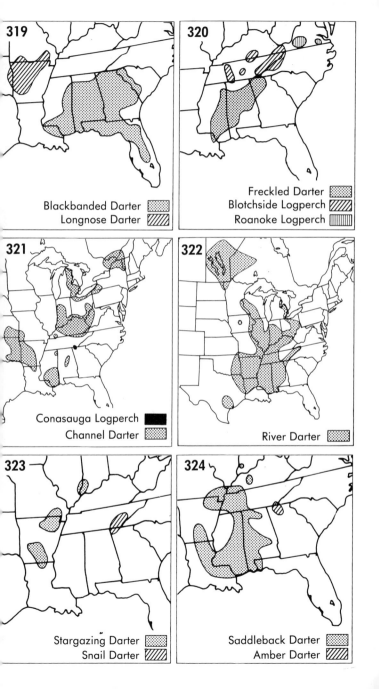

319

Blackbanded Darter [shaded]
Longnose Darter [hatched]

320

Freckled Darter [shaded]
Blotchside Logperch [hatched]
Roanoke Logperch [vertical lines]

321

Conasauga Logperch [black]
Channel Darter [shaded]

322

River Darter [shaded]

323

Stargazing Darter [shaded]
Snail Darter [hatched]

324

Saddleback Darter [shaded]
Amber Darter [hatched]

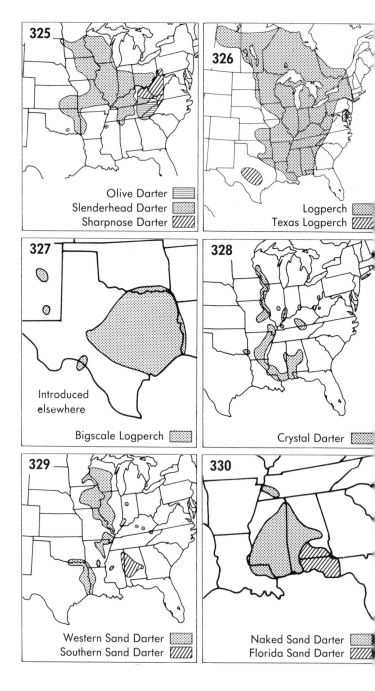

325
Olive Darter
Slenderhead Darter
Sharpnose Darter

326
Logperch
Texas Logperch

327
Introduced
elsewhere
Bigscale Logperch

328
Crystal Darter

329
Western Sand Darter
Southern Sand Darter

330
Naked Sand Darter
Florida Sand Darter

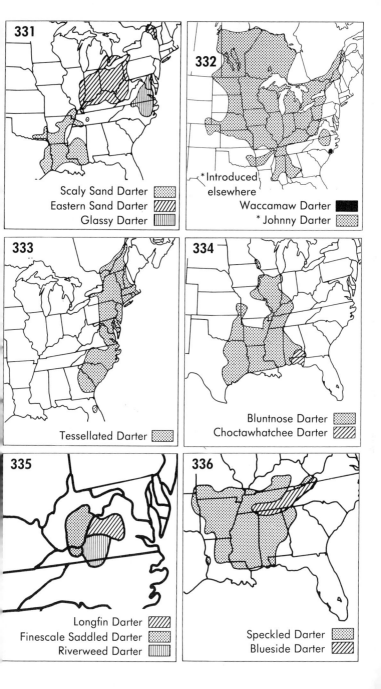

331
Scaly Sand Darter ▨
Eastern Sand Darter ▨
Glassy Darter ▨

332
*Introduced elsewhere
Waccamaw Darter ■
*Johnny Darter ▨

333
Tessellated Darter ▨

334
Bluntnose Darter ▨
Choctawhatchee Darter ▨

335
Longfin Darter ▨
Finescale Saddled Darter ▨
Riverweed Darter ▥

336
Speckled Darter ▨
Blueside Darter ▨

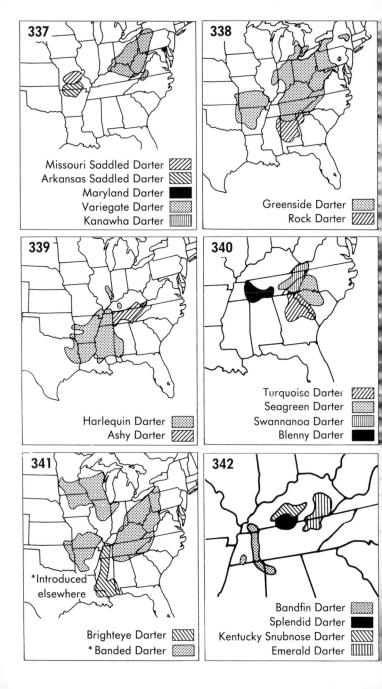

337

Missouri Saddled Darter ▨
Arkansas Saddled Darter ▨
Maryland Darter ■
Variegate Darter ▦
Kanawha Darter ▥

338

Greenside Darter ▦
Rock Darter ▨

339

Harlequin Darter ▦
Ashy Darter ▨

340

Turquoise Darter ▨
Seagreen Darter ▦
Swannanoa Darter ▥
Blenny Darter ■

341

*Introduced elsewhere

Brighteye Darter ▨
*Banded Darter ▦

342

Bandfin Darter ▦
Splendid Darter ■
Kentucky Snubnose Darter ▨
Emerald Darter ▥

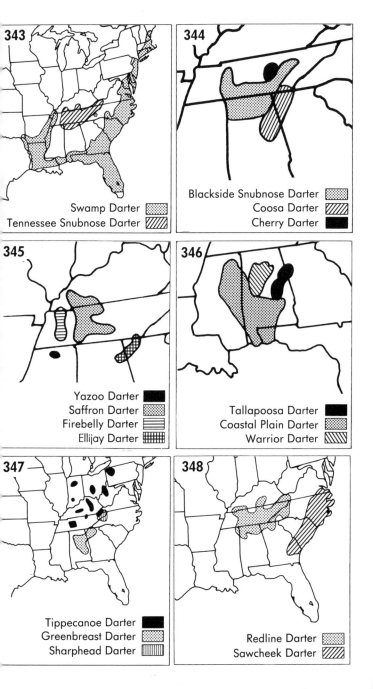

343

Swamp Darter
Tennessee Snubnose Darter

344

Blackside Snubnose Darter
Coosa Darter
Cherry Darter

345

Yazoo Darter
Saffron Darter
Firebelly Darter
Ellijay Darter

346

Tallapoosa Darter
Coastal Plain Darter
Warrior Darter

347

Tippecanoe Darter
Greenbreast Darter
Sharphead Darter

348

Redline Darter
Sawcheek Darter

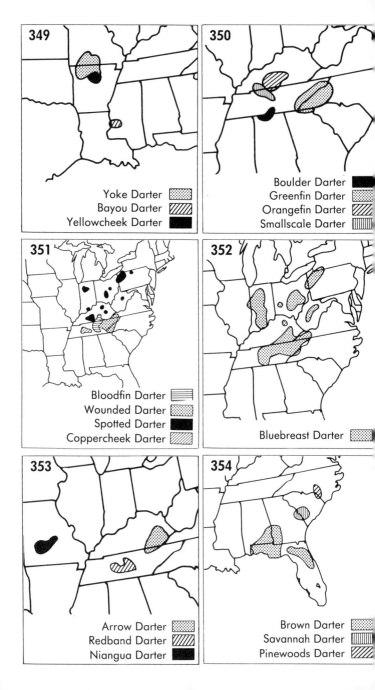

349

Yoke Darter
Bayou Darter
Yellowcheek Darter

350

Boulder Darter
Greenfin Darter
Orangefin Darter
Smallscale Darter

351

Bloodfin Darter
Wounded Darter
Spotted Darter
Coppercheek Darter

352

Bluebreast Darter

353

Arrow Darter
Redband Darter
Niangua Darter

354

Brown Darter
Savannah Darter
Pinewoods Darter

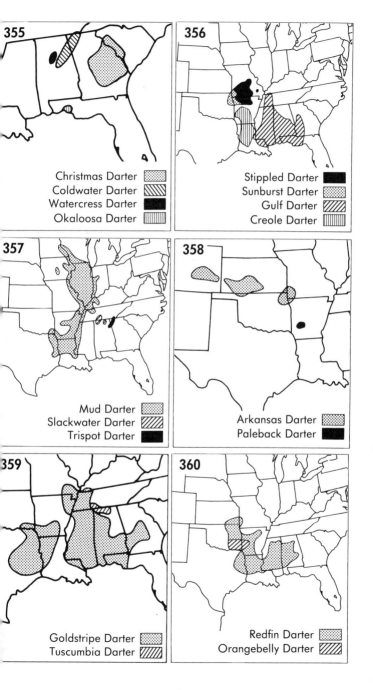

355
Christmas Darter
Coldwater Darter
Watercress Darter
Okaloosa Darter

356
Stippled Darter
Sunburst Darter
Gulf Darter
Creole Darter

357
Mud Darter
Slackwater Darter
Trispot Darter

358
Arkansas Darter
Paleback Darter

359
Goldstripe Darter
Tuscumbia Darter

360
Redfin Darter
Orangebelly Darter

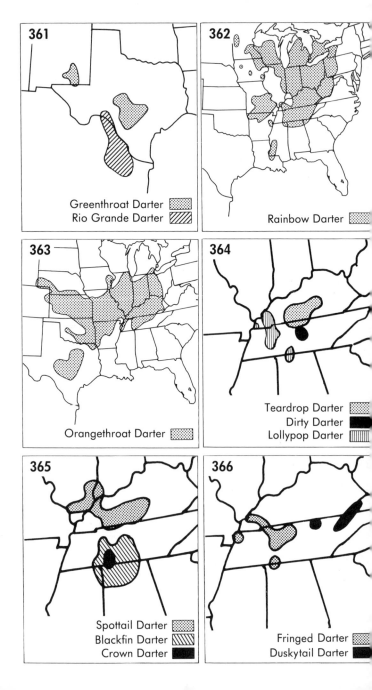

361

Greenthroat Darter
Rio Grande Darter

362

Rainbow Darter

363

Orangethroat Darter

364

Teardrop Darter
Dirty Darter
Lollypop Darter

365

Spottail Darter
Blackfin Darter
Crown Darter

366

Fringed Darter
Duskytail Darter

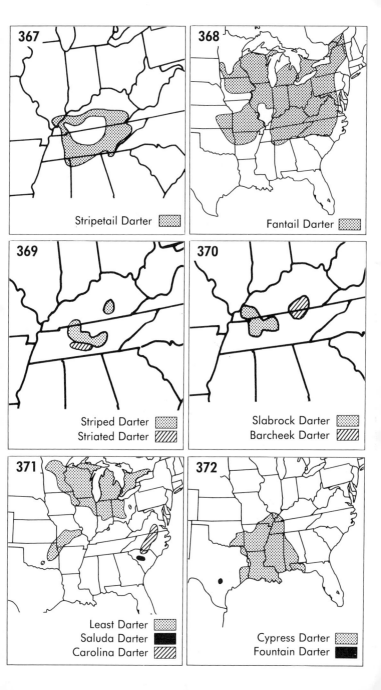

367 Stripetail Darter

368 Fantail Darter

369 Striped Darter
Striated Darter

370 Slabrock Darter
Barcheek Darter

371 Least Darter
Saluda Darter
Carolina Darter

372 Cypress Darter
Fountain Darter

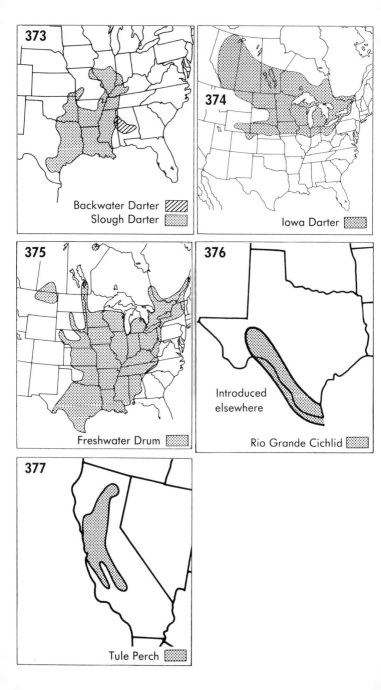

373
Backwater Darter
Slough Darter

374
Iowa Darter

375
Freshwater Drum

376
Introduced elsewhere
Rio Grande Cichlid

377
Tule Perch

INDEX

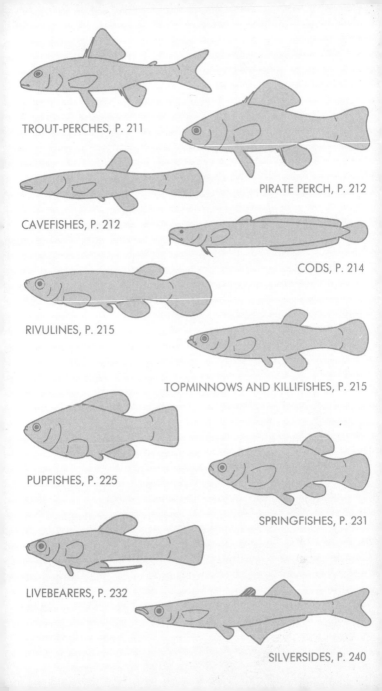

TROUT-PERCHES, P. 211

PIRATE PERCH, P. 212

CAVEFISHES, P. 212

CODS, P. 214

RIVULINES, P. 215

TOPMINNOWS AND KILLIFISHES, P. 215

PUPFISHES, P. 225

SPRINGFISHES, P. 231

LIVEBEARERS, P. 232

SILVERSIDES, P. 240